The Wines of Europe

FABER BOOKS ON WINE
General Editor: Julian Jeffs

*

Sherry by Julian Jeffs
The Wines of Europe by Julian Jeffs

The Wines of Europe

JULIAN JEFFS

FABER AND FABER LIMITED

London

First published 1971
by Faber and Faber Limited
3 Queen Square, London W.C.1
Printed in Great Britain
by Ebenezer Baylis and Son Limited
Worcester, and London
All rights reserved

ISBN 0 571 09510 0

© *1971 by Julian Jeffs*

this book
is affectionately dedicated to my father
Alfred Wright Jeffs
who brought me up on the bottle

Contents

9

CONTENTS

Maps

Introduction

Anyone setting out to write a book on the wines of Europe is instantly faced with the problem of what to leave out. It is a problem that admits of no tidy solution. This book does not pretend to be an encyclopaedia listing *all* European wines. No doubt I have omitted some which their admirers consider to be exquisite and have included others which their detractors would say are negligible. This is often simply a matter of personal taste. And since every year sees changes in the vineyards and techniques of the wine growers, one can never be completely up to date, particularly with regard to some of the lesser wine-growing countries and districts, some of which are very briefly mentioned only to show that they have not been overlooked.

I should explain my use of capital and lower case initial letters for the names of wines. Authorities differ in their approach to this and what ever one does is wrong. In this book I have used capital letters when referring to geographical districts and lower case for the names of wines, even if the words happen to be the same. Some of those district names have become current words in English: sherry and port, for example, yet no words could be more geographical than these. If such words are to have lower case initial letters, then one might as well be consistent and use them for the others as well. Thus bordeaux comes from Bordeaux and burgundy from Burgundy.

Many of my friends and acquaintances in the wine trade have given me invaluable help. Their names would make an impressive list, but as the help has extended over such a long period I fear there would bound to be omissions, so I shall omit them all and thank them collectively. I only hope that they will approve of the book. But some of my friends have given more direct aid by reading parts of the manuscript. They are: Gerald Asher; Thomas Blanco White, Q.C.; Paul Bouchard; John Boys, M.W.; Patrick Forbes; Heinz Frank; Edward Hale, M.W.; Peter Hasslacher; John Lockwood; David Peppercorn, M.W.; Robin Reid; the late Allen Sichel; and Michael Symington. My wife Deborah has been so kind as to read the proofs. Such mistakes as remain after their helpful scrutiny are entirely my own.

I must also thank two ladies who have had a lot to put up with: Celia White, who typed the first half of this book, and Joan Young, who typed the rest and had to cope with innumerable illegible corrections. Finally I must thank my publisher Charles Monteith for his continual encouragement and almost unbelievable patience.

CHAPTER 1

The Vine

The vine is as old as the hills—or nearly so. As a natural, wild plant it was growing when man was merely an ape. And if the vine is older than man, then so is wine: for wine is a product of nature. When a grape falls from a vine and ferments in the sun, wine is made; not wine as we know it, of course, but wine of a sort. It was not such a very great step forward for mankind to press the grapes, to watch the must ferment, and to drink the wine. It is a much simpler process than grinding corn to make bread, or fashioning a wheel to make a cart. Wine growing goes back to the earliest civilizations, and it is recorded in the books of all ages. In the Bible it is accepted as an every-day thing which the Mediterranean peoples assumed to be part of their lives. After the flood, when the waters left the face of the earth and the ark settled on the mountains of Ararat, the first thing that the legendary Noah did, after making his sacrifices, was to grow wine:

'And God blessed Noah. . . . And Noah began to be an husbandman, and he planted a vineyard: And he drank of the wine, and was drunken. . . .'

Genesis: Ch. 9, vv. 1, 20–21.

The name of the first man who made wine deliberately will never be known—nor that of the first drunkard. The Bible gives the honour to Noah, but Charles Tovey, the Bristol wine merchant, who was one of the best writers on wine in the last century, had another story. Jam-Sheed, the founder of Persepolis, was immoderately fond of grapes, and he preserved them in great jars for eating out of season. Some of them got crushed, and the fermented juice tasted so unlike grape juice that he wrote 'poison' on the jar and set it aside to be thrown away. One of his favourite hand-maidens was tired of life, and drank the poison to do away with herself. The effect was not quite what she expected. When she came round, she drank some more, and yet more, until there was none left. Then she confessed her crime. Thus was wine dis-covered, and it became known in Persia as Teher-e-Kooshon—the delightful poison.

Despite the ease with which a crude wine can be made, however, grape wine may not have been the first fermented drink to become popular; mead and beer probably came even earlier, whilst the Chinese credit their Ling Ching Noung with the art of making wine from rice in about 2000 B.C. The earliest fermented fruit juice recorded in literature was date wine. Xenophon described it rather discouragingly as 'a pleasant drink causing headache', despite which it was very popular. The vine, however, was cultivated, and grape wine was prepared, as early as the prehistoric Djemdet-Nast period in Mesopotamia, and it was brought into Egypt before 3000 B.C.—a thousand years earlier than the Chinese rice fer-mentations. In later ages, when the vine was already cultivated north of the Mediterranean, in the areas that are still famous today, these North African wines found little favour: Martial preferred vinegar, though Strabo claimed that Libyan wine tasted well when mixed with sea water. The wines of the countries around Palestine, however, are frequently praised in the Bible, and books of the Old Testament mention the wine of Helbon, in Syria, and the fragrant wine of the Lebanon. The Greeks, as one might expect, practised viticulture as an art, and the earliest detailed essays on the subject are those by Theophrastus of Eresos, the pupil of Aristotle. An earlier treatise by Democritus of Abdera is unfortunately lost.

The wild vine, in its various species, was widely distributed throughout the temperate regions of the world, and fossil remains have been found as far north as Iceland. It even flourished in Siberia during tertiary times, when that ill-starred region enjoyed a hot climate. But although the genus *Vitis* grew upon the earth long before *homo sapiens*, it does not follow that the grape as we know it was a common fruit. Some wild vines bore no fruit at all and others gave berries that were of little practical use. Like so many familiar plants, the vine, in all its varieties, came as a result

of selection and cultivation by man. It was probably first
methodically cultivated in eastern Europe, in the regions of the
Caucasus and the Caspian Sea, about ten thousand years ago,
whence it spread westwards. Phoenician and Greek traders
are credited with carrying it to the remainder of the Mediterranean
shores. Today, wine vineyards are cultivated over a very wide area
that is limited only by the climatic conditions under which the
vine will flourish. If there is too little sun, the grapes will not
ripen, but in the tropics there is too much, and the vines are burnt
up. A heavy frost in the spring may kill them, and even quite a
light frost will kill young shoots. There must be enough rain to feed
the vines and to fill the fruit with juice, but heavy rain when the
grapes are ripe will turn them rotten and may spoil the vintage
completely. The climate has a profound effect on the quality of the
wine that can be made. The most northerly of the major vineyards
are those of Germany, where the growers are faced with enormous
difficulties, for the crop is always uncertain and really outstanding
years are unfortunately few. The growers must always be on their
guard against sudden frost and the vintage is often so late that it is
imperilled by the onset of a severe winter. So the cost of the wines
is always comparatively high; but their grace and delicacy is
beyond comparison. Were it not for this, wine growing in such
latitudes would never be a commercial proposition. As it is, it only
succeeds owing to the immense skill and teutonic industry of the
growers. In the past there have been successful vineyards in
England. Wine growing as a major industry disappeared with the
dissolution of the monasteries, but it continued thereafter on a
small scale and the Hon. Charles Hamilton's vineyards at Painshill,
in Surrey, were famous for their sparkling wines at the end of the
eighteenth century. Those wines were so good that they commanded very high prices, but to make wine in England calls for
knowledge and enthusiasm. It appears that both were lacking, and
moreover in the nineteenth century the great continental wines
could be bought very cheaply. For three-quarters of a century
wine growing in England went into abeyance, and then, in 1875,
the Marquis of Bute made a noble attempt to resuscitate the lost
art by planting a large vineyard at Castle Coch in Glamorganshire.
Unfortunately, however, despite having produced some excellent
wine, the vineyard perished owing to lack of labour during the

First World War. There was another gap in the history of British wine until a band of enthusiasts re-started viticulture after the last war. Now there are successful vineyards in Hambledon and Beaulieu, and at the time of writing further vineyards are being planted. If wine growing in Britain becomes commercially successful our vineyards will be the most northerly in the world.

At the other extreme, great wines are grown in Madeira and such wines have been grown in the past in the Canary Isles, where the surrounding sea provides a temperate enough climate despite the latitude. Inland, wines are grown as far south as Marrakesh in western Morocco, and there are extensive vineyards along the North African coast; but the wines tend to be too heavy and are often coarse, unsubtle and even unpleasant *ordinaires*. Thus the effect of climate can be seen by comparing the wines of the most northerly and the most southerly vineyards. Further north or further south the crop would be too hazardous to be worthwhile, and the wines would be too weak and thin, or too big and coarse, to be worth drinking.

The climate, however, is only one out of four factors which determine the quality of the wine. The others are the soil, the nature of the vine and the method of vinification. For a good wine to be produced, the vinification must be meticulous and, above all, appropriate to the grapes that are grown. The greater wines can only be prepared in those areas in which nature has decreed that the climate and the soil form a perfect combination. And the position is often extremely critical. One slope of a hill may catch the sun from morning till night, whilst another falls slightly in the shade or is exposed to cold winds. In one vineyard the soil is exactly right; in the next it is too rich and the wine is coarse, or else it is so poor that not even the vine, which often flourishes in the poorest of soil, can be grown successfully. And the effect of the soil on the wine produced is not limited to the nourishment which the soil gives to the vine: the soil temperature also plays some part. This is not merely a function of the air temperature and sunshine, but is also related to drainage and soil composition. Thus it is that in France clear lines can be drawn on the maps of the vineyards. On one side of the line, the wine is a classic growth. On the other, it is a negligible *ordinaire*. The contrast can be as sharp as that.

There are innumerable varieties of vine, each somewhat different from the others. No one can tell how many, as when a vine is transplanted from one area to another it sometimes grows so differently as to appear to be another variety, and it may well be that vines known by different names in different parts of the world are fundamentally similar; moreover the same variety may be known locally by six or more different names. So the whole matter is very complicated. Whilst all vines belong to the genus *Vitis*, it is only one branch of that family, the *Vitis vinifera*, that yields the classic wines, and the cultivation of this has supplanted all the others that may have been indigenous to Europe. Indeed it is doubtful whether any other genus has grown in Europe since historic times until American native vines were planted here during the last century. Several species of *Vitis* were found growing wild in America, but none of these is capable of yielding a really good wine, and only three are of practical importance: the *Vitis berlandieri*, the *Vitis riparia* and the *Vitis rupestris*. All of these, and crosses between them, are grown today in practically all the great vineyards, because they are resistant to that deadliest of enemies, the phylloxera; but they are only grown as stocks on which the great native vines are grafted. There are also hybrid vines. The best of these are very hardy plants, being resistant to the phylloxera and to many of the diseases to which the vine is prone, but so far no cross has been achieved which is capable of giving a wine as good as that yielded by the native vines, and whilst they are grown in France, Romania, Russia and Italy to give adequate *vins ordinaires*, they may by law not be planted in the great wine areas, and in Germany it is utterly forbidden to grow them.

There appears to be no limit to the number of varieties in which the *Vitis vinifera* can exist. If one plants a pip, one never knows what sort of vine is going to come up. For the amateur, who just wants to grow a few bunches of grapes, there is a pleasant element of speculation, and there is always the chance that he may create a valuable new variety; but it is more likely to be a poor one. Nurserymen create new vine varieties deliberately in the hope that one will surpass all the rest, but for the wine grower this would be hopeless: long experience and much experiment has shown which varieties of vine yield the finest wine in each soil and climate, and vines have a remarkable way of acclimatizing themselves, changing their character slightly over the years when they are transplanted to a new region. To ensure continuity, therefore, new vines are grown from cuttings. Even then, though, the troubles are not ended, as occasionally a vine undergoes a spontaneous mutation, changing its style, or produces a shoot that is quite out of character: a black grape vine can suddenly produce a branch which grows white grapes. Although interesting, these 'bud mutations' are exasperating, as they are seldom of economic value and are usually retrogressive. I have even tasted a red wine vinified from black grapes that were grown on a vine that was a cross between a Riesling and a Sylvaner—both white. Or else a cutting fails to grow true to type, or grows into a disappointing vine giving a very poor yield. Then there is nothing to do but to grub it up and start again. In some vineyards, where the phylloxera has not yet penetrated, like those of England and Cyprus, or where it is kept under control by continuous effort, as it was until recently in some of the great German vineyards, the problem is somewhat easier: if a vine fails yet has a strong and successful vine as a neighbour it may be replaced by 'layering'. In the spring a sound cane from the strong vine is bent downwards and its end is planted in the ground. By the end of the summer it will have taken root; it can then be cut off from the parent vine and will grow independently. That is the easy way; but of course it is useless where the native vines have to be grafted on to phylloxera-resistant American roots, and it is now forbidden in Germany where only grafted vines may now be planted.

Like so many cultivated plants, vines are delicate: they are easily attacked by disease, fungi and noxious insects. The grower has always to be on the alert. And in cultivating a vine he is up against a difficulty that perhaps no other market gardener is faced with: the quality of the wine is dependent entirely on the grapes, and it has already been shown that minute variations in their composition, caused by slight changes in the soil or climate, which produce no visible change in the fruit, can affect the wine profoundly. Such variations can also result from changes in cultivation, such as pruning, fertilizing and spraying. So the grower must take great care. The remedy could too easily be worse than the disease. If the wine is to be great, everything must be exactly right.

All the most serious of the plagues afflicting vines were un-fortunately imported from America on plants brought over as experiments. Vines have three principal fungoid enemies. To give them their English names, they are: powdery mildew, downy mildew and black spot.

Powdery mildew, or *oidium*, used formerly to be known as *oidium tuckeri*, and by scientists it is called *uncinula necator*, *uncinula americana*, or *uncinula spiralis*. It is indigenous to North America, and was first observed in Europe by one Tucker, who found it in a hothouse at Margate in 1845. A London gardener named Kyle found the remedy a year later. From 1852 onwards it has been attacking all the vineyards of Europe and it seems that it will be with us for ever more, waiting to lay waste a vineyard when ever the grower is negligent and does not take the right steps to prevent it. It spreads rapidly, and it develops in conditions of humidity and warmth—conditions that are found at some seasons in every vineyard. It is particularly prevalent in close weather in those vineyards that are very well sheltered from the refreshing wind.

Oidium can attack all the green parts of the vine, and it is worst when it attacks the grapes themselves. It appears as a fine, light-grey film with a mouldy smell; it looks so much like ash that it is known colloquially in Spain as *ceniza* and in Germany as *ächerich*. Whilst growing on the outside of the plant it passes suckers through the skin that draw out all the goodness and ultimately cause death; and if it grows on the grapes it turns them sour and rotten. The only remedy, as discovered by Kyle, is to spray the vines with very finely divided sulphur, which is sometimes used in conjunction with lime.

Downy mildew is *plasmopara viticola*, formerly known as *peronospora viticola*. It grows under similar conditions to oidium, but requires more than mere moisture: an actual droplet of water is necessary for it to germinate. When it attacks vines, white stains like icing sugar appear, often at the edges of the leaves, and gradually spread inwards. Oily patches follow and the leaves gradually become yellow. It also affects the grapes, producing different colorations depending on the size and development of the fruit, and it is essential to destroy it before it gets this far. On young fruit it is known as 'grey rot', but on fruit that is almost ripe it is 'brown rot'. Unfortunately there is no sign of infection of the grapes until it has taken firm hold, and by that time it is incurable, as it grows inwardly and is beyond the reach of fungicides. Mercifully, however, it is very rare today, as it is prevented by spraying the vines with Bordeaux Mixture, or with one of the new, and better, commercial preparations, at intervals throughout the dangerous summer months. Bordeaux Mixture consists of copper sulphate and lime dissolved in water, though copper oxychloride is often used as an alternative, and there are many famous and effective proprietary sprays, of which the best known is Cuprosan. Only when the weather is particularly damp and sunless, as it was in many French vineyards during 1963, does the treatment fail.

Black spot, or anthracnose (the scientific name for which is *gloeosporium ampelophagum*) is, by way of a change, a native European fungus that can be recognized in ancient Greek and Latin essays on viticulture. As becomes a European fungus, it flourishes at a somewhat lower temperature than the other two and its presence is manifested, as its name would suggest, by small dark spots which grow into black, open scars. It also attacks the bunches of grapes when they are at a very early stage in their development, and reduces them to black, withered stalks. Like downy mildew, the fungus germinates in water and grows inwardly, so that once it gains a hold it is hard to get rid of, but it is kept in control in the same way by regular spraying.

Of all the plagues that can attack the vine, by far the worst is the insect phylloxera, which was first described by Dr. Asa Fitch in his *Noxious Insects of New York* (1856). It is an aphid, generally known as *phylloxera vestatrix* (the devastating leaf-dryer), though the names *viteus vitifolii*, *aphis phylloxera*, *pemphigus vitifolii*, *xerampelus vitifolii*, *peritimbia visitana*, or (very loosely) 'vine louse', are also found. It is thought to have been brought over to Europe on American vines which had been imported in the hope that they would be resistant to the then regnant plague of oidium. Unfortunately the cure was much worse than the disease. The American vines gave atrocious wine and brought the phylloxera with them. It was first noticed in hothouses at Hammersmith in 1863 and was described entomologically by M. J. E. Planchon in 1868.

It is yellow-brown in colour and horrible to look at through a magnifying glass, but it cannot be seen very clearly otherwise, as it is only a half to one millimetre long. Its life cycle is extremely complicated and varies according to the conditions under which it lives, but it breeds and multiplies at a prodigious rate. The female lays a single egg in the stem of the vine during the autumn; this hatches out in the spring to give a fundatrix, which may lay anything up to thirty eggs; these in turn hatch out and multiply, so that it has been estimated that one fundatrix born in April could give rise to twenty or thirty million insects by November.

The phylloxera vestatrix exists in five different forms, each occurring at a separate point in the life cycle. The winter egg is laid under the bark of the vine and hatches in the spring to give a phylloxera of the *gallicola* form; this lives on the vine leaves, on which it forms galls. It is self-fertilizing and lays eggs which produce larvae of two kinds: one half become *gallicolae* and continue to live on the leaves, while the other half pass down into the roots and are known as *radicolae*. This form also multiplies indefinitely by parthenogenesis and can hibernate as nymphs during the winter, but some of its larvae hatch out to give a third form of phylloxera: *sexuparae*. These have wings and fly to the higher parts of the vines where they lay eggs of two kinds, the larger hatching out as females and the smaller as males. The two then mate and the female lays a single large over-wintering egg which hatches during the following spring to give a fundatrix, thus completing the life cycle.

Gallicolae are rarely seen on European or grafted vines, and for that reason the full cycle of the phylloxera is seldom completed. On the other hand, the radicolae can perpetuate themselves indefinitely, causing debility, and ultimately the death of such vines as are vulnerable to them. They produce lesions which result in abnormal growth of the part attacked and also allow other parasites to get in, such as fungi and bacteria. Eventually the whole of the root beneath the lesion is separated from the remainder of the vine and dies. The gallicolae, when they do appear, are relatively harmless, though they cause some damage through feeding on the sap.

When phylloxera attacks a vine, for the first five or even eight years there is no sign at all of its existence: if anything, the yield increases slightly. Then debility is noticed when the damage begins to take effect: the tendrils are less well developed, the shoots are thin and short, the bunches of grapes are small. Even so, the contrast is not great, but the phylloxera has taken hold and the vine is doomed. In the following years the same symptoms are seen, but they are more marked. At the end, the vine is clearly drying up and preparing to die.

Phylloxerae travel from vine to vine through the ground or over its surface, especially when helped by wind or rain; the sexuparae, in particular, can be blown to quite distant vineyards. They can also be spread by vineyard tools, machinery and clothing. Although many attempts have been made to exterminate them, none has been successful. The most drastic and dramatic remedy was to flood the vineyards during the winter, but this could only be done in suitable geographical areas and even then was never fully effective in eliminating the aphids, while causing considerable damage to the fertility of the soil. Viala proposed a remedy involving human urine, but this proved worse than the phylloxera; Eloy Martinez attempted to electrocute the pests, but his experiments were equally futile; and so were many other fanciful remedies. Fumigation of the roots and soil with carbon disulphide, organic acids and arsenic compounds has been tried with limited success, but it has been found impossible to control phylloxera on a large scale. The problem has been to find some form of soil insecticide that does not cause more mischief than it cures, by leaving undesirable residues in the vine. Moreover, it is doubtful whether any systemic insecticide, which is absorbed into the plant sap to attack the pest from within, could operate successfully against phylloxera, as the parasite produces galls which deaden the plant tissues and reduce sap flow just where it would be required. In fact there is no known remedy, and the only solution is to pull up all the vines and replant with American stocks that resist attack. This, however, does not cure the plague, but merely renders it innocuous. The wine growers have ceased from fighting the phylloxera and have learned to live with it.

A longer established pest, of European origin, was a species of coleoptera known to entomologists as *haltica lythri* Aubé, sup-species *ampelophaga*. This was the scourge of wine growers during the sixteenth and seventeenth centuries, and no doubt it would readily manifest itself again were it not for the fact that it has been virtually eliminated by insecticide sprays. In 1566, the people of Beaune petitioned the curé of Autun to excommunicate the pest, and in the chapter meeting of April 10th, 1603 in Jerez, a prominent landowner, Don Diego Caballero de los Olivos, who was tired of waging war against a noxious yellow-green coleoptera, likewise clamoured for its excommunication, saying there was a learned and godly friar called Francisco de Porras who had successfully excommunicated it elsewhere and was prepared to do so again. Whether or not the anathema of the Church worked as a deterrent is not recorded, but everyone faced ruin, and the mayor ordered a procession of the whole town to the convent of Our Lady of Mercy. The scientists of that time scorned the remedies of religion and ordered the vines to be painted with the blood of a bull.

It is an oval, yellow-green insect, measuring about four millimetres long by two millimetres wide. It used to appear in early spring after spending the winter concealed beneath the bark of the root of the vine, or in the crevices of brick-work, or in any similar hiding place. By the summer its eggs had hatched out and a vast swarm of tiny yellow grubs attacked the vines, eating the leaves and the tender shoots. They lived on the leaves and bred at a prodigious rate. Every vine had to be examined and the infected leaves burnt, but that was never more than a partial remedy. It was a terrible plague, and even after it was exterminated, the vines took two or three years to recover.

These are perhaps the most established pests and parasites, the universal menaces, but there are many others, for instance the red mite and the cochylis caterpillar. The enemy that the grower has to guard against depends entirely on the climate: the problems in the Moselle are manifestly different, for example, from those in Jerez. Moreover there is no hard and fast rule for any district. No two years are alike. In a wet year he must be continuously on guard against fungi, whilst dry, sunny weather favours the insects. He must always be vigilant. Every year, however, with the development of new sprays and insecticides, the problem becomes less worrying; though, as with disease in human beings, it looks as if the enemies of the vine will never be fully overcome. They develop their own resistance to sprays and insecticides, so that when they become immune to one, another has to be found.

The universal plague with the most far-reaching effect is

undoubtedly the phylloxera. It has now spread to all the major vineyards of Europe with the exception of Cyprus, and thanks to it, practically all the vines planted today consist of the classic native vines grafted on resistant American stocks. The only exceptions (apart from the Colares district of Portugal which has soil which the aphid cannot penetrate) occur in small pockets of vineyards, notably some in Germany and part of Quinta do Noval in the Douro, where, with untiring effort, the phylloxera is still kept at bay, and in those humble areas where 'direct producers' (hybrid vines) are grown to give *vins ordinaires*. Apart from the latter, there are hardly any ungrafted vines now growing in France. Even the exquisite Domaine de la Romanée-Conti, which held out as long as possible, had to succumb in 1946. Like so many of the German vineyards it fell a victim to the war, when manpower and materials were very short and there were not enough left to combat the phylloxera.

It is hard to evaluate what difference grafting has made to the wine that is produced. The wines from the ungrafted vines of the Romanée-Conti were undoubtedly exquisite; but so are those made from the grafted vines today. A short time ago I had the honour of being shown some pre-phylloxera wines at a château in the Médoc. They were wonderful and vigorous in their old age; but so are some of the post-phylloxera clarets, the 1924s, 1926s, 1928s and 1945s, for example, some of which may live just as long. Claret vintages are notoriously capricious. Sometimes there are a great many good years in rapid succession, as in the 1940s, 50s, and 60s, whilst at other times there is a succession of rather poor to average years, as in the first twenty years of this century. This succession of uninspiring years followed soon after the vineyards were replanted. Every claret produced seemed dim in comparison with the legendary 1864s and 1871s; and it may well be this which gave the grafted vines a bad name. Since the last war there has been the further complication that the method of fermentation has been modified to produce wines which mature more quickly. They develop so quickly, in fact, that they frighten the older wine lovers who were used to waiting fifteen years before they considered their wines fit to drink. All this has helped to damn the wines from the grafted vines in the eyes of the older generation. But I am not sure that the older generation is right. It may well be that there is not really a great deal of difference. In the sherry area, where the wines develop in the wood more rapidly and more regularly than bottled table wines, so that a direct comparison is easier, the general opinion of growers is that wines from the grafted vines are slightly better than those produced before, though that exquisitely delicate style known as *palo cortado* is harder to come by. There is probably no general rule: some areas take readily to the grafted vines and produce slightly better wines, whilst those in other areas are slightly worse—or at any rate appeared slightly worse after the first replanting; but this was generally before the art of selecting the most suitable American stock was fully understood, and with present-day knowledge practically all of the past difficulties have been overcome. The selection of the right stock is now simply a routine matter.

Quite apart from this, the need to graft had one wholly bene-ficial effect: it gave the growers the opportunity to select the finest vine varieties from the many that they used formerly to grow, often in a most haphazard way, in their vineyards. Selecting the right variety often produced a dramatic improvement in quality, while selecting the healthiest vines of that species to provide the cuttings had a correspondingly good effect on the yield. This has now been yet further increased by modern sprays, which almost completely control the old pests and diseases, and by modern fertilizers, which greatly strengthen the vines without endangering in any way the flavour or quality of the wine. If this had not come to pass, wine today would be in short supply and astronomical in price.

One thing is certain though: the grafted vines have a shorter life than the native vines grown on their own roots. But this probably has nothing to do with the grafting. Modern viticulture gives high yields, and high yields reduce the span of life. It is impossible to say what the life of a vine is. So much depends on the soil and the climate. A variety of vine that lives for only thirty or forty years in one place may make a hardy centenarian in another. A healthy vine grown to bear fruit for eating can undoubtedly live, given suitable care, for several hundred years. Pliny wrote of vines six hundred years old, and in Jerez there is a venerable Beba vine said to be over three hundred years old; its trunk is eighteen inches wide and it is ten feet high. The doors of Ravenna Cathedral are made of wood from a giant vine, and vines planted at Santa

Barbara by the first Californian settlers grew to have a base circumference of eight feet; in 1895 one of them yielded nine tons of fruit. There were certainly vines over a hundred years old at Sanlúcar until the time of the phylloxera, and the great Black Hamburg at Hampton Court, which was planted in 1768, is still giving a full yield of fruit. In fact, if carefully tended, a vine goes on almost for ever, but if the grapes are to be made into wine, a concentration of goodness and flavour is necessary that can only be obtained from vines that are relatively young. Before the phylloxera, the useful life of vines varied between approximately fifty and a hundred years. Now it is about half that. To offset this a little, grafted vines with modern fertilizers and viticultural techniques give at least twenty per cent and sometimes as much as five hundred per cent more must[1] and produce as good wine at a much earlier age.

The method of grafting varies greatly between the various districts. In all the northern vineyards, and as far south as Bordeaux and Burgundy, the winters are inclement and there is the danger of a frost which would kill very young, newly grafted vines. To avoid this risk 'bench grafting' is practised. During the winter—usually in January—a cutting of the stock, about three or four buds long, is grafted with a shorter cutting of the native vine, or *scion*, which only has one bud. The grafts are then buried in sand and kept in a hot, humid atmosphere until the weather is warm enough for them to be planted out of doors in the nursery, where they are kept for two years before being transplanted into the vineyard. In the vineyards around the Mediterranean, however, frost is so rare that it becomes a commercial proposition to practise 'cleft grafting' with the vines *in situ* in the vineyards. More and more of the Bordeaux growers, too, are adopting this method, as it saves them a year when it succeeds—as it usually does. The stock is first planted and when it is strong enough, generally in the second year, the scions are grafted on. In Jerez this is done in about August, and if the graft at first fails a second graft is attempted between December and February. But the proportion of failures is not normally high, and this is as well, as the second grafts are never as satisfactory as the

[1] *Must*, derived from the Latin *mustum*, is the name given to fresh grape juice before it has fermented.

first: the weather is less favourable, and the stock will have grown, so the graft is higher up and there is more trouble with suckers growing from the American root. In the Douro the grafting is somewhat later—in February—and it varies from place to place according to the climate.

Apart from the diseases considered above, and brought about by fungi and insects, vines are also susceptible to attack by viruses. One of these produces the disease of *court-noué* which is at present causing consternation in Burgundy and Champagne. When this attacks, the growth of the vine is stunted and the yield is drastically reduced, though happily the quality of the wine is not affected. Unfortunately no cure is yet known.

Farmers and fruit growers are hard working men; and the wine grower is perhaps the most hard working of them all. At no time of the year can he be idle. Throughout the warm, wet seasons he must spray against fungoid attacks. He must continuously be on his guard against insect parasites. And on top of all this, he must cultivate his land. There is no set routine: the work to be done depends a great deal on the weather, and the general nature of the work varies widely between one area and another. The care taken in the Mediterranean vineyards to trap every drop of the limited rainfall, for example, would obviously be irrelevant in the north. A full description of all known methods of viticulture would fill a book far longer than this. Suffice it to say that the ground must be tilled to destroy weeds and unwanted shoots. At the same time, this tilling enables the rainfall to penetrate to the deep roots, it augments the humidity, admits air to the soil, helps in the control of insects, and levels the soil around the vines.

Whilst the climate is obviously one of the great factors which governs the wine growers' work, the fundamental approach depends on how the vines are to be trained. Practically no vines used for wine making are grown along walls or up trellises (save in the Minho district of Portugal)—both of which are methods that are very suitable when the grapes are to be eaten as fruit. Instead there are three ways in which vines are commonly cultivated: along wires, up posts, or like bushes, close to the ground. The first of these methods is said to be that of the Romans and is commonly used where the vineyards are fairly flat. The second method is ascribed to the Greeks and is found in precipitous vineyards, like those in the Moselle. The third is really only a variant on the second, and supporting stakes are often used near the vintage time when the vines are heavy with fruit and foliage; it is most common in the Mediterranean countries.

A task which is universal throughout all the vineyards is the pruning, but methods differ substantially from one area to another. Vines are immensely energetic plants. If left to themselves they will grow to be enormous, yielding an immense amount of wood and very little fruit. Moreover, fruit never grows on the same wood for two seasons in succession, so that the wood from one season is cut down to leave only a few buds from which the next season's wood is grown. That is why vineyards which look so green and prolific in summer show nothing but gnarled, dead-looking stumps during the winter. Most vines are grown in conditions that are far from ideal. Around the Mediterranean, vines are immensely strong: they need not be pruned too closely, and their yield is very large. In the north, however, where they yield their most delicate wines, they are less at home. If they are to contend with so un-natural a climate they must be very closely pruned so that all their energy is conserved. Of all the many tasks in the vineyard, it is pruning which calls for the most skill. If badly pruned, the life of a vine is futile and short. If it is well done, the vine will develop to exactly the shape and size which the grower wants, and it will give the finest possible quality of fruit year after year. There is no set routine. Each vine must be examined individually and pruned in accordance with its age, strength and shape. The pruner has to think further than fruit and considers the nature of the wine he wishes to produce. Thus in the sherry vineyards the vines are pruned long if the emphasis is to be on delicate *fino* wines, and short if a higher proportion of *oloroso* is required. The time for pruning varies, too. In the autumn, after the leaves have fallen, the branches still contain nourishment which sinks back into the roots, and the ideal time to prune is in the depth of winter, when there is little of value left in the wood. But if there is a severe frost soon after pruning, the vines may be killed, so in some areas it is delayed until after the optimum time to avoid this hazard, even though nourishment is once more rising from the root and some of it will be lost. If pruning is left too late, however, the vines will 'bleed', and sap will flow out in alarming quantities.

When the grapes are first formed, they are small, hard and acid. Chemically they consist of tannin, chlorophyll, malic acid and tartaric acid, with the merest trace of glucose; in fact, at this time, there is often more sugar in the leaves than in the fruit. That is why, if the leaves are attacked by fungi at an early stage, the grapes never grow sweet and ripen. As the berry grows it draws nourishment from the roots and leaves of the vine and gradually eliminates the chlorophyll and starch; it then becomes soft and is the centre of many chemical reactions, most of which are brought about by photosynthesis. Pectin and sugars accumulate while the acids are gradually eliminated: the first sugar to appear is dextrose, and then laevulose, while practically all the tartaric acid is converted into cream of tartar, and the malic acid is mostly destroyed by oxidation, though some of it reacts with bases derived from the soil. If it should rain for a few days while the grapes are nearly ripe, the proportional sugar content stops rising and may even fall slightly, while the proportion of acids decreases substantially during the rain, then increases, and then begins to fall again. Eventually the berries grow to their full size and receive nothing more from the leaves, but the process of oxidation continues until they are ripe, when the fruit consists essentially of sugar (in the form of both laevulose and dextrose) and tartaric acid, with vitally important traces of other organic compounds. There are also live yeasts on the skin. It is these additional compounds that give each type of grape its characteristic flavour and it is the yeasts in the 'bloom' of the grapes that start the fermentation when the fruit is crushed. The ultimate stage in the development of the grape, when it is over-ripe, is the attack of the fungus *botrytis cinerea*. But this time the attack is a beneficial one, and it only occurs in certain vineyard areas—those producing the finest sweet wines. The skin becomes less firmly attached to the pulp; malic and tartaric acids are reduced, but gluconic acid is created; the grapes shrink, losing water, and the proportional concentration of sugar and flavour goes up. Wines produced from such grapes are very sweet and of tremendous flavour, but the yield is low, and so the price is high. Thus in France it is called *pourriture noble*, or noble rot, and it is this which makes possible the great sweet wines of Sauternes and Barsac, while in Germany it gives the incomparable *beerenauslese* and *trockenbeerenauslese* wines.

31

CHAPTER 2

Pressing and Fermentation

To make wine, the juice must be extracted from the grapes, and it is clear to anyone that there must be two ways of doing it: crushing them beneath a weight or squeezing them in a bag. These were the methods of the earliest wine growers, and they are still the only ones found in European vineyards. It probably needed little experiment to discover, also, that the pressing must be gentle. If it is not, and the stalks and pips are crushed, unpleasant oils enter the wine that quite spoil the flavour; and once there they can never be got rid of.

The simplest method of all is to crush the grapes with the human foot. Ancient Egyptian wall paintings dating as far back as the late fifteenth century B.C. show the grapes being trodden in wooden or stone vats. Men and boys did the work to the rhythm of music, supporting themselves by holding on to straps or a horizontal bar placed above the vat, and the juice flowed out to ferment in separate containers, which were kept in cool cellars and dark buildings where the wine could ferment slowly. In Greece the vats sloped down towards one corner and were generally made of cement, or occasionally of acacia wood. At the start of the vintage, a boy sang the song of Linus, the god of the harvest, to the music of a lyre, surrounded by a circle of children, dancing, shouting and beating the ground with their feet. Until cheap and efficient mechanical presses were devised in the nineteenth century, treading was still the common method throughout the vineyards of Europe. Even today, an ancient Greek wine grower, suddenly finding himself at a remote *quinta* up the Douro during vintage time, would feel perfectly at home[1] though he would feel

[1] Foot pressing is still seen very occasionally in the sherry and burgundy vineyards.

far less at home in the other major vineyards, all of which have become mechanized. This change is comparatively recent, though, and dates from the second half of the last century. When Redding wrote his great book, *A History and Description of Modern Wines* (1833), he described how 'In some parts of France a labourer with sabots treads the grapes out as they come from the vineyard in a square box, having holes in the bottom, placed over a vat' and he went on to describe it as 'a very barbarous method', though one wonders why. He was certainly more favourably disposed towards the screw press, which probably made poorer wine. At least thirty years later boys in tubs were still treading grapes on the Rhine, though mechanical presses were already being used there. In Cyprus there used to be an interesting alternative to treading: the grapes were put on an inclined plane of marble and beaten with mallets.

Treading the grapes by foot is certainly picturesque, but it is also laborious. Both the ancient Greeks and the ancient Egyptians soon brought their ingenuity to bear. They devised methods of making the work easier, and, at the same time, of extracting more juice by exerting a higher pressure. The Greek contribution was the beam press, using the mechanical principle of the lever. A great beam of wood, twenty or thirty feet long, was pivoted at one end between a pair of upright pillars. A strong container for the fruit was built near the pillars, and the beam bore down on a wooden lid which did the crushing. In the earliest presses, the far end of the beam was pulled down by leather straps and the pressure was increased by weighting it with stones. The ultimate development came with the invention of the screw in about 300 B.C. and a screw press is described by Pliny the Elder, who died in the catastrophe at Pompeii in A.D. 79. In this form of the beam press, the weights were replaced by a screw which was rotated by levers. Presses of this kind were used certainly until the nineteenth century in many of the major wine-growing areas, and it would not be at all surprising to find one still in use in some remote spot. Examples may be seen in the wine museums at Beaune and at Villafranca del Panadés in Catalonia.

The next important development was the screw press in which the screw operated directly on to the pressing platform. This invention has also been attributed to the Greeks. In its many variant forms, it was soon established as the principal wine press throughout the world, and it remains so to this day. The usual version consists of a straight-sided barrel with a small gap between each of the staves, which are fastened to the hoops. The lid of the barrel is connected to the screw, and when it is wound down the grapes are crushed and the juice is expelled through the gaps between the staves, which are sufficiently narrow to keep the solid matter in. Many of these presses in use today are over a hundred years old, and older examples are found in all the wine museums, particularly in Rüdesheim, where one can see that until the end of the eighteenth century the screws were wooden, and thereafter they were made of steel. Steel in such applications is quite harmless, as there is very little of it in relation to the quantity of fruit and it only makes contact with the acid fruit juice for a very short time.

The construction of these presses has changed very little in two thousand years, and they are still seen in use in their original form, particularly in Spain. During the technological revolution of the nineteenth century, some were adapted to hydraulic operation, but these often proved too vigorous: the stalks and pips were crushed together with the grapes, and the wine was of very poor quality. Such presses are only useful for extracting the last trace of juice out of the fruit, making wine that can be distilled or sold very cheaply for local drinking, though this criticism does not apply to modern hydraulic presses. A more important variant was turning the whole press on its side, so that the barrel became horizontal and both ends were wound in simultaneously on a screw. This form of press is now the most popular in the white wine areas of France, where it is invariably operated by an electric motor, and the pressing is further improved by arranging a series of chains between the two ends. Through carefully arranged gearing, the pressure exerted can be very gradual and first-class wine is produced. The presses are commonly operated two or three times at their lowest pressure to produce the first pressing of the grape. Between each operation the screws are unwound and the chains effectively rearrange the fruit so that nothing is missed. Finally the full pressure is exerted to give a wine comparable to that from a hydraulic press.

Until the end of the last century, beams and screw presses were

34

often used side by side, the screw presses producing the finer wines and the beam presses being used to extract the last of the juice from the fruit and to produce a cheap and inferior wine after the good wine had been pressed in screw presses or by foot.

While Greeks employed the lever and the screw, the Egyptians discovered an alternative solution: they used torsion, and extracted the juice by wringing the grapes in a bag made of cloth or plaited matting. Either end of the bag was attached to a strong rod which was rotated by the workers. This was almost certainly the first kind of press to make use of a mechanical principle. It was invented at the very beginning of Egyptian history (3000 B.C.) and by the Third Dynasty (2700 B.C.) it existed in a more sophisticated form in which the bag was slung horizontally between uprights against which the poles revolved. In another form the bag was vertical with the lower end fixed and the upper end attached to a horizontal lever. This principle is still employed and the *pie*[1] method of pressing, as used in Jerez, is directly descended from it.

Of all the presses available at the present time, the modern German pneumatic machines are universally acknowledged to be the best for making the highest quality wines in vineyards of moderate size, and they are gradually being installed throughout Europe. This form of press consists of a horizontal stainless steel cylinder in the centre of which is a strong rubber bag. The cylinder is filled with grapes and then the bag is blown up by air pressure, squeezing the grapes against the side. After a while the pressure is released and the cylinder is rotated rapidly, which rearranges the fruit so that a further pressing can be performed. This process is repeated several times until no juice is left, and the soft, resilient nature of the rubber bag prevents any pips or stems from being accidentally crushed. At last the engineers have invented a practical alternative to the human foot.

Finally there is the simplest method of all—to allow the grapes to be crushed beneath their own weight. Very little juice, of course, can be extracted in this way, but it comes from the ripest fruit and it is as rich as can be in sugar. The Greeks called it *prodomos* or *protopos*, and valued it very highly, as it could be kept for longer than their other wines. One modern wine is still made by this method: the fabulous tokay essence. Hand picked berries are

[1] See p.388.

35

stored in small tubs and a minute proportion of their juice collects
in the bottom, giving a remarkably rich wine which only very rich
people can afford to buy; and even they are lucky if they can find
any. A similar method is also traditionally used for the preparation
of the sweeter form of Malaga wine called *lágrima*, though little if
any of the wine sold under this name is so made today. But to give
a good wine, the grapes must be of a suitable variety and very ripe
with a sufficient weight to assist the extraction by what amounts
to a gentle pressing; for in contrast to tokay essence, the must
that runs from the presses in red wine vineyards before the press
is commenced is found to give a very inferior and short-lived wine,
lacking in tannin; called *vin de goutte*, it is generally given away
to the workers.

As far as wine is concerned, the most important thing in grape
juice is sugar, for it is this which ferments to give alcohol. Natural
grape sugar consists of roughly equal amounts of glucose and
fructose. Each is chemically similar, having the formula $C_6H_{12}O_6$,
and the difference between them is a matter of structure: the
configuration of the atoms within the molecule. This difference,
however, can be forgotten, as both sugars ferment in exactly the
same way. In 1810 the French chemist Gay-Lussac summed up
the chemical change that takes place during fermentation by the
simple formula:

$$C_6H_{12}O_6 \rightarrow 2C_2H_5OH + 2CO_2$$

In other words, each molecule of sugar splits up to give two
molecules of alcohol and two molecules of carbon dioxide gas.
That is as much as readers of this book are likely to want to know.
It is, however, a far cry from the whole story, which is still not
fully understood. The fermentation is brought about by yeasts, or,
more accurately, by the ferments that are contained within them.
The air of a vineyard is laden with yeasts, and they collect in vast
numbers on the grape skins to give them their natural 'bloom'.
Of all the many varieties, two are of outstanding importance:
saccharomyces apiculatus, or 'wild yeast'; and *saccharomyces
cerevisiae* variety *ellipsoideus*, usually abbreviated to *saccharomyces
ellipsoideus*, or 'wine yeast'. The former greatly outnumber the
latter, and it is the wild yeasts which start the fermentation; but
they are comparatively weakly things and when the alcohol rises to

about four per cent they are overcome and die. It is then that the wine yeasts take over. Once they get going, the fermentation is very vigorous, but when the alcohol rises to about twelve per cent they slow down, and at about sixteen per cent they, too, die. In many musts there is not enough sugar to give anything like this strength of alcohol, and these ferment straight out to give completely dry wines. Sweet white grapes which are left on the vines until they get the 'noble rot' and are full of sugar, as in Sauternes and Germany, or which are shrivelled in the sun as they lie on mats, as in Spain, give musts which still have plenty of sugar left when the yeasts are killed; and it is these that give the great natural sweet white wines. Sweet wines can also be made artificially by deliberately killing the yeasts with an addition of alcohol before the sugar has fermented away, as in the Spanish *mistelas*. Or the yeasts may be killed by heating or filtration to make the German 'sweet reserves'.

On the other hand, there is often a shortage of sugar so that the wine is thin and deficient in alcohol even when it has completely fermented out. The remedy is to add a little pure cane sugar to the must at the beginning of the fermentation, when it behaves exactly as if it were derived directly from the grape, and the deficiency is made up. The amount required can easily be calculated once sugar already in the must has been estimated; and this can be done in a few seconds using a hydrometer. Just occasionally one feels that a little too much is used, producing a wine that is unnaturally alcoholic in relation to its flavour, but this is the exception rather than the rule. Generally it serves to give thoroughly drinkable wines in years which would otherwise yield wines too thin to be pleasant. The process is practised in many districts and is known as *sucrage*, or *chaptalization*, after the remarkable French-man Comte Jean-Antoine Chaptal de Chanteloup, who became Minister of the Interior and president of the Academy of Science. He was one of the first to investigate wine scientifically but he did not in fact invent the process which bears his name. It was described by Macquer in 1776, and it was not until 1800 that Count Chaptal gave it his blessing; but it was under his patronage that it became established as a boon to wine growers.

The wild yeasts are merely a nuisance: they delay the fermenta-tion that really matters and it is said that they sometimes work

37

perversely to give the wine a false flavour. This hazard naturally displeases the wine growers, and chemists set to work to do something about it, particularly in Germany, where the wines are so delicate. The easiest remedy, and one that is almost universally adopted, is partially to sterilize the must by adding a small and carefully regulated dose of sulphur dioxide, which kills the delicate wild yeasts and leaves the wine yeasts free to do their work. It also kills many undesirable bacteria and moulds, but the grower has to be careful not to use too much as this can give the wine a positively infernal taste—much worse than the wild yeasts. In some districts this is carried a stage further by artificially cultivating the desirable wine yeasts and injecting them into the must. In the extreme form of this treatment, the must is completely sterilized as soon as the grapes are pressed and the fermentation is then started using nothing but artificially cultivated yeasts. Wine is made by this method on a commercial scale in the U.S.A., but it has so far only been tried experimentally in Europe.

It is the ferments or enzymes within the yeasts that do the actual work inside the fermentation vats. These enzymes are extraordinary and fascinating things. They are highly complex proteins that act in specific ways to bring about various chemical changes. Their activities are by no means confined to wine: they are found throughout nature; they perform vital functions in our bodies; and when isolated they are used industrially to effect chemical syntheses. There is an enormous number of them and many more will be discovered in the future. They all have two features in common, however: they will each bring about one, often very complicated, chemical change—and only one; and they each require a co-enzyme to be present with them if they are to work. Nowhere in industry are the restrictive practices so perfectly organized.

Gay-Lussac's simple equation gives, in broad outline, what happens when the must ferments, but its over-simplification falls laughably short of the truth. Amerine and Cruess[1] list twelve different reactions, and the most common by-products are glycerol, lactic acid and acetaldehyde. There is no shortage of

[1] See *The Technology of Wine Making* by M. A. Amerine, Ph.D. and W. V. Cruess, Ph.D., Connecticut, 1960. A somewhat simpler and very lucid account is given by A. Massel, *Applied Wine Chemistry & Technology*, London, 1969.

ferments in the wine yeasts, and every one of these reactions is brought about by a different one. The wine produced at the end, however, is the direct product of the fruit that gives the must. The flavour ultimately depends on this and this alone: the precise strain of the wine yeast makes very little difference. It would be idle, for instance, to ferment the must from Burgundian Pinot Blanc grapes using yeasts obtained from Spanish Palomino grapes in the hope of making sherry. The wine would taste quite different. In fact it would still be a kind of white burgundy.

Sometimes after the fermentation, even as much as two years later, an additional malo-lactic fermentation may take place, which is brought about by the *Bacterium gracile* and results in malic acid in the wine being converted into weaker lactic acid, with the evolution of carbon dioxide. It is this that helps to give the *spritzig* quality, which is so admired when it happens to young moselles in bottle. When it happens in cask, the carbon dioxide goes harmlessly away, but when it happens to red wines in bottle it gives a *pétillance* that can be objectionable; but provided not too much carbon dioxide is evolved it generally disperses and the wine tastes all right again after a time.

Chemistry can satisfy one's curiosity by helping to explain fermentation, and chemists can help wine growers to avoid making mistakes, but the flavour of the wine still rests upon the whims of nature: on the soil, the climate, and the vine.

Red Wines

Red wines derive their colour from pigments contained in the skins of black grapes, and the must is therefore fermented in contact with the skins. White wines can, of course, be made from black grapes—champagne is an example—but for this to be achieved, the must is separated from the skins immediately on pressing. As red wines are made throughout the European vineyards, it goes without saying that there are variations in technique from country to country and from district to district. There are even very substantial differences between neighbouring growers in the same district. The surprising thing is that there are not more. The timing of the various stages of the fermentation varies widely; different styles of presses and fermentation vats are used; some growers leave as much as possible to nature, whilst others employ the aid of science by using cultivated yeasts and by careful control of the temperature during the fermentation; but the striking thing is the similarity of the methods used in vineyards that are geographically far apart and which produce wines having totally different flavours. So a general description will suffice as an introduction for the whole of Europe. There is only one exception: the Douro. But port wine has always been a law unto itself, and nothing written in this section applies to it.

When the ripe fruit is brought in from the vineyard to the winery[1] the first task is to separate the grapes from the stalks. This is the *égrappage* and the simplest (but by far the most laborious) way of doing it is by hand, when the bunches of grapes are rubbed over a sieve which allows the fruit to fall through but which keeps the stalks on the outside. This may still be seen in some of the more traditional and conservative vineyards. Small peasant growers put the grapes in a tub and stir them with a wooden trident that looks like the legs of a stool attached to a pole. By the second half of the nineteenth century, simple but effective machines were available in which the grapes were put into an open-bottomed trough which was attached to a cage. Inside the cage there was a stirrer worked by a handle. This pushed the grapes through the cage but kept the stalks inside, and these were eventually expelled through a separate orifice at the end. Modern machines still work on the same principle but are electrically operated.

The separated grapes next have to be crushed. Perhaps it would be be better to say 'mashed', as the crushing is far from complete, and wine presses are not used at this stage. The traditional method was to give them a light pressing by foot, and this may still be done by some isolated growers, but the use of some form of grape mill, or hopper, is now practically universal. The simplest form of this device consists of two toothed rollers, looking like very elongated cog wheels, and geared so as to rotate in contrary

---

[1] The English term seems depressingly inelegant. In French it is the *cuvier* or *cuverie*, in German the *gärkeller*, in Italy the *tinaïa*, in Spanish the *cocedero*, and in Portuguese the *adega*. All these words cover the relevant part of the winery. 'Winery' itself is translated *cave de vinificacion, gärkeller, cantina di elaborazione, bodega,* and *adega* respectively. For reasons of space, equivalents in other languages will no longer be given but may be ascertained from *Lexique de la Vigne et du Vin* (O.I.V., Paris, 1963).

directions. The rollers were originally made of wood, but are now made of stainless steel or bronze, which is resistant to the acids in the fruit and is perfectly satisfactory. The two rollers are, however, not in close mesh but are adjusted so that there is a gap between them which is wide enough for the partially crushed fruit to fall through. Like the *égrappoirs*, they are now also generally operated by electricity.

For a grower operating on a fairly small scale, these machines are all that is necessary, and they are all that will be found in many of the greatest vineyards. The grape mill is placed over the fermenting vat, the handle is turned or the motor switched on, and nothing else is called for at this stage. Such methods, however, would obviously be uneconomic in the vast vineyards that make cheap wine, or in co-operatives where wine is made in large quantities for many small growers. In such places some degree of mechanization is essential not only to ensure that the wine is made economically but also to ensure that it is made well. Unless an enormous labour force were employed, each team of men dealing with a small quantity of grapes, there would be far too much delay in getting the fruit inside the fermenting vats and the wine would suffer. Traditionalists always shudder at seeing machinery of any kind in a vineyard, but there is no harm in it provided it is properly designed. And it usually is.

When red wine is being made in larger quantities one of the modern machines is employed which remove the stalks and crush the grapes in one operation and which are, of course, electrically operated.[1] The principle on which they work is identical with that described above. The mash of juice, skins and partially crushed grapes from these machines is sometimes pumped straight into the fermentation vats through a corrosion-resistant pipe and sometimes it is carried up on a conveyor belt.

Very soon after the crushing, on the way to the vat or immediately after it gets there, the mash is mixed with a small dosage of sulphur dioxide to prevent the fermentation from being started by the wild yeasts. This is carefully controlled so that the wine yeasts are not affected, but the exact amount used varies from year to year. It is increased if the grapes have been suffering from mildew or if the temperature at the time of the vintage is exceptionally

[1] In French this type of machine is known as a *fouloir-égrappoir*.

41

high. Conversely it is reduced if the weather is cold. After this treatment some growers leave the rest to nature; others add an appropriate quantity of cultivated wine yeasts. The fermentation vats themselves vary a great deal in size and in the materials used. The traditional material is wood, and this is still used to a very large extent, but some vats are made of concrete, of stone, of plastic, or of metal that has been treated with a specially resistant form of enamel. Best of all (and most expensive) is stainless steel. All of these work perfectly well, but wooden or stainless steel vats are used for nearly all the finest wines. Some growers have presumed to attempt fermentation in plain metal vats, but the less said the better. In size, they may be very small; peasant growers make excellent wines in ordinary casks. There does, however, seem to be an upper limit, which is about six to seven thousand gallons. Above this it is very difficult to control the rate of fermentation and it may get out of hand. Most of the vats are a good deal smaller, and in the great wine districts they generally hold a thousand gallons or so.

The time that the must is left in the vats in contact with the skins varies a great deal, and just how long this should be is hotly disputed. The shortest time is about four days and the longest about three weeks. The amount of time spent in the vat has a profound effect on the style of the wine that is produced: if it is long, the wine absorbs a great deal of colouring and tannin, so that it takes several years to mature in the bottle before it is fit to drink; and the opposite applies if the time is short. The latter course is obviously the more attractive commercially, but it has incurred the wrath of many old wine drinkers who believe that wines which mature quickly will not live for so long, and that occasional greatness is being sacrificed to consistent mediocrity. They may or may not be right; wines have not been made in this way long enough for us to be sure.

The fermentation vats are not filled to the brim, but a gap is left equal to about twenty per cent of their capacity. This is necessary as the heat developed during the fermentation causes the must to expand, whilst the carbon dioxide makes it froth vigorously and a deep strong layer of grape skins, pips and similar residue is formed on the top. The temperature of the fermentation is all important. If it rises to 95° F. the yeasts are seriously weakened. If it rises a few more degrees they are killed and the vat is said to 'stick'. It can be started again, once it has cooled down, by adding fresh yeast, but a really good wine will never result. To avoid this disaster, the temperature should not be allowed to rise to above 85° F., and it should preferably be a few degrees lower. In hot climates this means that the vats may have to be cooled, even when they are housed in tall, cool buildings. As far north as in Burgundy, for example, the fermentation can easily get out of control, and devices resembling radiators are kept handy in case there is any sign of this happening. They are made of bronze or stainless steel, and when necessary they are lowered into the vats and cold water is passed through them to take away the excessive heat. As an alternative, some *cuviers* have cooling radiators outside the vats, and the must is pumped through them. On the other hand, if the weather is too cold it is hard to get the fermentation going at all, as wine yeasts do not work at below about 40° F. If this happens it is usual to take a proportion of the must out of the vat, to warm it, and then to put it back. Alternatively, warm water may be passed through the cooling radiators, and in exceptionally cold weather the whole building is warmed. When stainless steel vats are used they can be cooled by running cold water over the outside. Once the fermentation does start there is normally no more trouble owing to the heat that is given off.

The cap which forms at the top of the vat includes most of the grape skins whose presence within the wine is so essential, and if left to itself the cap becomes so solid and so separate that little intermingling occurs. It must regularly be pushed back into the wine and this is usually done by men using wooden poles with trident or similar ends. Owing to the depth and toughness of the cap, and to the fact that it is buoyed up by the continually rising carbon dioxide gas, this is extremely hard work, and an alternative is for the men to tread on the cap as if they were crushing the grapes. In large vats it will almost bear their weight, but not quite, and they keep themselves afloat by holding on to a support. There are easier ways of overcoming this difficulty, and they would doubtless be used universally if they gave equally good results; but unfortunately they do not. One method is to pump some of the fermenting must out of the bottom of the vat and to spray it over the top. This also cools the must: an advantage in some districts. Another is to install a grid at a carefully chosen depth within the cask. The grid is sufficiently open to allow the gas to escape but sufficiently closely meshed to keep the cap down, so that it is completely immersed in the wine. It does not, however, mix with the wine to the same extent as if it were agitated, and it has been found that the open surface of the wine is liable to be infected by disease-bearing yeasts and bacteria.

After the must has been in contact with the skins for long enough, it is run off and the last of the fermentation is completed in another vat. The *marc*[1] or residue, is then passed to the wine presses where it is finally crushed to remove the remainder of the juice. This is done in two stages: in the first it is pressed lightly and the resultant wine, which is rich in flavouring and tannin, is generally mixed with that drawn from the fermentation vat. The second pressing is conducted far more vigorously, so that as much juice as possible is extracted, but it is of such inferior quality that it can only be used for making coarse wine or for distillation to give the famous *Eau de Vie de Marc* or *Grappa*. Any of the presses already described may be used for this, though the final stage is usually accomplished by means of a very strong mechanical or hydraulic press.

After a period of time, which varies considerably from one district to another, the new wine is racked off the lees into the casks in which it will be left to mature. It is essential that these casks are full to the bung, to avoid attack from hostile bacteria and fungi; and the cellar where the wine matures should be cool and safe from any atmospheric extremes. The wine is generally allowed to mature between one and three years in the wood before being bottled, but in some districts the period is much longer, and everywhere it necessarily depends on the style of the vintage and when the bottler thinks it is ready.

Very recently an entirely new method of making red wine has come into use in France; it originated in the Rhône valley and is also used by the renowned firm of Sichel & Co. in their *Cave de Vinification* at St. Maixant, and by one or two other growers in the lesser areas of Bordeaux making wines for early consumption. In such areas the old method (even if the must was not left long in

[1] American growers use the term *pomace*.

44

contact with the skins) tended to give over-tannic wines that took too long to mature and which frankly were not worth waiting for. To overcome this the method of *maceration carbonique* was invented. The whole bunches of grapes, stalks and all, are put into the vat in an atmosphere of carbon dioxide. A slow fermentation begins and after three or four days, when it is far from complete, the grapes are pressed and the must is fermented out of contact both of the stalks and skins. The wine that results has no pretentions to greatness but it is good, fruity and soft, so that it can be drunk with pleasure after only a few months. It is also light in colour. If a heavier and darker wine is required (especially for the export markets) the new system can to some extent be combined with the old by letting the must have some contact with the skins and stalks.

There is endless controversy as to whether wine should be bottled at its place of origin or exported in bulk, and there is much to be said on either side. Château or domaine bottling may be a guarantee of authenticity, and on the whole wines bottled where they are grown travel better, but some growers do not seem to understand bottling at all, while British merchants have had years of experience at it and do it very well. There is no hard and fast rule.

White Wines

It is a common fallacy to believe that all white wines are made from white grapes. Most, in fact, are; and these are sometimes called *blancs de blancs*; but others are made from black grapes and are described as *blancs de rouges*. The colouring matter in black grapes is derived from cells just beneath the skin and most of them, if they are pressed gently and swiftly, give a must that contains practically no pigment. A great deal of white wine is made in this way, notably champagne, which is a blend of *blancs de blancs* and *blancs de rouges*.

In making a *blanc de rouges*, speed is essential. If the must is left in contact with the grape skins for any length of time it will absorb some of the colouring matter and will become pink. As soon as the grapes are brought in from the vineyard, they are pitched into a rectangular wooden container, so that the must that seeps out of them, owing to their ripeness and the bruising they suffer in transit, can be collected and run off into a vat right away. It is surprising to see what a large volume of must, known as *moût de goutte*, is collected in this way. Each container holds enough grapes to charge the press, and the pressing is done with a minimum of delay. In many districts the fruit is not separated from the stalks. If the pressing is sufficiently gentle, very little wood tannin is absorbed; and a little is beneficial as the wine gets no chance to absorb tannin from the skins. Moreover, the stalks help to separate the bunches and the presence of something solid makes the pressing easier. Particularly when very large presses are used, *drains assécheurs* are put in with the fruit. These consist of troughs in the shape of a double V and, apart from providing something solid in the midst of the slippery pulp, they give the juice somewhere to collect and help it to leave the press more rapidly. Any of the presses already described may be used, though the German pneumatic presses are rapidly gaining favour, particularly for very high quality wines. Hydraulic presses are also widely used and these are sometimes of enormous size. Large presses are generally found to give the best result, as the pressure is more evenly distributed. Particularly fine examples may be found in Champagne, many of which date from the last century. In Bordeaux and Burgundy, on the other hand, horizontal screw presses are often used, especially in those vineyards where red wines are also made.

There are usually several pressings: often as many as five, and in between each pressing the marc is disturbed so that none of the fruit is missed. In the horizontal screw presses, this is done automatically by the chains, and in the German pneumatic presses it is achieved by rapid rotation after the pressure has been released. When the older kinds of press are used, however, it is common to unload the press and to load it up again, especially when white grapes are being pressed. With black grapes this would tend to encourage the absorption of colouring matter. The first two or three pressings, which are very light, give must of the highest quality. This *moût de presse* is mixed with the *moût de goutte* and used for making the finest wine—*vin de goutte*.[1] The must from the remaining pressings, which are far harder, is fermented separately to provide an inferior wine—*les suites*. The later pressings from

[1] cf. p. 36. The term therefore can mean quite different things, depending on whether it refers to red or white wines.

black grapes are pinkish. They can either be used for making *vin rosé* or, very occasionally, are discoloured by being passed through carbon filters: this process is of academic importance to the writers of textbooks rather than of practical value to wine growers.

White wines are by nature more delicate than reds: they are more prone to disease and to infection by hostile bacteria. The must is accordingly sulphured immediately after the pressing and approximately twice as much sulphur dioxide is used as when making red wines. Sometimes it is obvious that far too much has been used, and the unpleasant taste that results is only too familiar to wine drinkers.

What happens next depends very much on the quantity of sulphur dioxide that has been used. If the dosage has been very small, with a view only to killing off the wild yeasts, the fermentation will be delayed but not prevented. This delay is valuable, as it enables the must to accumulate for a time in a tall vat. It is generally left there overnight, and by morning much of the solid matter will have fallen as sediment. The clear must can then be run off into smaller casks for fermentation. The size of cask used varies, of course, from place to place, but they are invariably much smaller than those used for the fermentation of red wines, and they often hold no more than fifty or a hundred gallons, though casks containing as much as five hundred gallons are found in some districts. This ensures that the fermentation proceeds slowly, which is essential if a good quality white wine is to be produced. In larger casks there is too great a tendency for the temperature to rise. For the same reason the cellar or building in which the fermentation takes place is kept as cool as possible, especially in Germany, where a very slow fermentation is essential if the wine is to retain in solution a little of the carbon dioxide gas that is evolved. This helps to retain in some moselles their *spritzig* characteristic that tickles the palate so delightfully, and a smaller amount of gas dissolved in hock—a third or a quarter of the quantity—gives it a freshness that is much sought after. Moreover, a very slow fermentation results in the yeasts being less enthusiastic to convert the last traces of sugar into alcohol so that a softer wine is produced even when the initial concentration of sugar has not been particularly high.

When the sulphuring has been extensive enough to kill off all

47

the yeasts, it is, of course, necessary to seed the must with cultured yeasts for the fermentation to take place, and in extreme cases some of the sulphur has to be removed before this is done. It is achieved by thoroughly aerating the must, when the air that is bubbled through—in theory, at least—takes away the dissolved sulphur dioxide. One looks somewhat askance at this method and it is generally used only for making the cheaper beverage wines, particularly in hot climates such as in the south of France, where the danger of the wine 'going wrong' is greater.

Ten or fifteen years ago another method of achieving a slow fermentation became quite popular. The must was fermented in sealed vats, in which a high pressure of carbon dioxide was built up which inhibited the action of the yeasts. At first this method seemed very promising, but it was not a great success and better results have been achieved by using small casks in cool cellars. It has now more or less died out.

Pink Wines

Pink wine—*vin rosé* or *vin gris*—is a popular drink throughout the world, especially in summer when it is so refreshing, slightly chilled, with a salad, or drunk by the litre in a pavement café. A few pink wines are of considerable quality and character, but most of them are from the humbler areas, or afterthoughts from the greater ones. The best are made from black grapes, the skins of which have been allowed to remain in contact with the fermenting must for a limited time so that just a little of the colouring matter has been absorbed. There are, of course, variations and the wine may be made by the white wine method but using black grapes of a variety which gives slightly coloured must. Sometimes pink and red wines are made from the same pressing, the must intended for the former being run off first. Or the musts separately pressed from red and white wine grapes may be mixed before fermentation, as is done in Valdepeñas. The difference between a *vin gris* and a *vin rosé* is that the former will have been made as if it were a white wine, so that only a very slight coloration from the must or from the skins might be expected, whereas in the latter the coloration is deliberate and results from the fermentation of the must in contact with the skins, the degree of colour being in proportion to the time of contact.

That, at any rate, is how *vin rosé* ought to be made. Sometimes, alas, it is far from the truth. Very cheap beverage pink wines are undoubtedly blended in France by wholesale merchants using a mixture of red and white wines. And one has also heard terrifying references to cochineal. But the finest *vins rosés* are excellent wines in their own right; and they are not particularly cheap. The best of these wines are not the afterthoughts of the great red wine districts, but rather the products of areas which specialize in them, such as Tavel and Anjou.

There is also a style of wine, intermediate between pink and red, known as *vin de café*. This is a comparative newcomer and dates only from the 1920s. It is grown principally around Montpelier and its purpose, as its rather odd name suggests, is to produce a light style of red wine that is popular in some of the French cafés. The vinification is much the same as that of red wines, but the *cuvage* only lasts from between twelve and twenty-four hours; hence these wines are often known as *vins de 24 heures* or *vins d'une nuit*.

Sparkling Wines

To make a wine that sparkles is one of the easiest things in the world: to make a really good sparkling wine is one of the most difficult and one of the most expensive. The sparkle in wine, just like that of soda water, comes from bubbles of dissolved carbon dioxide gas, and carbon dioxide is, of course, one of the natural products of fermentation. To get a wine that sparkles, therefore, it is only necessary to bottle it before the fermentation is complete. Unless the bottle explodes or the cork blows out, a sparkling wine will result. The phenomenon was well known to Our Lord:

'Neither do men put new wine into old bottles; else the bottles break and the wine runneth out, and the bottles perish: but they put new wine into new bottles: and both are preserved.'

St. Matthew: Ch. 9, v. 17.

Bottles as we know them did not exist in New Testament days, and the Revised Version prefers to translate 'bottles' as 'wine-skins'. This is almost certainly correct, as skins were used by Mediterranean peasants to transport wine until quite recent times, and specimens may be seen in the wine museum at Villafranca del

Panadés. If the skin were tightly sealed it would need real flexibility to withstand the pressure of gas.

Effervescent wines, frothing in their first fermentation, have presumably been drunk ever since wine has been known. In some districts they are still local specialities sold in the bars—sweetish, sparkling, peculiar, rather enchanting, and highly laxative—but quite unsuitable for anything other than local drinking. It was no mere chance that the earliest known sparkling wines that were bottled came from the comparatively cold wine-growing regions in the north of France, as winter temperatures would inhibit the action of the ferments, and if this happened before the fermentation was complete it would start again in the warm spring weather. The invention of the greatest of all sparkling wines—champagne—is often credited to Dom Pérignon, the immortal cellarer of the Abbey of Hautvillers, though he in fact perfected the wine rather than invented it. Sparkling *vin gris* from Champagne was drunk in London during the 1660s and credit must be given to the English vintners who were amongst the earliest to use corks and who evidently contrived to put them in the bottles at exactly the right time: when the fermentation was dormant and about to start again. Sparkling wines are still made by this method. They are cheap and some of them are quite enjoyable. Unlike the many wines that set out to imitate champagne, they do at least have the virtue that they are individualists. The champagne process produces an overtone of its own flavour which mingles with that of the wine; and the combination is only quite perfect in the genuine article. Wines that are bottled before the fermentation is complete, on the other hand, retain their own flavours more or less intact and do not conform to any particular style.

The *méthode champenoise* is the one used for making the finest and most expensive sparkling wines throughout the world. It is complicated and it takes a long time. It is therefore necessarily expensive. But it is well worth while. After the must is fully fermented a blend is made by selecting wines from various areas and sometimes also of various vintages, so that each makes up the deficiencies and excesses of the others to give a final blend, or *cuvée*, of exactly the style which the shipper requires. The *cuvée* is bottled generally during the late spring or early summer following the vintage, and a second fermentation in bottle is provoked by adding a dose of syrup, called *liqueur de tirage*. This consists of sugar dissolved in wine to which a cultured yeast of the finest strain has been added. These cultured yeasts have been a great blessing. Before they became available, the second fermentation was haphazard, depending on what ferments remained in the bottle and in the added wines. The cultured yeasts are entirely natural, being simply the champagne yeasts that have been grown for their own sake, and their use makes certain what before was only probable. The dosage of sugar used depends on the pressure of gas that is required. At a cellar temperature of 50° F., four grams of sugar fermented in a bottle results in a pressure of one atmosphere, and the usual pressure required varies between five and six atmospheres. If there is any natural sugar in the *cuvée*, proportionately less is added.

As soon as the dosage has been added, the *cuvée* is bottled and the bottles are tightly sealed either with a large cork held in place by a metal *agrafe* or else with a plastic stopper held in place by a crown cap. This method, which works just as well as the old one and which is much cheaper, was invented in Germany when corks were scarce during the Hitler war, and is now used by a great many of the greatest champagne shippers. It is easy to see whether a crown cap or a cork has been used by looking at the top of the bottle. If it has a lip like a beer bottle, then it has been sealed by a crown cap.

This second fermentation takes two or three months, but the bottles are left, binned horizontally, for a much longer time. Even the cheapest sparkling wine should be left for at least a year in bottle, and the best champagne needs four years or more. Fermentation produces a deposit, and this is no exception. That formed in champagne bottles is very fine, consisting largely of dead yeast cells, and such a deposit in a crystal clear sparkling wine would be utterly inappropriate. But, being so fine, it is frightfully hard to get rid of. It tends to remain suspended in the wine and will not fall to the bottom of its own accord, like the heavier deposit of a normal table wine. The classic way to get rid of it is the method of *remuage*, with the bottles held in *pupitres*; and this method, despite its expense, is still almost universally used. The *pupitres* consist of two wooden rectangles, joined together so as to form an inverted V, with the open end on the ground. Each rectangle is pierced with holes of a suitable shape to hold the neck of a heavy champagne bottle, and the bottles are at first inserted in an almost horizontal position. The *remueur* then walks along the rows of *pupitres* taking a bottle in each hand, shaking them vigorously, and moving them into a more vertical position. A good workman can do this to thirty or forty thousand bottles a day. At the end of several weeks the bottles are vertical, neck downwards, with all the deposit collected as a compact little cylinder next to the cork.

The bottles are then stored vertically, upside down, pending the final stage of *dégorgement*. Until a few years ago, this latter process was extremely tricky and called for great skill. It is not easy even today. The old method was to hold the bottle vertically upside down and to withdraw the cork slowly, using pincers. As soon as the *dégorgeur* felt that the cork was about to leave the bottle, he quickly turned it upwards, when the cork, together with the cylinder of sediment, was shot out by the pressure of the gas. Such a process is obviously impossible if crown stoppers are used, and it was somewhat hazardous at the best of times. Nowadays the neck of the bottle is frozen in a freezing mixture and the deposit is neatly removed in the middle of a little cylinder of ice.

The classic method of *remuage* is obviously time consuming and expensive, so it is not surprising that those who make sparkling wines—especially the cheaper kinds—have found an easier alternative, and one that works quite well. It originated in Germany and is known as the transfer system. After the second fermentation, which still takes place in bottles, the wine is emptied into a tank. This is achieved by means of a special apparatus which maintains the pressure practically intact. From the tanks, the wine is filtered, still under pressure, and re-bottled.

Finally comes the *dosage*. After the deposit has been removed a small dose of *liqueur* is added to each bottle before it is recorked. The formula of this is a closely guarded secret of each house, but it consists mostly of sugar dissolved in wine, and sometimes a little brandy is included. The wine is then kept for another six months or so before it can be sold, so that the wine and liqueur can 'marry'.

The whole champagne process is an extremely expensive one, and it hardly seems justified unless a high quality wine is to be made. For cheaper wines there are two other methods, and the first of these gives a product that is very similar to a wine made in the classic way. It is called the method of *cuves-closes*, otherwise known as the Charmat, Chaussepied, or tank method. It consists of arranging the second fermentation in large enamelled metal containers. The wine is often pasteurized to destroy any natural ferments that remain before it is run into the pressure tanks. A cultivated yeast is used, and the tanks are equipped with internal mixers to ensure an even distribution. The deposit, which collects near the bottom, is easily filtered out and the wine is bottled under pressure into bottles which have previously received their dosage. The process is not so very far removed from the traditional one, save in the size of the containers for the second fermentation, and if the *cuvée* is good, an excellent wine can be made. What difference there is probably results, for the most part, from leaving the wine in contact with the yeast for a far shorter period. It is this contact which helps to develop the characteristic flavour that all *méthode champenoise* wines have in common.

A form of slightly sparkling wine known as *perlwein* is extremely popular in Luxembourg and is becoming increasingly popular in Germany. To make wine of this kind the initial fermentation in tanks is allowed to proceed until most but not all of the sugar has been used up, and the temperature is then drastically lowered so that the fermentation only proceeds very slowly. The carbon dioxide that is produced is absorbed in the wine which is then filtered under pressure and bottled, leaving the wine slightly effervescent but only with a small pressure, so that a champagne cork and wiring is not called for. This method gives sparkling wine even more cheaply than by the *cuves closes* and very pleasant wine it is, too, though not pretending to compete with wines made by the *méthode champenoise*.

Finally there is the impregnation method, which consists simply in taking a cheap white wine and aerating it with carbon dioxide. Other writers in the past had the awful vision of taking a bottle of bad graves and putting it in a Sparklets syphon. A friend of mine once did it at a party when the champagne gave out at midnight, and he assures me that no one noticed, but happily I was not there. Now the nightmare has become a reality, and it is practised on a substantial commercial scale; but not, of course, in Champagne. A fairly alcoholic white wine is used, and after it has been cooled to a low temperature, carbon dioxide is forced in under fairly low pressure. It is then bottled, still under pressure, and when it thaws out it is suitably effervescent. All it requires is an attractive label and a pretty name, and it can be sold to the ignorant at a great profit to its manufacturer. Once it has been poured into the glass, however, the sparkle rapidly disappears. In wines made by the *méthode champenoise* some of the carbon dioxide is combined chemically with the alcohol to give an unstable compound called *ethyl pyrocarbonate*, which decomposes gradually so that the sparkle lasts a long time in the glass—longer than it takes to drink the wine—but this compound is absent from wines which have been impregnated.

Diseases of Wine

Like all living things, wine is vulnerable. It is liable at any time to be attacked by bacteria, and the danger is increased if it is ill-balanced or deficient in any characteristic—in alcohol, acid, or tannin. If the wine is perfectly made and then carefully stored in ideal conditions, it will never be infected. But that is a counsel of perfection that cannot be achieved. Bad weather gives bad fruit and this in turn gives an unbalanced must that is liable to attack. Nothing will prevent people from being careless occasionally. Sometimes the infection will appear mysteriously and unexpectedly, as it does in a healthy person. So the wine grower needs to be continuously on his guard. Things now are easier than they have ever been in the past, though. Enological research has provided remedies for most of the defects. Even peasants have overcome their distrust and take samples of their ailing wine for analysis. This has resulted in nothing but good. Admittedly, scientific treatment can produce no wine finer than the great wines that nature, unaided, has given us in the past; and such wines still need no aid. But it can, and does, help to do away with those manifestly inadequate and defective wines which have so often hitherto insulted palates.

Of all the many diseases brought about by harmful yeasts and bacteria, the most dramatic (though by no means the most common) is acetification—when the wine turns to vinegar. This is the work of the *mycoderma aceti*, which oxidizes the alcohol to form acetic acid:

$$C_2H_5OH + 2[O] \rightarrow CH_3COOH + H_2O$$

The first sign of this is that the wine becomes 'pricked' or *piqué*, and has an unpleasant touch of vinegar about it. If it is caught early at this stage it is not a total loss. The wine can be disinfected with sulphur dioxide or sterilized by pasteurization, and the progress of the disease will be halted. But the acetic acid will still be there. The remedy is to neutralize it with an alkali such as calcium carbonate. When wine was drawn from the wood, before bottling became common in the eighteenth century, this catastrophe was an everyday experience of English vintners, and the old books are full of explanations and remedies, some of which were bizarre. When Walter Charleton wrote his *Two Discourses* in 1692, he suggested as causes of acidity:

'Among the External are commonly reckoned . . . immoderate Heat, Thunder or the report of Cannons, and the admixture of any exotick body, which will not symbolize or agree . . . especially the flesh of Vipers. . . .'

He also quite rightly pointed out that lack of alcohol made infection more likely, but he rather alarmingly added:

'The Spirits of Wine may be Exhausted . . . Suddainly by Lightning; which doth spoil Wine . . . not by Congelation or Fixation of its Spirits . . . but perhaps by Disgregation and putting them to flight. . . .'

One wonders about the flesh of vipers, and it is too late to experiment with cannons, but he was certainly right about heat, which encourages the bacteria; and the talk of thunder is merely another version of the old wives' tale that it turns the milk sour. It is the heat again that is really responsible. In the olden days, lime was commonly prescribed as the alkali, and even the great Sir John Falstaff, through the pen of Shakespeare, was moved to complain:

'Give me a cup of sack, rogue—
Is there no virtue extant? . . .
You rogue, here's lime in this sack too.'

But the remedy is only useful if the wine is to be sold off cheaply, as the alkali also destroys the desirable acids which help to give the wine its flavour. Even if it becomes only slightly pricked it is spoilt. Perhaps the best thing to do with a cask of wine in this condition is to take it away to some place where it cannot infect its neighbours and there to let it quietly turn into a good wine vinegar. It should never happen, though; and it very seldom does. The *mycoderma aceti* require air in order to live and will never gain a hold if the barrels are steadily kept topped up. That is why such care is taken to replace wine lost through evaporation or seepage. The only wines that can safely be left on ullage are the strong wines of Jerez and others growing *flor*, which is a protective layer of yeast cells that are found growing naturally in various places, notably the sherry area, Valdepeñas and the Jura. All others need to be airtight, and if a cask of wine does turn to vinegar it is pretty safe to say that the grower has been careless.

Fleur is somewhat different. It is perhaps the most common disease of all, but it is also the mildest of all, and it is brought about by microbes which are known as *mycoderma vini*. Like the *mycoderma aceti*, these need air for their growth, and they develop very rapidly on the surface of the wine to produce a greyish scum that looks not unlike the entirely healthy *flor* of saccharomyces that grows on the surface of fino sherries—a fact that has caused considerable confusion in the minds of some writers on wine in the past. Unlike the sherry *flor*, *la fleur* is usually found on wines possessing low alcoholic strength. It produces a 'flatness' of flavour and sometimes also a slight yellow tinge. As with the *mycoderma aceti*, this disease may be regarded as purely voluntary, for it will never occur if the casks are kept full. When it does occur, however, if it is alone, it can be cured by separating the wine from the scum, filtering, and running it into a clean, well-sulphured cask. Unfortunately, however, it seldom is alone, as the two forms of mycoderma tend to arrive together; and when this happens the *fleur* is a mere detail.

Another form of bacteriological infection produces *mannite* or *la peste*. The sugar in the wine is decomposed to form short, rod-like crystals of mannitol that give the wine a 'bitter-sweet' taste. At one time it was thought that this disease was characteristic of wines made from figs and that its presence in grape wine was a sure sign of adulteration; but this is quite untrue. It can happen to the purest wines but only if weather has been hot at the time of the vintage. *Scud*, or *la tourne*, sometimes referred to as *pousse*, shows up in wine as a suspended cloud, rather like steam, accompanied by an unpleasant smell. Carbon dioxide is evolved, too, and sometimes with such force that if the wine is in bottle the cork is pushed out. *La graisse* or *hilo* makes the wine 'ropey' or viscous. When it is poured out it looks like oil, and it tastes insipid and flat. All three diseases are bacterial but it is hard to say how they occur or what exactly happens. Several bacteria are involved, and what happens varies greatly according to the deficiencies in the wine and the conditions under which it was made. The remedy is first to kill the bacteria by sulphur dioxide treatment or by pasteurization and then to make up any deficiencies in so far as this is possible.

These are not the only bacterial diseases. There is *amertume*, for instance, which produces a bitter taste in old red wines. This is treated in the same way. But far more common, and far more important, are the various forms of *casse*: *casse ferrica*, *casse oxidasica*, *casse cuprica* and *white casse*. The first, which is also known as *blue casse*, is caused by an excess of iron and tannin which react together to produce a coloration—a phenomenon well known to manufacturers of ink. When it happens it usually means that someone has been clumsy with a mechanical press. A partial remedy can be effected by adding citric or tartaric acid, but the only complete answer is to use 'Moeslinger finings', otherwise known as blue finings, in other words potassium ferrocyanide. Used in an exactly calculated proportion, this precipitates the iron which can then easily be filtered out; but it is very highly poisonous and its use is prohibited in some countries. The imagination boggles at the slaughter which might follow its application by a slap-happy peasant. It is only possible where full laboratory facilities are available, and it is most common in Germany and France. *Casse oxidasica*, or *brown casse*, occurs as a result of excessive oxidation, and it used often to be found when wine was made from rotten grapes, but it is rare today owing to the use of sulphur dioxide during fermentation. When it does occur, it is best treated by pasteurization, which destroys the organic oxidizing agents. *Casse cuprica*, which is seen in the form of a reddish-brown haze, results from over-enthusiastic use of the copper sulphate spray in the vineyards and is removed in the same way as *casse ferrica*. *White casse*, which is found particularly when wines are made from grapes having an abnormally low natural acidity, shows up in the form of a milkiness that cannot easily be filtered out. It is another result of an excess of iron, and the white film consists of ferric phosphate. It is dealt with in the same way as *casse ferrica*.

So that is how wine is made. Basically it is easy: one just crushes some grapes and lets them ferment naturally. But in practice that is only a very small part of the story. There are an infinite number of variations on the theme, and each stage calls for skill and care. Consistently to create a fine wine calls for an immense effort; but few efforts can be more worth while.

Finally, before coming to the individual districts, a mention should be made of the way that wine develops in bottle. The chemistry of this development is not yet fully understood; and in so far as it is understood at all, it is so complex as mercifully to be beyond the scope of this book. The practical effect of ageing varies greatly from one wine to another and will be mentioned in individual chapters, but nevertheless there is a general over-all pattern that is common to all wines.

Young red wines tend to be loaded with tannin and natural acid so that they shrivel the mouth and are undrinkable: generally speaking, the finer the wine the more this is apparent. It is also noticeable that the components which give the wine its flavour are not intermingled, so that it tastes of many things rather than having a real taste of its own. With age the wine mellows so that the flavours mingle into one, the aroma increases, the sugar (if any) is slowly used up so that the wine tends to become drier, it also gets lighter in colour, and a deposit is formed. In my experience the ignorant detest deposits and many merchants unhappily go out of their way to prevent the wine from 'throwing'. Real wine drinkers delight in deposits for they suggest that the wine has not been tampered with, and they can easily be decanted off. Left too long in bottle, however, the wine becomes over mature; it loses its character and flavour, tending to taste insignificant and flat.

White wines follow the same course but more quickly and some, like fino sherries, do not like bottles at all. The colour, however, tends to get darker rather than lighter. When a white wine gets too old, it undergoes a particularly unfortunate change: it becomes maderized. When this happens the colour goes brown and the aroma becomes pungent and odd—somewhat resembling madeira, hence the name. Sparkling wines, apart from the other aspects of development, become less sparkling and eventually go flat, by which time they are spoilt.

CHAPTER 3

Bordeaux

Claret is the most fascinating wine in the world. Those whose first love is burgundy or hock are welcome to protest. Claret drinkers will hear no argument: we are unrepentant and unashamed. To say that it is the most fascinating wine in the world, though, is not to suggest that it is the greatest. There is no such thing as a 'greatest wine': all the great wines have their places in the hierarchy. They stand alongside each other, each quite different from the others, and each exquisite in its own way. To select any one as being greater than the others would be as meaningless and unfair as to choose a beauty queen in a competition where the girls represent all the races of the world. But of all the wines, no other presents so many subtle distinctions and variations. And that is only a part of the story. The white wines of Bordeaux can also hold their own with any, and these, too, exist in a bewildering variety: from the immensity and glory of Château d'Yquem to the humble little wines of Entre-Deux-Mers.

Bordeaux, moreover, has a special place in the history of wine drinking in this country, for the vineyards were once on English soil. In 1152, Eleanor, who was Duchess of Aquitaine in her own right, married Henry Plantagenet, Count of Anjou. When he succeeded to the throne of England two years later, the whole of Bordeaux, Gascony and Guienne became English possessions and Bordeaux was not lost until 1453. During the English domination the wine growers achieved a splendid prosperity, but the origins of their trade lay much further back.

Bordeaux first became important when it was a great Roman city, famous throughout the Empire for its university. It was also

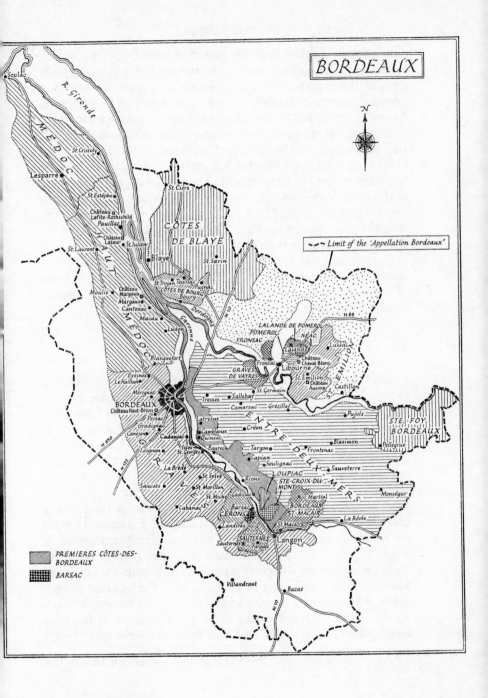

BORDEAUX

N

Limit of the 'Appellation Bordeaux'

R. Gironde

Soulac

MÉDOC

St. Cristoly

Lesparre

St. Estèphe

Château
Lafite-Rothschild
Pauillac

St. Ciers

CÔTES
DE BLAYE

Château
Latour

St. Julien

HAUT

Blaye

St. Savin

St. Laurent

St. Troyan Teuillac Pugnac
CÔTES DE BOURG
Bourg
Château
Margaux

Moulis

Margaux

Cantenac

Macau

Ludon

N 89

Dordogne

LALANDE DE POMEROL

POMEROL
FRONSAC

NÉAC

Lalande

Lussac

Blanquefort

Garonne

Eysines
Le Haillan

GRAVES
DE VAYRES

Fronsac

Château
Cheval Blanc

MILION

Mérignac

Libourne

St. Germain

St. Émilion
Château
Ausone

Castillon

BORDEAUX
Château Haut-Brion

Tresses

Salleboef

Camarsac

Grézillac

Pessac

Latresne

Camblanes

Créon

Pujols

STE.-FOY
BORDEAUX

Gradignan

Quinsac

Blasimon

Pellegrue

Canéjan

Cadaujac

Baurech

Targon

Frontenac

Leognan

Isles
St. Georges

Capian

Souligniac

Sauveterre

La Brède

ENTRE-DEUX-MERS

St. Selve

Klons

LOUPIAC
STE.-CROIX-DU-
MONT

Monségur

Saucats

St. Morillon

Cadillac

St. Michel

Martial

Cabanac

Barsac

BORDEAUX
ST.-MACAIRE

La Réole

CERONS

St. Macaire

Landiras

SAUTERNES

Langon

Sauternes

Fargues

N 10

PREMIERES CÔTES-DES-
BORDEAUX

BARSAC

Villandraut

Bazas

N 10

a major port, involved with the import of wine from Italy and its re-export to the north. A Roman inscription dating from the great days of the Empire, refers to a *negociator britannicus* operating between Bordeaux and this country. The history of its vineyards, however, begins rather later, for in A.D. 92 the emperor Domitian ordered all the vineyards of Gaul and Spain to be rooted up, and his decree stood until its repeal by Probus in A.D. 282. It is doubtful to what extent the prohibition was enforced, especially in Spain, but there appears to be no record of wine growing in the Gironde at this time. Very soon afterwards, however, wines of the province became famous. One of their earliest eulogies was written by the Roman poet Ausonius, who himself was born and died in Bordeaux; and there is an attractive legend that Château Ausone, at St. Emilion, stands on the site of his country villa. His gastronomic interests were evidently divided between a love of wine and of fish, for just as he praised the wine and the trout of the Moselle, he also praised the wine and the oysters of Bordeaux:

> Ostrea . . .
> Non laudata minus, nostri quam gloria vini.

After the Roman rule ended, and despite attacks by the Vandals, Goths, Moors, Franks and Normans, the Bordeaux wine growers continued to flourish; but although their wines were far famed they were by no means predominant. In 1189, after thirty-five years of English rule, Gascony was not the principal supplier of wine to England. The wines of Anjou, shipped from La Rochelle (which was also English territory), were more popular. Bordeaux wines were introduced to England on a large scale in the reign of King John (1199–1216), who rewarded the Bordelais for their loyalty and support during his wars with the kings of France and Castile by becoming their patron. Claret was soon firmly established in English favour. The Bordeaux merchants and growers relied for their prosperity on the great trade with this country, and some idea of its magnitude may be gathered from the fact that in 1307 Edward II ordered a thousand tonneaux[1] for his coronation feast. By the end of the fourteenth century, nine-tenths of the wine coming into England was sent over from Bordeaux and about a

---

[1] A tonneau is a large cask, equivalent to about four hogsheads, i.e. 900 litres.

thousand ships were employed in the trade. So much gold was exported to pay for it that Parliament became seriously concerned; and land suitable for vineyards became of immense value. By no means all the wine exported from Bordeaux was grown there: much of it was shipped down the rivers from vineyards further inland. But the fame and prosperity of Bordeaux was already clearly sealed, and it continued until the English were finally driven out in 1453. By then, of course, the two races were intermingled and many of the Bordelais were of English descent. Even after the English were expelled it was only a matter of time before they returned as merchants instead of overlords, for we are proud of our tradition as a nation of traders if not of shopkeepers, and in every port where good trade is to be found, especially if the trade is in wine, there is sure to be a British colony. Bordeaux is no exception, and today many growers, brokers and merchants are British or have British names.[1]

The change of rule, however, naturally brought in its wake many difficulties for the traders, and for several hundred years the state of tension and the many wars that existed between the two countries did little to help. But if the English politicians sought to deprive the squirearchy of its claret, the Scots had more sense. Throughout the centuries they continued to import large quantities of good wine and Edinburgh became the centre of enlightened claret drinking in Britain. There are those who claim that it still is, but one feels that they do so with patriotism rather than with reason, as many delicate palates have succumbed before the onslaught of all-conquering whisky.

Relations were at their very worst from the accession of William and Mary in 1688 until the beginning of the nineteenth century. Successive ministries regarded it as their duty to do as much mischief as possible to the prosperity and trade of France. And they did so regardless of the effect their policy might have on the health and morals of their own people. Wine was one of the chief articles of commerce between the two countries, and it was very vulnerable to attack. Already taxed, they decided that the trade in French wines could be done away with by imposing a tax that was

[1] A more detailed account of the history and every other aspect of the Bordeaux wine trade is to be found in Edmund Penning-Prowsell's admirable *The Wines of Bordeaux*, London, 1969.

altogether prohibitive; and if any trade did remain, its evil would be mitigated by the benefits it brought to the disastrously depleted exchequer. In its unparalleled ignorance, the official mind evidently thought that one wine was very much like another, for it sought to supplant French wines with those of Portugal. The rise of the port wine trade will be described in the appropriate chapter: suffice it here to say that in 1693 an extra duty of £8 per tun was imposed on French wines and that in 1697 the differential was increased to £30, French wines paying 4s. 0½d. per gallon, whilst the Portuguese only paid 1s. 8d. The next blow was the famous Methuen Treaty of 1703, which provided for Portuguese wines paying one-third less duty than French in exchange for the importation into Portugal of British woollens. In fact the differential imposed was far higher; Portuguese wines were paying £7 per tun whilst the French paid £55. Port as we know it today, however, had not been invented, and the blessings of the Government were ineffectual in selling inferior wine. The Government did, however, succeed in putting honest French wines beyond the pockets of all but the wealthiest drinkers, and the results were disastrous. As the recent efforts at prohibition in America have clearly shown, if the people cannot get decent and harmless drinks at a price they can afford, they will drink all the same; but they will drink raw and terrible spirits, to their infinite detriment. It happened here in England. In the first year of Queen Anne's reign, just before the Methuen Treaty, an act was passed which was declared to be: 'An Act for the incouraging the consumption of malted corn and for the better preventing the running of French and Foreign Brandy.' The result was as inevitable as it was quick. Before long a Southwark innkeeper put up his infamous sign which read:

> Drunk for 1d.
> Dead drunk for 2d.
> Clean straw for nothing.

The masses were besotted and soaked in gin. And not only the masses. Young people could well afford to get dead drunk and the degradation soon spread to the educated classes, as any student of Hogarth will know full well. In 1680 *A Person of Quality* was moved to verse:

THE CLARET DRINKER'S SONG[1]
or
THE GOOD FELLOW'S DESIGN

A pox on the fooling and plotting of late,
What a pother and stir has it kept in this state?
Let the rabble run mad with suspicions and fears;
Let 'em scuffle and fan, till they go by the ears;
Their grievances never shall trouble my pate,
So I can but enjoy my dear bottle at quiet.
A friend and a bottle is all my design,

Has no room for treason, that's top-full of wine,
I mind not the members and makers of laws,
Let 'em sit or prorogue as His Majesty please,
Let 'em damn us to woollen, I'll never repine
At my lodging when dead, for alive I have wine.
Yet oft in my drink I can hardly forbear
To curse 'em, for making my claret so dear.

A great political battle raged between the friends and foes of France in this country, but the friends lost the day, and French wines remained beyond the pockets of all but a few. Every kind of propagandist, in the absurd name of patriotism, did his best to denigrate French wines and boost Portuguese. Fortunately, however, there were noblemen and wine-loving squires who were strong-minded enough to resist the propaganda and rich enough to indulge their own tastes, so even in the darkest years claret never disappeared. In his fine book on wine in the eighteenth century—*Bottlescrew Days*—André L. Simon quotes purchases made by John Hervey, first Earl of Bristol, between 1703 and 1725, and he bought the best: Château Margaux, Château Lafite, Château Latour and Château Haut-Brion. Such wines were happily by no means confined to noblemen: that country gentlemen still enjoyed fine claret is amply illustrated by *The Purefoy Letters*, which cover the period 1735 to 1753. The fact that claret had never lost its following is even better demonstrated by the tone of the propaganda that was directed against it; for even

[1] From a 'Complaint'. The original was presented to the *Conseil Interprofessionel du Vin de Bordeaux*. The above lines are copied from *The French Vineyards* by Denis Morris, London, 1958.

political poetasters will not lavish their dim verses on denigrating something that is already dead.

The partial eclipse of the English market at least had one good effect, and that was to raise the quality of the wine imported. Faced with such excessive duties, there was no point in saving a mere fraction of the selling price by importing cheap wine; and the claret that *was* imported had to appeal to educated drinkers if it was to be sold at all. So the finest growths became the rule rather than the exception, and when trade eventually did become easy again in the second half of the nineteenth century, the standard had already been set for the vintners to maintain. The cheap wines that had been sold vaguely as Gascony, Guienne or Bordeaux practically disappeared and their place was taken by wines that bore the proud names of their châteaux, or at least of their district. Sometimes, too, the names of their growers were specified. Thus the Earl of Bristol bought 'Pontack Clarett', evidently grown in one of the many estates of the great Pontac family, which at one time included Château Haut-Brion.

The collapse of trade with this country, although gastronomically disastrous for our ancestors, did not greatly affect the Bordeaux growers and merchants, who were enjoying a period of boom. In the first quarter of the eighteenth century, in fact, the vineyard area greatly increased, the wine being exported to the prosperous French colonial empire in Africa and in the West Indies. From the end of the seventeenth century, the Netherlands was also a major customer, taking over the lead from the English. The Netherlands merchants, however, bought mainly cheap wines, especially white wines, and it was this that led to a great increase in white wine production. Many of these wines were blended (to the displeasure of the Bordelais) and there was a large re-export trade.

One hears today a great deal about blending and adulteration. The popular press is at last taking an interest in wines, and anything smacking of dishonesty or corruption is more likely to attract its attention than the great mass of completely honest trade, just as one thoroughly unwholesome divorce will make the headlines whilst a million happy marriages pass unnoticed. Consequently people have come to think that merchants' blends are new things, whereas they are as old as the wine trade itself; and they are not necessarily evil. This aspect will be discussed in the next chapter. But it must be admitted that foreign merchants have always been tempted to foist off their worst wines on the British, who, having no vineyards of their own, are assumed to be ignorant. Happily British wine merchants and wine drinkers are usually far from ignorant, and we are now regarded as a difficult market. Those who have attempted to exploit them have usually brought about their own undoing. Thus, although in the sixteenth century Bordeaux was the greatest wine port in the world, a century later it had lost its position. Too often did the wines displease, and a considerable portion of the trade was captured by the Dutch, who were prepared to pander to the English taste by blending wines to suit it. Known generally as *remontage* or *coupage*, the process also enjoyed the far from flattering name of *travail à l'anglaise*. But the practice was much older than that. As early as the reign of Philip V, at the beginning of the fourteenth century, there is a charter that reads: *vinorum tinctorum quae soium addendum colorem aliis vinis sunt necessaria*. And it has been going on ever since. Good wines need no treatment, but if inferior wines are sold, the customers rebel. If such wines are skilfully blended they become stronger in flavour and alcohol, and hence more palatable. But once the corrupt taste for them has been established, the finest of natural wines appear too weak, and a vicious circle has been started.

One thing at least is clear: the clarets imported into this country during the eighteenth century were often not absolutely 'straight' Bordeaux wines, even when they were sold under the names of great châteaux. The blending that was done was to satisfy the English taste for big, heady, dark wines. These wines were quite different from those that had been imported into this country previously. The *Oxford English Dictionary* traces the word *claret* back to a French source in 1396, which contrasted *vin claret* with *vermeille et blanc* while in England it states that 'French claret wines' were referred to in 1533, though the usage is certainly much older than that. Shakespeare also mentioned them, in a very odd context, through the mouth of the infamous Jack Cade:

'Now is Mortimer lord of this city. And here, sitting upon London-stone, I charge and command that, of the city's cost, the pissing-conduit run nothing but claret wine this first year of our reign. And

now, henceforward, it shall be treason for any that calls me other than
Lord Mortimer.'

2 Henry VI, act iv, scene vi.

While soon afterwards, in 1623, Gervase Markham, in his *English
Housewife*, described what good claret should be like:

'See that in your choice of Gascoine wine, you observe, that your
Claret wines be faire coloured, and bright as a Ruby, not deep as an
amethest; for though it may show strength, yet it wanteth neatness.'

As a name for red bordeaux, claret does not exist in the French
language, but it appears that the wines originally sold as such in
this country were what the French still call *clairet*, and such wines
can still be found in Bordeaux. They are comparatively light in
colour—darker than a rosé but certainly much lighter than the
wines we know today. And the wines we know today are lighter
than those which were being imported during the eighteenth
century. In those days it was the common practice to give clarets
more body and colour by blending them with the strong wines of
Roussillon, the Spanish benicarlo and alicante, or (for the best
clarets) hermitage. This could hardly have been done, as is often
suggested, merely to 'stretch' the wines and to increase the
shippers' profits, though this factor was undoubtedly present in
the minds of some of the lesser shippers who avoided the more
expensive wines from Hermitage and made do with benicarlo.
Even then, however, anomalies occurred and in 1804, when the
benicarlo vintage had failed, a Cork wine merchant complained
that the Spanish wine was more expensive than the claret it was
destined to 'help'.

The English taste became so firmly established that even the
great growths were blended, and the letter books of Nathaniel
Johnson, who was one of the best and most respected Bordeaux
merchants of his day—a position that is well maintained by his
successors, for his firm is still a flourishing one—record that 'The
Lafitte [*sic*.] 1795 which was made up with Hermitage was the
best liked wine of any of that year.' In 1801, which was a decent
average vintage, Johnson wrote to his partner Guestier a letter
that is quoted by H. Warner Allen in his *A History of Wine*:

'If the wines have the body and colour which others represent more
favourably than you do, I think they ought to be made up very lightly

68

this year—the first and even good second growths with not more than three or four gallons of Spanish wine and about three gallons of Hermitage, and the other wines not to have more than five gallons of Spanish wine.'

The habit died hard. When Cyrus Redding wrote *A History and Description of Modern Wines* (3rd edition, London, 1851) he described how:

'The first growths of the Medoc are hardly ever sent to England in a perfect state, but are, when destined for that market, mingled with other wines and with spirit of wine. . . . This is called "working them". By this means much of the delicate flavour is destroyed, to give it a warmer and more intoxicating effect. . . . It is often too artificially flavoured. Wines so treated never recover their natural bouquet. . . . Orris root is employed to give the perfume destroyed by mixing, and sometimes a small quantity of raspberry brandy is used, two ounces to a cask, in order to flavour it factitiously and replace the natural flavour it has lost. . . . Natural wines, the genuine offspring of simple fermentation, are not the fashion in England. . . . The Dutch import these wines on the lees and treat them as they are treated in France, drinking them pure and unmixed.'

The trade between Bordeaux and England at the end of the eighteenth century was still difficult and relatively small: it did not recover until after the Napoleonic wars, though it was ten times what it had been in the first quarter of the century, and it was greatly helped when Pitt slashed the duty on French wines from £90 to £43 a tun in 1786. But mercifully wars were not total wars in those days, and the history of the wine trade—especially the sherry trade—shows how merchants continually pitted their wits against those of the politicians. Happily the merchants generally won. Their lives were very difficult, their losses were heavy; but the wine got through. The machinations of the Bordeaux merchants during this time were in the best tradition. Let statistics speak for themselves: in 1812, 135 pipes of port were shipped from Oporto to Guernsey, and 2,545 pipes of port were shipped from thence to London, where they were admitted at the preferential rate of duty. Any comment would be superfluous. Other ships sailed first from Bordeaux to Oporto, and then to England, officially carrying cargoes of port. During the Napoleonic wars, on the other hand, the usual method of importing French wines was by means of neutral ships, though the trade was so precarious that the rates of freight and insurance were astronomical. To make the picture more complete, and perhaps more exciting, one should add that throughout the centuries a vast amount of wine was smuggled. Some of the evasions of customs duty were operated with the aid of the privileges extended from time to time to ambassadors, bishops, noblemen, members of Parliament and others to import wine for their own use. From the figures available, it looks as if some of them swam in it. And for smaller quantities there was always the diplomatic bag. Moreover seafaring men had certain privileges of their own, and as early as the fourteenth century it is recorded that penurious mariners made arrangements with Bordeaux merchants to import wine duty-free as their own 'adventure'.[1] But to embark upon a detailed history of evasions would fill a book many times the length of this.

It was as well for the Bordelais that the trade in wine with England had never been lost and that, by the end of the eighteenth century, it was improving. For by May 1790 the French Government brought about a far-sighted and generous liberal reform that proved disastrous to the Bordeaux trade: it liberated the negroes in the colonies. Immediate ruin followed. The colonial trade collapsed, and the internal trade was disrupted by the Napoleonic wars. But salvation was near at hand, and it was brought about by three things: the cork, the bottle and the eventual peace. Of these, the first two were by far the most important.

Bottles, neatly sealed with corks, are such familiar things that it is hard to realize that they have not always been with us; but they are comparatively newcomers. It is all the stranger since cork is a natural product, stripped from the bark of a tree, that has been known for centuries. Phoenician traders used it and so did the ancient Egyptians. The Romans sealed the mouths of their amphoras with it; and the longevity of some of their wines—like the fabulous Opimiam Falernian—is legendary. But the decline of the Greek and Latin civilizations brought with it a decline in all the appendages of gracious living. Wine was amongst the finest of these and, like the rest, it suffered. Great vintages were heard of no more. For centuries wine was shipped in casks and drawn from the wood as required. It was the young wine that was prized in

---

[1] See Neville Williams, *Contraband Cargoes*, London, 1959.

England, as it became thin, acid and nasty if it were left too long. If the worst came to the worst (as it often did) it actually turned into vinegar. Books written for merchants in Elizabethan times are full of remedies for destroying the acidity. When the great Falstaff was reduced to complaining that there was lime in his sack, wine had reached its nadir.

The use of cork had to be re-invented, and it is an extraordinary thing that the earliest references suggest that it was pioneered by the English. It came into use during the reign of Elizabeth I, and by Shakespeare's time it was clearly established. But it was still many years before its full significance was realized. By the 1660s, sparkling wine from Champagne was on sale in London—about two decades before champagne as we know it was first made—and this was achieved by cunning wine merchants who tightly corked their bottles before the secondary fermentation began. But the corks were quite different from modern ones: they were tapered, and one end stuck out of the bottle, so that there was something to hold when the cork was pulled out—just as there is in the modern 'stopper' cork. Before it became possible to store wine for long in bottle it was necessary to invent the corkscrew—or bottlescrew as it was called at first—and this did not happen until the eighteenth century.

Simultaneously the bottle was gradually being developed. It began as a broad-based, lop-sided decanter. Gradually it got nearer and nearer to the modern shape, and by about 1770 the bottle as we know it had come into being. It was perfect for its job: safe and steady on the table, and easily binned. The earlier, misshapen bottles could only be stored standing upright on shelves so that when Pepys visited Mr. Thomas Povey in Lincoln's Inn Fields on January 19th, 1663, he saw that:

'Upon several shelves there stood bottles of all sorts of wine, new and old, with labells pasted upon each bottle, and in order and plenty as I never saw books in a bookseller's shop.'

In those days some bottles still had glass stoppers, sealed over with wax, and those that Pepys saw may well have been of this kind. It is to be hoped that they were; otherwise the wine would not have survived for long, and the 'old' wine would have been vinegar. To keep a wine in bottle for a period of years—which is essential if a vintage wine is to mature as such—the bottles must be binned on their sides, so as to keep the corks moist. The old way of storing wine is today only suitable for spirits, which eat away the cork and should be kept upright. The new era of vintage wines therefore did not dawn until towards the end of the eighteenth century, when well-made bottles, firmly corked, could be stored away on their sides. The first order for vintage claret in bottles that occurs in Nathaniel Johnson's letter books came from a Guernsey wine merchant in 1798; but Mr. Johnson, like nearly all wine merchants, was a conservative, and he took some convincing that the change was for the better. As late as August 18th, 1801, despite the success of his earlier shipments, he wrote to his partner in Bordeaux: 'It appears to me this wine is meant to be in the wood', though he was already experimenting by putting a few bottles on one side to see if the wine would improve, like port. By 1802, however, bottled claret had become so popular in Dublin that it was in short supply. By 1811, the bottling of vintage clarets was well established. The date is significant, for this was 'the year of the comet'—one of the greatest vintages of all time. The longevity of its wines is famous, and we can attribute the advent of claret as we know it today to the success of this vintage. But the change did not come suddenly. Even by the end of the nineteenth century wholesalers in this country were quoting vintages that had been in the wood for five or six years, and merchants commonly kept their wines in the wood until they were 'ready' before bottling them—as is still done in many districts, such as Rioja, to this day.

The discrimination against French wines was finally ended, and a great fillip was given to the Bordeaux trade, by Gladstone's budget of 1860, which reduced the duty on table wines from a shilling to twopence a bottle, and which ended Empire preference, thus effectively killing the new trade in South African wines, which had become serious rivals to the French. The budget was followed by Gladstone's 'Single Bottle' Act of 1861, which brought off-licences into being and threw the wine trade open to grocers. Rather surprisingly, the reduction in duty was not particularly popular with some of the old-established wine merchants, and the Single Bottle Act was even less so. The new policy wrought a revolution in a notoriously conservative trade. The classes who had had to do without wine for years were able to buy it again, and the stuffy merchant who sold expensive wine in his mahogany-laden office had suddenly to compete with the stores round the corner. Many were outraged by the ignorance of their competitors, and certainly some very strange things happened. Charles Tovey, the old Bristol wine merchant, whose horror was second to none, recorded[1] how a grocer advertised '*Sherry* direct from *Bordeaux*', and quoted the following prices:

Sherry, Chateau d'Yquem	40s. per dozen
Ditto, Finest Sauterne	34s. per dozen

And there were plenty more absurdities and there were also social consequences; for surreptitious drinkers could at last buy the odd bottle with their groceries. G. K. Chesterton knew all about it:

> The wicked Grocer groces
> In spirits and in wine
> Not frankly and in fellowship
> As men in inns do dine:
> But packed with soap and sardines
> And carried off by grooms,
> For to be snatched by Duchesses
> And drunk in dressing-rooms.

But the overall effect was unquestionably good, and the effect on the Bordeaux trade was very good indeed, even though the ignorant saw fit to sneer for many years at the so-called 'Gladstone claret'.

The good that was done by Gladstone's budget, however, was swiftly followed by a disaster that struck the Bordeaux shippers on their own soil: the arrival of the phylloxera. It was the worst thing that has ever afflicted wine growers, and at one time it was seriously feared that the European vineyards would be totally and irrevocably destroyed. It was even worse—much worse—than the oidium[2] that had already wrought havoc in the 1850s. The origin, the nature, and the appalling effects of the phylloxera have already been described.[3] On June 11th, 1869, the insect was discovered on the roots of vines at Floirac, but these had evidently been infected

[1] *Wine and Wine Countries*, 2nd edition, London, 1877.
[2] See *ante*, p. 21.
[3] See *ante*, p. 22.

about two years earlier. The spread was both inevitable and rapid. By 1875 it had reached the Médoc. In the early days the disease was little understood. The vines were just seen to wither and to die for no obvious reason, and when the phylloxera insects were discovered there was a debate as to whether they were the cause or the effect. Some blamed a blight in the atmosphere, and others said that it was God's Punishment for the Country's Abandonment of the Emperor. Great efforts were made to combat the plague. The palus vineyards alongside the river were flooded; but these, in any case, only gave poor wine, and it was impossible to flood the higher lands. Every possible insecticide was tried, and some benefit *was* derived from the use of carbon disulphide. But this is a dreadful substance; it has a horrible smell, is poisonous, and is highly inflammable. The more optimistic growers held on to their vines till the very end, and those who owned the great classified growths were especially loath to replant for fear that the wine might suffer, so that as late as 1907 there were no grafted vines at Mouton-Rothschild, Brane-Cantenac or Haut-Bailly, and few at Calon Ségur. Even now there are a number of native vines, especially at St. Emilion. There is, therefore, no clear dividing line before which claret was 'pre-phylloxera': each château has to be considered separately. Eventually even the most optimistic had to abandon hope: the vineyards were grubbed up and replanted with American stocks on to which the native vines were grafted.

The controversy about the rival merits of the pre-phylloxera and post-phylloxera clarets is as old as the phylloxera itself. Growers were naturally very worried at the time and writers of the 1920s and 1930s all declared that the post-phylloxera vintages were short-lived, poor things compared with those that had gone before. But it is notoriously hard to compare two vintages that are wide apart in time, and one has to rely on that notoriously unreliable instrument, the memory, which tends always to glorify things of long ago. In considering the phylloxera, things are even more complicated than usual. The grafting of the vines alone was enough to create a prejudice in the most honest mind, and just before the plague struck there was a whole series of outstanding vintages: 1858, '64, '65, '69, '70, '71, '74, '75, '77 and '78. Unhappily I must confess that I have only tasted two clarets that I know for certain to have been pre-phylloxera: the Château Rauzan-Gassies 1875

and the Château Palmer 1880. The first was superb. In the great
Professor Saintsbury's opinion: 'As long as the '74s and '75s
lasted, nothing quite touched them.' In 1919, André Simon wrote
of this vintage: 'Clarets exceptionally fine, and still in perfect
condition.' He could almost use the same words today. I was
privileged to taste it in 1962 while staying as a guest in a château in
the Médoc, where the private cellars are fabulous. My note on this
wine was made in the enthusiasm of the moment: 'Perhaps the
most wonderful claret I have ever tasted. The nose was musty,
faded and old. It was like going into the Prado and looking at a
Velasquez through dark glasses. But to drink! Too old, of course,
but how it has survived! A superb wine. So soft and exquisite. The
bouquet improved with every minute in the glass.' No doubt had I
kept it in the glass long enough the bouquet would eventually have
faded. But it did not get the chance. I was almost as enthusiastic
about the Château Palmer. That it had survived so well is really
remarkable, as 1880 was only a light and mediocre year. André
Simon has described it as providing 'Excellent champagne, the
only exception in a year of bad crops', and Saintsbury mentioned
no claret of that vintage. By then the phylloxera was already well
established in Bordeaux, and there was also continual trouble from
mildew. Many prophesied doom. The Château Palmer utterly
belied the reputation of its year. Unfortunately, however, something went wrong: I had it at the same dinner as the 1875 Rauzan-
Gassies, and as a result of an error with the decanters, the 1875
was drunk first. In comparison, the 1880 seemed dimmer and less
refined—but not very much. Had they been drunk the other way
round it would have received almost as high an accolade. So the
reputation of the pre-phylloxera wines for longevity and outstanding quality seems to be justified; but I am not sure that some
of the wines of more recent vintages—particularly the 1945s—
will not be every bit as good. The post-phylloxera wines got off to
a very poor start: at the beginning of this century there was a
whole series of bad vintages. It is not surprising that a pessimistic
view was taken of the wines, but perhaps the weather was to blame
as much as the vines. The reports are full of phrases like these:
'1903—Severe frosts in April did enormous damage to the vines,
and a severe hailstorm in July completely devastated a very large
area of vineyards'; '1905—Towards the end of August the fine

weather broke up, and there was practically nothing but incessant rain afterwards'. Such misfortunes had nothing to do with the phylloxera, and anyhow, fine wines are never given by young vines. So perhaps the deterioration was exaggerated; and the succession of fine vintages we have enjoyed in the 1940s, 1950s and 1960s proves that these things can still happen. If some new blight were to strike the vineyards, these great years would be talked of with nostalgia, and they would be declared unrepeatable. Even so, it can hardly be denied that modern clarets *do* mature more quickly— though this is largely the result of modified fermentation methods —and perhaps they do not live for quite as long as their great predecessors. But they have not lost all that much quality.

The phylloxera was the last truly dramatic event in the history of Bordeaux wines. Bordeaux, unlike Champagne, was well south of the battle lines in the two world wars, but nevertheless the Kaiser war had a more than temporary effect; for before 1914 Germany had been the principal market for the cheaper wines, and when the market disappeared after the war, so did some of the lesser growers.

One would expect wines grown over such a wide area to vary considerably in style and quality. From the northern tip of the Médoc to the southern extremity of the Sauternes is a distance not far short of ninety miles. Faced with so much territory one hardly knows where to begin, and the matter is made even more complicated by the fact that there is no clear-cut line between those areas in which red wines and those in which white wines are grown. Both may be grown side by side even in the greatest districts: Château Margaux has its Pavillon Blanc, and Château Haut-Brion, which also grows white wine as well as red, is in Graves. But it is most convenient to consider the two kinds of wine separately, even though the same communes will often occur twice.

Red Wines

Throughout all the many districts there are six varieties of vine: Cabernet-Sauvignon, Cabernet-Franc, Carmenère, Merlot, Malbec and Petit-Verdot. But all six masquerade under a great variety of different names: a source of confusion found in most of the great wine-growing districts. The Cabernet-Sauvignon is found as the

Petit-Cabernet, Vidure, Bouchet-Sauvignon, Marchoupet and Carbouet; the Cabernet-Franc as the Gros-Cabernet, Carmenet, Cabernet Gris, Grosse Vidure, Gros Bouchet and Petit Fer; the Carmenère as the Cabernelle; the Merlot as the Sémillon-Rouge, Vitraille, Bigney, Crabutet and Plant-Médoc; the Malbec as the Malbeck, Gourdoux, Etranger, Gros-Noir, Cahors, Prolongeau, Pied-Rouge, Pied-de-Perdrix, Pied-Noir, Côte-Rouge, Noir-Doux, Balouzac and yet more names; while the Verdot adds a further complication by existing in three distinct variants—the Petit-Verdot, the Gros-Verdot or Verdot-de-Palus, and the Verdot-Colon. These are the only varieties that are permitted by the laws of *appellation contrôlée*, and other varieties have been eliminated from all the vineyards producing quality wines. There were many of them in the past, though, and the 1883 edition of Cocks and Feret's *Bordeaux et ses Vins* lists fifteen additional ones, many of which enjoyed a multiplicity of names.

Of all these vines, the greatest is the Cabernet-Sauvignon; and if anyone wished to plant a vineyard with only one variety, it is at least to be hoped that it would be this. It gives a wine of ample body, tannin and colour; but unfortunately the yield is comparatively small. It is also perhaps the oldest variety grown in Bordeaux; in Graves it is still called the Vidure, and in the sixteenth century the commonest vine was named La Bidure, which may well have been the same thing. Could it be the same as Pliny's *Biturica*? A closely related vine is the Bouchet, grown in St. Emilion. The Cabernet-Franc gives a softer, lighter and slightly less aromatic wine with somewhat less tannin, but plenty of sugar (and therefore alcohol) and with a better yield. The Carmenère is another variant of the Cabernet, and it gives a rich, full and mellow wine, but it is rather more temperamental and is liable to be more affected by the weather: it has practically disappeared and is never planted. The Merlot gives a soft, light, fragrant wine that matures quickly and the grapes ripen earlier than those of the Cabernet-Sauvignon; it is grown in especially large proportions in St. Emilion and Pomerol. But as it flowers early, it is particularly susceptible to spring frosts and also suffers readily from rot if the weather is wet at vintage time. The Malbec gives a large yield of fragrant wine that is inclined to be rather light, but somewhat less so than the Merlot. Results, however, are very variable and depend greatly on the soil. The three varieties of Verdot are listed above in order of merit, and the last two are certainly on their way to oblivion. The Petit-Verdot gives a strong wine of quite good quality, but the bouquet is very limited, and the vine tends to fail in cold, wet years; there is also a tiresome tendency for the flowers to drop off without forming grapes: the disease of *coulure*, to which the Malbec is also prone.

In providing the varieties of the wine, nature has been kind, but not too kind: all have their advantages, but none by itself is perfect. To get exactly the style of wine that the grower wants, he generally has to plant three or four varieties and blend the wines obtained from them. The particular choice and proportion of vines adopted is known as the *encépagement*. Years of experience show just what should be grown in a given vineyard—but even then there is an element of hazard. In one year, one variety may do particularly well and another badly; whilst in the next year the order may be reversed. In the really good years, all the vines do well and the châteaux show up in their true form. In mediocre or bad years, however, odd things can happen, and the fact that there are usually several varieties of grape to choose from helps a little to explain why in an off-vintage year a few châteaux produce remarkably good wines, whilst in a mediocre, and sometimes even in a good vintage, châteaux with great names occasionally prove disappointing.

The *encépagement* not only greatly influences the style of the wine but also the rate at which it matures. At the moment, the great vine in the Médoc is the Sauvignon, which yields slowly-maturing wines, while the Merlot is the most widely planted vine in St. Emilion and this, quite apart from the soil, helps to explain why the wines of St. Emilion mature more quickly. The present tendency is to plant more Merlot in the Médoc. Thanks to small differences of soil, subsoil and aspect, neighbouring vineyards would never produce identical wines but these differences are accentuated by different methods of vinification and especially by differences in *encépagement*. For instance the vineyard of Château Mouton-Rothschild, with its great robust wines, is planted with 90 per cent Sauvignon, 5 per cent Cabernet-Franc, 3 or 4 per cent Merlot and the rest Petit-Verdot. In contrast, its neighbour Château Lafite, growing a lighter, more delicate style of wine, is

planted with 67 per cent Sauvignon, and 16 per cent each of
Cabernet-Franc and Merlot with the rest Petit-Verdot. Château
Margaux goes a step further, with 50 per cent Sauvignon, 10 per
cent Cabernet-Franc, 35 per cent Merlot and the rest Petit-Verdot.
And so on. Edmund Penning-Prowsell gives the *encépagement* of a
typical vineyard in the Médoc as 55 per cent Sauvignon, 20 per
cent Cabernet-Franc, 20 per cent Merlot and 5 per cent Malbec,
whereas a St. Emilion vineyard might include as much as 60 per
cent Merlot.

The grape varieties, however, are only one of the natural factors
that govern the quality and style of a wine, and all six are available
throughout the region. The other factors are the climate and the
soil. Over such a wide area, both differ considerably. There are
six principal kinds of soil: the alluvial or palus lands; the rich
soils, known as *terres fortes*; marly calcareous soils; gravelly soils;
siliceous soils; and, lastly, sablo-argillaceous, or sandy clay soils.
The alluvial soil is found beside the river, or where rivers used to
run, particularly in the old marsh, or *palus*, lands which have long
since been drained. It is too rich, and gives coarse wines. The
terre forte is rather hard, clayey, and difficult to work. Marly
calcareous soil is widely dispersed and good for viticulture. The
gravelly or *graves* soil, however, is the best of all for the vine, and
it is found in all the finest vineyards, where it is up to a yard deep,
and full of stones or quartz, with a sand or stone sub-soil. Other
areas, where the sub-soil is clay, are too humid and much inferior.
The siliceous soil is the most widely distributed of all, covering
about half of the total area. It is quite good for viticulture without
being outstanding. The sablo-argillaceous soils are not so good,
tending to be too damp.

Vines grow deep, and the effect of the sub-soil has already briefly
been mentioned. To grow the very finest wines, the soil has to be
right, through and through, and the formation of the earth is
notoriously irregular, consisting of folds and layers. Hence it is
that while most of a vineyard may be excellent, one corner of it is
hopelessly inferior, and vineyards on opposite sides of the road
grow very different wines.

In contrast with the practice in Burgundy, in Bordeaux chaptalization is only permitted in the very worst years, so that the
wines tend to be drier and more austere, with a very pronounced

bouquet; nevertheless in the off-vintages chaptalization is both practised and easily detected.

Yet another factor that influences the wine is the time of bottling. This may vary between eighteen months and three years —the shorter period for a light wine and the longer for a great wine of a good year. Timing calls for great skill and judgment.

The meaning and the merits of the laws of *appellations contrôlées* will be considered later. At this stage suffice it to say that they enable each region to be broken down into geographically exact and convenient areas. The red wines of Bordeaux are grown in the Médoc, Graves, Premières Côtes de Bordeaux, Blayais and Bourgeais, Fronsac, Entre-Deux-Mers, St. Emilion and Pomerol. Most of these, as will be seen, can be further divided into more exact *appellations*. The greatest wines come from the first two and the last two named.

Of all these districts, the Médoc is the greatest for red wines, and of the great regions it is certainly the youngest, for it did not gain real importance until the seventeenth century. Previously the name of Graves had been synonymous with red bordeaux. As the map shows, the Médoc adjoins the Graves and begins at a point a few miles north of Bordeaux, extending along the west side of the Gironde almost to where it flows into the Atlantic. On the west, it is bordered by the forests, meadows, lakes and sand dunes of the Landes. The Médoc is a delightful place, in a quiet, unobtrusive sort of way. It is gently undulating countryside—certainly not hilly—and where the ground is unsuitable for growing good wines it is cultivated as ordinary, mixed farms; and it is well wooded. Moreover it became prosperous when French domestic architecture was in its most delightful phase. Most of the famous châteaux date from the first half of the nineteenth century; and they are as beautiful and full of character as the wines that grow around them.

The Médoc is divided about half-way along into two parts: the southern end, where the greatest wines are grown, is called the Haut-Médoc (and that is its *appellation*), while the northern end used to be known as the Bas-Médoc; now it is just plain Médoc,[1] since its inhabitants successfully petitioned during the Hitler war to have 'Bas' deleted. The dividing line passes just north of St.

[1] Officially, Médoc Maritime, but I have never heard it so described.

Seurin-de-Médoc, and it is surprising how clearly it can be drawn. The bourgeois growths just north of St. Estèphe tend to be rather hard and dull on the nose; but just as it is clear that they are approaching the Bas-Médoc, it is equally clear that they are not in it. On the other side of the line the wines are distinctly coarser. They are still good, they are still Médoc wines; but they have none of that supreme subtlety and delicacy that is notable in their neighbours, and no really great wines grow there. The Haut-Médoc is in part further sub-divided into six smaller *appellations contrôlées*. Travelling north up the Médoc from Bordeaux, these are reached in the following order: Margaux, Moulis, Listrac, St. Julien, Pauillac, St. Estèphe. It is in these areas that most of the finest wines are to be found—particularly in the first and in the last three—but they are all included in the great general classification of Haut-Médoc, and they certainly do not have a monopoly of the fine wines. Wines bearing broad *appellations* are often further defined by the names of the distinguished communes where they are grown when these communes do not have separate *appellations* of their own.

The French have a tidy passion for classification. In a guide book, one is alarmed to see even the cathedrals and churches neatly classified with a system of stars, as if they were A.A. recommended hotels: it seems somewhat blasphemous. Even the famous chickens of Bresse are protected by an *appellation contrôlée*, and what can be done for the fowl can obviously be done for the wines. But wines, unlike cathedrals, are capricious. A Gothic church will not change from one year to the next, save in its minor embellishments, but a wine of one vintage may differ radically from its predecessor; and over a period of years the whole character of a vineyard may change owing to altered viticulture. Moreover, because wine is so capricious in its development, anyone who attempts to classify the vineyards with any sort of precision is trying to outwit nature, like a handicapper at a race. His efforts will always be foiled when a great vineyard proves disappointing or when a lesser growth produces an outstanding wine. Even so, a classification is valuable provided it is used intelligently. Since the quality of a wine depends ultimately on the soil and the climate, it will be consistent if taken over a sufficient period of years. It is in the light of this that one must consider the great classification of the wines of

F

81

the Médoc in 1855, when the leading growths were divided into the *Cinq Crus Classés*. This final, official classification, however, was no new thing. Morton Shand[1] referred to previous classifications in 1641, 1647, 1698 and 1767. In 1707 an advertisement in the *London Gazette* had already mentioned the first growths of the Médoc by name: 'an entire Parcel of New French Claret ... being of the Growth of Lafitt, Margouze, and La Tour.' A detailed and fascinating account of the early classifications is given in, Edmund Penning-Rowsell's book. The earliest classifications however, were vague things—by parishes and districts rather than by individual vineyards. When Thomas Jefferson visited Bordeaux in 1787 the status of the first growths was already recognized, as were some well-known châteaux in the second and third growths— the latter including Mouton! The first of the more precise classifications was made in 1803 by Mr. William Lawton, a broker of Irish descent,[2] who divided some of the greater wines into three classes. Books published in the 1820s[3] already contained the essence of the classification, and by 1846[4] it was almost complete. Between 1835 and 1840, a viticultural journal *Le Producteur* pursued a study of the wines of the Médoc and published a classification which has been rather delightfully described as 'tainted sometimes by a spirit of opposition to the conception of commerce'.[5] In 1855, the question of classifying the wines of the Gironde was at last brought to a head: there was to be a World's Fair, and the authorities of Bordeaux were anxious that only their finest wines should be chosen to represent the region. The syndicate of wine brokers was asked to propose an official list, and it did so, based on experience over the years, and the prices that the wines would fetch. Really they did little more than to give the earlier classifications the blessing of the authorities, and they were the only people who could do the job. All the wine of Bordeaux is sold through brokers. It is they who negotiate the price between the grower and the merchant, so that their knowledge of the trade

---

[1] P. Morton Shand, *A Book of French Wines*, London, 1960.

[2] The Lawton family is descended from Abraham Lawton, a native of Cork, who came to Bordeaux in 1739.

[3] Wm. Franck, *Traité sur les Vins de Médoc*, Bordeaux, 1824, and *Notice Sur les Vins de Bordeaux*, Chez Fillastre et Neven, Bordeaux, 1827.

[4] C. Cocks, *Bordeaux: Its Wines and the Claret Country*, London, 1846.

[5] P. Joseph Lacoste, *La Route du Vin en Gironde*, Bordeaux, 1948.

is second to none. There are about five hundred of them and most were born to the trade.

The Classification of 1855

Château	District	Average Production in Tonneaux[1]
FIRST GROWTHS		
Lafite	Pauillac	180
Margaux	Margaux	150
Latour	Pauillac	200
Haut-Brion	Pessac (Graves)	120
SECOND GROWTHS		
Mouton-Rothschild	Pauillac	135
Rausan-Ségla	Margaux	120
Rauzan-Gassies	Margaux	100
Léoville-Las-Cases	Saint Julien	225
Léoville-Poyferré	Saint Julien	160
Léoville-Barton	Saint Julien	70
Durfort-Vivens	Margaux	70
Lascombes	Margaux	175
Gruaud-Larose	Saint Julien	185
Brane-Cantenac	Cantenac	250
Pichon-Longueville	Pauillac	70
Pichon-Longueville-Lalande	Pauillac	150
Ducru-Beaucaillou	Saint Julien	130
Cos-d'Estournel	Saint Estèphe	210
Montrose	Saint Estèphe	125
THIRD GROWTHS		
Kirwan	Cantenac	60
Issan	Cantenac	75
Lagrange	Saint Julien	110
Langoa	Saint Julien	75
Giscours	Labarde	245
Malescot-Saint-Exupéry	Margaux	50

[1] One tonneau contains four Bordeaux hogsheads, i.e. 900 litres, or twelve hundred bottles.

The Classification of 1855

Château	District	Average Production in Tonneaux
Cantenac-Brown	Cantenac	90
Palmer	Cantenac	110
La Lagune	Ludon	230
Desmirail[1]	Margaux	0
Calon-Ségur	Saint Estèphe	250
Ferrière	Margaux	10
Marquis d'Alesme-Becker	Margaux	22

FOURTH GROWTHS

Saint-Pierre-Sevaistre	Saint Julien	40
Saint-Pierre-Bontemps	Saint Julien	40
Branaire-Ducru	Saint Julien	120
Talbot	Saint Julien	75
Duhart-Milon	Pauillac	60
Pouget	Cantenac	30
La Tour-Carnet	Saint Laurent	20
Lafon-Rochet	Saint Estèphe	50
Beychevelle	Saint Julien	230
Prieuré-Lichine	Cantenac	60
Marquis-de-Terme	Margaux	130

FIFTH GROWTHS

Pontet-Canet	Pauillac	200
Batailley	Pauillac	60
Haut-Batailley	Pauillac	60
Grand-Puy-Lacoste	Pauillac	100
Grand-Puy-Ducasse	Pauillac	35
Lynch-Bages	Pauillac	160
Lynch-Moussas	Pauillac	20
Dauzac	Labarde	40
Mouton-d'Armailhacq[2]	Pauillac	125
Le Tertre	Arsac	25
Haut-Bages-Liberal	Pauillac	40

[1] This château is extinct as a separate entity but the vineyard is incorporated into that of Château Palmer which it adjoins.

[2] Now renamed Château Mouton-Baron-Philippe.

The Classification of 1855

Château	District	Average Production in Tonneaux
Pédesclaux	Pauillac	35
Belgrave	Saint Laurent	90
Camensac	Saint Laurent	25
Cos-Labory	Saint Estèphe	55
Clerc-Milon	Pauillac	30
Croizet-Bages	Pauillac	90
Cantemerle	Macau	70

The production figures, of course, are only very approximate: they vary greatly from year to year. Those quoted are taken from Alexis Lichine's magnificent *Encyclopaedia of Wines and Spirits* (London, 1967). I believe them to be accurate and it will be seen that they differ considerably from figures previously published.

One anomaly will be noticed immediately: the first growths include Château Haut-Brion, which is not from the Médoc at all, but from Graves. Some say that the classification was only meant to cover the Médoc and that Château Haut-Brion had to be included because it just could not be left out, but the better view appears to be that the classification was supposed to cover the whole of the Gironde and that all save one of the great red wines were at that time grown in the Médoc. It was before St. Emilion and Pomerol came into their own.

In preparing lists of the individual growths, the brokers endeavoured to list the various wines in order of merit within the five categories. This was perhaps brave rather than wise, as it would be very difficult to justify a strict order between wines that come from opposite ends of the Médoc and which are of quite different styles. The choice is essentially a matter of taste. It would have been better to have listed the châteaux in alphabetical order as there is no way of assessing wine gradations. Indeed there is no very pronounced falling off in quality from one growth to the next. The fifth growths are by no means fifth-rate: they are very good wines indeed, and it seems a pity that the fourth and fifth growths were not included in a single classification, as there is no real difference between them. Recent attempts have been made to produce a new classification, and this has very rightly included great wines from districts other than the Médoc. For that reason, it will be discussed later in this chapter after those districts have been described. Moreover, since 1855 good viticulture has given some châteaux such standing that they would today undoubtedly be upgraded and other bourgeois châteaux would be included for the first time. Conversely some of the great names ought to be down-graded, but their proprietors will undoubtedly fight to the last ditch before succumbing to such an indignity. It is this, more than anything else, that will probably delay the publication of a new official classification. At best, the classification is there to guide and assist, never to dictate. Apart from the *cinq crus classés* there are the *crus bourgeois exceptionnels*, *crus bourgeois supérieurs*, *crus bourgeois*, *crus artisans* and *crus paysans*. As terms, they are hardly translatable, though Charles Tovey tried hard with 'Burgesses and Superior Burgesses; Peasants and Superior Peasants'. There are excellent wines amongst them—even amongst the 'Peasants'. The idea of a wine being classed as *bourgeois* may at first sight seem odd, but it is a very old term, of feudal origin. During the English domination the bourgeois citizens of Bordeaux were given certain privileges of land tenure which were continued by the French and which helped to create the great tradition of viticulture that went with the ownership of land. When a great wine is required, one must have a *cru classé*; but the lesser known wines often represent wonderful value, and they must be well made if they are to be sold at a good price, as they have no great name or convenient classification to help them, whereas one suspects that some of the *crus classés* fail to live up to their reputation simply because the proprietor knows full well that he can get a good price, at least for a time.

The 1855 list includes châteaux from all over the Haut-Médoc, but the majority of them belong to the six special *appellations* that have already been mentioned. The most southerly of these, and that nearest to the city of Bordeaux, is Margaux. It is here that the lightest and most delicate of all the clarets are grown. They have been described as: 'Gifted with great finesse, a beautiful colour and an aroma which lingers on the palate. They are generous without being heady, stimulating digestion without affecting the head.' The greatest of them all, of course, is Château Margaux itself, but ten other châteaux are included amongst the classified growths, and apart from these the following *bourgeois supérieurs* châteaux produce fine wines: de Labégorce, de l'Abbé-Gorsse-de-Gorsse, de Lamouroux and la Colonilla.

Closely associated with Margaux—so closely, indeed, that it is difficult to draw any valid distinction between the two—is Cantenac. If there is any difference at all it is that the wines are slightly 'bigger'. Some vineyards, including the great Château Margaux itself, have part of their land in each commune, and it shares the *appellation* of Margaux. Apart from its seven *crus classés*, good *bourgeois* wines include Châteaux d'Angludet and Montbrun. The *appellation* is also shared by part of the commune of Arsac, with its *cru classé*, and by part of Labarde, with its two *crus classés*, and notable *bourgeois* wines such as Château Siran.

The commune of Moulis, although enjoying a special *appellation*, produces no *cru classé* wines; but its *bourgeois* growths are of real distinction, though rather big-bodied compared with those of the finer areas of the Médoc, and some of them perhaps somewhat lacking in finesse. It is rather as if a Médoc were crossed with a St. Emilion though so far as the best are concerned it would be fairer to say they taste like a cross between Margaux and Pauillac. They include Châteaux Chasse-Spleen, Poujeaux-Theil, Gressier-Grand-Poujeaux, Dutruch-Grand-Poujeaux, Pomys and Duplessis. These (and some would certainly figure as classed growths in any new classification) are the leaders in a considerable list, and there are several other serious challengers for the leadership. Despite the absence of anything truly and consistently great, one can understand why the commune has the dignity of its separate *appellation*.

Much the same remarks apply to Listrac. The wines are robust like those of Moulis, with a little more bouquet and breed. At least two of the leading *bourgeois* growths have acquired a considerable following in this country: Châteaux Fourcas-Dupré and Fourcas-Hostein. Other notable names are Châteaux Fonréaud, Lestage, Sémeillan and Clarke. Château Clarke, although not much known in this country, is said to possess much body and to last for years.

With St. Julien, we come again to an area where wines of the very highest quality are grown: wines, moreover, of great individuality, having a bouquet all of their own, that has been described, in a somewhat far-fetched way, as resembling crushed ivy. It is the soil, of course, that can be thanked for this: it is gravelly, like that of Margaux, but it is just a little richer, and the wines, in consequence, are bigger. It includes no less than twelve *crus classés*, and two of the *bourgeois* growths—Châteaux Gloria and Moulin Riche—are practically as good as some of their more famous neighbours.

Pauillac is the greatest of all the communes, in every sense of the word. The quantity of wine produced is enormous, and the quality is positively second to none. Being just a little further up the Médoc, the soil is slightly richer than that of St. Julien, and the wines accordingly have even more body. But despite that, they are soft, delicate and delightfully aromatic. To head the list, there are three of the greatest Châteaux of all: Lafite, Latour and Mouton-Rothschild. This is only the beginning, though, and these great wines are followed by fifteen other *crus classés*. What a piece of land! And apart from the *crus classés* there are a considerable number of excellent *bourgeois*, amongst them Châteaux La Couronne, du Colombier-Monpelou, Malécot, Fonbadet and La Tour-Milon. The local co-operative also makes an excellent wine which sells as La Rose Pauillac.

By the time one has reached St. Estèphe, the soil has become perhaps a trifle too rich. The wines tend to be fuller while none has quite the distinction or exquisite bouquet of the Pauillacs. They are not particularly 'big' wines but from the point of view of 'vinosity' they easily top the list. The best of them are very good indeed, and there are five *crus classés*. Amongst a considerable number of excellent *bourgeois* growths there are Châteaux Tronquoy-Lalande, Meyney, Le Crock, de Marbuzet, Beau-Site, Fatin, Phélan-Ségur, Canteloup, Capbern, Beauséjour, Les Ormes-de-Pez, de Pez, Haut-Marbuzet and several others that might well be mentioned.

Apart from these communes that are entitled to *appellations contrôlées* of their own, there are several others throughout the Médoc that produce excellent wines. For the sake of readers who wish to use this book as a work of reference, these will be listed. Other readers will very probably choose to skip over the next page. Amongst the most southerly of the communes of the Haut-Médoc, is that of Blanquefort, producing light, quickly maturing wines including that of Châteaux Dillon. At Le Taillan there is the château of that name (one of the Cruse properties) that grows both red and white wines—the latter being sold as La Dame Blanche. Then come Parempuyre, with Châteaux de Parempuyre (which is divided into two), Ségur-Bacqué and Ségur-Fillon; and Le Pian-Médoc, with Château Sénéjac. One then gets to Ludon, with the most southerly of the classified growths and several good *bourgeois* growths such as Châteaux Pomiès-Agassac, and Nexon-Lemoyne. Before arriving at Margaux, there are Macau, with its excellent classified growth and several *bourgeois* growths including Châteaux Maucamps, Cambon-La-Pelouse and Priban; and, on much the same latitude but further west, Arsac, with its classified growth and several *bourgeois* growths. To the west of Margaux is Avensan, with Châteaux Villegeorge and Citran-Clauzel. Just north of Margaux is Soussans, with notable *bourgeois* growths that include Châteaux Bel-Air-Marquis d'Aligre, La Tour-de-Mons and Paveil. To the west of St. Julien is St. Laurent-de-Médoc, with three classified growths and several *bourgeois* growths including Châteaux Caronne-Sainte-Gemme and Barateau; while to the south of St. Julien is Cussac, with Château Lanessan. To the west of Pauillac is St. Sauveur, whose *bourgeois* growths include Châteaux Liversan and Fontesteau, just north of which is Cissac with its *bourgeois* Châteaux du Breuil, Hanteillan, Cissac and La Tour-du-Mirail. Finally, to the north of St. Estèphe, but still within the Haut-Médoc, comes St. Seurin-de-Cadourne. By now one is certainly approaching the Bas-Médoc, and the wines tend to be a trifle dull on the nose; but they have an immense amount of body and often develop unexpectedly well over the years. There are no classified growths, but notable amongst the *bourgeois* are Châteaux Verdignan, Pontoise-Gabarus-Brochon, Sociando and Bel-Orme-Tronquoy-de-Lalande. Already the reader has been burdened with a catalogue of châteaux, all of which produce worthy wines and some of which are certainly obscure. To give a similar list for the Bas-Médoc would be superfluous, not to say tedious. The reader who wishes to obtain more names, or to check the whereabouts of châteaux whose wines he enjoys, should consult the standard works, such as Cocks et Feret[1] or Roger.[2] But even if a list of the communes of the Bas-Médoc cannot be included in a book of this size, their wines should not be forgotten. Many of

[1] *Bordeaux et Ses Vins*, 11th edition, Bordeaux, 1949.
[2] J. R. Roger, *The Wines of Bordeaux*, London, 1960.

them are very good indeed and some, such as Château Loudenne, are well established as favourites in this country: amongst its many admirers was the late Maurice Healy, and it was his mother's favourite claret.

The name 'Graves' in England is generally taken to signify the pleasant, if scarcely inspiring white table wines that are grown in that district. Apart from them, however, it also yields red wines of exceptional quality and of a most distinctive character; so much so, in fact, that when the wines of the Gironde were classified in 1855, the greatest of all the graves, Château Haut-Brion, was included amongst the first growths: the only wine to be classified outside of the Médoc. Until the beginning of the last century practically all the wine grown in Graves was red, and about a quarter of it still is. The red graves tend to have a rather earthy taste, lacking the finesse of the médocs, but much nearer to them in style than to the wines of St. Emilion and Pomerol. In speed of maturing and length of life they tend to come between the two.

Graves takes its name from the *graves* soil on which the finest vineyards are found. It is of the gravelly kind but with plenty of flinty pebbles, and a little clay; and although such soil is quite widespread—being also found in the red wine districts of the Médoc, St. Emilion and Pomerol—it is most common in Graves and is generally considered to be characteristic of that region. This is the very best kind of soil for red wines. In some parts of the area, however, there are sandy soils, and these are devoted to growing the humbler kinds of white wines.

At its northern edge it borders the Médoc and extends southwards for some thirty-five miles, encompassing the city of Bordeaux. While red wines are grown throughout the region, they are at their best in the northern half where the best *graves* soil is found, and the two most notable communes are undoubtedly Pessac and Léognan. The former, indeed, is a suburb of Bordeaux, and unfortunately the vineyards are receding as the city encroaches. Already some of the vineyards that were highly praised in the eighteenth century have totally vanished. The only hope for the future lies in the fact that the suburbs in this direction are rather seedy ones, and the vineyards are valuable, so one prays that the city will be forced to grow upwards instead of outwards. The greatest name in Pessac is, without doubt, Haut-Brion, but it is

by no means alone. Just across the main road that leads to
Arcachon is the admirable Château La Mission-Haut-Brion, and
a little further out lies Château Pape-Clément. The commune of
Léognan, further south, includes a galaxy of excellent growths that
are rightly popular in this country, amongst them Châteaux Haut-
Bailly, Malartic-Lagravière, Domaine de Chevalier,[1] Fieuzal,
Carbonnieux and Larrivet-Haut-Brion. But if these be the prin-
cipal communes, they are by no means the only ones of note. For
instance one should mention Château La Tour Haut-Brion at
Talence, Château Couhins at Villenave d'Ornan, Châteaux Smith-
Haut-Lafitte, La Tour Martillac and La Garde at Martillac;
Château Bouscaut at Cadaujac; Château du Tuquet at Beautiran;
and one could reasonably name many others. Châteaux in the
Graves commonly grow red and white wines in different parts of
the same vineyard.

The district of St. Emilion lies well to the north-east of Bordeaux, on the far side of the River Dordogne, beyond Libourne;
and it is one of the very greatest districts both for quantity and for
quality. Next to it lies the smaller but also very important district
of Pomerol. There is a distinct difference in the style of their wines
—a difference that can only be appreciated by tasting them—but
they also have a lot in common: they are big, strong, heady wines
which in blind tastings are often mistaken by the unwary for
burgundies. Yet despite this they have the subtlety and delicacy
that is unique to claret. The wines of Pomerol have been described
as having a 'rich truffle scent', and the district is fortunate in that
the phylloxera does not take kindly to the soil, so that there are still
a considerable number of native vines. But despite this the wines
mature relatively quickly, though their rapid development is by
no means followed by a rapid decline. The town of St. Emilion is
a sheer delight; a town whose origins are lost in antiquity and
whose ancient remains are unique in this part of France. It is a
place that every traveller should visit, though preferably not on a
Sunday in summer, when it is crammed to overflowing. The early
Christians there lived a somewhat troglodyte existence, as their

---

[1] This château is peculiarly good at making fine wines in off-vintage years.
The 1954, for instance, was memorable. It appears that a large local labour force
is available to swoop on the vines at precisely the right moment, and this at least
partly helps to account for its repeated successes.

great underground church clearly shows, and the ground beneath the town is hollowed out to give acres and acres of cellar space. Set high up on its hillside, overlooking some of the greatest vineyards in Europe, there is nowhere quite like it; and it is a town with a very English history—a frontier post in Guienne that remained loyal to England despite every siege and assault until it was obliged to capitulate in 1433, when John Talbot, Earl of Shrewsbury, was defeated and slain at the Battle of Castillon, seven miles away. The vineyards in St. Emilion and Pomerol are as old as the town. They may have been planted by the Gauls, or perhaps by the Romans, and they were famous long before the Médoc was heard of. Those of St. Emilion, moreover, were the subject of perhaps the earliest attempt to secure an *appellation contrôlée*, by royal letters patent of Edward I in 1289; and the delimitation then was much the same as it is today. Unfortunately, however, they have not always been cultivated with that degree of care which they deserve. One can too easily understand why: in such a pleasant, lazy place, where it is easy to grow a fine wine that will command a high price, why bother to grow an even better one? When, in 1855, the wines of the Gironde were classified, those of St. Emilion and Pomerol were ignored. It was not until after the holocaust of the phylloxera that, in comparatively recent times, they came once more into their own—Pomerol even later than St. Emilion. The Pomerol vineyards lie near the town of Libourne, a rather dull town in everything save gastronomy. It was named after Sir Roger de Leyburne, whose English castle was at Leybourn in Kent.

A wide range of soils are found in various parts of the two districts, but most of the finer wines come from gravel soils with more or less clay. The district of St. Emilion can be broadly divided into two areas: the Côtes, where the vines are grown on the hillsides, and the Graves, where the soil is flat, towards Pomerol. The *appellation* St. Emilion includes eight communes: St. Emilion, St. Laurent-des-Combes, St. Christophe-des-Bardes, St. Hippolyte, St. Etienne-de-Lisse, St. Pey-d'Armens, St. Sulpice-de-Faleyrens and Vignonet. Most of the finest wines of the district are grown within these communes, but excellent wines that equal some of them come from five further communes which are permitted to add St. Emilion after their own names. These are:

St. Georges, Montagne, Lussac, Puisseguin and Parsac. There is a further *appellation* Sables St. Emilion which is applied to some rather light wines grown near Libourne.

Although the St. Emilion wines were omitted from the classification of 1855, the wines of the first eight communes were classified into four categories in 1954. Previously to this classification, it was the habit of many relatively insignificant growths proudly to label their bottles with the words *Premier Cru Classé*, which caused mixed ribaldry and indignation amongst the proprietors of the Médoc. The present classification has at least put an end to that; but it must be remembered that it only purports to compare wines grown in one area, and there is no suggestion that the first and second growths of St. Emilion are comparable with those of the Médoc. The classification is as follows:

Saint Emilion Premier Grand Cru Classé
(a) Château Ausone
    Cheval Blanc
(b)   Beauséjour (Duffau)
    Beauséjour (Fagouet)
    Belair
    Canon
    Clos Fourtet
    Figeac
    La Gaffelière Naudes
    Magdelaine
    Pavie
    Trottevieille

Saint Emilion Grand Cru Classé
Château L'Arrosée
    L'Angélus
    Balestard la Tonnelle
    Bellevue
    Bergat
    Cadet Bon
    Cadet Piola
    Canon la Gaffelière
    Cap de Mourlin
    Chapelle Madeleine et Clos la Madeleine

93

Saint Emilion Grand Cru Classé—continued

Chauvin
Corbin (Giraud)
Corbin Michotte
Curé Bon de la Madeleine
Fonplégade
Fonroque
Franc Mayne
Grand Barrail Lamarzelle Figeac
Grand Corbin d'Espagne
Grand Corbin Pegresse
Grand Mayne
Grand Pontet
Grandes Murailles
Guadet Saint Julien
Jean Faure
Clos des Jacobins
La Carte
La Clotte
La Clusière
La Couspaude
La Dominique
Larcis Ducasse
Lamarzelle
Larmande
Laroze
La Serre
La Tour du Pin Figeac (Belivier)
La Tour du Pin Figeac (Moueix)
La Tour Figeac
Le Chatelet
Le Couvent
Le Prieure
Mauvezin
Moulin du Cadet
Pavie Decesse
Pavie Macquin
Pavillon Cadet
Petit Faurie de Soutard

Saint Emilion Grand Cru Classé—continued
Petit Faurie de Souchard
Ripeau
Sansonnet
Saint Georges Côte Pavie
Clos Saint Martin
Soutard
Tertre Daugay
Trimoulet
Trois Moulins
Troplong Mondot
Villemaurine
Yon Figeac

A similar classification has been prepared for Pomerol:

Appellation Contrôlée 'Pomerol'

I ÈRS CRUS
Ch. Pétrus
Vieux Ch. Certan
Ch. l'Evangile
Ch. la Conseillante
Ch. Lafleur
Ch. Certan
Ch. Petit Village
Ch. Trotanoy
Ch. Latour Pomerol
Ch. Gazin
Clos l'Eglise
Clos l'Eglise Clinet
Ch. la Grave Trigant de Boisset
Domaine de l'Eglise
Ch. le Gay
Ch. Rouget
Ch. la Fleur Pétrus
Ch. Beauregard
Ch. Guillot
Ch. Nenin
Ch. Lagrange

I ÈRS CRUS—*continued*

Ch. Certan-Marzelle
Ch. la Pointe
Ch. la Croix de Gay
Ch. Clinet
Ch. la Croix
Ch. Gombaude-Guillot
Ch. Vraye Croix de Gay
Ch. Feytit-Clinet
Clos du Rocher
Ch. la Commanderie
Cru de la Nouvelle Eglise
Ch. Plince
Ch. Taillefer
Clos Beauregard
Ch. la Croix St.-Georges
Ch. la Cabanne
Ch. Bourgneuf
Ch. le Caillou
Ch. l'Enclos
Clos René
Ch. Pignon de Gay
Clos du Roy
Ch. de Sales
Ch. Moulinet
Ch. l'Enclos du Presbytère
Ch. Grate-Cap
Clos des Templiers
Clos de la Gravette
Ch. Haut Maillet

DUEXIÈME I ÈRS CRUS

Clos du Commandeur
Ch. la Providence
Vieux Ch. Groupey
Les Grandes Vignes Clinet
Domaine de Haut Tropchaud
Clos Tropchaud
Ch. la Violette

DUEXIÈME I ÈRS CRUS—*continued*

Ch. le Carillon
Domaine de Haut Pignon
Ch. Chêne Liege
Ch. la Fleur du Gazin
Ch. Bel Air
Ch. Rêve d'Or
Clos Lacombe
Ch. Cantereau
Ch. Ferrand
Ch. Mazeyres
Enclos du Haut Mazeyres
Ch. Beauchêne
Clos Mazeyres
Ch. Trintin
Clos Bonalgue
Ch. Couprie
Close du Seigneur
Cru Grands Champs
Ch. des Grands Champs
Ch. Tailhas

2 ÈMES CRUS

Ch. Franc Maillet
Ch. Vieux Maillet
Ch. Thibaud Maillet
Ch. le Bon Pasteur
Cru la Rose
Clos Pince
Ch. la Croix Taillefer
Ch. la Patache
Clos la Patache

The above four districts of the Médoc, Graves, St. Emilion and Pomerol, with their classified and *premier bourgeois* growths, produce all the greatest clarets; but nevertheless a great deal of very worthy and enjoyable wine is grown in the other districts that have already been referred to on page 80. The Premières Côtes de Bordeaux consists of a long, narrow strip of sloping ground on the east bank of the Garonne. The soil, for the most part, is marl, but there is a little gravel, and the wines are full-bodied and pleasant, but not at all distinguished. Most of the vineyards grow both red and white wines, but the emphasis is on red in the north and white in the south.

Blayais and Bourgeais wines are grown on the eastern bank of the Gironde, to the north and west of Pomerol. There are three *appellations contrôlées*: Bourg, Bourgeais and Côtes de Bourg—names that are becoming increasingly well known and respected in this country. Owing to the high prices fetched by even the humble growths in the greater districts, wine merchants are increasingly looking towards Blayais and Bourgeais for their cheaper clarets, and many good, well-made wines from single châteaux in this area are sold at prices directly competitive with those blended wines that are available under rather vague district names or under the attractive trade marks of the merchants who blend them. Such château wines often represent excellent value and mature relatively quickly. If it can be said of the wines of St. Emilion and Pomerol that in blind tastings they are often mistaken by the unwary for burgundies, the same can be said far more strongly of the wines of these districts. This was pointed out long ago by Franck in his *Traité des Vins du Médoc*. Shortly before writing this chapter I was having lunch with a friend of mine who is a Master of Wine and whose palate, especially for claret, is renowned in the wine trade. We shared a bottle of simple wine from the commune of Villeneuve and we both knew exactly what it was; but we agreed that had we been tasting it blind we should almost certainly have identified it as a burgundy.

Fronsac is right next door to Pomerol. Scenically, it is one of the most pleasant areas of the Bordeaux country, and the wine it produces is of admirable quality, resembling that of Pomerol but with more body; in fact some of the lesser growths are so 'big' that they tend to be coarse. For the purposes of *appellations contrôlées* the area is divided into two parts: Côtes-Canon-Fronsac and Côtes-de-Fronsac, of which the former is the more distinguished.

A certain amount of red wine is also grown in the Entre-Deux-Mers area. It is of very ordinary quality and it has no *appellation contrôlée* of its own, being sold simply as *bordeaux* or *bordeaux supérieur*.

The classification of 1855 is far more than a useful guide: it is still very accurate. But although the quality of which a vineyard is capable depends ultimately on geography, there are also more transitory factors, such as the vines that are growing there and the skill with which the wine is made at any given time. Thus, looking at the list today, some growths may appear a trifle over-rated, whilst others consistently belie their humble classification. A few more, which are not included in the classified growths at all, should certainly be amongst them. The most powerful criticism of all is that a classified list of great clarets should not be virtually confined to the châteaux of the Médoc. Viewed through the eyes of a négociant living in 1855, such a limitation may well have been justified, but it certainly is not so today. It is therefore not at all surprising that for many years there has been an agitation to bring the list up to date. Such a revision may well be in the interests of the public, who tend to pay more attention to such things than perhaps they deserve. One cannot expect casual wine drinkers, who nevertheless thoroughly enjoy their glass of claret, to acquire a specialist knowledge, and one must give them such concise and comprehensible guidance as one can. A revised list would not greatly affect the skilled merchant who buys his wines according to his own deep knowledge; but it would undoubtedly help the public. On the other hand its preparation is fraught with the difficulties that have already been outlined. Those proprietors whose wines were down-graded would fight furiously, and if the list were ever to be officially published they would deny its authenticity and would still sell their wines under the 1855 classification. Despite these obstacles, however, a great deal of work has already been done, and a new list has been provisionally prepared. So far the only official list that has been published has been tentative and confined to the wines of the Médoc, but Alexis Lichine, the famous wine grower and writer on wine, has shown splendid enterprise and has prepared a list of his own. It has changed somewhat over the years as will be seen in the various editions of his *The Wines of France* and his recent massive *Encyclopaedia of Wines and Spirits*, and it is more far-reaching and enterprising than that of the *Institut National des appellations d'origine* which was published in 1962.

With his immense experience and knowledge of Bordeaux, he

should know how to classify wine if anyone does. But his new classification is not yet by any means definitive and is undergoing constant revision: this in itself indicates the immensity and difficulty of the task. And with the utmost diffidence (for I am an amateur criticizing a supremely successful and knowledgeable professional) I differ from him in some of his assessments, for I have consistently had fine wines off some of the châteaux he places low on the list and have scant respect for one or two of the mighty. If ever a new list does achieve official recognition one thing is certain: not a soul will agree with every detail of it.

There are some reassessments, though, that no one would seriously dispute. In the first place, if five classes are to remain, practically all the châteaux at present classed would be in the first four, and the fifth would bring in several more that are at present unjustly omitted. Secondly, each of the various classes would list wines of equivalent merit from other districts alongside those of the Médoc.

For some wines there must obviously be promotions. Château Mouton-Rothschild joins the first growths, with Château Cheval-Blanc from St. Emilion and Château Pétrus from Pomerol. Amongst the third growths, Château Palmer and Château Calon-Ségur should surely be promoted to the seconds with leading growths from St. Emilion, Pomerol and Graves. In the 1855 classification, Château Beychevelle is clearly far too low down as a fourth growth: it should rightly be regarded as a second, and Château Cantemerle should equally be promoted from its indefensible position at the bottom of the fifth growths right up to the seconds. Alexis Lichine would also promote Château Lynch-Bages from the fifth growths to the seconds, and on both price and fame he is obviously right, but with the greatest respect for his judgment I should personally not promote it quite so steeply, as its wines, perhaps owing to the method of vinification, have a style of their own which gives them remarkable individuality but which, to my taste, is not the classic style of the Médoc. Quite apart from these, there are several other arguable promotions and one or two demotions: that is where the trouble starts. But the remarkable thing is how accurate the old classification as a whole remains.

Amongst the wines of the Médoc that should certainly be

BORDEAUX

brought into the classification are Châteaux d'Angludet, Capbern, Fourcas-Dupré, Fourcas-Hostein, Lanessan, de Pez and Phélan-Ségur. There are several other strong candidates. A curious aspect of the classification is that it passes with the château and not with the vineyard, thus in recent years there has been a considerable amount of consolidation and rationalization—scattered pieces of vineyard having been exchanged for adjacent pieces, and so on. An example of where this has been done is Château Lascombes, but there are many others. Notably Château Palmer has absorbed Château Desmirail. This in itself, of course, is a very good thing: a properly consolidated vineyard is more likely to run true to form than one which has several remote fragments, but the fact that this is possible does help to make nonsense of the classification.

The fundamental question, though, is: should there be a classification at all? This is academic, as in France it is inevitable, moreover it does generally help the public. At times, though, it can be misleading, as for instance when a vineyard is mismanaged for a period. And there is the further difficulty that vineyards which are left out or rated in a low position may find themselves in a vicious circle. Their wines will not fetch the high prices of those grown by their neighbours and the only way to make a profit is to increase the yield; but this in itself will keep the quality down. Once the wine has been given a bad name, it needs a lot of capital as well as enthusiasm and patience before it can retrieve itself. On the whole, the classification is a blessing but a mixed blessing.

When planning this book, I entertained the pious hope that I would be able to include a few paragraphs on each of the classified growths, giving something of their history and trying to describe their wines. But it is a vain and rash man who attempts to describe the bouquet and flavour of any wine. Only a lunatic would try to convey those subtle differences that distinguish the great growths. There is only one way for the reader to do it: to taste them and see for himself. And to write of each château in turn would fill the whole of a book bigger than this. The first growths, however, stand apart even from their great rivals, and each of these châteaux must be described. But only their histories. To write of their vintages and to indulge in reminiscences of past dinners would fill a small book, and to limit oneself to the great growths would be unfair to the slightly lesser ones, which have given almost as much pleasure.

To try and draw fine distinctions between them, to pretend that one or other is 'the best', would be impossible. Sometimes they disappoint one, even tragically. In occasional vintages, one or other of their humbler rivals will produce a wine so outstanding that perhaps it excels all the first growths. The late Maurice Healy, whose judgment was second to none, declared that in 1920 Château Latour made the finest wine, but Château Giscours came second and Léoville-Poyferré third. Similar strange stories may be told of many other vintage years. Sometimes, then, the first growths prove not to be the greatest clarets of them all. Occasionally there is a complete catastrophe. An example of a disappointing wine from a first growth was Château Margaux 1933. Sometimes, too, a first growth may pass into a prolonged decline, as Château Haut-Brion did in the 1920s. But these odd years and bad periods are mere aberrations: over a period of time the first growths will win. These are the vineyards in which absolutely everything is exactly right. They are the kings of their districts, and their districts are the kings of Bordeaux.

The name of Château Lafite is said to be derived from an old French word *lafitte*, meaning a hillock, and until recently the number of fs and ts in its name seems to have varied as a matter of whim. It is at present owned by the Barons de Rothschild, whose ancestor, Baron James de Rothschild, bought it for more than four and a half million francs—an astronomical price at the time—in 1868. It also has the distinction, unique among châteaux, of being the subject of a complete book, Cyril Ray's *Lafite*:[1] a work of outstanding interest on the subject of claret in general, quite apart from the château.

Lafite has one of the longest and most interesting histories of all the châteaux, and it was famous before many of its rivals even existed. In the eighteenth century it was owned by the Ségur family, who were once amongst the most important wine growers in the Médoc and whose name is immortalized by Châteaux Calon-Ségur and Phélan-Ségur. Afterwards it came into the hands of a M. de Pichard, who was head of the Guienne parliament. Although he was said to be highly popular in the Médoc, he was evidently less so with the Parisian mob, and he was guillotined in

[1] London, 1968.

1794. All his possessions were confiscated by the state, and the château became national property until it was bought by a Dutch syndicate in 1797. In 1803 it was bought from the syndicate by a French merchant named Vanlerberghe. He was an international speculator and financier who made a fortune as a supplier to the French army; but perhaps his methods were not too scrupulous. In 1808 he went bankrupt and with the changing political climate he had to make a very quick exit in 1818. There was a little matter of some twenty million francs which the state claimed was owing on his army contracts, and his property was forfeit. However his cunning prevailed to the end, and he indulged in a series of ruthless manœuvres that would delight the heart of any lawyer. First of all, he and his wife divorced one another by mutual consent. He was then liable to repay her dowry of a million francs, which he did by giving her Château Lafite. Thus she appears in the list of owners under her maiden name, Mlle. Barbe-Rosalie Lemaire. Then, in 1821, the figure of Mr. Samuel Scott, an English banker, comes into the picture. The wife, with rare brilliance, sold him the château for the exact sum of her dowry—a million francs. For ten years the state struggled to prove that the divorce was fraudulent and void until it was eventually declared a nullity in 1827. But it was all to no avail. Mr. Scott and his successors only held the property as trustees, but they continued to hold it, and very good trustees they were, too, for it was during this period that the Carruades vineyards were acquired. Both the family and the trustees exercised so much discretion that it was locally thought that the Vanlerberghe heir had been wrongfully dispossessed. In his *Bordeaux*, Malvezin relates how 'He used to walk among the vines in the blazing sunshine of August, doing his best to protect himself from its heat under the shade of a vast parasol of red silk, only to die after many years either of apoplexy or melancholy.' Presumably he was keeping a careful eye on his valuable property, which was being managed by a famous *régisseur* Emil Goudal. The château was eventually sold by auction in 1868. It was bought by Baron James de Rothschild for a total of 4,840,000 francs—about £193,000.

It was Vanlerberghe, in 1797, who started the great 'library' of wines that includes every vintage from that year. Seventeen ninety-seven itself was a very poor vintage, and it is probable that the

wine has been undrinkable for years. But the 'library' was started
in ample time to include what was perhaps the greatest vintage
ever: 'The Year of the Comet'—1811. It was one of those immortal
vintages in every sense of the word: immortal because its quality
will never be forgotten, and immortal because the wine seems to
last for ever. In 1926, Maurice Healy, with some three hundred
other guests, was entertained to a special luncheon in the château,
and I will let him speak for himself:[1]

'Magnums of Château Margaux 1907 competed with the Latour 1900
in bottles, to the great improvement of our Filet Mignon; and then with
the Poularde came Château Lafite 1870, also in magnums. . . . It was
perfect. Elegance, dignity, charm; bouquet, colour and fruit; all were
present, and none over-weighed the others. After that what could be
served that would not be an anti-climax? There was a hush, as the
sommeliers began to announce "Le Vin de la Comète"; and to more than
three hundred guests was served a generous measure of the Lafite of
1811! In 115 years it had only once been re-corked; save for the
re-corking it had never been moved. (I brought a little flask home for
George Saintsbury; he was charmed). . . . On the occasion I am
describing there must have been five dozen bottles served; not one
received a word of criticism. I can only speak personally of my share
of one, but my opinion coincided with all the others I heard. The
colour was a little pale; the bouquet was very delicate, but there was
plenty of it. On the palate it tasted just a wee bit tired; some 1920s are
much more tired today. I said to my neighbour, as we played with the
1870 and its ancestor: "The image in my mind is that of a distinguished
lady, herself no longer young, saying to those who have gathered to pay
her court, 'My mother would like to come amongst you for a few
minutes'; and then there enters, leaning slightly on her stick, a very old
lady, but with a young heart, who speaks a few bright words to each
guest, and then departs." I do not wish to alter the image. In the
'thirties and 'forties of the last century it must have been a wonderful
wine.'

Can there ever have been a greater claret?

Compared with many of the other growths of Pauillac, Lafite is
remarkably light and delicate. This is perhaps at least partly
attributable to its *encépagement* which has already been mentioned.
This delicacy helps to give it some of its unique charm, and the
influence of the various vines can be seen particularly clearly when

---

[1] Maurice Healy, *Claret and the White Wines of Bordeaux*, London, 1934.

one of the varieties fails, as in 1947 and 1957, when the Merlot fell victim to *coulure*, the flower falling from the vine without forming fruit. In those years the wine lacked the Merlot's softness and was uncharacteristically hard. But the choice of vines hardly accounts for all of it. Techniques of vinification play their part and so, very significantly, does the soil. Outlying parts of the Lafite vineyards are actually in the commune of St. Estèphe, and they lie between two vineyards producing notably 'big' wines—Mouton-Rothschild and Cos d'Estournel—yet Lafite is unique, and quite unlike its neighbours.

Mention has been made, very briefly, of the Carruades de Château Lafite. The vineyards originally known as Carruades were on slightly rising ground adjoining the Lafite vineyards, and dovetailing into the Mouton property. They were bought for the elder Scott by his manager Goudal at some time between 1830 and 1849. Subsequently the younger Scott was minded to sell them again, but Goudal was insistent that he should not do so. He was naturally anxious that vineyard land of such superb quality should not be lost to the property, but he also appears to have been motivated by an intense desire to keep them out of the hands of the owners of Château Mouton; for as long as history relates there has been an intense rivalry between the two properties, dating back to long before they were owned by cousins. Whatever his motives, however, there can be no doubt that Goudal was right, and after a considerable struggle his counsel prevailed. These vineyards have now very properly been integrated with the remainder of Château Lafite and the name Carruades de Château Lafite is used to designate wines made on the property from vines that are less than twelve years old—a good five years older than the minimum imposed by most other growers. It is a fine wine, but not, of course, up to Château Lafite standards. In the best years, and only in France, a third wine is marketed, known as Moulin des Carruades, made from young vines and second pressings. But there is very sensibly some latitude as to the manner in which the first two names are used. In 1950, for instance, the whole of the wine produced by the younger vines was *déclassé* to *bordeaux supérieur*, the best wines made from the old vines being sold as Château Lafite and the poorer wines being sold under the name of *Carruades*. In 1950, therefore, the difference in the wines was one of quality rather than of style, and it was not very great. A similar policy had been followed earlier, in 1921. The *Carruades* generally disappear entirely in the poorer years such as 1963, 1965 and 1968.

The name of Latour is as inseparable from that of Lafite as Toulouse is from Lautrec. They both belong to the same commune, and they are as alike in their greatness as they are individual in their subtleties. The history of Château Latour as a property goes back far further than its history as a vineyard. The *chais* occupies the site of an old castle: one of a line of fortifications erected during the English rule to protect Bordeaux from the pirates of the Gironde. There is a legend that when the English were at last expelled from Gascony, their commander, Lord Chandos, had to leave this castle in a great hurry. He was unable to take his possessions with him and buried a treasure of gold coins in what is now the vineyard. There have been many attempts to dig them up again, but so far no one has succeeded. Little now remains of the original castle: only a few foundations; but during the reign of Louis the Just, in about 1611, some of the old stones were used in building La Tour, the charming little domed tower that gives the château its name. Its known history as a vineyard begins some years later, in 1670, when it was bought by a M. de Chavanas, who was secretary and counsellor to the king. Seven years later it was acquired by the Clauzel family from which it passed by marriage to the great Ségur family. It is still partially owned by members of that family, but a few years ago they sold three-quarters of their holdings to English companies. At the present time Lord Cowdray's interests hold fifty-one per cent of the equity and Harveys of Bristol hold twenty-five per cent. When the new proprietors took over, they found that several small parcels of vineyard had made their way into the hands of peasant proprietors and one speculates as to what sort of wines they made; but these parcels have now been bought in.

The soil of Latour is unique; it is full of pebbles and very arid, giving a low yield of superb wine. Its *encépagement* is seventy per cent Cabernet Sauvignon, ten per cent each of Merlot and Cabernet Franc, and five per cent Petit-Verdot. Perhaps more than any other château, Latour is remarkably reliable even in the oddest off-vintage years. Until very recently it was also notable as being by far the most conservative of all the châteaux. A hand *égrappoir* was used, and afterwards the grapes were crushed under foot before being lifted in barrels into the great oak fermentation vats. The method was utterly reliable, extremely picturesque and wholly uneconomical. Even despite this rather sordid failing, however, it would still have been kept on, had it been better for making wine than the methods of its more mechanized rivals; and the extra costs could easily have been absorbed in the very high prices that the wine fetches. Experience, however, has shown that when a château has been converted to slightly more modern methods no deterioration whatsoever takes place in the quality of the wine. If anything, the reverse is true. The real snag became only too clear in the 1963 vintage, which was a very late one. Much of the casual labour needed for the vintage was provided by Spaniards, holiday-makers and schoolboys, but when it was so late they had all gone away and there were no people to do the work. A mechanical *égrappoir* had to be borrowed very hastily and the mash was pumped up into the vats: a method which all the other châteaux had been using for years. The wine was none the worse for it. Moreover the new proprietors found that much of the equipment was worn out and beyond repair. Of the twelve great fermentation vats, six were useless and the others were becoming distinctly rickety. They had been made of Hungarian oak, which was by far the best for the purpose, but it is now practically unobtainable. After much heart-searching it was decided that they could not be replaced, and a series of stainless steel fermentation vats were installed in 1964. Stainless steel is perhaps the very best material of all; and it is also unfortunately the most expensive. Being practically inert, chemically, it is a very different proposition from ordinary steel, and it will probably become adopted by more and more of the vignerons who can afford it. Moreover, of course, the must only stays in the vats for about a fortnight, whilst it is fermenting. The very successful pioneer installation is at Château Haut-Brion. The new vats are fed from a new *égrappoir* and new presses of the latest pneumatic kind are being installed to replace the primitive and wasteful hydraulic presses that were made in about 1870. There will be many who will regret the passing of the old days, and the régime of M. Bougière, who managed the property from 1928 until he retired in 1963 at the age of eighty-four. But no one need have any fears for the quality of the wine.

His successor is M. Henri Martin, himself the proprietor of Château Gloria, who is mayor of St. Julien and Le Grand Chancelier of the Commanderie du Bontemps-de-Médoc et de Graves. He is a native of the Médoc who knows all that is to be known about wine.

In writing of Latour immediately after Lafite, I have already abandoned the established order of listing, but it seems more logical to describe all the first growths of one commune before passing on to the next, so now it is the turn of Mouton-Rothschild. It seems extraordinary and even eccentric that this great château was ever classified with the second growths. Admittedly it was placed at the very top of the list, but a miss is as good as a mile. It would have been more reasonably placed as the fifth of the first growths rather than as the first of the seconds, though of course this is by no means the only apparent eccentricity in the list. Perhaps those responsible for the classification were divided amongst themselves and reached the sort of compromise that would be expected of the English but which comes as a surprise from the French. For years Mouton has been commanding a price comparable with that of the great first growths, and it has devised a slogan that aptly sums up the situation: 'First I am not, second I do not deign to be, I am Mouton.' In any future classification it will be rated as a first growth. That is absolutely certain.

The great value that has long been attached to Mouton is illustrated by a story told by Paul de Cassagnac.[1] In the 1830s the British Consul in Bordeaux was a Mr. T. G. D. Scott, who was a gourmet, a *bon viveur* and above all an English gentleman, much addicted to society. Everything in his dining-room had to be perfect. The glass and china were the best available. Even the carving knife and fork were kept in boiling water so that the meat would not be injured by contact with the cold steel. And the wine, of course, had to be superb. One day he was entertaining the mayor, a M. Duffan-Dubergier, who was known as 'The King of Aquitania'. One great wine followed another until the butler presented the wine that was to crown the banquet.

'This wine,' said Mr. Scott, 'is Mouton 1828.'

'Have you much of it left?'

'Alas! only a dozen bottles.'

[1] *French Wines*, London, 1936.

'I'll make you a proposition. Twelve bottles, twelve thousand francs.'

The company was astounded. A hundred dozen wine at that price was equal to the whole value of Château Lafite, as claimed by the state in its litigation with the Vanlerberghes.

'Sorry! I can't do that. But I'll split it with you as a favour. You can have half a dozen bottles for six thousand francs.'

'My dear Scott,' replied the king, 'if I buy a wine at that price it is on the assumption that my friends can drink it only at my table.'

'Right, we'll say no more about it.' He turned to his butler. 'Bernard, decant us two more bottles of the Mouton '28.'

Is there any more perfect example of the *flegme britannique*?

By the standards of the Médoc, as indeed by any standards, Mouton is a vineyard with a very long history, and it has had a whole series of illustrious owners. In 1350 it was owned by le Seigneur de Pons, then, in 1430, it passed into English hands as the property of the Duke of Gloucester. Following his fall it was owned by Jean Dunois, the Bastard of Orléans, and then by Gaston de Foix. From 1740, for ninety years, it was owned by one of the great Bordeaux families, the Barons de Brane, whose name, like that of the Ségurs, is immortalized by a château: Brane-Cantenac. During the time of the Barons de Brane, the château was called Brane-Mouton, and it was they who brought it to its glory. The last of them was known as 'The Napoleon of the Vines'. In 1853 it was bought by Baron Nathaniel Rothschild and its present enthusiastic owner is his great-grandson, Baron Philippe, who, incidentally, has translated the works of Christopher Fry into French.

Mouton is one of the most beautiful and most delightful places to visit. Both the Baron and the Baroness are intensely interested in the arts, and they have achieved a décor that is as near perfect as any can be. The *chais* is a sheer joy, with cask after cask of exquisite wine in perfect order, and subdued lighting that shows the whole to the very best effect. There is also a museum that can be seen on written application. It is a very individual affair, not at all like the other museums of wine. It is not a place of crooked bottles and dismembered antique wine presses, but a museum of the fine arts, with this qualification: that each work must have some connection with wine or the vine. There is, for example, an ancient Roman bust of Silenus, crowned with ivy; a gold jug and beaker from Iran dating from the ninth or eight century B.C.; a Rhineland pitcher with English silver-gilt mountings dated 1591; a gilt wood bed decorated with vine leaves and clusters of grapes that was made for the last Doge of Genoa. These are just a few of the things. There are tapestries, sculpture, glass, china and precious metals to delight a collector's heart.[1]

When Mr. Denys Sutton was shown the museum, he recalled the words of Pater in his essay on Dionysus:

'He (Dionysus) comes at last to have a scope equal to that of Demeter, a realm as wide and mysterious as hers; the whole productive power of the earth is in him, and the explanation of its annual change. As some embody their intuitions of that power in corn so others in wine. He is the dispenser of the earth's hidden wealth, giver of riches through the vine, as Demeter through the grain. And as Demeter sends the airy, dainty-wheeled and dainty-winged spirit of Triptolemus to bear her gifts abroad on all the winds, so Dionysus goes on his eastern journey, with its many intricate adventures, on which he carries his gifts to every people.'

What better inspiration could there be for artists?

But why is it called Mouton? That remains a mystery, but one explanation at least can be denied. Charles Tovey tells the following story:[2]

'The day previous to my leaving London, in the course of conversation upon Claret, I was informed by a member of the Reform Club, where he drank Château Mouton, that the wine had a decided taste of *wool*, which it derived from the vineyard being manured with sheep's dung. From this peculiar character I was told it derived the name of Mouton. This statement was supported by others present, and anything I could say in refutation of such an absurdity was treated with contempt, and the discussion waxed warm. But I kept the statement in mind, and when I visited the Mouton Chais I narrated the discussion to Mr. Daniel Guestier; he, suppressing his laughter, communicated it to the chef, who related it to the workmen engaged in drawing off the new wine. The merriment which such nonsense created was a sufficient answer to my opponent. The vines are manured in the ordinary way from oxen and the usual stable refuse.'

[1] Anyone wishing to know more should consult the beautifully illustrated article by Denys Sutton in the September 1963 issue of *Apollo*.
[2] *Wine and Wine Countries*, London, 1877.

Of the many explanations that have been put forward from time to time, two sound more probable than the rest: it could be derived from the old French word *mothon*, meaning hilly land, or it could simply be the place where sheep grazed in the olden days. Mouton Rothschild must not be confused with Mouton Cadet. Unlike the Carruades de Château Lafite, which do in fact come from the Lafite vineyards, Mouton Cadet is merely a blended wine. That is not to say that it is a poor wine. On the contrary, of its class it is admirable, but its class is a very different one from that of Mouton Rothschild. It is bought in from the local co-operatives and small growers, and is blended to give a pleasant wine of consistent quality that is intended for early drinking.

The word 'château' conjures up visions of castellated architectural magnificence; of enormous, impressive, and beautiful buildings like the châteaux of the Loire that are so familiar to English tourists. Those who visit the Médoc hoping to see something similar are bound to be disappointed. As a great vineyard area, the Médoc is a comparative newcomer, and few of the buildings date from before the end of the eighteenth century; Château d'Issan is the chief exception. If one wants a real castle one must go to Graves, to Château Olivier or Château de la Brède, which date from the fourteenth century. The former was once a hunting lodge of the Black Prince. Not only are the other châteaux comparatively modern, but most of them are relatively small, and many were only intended to be lived in during the summer months. Most of the buildings are quite delightful, but in no way memorable. Some of the famous 'châteaux', like Léoville Barton, have no house at all; the proprietor, Ronald Barton, lives in Château Langoa, close by, and the two growths share the same *chais*. Château Margaux is an exception, though: a place of pilgrimage to students of architecture and to students of wine alike. The history of the site goes back further than that of the vineyard. In the fifteenth century it was a fortified castle named Lamothe, and legend has it that it once belonged to an English king: Edward II, Edward III and Henry IV have been suggested. Its history as a great vineyard begins more recently, at the end of the seventeenth century. In 1802 it was bought by the Marquis of La Colonilla who held it until 1836. It was he who pulled down the old château and built the present one. It is a most impressive place to visit. One passes through wrought-iron gates, along a private drive, and there it is, standing four-square, with its vast *chai*, in the middle of a six hundred acre estate. It is enormous; it is imposing; and it has a portico supported by four pillars. It is a magnificent house of its period. But to my taste it is rather forbidding: somewhat undistinguished in its proportions. If only the marquis had moved in thirty years earlier!

If the château building is perhaps a trifle unsubtle, the wine is certainly not. It is a big wine, as one would expect a first growth to be, but it is lighter than the Pauillacs; and it has a special delicacy, all of its own, so that vintages such as 1934 which, coming from other comparably great vineyards, tend to be rather hard, show exceptionally well. Some indication of the care that is taken in growing the wine may be gathered from the fact that out of the whole estate, only about a quarter, on the best gravelly ridges, are planted with vines used for the great château wine. The second wine of Château Margaux is sold as *Le Pavillon Rouge, Margaux*.

Château Margaux has long been a favourite in England, and the account books of the Earl of Bristol show that he bought it regularly from 1703 onwards. Unhappily, however, he could not spell it, and tried at least six variations, of which the most enchanting is 'Margoose'. Morton Shand[1] tells a story that shows how well it is appreciated in its home country:

'Phillipe Egalité possessed some superb Château Margaux which he rarely produced even for his most intimate friends. On his death, what was left of it was bought by the chef of the Rocher de Cancale—a Parisian restaurant that will be familiar to readers of Balzac—who sold it to his customers for the then un-heard of price of eight francs the bottle. Moreover it was the only wine he allowed to be served with *Perdreaux rouges farci aux truffes*.'

What a wine! And what a restaurateur!

To reach Château Haut-Brion, one crosses to the other side of Bordeaux, to Graves, which was once the very centre of the Bordeaux trade before the Médoc came into its own. Amongst the red wines of Graves, Haut-Brion has always been far more famous than the rest, and it was the first of the great clarets to be mentioned by name in English letters; for it was on April 10th, 1663, that Pepys wrote in his diary:

[1] *A Book of French Wines*, London, 1960.

'. . . to the Royall Oak Tavern in Lombard Street and here drank a sort of French wine, called Ho Bryan, that hath a good and most particular taste that I never met with.'

Pepys was by no means alone in his taste. It was praised by Dryden, Defoe and Swift; and everyone who writes of wine today must join in their praises.

The history of the vineyard can be traced back to the close of the Middle Ages, and Morton Shand tells us that there are references to it in the old chronicles prior to 1480, when it was a wine much loved by the Flemings. It would seem that there was once a *seigneurie* de Brion, and it was later called d'Aubrion, and then Hault-Brion, before becoming Haut-Brion, as we know it today. Maurice Healy, as a patriotic Irishman, had another theory. He suggested that its name was a corruption of John Brian, or O'Brien, a sixteenth-century wine merchant of County Cork. Good counsel that he was, he certainly made out a case to go to the jury; but in view of the earlier references discovered by Shand, I fear that the jury would have rejected his case. It is a pity, as one would like to think of there being a first growth with an Irish name.

The property is so ancient that even the château itself has no additions later than the seventeenth century; and its many illustrious owners include Talleyrand. Since 1935 it has been in American hands—those of Mr. Dillon—and although some would suggest that the wines grown there during the 1930s were not the finest it has produced, there can be no doubt that recent vintages have been superb. And like the other great growths, it sometimes yields a good wine in a humble year, or even a rank bad year like 1910. For a few years, though, its quality did collapse. In 1923 it passed out of the hands of the family of Larrien, which had held it since 1836, and was bought by a M. Gilbert. Something went wrong, and the vintages of 1926, 1928 and 1929 were frightfully disappointing though I have greatly enjoyed the 1934. Mr. Dillon at once set to work to return it to its former glory. The vintages from 1943 onwards have been excellent and fully up to the old form.

One of the wonderful things about the four first growths is the way they have kept their character over the years. To summarize their differences today one can hardly do better than to quote the words of Alexander Henderson, published in 1824:[1]

[1] *The History of Ancient and Modern Wines*, London.

'Of the RED wines of the Bordelais, the Lafitte, Latour, Château Margaux, and Haut-Brion, are so greatly esteemed, that they always sell from twenty to twenty-five per cent higher than any others of the province. The first-mentioned is the most choice and delicate, and is characterized by its silky softness on the palate, and its charming perfume, which partakes of the nature of the violet and the raspberry. The Latour has a fuller body, and, at the same time, a considerable aroma, but wants the softness of the Lafitte. The Château Margaux, on the other hand, is lighter and possesses all the delicate qualities of the Lafitte, except that it has not quite so high a flavour. The Haut-Brion, again, has more spirit and body than any of the preceding, but is rough, when new, and requires to be kept six or seven years in the wood; while the others become fit for bottling in much less time.'

If Château Haut-Brion nowadays spends no more time than the others in the wood, it still tends to mature rather slowly though less slowly than Château Latour.

Alexis Lichine's proposed new classification happily includes two of the great wines of St. Emilion—Château Cheval-Blanc and Château Ausone—and one from Pomerol—Château Pétrus. These wines are certainly worthy to be ranked with the other first growths from the Médoc and Graves even though the full capabilities of Château Ausone do not appear to have been realized in recent vintages. The name of Cheval-Blanc is a trap for the unwary: it suggests a white wine, and at least one unfortunate novelist has made that mistake. It is, on the contrary, a splendid claret—big in body and flavour, yet not excessively so: it is delicate and well-balanced, so that it ages well. The soil of the vineyard is predominantly gravelly, but it is also peculiarly mixed, and varies widely in its constituents from one part to another. Its cultivation, therefore, calls for particular care, the most appropriate style of vine being planted in the appropriate place. Perhaps this peculiar characteristic, and the corresponding care taken in the planting, helps to give the wine its excellent balance. By about 1920 its opening price caught up with that of Château Ausone. Not so long ago, however, this great vineyard suffered tragedy. In February 1956 a terrible frost struck St. Emilion and Pomerol, and at first it was feared that a large proportion of the vines had been destroyed. In June, the vineyard of Cheval-Blanc looked like a cemetery of vines, and hardly any wine was made in that year.

Happily, however, things were not quite as bad as they seemed. Many of the vines that appeared to be dead recovered, and the others were soon replanted; but young vines do not make great wines, and it was not until 1961 that Cheval-Blanc (and many of the other vineyards of St. Emilion and Pomerol) were able once more to grow top quality wines in anything like the old quantities.

Legend has it that on the site of Château Ausone stood the villa of the poet Ausonius. It is certainly an attractive legend, and it may even be true but, to say the least, it has never been established.[1] However it has the authority of a very old tradition, and there can be few sites more perfect for building a country villa. It is high on the slopes of St. Emilion, with a marvellous view over the vineyards, and its cellars are amongst the most spectacular in the whole of Bordeaux. They penetrate deep into the hillside and it would be possible to walk through them for about four miles, until one comes to Clos Fourtet in the town of St Emilion, had the passage not been blocked up. The wines have long been acknowledged as the equals of the great châteaux of the Médoc, and Ausone might well have been brought into the 1855 classification. Anyone who has read André Simon's *Tables of Content* will remember how often the old vintages accompanied his matchless meals. It was also a great favourite of King Edward VII. One of the best off-vintage clarets I have ever tasted was Château Ausone 1938 in 1965. It was a magnificent, big wine and there was no sign of a decline. Post-war vintages have tended to be disappointing in comparison, though I am told that it is now returning to its old form. Some vintages achieved the curious combination of being light in colour but hard in flavour.

Until quite recently, Château Pétrus was comparatively little known in this country, although its quality was beyond question. Consequently it was often sold at a bargain price in comparison with the first growths of the Médoc. Those days, alas, are no more, and the wine now invariably fetches the price that it has long deserved. The fame of pomerols is said to date from when Château Pétrus won a gold medal at the Paris Exhibition of 1878. For many years it was owned by one of the great widows of the wine trade— the redoubtable Mme. Loubat, who died only a few years ago at a great age. No doubt she is now drinking nectar with the widow

[1] See H. Warner Allen, *The Wines of France*, London, 1924.

Cliquot, and certainly during her lifetime she grew wines which were second to none: a tradition that is being well maintained by her successors.

So much for the first growths. Unhappily there is not space enough to write in detail of the others. All the classified growths are great wines. Many of them have long and interesting histories. Some châteaux are worth mentioning for their architecture as well as for their wine. Each has something to offer. The complete study of Bordeaux is more than a life's work, and one can imagine no better way of enjoying life.

At the other end of the scale there are the humble district wines, falling within the broad, general *appellations contrôlées* that have already been given. Any vineyard within the stipulated area is, of course, entitled to sell its produce under the area name, and even the greatest of châteaux do so in poor years which would disgrace their great reputations. Most of the peasant growers invariably sell their wines in this way, and they are served by co-operatives, where the vinification is carried out under expert supervision. Consequently, the humble wines have improved immeasurably in quality, and one of the co-operatives—that at Pauillac—has registered its own trade name that has deservedly become popular in this country: *La Rose-Pauillac*. These various district wines are bought by the shippers and are blended together to give the product they require, to be sold either as a district wine or else under some fancy trade mark. In the nature of things, none of these wines is ever great, but many are excellent within their limitations. Sometimes they are very good indeed. In 1961 I was given a bottle of 1933 st. emilion shipped by Sichel and Co. It was too old, of course, but it was still quite remarkably good; and it surprised me by having lasted so long and so well. By that time most of the classified growths were already long past their best. I have also been repeatedly impressed by district wines shipped by Avery's of Bristol.

The district wines most commonly found in this country are those three admirable saints: St. Julien, St. Emilion and St. Estèphe. Unhappily many of these wines are vinous blasphemies, as they have little or nothing in common with the saints that they purport to represent. One also comes across a great deal of margaux, of which much the same may be said, even if one cannot accuse it of blasphemy. When Professor George Saintsbury published his immortal *Notes on a Cellar Book*, in 1920, he wrote that 'Perhaps no wine's name has been more taken in vain in England than Saint Julien's. He must be a fortunate claret-lover who has not sometimes made grimaces over a bottle so labelled at the average British hostelry. Exactly why this poor district has been so abused I do not know.' The abuse certainly continues. When I was in Bordeaux in 1962, a famous and highly reputable shipper, in a moment of post-prandial candour, gave me the formula for his current blend of 'St. Julien'. It was as follows: forty per cent from the co-operative of St. Savin, 1960 vintage; twenty per cent from the co-operative of St. Yzans, 1960 vintage; twenty per cent from the co-operative of St. Yzans, 1961 vintage; and twenty per cent of a famous bourgeois Château of St. Estèphe, 1960. It was an admirable blend for the table, but it contained no wine whatsoever from St. Julien. Nor could it have included much at the price. But at least it was a genuine claret and not a *grand vin d'Algerie*.

It is the district, then, that determines the style of a wine, and it is the precise piece of ground within the district that supplies its finer qualities. But the year matters far more than the château. If the weather is very bad, the greatest vineyard in the Médoc will produce a dreadful wine. If, on the other hand, there is enough rain and plenty of sunshine at exactly the right times, so that the year is a truly great one, even the humbler artisan growths will give good wine, and the wine from the bourgeois growths will be excellent. Most years, of course, lie somewhere between the two extremes, and in no year are the wines given by the different châteaux entirely consistent. In the worst of off-vintage years there are usually a few that escaped the hail storm, or the frosts, or that seemed to catch what little bit of sun there was; and to find good wine in off-vintage years is one of the joys of claret drinking. Maurice Healy was an adept at it, and readers of *Stay Me With Flagons* will remember that his finds included such wines as Châteaux Haut-Brion Lassivet and Carbonnieux 1925, and Château Léoville Lascases 1906. Conversely, in some good vintage years a great château produces a complete failure, as Lafite did in 1921, whilst in many others quite humble growths have proved to be more than the equals of their leaders.

Claret matures very gradually in the bottle and more quickly in the wood. Since the last war it has been accepted as the universal practice that claret should be left from two to three years in the wood and then bottled. Before the war, the more powerful wines were often kept from three to four years, and I have seen whole-sale merchants' lists dating from the turn of the century in which clarets five or six years old were quoted both in the wood and bottled. The modern practice, however, is probably the best one. Given patience, the wine can be left to mature slowly and in peace. A bottle can be opened from time to time, to see how it is getting on, and then the bulk of the wine can be drunk when it is at the peak of its development. Unhappily one seldom sees really old and mature clarets on restaurant wine lists: they have succumbed to the infanticide greed and ignorance of expense account diners who insist on trying to impress their guests by giving them first growths and great vintages long before they are ready to drink. Indeed, they are often so young as to be positively nasty, and much inferior to a good *ordinaire*. It infuriates me to see such wines on restaurant wine lists at all.

It is impossible to give any general rule as to how soon a claret will be ready, save that a 'big' wine—a leading growth of a great year—will take far longer to mature, and will last far longer, than an off-vintage wine or a very humble one of a vintage year. A lot, too, depends on the cellar. In a cool, dark cellar, claret will mature, most perfectly and most slowly, especially if it spends its whole life there without being moved. Moving certainly hurries it along, and may even spoil it. The same wine will never mature in exactly the same way in two different cellars, and when a wine grows really old—after a quarter of a century or so—wide differences may be noticed between individual bottles that have spent the whole of their lives side by side. It may also make a difference as to whether a claret was château or English bottled. We can ignore the pos-sibility of dishonest 'stretching' with inferior wine. This can happen on either side of the Channel, though it seldom does, and there is no possibility of it if one buys from a thoroughly reputable wine merchant. Unfortunately, however, some merchants who are perfectly honest are not very skilful at bottling: they treat the wine incorrectly and quite spoil it. Again, there is no danger of this with the really great firms, but everyone who drinks claret regularly could quote examples where it happened. It is a very controversial point as to whether château bottling or London bottling is best. Bordeaux growers have been doing it for long enough to be good at it—unlike some of the growers in Burgundy. Nevertheless, some are better than others. Bottling tends to be done in odd moments when there is nothing better to do, and the result is that it is spread over a considerable period so that the bottling that is done at the beginning tastes somewhat different from that at the end: wine that has been a relatively short time in cask tends to take longer to mature in bottle than wine that has been a long time— and the difference can be quite apparent, particularly when the wine is young. It may well be that the best English merchants bottle their wines better than those of Bordeaux—and that is certainly their claim. I have several times tasted château bottled clarets against British bottled, and although just occasionally I have preferred the latter, in the great majority of instances the former has been better. It may well be that a long journey in the wood does little to improve the wine. Nevertheless, the matter is by no means beyond doubt. The difference is not a great one, and the extra expense of château bottling is only justified when really good clarets are brought for laying down.

Sometimes the development of a claret will fool even the greatest experts. The wine may spend years in the doldrums and then emerge to be magnificent, or it may appear to have reached its perfection and then pass into another and even finer state: that seems to have happened to some of the 1953s. As an example of wines that spent a period in the doldrums, one may quote the 1920s, which even succeeded in fooling the late Maurice Healy. In 1934, in his admirable little book *Claret and the White Wines of Bordeaux*, he wrote:

'Nineteen hundred and twenty has disappointed a great many of us. I confess that when I first met the '20s, the 1914s were still in their best days; and I was surprised that wines so full of tannin as were the 1920s should have been appraised so highly. But, having come to scoff, I remained to praise; I developed a firm belief that is we only would wait until 1935 these would develop into splendid wines. In 1930 Warner Allen shocked me by suggesting that they were nearing their end. At first I laughed at him; I did write to Bordeaux for reassurance (which was not wanting), but I could see no grounds for his suspicions. I am sorry to say that they were only too well founded; and, while big wines like Latour will probably be good drinking for a long time yet, I should advise the immediate consumption of all the 1920s before it is too late. This affords an excellent example of how the body of instructed and expert opinion may be wrong. Of course, I am speaking of English cellaring; the Marquis de Polignac tells me that his Mouton, cellared in the chalk of Reims, is admirable. Mine, alas, has gone downhill.'

We who presume to write about wine must always be ready to eat our words. In his later and greatest book, *Stay Me With Flagons*, published in 1940, he entirely revised his opinion. And being a big man (in every sense of the word) he did so with the utmost grace:

'I owe Mouton an apology. The 1920 Bordeaux vintage was trumpeted at the time as likely to be one of the outstanding vintages of the century; and we patiently awaited their development. . . . But to my horror about 1930 I began to see a presage of wear in them; I had bought some Mouton 1920, and I began to drink it, unwillingly but hopefully. Alas! not a single bottle had yet ripened and still each tasted as if it had gone over the edge. So that I . . . sang the swan-song of my Mouton, and indeed of all the 1920s, lamenting them as Mary and Martha may have wept for Lazarus. For lo and behold! the 1920s were not dead; they were sleeping. Last spring Robert Speaight gave me dinner one night at the Savile Club; and he crowned the feast with a Claret that summed up all the glories of the wine. It was the 1920 Mouton. . . . For the wine had "come out on the other side", and was at last showing the beauties so long hidden; and the only fit deed was to "hush and then bless myself with silence". . . . The 1920s seem all to have come back.'

At the time he was writing, the 1924s were undergoing a similar strange development. If a claret of a leading growth and an acknowledged vintage year proves to be disappointing, there is never any point in drinking it off as if it were an *ordinaire*. It will remain drinkable for years, and there is always the hope that it will eventually come into its own.

In writing of individual vintage years, another matter has to be borne in mind: clarets tend now to mature more quickly than they did. After 1945, most growers made their wines lighter by reducing the time that the fermenting must spends in contact with the skins. The pre-war vintages were almost exhausted and things were made worse than they might have been by the shortage of good vintage years during the 1930s. The growers wanted to meet the demand for wines that would soon be ready to drink, and they succeeded admirably. The older connoisseurs, however, had misgivings. Could wines that were ready so soon possibly last? Was occasional excellence being sacrificed to regular mediocrity? Their doubts were not without foundation, but one feels that they were less justified than the similar doubts voiced about burgundy. Some of the younger claret vintages seem to be lasting very well, and I wonder just how much has really been lost? Time will tell. The clarets of St. Emilion and Pomerol, of course, have always been ready for drinking sooner than those from the Médoc, and yet they have generally lasted just as long. At least the vintage dates on claret labels can nearly always be relied on. I say 'nearly always' because of course there is always an occasional rogue; and one malpractice that horrifies the reputable growers is to increase the yield of a fine vintage by adding a proportion of a preceding lesser vintage to the fermentation tanks.

The new techniques in vinification are particularly valuable in the more difficult years. For instance, 1921 ought to have been a very great claret vintage, but it was not. It produced some magnificent sauternes but the clarets were often highly alcoholic and aggressive. A more scientific approach in 1961 resulted in very fine wines being produced under comparable climatic conditions. But vinification is still an art aided by science rather than an exact science, and many things have still to be learnt. Happily, too, the growers are becoming more willing to learn and to experiment so that the quality of the wines on average tends to go up year by year. One of the more recent interesting experiments is to warm the must while it is still in contact with the skins, which extracts the colouring without extracting relatively as much tannin, providing a fruity and soft wine whereas long vatting would give a hard wine. This practice is being tried in several châteaux. And conversely, many growers never have departed from the old methods and never will.

The great clarets are famous for their longevity, particularly the pre-phylloxera wines. To drink such wines in the glory of their old age is a memorable experience. The oldest claret I have ever tasted, as I have already mentioned, was the Château Rauzan-Gassies 1875 which was still superb in 1962. And the Château Palmer 1880 was almost as good. In fairness to anyone who might have the good fortune to be offered so old a wine, perhaps I should add that my host, when I drank these two wonderful old clarets, had to open several bottles of each before he found a good one.

The oldest pomerol I have tasted is Château Pétrus 1895—a vintage year, but by no means a great one. The wine was memorable. Once, it had obviously been fabulous, but when it was first decanted, the nose was hard, dead and musty. The mustiness was not seriously objectionable, though, and it steadily improved in the glass, though it never quite vanished. Despite its nose, the wine was a delight to taste: beautifully subtle and delicate in its old age.

There is nothing more tedious to the reader than a long account of the glories of vanished vintages. Not that any of the above have vanished: I tasted all three of them in Bordeaux as recently as 1962, and there are several more bottles where they came from, but they are certainly unobtainable commercially. I mentioned them simply to demonstrate how well and for how long a great claret can age. There is no point in dilating on the glories of other ancient vintages. Anyone who is interested in them can read descriptions in the old books. From 1920 onwards, however, it is a different story, and every vintage year is relevant. Representatives of pre-war vintages can be found in many private cellars and occasionally on the wine lists of the best restaurants. The years are as follows:

1920: Maurice Healy's remarks on this vintage have already been quoted. The wines spent a period in the doldrums and did not come into their own for about twenty years. According to him, Latour was the first wine of the vintage, Giscours came second, Léoville-Poyferré third, and Lafite fourth. Many of the finer wines are still excellent, though the time has certainly come to drink them. Recently I have tasted three examples: Châteaux Lafite, Ducru-Beaucaillou and Smith-Haut-Lafitte. The Lafite could only be described as exquisite. Until I tasted the Château Rauzan-Gassies 1875, it was certainly in the running for the title of the best claret I have ever had in my life. It was indescribably soft and beautiful. The Ducru-Beaucaillou was also excellent but not in the same class as the Lafite. The Smith-Haut-Lafitte was a beautiful old graves that was tawny in colour, and which tended at first to fade in the glass, but somehow survived a remarkably long time afterwards. Another bottle of the same wine, however, which I tried later, showed very badly. It had been re-corked and I am not sure of its history. None of them showed any particular amount of tannin, and it seems to be one of those vintages that ends up by consuming its excess of tannin and realizing its high initial promise.

1921: Rather a mixed year. There was excessive heat at the time of the vintage and some of the great growths of the Médoc, including Château Lafite, went wrong to such an extent that they had to be sold off as district wines. The st. emilions did well and the Cheval-Blanc was superb. Any wines that remain are likely to be well past their best.

1922: A poor year giving quantity rather than quality; in fact the yield remains a record. A few châteaux, however, did give pleasant wines, including Latour.

1923: A somewhat better year than 1922, and not unlike 1933; it produced some excellent wines—amongst them Ausone and Lafite—but by now most are probably well past their best, though I have heard good reports recently of Châteaux Margaux, Palmer and Gruaud-Larose.

1924: Despite poor weather during the summer this was an excellent vintage that has worn very well. Although most of the wines should have been drunk by now, there are exceptions. I remember drinking some 1924s a few years ago with very great pleasure, but unfortunately I have no notes. To judge by the one wine of this vintage I have tasted recently, the leading growths must still be admirable if anyone has any and has kept them well. Châteaux Lafite, Haut-Brion and Léoville-Poyferré were certainly very good. The wine I tasted was a Château Bel Orme, quite a humble growth from St. Seurin de Cadourne, at the northern end of the Haut-Médoc. Despite its only being a *cru bourgeois*, it produces admirable wines that last so well that they seem to belie their classification—as do several of the other generous wines from that end of the Médoc. The 1924 was first class; in fact it was staggeringly so. Dark in colour, it had plenty of body and was perfectly balanced. The most astonishing thing about it, though, was that it was nowhere near ready. I could hardly believe the label. Tasting it blind, I should probably have identified it as a much younger, leading classified growth: it was that good. I tasted it in London in 1963, but perhaps the clue to the whole thing lay in the fact that it had rested in the cellars of the château until 1961. One feels, though, that it would have been a great wine wherever it had been kept.

1925: A rather ordinary vintage. Some good wines were made, such as Lafite and Cheval-Blanc, but they are long past their best.

1926: Generally speaking, this was a very good year, though most of the wines were inclined to be hard and tannic, so that they took a long time to mature, and in some of them the hardness has persisted to the end. Others were inelegant and disappointing from the very beginning, and never did become much good. Recently I have tasted Châteaux Léoville-Poyferré, château bottled; Léoville-Las-Cases, Bordeaux bottled; and Bel Orme, château bottled. The two Léovilles were excellent, but I think the Poyferré had the edge. It was faultless and on top of its form, whereas the Las-Cases was just a trifle hard. The Bel Orme also had a touch more tannin and slightly less fruit than perfection would demand, but it was very good and vigorous. The better wines certainly make excellent drinking, but it is not a vintage to keep any longer.

1927: Very poor.

1928: Many wines of this vintage are disappointing, but others are excellent. Of the thirteen that I tasted during 1961–1970, eight were really good, and five quite good, but I tasted several bottles of one or two; three bottles were downright bad. Most of them tended to be hard, having too much tannin, and the worst examples had little else: the flavour and bouquet were old and faded, leaving only the hardness behind. As one would expect with claret of such an age, there was often quite a difference between individual bottles. The most striking example of this was the Gruaud-Larose. At a dinner party I tried two bottles that had been maturing side by side ever since the wine was shipped. The first was excessively hard and tannic, whereas the second was much better balanced; it was a beautiful old wine. The Château Lascombes also differed considerably from bottle to bottle, but all were very good, if lacking in real delicacy. The Léovilles, as usual, were admirable, and had plenty of life left in them. I have only tried two of the three—the Poyferré and the Barton—and of those I slightly preferred the former, which had less of the characteristic 1928 hardness. At Bordeaux I tried what one would expect to be a rank outsider in such a year—the Château Loudenne. In fact, it was excellent. It was a very big wine, and strikingly dark in colour, but it was beautifully balanced and without excessive tannin. I shall be happy to drink it (if ever I get the chance again) for years to come. The best claret I have drunk of this vintage was, however, without any doubt at all, the Château Mouton Rothschild. On decanting it, the first thing I noticed was its enormous deposit; but it proved to be a veritable giant of a wine in every way. Yet nevertheless it had remarkable finesse and delicacy—a combination of features that can only be found in the very greatest growths; and its balance was perfect. It was absolutely on top—as good as ever it will be—but it will last for years and years. Other good wines were Châteaux Beychevelle, Calon-Ségur, Margaux, Palmer and Pontet Canet. Amongst the failures was Lafite, which was pasteurized, and Haut-Brion.

1929: This was a truly delightful vintage, giving well-flavoured, delicate and balanced wines. Most of them reached perfection in about 1950, when I had the good fortune to drink a great many bottles; and no vintage has been more enjoyable. I remember with particular pleasure the Château Talbot, of which my father had a large stock. Latour was the best of the first growths; Mouton-Rothschild, the Léovilles, Beychevelle, and Pontet-Canet were excellent, as were most of the other classified growths. In 1963 I refreshed my memory by tasting three wines. A bottle of Gruaud-Larose, château bottled, was pleasant, although it was very much showing its age. Nevertheless it was so well balanced that it was still delightful to drink, and I think I enjoyed it every bit as much as I would have done when it was in its prime. Château Duhart-Milon was even better—a beautifully balanced wine that showed no signs of a decline. The Latour was in a different class altogether. Yes, if one must be hypercritical it was perhaps just slightly past its best, but it was such a massive wine that it will still be beautiful for many years to come. It was not really a vintage for the first growths, though, and the others tended to be very disappointing, especially the Haut-Brion. A magnum of Château Margaux, drunk in 1968, was magnificent, but this wine has a very mixed reputation and it seems that some of it was not up to standard.

1930: Bad.

1931: Bad, though I would mention one honourable and un-expected exception: Château Loudenne. Tasted at the château in

1962, it was surprisingly good, and it would have been even better, though by no means great, had it been drunk a few years earlier.

1932: Rank bad.

1933: The clarets of this year were a thoroughly mixed bunch. In France the year never seems to have been a popular one, and in this country the 1933s were overshadowed by the 1934s. To my taste, however, the best of the 1933s were far more enjoyable than any of the 1934s. They were exquisitely subtle and delicate wines, whereas those of the latter year tended to be hard. But I use the past tense advisedly. Some that were delightful in their day were far too light to last, and others never were any good, including at least one of the first growths—Château Margaux. When my maternal grandfather died some years ago I found half a dozen bottles of it in a bin in his cellar. I cannot blame him for not having drunk them. I would willingly name the Margaux '33 as the most disappointing claret I have ever tasted. I was especially disappointed because, at that time, we were regularly drinking the Château Beychevelle at home, and it was a truly beautiful wine—a claret that I shall always remember with joy, but one that is now, alas, well past its best. My father bought it from Berry Bros., who had very wisely acquired the whole of the Beychevelle of that vintage. The last time I tasted it was in 1961, and although it was still very good I suspect that part of the pleasure it gave was to bring back memories of earlier bottles. During the same year I tried two bottles of Château Talbot. One admittedly was on the light side and somewhat beyond its prime, but the other was outstandingly good. It was a great wine and actually still seemed to be developing. It certainly had several years of life ahead of it; but with a rather light vintage of such an age one must expect considerable variations between bottles. And the Château Talbot was not alone in its longevity: in 1964 I drank the Châteaux Latour and the Mouton-Rothschild, both of which were beautiful and fully mature clarets—very robust and good—while more recently, in 1969, I enjoyed the delicate elegance of the Château Pontet-Canet. But these are the exceptions: most of the 1933s are quite dead.

1934: The 1934s are less stimulating to the memory than the 1933s, but they are currently more pleasing to the palate. The only trouble with them is one that has been present from the very beginning: they have a slight excess of tannin that seldom quite wears off, leaving them rather hard. There are exceptions, and some that I have particularly enjoyed include Châteaux Cheval-Blanc, Haut-Brion, Lagrange and Durfort-Vivens, all of which were absolutely beautiful and truly delicate. The Cheval-Blanc was especially good: just what old claret ought to be, and there is not a trace of the 1934 hardness. Two bigger and less delicate wines, but ones that were well balanced and thoroughly enjoyable, were Château Léoville-Poyferré and Château Pontet-Canet. Apart from the Haut-Brion I have tasted two of the first growths recently: Lafite and Margaux. The Lafite was magnificent but not particularly elegant; although it appeared to be fully developed it was distinctly hard. I preferred the Margaux. It was fully developed in about 1960, and made excellent drinking, though it was certainly not a great claret. Nineteen thirty-four was a year in which the first growths by no means stood head and shoulders above their rivals. The other leading growths of the Médoc closely followed their style, and my tasting notes recall a great many of them. I have enjoyed them all but have been inspired by few. It was the rather fruitier wines from St. Emilion and Pomerol that gave me the most pleasure.

1935: A poor vintage, though a few pleasant, if transitory, wines were made.

1936: Much as 1935.

1937: Will the 1937s ever be fit to drink? They were so laden with tannin that some of them seem to have consumed their fruit and sugar, leaving nothing but tannin behind. But the 1920s also had lots of tannin and we have seen how they pulled round. One can only say that if the 1937s *are* going to mend, they are taking their time about it. Many of them are positively unpleasant at present and I think that those showing any quality should be kept in the hope that they will improve. That was the impression given me, for example, by the Château Cheval-Blanc, which I tasted in 1962. With such a backward and hard vintage it is not surprising that the only wines to have matured so far are the comparatively humble growths which, in a more normal year, would long since have been dead. The only 1937s that I have really enjoyed recently were Château Haut-Bailly, from Graves and a humble district wine, from St. Georges, St. Emilion, which were fruitier and less

tannic than any other wines of that vintage I have tried. Of all
the clarets, those from Graves, St. Emilion and Pomerol seem to
hold out the most promise.

1938: Some quite pleasant wines were made, but they are not
very interesting today. I have recently tasted two: Château
Mouton d'Armailhacq and Château Langoa-Barton. The first was
a very thin and *passé*. The second was much better, but that might
have been because it had never been moved from Bordeaux. Even
so, it only served as a pleasant introduction to show off greater
things.

1939: A poor year, but a few wines were successful. In 1961 I
tasted a half bottle of Château Cos d'Estournel which proved to
be well balanced and quite unexpectedly good. Another success in
a poor year was the Château Latour. These wines reached their
best form many years ago and should all have been drunk.

1940: A slightly better vintage that was acclaimed with wholly
unjustified enthusiasm just after the war. In 1962 I tasted the
Château Durfort-Vivens. It began by tasting distinctly odd in a
way that I have never come across before or since, but after it had
breathed a bit in the glass it developed into a very pleasant and
fully mature but not notable claret. The Latour 1940 was a pleasant
but light wine. These should, by now, have been drunk.

1941: Bad.

1942: Not by any means a great year, but pleasant wines were
made, notably by Châteaux Margaux and Latour. This is one of
the under-rated vintages. It would have been praised much more
had the wine merchants after the war not spent all their available
currency on buying 1943s. Most of the wines are now too old,
though.

1943: This vintage reminds me somewhat of the 1933. The wines
were light, elegant, charming and relatively short-lived. Many are
now dead, most of the remainder are in a decline, a few are at the
top of their form, and none is improving. All the first growths did
well and, amongst the st. emilions, the Château Cheval-Blanc
was outstanding, as was Château Pétrus in Pomerol. In 1963 I
tasted the Château Léoville-Poyferré and it was a revelation. It
was a wonderfully big, vigorous wine, at the peak of its development and without the least suggestion of a decline. Shortly afterwards I tasted Château Latour, and it may be that this wine is even

better: I should like to taste the two side by side. The other two 1943s that I have tried lately—Châteaux Pichon-Longueville and Calon-Ségur—were both very elegant and elderly.

1944: An abundant yield mostly of light wines that were at their best a few years after the vintage. A few of the leading growths had staying power, however, and although they are now perhaps getting past their best, they are still good to drink. Amongst them are Châteaux Lafite, Latour, Haut-Brion, Calon-Ségur and Pontet-Canet. This vintage was under-rated for the same reason as 1942.

1945: It has often been said that this was the last of the classic vintages, though that of 1961 bids fair to rival it. The quality was superb although the quantity was small. It was certainly the last in which the old methods of vinification were universally used. At the same time it was a distinctly big vintage, with plenty of tannin in massive, fruity wines; and many of the finer growths have been slow to show their undoubtedly great qualities. Some of the *bourgeois* growths, on the other hand, made good drinking after about twelve years, and a few of the lighter classified growths are ready now. I have recently enjoyed Châteaux Beychevelle, Batailley and Canon. But it is a shame to drink the really great growths yet, especially as the later, lighter vintages are so much more ready; indeed many of them are past their best. The vintage was almost universally successful, although there were one or two mishaps. These were generally caused by excessive heat during the vintage, and some growers had to put lumps of ice in the fermentation vats. Something went wrong at Château Cheval-Blanc, for instance, and half the wine was pasteurized, whilst in the Graves, Château Carbonnieux suffered terribly from early frost. There are pessimists who say that the 1945 will disappoint in the same way as have some of the 1928s—finishing up with nothing but tannin. This may apply to a few, particularly to some that were bottled in England too late owing to post-war conditions, but I personally am a patient optimist.

1946: Generally speaking a bad year, owing to lack of sun, though there were some quite good wines such as Châteaux Latour and Lafite, which were excellent to drink in 1964. But most of their lesser brethren have long since expired, and many had a peculiarly unpleasant metallic taste.

1947: An excellent vintage. The weather was so favourable

that it was proclaimed as 'The Vintage of the Century' before any wine had been made. In the event, the forecast proved over-optimistic. Although the wines were superb at the beginning, the médocs have not shown the staying power that was expected of them and now tend to be disappointing. Although all the leading growths did well, it is those from St. Emilion and Pomerol that did best of all, and these are the only ones that are fulfilling their promise. One of the outstanding ones was Château Cheval-Blanc, and it is hardly ready yet.

1948: This vintage was run down most unfairly, falling, as it did, between the outstanding vintages of 1947 and 1949. Had it not been for that it would have been acclaimed. The merlot grapes suffered a lot from the damp, but the others did well, and many of the wines, at the beginning, were full-bodied and rather too hard. They are now showing very well though, and some of them are great. The Château Cheval-Blanc again is particularly good, and nearing its peak. The Château Latour has the makings of a great wine, but it is overloaded with tannin, and it will be years before it is ready. I should like to taste it again in about 1975. The Château Calon-Ségur is also exceptionally good and only just ready. Amongst the wines for earlier drinking, the Château Brane-Cantenac and Château Léoville-Lascases are delightful, as are many others. The more robust growths will clearly outlive the 1947s.

1949: Another excellent vintage, though somewhat mixed. It was a very hot summer and some of the wines have a *rôti*, or scorched taste, with so much tannin that it took ages before they began to come round. Others, on the other hand, are most elegant: amongst them the Cheval-Blanc, which is ready. Another château which is very pleasant to drink now is the Pichon-Longueville. The Châteaux Léoville-Barton and Langoa are enormous wines that merit keeping, as do the first growths, of which the Château Latour and Château Haut-Brion are outstanding, as are those contenders for first growth status, Châteaux Mouton-Rothschild and La Mission Haut-Brion; indeed some maintain that in this year they clearly take the lead. Of these wines, I think Château Margaux will want drinking first.

1950: This proved to be a pleasant—if fairly light vintage throughout Bordeaux, even though people were sceptical at the time because it was so abundant. The st. emilions and pomerols were particularly successful and Château Cheval-Blanc again was outstanding. Amongst wines from the Médoc, I have recently tasted Châteaux Lafite, Latour, Margaux, Beychevelle, Gruaud-Larose and Rausan-Ségla, and they were excellent; but there were some disappointments, too. Most of the classified growths were at their best after ten to twelve years, though a few, like Château Léoville-Barton, took longer.

1951: A very bad summer resulted in a lot of disease amongst the vines, and it was a poor vintage, but some very pleasant light wines were made, nevertheless, including Châteaux Haut-Brion, Mouton-Rothschild and Bel Air. The Château Latour was a surprisingly attractive wine as late as in 1963, but most wines of this vintage are now well past their best.

1952: This was acclaimed as a major vintage, but at first I found the wines disappointing. The 1952s seemed to bear the same sort of relationship to the 1953s as the 1934s did to the 1933s, but although some of them are a trifle too hard to be really elegant others have softened and are developing beautifully, though I doubt whether many will have the great staying power that was once predicted. Despite its having been a very hot summer, some growers clearly picked their grapes too late. Although some very fine wines were grown in the Médoc, the st. emilions and pomerols are generally the best. Châteaux Lafite, Latour and Léoville-Barton deserve keeping, as do many others.

1953: Generally speaking a very elegant and delightful vintage. The wines were not particularly big, and many of them were ready to drink surprisingly early, so that a short life was predicted. This proved to be true of some, but others seem to be entering a further admirable phase of their development and they may last a good few years yet. An example of a wine that developed rather quickly was the Château Palmer, which was absolutely delicious in the early 1960s. Wines that are still showing well, or even improving, include Châteaux Lafite, Margaux, Mouton-Rothschild, Léoville-Barton, Cantemerle, La Mission Haut-Brion and Rausan-Ségla. Château Latour was at first disappointing, but now it seems to be coming into its own. It is not an easy vintage to give general advice about, and several of the other leading growths were disappointing, but those that did well did very well indeed, and gave wines that were the most elegant of the decade. It was better for médocs than for st. emilions and pomerols.

1954: This vintage was not very well received, but personally I think it is under-rated, partly because it falls between the excellent 1953s and 1955s, but principally because the weather was bad, which shook confidence. The wines, generally speaking, were light and became excellent to drink after six to ten years; most are now far too old, but a few are still lasting. Probably all were chaptalized. I have enjoyed such wines as Châteaux Cheval-Blanc, Calon-Ségur, Cantemerle, Lynch-Bages, Domaine de Chevalier, Pontet-Canet and Loudenne. By far the most notable 1954s I have tasted, however, are Châteaux Latour and Pétrus. These are the exceptions, though, and it must be admitted that many of the wines were poor.

1955: An abundant vintage, producing wines of consistently good quality but few, if any, that were really great. The lighter *bourgeois* growths were pleasant to drink after six or seven years, but the class wines are only now reaching their peak. They are thoroughly sound and have given a lot of pleasure but no excitement.

1956: Many vineyards, particularly in St. Emilion and Pomerol, were wrecked by February frosts—so much so that I look on all subsequent vintages from these districts with suspicion until 1961, though those on the slopes beside the town of St. Emilion, such as Château Ausone, largely escaped. The result was a very small crop of very poor quality, though one or two quite enjoyable wines were made, such as those of Châteaux Latour, Ducru-Beaucaillou and Montrose.

1957: This vintage at the time was highly praised by the trade—one feels perhaps too highly. Other critics were rather too unkind. The wines were hard, with plenty of tannin, but they tended to lack body. Many will take a long time to come round, and one is inclined to compare them to the 1937s and to wonder whether they will ever be really good. The first growths, and many of the lesser ones, were quite unready to drink in 1969. Wines that seem to have a promising future, however, include Châteaux Beychevelle, Cos d'Estournel, Ducru-Beaucaillou, Lynch-Bages, Palmer and Rausan-Ségla. Production was very small, partly owing to frosts.

1958: A very second-rate vintage, and many of the wines had a peculiar and characteristic taste when young. They served a useful purpose, though, by maturing quickly. One or two châteaux, such as La Mission Haut-Brion, Haut-Brion and Latour, produced agreeable wines.

1959: After the poor vintages of 1957 and 1958, 1959 *had* to be good, and it would have been praised regardless of what it was like. Owing to good weather, the wine was bought wildly in advance, and it fetched alarmingly high prices. Happily, in the event, the vintage actually *was* a very good one (though less good than the 1961) and it succeeded everywhere though the quantity produced was relatively small. But the weather was actually *too* hot and the lives of many of the wines will be limited by lack of acid. There was a great deal of sugar, and the wines had to be racked regularly to wake up the yeasts. Some growers were not as skilful as others, and a few of the smaller ones got into trouble with excessive volatile acidity. District by district, then, the vintage was an admirable one, but individual châteaux have to be picked with care. The wine is maturing somewhat more quickly than was first expected; the *bourgeois* growths are already mature and the better-class growths will probably reach maturity in the 1970s.

1960: A mediocre vintage, but a useful one, as the wines matured quickly. It was a very wet summer and the vintage was late. Some growers gambled on having good weather in October; and they won. Some humble *palus* wines did quite well, and they were pleasant to drink young, while the more successful classified growths are now most enjoyable. Château Latour is still actually improving.

1961: A very good vintage indeed—certainly the best for clarets since 1929. Some would acclaim it as 'The Vintage of the Century', though one wonders what such a phrase can mean. The yield was very small, though, thanks to early frosts, and the prices were astronomic. Happily, however, the vintage was so very good that even the humblest of growths made first-class wine. Wine lovers of modest means will find the *bourgeois* growths very rewarding. And thanks to inflation the prices now seem actually reasonable.

1962: Despite uninspiring summer weather this was a thoroughly useful, if not great, vintage year, and the yield was good. The wines are rather elegant and put me in mind of the 1953s in style, though they are lower in quality. The classified growths should take about ten years to mature. The lesser wines are ready now. It was a better vintage in the Médoc than in the other districts.

1963: The weather was dreadful, and not all the spraying in Bordeaux could overcome the problem of mildew. This vintage has only proved one thing: that all the science of the enologists is in vain if the sun does not shine. In 1964 some of the experts were saying that the '63s would be comparable with the '60s but this assessment proved to be wildly optimistic. Only a very few châteaux managed to grow decent wines, amongst them Latour, Montrose and La Mission Haut-Brion. Most of the wines were ghastly and some châteaux which sold wines under their own labels tried to recall it.

1964: The wines of this vintage must be selected with especial care. To choose between the great names is almost a toss up. It was a hot year, and at first the prospect seemed very good indeed with wines like the 1959s, but half-way through the vintage the rain came down, and fell, and fell. Most of the châteaux which picked before the deluge made excellent wine, and these included many of the *bourgeois* growths, but some of the great names, which habitually pick late, picked too late, and their wines are very poor in consequence. Not all the châteaux that picked early made good wine, though: there had earlier been a shortage of rain that particularly affected young vines with short roots especially in well-drained gravel soil. Those that are good have plenty of fruit but not much acid, and will probably develop quite quickly. The wines of St. Emilion and Pomerol generally escaped the disaster and are better than those of the Médoc.

1965: A poor vintage, but some quite nice light wines were made which are pleasant for early drinking, thanks largely to lessons learnt in 1963, especially with regard to careful selection of grapes.

1966: One of the most universally successful of recent vintages, this year has been likened to 1962. Its wines promise very well, and should have substantial lasting power.

1967: A rather lighter vintage than 1966, and the wines should develop more quickly. Production was very large and careful selection is necessary particularly of the médocs. The st. emilions and pomerols appear to be the most promising, especially the latter. It is still a little early to assess the 1966s and 1967s accurately, and the latter year at present appears to be rather over priced. As it is also likely to mature more quickly, it seems the poorer buy for the purposes of laying down.

1968: Bad.

1969: One thing is certain: the yield was very low. September weather was the worst on record, and although October was very fine it could not put right the damage that had been done. By no stretch of the imagination will this be rated as anything more than a second-rate vintage but it is still too early to assess it more accurately. Undoubtedly some good wines were made by the most skilful growers but these will call for even more careful selection than the 1964s.

White Wines

If the red wines of Bordeaux are legion, the range of white wines is perhaps even greater, and the differences between the various white wines are more immediately apparent. The red wines differ in their subtleties: one needs considerable experience before one can regularly distinguish between a médoc, a st. emilion and a graves. To place a médoc within its commune with any certainty one has to be an expert indeed; and even the experts are often caught out. To assign a white wine to its exact area is often just as difficult, but the white wines do have one feature that can be assessed by the veriest amateur: their sweetness. In this they differ widely. Most of the white wines of the Médoc, and some of those from Graves, have only the barest touch of sweetness, particularly when there has been a shortage of sun to ripen the grapes. In our rather loose English parlance they can justly be described as 'very dry'. The wines from Sauternes are the very opposite: they are laden with sweetness, and the greatest of them all—Château d'Yquem—is practically a liqueur. To put the *d'* before its name, by the way, is perhaps pedantic, and from now onwards it will be omitted.

The white wines do not only differ in their degree of sweetness, though: they also differ enormously in quality. This is obvious to anyone who tastes them. When one talks of the 'quality' of a wine the uninitiated at once ask what one means, and they seek for a definition, much as the unbelieving Israelites looked for a 'sign'.

The trouble is that one can no more define the quality of a wine than that of a beef steak. It is easy to say whether the meat is tender or tough, or whether the wine is sweet or dry. To describe its flavour is far more difficult. In the end one is usually reduced to saying that one likes it or else one doesn't. With wine things are somewhat easier than with meat, and the experts have developed a specialist vocabulary that is reasonably precise. But it is really a language in itself, and one can only learn to speak it fluently by tasting wines and by talking about them with people of experience. I hope, nevertheless, that some of the terms will become clear in the course of this book.

This, of course, is the lamentation of an author who is about to condemn, and who feels slightly guilty about it. The fact is that, with a few notable exceptions, I can stir up little enthusiasm for the dry and medium-dry wines of Bordeaux. For the most part they are dull little things: pleasant luncheon wines but not much more. The worst of them are by far the most nondescript wines to be grown in any really great district, and many are ruined by too much sulphur, a sin not confined to small growers or cheap wines. In the right proportions, sulphur is an invaluable aid: it protects both vines and wines from infection. But if too much is used, the wine becomes positively infernal. There are certainly some exceptions to the rule of mediocrity—wines that are good by any standards—but even the best fall short of greatness. I have never tasted a dry white bordeaux that really compares with a great white burgundy, and the slightly sweeter wines are outclassed by those from Germany. It is only the very sweet wines that can hold their own with any. As dessert wines, the great sauternes, with the German beerenauslesen and trockenbeerenauslesen, are in a class by themselves. But I refer to the great wines. The lesser growths have too often been badly made, while a great emphasis on alcoholic strength combined with sweetness has led some of the lesser proprietors to add sugar and produce strangely unbalanced wines which peasant vinification has made even worse than they need be. One cannot altogether blame them, though, as the market price for such wines is related to their strength. Recently there has been a move towards reform, helped by an agreed minimum price. Let us hope that this will bring about an improvement and restore the fortunes of the growers; for it cannot be denied that the mediocrity of their wines had done much to help the eclipse of sweet wines in recent years, and the poor ones have taken the good down with them.

Throughout Bordeaux, three varieties of vine are grown for white wines, though in widely differing proportions. They are: the Sémillon, otherwise known as the Cruvillant or Colombier; the Sauvignon, otherwise known as the Douce-Blanche or Blanc-Doux; and the Muscadelle, otherwise known as the Muscadet-Doux, Raisinotte, Muscade, Colle-Musquette, Catape or Guépié. There used to be many more, and a few are still found in some of the older of the less important vineyards. The 1883 edition of Cocks and Feret lists a further seven varieties that were then being grown, and outside species have also been tried. For instance one enterprising nineteenth-century owner of Château Rabaud—a very ancient and beautiful property—imported riesling vines from Germany; but grown in Bordeaux they gave a typical sauternes; the wine did not at all resemble hock and the vines apparently changed their ways to conform with their neighbours. As with the varieties grown to yield red wines, each kind of vine has its merits and limitations. The Sauvignon gives a good but not large yield of fine, highly flavoured and aromatic wine—perhaps too highly flavoured, sometimes, and blending with the lesser wines from the Sémillon improves them; but it is also the Sauvignon that attracts the *pourriture noble*. The Sémillon gives a larger yield of more delicately flavoured but less distinguished wine. The Muscadelle, which may be translated into English as the muscatel, is a law unto itself. It is the most ubiquitous of all vines, and it seems to be at home anywhere; it can be found flourishing as far south as Andalusia and as far north as Germany. Apart from its value in making wine, its sweet, juicy grapes are admirable for the table, and everyone knows their unique flavour. It is one of the few vines that can be identified with certainty in the writings of the ancients, including those of Pliny, its name being derived from the Latin *musca*, a fly, because flies are greatly attracted by its grapes. Its most remarkable characteristic is that its unmistakable flavour always comes out in the wine. For this reason it is not one of the major vine varieties in Bordeaux, and it is declining in popularity, but it is mixed with the others in small quantities, just to give a trace of its savour. A typical vineyard in Sauternes may have about twenty-five per cent Sauvignon, seventy per cent Sémillon, and five per cent Muscadelle.

White wines are grown in the following districts: Graves; Sauternes, which is surrounded on three sides by Graves, and which comprises the five communes of Sauternes, Bommes, Preignac, Fargues and Barsac; Cérons, which is adjacent to Sauternes and also within Graves; the Médoc; St. Emilion; Bourgeais and Blayais; Entre-Deux-Mers; Bordeaux Sainte-Foy, forming an extension of Entre-Deux-Mers to the north-west; Graves de Vayres, which is to the north of Entre-Deux-Mers and surrounded by it, just as Sauternes is surrounded by Graves; the Premières Côtes de Bordeaux, which is a strip taken out of the south-west of Entre-Deux-Mers; Sainte-Macaire, which adjoins the south-eastern end of the Premières Côtes; Loupiac and Sainte-Croix-du-Mont, which are adjacent and which are in turn surrounded by the Premières Côtes de Bordeaux. It is all terribly confusing until one looks at the map; then it will be clear that the first-named areas are broadly south-west of the Gironde; the next to the north-east; and those last named lie between the rivers Garonne and Dordogne. Since one must mention them in some sort of order, this seems as good as any; but it is less than satisfactory. The rivers form convenient geographical boundaries, and they obviously determine the lie of the slopes, but they do not necessarily coincide with the divisions in the soil. Looking at the map again, it will be seen that Loupiac and Sainte-Croix-du-Mont on the right bank of the Garonne face Cérons and Sauternes on the left bank. Geographically it would be just as logical, or more so, to draw a circle around them and discuss them as a single area.

The position of Graves has already been discussed, and so have its excellent red wines. Its cheap white wines, with their gentle sweetness, so beloved of maiden ladies who buy occasional bottles surreptitiously from their grocer, are amongst the most famous and popular wines in the world. To some extent their popularity has been their undoing, for many of the cheap wines that are sold as graves in this country, and which bear the name of no château to vouch for their authenticity, do not come from Graves at all. Most of them are rather unpleasant, but as the district is innocent of their production it cannot be blamed. Many of the genuine wines are dry, but hardly any of them are absolutely dry: they nearly all have their *pointe de douceur*, and some are quite sweet. Some, indeed, such as those with the *appellation* cérons, are made in the sauternes way and can be sweet. The dry wines are to my taste the most attractive: slightly chilled, they make excellent aperitifs, and they are pleasant with the fish course. Although none is truly great, many are certainly good, and even the humblest of the dry wines are free from that unpleasant astringent acidity that sometimes spoils similar wines grown in other places. Thomas Heywood was certainly not thinking of such wines when he made his jest that 'None but clerks and sextons love grave wines'.[1] Another feature of these innocent-seeming wines is that they have plenty of alcohol. To receive the *appellation contrôlée graves supérieures* they must have 12° of alcohol. There is seldom any difficulty about this, and they usually have quite a bit more. This combination of plenty of sugar with plenty of alcohol gives them another virtue: their longevity. Unlike some of the more delicate whites, they do not spoil quickly in the bottle, and there is normally no hurry to drink them. They do not last nearly as long as their red neighbours, of course, but for the first three or four years in bottle the best of them actually improve, and then they remain good for another four or five years before there is any real risk of their going off and becoming unpleasantly maderized.[2]

Many of the châteaux grow both red and white wines in different parts of their vineyards, and one of the very best for white wines, as it undoubtedly is for red, is the great Château Haut-Brion. Maurice Healy sadly underestimated some of its neighbours when he said that it was the only white graves that he would acknowledge as being good. But it certainly is good: very good indeed. It is a dry wine with a particularly fine aroma that puts one in mind of a sauternes. Perhaps this is not entirely a fancy, as it has an amusing link with the great Château Yquem. In the early years of this century, the then proprietor of Yquem was entertained to dinner at Haut-Brion, and his host complained that although Haut-Brion grew red wine that was second to none, he still had to get his dessert wine from Sauternes. The next day, some vines from Yquem were sent to Haut-Brion, but things did not turn out quite as they were planned. The proprietor of Haut-Brion must still go

[1] *Fair Maid of the West*, 1631.
[2] See p. 58.

to Sauternes for his dessert wine, but his own dry white wine is perhaps the best in Bordeaux.

Apart from this outstanding wine, the best graves are grown by the following châteaux, which were officially classified in 1959:

Château Bouscaut	Cadaujac
Château Carbonnieux	Léognan
Château Chevalier	Léognan
(Domaine de Chevalier)	
Château Malartic Lagravière	Léognan
Château Olivier	Léognan
Château Latour-Martillac	Martillac
Château Laville-Haut-Brion	Pessac
Château Couhins	Villenave d'Ornon

Château Laville-Haut-Brion is the name given to the white wine of Château La Mission Haut-Brion.

It will be seen that all these classified growths come from the northern half of Graves. Further south the quality becomes much poorer until suddenly things are completely reversed, and one gets to the glory of Sauternes. Nearly all the above châteaux are equally noted for their red wines, and one of them—Carbonnieux—should also be mentioned for its ancient Christian cunning. This legend is given by Franck:[1]

'The estate of Carbonnieux once belonged to the Abbey of St. Croix, of Bordeaux. The holy fathers found an enormous profit in sending their wines to Turkey, for the Church has a strong feeling for getting money, but the Mussulman law operated against making a satisfactory gain. To mystify Mahomet was a worthy and holy work for the children of the popish St. Bennet. So they exported their white wine, of which the limpidity was remarkable, as "The Mineral Waters of Carbonnieux". Under this entry at the Mohammedan custom-house, the wine escaped the anathemas of the holy men of the Ottoman Empire, with their prophet guiding them. The children of the triple crown of Rome triumphed, for the trick succeeded; the Benedictine beat the sun of the Koran, just as the triple-crowned sovereign of the Vatican would have foretold, had he been consulted. A sagacious Frenchman hereupon remarked, "that it was much better to give wine for water, than to pass off water for wine", as too often happened in his own country at all times.'[2]

[1] *Traité sur les Vins du Médoc*, Bordeaux, 1845.
[2] Quoted in *French Wines*, by Cyrus Redding, London, 1860.

The truly great white wines of Bordeaux are all grown in
Sauternes—an enclave of specially good soil towards the south of
Graves. The soil has a somewhat reddish tinge, though it is far
removed from the striking deep red of the Valdepeñas vineyards,
and in this rather flat, sun-drenched area the grapes often attain
their ultimate degree of ripeness. They experience the *pourriture
noble*, or noble rot, and the shrivelled grapes are full of sweetness.
To help them on their way, when the fruit is fully formed and
approaching ripeness, the leaves are plucked from the vines to let
every possible ray of sunshine do its work. The result is a strong
wine laden with sugar. It is more than sweet: it is *liquoreux*. And
its sweetness is balanced by an intensity of flavour with a unique
fruitiness. To create such a wine, however, the harvest needs to be
long, and it is therefore hazardous and expensive. Only the rotten
grapes can be picked, and the vintagers have to go over the vines
as many as a dozen times. Sometimes the vintage is not finished
until very late indeed, and once, at Château Filhot, it lasted until
Christmas. Only with such care as this can the sweetness of a great
sauternes be achieved. And the delay creates a grave risk, for the
grapes can be destroyed only too easily by harsh winter weather.

Apart from its sugar sweetness, the wine is also laden with
natural glycerine, which gives an impression of sweetness that is
really more of a softness, even when it is found in wines that are
fully fermented out and which contain no natural sugar, such as the
unblended solera *olorosos* of Jerez. In the sauternes, with their
great natural sweetness, the glycerine helps further to add to their
liqueur-like appeal. They are so instantly likeable that they are
enjoyed by many who are not normally wine drinkers at all; but
the ladies who enjoy them so perversely throughout their meals
would probably be horrified to learn how strong they are. With so
much sugar and alcohol they are almost unwholesome. A small
glass of a fine sauternes, taken with a fruit salad or dessert, is a
marvellous and unique gastronomic experience; but such wines
should not be drunk in large quantities. The humbler growths of
sauternes, particularly in off-vintage years, although still sweet,
are much lighter and less deadly, just as they are much less
delicious. I remember once being invited to lunch in a restaurant
by a northern industrialist who told me that he liked a dry white
wine at mid-day. He then astonished me by ordering a sauternes.

Happily it was one of the humbler kind, and I thoroughly enjoyed my meal, though I left the restaurant feeling slightly sick.

Sauternes covers five communes: Sauternes itself, Bommes, Preignac, Fargues and Barsac. These were listed earlier so as to include the name of Barsac—a name almost as renowned as that of the larger region which contains it. The soil is somewhat different from that of Sauternes. In the north it is gravelly on a limestone sub-soil, whereas in the south, where the finest wines of the district are grown, it contains more red marl on a calcareous, stony sub-soil. Barsac enjoys a double *appellation*, being sold either as sauternes or as barsac, and its wines differ somewhat from those of the other parts of the region in that they have slightly less sugar; but they have at least their fair share of fruitiness, and they are noticeably more delicate. Just as Château Yquem is the undoubted king of the whole region, Château Coutet and Château Climens are the leading growths of Barsac, and many would say that they run Yquem a close second, having an appeal all of their own. The wines of Bommes resemble those of Sauternes very closely, as do those of Preignac, with the exception of some that are grown in the very centre of the district, where the *graves* soil is modified with clay, flint and gravel, over a calcareous sub-soil, giving a larger yield of rather less distinguished wines. In Fargues, too, the soil is some-what modified with marl, gravel and sand, giving wines that for the most part are somewhat like those of Preignac.

The white wines of Sauternes, like the red wines of the Médoc, were classified in 1855:

1st Great Growth

Château Yquem	Sauternes

1st Growth

Château La Tour-Blanche	Bommes
Clos Haut-Peyraguey	
Chateâu Lafaurie-Peyraguey	Bommes
Château Rayne-Vigneau	Bommes
Château de Suduiraut	Preignac
Château Coutet	Barsac
Château Climens	Barsac
Château Guiraud	Sauternes

Château Rieussec	Fargues
Château Rabaud-Sigalas	Bommes
Château Rabaud-Promis	Bommes

2nd Growth

Château de Myrat	Barsac
Château Doisy-Dubroca	Barsac
Château Doisy-Daëne	Barsac
Château Doisy-Vedrines	Barsac
Château d'Arche	Sauternes
Château Arche-Lafaurie	Sauternes
Château Filhot	Sauternes
Château Broustet	Barsac
Château Nairac	Barsac
Château Caillou	Barsac
Château Suau	Barsac
Château de Malle	Preignac
Château Romer-Lafon	Fargues
Château Lamothe-Bergey	Sauternes
Château Lamothe-Espagnet	Sauternes

Château Yquem, then, stands alone; it is in a class by itself; and its glorious isolation is fully justified by its quality. Maurice Healy described it thus:[1]

'My first bottle of Yquem was a 1906: a fairly good year. I decanted it; and the room was filled with a perfume that recalled the Arabian Nights. There is nothing that is exactly like the bouquet of Château Yquem; no garden could do it justice, and to talk of spices were an impertinence, or I would say that it embalms the air. There is nothing like it; nothing; nothing. It is the most beautiful wine God ever allowed man to make; and it ought never to be drunk profanely.'

Elsewhere[2] he said: 'I am convinced that the miracle wine of the Marriage Feast at Cana was a prophecy of Château Yquem.' And what more could any man say? Apart from the splendour of its wine, Château Yquem is a most beautiful piece of architecture—a fine old castle dating from the fifteenth century, that stands

[1] *Claret and the White Wines of Bordeaux*, London, 1924.
[2] *Stay Me With Flagons*, London, 1940.

magnificent at the top of its vineyard slopes. Its proprietor is the Marquis de Lur-Saluces, whose family have owned it since 1785. He has worked tirelessly in a number of official capacities to further the cause of good viticulture and in his own vineyards he puts quality before everything. The yield is therefore about as small as it is possible to get: it never exceeds two barrels per acre, and a particularly sad story is told of the fabulous vintage of 1921. At that time the château was under contract to supply a certain quantity of wine to one of the great market houses at 6,000 francs per *tonneau*. The yield in 1921 was so small that the market house had practically the whole of it. The opening price was 26,000 francs, and it soon rose to 50,000. . . .

The mention of the 1921 brings one to the other great years of Yquem. There are many of them, but the greatest were 1847, 1859, 1861, 1869, 1874, 1884, 1890, 1893, 1900, 1904, 1914, 1921, 1924, 1928, 1937, 1945, 1947, 1949, 1955, 1959 and 1962; and of all these perhaps the greatest of all was 1921. Such few bottles that remain are still magnificent; and they are not even particularly old by Yquem standards. Château Yquem is fabulous in every way, and it breaks all the rules for white wines: the great vintages remain excellent for fifty or sixty years. Even at Yquem, though, not every year is good, and those that would hopelessly let down the reputation of the château are sold off as simple district wines. Until 1921 bottles from the most exceptional casks used to be sold separately as the *crème de tête*. Now the problem of differing qualities is faced from the opposite direction: only the best wines are sold under the château label and the others are disposed of elsewhere. One would be happier still if, like some of the châteaux in the Médoc, it possessed a second name under which the secondary vintages could be sold, since just a few of the vintages that *have* been bottled are not as magnificent as one might wish.

Château Yquem does in fact have a second name—Château Ygrec—but that is another story. The very late sauternes vintage is extremely vulnerable; a hail storm or heavy rain can wreck it. To provide a safeguard against total loss, some of the grapes at Yquem are picked before the main crop and are used for making Château Ygrec. It is a pleasant medium style of wine, and in a different context one would willingly praise it; but it seems extremely sad that grapes which could go into the making of anything as great as Yquem should be used for any other purpose at all, whatever the economic advantages. The same commercial considerations, together with an increasing demand for dry wines at the expense of sweet ones, are now causing other great châteaux formerly famed for sweet wines to vinify part of the vintage to be dry, notably Château Filhot.

The soil of Château Rayne-Vigneau is one of the phenomena of Bordeaux, and not solely for the fine wine it yields; though this, in all conscience, is superb. At the Paris Exhibition of 1867 the Germans challenged the French to pit one of their white wines against a fine wine of the Rheingau. The French chose Château Vigneau-Pontac (as it was then called) 1861, and they won. Such competitions are meaningless, of course, but nevertheless it must have been a very good wine indeed. In 1964 I tasted the 1929 vintage. It was so dark in colour that one of the guests at the luncheon party, looking at his glass, thought it was a very old tawny port. It certainly resembled the colour of a light oloroso sherry rather than a sauternes, and yet the wine did not taste the least bit maderized. It still had plenty of sugar and the flavour was exquisite. But the earth at Château Rayne-Vigneau gives even more than a fine wine: it is full of jewels; real jewels; semi-precious stones. The happy proprietor has extracted more than twelve thousand of them: agates, amethysts, chalcedony, cornelian, jasper, onyx, opals, sapphires and sardonyx, many of which were excellent examples. It is an unexplained geological phenomenon that sounds more like an Old Testament miracle. Semi-precious stones have also been found in the graves at Château Carbonnieux.

As with the red wines of the Médoc, the classification is a good guide, but it must not be taken too categorically. In particular one wonders what that distinguished sauternes, Château Filhot, is doing down amongst the second growths. Apart from the classified growths, there are a number of thoroughly worthy bourgeois châteaux, but much sweet white wine is sold simply under the district names of Sauternes and Barsac. Some of it, of course, is genuine. Some is not.

The appellation contrôlée cérons is applied to white wines grown on the plain beyond Barsac in the communes of Cérons, Illats and Podensac. Such wines are also entitled to use the appellation graves, and in character they fall midway between a graves and a sauternes.

As in the area of Sauternes, the vines are pruned short and the vintage is late, after the noble rot has set in, but the wines are lighter, with less sugar.

A considerable amount of white wine is grown throughout the Médoc—more than is sometimes realized—but the name *médoc* is reserved exclusively for red wines, and white ones are sold as *bordeaux* or as *bordeaux supérieur*. During the last century the area was better known for white wines than it is today, particularly the commune of Blanquefort, but after the phylloxera few of the white vines were replanted and production suffered a partial eclipse. Now it is rising again. The wines are lighter in body than a graves, and less sweet; some, indeed, are almost completely dry. All of them are pleasant table wines, and a few rise to greater heights.

St. Emilion has its white wine vineyards just as does the other predominantly red wine area, the Médoc. They are also sold under the *appellations* of *bordeaux* and *bordeaux supérieur*, the principal area of production being in Lussac-Saint-Emilion, though white wines are also found in the main traditional red wine area, as at Châteaux Maurens and Saint-Hippolyte. Most of the wines are drunk locally. They are pleasing without being in any way notable, and rather resemble the better-known wines of Entre-Deux-Mers.

Bourgeais and Blayais grow a substantial proportion of white wines, those from the latter area being somewhat superior to the former. The white wine vineyards are old established and contain some of the rare vine species that are no longer encouraged and that are practically extinct elsewhere. Like the reds, the white wines are big in body and lacking in subtlety. In sweetness they vary between dry and medium.

No one knows how Entre-Deux-Mers has come by its name: it is not between two seas but between two rivers, the Garonne and the Dordogne. All its wines are perfectly acceptable, but none, by any stretch of the imagination, is any more than that. Those areas which do grow more interesting wines are separated from it and have *appellations* of their own. The quantity of wine produced, on the other hand, is enormous, and this alone is a useful feature, as it does help to fill the demand for pleasant, commercial white bordeaux. It is as if the Languedoc had established an outpost in

Bordeaux. The soil is richer, the vines grow higher, and the yield is large.

Graves de Vayres forms an enclave in the north of Entre-Deux-Mers, notable for its gravel soil. Its wines are somewhat sweeter than the usual run of Entre-Deux-Mers, and they are substantially better, but their quality does not approach that of a genuine graves, with which they must not be confused, and some of the more delicate wines, which are delightful to drink on the spot, do not travel well. Another segment cut out of Entre-Deux-Mers is called the Premières Côtes de Bordeaux, where the white wines are more fragrant and of distinctly finer quality, particularly those grown in Cadillac. The best wines are dry or medium, but some very sweet ones of acceptable quality are also grown. Saint-Macaire forms an extension of the Côtes to the south-east, where white wine is grown in ten communes. The vines are confined to the marl and gravel slopes of the hills, the rich soil of the plains being avoided. The wine is generally of medium sweetness and of quite good quality. Loupiac and Saint-Croix-du-Mont are areas adjacent to the river and divided off from the rest of the Côtes, just as Sauternes is divided off from Graves on the opposite bank. These are by far the finest white wine areas of the right bank. Careful viticulture, with the aid of the noble rot, gives rich *vins liquoreux* that are excellent for drinking with the dessert and second only to sauternes in quality. Many of them are, without doubt, sold under the label of the more illustrious area.

The quality and style of the white wines, as with the red wines, varies considerably from vintage to vintage. With white wines, the sweetness is particularly liable to vary; it depends directly on the ripeness and sweetness of the grapes, and it is therefore high when there has been plenty of sunshine and low when there has been a shortage of it. The vintage years since 1920 for sauternes are as follows, and the other white wines follow the same pattern:

1920: Quite good, with a fair amount of sugar.

1921: One of the greatest vintages ever. Many of the wines are still excellent, particularly Château Yquem, which was a classic.

1922: Quite a fair year, but of no interest today.

1923: A good year but not outstanding; the wines tended to be rather thin and are of little interest now.

1924: A great vintage. Many of the wines are still excellent.

1925: Poor, though a few quite good wines were made.

1926: A very good year in its day but the wines are now mostly past their best.

1927: Average.

1928: A great vintage. Many of the wines are still excellent.

1929: This was a fine vintage which some compared with the 1921, and many of the wines are still good, but they have not proved to be quite as good as was thought at first, and they are not holding up as well as the other fine vintages of the 1920s.

1930: Bad.

1931: Bad.

1932: Bad.

1933: A pleasant year with a short life.

1934: A very good vintage. Many of the wines are still excellent.

1935: Poor.

1936: Poor.

1937: A very great vintage. The leading growths were at their best in the early 1950s and will last for several years more.

1938: Poor.

1939: A tolerable year, but the wines did not live long.

1940: Similar style to 1939 but somewhat better.

1941: Poor.

1942: A very good year.

1943: A fine year with well-balanced wines, the best of which were excellent to drink in the early 1960s.

1944: Poor.

1945: The vintage in Barsac was spoilt by spring frost, but that in the rest of Sauternes was excellent. The wines were very big and sweet, but they are now tending to go rather dark and they want drinking.

1946: Poor.

1947: A classic vintage that produced beautifully balanced wines which will be good for years to come.

1948: A good year, but one that is not likely to live as long as the '47s and '49s.

1949: A fine big vintage with sweet wines, but some of them are tending to darken and may not live as long as the 1947s.

1950: Light but good wines that are fully ready for drinking.

1951: Poor.

1952: A very fine year for quality but the quantity was sadly reduced by a violent hail storm. The wines are reaching their peak.

1953: Another fine year, similar to 1952.

1954: Poor.

1955: A great vintage with well-balanced wines that will probably be at their best in the 1970s.

1956: Bad.

1957: Generally speaking, the wines were well balanced but light and are making good early drinking. Very low yield.

1958: Quite a successful year. The wines were (rather surprisingly) bigger than the 1957s but not so fine in style and they will not repay keeping.

1959: A very fine vintage that promises well but the yield was low.

1960: Light but pleasant wines.

1961: An average year for quality but the quantity produced was well below average.

1962: A very high yield of good wines. Better for white wines than 1961.

1963: Bad.

1964: A few quite good dry wines were made but the great sweet wines were largely (though not entirely) wiped out by the late rains.

1965: Bad.

1966: A very promising vintage.

1967: A promising vintage but unlikely to be as good as 1966.

1968: Bad.

CHAPTER 4

Burgundy and Rhône

I f the red wines of Bordeaux appeal to the intellect, then those of Burgundy go straight to the emotions. Claret is a delicate and austere wine. The great châteaux are each single entities, so the origin and pedigree of clarets can be clearly established, and it is the recreation of a trained palate to identify them blindfold. There are plenty of hard facts for the intellect to bite on, and the austerity of the wines flatters the puritan that hides within even a *bon viveur*. With burgundies all this is reversed. They are great, big, smooth wines that warm the body and soul. They are not wines for puritans: they are too bluff and cheerful. That is not to say, though, that they are unsubtle or lack delicacy. Far from it! A great burgundy has a remarkable delicacy all of its own: the sheer volume of its bouquet and flavour is made up subtly of many parts that form a perfect whole. The great wines, too, are in no way shy of their origin: they have no need to be. And they are expensive. With the cheaper wines it is otherwise. They are as shy of their pedigree as a wealthy and ambitious bourgeois is vague about his ancestors; and the more ambitious the bourgeois is in his claims, the more suspect he becomes. So it is with burgundy. Far more chambertin is sold than is ever grown in the *climat* of Chambertin. Unhappily nearly all the great names have been debased, and the lesser ones never did mean much. This makes things far too easy for the claret fancier who chooses to sneer at burgundy. A good Burgundian will say of a Bordelais that his red wines are tannic and flat, while his white wines are syrupy and sulphured; and if he wants to be really unpleasant he will add, inaccurately, that the wines of Bordeaux grow in marshes. The Bordelais, for his part, will castigate his friend for making a dim and scentless red wine by fermenting a mixture of grape juice and sugar, and he will suggest that the Côte d'Or stretches right across the Mediterranean and far into Algeria. If they take the trouble, both can make out quite a convincing case. A wiser man will hit their heads together and drink the best that each can provide. Nor does skill in selecting wines from one area preclude an equal skill with those of the other; at least one great shipper—Calvet—is equally famed in each place.

To include such a vast area of vineyards as those of Burgundy, the Beaujolais and the Rhône, in a single chapter is perhaps perverse, but there is one link between them: they are all, except those of Chablis, on the hillsides that rise above the valley of the Rhône and of its northern tributary, the Saône. And they have more than the physical link of the rivers to unite them. Unfortunately some of the less scrupulous shippers have a sense of geography as vague as that of a house agent. In London, a Fulham slum is advertised as being in a select area of Chelsea. In Burgundy, the wines tend to come from many miles further south than their labels would suggest, while many a cross-breed passes as a thoroughbred.

Chablis has long been thought of as being part of Burgundy, though its wines are very different from the bigger wines from further south. In the French laws of *appellation contrôlée*, moreover, if chablis is declassified it may be sold as *bourgogne* or *bourgogne grand ordinaire*. Chablis stands apart from the rest of the burgundy country: a little oasis, and quite isolated. It is the most northerly of all the districts being considered in this chapter. Then, some seventy miles to the south-east, comes the long strip of hillside with the greatest vineyards of Burgundy: the Côte d'Or. It begins about five miles south of Dijon, just before the village of Fixin, but there are also burgundy vineyards to the west of Dijon, and others to the south, between Dijon and Fixin. These used once to be described as the Côte de Dijon and they were considered part of the Côte d'Or, but those that survive are unworthy or undistinguished, and they are now known as the Arrière Côte et Sud de Dijon. The best have unhappily long since been absorbed by the growing suburbs of the city. The Côte d'Or is itself divided into two parts: the Côte de Nuits and the Côte de Beaune. The Côte de Nuits comes first, and runs in quite a narrow strip on the hillsides to the west of the main N.74 road, only crossing it in one place,

near the village of Gevrey-Chambertin. But if you happen to be
that way and want to see the vineyards it is better to leave the
main road and drive along the Route des Grand Crus. Then every
village you pass through has a glorious name: Gevrey-Chambertin,
Morey-St.-Denis, Chambolle-Musigny, Vougeot, Vosne-Romanée
and so to Nuits-St.-Georges which gives its name to the whole
Côte. As far as the great wines are concerned the vineyards are in
fact even narrower than they look, for the finest wines can only be
grown in the middle slopes.

The Côte de Nuits comes to an end. There is a short stretch of
flat country with some quarries. Then the hills rise again as the
Côte de Beaune begins. If the Côte de Nuits is the home of the
greatest of all the red wines, then the Côte de Beaune competes
for glory with its white wines, for it includes the villages of Meursault, Puligny-Montrachet, and Chassagne-Montrachet. In the
pleasant hills behind the two Côtes are the Arrières-Côtes, with
their worthy, but humbler burgundies.

The Côte d'Or is a golden slope indeed, and happily this has
been so well recognized that its name has been given to the whole
département of which if forms only so small a part. The soil is
perfect for the vine, but the soil can do little without the sun, and
the orientation of the slopes of the Côte d'Or is exactly right: they
catch every bit of sunshine. Even so, the vines have to be hardy,
for the climate is a continental one: it is hot in the summer, but in
the winter it can be very cold indeed, with great frosts and lots of
snow. It is a fine country for growing wines, but there are better
places to live in.

After the Côte d'Or there is a gap of a few miles, until the Côte
Chalonnaise is reached on the other side of Chagny, where there is
another outcrop of fine burgundies around Rully and Mercurey.
Then there is another gap until one reaches Givry, and yet another
before the vineyards of Montagny—the most southerly to produce
a burgundy of the classic style.

The name 'burgundy' is rather a vague one, though. If chablis be
a burgundy, then so certainly are the more southerly wines from
the Mâconnais and the Beaujolais. All are entitled to the *appellation*
'bourgogne'. The Mâconnais vineyards, where the popular and
pleasant mâcon wines are grown, begin soon after Montagny, but
there are no wines of any great distinction until one gets to the

area of Mâcon itself, and the vineyards that produce pouilly-fuissé, pouilly-loché and pouilly-vinzelles. Next after the Mâconnais comes the Beaujolais: a country of scenic beauty and delightful wines. The vineyards extend to Villefranche-sur-Saône, and then there is a substantial gap before one comes again to any vineyards of real importance, which are right the other side of Lyons. And then one has definitely left Burgundy. The major vineyards of the Côtes du Rhône begin with the Côte Rôtie, just south of Vienne, which extends to St. Péray, just south of Valance. Further to the south, there is an outpost of good vineyards around Livron, but apart from that, no notable wines are grown until the next substantial area. This begins along a line drawn roughly between Bollene and Nyons, and it continues until south of Avignon. It includes the great Châteauneuf-du-Pape. Finally there is Tavel, with its famous rosé.

The white wines from throughout these areas are all dry, and they are the finest of their kind grown anywhere. Chablis is in a class by itself: to include in it a classification with the white wines of the Côte d'Or would be almost as meaningless as to include the red wines of Burgundy with those of Bordeaux. The white wines of the Côte d'Or, however, may be classified amongst themselves without very much risk of contradiction. Montrachet comes first and then chevalier-montrachet. Third come the finest growths of meursault, puligny-montrachet, chassagne-montrachet, bâtard-montrachet and corton-charlemagne. Fourth come the remaining growths of meursault, puligny-montrachet and chassagne-montrachet. But they are all great wines: the fourth group are no more fourth-rate than the fourth growths of the Médoc are.

To classify the red wines of the Côte d'Or poses a harder problem. The greatest authorities on burgundy[1] have adopted a classification drawn up in 1888 by an amateur of wine. I can only quote it:

The Royal Family of the Wines of Burgundy
  The King: Le Chambertin.
  The Queen: La Romanée-Conti.
  The Regent: Le Clos-de-Vougeot.
  The King's First Cousin: Le Richebourg.

[1] Pierre Poupon and Pierre Forgeot, *A Book of Burgundy*, London, 1958.

Princes of the Blood: Romanée, Clos-de-Tart, Musigny, La Tâche, Echézeaux, Bonnes-Mares.
Royal Standard Bearer: Le Corton.
Dukes and Duchesses: Volnay, Nuits, Pommard, Beaune, Savigny-Vergelesses, Aloxe-Corton, Chassagne.

That the genealogist should have needed to create a special place for the king's first cousin shows how difficult he found his task, and he also had to include a regent, although there is no suggestion that the king is under age or unfit to govern. Poupon and Forgeot, moreover, rightly indicate that there are many other wines that deserve a place in the 'Royal Family', such as gevrey-chambertin, vosne-romanée, chambolle-musigny, morey-st.-denis, santenay, auxey-duresses, monthélie, etc. And the list could be much longer.

Today nearly all the growers and shippers concentrate on producing these great red and white wines, though there is also a certain amount of *vin rosé*, and some sparkling wines are made by the *méthode champenoise*. But of the latter, the less said the better. In the past there were other wines as well. During the thirteenth century, and probably for some centuries thereafter, the growers at the time of the vintage used to put aside some of their must which they boiled in great copper basins, to produce a cooked wine known as *galant*. Such wines would be similar to the *sancocho* and *arrope* that are still made in the sherry country, where they are used in blending, to add colour and sweetness to the natural wines. Their history, however, goes back much further. In the days of the Roman Empire there were two such wine syrups known as *sapa* and *defrutum*, which are mentioned by Pliny, Columella and others, while the Greek comedians of the fifth and fourth centuries B.C. spoke of boiled-down must as *hepsema*. Such wines, or syrups, ceased from being made in Burgundy a very long time ago, though.

Another wine of the past was *vin fou*, or crazy wine, which should not be confused with the wine that is today produced in the Jura and sold commercially under that name. Originally this was a sparkling wine prepared by fermenting the must in a tightly sealed and strongly bound barrel, so that the gas evolved during fermentation could not get out. There used also to be sweet wines, known as *vins de paille*, or straw wines, so called because the grapes were left for several weeks on a bed of straw, so that they shrivelled and lost part of their water before being pressed, to give strong, sweet wines. They were also, incidentally, rather like straw in colour. Such wines are still made at Château Chalon, in the Jura, and at Beaulieu in the Dordogne, but not in Burgundy.

The origin of viticulture in Burgundy is lost in antiquity. Historians have devoted much energy and some spleen to the subject, but without any very definite result; nor does it really matter. It is so old that a few hundred years more or less makes no difference. It may even pre-date the Roman conquest, and that started in 58 B.C. Very probably vines were grown there as far back as the fourth century B.C. The inexcusable and churlish decree of Domitian, which ordered the uprooting of vines in the Roman provinces, has already been mentioned in earlier chapters, and such a decree would have been quite superfluous had there been no significant vineyards to uproot. As it is, it is doubtful to what extent it was carried into effect, and it seems that wine growing never actually ceased in Burgundy. Possibly the vignerons were granted special privileges, or else the authorities looked the other way, as the vineyards must have been very useful. They were strategically placed on the great trade route that linked Rome with her Rhenish garrisons—the same route which now links Paris with the Côte d'Azur. In the year 312 the citizens of Autun addressed a memorandum to the Emperor Constantine which showed that vines of 'immemorial age' were growing on the Côte de Nuits, then known as the Pagus Arebringus. They were so old, in fact, that they were useless for all practical purposes. But if the Romans did not kill viticulture, they certainly throttled it; and the vine could not come into its own until the decree was repealed by Probus in 281.

Once the decree had been repealed, viticulture was soon flourishing again on a large scale. The first of the great wine growers were the monasteries, which became established throughout the area from the end of the fifth century. Notable amongst them was the abbey of Bèze, dating from the end of the seventh century, which owned vineyards at Beaune, Chenôve, Conchey, Gevrey, Marsannay and Vosne. Throughout the centuries, the Church steadily gained notable vineyards, and it is said that the prosperity of the monks caused them to indulge in 'a life of deplorable abandon'. But their riotous living probably helped to encourage the vine, even if they became distracted from their more pious purposes. Inevitably, however, their decadence led to a reaction. Amongst the later monastic orders was that of the Cistercians, a simpler, purer and stricter observance of the rule of St. Benedict, which was founded at Cîteaux, near the village of Nuits, during the eleventh century: a monastery that was to play its own part in viticulture, and whose vineyards have been famous since the twelfth century. Other important abbeys included those of St. Bénigne at Dijon and Cluny near Mâcon. In the little town of Beaune it is said that there were at one time as many as twenty religious foundations. It is unfortunate that viticulture is not still concentrated in these good hands: it was the eventual downfall of the religious orders, following the French Revolution, that led to the division of the great vineyards between innumerable small proprietors. Paul de Cassagnac's phrase that the Côte d'Or is the 'wine democracy of France' sounds very fine; but in fact it has been disastrous. It has debased the quality of the wine and has encouraged fraud.

Since the quality of a wine ultimately depends on the soil and the climate, the wines were probably good from the very beginning. Burgundy was served on the royal table of Philip le Bel (1285–1314), and by the end of the fourteenth century, beaune was considered to be one of the greatest of all wines: it was already established as the 'wine of kings'. The removal of the Papacy to Avignon in 1308 brought it new fame, for the papal court consumed a prodigious amount of wine, and it had to be good wine. Indeed, the excellence of beaune was later used as an argument against returning the papal see to Rome. Then, in 1363, Philip the Bold established the Valois dynasty as Dukes of Burgundy and provided another court of almost royal importance to patronize the local wine growers; while the dukes themselves, as landowners, became growers in their own right, and they, with the monasteries, set a standard for others to emulate.

Although burgundy had become famous, it remained for many years a comparatively local drink. Some was exported to Italy but little elsewhere. This was entirely owing to geography: it could easily be taken southwards, along the waters of the Saône and Rhône, but transport to the north and west was far more difficult. Consequently the wines of the Seine valley, shipped from Auxerre, and those of Champagne, were far better known in Paris, while in England we relied on wines from Bordeaux and La Rochelle. Such burgundy as did reach Paris was generally taken via the Yonne. Thence it was occasionally brought to England. Only wealthy connoisseurs could afford to import burgundy. For instance, between 1700 and 1739, John Harvey, first Earl of Bristol, imported both red and white burgundies, but in very small quantities as compared with claret.

Burgundy did not become established at the French court until the reign of Louis XIV (1643–1715), to whom it was recommended by his physician Guy-Crescent Fagon. The king lived to be almost seventy-two, and the doctor eighty, so let others take heart. But it must be admitted that burgundy had its enemies at court as well as its friends. One writer has suggested that the royal stomach was so debilitated that it could only take its burgundy well diluted, and that the king consoled himself for its tastelessness by laughing at the noblemen who sought the honour of sharing his special wine.[1] The chief opponents of burgundy at that time were the admirers of champagne, which had not yet become sparkling. It was made from the same grapes as those grown in Burgundy and had a strong family resemblance.

The physician can be thanked for giving burgundy its official acclaim, but a peasant from the Mâconnais did almost as much to help it on its way. Claude Brosse was a veritable giant of a man. In 1660 he decided to take two casks of his wine by cart to Paris, in the hope of gaining a new and profitable market. He was strong enough to protect it from the robbers that infested the roads, and having safely reached Versailles, he went to mass. This almost led to his undoing. It was a royal mass, and at a solemn moment when the whole congregation knelt, the Sun King chanced to look around, and he saw a peasant still standing. Scandalized, he sent one of his courtiers at once to bring the fellow to his knees. But when the courtier reached him, he found that Claude Brosse was indeed kneeling: it was only his massive size that made him tower over the congregation. The king was intrigued, and after the service he commanded that the giant Brosse be brought to him. His Majesty graciously enquired what brought so fine a peasant

---

[1] St. Simon's Memoires quoted by H. Vizetelly in *A History of Champagne*, London, 1882.

all the way from the Mâconnais to Versailles. He was told of the wine, and he tasted it. He liked it. He liked it far better than the thin wines that were then in vogue; and his courtiers were only too pleased to gain royal approbation by acclaiming his taste. He and his court continued to taste and drink it for ever more. Claude Brosse spent the rest of his life carting his wines to Versailles, and his fortune was made. It was thus that the wines of southern Burgundy came into their own, and if they were late starters, they have certainly made up for it since. Production is enormous, and it is more than matched by the demand. The wines flow into Paris like a river. They are perhaps the most popular beverage wines in the world.

By the beginning of the eighteenth century claret, champagne and burgundy were invariably listed in England as the great wines of France, in that order. It was thus that Swift referred to French wines in his *Journal to Stella*, and Pope, writing to Congreve, described how 'I sat up till two o'clock over Burgundy and Champagne'. When that invaluable book *The Vineyard: being a treatise. Being the observations made by a Gentleman in his Travels* was published in London in 1727, the author expressed his preference for champagne and burgundy, but he was principally concerned with growing wine in England, and it is therefore not surprising that he devoted most of his attentions to the more northerly wine. To him, burgundy was red and champagne white, but he added 'And now they make yearly in Champagne, great quantities of Red Wine, after the manner of Burgundy, which they export and send to Foreign Countries, and there sell for Burgundy' or 'Again the natural wine of *Burgundy* is Red, notwithstanding they do frequently make a White Wine, in imitation of the *Champagners* which they will sometimes sell for Champagne, and at other times for white Burgundy.'

Surprised and grieved that the wines of his native Burgundy were so little known in this country, a Monsieur Arnoux, who was a French tutor in London, wrote in 1725 a little book with an astonishingly long title, even by the standards of those days: DISSERTATION SUR LA SITUATION DE BOURGOGNE, SUR LES VINS QUELLE PRODUIT, SUR LA MANIERE DE CULTIVER LES VIGNES, DE FAIRE LE VIN ET DE L'EPROUVER, SUR LES QUALITEZ, FINESSE, COULEUR, & DUREE DES DIFFERENS VINS

QUE PRODUIT LA COTE DE BEAUNE AVEC LE NOM DE TOUS LES
BONS COTEAUX GRAVES EXACTEMENT DANS UNE CARTE
GEOGRAPHIQUE DES COLLINES DE LA HAUTE BOURGOGNE;
SUR LA FACILITE D'AVOIR DE CES VINS, A QUI IL FAUT
S'ADDRESSER POUR CELA, DEUX MOYENS POUR LES FAIRE
VENIR A LONDRES SANS ALTERATION ET A BON MARCHE, LE
TOUT PRECEDE D'UNE ODE LATINE QUI FAIT L'ELOGE DU VIN
DE VOLNET ADRESSEE A UN DES PLUS SCAVANTS HOMMES DE
L'EUROPE, AVEC LA COPIE DE LA LETTRE QUE CE SCAVANT
ENVOYA A L'AUTEUR DE CETTE ODE ET DE CETTE DISSERTA-
TION. PAR MR. ARNOUX, PRECEPTEUR DE MSS. LES FILS DE
J. FREEMAN, ESQ. MODICUS SED UNICUS. A LONDRES.
IMPRIME CHEZ SAMUEL JALLASSON, EN PRUJEAN'S COURT,
OLD BAILY & SE VEND P. DU NOYER, A LA 'TETE D'ERASME',
ET CHEZ N. PREVOST, VIS A VIS SOUTHAMPTON STREET,
DANS LE STRAND. M.DCC.XXVIII.

The greatest difficulty the good Frenchman faced was the 'Les
faire venir à Londres' part; for it was still long before the coming
of the railways, and the overland journey was extremely expensive.
Moreover it was often disastrous to the wine, as the carriers helped
themselves whenever they felt thirsty, and what wine was left,
after its long journey on ullage, would be damaged if not ruined.
The answer he suggested was for the noble lord or gentleman
concerned to import the wine already bottled by the car-load—
which consisted of a thousand bottles. Few, even in those days,
would have been able to take his advice. And that very same year
the importation of wine in bottle was prohibited in his country,
so his good scheme came to nothing. It was not until a century
later that burgundy became a popular and economically possible
drink in this country, and its introduction was helped not only by
the railways but also by the establishment of great mercantile
houses in Burgundy towards the end of the eighteenth century.
These houses were soon handling practically the whole of the
burgundy exports, as they and their successors still do to this day.
It was no doubt owing to transport difficulties that during the
early years of the eighteenth century there was actually over-
production in Burgundy, and in 1732 the inhabitants of Beaune
petitioned the king to have the vineyards that were planted on the
hilltops and plains torn up, in the hope that the removal of the

inferior growths would improve the value of their fine wines. They were unsuccessful and the lesser vineyards are still there.

In Burgundy, as in all the other great wine countries, the tragedy of the nineteenth century was the coming of the phylloxera. It was found in the south of France as early as 1863. By 1866 it was established at Orange, in the southern vineyards of the Rhône; and it slowly worked upwards. By 1874 it had reached Villé-Morgon in the Beaujolais; in 1875 it reached Tournus, and was well on the way to the Côte d'Or; three years later it was found at Meursault. Some years before it arrived, at the Viticultural Congress at Beaune, in 1869, the only practical remedy had already been proposed: to graft the native vines on to American roots; and in 1886 the use of American stocks was authorized in the Côte d'Or.

Inevitably one is faced again with the question as to whether the wine from the grafted vines is as good as that from the native vines growing naturally; and the answer in Burgundy, as in Bordeaux, appears to be that there is really very little difference, if one thing is remembered: that great wines are only produced by old vines, and newly replanted vineyards are therefore always at a disadvantage. Unfortunately, though quite understandably, the growers were anxious to get into production again as soon as possible, and some wines were certainly sold that were a disgrace to their famous names. Even so, the greatest burgundies maintained their reputation. Since the invasion of the phylloxera and the consequent replanting were both gradual, it is not easy to draw a clear dividing line between the pre- and post-phylloxera vintages, but it is probably not far out to say that it occurred at about the turn of the century. The vintages of 1904, 1906, 1911, 1915 and 1919, however, were quite able to hold their own with the earlier vintages of 1881, 1885, 1886, 1887, 1894 and 1898. Until quite recently, moreover, there were ungrafted vines in the great vineyard of Romanée-Conti, but again the replanting does not seem to have made much difference, and there are now no ungrafted vines left anywhere in Burgundy or the Rhône. There seems to be no truth, either, in the legend that the pre-phylloxera wines lasted longer in bottle. In 1860, Cyrus Redding wrote that:[1]

'The endurance of those wines of the finer class, which keep

[1] *French Wines and Vineyards*, London, 1860.

best, is not more than a dozen or fifteen years from the vintage, for then they become bitter. They still sustain themselves, it is true, some years more, but they will decline rather than improve. After being ten years in bottle the strongest will have attained their greatest perfection.' Modern wines regularly last longer than that, and some of the great 1945s are now only reaching their best, after more than twenty years.

Unfortunately the plague gave a wonderful opportunity to the unscrupulous. When production of genuine burgundy was at its lowest, the demand remained unaffected, and large quantities of young wines were brought in from other areas, to be matured in the cellars of the Côte d'Or and sold as burgundy. It is not surprising that the public became suspicious. Until the twentieth century there were very few laws controlling the sale of wine, especially as regards nomenclature, which became more and more elastic. To make matters worse, after the Kaiser war the demand grew and was hard to satisfy, so the temptation towards fraud grew worse. After the Hitler war the situation was worse than ever, and in 1946 the laws of *appellation contrôlée* were finally tidied up and applied throughout Burgundy, although, it must be confessed, with only a limited measure of success. Even so, they are better than nothing, and they have done some good. Unfortunately, however, they are without legal force in Britain and until they can be enforced in all wine importing countries they will never be wholly successful. We are the main culprits.[1]

In the delightful and ancient little town of Beaune, which is the wine capital of Burgundy, there is one day in practically every year that is more exciting, more entrancing, and more hectic than any other: the third Sunday in November—the day of the great sale at the Hospices de Beaune. This great home for the aged, poor and sick, was founded in 1443 by Nicolas Rolin, a pious *parvenu* lawyer who became rich and powerful as Lord Keeper of the Seal in the court of the great Duke Philip the Good. Its beautiful old buildings, designed in the Flemish style, with high, steep roofs and an immense cobbled courtyard, provide the greatest tourist attraction of the Côte d'Or. And unlike so many tourist attractions, it really is well worth a visit. The endowment he provided consisted of a number of vineyards, and these have been added to by

[1] See Appendix.

the posthumous generosity of a number of testators. The wines are generally well made, and no doubt it was this that originally caused them to be sold at a premium. Nowdays they fetch even higher prices, but not entirely for the same reason: there is the glamour of the name *Hospices de Beaune*, and the certainty that the wines will command a high price throughout the world. Every leading shipper has to buy some, against direct bidding from foreign importers and restaurants, and so the price rises out of proportion to the quality; for the wines themselves, although excellent, are in no way unique, and none is in the very top class. It is a sad reflection on other growers, though, that they often surpass wines grown on superior sites.

Before the auction there is a tasting of samples, for which a charge is made, to enhance the charity's revenue. Then the sale is conducted by the old method of *à la chandelle*—by the candle. It is a very effective method that is virtually extinct in this country, but it certainly gets things moving. A short length of taper is lit, and the last bidder to make his offer before the flame flickers out gets the wine. It is all so picturesque that somehow one always assumes that the auction has been going on every year since the Hospice was founded, but it has not. The first was held in 1850, when 189 lots were sold for 19,247 50F.

Apart from its charitable virtue, the auction serves two useful purposes: it enables the merchants of the Côte d'Or to assess the merits of the vintage by a fairly comprehensive and open tasting, and it sets the level of prices for the rest of the year. Only in the very worst years such as 1956 and 1968, when no wines were made that were considered worthy of the Hospices, is the sale not held. In normal years both red and white wines are sold from various *communes*,[1] wines from the many *crus* owned by the Hospices being made up into the following *cuvées*:

Red Wines

Communes	Cuveés
Aloxe-Corton	Charlotte Dumay
	Docteur Peste
Auxey-Duresses	Boillot

[1] In Burgundy, a commune is sometimes referred to as a *finage*.

Red Wines

Communes	Cuvées
Beaune	Bétault
	Brunet
	Clos des Avaux
	Dames Hospitalières
	Estienne
	Guigone de Salins
	Nicolas Rolin
	Pierre Virely
	Rousseau-Deslandes
Meursault	Henri Gélicot
Monthélie	Jacques Lebelin
Pommard	Billerdet
	Dames de la Charité
Savigny	Cyrot
	Arthur Girard
Savigny-Vergelesses	du Bay-Peste
	Forneret
	Fouquerand
Volnay	Blondeau
	General Muteau
Volnay-Santenots	Gauvain
	Jehan de Massol

White Wines

Communes	Cuvées
Meursault	Baudot
	Goureau
	Jehan Humblot
	Loppin
Meursault-Charmes	Albert Grivault
	de Bahèzre de Lanlay
Corton-Charlemagne	François de Salins

It is a fine and extensive list, many of the *cuvées* being named after vineyard donors, and no one need be apprehensive about the corton named after Docteur Peste. It is perhaps unfortunate that the name which must have plagued him throughout his life has now been immortalized, but the wine is admirable.

These wines are authentic beyond doubt, but they are all sold in cask, and their fate is in the hands of those who buy them. Thanks to the high price and kudos they command, it is not unlikely that some of the less scrupulous merchants succumb to the temptation of 'stretching' them, for there is no control over the issue of labels. Others are bought by restaurateurs and small merchants whose bottling ability may not be above suspicion. But if a Hospices de Beaune wine is bought from an honest shipper it will be a well-made wine and as authentic as a *domaine*-bottled burgundy.

Although the phylloxera may not have done the quality of the wine much harm, nevertheless it is generally agreed that burgundy is not what it used to be, or at any rate that shippers' burgundies are not what they used to be. My father's cellar still contains, apart from the great burgundies he bought, some humble district wines of pre-war vintages shipped by some of the leading burgundy houses. Their vigour and longevity are astounding, and they are incomparably better than anything sold by the same shippers under the same labels of recent similar vintages. But the story of the decline really begins much earlier: at the time of the French Revolution when the property of the monasteries was confiscated and divided. The situation has since become even worse than it was then, thanks to the French law of inheritance, which favours equal shares, unlike the law and custom of England which, favouring the eldest son, kept many of our great estates intact until they were ruined by death duties.

The result has been chaos. Thus the great vineyard of Clos Vougeot alone is split into about seventy pieces. This is the worst example, but there are others nearly as bad, and only comparatively few of the great names—names like Romanée-Conti and Clos de Tart—are still intact. Most of the growers, it must be said, make their wine to the best of their ability; but some are more able than others. And unfortunately a few have chosen to produce quantity rather than quality. It is hard to blame them: there is little pride in a great name when you only own one per cent of it. The temptation is to make as much as possible; to cash in on the name and leave the quality to someone else. Even in those places where everyone does his best there is often a wide variation between the wines of different growers, and this alone is enough to render a label practically meaningless, even where the wine in the bottle is authentic. Pierre Poupon[1] has summed up the situation graphically: 'If ten or twelve writers were given, in a few words, the subject for a novel, we should have ten or twelve different works, even though the theme would be the same. Vignerons likewise work on a common theme—the same type of vine, the same earth, the same climate—and nevertheless each of the proprietors in Chambertin or in Montrachet, for example, makes a chambertin or a montrachet of a personal character that is not like those of his neighbours. . . .' Despite all the science of modern enologists, wine remains a very personal thing. Sometimes the small growers get together to produce wines in commercial quantities, while others are content to make their odd cask or two. In three areas—Chablis, the Beaujolais and the Mâconnais—they rely on large and active co-operatives. There are also co-operatives in the Côte d'Or, but they are relatively less important. I have never tasted a bad wine from a co-operative, but I have never tasted a great one, either.

That is part of the story, but there are several more factors. Firstly some growers have increased their vineyard production by choosing only cuttings from the most prolific vines for grafting, and then pruning them long, which gives the greatest possible yield at the expense of reduced flavour. In some instances the pruning has been too long to comply with the laws of *appellation contrôlée*. Supervision can never be complete. Admittedly, under the laws of *appellation contrôlée* the maximum output of each vineyard is stipulated, and only that amount can be sold under the great name. But the rest can still be sold. And it is. Where there is over production, the quality of the *whole* suffers.

Secondly, the method of vinification has gradually been changed. In the past, when red wine was made, the must was left to ferment in contact with the skins and with some of the stalks for eight to fifteen days. Now it is only left for about six days, and sometimes even less. The result is a wine with a lighter colour, less tannin, and less body, that is pleasant, if unexciting, to drink, and which matures much more quickly. In short, it is a far better commercial

[1] *Pensées d'un Dégustateur*, 1957.

proposition. And the enologists know exactly what they are about. In the old days some of the wine turned out to be superb and some was worthless. Nowadays very little of it fails, but much of that which is made is uniformly second-rate. Happily, however, there are still a few growers and shippers who are not so commercially minded, and who still make their wines in the old way. But such wines do take time to mature: at least five and sometimes thirty-five years. Wine merchants no longer have the capital to lay them down, for the return is low; and few private buyers have either the capital or the inclination. Scarce and expensive as these great wines are, far too many of them suffer infanticide in the glasses of the ignorant. The modern style of shippers' burgundies is easier to make and easier to sell profitably.

Thirdly, many of the wines are over-chaptalized. The purpose of chaptalization (that is to say the addition of sugar to the must before fermentation) has already been discussed. Within limits, the idea is an excellent one, and it often enables a drinkable wine to be produced in an impossibly bad year. But it is too often used only as a safety precaution: to produce wines so strong in alcohol that they are artificially protected against the diseases that attack weaker wines. Such wines, moreover, have their public following. And it also helps to produce vigorous and characterless wines from feeble grapes grown on vines that have been underpruned.

Most commercial burgundies, moreover, are blended wines. If a great shipper lists a 1959 beaune, his customers all expect to receive the same wine; and they do receive the same wine. He buys wine from innumerable little growers whose wines are entitled to be sold as beaune, mixes them to make a single *cuvée*, matures them for the appropriate time in the wood, and then sells them. With a humble name like beaune (as distinct from the leading *climats* in the *commune*), where the wines are in any case inexpensive, this is no bad thing. Without this system the merchants would have to list the individual names of all the vineyards, and they would soon be in the same position as the shippers in Germany. The public would find their labelling confusing if not incomprehensible, and trade would suffer. Moreover, the extra work involved would cause prices to rise; and the wine would be no better. Anyone who has been to Burgundy will have tasted some of the thin, dim little wines that are perfectly entitled to bear famous names. They are not what the public wants; nor, indeed, what anyone wants. A good shipper will make up their deficiencies by skilful blending. He will take a wine deficient in tannin and blend it with another that has too much; he will take a thin wine and blend it with another that is over-robust; and so on. And if he is making a cheap blend, he may be none too scrupulous as to where his wines come from. In the past it was often alleged that half the cheap burgundy was grown in Algeria. Today it is more likely to come from the Rhône or from the Languedoc, which suffers from a chronic over-production of cheap, coarse wines. Such blends are often far more palatable for everyday drinking than a poor but honest burgundy. It is thus, too, that wines from the south are promoted and sold under more august names from further north. The shippers tend to be consistently fifty or sixty miles out in their geography.

These are the cheap wines, where the problem is to satisfy the enormous and growing demand, and at the same time to produce the smooth, full wines that sell so readily over the grocers' counters. For such wines, blending is at least harmless and even desirable. It is otherwise when the wines bear great names. But here again the hapless shipper finds himself in a difficult position. The public expects its burgundies to be big, full wines. It does not understand that some burgundies are truly delicate, and that others need maturing for a long time. Understandably, many of the shippers pander to the popular taste, which was originally largely of their own creating. To the purists amongst us, this would seem unfortunate. As an example, here is a blend used by a well-known shipper, which he sold as his clos-de-vougeot 1961:

clos-de-vougeot, first supplier	7 parts
clos-de-vougeot, second supplier	3 parts
savigny	1 part
châteauneuf-du-pape	1 part
	12

It was undoubtedly a very nice wine indeed, and commercially it was probably more acceptable than either of the clos-de-vougeot wines would have been alone. A small infusion of good wines such as savigny and châteauneuf-du-pape, moreover, made little difference to its cost, so that there was no profit motive. But it was no longer, to my mind, a genuine clos-de-vougeot. Another of his blends was being sold as vosne-romanée, les malconsorts. Two-thirds of it were just that. The other third consisted of château-neuf-du-pape. And it purported to be a single-vineyard burgundy.

Art has been said to be the product of the human mind working on nature; or a dream combined with reality. The blending of burgundy is certainly an art; and within its limits it is a useful one: poor wines can be improved, and acceptable everyday wines can be prepared cheaply for sale under meaningless brand names. But such things should not happen to great wines. La Rochefoucauld remarked: 'There are good marriages, but there are certainly not delicious ones.' And the greatest of all wines are best if they are allowed to be celibate. Anyone who desires the very best must go to a wine merchant of unimpeachable integrity and vast knowledge who, in turn, will buy only from the most honourable shippers: names like Louis Latour or Drouhin, with perhaps half a dozen others. If he wants to be even safer he will buy *domaine*-bottled wines. Whichever he does, he must not care about the price. Such wines are worth every penny of it.

As a final degradation, two of the houses in Beaune, and probably some others elsewhere, pasteurize their wines—heating them until the ferments are dead, and the wines therefore are perfectly safe. They are quite good. They stay good. But they can never attain greatness.

Throughout the burgundy area, for growing red wines there are basically two varieties of vine: the Pinot and the Gamay. For white wines, there are the Chardonnay, the Aligoté and the Melon. Further south, as one gets to the Côtes du Rhône, one not surprisingly finds other species more appropriate to the hotter climate, though the great burgundy vines also grow there in some places. The greatest of all the vines in the Rhône vineyards is the black Syrah. Other black varieties include: Carignan Noir, Cinsault, Clairette, Grenache Noir, Mourvèdre, Picpoul Noir and Terret Noir. White species include: Marsanne, Mauzac Blanc, Rousanne de Tain and Viognier. But there are many others besides, some of them permitted by the laws of *appellation contrôlée*, and some not.

The Pinot Noir is also known as the Noirien and (anciently) as the Beaunois. It was first heard of in the fourteenth century, when Philip the Bold, Duke of Burgundy, sent a quantity of *vin de pinot vermeil* to Bruges, and from that date onwards it has been lauded continually as the great vine of Burgundy. In all probability it was established long before that time. Its name may well have been derived from the shape of its bunches of grapes, which rather resemble that of a fir cone (pomme de pin). It is a vine for quality rather than quantity, and its yield is not great. This has recently been increased by selective cultivation; but as to whether such a change is a good thing, one can only express doubt. Apart from its basic form of Pinot Noir, it exists in at least three other variants: Pinot Gris, or Beurot; Pinot Renevey; and Pinot Maltais, or Pinot de Morgeot. The Pinot Gris, so called because of its ash-grey colour that is said to resemble the home-spun habits worn by monks, produces somewhat larger bunches of grapes than the Pinot Noir, but fewer of them, so that the yield is less. Moreover the skins are very thin, making the grapes more vulnerable to attack and disease. However, the wine they give is second to none, and although the Pinot Gris is never grown alone, a small proportion is often grown alongside the Pinot Noir to enhance the quality. The Pinot Renevay was selected in 1765 by one Pierre Renevey, and the Pinot Maltais was cultivated by the Knights of Malta on their property at Morgeot. Both these latter give a large yield, and the wine is of good colour, but the quality is inferior, and these variants are more or less extinct.

The history of the Gamay vine goes back almost as far as that of the Pinot, but it is far less glorious. In its early days the Gamay excited nothing but official opprobrium. It was roundly condemned; and it still is, as far as the Côte d'Or is concerned. But it still grows there. It was introduced into Burgundy by a crusader from the little hamlet of Gamay, near Meursault, who brought it back with him when he returned from the East. The exact date it arrived is unknown, but by 1395 it was evidently well established— only too well established, in fact. Philip the Bold, who was a great champion of his duchy's fine wines, issued a proclamation, and ordered the Gamay vines to be uprooted within a month. His edict is a minor masterpiece of anathema: '. . . vignes d'un très mauvais et très déloyaud plant nommé gaamez, duquel mauvais plant vient très grande abondance de vin, et pour la plus grande quantité desdits mauvais vins ont laissé en ruine et désert les bonnes places où l'on fait venir et croître le bon vin. Et lequel vin de gaamez est de telle nature qu'il est moult nuisible à créature humaine, mêmement, que plusieurs qui au temps passé en ont usé, en ont été infectés de grièves maladies, si comme entendu avons; car ledit vin qui est issu et fait dudit plant, de sadite nature est plein de très grand et horrible ametume, et devient tout puant. . . .'

The proclamation did not, however, work. The wine might well have been inferior—indeed it undoubtedly *was* inferior—but the instinct of the French peasants was all in its favour. They had more to sell; and that was all that mattered. The proscription was re-enacted in 1441. In 1485 the battle was still raging, but the Gamay was still there. In the first quarter of the seventeenth century, the growers of Mâcon enjoyed a tempest of righteous indignation against those of the Beaujolais, who were daring to grow this dangerous vine. And there were further attempts to suppress it later in the century. But it never was suppressed. It is with us yet; and in some places that is no bad thing. Just occasionally it is found growing on the great slopes of the Côte d'Or; and that is damnable. But it is harmless enough in the plains, where fine wines cannot be grown, and there the Gamay yields abundant and perfectly good *ordinaires*. Above all, it is supreme in the Beaujolais, where a fine strain has emerged which perfectly suits the soil and climate. Taken that far south, and grown on the granite soil, it undergoes a transformation comparable with that of the Traminer, when it is planted in Alsace rather than in Germany. Even in the Palatinate it gives a rather dull sort of wine compared with the Riesling, but in Alsace it comes into its own and provides a wine with an exquisite bouquet that no other vine can match. Similarly, in the Beaujolais the Gamay surpasses the great Pinot.

Thanks to evolution and selection, the Gamay is now found in several forms. It can be white, or grey, or black with colourless juice, or black with coloured juice. The principal varieties are the Petit Gamay de Beaujolais, which gives black grapes but a colourless juice; the Gamay Rond and the Gamay de Bévy, which are similar in this respect but which grow in the Côte d'Or, and which are selected for the comparatively high quality of their wine when grown there; and the Gamay d'Arcenant, which is only good for quantity.

The Syrah is unknown in Burgundy, but it is the greatest vine for the hotter climate of the Côtes du Rhône. Also known as the Serine, there is a legend that, like the Gamay, it was brought back from Asia Minor by a returning crusader, and that it originally came from Shiraz in Persia. It gives a good yield, and its wine has a fine colour. The only snag is that in some areas, particularly in Tain, they are susceptible to *coulure* if the weather is bad at the time of the flowering.

The great vine for white wine throughout Burgundy is the Chardonnay, which is sometimes (but improperly) called the Pinot Blanc. In Chablis it is known as the Beaunois. It is used for making all the finest white burgundies. For the somewhat cheaper wines, the Aligoté is generally grown. It does well on the Arrières-Côtes and it is also found on the Côte d'Or growing at the tops of the slopes that are too high to be used for anything better. A third species, the Melon, also known as the Gamay Blanc à Feuille Ronde, is only grown in the plains. It is said to be so called because its large leaves resemble those of the melon. Although it is liable to be attacked by rot, it gives a vast yield, but the quality is such that the wines are only fit for local consumption. When it is grown in the Loire valley, however, it undergoes a complete transformation. There it is known as the Muscadet and provides a delightful, very refreshing wine.

In the more southerly vineyards of the Côtes du Rhône different varieties are favoured for white wines, as they are for reds. Here the principal vine is the Viognier. It has been grown there from time immemorial, and it is probably of local origin, as it is not found elsewhere. Other vines include the Marsanne, Mauzac Blanc and Rousanne de Tain.

The great names of the burgundy areas are as familiar as they are misapplied. Apart from these there are more general names applied to the wines that are intended for everyday consumption and which have no pretensions to real quality. These are all clearly defined by the laws of *appellation contrôlée*, and they will be considered in that light, but always bearing in mind Gilbert's prudent couplet:

'Things are seldom what they seem,
Skim milk masquerades as cream.'

At the bottom of the hierarchy comes the humble *bourgogne ordinaire*. It may also be called *grand ordinaire*, but this is a matter of choice rather than a sign of distinction. It may be red, rosé or

white, the rosé sometimes being sold as *bourgogne clairet*. It must
have a minimum alcoholic content of 9° for red wines and 9·5° for
whites, and it must be fermented from one of the authorized vine
varieties, which include the Gamay, but it may come from anywhere in the Burgundy-Mâconnais-Beaujolais area. One step
higher is the plain *bourgogne*. Like the *ordinaire*, it may be red,
rosé or white, and it comes from the same wide area, but the vine
varieties are more limited. For red wines, the Pinot must be used,
save in certain areas of the Mâconnais and Beaujolais, where the
Gamay is allowed, and in the Yonne, where the César and the
Tressot can be grown. White wines must be from the Chardonnay.
It must be a degree higher in alcohol. A wine that does not meet
these requirements is declassified as an *ordinaire*.

A red wine of no great distinction, but which nevertheless is
often good value for money, is *bourgogne passe-tout-grains*. This
may come from anywhere in the area, but it is made from a
mixture of grapes: two-thirds Gamay and one-third Pinot. An
undistinguished white wine which has a pleasant enough character,
and which is becoming quite popular in England is *bourgogne
aligoté*. This may also come from anywhere in the area and is
fermented, as its name would suggest, from Aligoté grapes, which
may or may not be mixed with Chardonnay. If either of these fail
to meet the requirements of their *appellation contrôlée* they are
declassed to an *ordinaire*. A certain amount of rather undistinguished sparkling wine is also made and is entitled to the
appellation bourgogne mousseux.

Chablis

The most northerly vineyards in the vast area being considered
in this chapter are those of Chablis. Chablis is a pleasant little old
town, built on the banks of the River Serein—a small river that is
a tributary of the Yonne, which is itself a tributary of the Seine.
One can still enter the town through the twin round towers of the
Porte Noël, which gives a fine impression of the antiquity to come.
But the impression is a somewhat false one, and Chablis is one of
those towns that looks its best by night; for it is only then that all
the stone looks old. In daylight, rather too much of it is new; for
some inscrutable reason the town was bombed during the last war
and part of the centre had to be rebuilt. Being further north than

the Côte d'Or the climate is far from agreeable, and although it can be quite hot in summer, it is inclined to be cold and damp in winter. It is this that helps to give the wines their northern delicacy.

Exploring the vineyards around Chablis is rather a depressing experience: there is so much good vineyard land lying fallow. This is partly caused by the nature of the soil: it is incredibly un-fertile, even by vineyard standards, being only a few inches thick before you come to the barren rock. Once a vineyard has been uprooted, it cannot be replanted again for fifteen or twenty years. But that is not the only reason why there is so much fallow ground. Chablis is a little too near Paris. There is not a very good living to be made out of viticulture, and too many of the workers have been attracted to the easier life of the city. Before the war, in particular, it was not worth while to replant the lesser vineyards when the vines became too old. In some the soil was good enough to grow other crops; others just went to waste. Chablis, in those days, was not commanding the price that it does today, and the market was ruined by spurious wines and cheap imitations. Moreover, owing to the precarious climate, a wine grower needed iron nerves and sufficient capital to tide him over bad years. And such years are more common in Chablis than they are in the more southerly parts of Burgundy: in 1945 and in 1951, for example, the vintage was reduced practically to zero by late frosts. Nowadays, happily, the trend has been reversed, and production is rising again, while the frost risk has been greatly reduced by the installation of modern oil burners in the vineyards. But chablis remains the most blatantly imitated of all wines. Apart from the totally spurious wines from other countries that do not even pretend to be real chablis, the burgundy shippers themselves seek to satisfy the demand by imitation and blending. Perhaps one or two importers are no better. Some of them add insult to injury by obtaining higher prices for their imitations than those received by the growers in Chablis for the genuine wine. If you buy a cheap chablis, it will not be a chablis. It might be almost anything from a pouilly-fuissé to a pouilly-fumé, but it will not be a chablis. Far more is drunk throughout the world than ever is grown. And the deception is of long standing. Charles Tovey, in 1877, remarked on the then rarity of pouilly-fuissé in England and added that most of what did find its way here was sold as chablis.

The history of chablis begins in the ninth century, when Charles the Bald presented land in the Yonne to his uncle Eudes, who was abbot of St. Martin at Tours. It would appear, however, that the monks of St. Martin were not particularly good viticulturalists. The wine owes its greatness principally to the Cistercian monks of Pontigny, who coveted a vineyard that could be compared with Clos de Vougeot, which was then held by the monks of Cîteaux. They obtained a concession in 1118, but they had to pay six hogs-heads of wine per annum to Tours, by way of rent. Thanks to its position on the banks of a river, chablis could be exported far more easily than the wines of the Côte d'Or. For centuries it was popular in Paris, and it may well be that chablis was the first burgundy to be known in England; for wines from nearby Auxerre were imported here as long ago as the reign of King John. In the eighteenth century, however, chablis apparently fell out of favour. Arnoux, in his little book with the enormous title which has already been quoted, said that chablis did not approach in quality or style the wines of the Côte d'Or; and when D. McBride published a book entitled *General Instructions for the Choice of Wines and Spirituous Liquors*, in 1793, he wrote: 'Vin de Chable [sic] is a light pleasant wine, and not unwholesome to be used at the table instead of Beer.' It is hard to see why chablis was not esteemed in the eighteenth century, but happily it became honoured and popular in the nineteenth. In 1875, James L. Denman[1] was able to write that: 'its stirling merits have secured for it a permanent place in general estimation'. In fact it became so popular that the frauds which disgrace its name came into being. At that time, though, the greater part of the wines grown were still destined for the Paris market.

The soil in the chablis vineyards is very light grey in colour, almost white, and consists of marl with a high proportion of calcium—generally about fifty per cent—including fragments of grey and pink marble. The vine grown is the Chardonnay. It is the same species which gives the great white burgundies of the Côte d'Or, but in Chablis the vines are planted further apart, there being about five to six thousand vines to the hectare[2] as compared to ten thousand in Burgundy.

[1] *The Vine and its Fruit*, London.
[2] 2.471 acres.

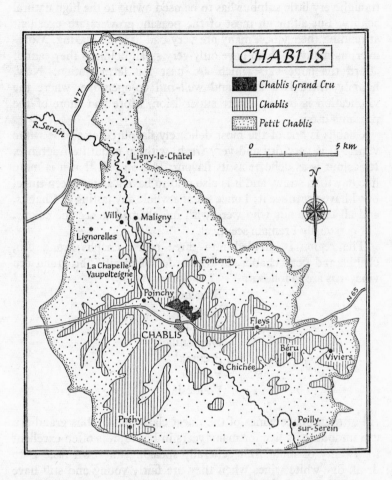

The method of vinification is the normal one for white wines, though very little sulphur has to be used owing to the high natural acidity. But although most of the peasant growers are excellent at tending their vines, many are very bad at wine making. Moreover, as many of them have only very small holdings they cannot afford the large vats which are best for fermentation. Now, happily, there is a large and well-run co-operative, where the vinification is under expert supervision. More and more of the peasants use it.

Chablis is one of the most delicately flavoured of all the white wines. It is very dry and very fresh, with an exquisite fragrance. Its colour is as delicate as its flavour. It is so pale that it is more like hay than straw, and it is also said to have a slight green tinge, but I have yet to see it: I once spent a whole day tasting in Chablis, and all the friends who were with me claimed to see the colour, but personally I remain sceptical.

The region is divided into three parts: chablis grand cru, chablis and petit chablis, in that order of merit. The grand cru vineyards are as follows:

Blanchots
Bougros
Les Clos
Grenouilles
Preuses
Valmur
Vaudésir

All of them make wines of the finest class, and chablis grand cru can undoubtedly live for many years in bottle; it is often excellent for twenty or more. But generally speaking, my own taste is to drink dry white wines when they are fairly young and still have their full freshness. This is especially true of chablis. It needs a little time to settle down happily in the bottle and to develop perfectly, but there is no point in keeping it any longer. By these standards a grand cru wine should be drunk after about five years, while a petit chablis is excellent after a year or two.

Chablis is an individualist in everything. Even its casks are different: a chablis *feuillette* is narrow and long, like the casks used at Cognac, and it holds 136 litres, whereas a burgundy *pièce* is short and pot-bellied, holding 228 litres; though its exact size varies from place to place.

Moving south-east from Chablis, the next region is the greatest of all: the Côte d'Or. It rises at the extreme eastern edge of the Massif Central and, being at the edge, it is open to the sun and ideal for vines. Some of the hills immediately behind the Côte d'Or also give very drinkable wines, but none that rise much above the class of an *ordinaire*. Beyond the slopes, to the east, the vineyards extend for a few hundred yards into the plains, again giving, for the most part, second quality wines. The great valley that lies between the foot of the Côte d'Or and the Jura mountains used once to be a lake, and many fossilized shells are found there, but this flat earth is far too rich and fertile to give good wines, and it lies wholly outside the burgundy area.

If the Golden Slope is narrow, it is also long, and although all its wines have a strong family likeness, they vary greatly in character as one moves from north to south. Since it is the climate as much as anything that makes the difference, it is not surprising that a very slight difference in orientation, giving slightly more or less exposure to the sun and wind, may make a very real difference to the wine. Thus, in Chambolle-Musigny, the great vineyard of Les Musigny adjoins the humbler vineyard of Les Barniques and, where the slope turns slightly to the north, it adjoins the far humbler vineyard of Les Argillères. It is natural, therefore, that in the language of the Burgundian, each separate vineyard is known as a *climat*; for it is this, as much as the soil, that distinguishes one from another.

The soil naturally varies from place to place, but all the finest wines of the Côte d'Or are grown in places where it is predominantly calcarious marl with some sand, and the following analyses are typical:[1]

Growth	Silicon	Clay	Chalk	Iron Oxide
Clos-de-Vougeot	47·1	36·7	12	3·2
Montrachet	33·7	28·1	31·6	0·0

Neither analysis adds up quite to a hundred per cent, but they are near enough, and whether the discrepancy arises from experimental error or is due to 'miscellaneous' undefined constituents,

[1] Poupon and Forgeot, *Les Vins de Bourgogne*, 1959.

matters little. Owing to the presence of so much chalk, the soil is light in colour, and that in the finest vineyards is very stony. It is the stones that account for a good part of the silicon. Where there is an excessive amount of silicon, in the form of sand, the wines tend to be light, and where there is more clay they are strongly alcoholic, coarse and tannic.

And now the districts of the Côte d'Or may be considered one by one. In each instance, the finest vineyards—those that are classed as *têtes de cuvées* or as *premières cuvées*—will be listed. These wines alone are likely to be sold as single vineyard wines, those classed as second or third growths generally being blended into wines sold under the district name. But a *tête de cuvée* must be considered in the context of its *commune*. A wine classified as a *première cuvée* or even as a *deuxième cuvée* in one of the great *communes* of the Côte de Nuits is often a finer burgundy than the best wine of a humble *commune* in the Côte de Beaune.

Côte de Nuits

It is here that the greatest red burgundies are grown. They are fine big wines yet of great finesse, maturing more slowly and lasting longer in bottle than those grown further south.

Fixin
Leaving Dijon in the north, one comes first to that area formerly known as the Côte de Dijon, which has declined in importance. Then comes the Côte de Nuits. The first *commune* is Fixin, one of the oldest villages of the whole Côte, with a history dating back to at least the year 895. For some reason—perhaps because the name is hard to pronounce—its wines are seldom heard of in this country, which seems strange, as they are comparable with those of its more famous neighbour Gevrey-Chambertin, and they often attain a great age in bottle. The outstanding growths of this *commune* are:

Tête de Cuvée	*Acres*
Clos de la Perrière	11·8

Premières Cuvées

Clos du Chapitre	11·8
Les Arvelets	8·2
Aux Cheusots	3·5
Les Hervelets	9·3
*Les Meix-Bas	1·2

The *climat* marked * occupies an area that extends beyond the best portion of the slope, and therefore grows wines of less notable quality in addition to its finest wines.

Gevrey-Chambertin

Now the great names come one after another. The next village is Gevrey-Chambertin. Originally it was just plain Gevrey, but in 1847 it succumbed to a vainglorious fashion of the time and tacked on the name of its most famous vineyard. It therefore goes without saying that the man who boasted to his guests that 'This wine is not merely a chambertin; it is a gevrey-chambertin', was an ass.

In the seventh century, when Gevrey was called Gibriacus, some land was ceded by the then Duke of Burgundy to the abbey of Bèze, and the monks planted vines. Today it is one of the most famous vineyards in the world: Le Clos de Bèze. Other early wine growers included the abbey of Cluny. According to tradition, the greatest vineyard came by its name in an interesting way. One Bertin owned a field next to the Clos de Bèze. Wondering whether his field would produce as fine a wine as that of his neighbour, he planted it with vines and found, no doubt to his delight, that it was not only as good, but, if anything, even finer. It was called *le champ de Bertin*, then *le Champ-Bertin*, and finally Le Chambertin. Who M. Bertin was, and when he lived, remains a mystery. He certainly lived a long time ago, though, as the name is found in a document of 1219. Wines from anywhere in the *commune* may be sold as gevrey-chambertin, but only wines from Le Chambertin or Clos de Bèze may be sold simply as chambertin, and the latter may also be sold as chambertin-clos-de-bèze. The outstanding growths of the commune are:

Têtes de Cuvée

	Acres
Le Chambertin	32·1
Le Clos de Bèze	37·1

Premières Cuvées

	Acres
†Charmes	30·4
†Chapelle	19·5
†Griotte	7·2
†Latricières	17·2
†Mazis	21·2
†Mazoyères	36·4
†Ruchottes	8·4
Cazetiers	20·0
Clos Saint-Jacques	17·3
Étournelles	4·8
Fouchère	2·5
Varoilles	14·8

The *climats* designated † may sell their wine under their own name hyphenated with the name of chambertin. Unlike the name gevrey-chambertin, these hyphenated names really mean something: they are amongst the very best burgundies, but they do not share the same fine soil that gives the *têtes* their quality. The five last named of the *premières cuvées* are far removed geographically and on a distinctly less propitious slope.

Chambertin is an inexpressibly fine wine, with incomparable body and vigour. One can only feel sympathy with the old man who had almost, but not quite forgotten a certain glorious night of his youth. He had forgotten exactly where it happened. He could not quite remember the year. There was a girl with him, but he could not remember her name. 'But—by God!—the wine was chambertin!' It must have been a genuine chambertin. Alas, today too many of the wines sold under this great name are *not*, and some of them are very odd indeed: vast and coarse, without a trace of breeding.

Morey-Saint-Denis

The next *commune* to the south is Morey-Saint-Denis. Originally it used to be simply Morey but, following the fashion of the Côte d'Or, in 1927 it saw fit to append the name of one of its greatest vineyards. And what a perfectly spendid *commune* it is! In Gevrey-Chambertin the greatest vineyards form an oasis amongst the lesser growths. They are admittedly the greatest of all; but they are alone. In Morey-Saint-Denis begins the continuous line of great

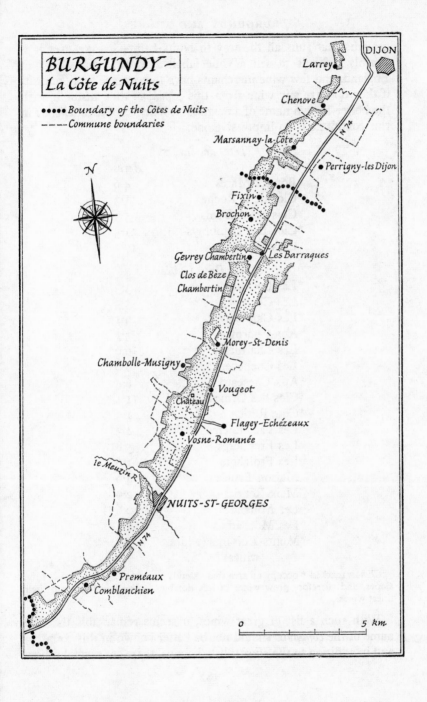

BURGUNDY –
La Côte de Nuits

•••• Boundary of the Côtes de Nuits
–––– Commune boundaries

N

DIJON

Larrey

Chenove

Marsannay-la-Côte

Perrigny-les Dijon

N 74

Fixin

Brochon

Gevrey Chambertin

Les Barraques

Clos de Bèze
Chambertin

Morey-St-Denis

Chambolle-Musigny

Vougeot

Château

Flagey-Echézeaux

Vosne-Romanée

le Meuzin R.

NUITS-ST-GEORGES

N 74

Preméaux

Comblanchien

0   5 km

growths that runs all the way to Nuits-Saint-Georges. Yet it is terribly difficult to sell a wine labelled Morey-Saint-Denis in England, and few wine merchants have the courage to attempt it; if they do have any wine from this *commune* they insult it with the better-known name of a neighbour. The list of great *climats* in this commune is an impressive one:

Têtes de Cuvées

	Acres
Bonnes-Mares	4.6
Clos de la Roche	11·3
Clos Saint-Denis	5·3
*Clos Les Lambrays	21·5
Clos de Tart	17·3

Premières Cuvées

*Les Bouchots	3·3
Les Chabiots	5·3
*Les Chaffots	3·1
Aux Charmes	3·1
Les Charnières	6.0
Les Chenevery	8·0
*Aux Cheseaux	6·4
*Clos des Ormes	11·1
*Côte Rôtie	1·3
Les Faconnières	4·3
Les Fremières	5·8
Les Froichots	1·6
Maison-Brûlée	4·6
Meix-Rentier	2·9
Les Millandes	10·6
Les Mochamps	6·2
*Monts-Luisants (white wines)	7·7

Climats marked * occupy an area that extends beyond the best portion of the slopes, and therefore grow wines of less notable quality in addition to their finest wines.

With such a list of great wines, it seems remarkable that the name of the *commune* should not be better known in this country; and in addition to the *climats* listed above, there are several others which are justly well known, such as Clos Sorbet and Morey. Some good white wine is also grown.

Of the five *climats* classified as *têtes de cuvée*, two have the advantage of being owned throughout by a single proprietor: Clos Les Lambrays and Clos de Tart. Clos de Tart, perhaps rather suggestively, used once to be the property of a female religious order. It has a history going right back to the twelfth century, when it was known as Climat de la Rorge. There are many who would say that Clos de Tart should be at the top if the *climats* were listed in order of quality. It is now owned by the famous House of Mommessin at Mâcon, and I have certainly enjoyed some very fine vintages of it in the past; but just lately they have seemed a shade disappointing. Most great vineyards suffer short periods of decline at one time or another, and soon no doubt it will be entirely back to normal again. Even when it is 'not what it was', it still grows some of the finest wines in Burgundy.

Another *climat* that deserves special mention is Bonnes-Mares. The wines, at their best, are admirable, but it is shared between a number of proprietors, and their products differ somewhat. The really confusing thing, though, is that it straddles two *communes*: part is in Morey-Saint-Denis, but most of it is in Chambolle-Musigny. Such geographical facts confirm one's suspicions of connoisseurs who occasionally claim infallibility in identifying the *commune* of a wine.

Chambolle-Musigny

Chambolle-Musigny was one of the pioneers of the doubtful fashion of tacking the name of a vineyard on to that of a village: until 1878 it was just plain Chambolle. And a most charming village it is, standing in a valley half-way up the hillside. Before it lie its great vineyards; behind it there is nothing but rock and desolation. The ground on one side is deservedly amongst the most valuable in the Côte d'Or; on the other it is worthless. The greatest *climats* are:

Têtes de Cuvées

	Acres
Le(s) Musigny	24·8
Les Bonnes-Mares	33·9

Premières Cuvées

	Acres
*Les Amoureuses	13·2
*Les Baudes	8·8
Les Charmes	14·4
La Combe-d'Orveau	12·6
*Les Cras	10·4
Derrière la Grange	1·8
Les Fuées	15·2
*Les Hauts-Doix	4·3
Les Lavrottes	2·5
*Les Sentiers	12·2

Climats marked * occupy an area that extends beyond the best portion of the slope, and therefore grow wines of less notable quality in addition to their finest wines.

Apart from these *climats*, there are many others that are very good, such as Les Gruenchers and Les Noirots. Amongst them all, Les Musigny stands supreme as providing one of the greatest red burgundies. A small amount of good, white musigny is also made.

Vougeot

Vougeot is a very small village indeed, named after the equally small River Vouge which passes through it. But it has given its name to a great vineyard: Le Clos-de-Vougeot. And in the vineyard stands a great château. The Clos-de-Vougeot was the creation of the Cistercian monks, but its history does not go right back to the foundation of the order in 1098. The Cistercian Order was founded as a reaction from the degeneration into which the Benedictines had sunk, and its first members had grave doubts as to whether they should embark on anything that might bring wealth and open the door to corruption. Happily, after much hesitation, they overcame their scruples and engaged in viticulture —to the delight of posterity. The first vineyard was given to them in 1110, and in 1162 the new statutes enabling them to grow wine were ratified by Eudes II, Duke of Burgundy. It was one of the last things he did before he died. Two years later the pope, Alexander III, took the abbey under his protection and specifically included the cellarer of Vougeot. The monks were given many parcels of land in the Clos-de-Vougeot, but by no means all of it, and they had to buy land at high prices before they gained complete control. They made their last purchase in 1336. In the meantime, they started to build an enormous wall to enclose their property. When it was all finished, the vineyard covered about 125 acres. As it was some distance from the abbey, it was under the control of a cellarer, and in 1551 the abbot decided to demolish the insignificant buildings that were then standing in the vineyard and to build instead the magnificent Renaissance castle which stands there today. But it could have been even better. One of the monks was a very able architect, and the abbot instructed him to draw up suitable plans. When these were ready, they were so fine that the hapless monk became puffed up with his own conceit. To abash him, the worthy abbot sent the plans to another artist, who completely wrecked them. As his penance, the unfortunate architect was made to adopt them and to carry them into execution. The wretched building has been giving trouble ever since, and the twentieth century has had to pay heavily for the piety of the sixteenth. The château still contains a unique wealth of ancient presses and similar vineyard equipment, but during the last war they were very nearly lost. It was used as a prison for captured Germans, and one day they attacked the old presses, intending to use them for firewood. But happily they were beaten off, and the presses were guarded with a barbed-wire entanglement, erected by command of the local American general.

In the days when the monks had the vineyard it was divided, according to legend, into three separate parts. Wine from the top part, which was the best of all, was never sold. It was reserved by the abbot to be given as presents to crowned heads of state and to princes of the church. The great wine served its purpose well. In 1371, the then abbot gave thirty *pièces*, each containing 228 litres, to Pope Gregory XI. Four years later he received his cardinal's hat. The second area was almost as great. Its fate is uncertain, but perhaps it could be obtained with difficulty. The third was merely very good and was sold for a very good price. It is a pleasing story, but it is doubtful if it is true: the upper slopes certainly produce exceptionally good wine, but a finer balance can be achieved by blending the best-made wines from various parts of the Clos.

It continued under the control of the monks until the decree of

1790 vested their goods in the state. The last cellarer had the delightfully appropriate name of M. Goblet, and when he handed over the property to the authorities in 1791 they gave him a present of two silver covers and—much more important—they allowed him to take away with him into his retirement at Dijon enough of his fine wine to last him for the rest of his life. There were still a few bottles left when he died in 1813.

In January 1791 the property was sold to a Parisian timber merchant for 643.710 livres, but he was unable to find the money. It then passed through various vicissitudes and changes of ownership until, in 1889, it was tragically divided up. Today there are over seventy separate holdings, and every good burgundian has the ambition to own a bit of it. Each proprietor makes the wine in his own way, and consequently at each vintage there is a plethora of styles, and this of course, makes it much easier to 'stretch' the wine. But, as a small compensation, it is at least entertaining to taste several examples side by side.

The Clos is accorded a rare honour: whenever a contingent of the French army pass by, the soldiers stop and present arms. Stendhal tells how the custom was started by General Bisson, who was marching from the army of the Rhine with his regiment. His spontaneous homage appealed to the gastronomic sophistication of the French, and they have followed his example ever since.

Unlike its neighbours, Vougeot needs no long list of *cuvées*. Nearly all of it is one great *tête* of 125·7 acres. But apart from the Clos itself, just outside its walls there is grown a fine white wine, entitled to the rank of a *première cuvée*: La Vigne Blanc, or Clos Blanche de Vougeot (4·6 acres), as is also part of Les Petits-Vougeots (14·4 acres).

Flagey-Echézeaux

The village of Flagey, unlike the other villages that give their names to the great *communes* of the Côte d'Or, is some distance from the vineyards that provide its fame and wealth. It is down in the plain, on the other side of the *route nationale*. In 1131 it was known as Flagiacum, and then as Flagey, until it added the name of its greatest vineyard in 1886. Like Morey-Saint-Denis, its name is less well known abroad than the quality of its wines would justify: for they are delicate and beautifully balanced. It may be that its name is so unpronounceable to foreign lips that the wine merchants avoid it. However, wines from this *commune* can also be sold under the better-known name of Vosne Romanée, and they usually are. When one of them appears under the name of its own *commune*, it often means that it is so good that the merchant is prepared to take a risk.

The *climats* are as follows:

Tête de Cuvée

	Acres
Les Grands-Echézeaux	22·6

Premières Cuvées

	Acres
Les Beaux-Monts-Bas or Beaumonts-Bas	13·6
Champs-Traversins	8·8
Clos Saint-Denis	4·5
Les Cruots or Vignes Blanches	8·1
Les Echézeaux-du-Dessus	8·8
Les Loachausses	9·3
*En Orveau	24·0
Les Poullaillières	12·9
*Les Quartiers du Nuits	6·4
Les Rouges-du-Bas	9·9
Les Treux	12·1

Climats marked * occupy an area that extends beyond the best portion of the slope, and therefore grow wines of less notable quality in addition to their finest wines.

Few of these *climats* are ever heard of, however, with the exceptions of Les Beaumonts and Clos Saint-Denis, as when their wine is not sold as vosne romanée, it is generally sold under the general *appellation* échezeaux to which all these *climats* with the exception of Les Beaumonts-Bas are entitled, though those marked * above may only use the name for wines grown in their better parts. Les Beaumonts-Bas is invariably sold as a vosne romanée.

Vosne Romanée

The *commune* of Vosne Romanée is sheer magnificence. The

village of Vosne can be traced back at least as far as 636, and it followed the example of its neighbours in adding the name of its most famous vineyard at the end of the last century. The vineyard itself obviously has an even older history. Was it planted by the Romans? Was it the site of a Roman camp? Were its wines particularly beloved of the Romans? Of the latter question there can be little doubt: everyone who tastes them loves them. But how it got its name will probably never be known for certain.

In past centuries, the history of the *commune* was inextricably tied up with that of the Croonenbourg family. Today its great wines are very much under the spell of the Domaine de la Romanée-Conti. For if the wines of the Romanée-Conti are the greatest of all, their neighbours are very little their inferiors, and the Domaine owns many of them: the whole of La Tâche, part of Le Richebourg and parts of Les Grands-Échezeaux.

The Croonenbourgs certainly owned property around Romanée in the fifteenth century, and probably earlier still, but the last of the line sold Romanée-Conti in 1760 to the Prince of Conti, over the head of Madame La Pompadour, whose covetous machinations for once proved futile. The price was a high one, but not out of proportion to the quality of the wine. Despite a short period in the doldrums around 1735, when the vineyard was neglected, its wines were famous then as they are now. The new proprietor fully kept up the standard. However, although he added his name to that of the great *climat*, he did not long enjoy its ownership, for, like so many of the great vineyards, it fell victim to the French Revolution. It was declared the property of the state, and finally it was sold. But unlike so many others, happily it was never divided, and it remains intact to this day, owned by a company that is controlled by M. de Vilaine.

Until 1946 it was planted with nothing but pre-phylloxera vines. But the fight against the phylloxera called for continuous hard work and effort, and when labour became scarce during and after the Hitler war, it became impossible to carry on. The vines were very old, and the yield became less and less. Ultimately the proprietor had to give in and replant: but the wine does not seem at all to have suffered. Thanks to the replanting, though, another vintage was not produced until 1952.

The leading *climats* are as follows:

Têtes de Cuvées

	Acres
Romanée-Conti	4·5
La Romanée	2·1
La Tâche	14·9
Le Richebourg	12·2
Les Verroilles or Richebourg	7·6

Premières Cuvées

	Acres
Les Beaux-Monts	6·0
Aux Brûlées	9·6
Les Gaudichots	14·3
La Grande-Rue	3·23
Aux Malconsorts	14·7
*Aux Reignots	4·15
La Romanée Saint-Vivant	23·6
*Les Suchots	32·41

Climats marked * occupy an area that extends beyond the best portion of the slope, and therefore grow wines of less notable quality in addition to their finest wines.

The list of *premières cuvées* is in alphabetical order. That is why Romanée Saint-Vivant appears so low down: many would list it with the *têtes de cuvées*. In 1232 it was given by the then Duchess of Burgundy to the religious order of Saint-Vivant, which continued to cultivate it until the French Revolution. It was then sold, and the whole of the monastic buildings were razed to the ground by the irreligious zeal of the new lay proprietor. For a comparatively large vineyard, it is divided into surprisingly few holdings, and its wines are undoubtedly very fine indeed. La Tâche and Le Richebourg were also owned by monastic foundations until the Revolution, but Les Malconsorts, whose wine is so well known and admired in this country, is a comparative upstart amongst vineyards: it was not planted until 1610. In the list of *têtes de cuvées*, Richebourg is divided into two separate *climats*, but they are adjacent, and for all practical purposes they are considered as one, so the name of Les Verroilles is seldom found.

Apart from the greatest vineyards of Vosne, there are others that are very good and famous, such as Aux Petits-Monts, Clos de Réas and Les Chaumes.

Nuits-Saint-Georges and Prémeaux

Nuits-Saint-Georges is the capital of the Côte de Nuits, which is named after it. Until, in 1892, it followed the unfortunate example of its neighbours in adding the name of its greatest vine-yard, it was just plain Nuits. The name has nothing to do with *night*: it is said to be derived from the tribe of Nuithons, who were closely associated with the Burgundians. Owing to its strategic position it has been sacked almost as many times as Cádiz, but by land rather than by sea; and inevitably the English, in the four-teenth century, were amongst the aggressors. Nuits-Saint-Georges, today, is one of the great centres of the trade, for apart from its own vineyards, it is second only to Beaune as a headquarters for merchants.

Next door to Nuits-Saint-Georges comes Prémeaux, the last of the *communes* where great Côtes de Nuits wines are grown, and these are so like those of Nuits-Saint-Georges that the two can best be considered together. Beyond them lie Prissey, Comblachien and Corgoloin, where the wines are worthy enough but in no way notable. Then the Côte de Nuits comes to an end. There is a gap, and the Côte de Beaune begins.

The principal growths are as follows:

Premières Cuvées

	Acres
†Les Boudots	15·8
†Les Cailles	9·4
Les Chaboeufs	7·2
Les Chaignots	13·8
Château-Gris	5·8
†Les Cras	7·7
†Les Murgers	12·5
Les Perrières and	
Clos des Perrières	7·6
†Les Porrets or Poirets	17·5
Les Poulettes	5·8
Les Procès	4·7

Premières Cuvées

	Acres
†Les Pruliers	17·5
La Richemone	5·5
Les Roncières	5·4
*Rue de Chaux	7·7
†Le Saint-Georges	18·6
†Les Thorey and	
Clos de Thorey	15·3
†Les Vaucrains	00·0

and those at Prémeaux are:

	Acres
Clos Arlot	10·0
Clos des Argillières	10·4
†Clos des Forêts-Saint-	
Georges	16·6
*Clos-de-la-Maréchale	23·6
Clos Saint-Marc	2·5
†Le Clos des Corvées	12·7
†Les Corvées-Pagets	5·8
†Les Didiers-Saint-Georges	7·0
Les Perdrix	8·3

Climats marked * occupy an area that extends beyond the best portion of the slope, and therefore grow wines of less notable quality in addition to their finest wines. Those marked † could properly be classed as *têtes de cuvées*; but such terms are necessarily relative and I would rather insult them with a pessimistic classification than insult the greater wines of the Côte de Nuits by suggesting that they are equals; though one at least—Le Saint-Georges—could certainly hold up its head in such company.

The appellation *Nuits-Saint-Georges* must not be confused with that of *Vins Fin de la Côte de Nuits*, otherwise *Côte de Nuits Villages*. These are blended wines (often excellent) from the communes of Fixin, Brochon, Prissey, Comblanchien and Corgoloin.[1]

[1] There are a considerable number of *appellations controlée* which are not considered in this chapter as they are thought to be beyond the scope of a book about European wines in general. Readers requiring detailed information should see *The Wines of Burgundy*, by Pierre Poupon and Pierre Forseot, Paris, 1964.

The Côte de Beaune

After Corgoloin there is a short break in the golden slope. Then it rises again as the Côte de Beaune. Generally speaking, the red wines grown on these more southerly slopes are somewhat lighter than their more northerly neighbours. They mature more quickly, and they do not last as long. They are often held to be somewhat humbler, in fact, though such a comparison is less than fair to some of the red wines grown in the *commune* of Aloxe-Corton. But although the greatest red wines of Burgundy are grown in the Côte de Nuits, the Côte de Beaune is by no means a poor relation, for it is here that the greatest white burgundies are grown, in the *commune* of Chassagne-Montrachet. The two ends of the slope are complementary: each provides wines that the other cannot.

The first *commune* of the Côte de Beaune is Ladoix-Serrigny. Its best *climats*, both of which are classed as *premières cuvées*, are on the slopes adjacent to the great vineyards of its neighbour Aloxe-Corton, and they can legitimately be considered as part of that *commune*, whose name they append to their own. The dividing line is academic rather than geographical. They are: Les Vergennes-Corton (3·5 acres); and Le Rognet-Corton and Clos des Cortons-Faiveley (22·7 acres).

Aloxe-Corton

Aloxe-Corton (pronounced aloss-corton) is without doubt one of the great *communes* of Burgundy, and it has the distinction of providing both red and white wines of the finest quality. Both le corton and corton charlemagne can be red or white, though the former is famed principally for red and the latter for white.

Providence has shaped a hillside that is exactly right for wine growing: it curves round, giving a southerly aspect with exceptional exposure to the sun. The top is wooded with the Bois de Corton, and beneath it lie a succession of noble vineyards. Not surprisingly, vines have been grown there ever since the days of the Romans, and there still remain the traces of a road known as Le Petit Chemin des Romains. The *commune* also has a link with the great Emperor Charlemagne, for he had vineyards there, which he presented in 775 to the religious community of Saulieu. They still perpetuate the glory of his name. In 1862 the village of Aloxe appended the name of its most famous vineyard.

Amongst the many great men who have enjoyed these wines was Voltaire, who wrote in 1759 to Antoine Le Bault, owner of Château de Corton-Grancey: 'Your good wine has become a necessity to me. I give a good enough beaujolais to my guests from Geneva, but in private I drink your Corton.' The recipients rather ungraciously scribbled in the margin 'The words of a cad'.

The principal *climats* are:

Têtes de Cuvées

	Acres
*Le Charlemagne	41·7
Les Chaumes	5·9
Le Clos-du-Roi	26·0
*Le Corton	27·9

Premières Cuvées

	Acres
Les Bressandes	42·2
Les Chaumes-de-la Voirosse	11·2
*Les Combes	21·4
Les Fiètres	3·3
Les Grèves	4·6
*Les Languettes	18·2
*Les Maréchaudes	16·5
*Les Meix	4·89
*Le Meix-Lallemand	1·56
*En Pauland	6·6
Les Perrières	26·9
Les Pougets	24·6
La Vigne-au-Saint	5·7

Climats marked * occupy an area that extends beyond the best portion of the slope, and therefore grow wines of less notable quality in addition to their finest wines.

Le Clos-du-Roi was formerly the property of the Dukes of Burgundy, who could presumably choose which vineyards they liked; and they chose well. From them it passed to the French royal family until it was eventually sold at the time of the Revolution. Today sadly it is split up between some fifteen proprietors.

Pernand-Vergelesses

Behind Aloxe-Corton, in a fold of the hills, likes the *commune* of Pernand-Vergelesses. Although it has its own *appellation* and grows some good wines, it is hardly ever heard of, as its output is relatively small and it is completely overwhelmed by its more august neighbours: Aloxe-Corton and Savigny-les-Beaune. Most of the wine grown there is sold under those names, and some of it is undoubtedly rightly so sold, for the *commune* includes part of the vineyard of Charlemagne (albeit not the best part) and of Corton. When this charming hill village chose to follow the current fashion and to add grandeur to its name, it is perhaps surprising that it did not call itself Pernand-Charlemagne, as Aloxe had opted for Corton; but perhaps the villagers were right in honouring their own great vineyard instead of the less notable part of the even greater vineyard that they share with the *commune* next door. The principal *climats* are:

Tête de Cuvée

	Acres
Ile-de-Vergelesses	23·1

Premières Cuvées

	Acres
*Basses-Vergelesses	44·2
*En Caradeux	49·7
*Creux-de-Net	12·4
*Les Fichots	27·5

Climats marked * occupy an area that extends beyond the best portion of the slope, and therefore grow wines of less notable quality in addition to their finest wines.

Savigny-Les-Beaune

Savigny-Les-Beaune, with its fine seventeenth-century château, built on fourteenth-century foundations, although ancient and quite large, is not of much importance as a commercial centre: for that purpose it is too near the town of Beaune. But as a wine-growing *commune* it is very important indeed, and it has a history

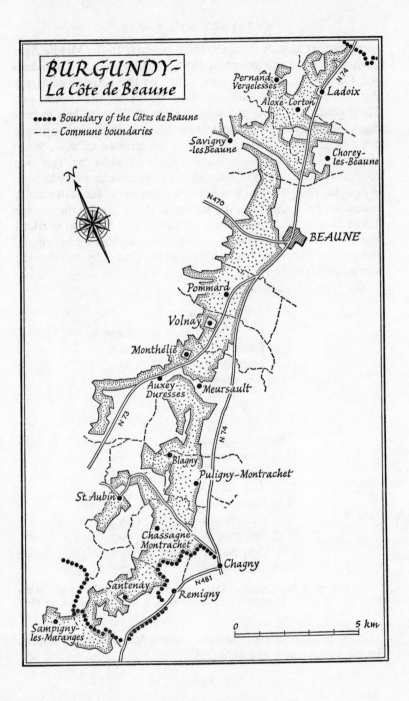

BURGUNDY~
La Côte de Beaune

•••• Boundary of the Côtes de Beaune
- - - Commune boundaries

N

Pernand-
Vergelesses
Ladoix
Aloxe-Corton
Savigny-
les Beaune
Chorey-
les-Beaune

N 470

BEAUNE

Pommard

Volnay

Monthélie

Auxey-
Duresses
Meursault

N 73

N 74

Blagny

Puligny-Montrachet

St. Aubin

Chassagne-
Montrachet
Chagny
Santenay
N 481
Remigny
Sampigny-
les-Maranges

0   5 km

going back at least as far as the tenth century. In the Middle Ages most of its wine was grown by the religious orders of Cistercians and Carmelites, who were later joined by the Knights of Malta. But the good monks did not have things all their own way. Throughout Europe it was the privilege of the local lord to proclaim the 'ban' of the vintage, and until it was proclaimed no grapes could be gathered. Legend has it that the great sweet white wines of Bordeaux and the Rhine were discovered when the 'ban' was accidentally delayed. But although there are sometimes advantages in delaying the vintage of white wines, there are no such advantages as regards reds, and in 1401 the monks chose to start the vintage before the ban was proclaimed. Unfortunately the local overlord was a woman, Marguerite de Mussey, who insisted on her rights, and presumably risked the anathema of the church by ordering the whole harvest to be forfeit.

The principal *climats* are:

Têtes de Cuvées

	Acres
Les Jarrons	22·7
Les Marconnets	23·4
*Aux Vergelesses	42·0

Premières Cuvées

	Acres
Basses-Vergelesses	4·2
*Les Charnières	5·1
Aux Gravains	15·8
*Aux Guettes	52·0
*Les Lavières	45·7
*Les Narbantons	25·2
*Les Peuillets	56·7
*Aux Serpentières	33·2
*Les Talmettes	7·8

Climats marked * occupy an area that extends beyond the best portion of the slope, and therefore grow wines of less notable quality in addition to their finest wines.

Other notable *climats* include: Aux Cloux, Grand-Picotins, Hauts-Jarrons and Les Pimentiers.

Beaune
One has only to set foot in the delightful little town of Beaune
to know how old it is. It may have been the Bibracte of Caesar's
Commentarii; its certain history goes back at least as far as the
fifth century. And how pleasant it is to find a town that is content
with its ancient name, alone and unadorned. This old home of the
Dukes of Burgundy has every reason to be self-assured. It has no
need to call itself Beaune-Les-Fèves, or Beaune-Les-Grèves. It is
just plain Beaune.

Like most of the old towns of the Continent, its history has
hardly been one of peace and tranquillity. The Romans were there,
and so were the Burgundians and the Franks. In 732 the Saracens
from Spain penetrated as far as Beaune, bringing pillage and ruin
with them, until they were finally repulsed by Charles Martel. It is
not surprising that it was a massively fortified city, triumphant
through many a siege. Many of its fortifications still stand, dating
from the fourteenth and fifteenth centuries, and at one of the
principal entrances to the town travellers can still pass through
the Porte Saint-Nicolas. To a remarkable extent, Beaune has
retained its original shape and plan as a walled city, and the most
superficial glance at a map of the town will show exactly where the
walls stood. But even when it was not repelling an invader, it was
not without its troubles. From 1347 to 1349 there was a terrible
famine—*le grand mort*—which decimated its population. In the
second half of the sixteenth century there were persistent religious
quarrels between the Roman Catholics and the Calvinists. As is
well known, the Romans won and the protestants went into exile,
taking much of the town's prosperity with them; for they were
the skilled cloth workers, and their industry, as much as that of the
wine growers, supported it at that time. The misery wrought by the
religious controversies was made even worse by the plague, which
broke out several times in the sixteenth and seventeenth centuries.

As was normal in the Côte d'Or, from the earliest ages until the
French Revolution, the vineyards were largely in the hands of the
monasteries, whose skill and industry made their wines world
famous. Others were, and still are, in the hands of the great and
historic charity of the Hospices. But that is a story that has already
been told.[1] As far back as 1512, Louis XII of France sent James IV

[1] See p. 161.

of Scotland a present of 30 puncheons of *Vin de Beaune Cléret*. But the great international trade of Beaune did not commence until later, when communications grew easier. At the end of the eighteenth and during the nineteenth century the great merchant houses of wine shippers were established, and by the nineteenth century Beaune had become indisputably the wine capital of Burgundy. The ancient towers (now somewhat truncated) which protected it from invaders in the past, were to serve another purpose: wine matures in their massive foundations, where the powder was once stored. Beaune, indeed, is built over a maze of cellars, and space beneath the ground is often more valuable than space above it: a very civilized scale of values. Above ground, it is appropriate that the palace of the old Dukes of Burgundy should house the wine museum of the Côte d'Or; it is one of the best there is, and any wine lover visiting Beaune should certainly see it.

A friend of mine some time ago offered me some wine with my dinner. His words failed to stir my enthusiasm. 'Will you have some of this?' he asked. 'It's only a humble beaune, I'm afraid.' It was a humble wine indeed, though pleasant enough. It may even have hailed from the Côte de Beaune. But how different it was from the best wines of Beaune! The name beaune in England has come so much to mean a humble wine from the Côte that the fine wines from the *Têtes* and *premières cuvées* have become hard to sell. Consequently they are often splendid value. They are not great or magnificent wines, like the leading growths of the Côte de Nuits, nor do they live so long in bottle, but they are beautifully balanced and delicate. Another friend of mine, who is a wine merchant, recently told me a horror story. He sold some beaune les grèves to a hotelier, who promptly asked him to change it because he wanted a wine with beaune on the label and nothing else—least of all graves. The same hotelier returned a truly beautiful nuits st. georges because it had had the impertinence to throw a deposit. . . .

The principal *climats* are:

Têtes de Cuvées

	Acres
Les Bressandes	45·8
Les Champimonts	41·0
Le Clos-de-la-Mousse	8·4

	Acres
Le Clos-des-Mouches	61·4
Les Cras, or Crais	12·5
Les Fèves	10·6
*Les Grèves	78·5
Les Marconnets	25·2

Premières Cuvées

	Acres
*Les Aigrots	46·1
Les Avaux	33·1
*Le Bas-des-Teurons	17·9
*Blanche-Fleur	22·7
Les Boucherottes	21·4
*Les Cent-Vignes	57·6
*Les Chilènes	42·0
*Clos-du-Roi	34·4
*Aux Coucherias	55·9
A l'Ecu	7·7
*Les Epenottes	33·7
En Genet	12·5
Sur-Les-Grèves	11·3
La Mignotte	5·9
*Montée-Rouge	41·1
*Les Montrevenots	19·9
En l'Orme	5·1
Les Perrières	8·0
Pertuisots	13·7
*Les Reversées	12·9
Les Seurey	3·1
Les Sizies	20·4
*Les Teurons	38·4
*Les Theurons	18·6
Tiélandry	4·4
*Les Toussaints	16·1
Les Vignes-Franches	24·6

Climats marked * occupy an area that extends beyond the best portion of the slope, and therefore grow wines of less notable quality in addition to their finest wines.

Other notable *climats* include: Les Beaux-Fougets, Chaume-Gaufriot and Les Choiceux.

In addition to the *appellation* beaune, which includes all the above leading growths and many lesser ones, there is another general *appellation côte de beaune* which covers practically the same area, though there is a small extension. It is one step down from *beaune* and is used as a declassification, particularly in years of over-production. On no account is it to be confused with the *appellation côte de beaune villages*. Wines sold under this *appellation* are all mixtures—and often very agreeable ones. They must be derived from specified areas which include parts of most of the *communes* of the Côte de Beaune, and extend into the Côte Chalonaise, but wines grown in Pommard, Volnay, Aloxe-Corton and Saint-Romain may not be included.

Pommard

Next to Beaune comes Pommard, a charming town lying beneath the slopes, with the little river L'Avant Dheune flowing through it. And it includes the Château de la Commaraine—one of the finest buildings in Burgundy, that dates from the twelfth century. Its name has been delightfully described by Rodier[1] as *savoureux et rabelaisien*, and its wines are amongst the most famous and popular of all the burgundies. But it has not always been so, and compared with some of their neighbours, the pommards are comparative upstarts amongst the internationally famous burgundies.

Pommard is mentioned as Polmaraeum as far back as 1004, though its real history goes back even further: old foundations have been found beneath the town, and many coins have been dug up dating from the times of Nero and Valentian the First. In the Middle Ages viticulture was, as usual, monastic. Later, a vineyard was also owned by the Knights of Malta. It was not until the Huguenots fled after the revocation of the Edict of Nantes in 1685 that pommard, and its neighbour volnay, became famous amongst the great wines of the world; for many of the Huguenots came from the Côte d'Or, and they carried the fame of their native wines with them.

There is a tradition that in the fourteenth century, a tiny vineyard, high on the slopes above Pommard, saved the whole of the

[1] Camille Rodier, *Le Vin de Bourgogne*, Dijon, n.d.

Côte d'Or. In 1349, the vines suffered from a dreadful plague—
la malade noire. Perhaps it was the first coming of the oidium; but
whatever it was, the vineyards were wiped out, and only an acre or
two of vines above Pommard were left. It was these that provided
the shoots that eventually filled the vineyards of the Côte.

In all, the *commune* contains not far short of eight hundred and
fifty acres of classified vineyards, but it is not only this that
accounts for its fame: the slope bends round rather to the south,
giving a particularly good exposure to the sun, so that the wines
are rather bigger than those of its neighbour Beaune, and they
have something of the lasting powers of the great burgundies of
the Côte de Nuits. In fact, they come somewhat between the two.
They are wines which everyone finds pleasant even though few can
become really excited about them. The principal *communes* are:

Têtes de Cuvées

	Acres
*Le Clos-Blanc	10·6
Les Epenots	25·6
Les Rugiens-Bas	14·5

Premières Cuvées

Les Argillières	9·0
Les Arvelets	20·9
Les Bertins	9·1
Les Boucherottes	3·7
*Les Chanlins-Bas	17·7
Les Chaponières	8·2
Es Charmots	14·2
Les Charmots	8·9
*Clos-de-la-Commaraine	9·8
Le Clos-Micot	6·7
Clos-de-Verger	6·2
*Les Combes-Dessus	6·9
Les Croix-Noires	10·5
Les Fremiers	12·2
Les Jarollières	7·9
Les Petits-Epenots	50·1
Les Pézerolles	16·0
*La Platière	14·3

Premières Cuvées

	Acres
Les Poutures	10·9
*La Refène	6·1
*Les Rugiens-Hauts	18·8
Les Sausilles	9·4

Climats marked * occupy an area that extends beyond the best portion of the slope, and therefore grow wines of less notable quality in addition to their finest wines.

Other notable *climats* include: La Chanière, Derrière Saint-Jean and Village de Pommard.

Volnay

Volnay is a wine to inspire affection. No other wine of the Côte d'Or has had quite as many little rhymes and proverbs composed about it—things like this:

En dépit de Pommard et Meursault,
C'est toujours Volnay le plus haut.

It is a light, delicate wine with a strong and beautiful bouquet; and if modern methods of enology seem to have made it even lighter of late, it is only returning towards what it used to be; from the thirteenth to the seventeenth centuries its wines were so *clairet* as to be almost *rosé*. And *vin de paille*, which is now extinct as far as the Côte d'Or is concerned, were also made here and in the neighbouring *commune* of Pommard.

When Maurice Healy published *Stay Me With Flagons* in 1940 he quoted the advice of his good friend John Bourke, who was also an acquaintance of the present author. The advice was that when he was confronted with an unfamiliar hotel wine list he would always pick a volnay, 'For it is not as widely known a name as beaune or pommard and thus not worth the faker's while!' Today I think the advice is only good in part, for the name of volnay has become very well known, and it would be idle to suppose that it is not faked; but as it is by nature a light and delicate wine, the shippers are less disposed to give it an artificial wealth of body and it seldom displays the more alarming manifestations of their art. So it is still a good bet.

The village has a history going back into Celtic times, and it is named after Volen or Velen, the Gaulish goddess of the springs. It has shown remarkable consistency in retaining the same name throughout the ages, and has not even succumbed to the temptation to hyphenate it with that of a vineyard. Its history as a centre of wine growing goes back probably almost as far, and the instruments of the ancient vintners are still sometimes found when the land is dug. In the Middle Ages it was the favourite summer residence of the Dukes of Burgundy. The dukes were also wine growers and the name of the greatest vineyard, *Les Caillerets*, is derived from *Caille du Roi*. When the duchy became united with the kingdom of France its wines retained their position in the royal favour, alongside those of Beaune and Pommard.

In addition to the *appellation* volnay, there is also an *appellation* volnay-santenots. The vineyards growing santenots are in fact in the neighbouring *commune* of Meursault, but as the wines they produce are red, unlike most in that *commune*, and as they are only just over the border, to group them with the volnays is perhaps less confusing then to group them with the meursaults.

The principal *climats* are:

Têtes de Cuvées

	Acres
Les Angles	8·6
Les Caillerets	35·5
Les Champans	28·0
Les Fremiets	16·1

Premières Cuvées

	Acres
*Les Aussy	7·5
La Barre	3·2
Bousse-d'Or	4·9
*Brouillards	16·9
*Carelles-Dessous	5·3
Carelles-sous-la-Chapelle	9·3
*Chanlin	9·7
En Chevret	15·0
Clos des Ducs	6·0
*La Gigotte	8·6
*Les Lurets	20·8

	Acres
Les Mitans	9·9
En l'Ormeau	10·7
*Pitures-Dessus	9·1
Pointes d'Angles	3·1
*Robardelle	10·5
En Ronceret	5·0
*Taille-Pieds	18·0
En Verseuil	2·0
*Village-de-Volnay	32·2

Climats marked * occupy an area that extends beyond the best portion of the slope, and therefore grow wines of less notable quality in addition to their finest wines.

Other notable vineyards include: Clos-des-Chênes (40·2 acres) and Grand-Champs (17·5 acres).

Monthélie, Auxey-Duresses and Saint-Aubin

The commune of Monthélie borders those of Volnay and Meursault. It occurs at the beginning of a fold in the hills, giving the vineyards a good exposure to the south, but the ground is very infertile, and there is a local saying that 'A chicken at Monthélie dies of hunger during the harvest'. Vines, in fact, are the only things that will grow there, and they are said to have been growing there ever since the decree of Probus. Much of the wine produced is of very ordinary quality, both red (including some Passe-Tout-Grains) and white, but some is good enough to be comparable with those of its neighbours, though having more body and less finesse. Before the coming of appellation contrôlée the best wines of Monthélie used to be sold as volnay. Four climats qualify as premières cuvées: Le Cas-Rougeot (1·4 acres), Les Champs Fuiliots (19·9 acres), Le Clos Gauthey (3·2 acres) and La Taupine (3·4 acres).

Further in the fold of the hills comes the little commune of Auxey-Duresses. Until 1924 the village was content to be known as Auxey-le-Grand, but it then decided to improve its status by adding the name of its best climat. And no doubt it was right to be proud of its climat, which produces a sound enough wine, even though it is only of the second category. The village of Auxey (pronounced Aussy) is a very ancient one. In the middle of the ninth century it was called Aulessiacum, and the monks grew wines there certainly from the thirteenth century. These were greatly esteemed and were allegedly exported to England in the fourteenth and fifteenth centuries. In those days, before table wines were bottled, the great wines could never come into their own, and no doubt those of Auxey could hold their own with most of those then available. But today they seem quite humble things—though by no means as humble as the complete obscurity of their name might suggest; for the best of them are usually sold as volnay or pommard. There are no *climats* worthy to be classed as *premières cuvées*.

Two other communes on the slopes behind the main vineyard area—Saint-Aubin and Saint-Romain—have *appellations* of their own, but neither produces wines of any particular note.

Meursault

Meursault is fortunate and unusual in having both red and white wines of very high quality. In the past, the red wines predominated, but now the emphasis is on the whites; and the greatest of its red wines, from Les Santenots, is sold as volnay-santenots. No doubt the use of the neighbour's name, famous as it is for red wines, avoids confusion, since today about ninety-seven per cent of the wines sold as Meursault are white; but even so, to allow the next *commune* to have the credit for such an outstanding wine suggests a rare degree of magnanimity. For it really is an outstanding wine. Like corton, it has something of the grandeur of the Côte de Nuits about it, and yet it has *finesse* comparable with that of a volnay. The white wines, too, are superb. They are second only to those from Puligny. They age very well, and their misfortune is to be overshadowed by their even more remarkable southern neighbours. The great vineyards of Meursault and those of Puligny-Montrachet run side by side.

The principal *climats* are:

For Red Wines:

Tête de Cuvée

	Acres
Les Santenots-du-Milieu	19·8

Premières Cuvées

	Acres
Les Cras	11·7
†Les Petures	27·0

† A portion of this *climat*, known as Désirée, gives white wines of *première cuvée* quality.

For White Wines:

Tête de Cuvée

	Acres
*Les Perrières	42·2

Premières Cuvées

	Acres
Les Bouchères	10·5
Les Charmes-Dessus	38·3
En Dos-d'Ane	7·1
Les Genevrières	
(Dessus and Dessous)	41·7
La Jennelotte	11·9
La Pièce-sous-le-Bois	27·8
Le Porusot-Dessus	16·7
Sous-Blagny	5·4

The *climat* marked * occupies an area that extends beyond the best portion of the slope, and therefore grows wines of less notable quality in addition to its finest wines.

Another notable vineyard for red wines is Les Santenots-du-Dessus (7·3 acres).

Le Montrachet: Puligny and Chassagne

Le montrachet is one of the very greatest white wines in the world. It has been called 'the divine montrachet' and 'the sublime montrachet'. It is a wine of superlatives, and it is worthy of them all. There is no other dry white wine to compare with it. The great *trockenbeerenauslesen* of Germany, and the great sauternes have their own glory; but they are sweet—very sweet indeed—and utterly unlike a great white burgundy. Montrachet is almost completely dry, and when it attains perfection, after some ten years in bottle, its glory lies in its bouquet and in the depth of its flavour, which is as immense as it is fresh. There is nothing quite like it.

In the *communes* of Puligny and Chassagne, the Côte de Beaune attains its apotheosis before trailing off into the anticlimax of Santenay. For not only do these *communes* produce the greatest of all white burgundies; they provide some very fine red wines as well.

Both *communes* are of Gallo-Roman origin, and their histories are well documented, though in somewhat less detail than those of some of their neighbours. Perhaps this is because the Church had less influence here and the land has long been held by private proprietors, though this has not prevented its being split up, as usual, into far too many small fragments. Chassagne, in 886, was known as *Cassaneas* and in 1321 as *Chaissaigne*; Puligny was *Puliniacus* in 1095. Within the *commune* of Puligny lies the hamlet of Blagny, which is perhaps even older than Puligny itself. It is justly proud of its wines, which are somewhat lighter than the montrachets and owe more to its neighbour Meursault, so that for its independent *appellation* it has the choice of calling itself either blagny or meursault-blagny, but not blagny-montrachet.

It was not until the end of the nineteenth century that the two *communes* created confusion by each tacking on the name of the great *climat* that they share. But even earlier, in the fifteenth century, when the Prince of Orange was the great landowner, Chassagne was being referred to as 'Chassagne Sous-le-Montrachet'.

There are three great montrachets: le montrachet itself, le chevalier montrachet, and le bâtard montrachet. They are listed in order of merit, or perhaps it would be fairer to say in the order of their magnificence, for the bastard is a royal bastard indeed! Le Chevalier lies entirely within the *commune* of Puligny, while the others spread across the line that divides the two. The sections within the *commune* of Puligny have slightly the edge on the others as regards quality, but it is in Chassagne that the best red wines of the area are grown, notably Clos-St.-Jean. The total production of le montrachet, however, is only about a thousand cases a year, and much, much more than that is sold. The demand so outstrips supplies that the price is necessarily high, and one generally gets the best value by paying the highest price and having a great domaine bottled wine of unimpeachable authenticity. If it is to be enjoyed at its best, moreover, it needs careful watching, as fine white burgundies have a distressing tendency to become maderized, when their quality is quite spoilt.

The *climat* next to the *chevalier*—a somewhat humbler but still very worthy neighbour—used once to be called Les Demoiselles, but jokes about Le Chevalier, Les Demoiselles and Le Bâtard eventually became so unbearable that its name was changed to Le Cailleret.

The red wines grown in these *communes*, if less distinguished than the whites, are none the less very good indeed, with a delightful fragrance that puts them amongst the finest of the Côte de Beaune, though they have nothing of the splendour or longevity found in their greatest rivals of the Côte de Nuits.

PULIGNY-MONTRACHET

White Wines:

Tête de Cuvée

	Acres
Le Montrachet (part)	9·8

Premières Cuvées

	Acres
*Le Bâtard-Montrachet (part)	24·0
Bienvenues-Bâtard-Montrachet	5·7
Blagny-Blanc	10·8
Les Chalumeaux	17·3
*Champ-Canet	11·4
Le Chevalier-Montrachet	15·1
Les Combettes	16·6
*Les Folatières	8·5
La Garenne	2·2

Red Wines:

Première Cuvée

	Acres
*Le Cailleret	13·4

A small proportion of this *climat* grows white wine.

CHASSAGNE-MONTRACHET

White Wines:

Tête de Cuvée

	Acres
Le Montrachet (the rest)	8.7

Première Cuvée

	Acres
*Le Bâtard-Montrachet (the rest)	31.6

Red Wines:

Têtes de Cuvées

	Acres
La Boudriotte and	
Clos de la Boudriotte	44·3
Le Clos-Saint-Jean	35·5
Le Clos-Pitois	—

Premières Cuvées

	Acres
Les Brussanes, Le Grand Clos,	
Le Petit Clos and	
La Vigne Blanche	44·0
Champgain	70·0
*Les Chaumées	2·8
La Maltroie	22·8

Climats marked * occupy an area that extends beyond the best portion of the slope, and therefore grow wines of less notable quality in addition to their finest wines.

As well as these leading *climats* there are certainly others that are fully worthy of note, for instance Les Pucelles amongst the white wines of Puligny-Montrachet; also En Cailleret amongst the red wines of Chassagne-Montrachet.

Santenay

Santenay, as a village, is one of the most interesting of the Côte d'Or; its wines, on the other hand, do not rank with their northern neighbours. They are good, though, and seldom adulterated. Like so many of its neighbours, it had a Gallo-Roman origin, and in the ninth century its Latin name was *Sentennacum*. At the end of the last century excavations brought to light a great number of relics going back as far as the Bronze Age, so it has certainly been a centre of civilization from time immemorial. There are still traces of an old temple dedicated to Mercury. Today it is unique amongst the towns of Burgundy in two respects: it has a small spa, fed by a mineral spring of foul-tasting water; and it has a small casino.

The style of its wines warns the drinker that he is approaching the Côte Chalonnaise: they are rougher and less finished than the greater wines of the Côte d'Or, and they mature quickly. Nevertheless those of the leading *climats* are often delightful.

Only one *climat* ranks as a *tête de cuvée*, but it is very large indeed: Les Gravières, of 72·6 acres. Part of the *climat* of La Comme (in all 80·1 acres) ranks as a *première cuvée*.

The Côte Chalonnaise

The Côte Chalonnaise is an extension of the Côte d'Or southwards into the neighbouring *département* of Saône-et-Loire. There is a gap between the Côtes, but the soils are much the same, so is the climate, so are the grape varieties, and so are the methods used by the wine growers. Naturally enough, then, the wines are similar in style. In the poorer years, those from the Côte Chalonnaise lack some of the breed and quality that those of the Côte d'Or, despite chaptalization, still possess; but in good vintages they rise to considerable heights. Overshadowed by the Côte d'Or, they are amongst the few great French wines that are under-rated. Theirs is the fate of the compromise, of the half-caste, of the second class in a railway with three classes. Despite their excellence, they are clearly not quite of the Côte d'Or, and they are equally clearly somewhere along the road that leads to Beaujolais. Hence they are neglected. The rich man buys his great wines from the Côte d'Or and the poor man is content with his beaujolais. But the wines of the Côte Chalonnaise are much nearer to the former than to the latter, in style as well as geographically.

The Chalonnaise wines come from three quite separate enclaves. The northernmost, which begins just south of Chagny, is Rully. Adjacent to it, but further to the south, is Mercurey. Then there is a gap before Givry, and another gap before Montagny, just south and west of the town of Buxy. Chalon-sur-Saône, which gives its name to the whole Côte, is some way over to the east, and no wines of any note are grown near it.

In Rully the only wines of any importance are white, and many of them are made into *mousseux* by the *méthode champenoise*. No doubt this is a wise move commercially, but as sparkling wines they are quite uninteresting whereas in their natural state they have considerable body, flavour and character.

The neighbouring, and rather larger area of Mercurey, grows some red and white wines of fine character and quality. It takes its name from a temple dedicated to Mercury, the site of which is now occupied by a windmill. The white wines are remarkably fresh and delicate, yet full of flavour, while the red wines are light and delicious. They are very like volnay, and indeed they are widely used to 'stretch' the far from adequate supplies of it. Amongst the many growers are Bouchard Ainé, the shippers from Beaune, whose mercurey wines have been favourites of mine for a long time.

Givry is a beautiful little town with vast and ancient cellars. It grows red wines almost entirely, though there are a few whites. In style and quality they are similar to the mercureys, though perhaps a little lighter, and, like them, they are unjustly under-rated. Before the wines of the Côte d'Or became so famous, those of Givry were more widely known and honoured: in the days of Philippe de Valois they had to pay a luxury tax, shared only by the wines of Beaune, on entering Paris. And they are said to have been amongst the many 'favourite wines' of Henry IV.

Montagny grows only white wines. Most of them are drunk in France, and although perhaps somewhat slight, they are certainly very pleasant.

The Mâconnais

The wines of the Mâconnais clearly and unquestionably belong to southern Burgundy. In style they are far removed from those of the Côte d'Or: they are slighter, rougher, and quick to mature, though delicious none the less. Though geographically nearer to the Beaujolais, they lack the beaujolais fruity generosity and are just as far away from it as they are from the Côte d'Or. The area is still within the province of Saône-et-Loire, beginning at Sennecey-le-Grand in the north and extending to just beyond Mâcon in the south. Just as in terms of wine, one is well on the way to the Beaujolais, in terms of architecture and scenery one is equally clearly on the way to the Midi, for the climate is hotter, and the earth in summer looks baked and parched, while the houses begin to assume the more casual proportions of the south, with curved Roman tiles in place of straight and formal tiles or slates. And mosquitoes are troublesome; in fact I have had more trouble with them there than anywhere else I have been with the possible exception of a pine forest in Andalusia. They like me. Once when I was sitting in Jean Mommessin's garden just outside Mâcon, I became so completely covered with them that one of his daughters had to be sent into the house hastily to fetch 'la bombe' (which happily turned out to be merely an aerosol spray) before 'Monsieur est totalement mangé'.

Like the Côte de Beaune, the Mâconnais has its generic classifications. Red wines may be called *mâcon* plus the name of the *commune* in which they are grown, or *mâcon supérieur*, or just plain *mâcon*. White wines may be *mâcon-villages*, *mâcon-supérieur* or just plain *mâcon*. The white wines (but not the reds) may be further declassified and sold as *bourgogne* or as *bourgogne grand ordinaire*.

Mâcon itself is an immensely old town, dating from before the Roman conquest, and the vine has been cultivated there ever since the decree of Probus. During the Middle Ages, viticulture came under the inspired eye of the monastery of Cluny, and although no degree of skill and care will make a truly great wine where the soil and climate are unsuitable, at least the Mâconnais has throughout this time produced great quantities of very useful red wine, and a white wine of real quality: the famous pouilly-fuissé. It bears the combined name of two *communes*—Pouilly and Fuissé—but it is also grown in others: Chaintré, Loché, Prissé, Vergisson, Vinzelles and Solutré. Some of the best comes from the last named. Loché and Vinzelles, however, despite their very small production, grow such distinctive and good wines that each has its own separate *appellation*: pouilly-vinzelles and pouilly-loché. All the true pouilly-fuissé is made from Chardonnay grapes, the vine originally native to the Mâconnais; and in its home territory it can be allowed to grow far higher than along the Côte d'Or or in Chablis, for the heat of the sun is so great that the grapes need none of the heat reflected from the ground, and the vintage is very late, so that they are slightly overripe. The resulting wine is rather heady, full but fresh-flavoured, and light golden with a characteristic yellow-green tinge: one of the best white burgundies. In addition to these wines, some red and white mâcons of more ordinary quality are grown from Gamay and Aligoté grapes respectively.

The Beaujolais

The Beaujolais begins where the Mâconnais ends. And what a splendid place it is! It must be one of the happiest, most scenically beautiful, and most delightfully casual places in the world. To sit in a simple inn, eating the local food and drinking glass after glass of the enchanting young village wine, is as good a gastronomic experience as I have ever had. For beaujolais, generally speaking, *should* be drunk young. Most of the wines are admirable after less than a year, and after three to five years in bottle they tend to go off. Only some of the greater growths repay keeping.

The vineyards lie just to the west of the N.6—the main Paris/Lyons road. It is a fast and deadly highway, packed full of cars careering madly towards the Riviera. Just to the west of this dreadful road lies one of the most beautiful stretches of country-side imaginable. Yet mercifully few of the tourists turn off, and the roads there are relatively quiet. To drive down the Route du Vin of the Beaujolais during summer is one of the happiest journeys it is possible to make. It is a land of innumerable hills and exquisite views—rich farmland, where vines are grown wherever the slopes face the right way. Elsewhere there are pastures and forests. The climate in summer is beautifully balanced like that of the Massif Central: it is hot but the land is not scorched; and everything is vividly green beneath the sun. Scenically it is not unlike the edge of the Vosges mountains, behind the vineyards of Alsace.

The countryside and its people have been immortalized in that wonderfully funny novel by Gabriel Chevalier: *Clochemerle*. Ronald Avery, the famous Bristol wine merchant, has said that *Clochemerle* has done more to make beaujolais popular in this country than all the wine merchants and wine writers put together, and he is probably right. There is even a village that claims to be the original: Vaux-en-Beaujolais. But it has grown vastly affected, and it does not wear its fame at all well; moreover, its claim is probably spurious. However, it has a useful public *pissoir*.

The vineyard area begins a few miles south of Mâcon, at

Chasselas, and it extends southwards as far as L'Arbresle, a distance of just over thirty miles. But although the vineyards entitled to the benefit of *appellation contrôlée* finish there, wines of the beaujolais style stop being grown only at the suburbs of Lyons, whilst in the north the *communes* in the *département* of Saône-et-Loire enjoy a dual *appellation* and may call their wines mâcon or beaujolais at will. So there is no clear dividing line between the Mâconnais and the Beaujolais. The width of the vineyard belt from east to west averages about eight miles. On the east side, it stops at the valley of the Saône, and only at three points, for a short way, does it cross the main Paris/Lyons road. On the west, it stops where the mountains become too high, at the edge of the Massif Central. The Beaujolais extends over two *départements*: the north-eastern tip is in Saône-et-Loire, and the rest is in the Rhône. The dividing line passes through the famous *commune* of Moulin-à-Vent, though not horizontally, and Juliénas is in the Rhône. The climate is distinctly continental: the summer months are pleasantly hot, and the winter is cold, often with a heavy snowfall.

The Beaujolais, like all the countryside around the Saône, was once under Roman occupation, the memory of which is perpetuated in names like Jullié, Juliénas and Romanèche. In the Middle Ages it was a barony—the fief of the ancient noblemen who have been described as 'the savage lords of Beaujeu'; and the description may well have been justified, for the hills of the Beaujolais must have been as insular and as resistent to invaders as were those of Wales. By the ninth century, the barony had become an apanage of the Count of Lyons and Forez. In 1531 the fief passed to the Bourbons, and the barony became united with the kingdom of France. During the reign of Louis XIV, it became a royal county. In the days of the barons, the capital was Beaujeu, an ancient little town that still bears the enchanting heraldic motto 'A tout venant—beau jeu'. But its importance, which at the most was only local, has passed to Mâcon, while the administrative capital is now Villefranche-sur-Saône. The focus of the whole area, though, is really the city of Lyons, and the restaurants of Lyons have always specialized in good beaujolais. There is a saying much repeated that 'Three rivers bathe Lyons: the Rhône, the Saône, and the Beaujolais'. The amount of beaujolais the locals drink is a standing joke; but how right they are! Like most wines, it tastes at its very best near the vineyards which produce it. The local housewives and restaurateurs, moreover, know just what foods it tastes best with. And no one in his right mind would think of drinking anything else in a Lyons restaurant.

The vine is old in Beaujolais, with a history going back to Gallo-Roman days, and yet as a major wine-growing area it is one of the youngest. In Roman times, the vineyards were very modest in size, and by the sixteenth century they were little, if any, larger; in those days most of the land was covered with forests, and farming came next in importance. It was not until the seventeenth and eighteenth centuries that the forests began to be cut down to make way for the vine. Even in those days the popularity of beaujolais was only local, and the main market was in Lyons, with the River Saône providing the highway that linked the city with the vineyards. Even a wine as popular today as Moulin-à-Vent was little known in the eighteenth century. According to Morton Shand[1] one of the earliest references to it occurs in the record of a law suit brought by one broker against another for selling at Mâcon a wine that was not, and could not have been, Moulin-à-Vent at the price. Despite the introduction of wines from the Mâconnais into the court at Versailles in 1660, the difficulties of transport effectively prevented those of the Beaujolais from reaching Paris, or from being exported overseas, until the advent of the railways in the nineteenth century. The demand was there, though: only the wine was missing; and as soon as quick transport brought it to the capital, it became as popular there as it had long been at Lyons.

Many of the vineyards are owned by peasants, and wine growing is still a family affair with everyone helping at the vintage. Sometimes, when the land is owned by a *rentier* landlord, it is cultivated by the method of *moitié fruit*—a semi-feudal system in which the produce and the expenses are shared between the owner and the peasant. Unhappily, though, there are already signs that the system is breaking up. Some peasants sell their grapes straight to a *négociant*, who presses them in his own *chais*, whilst others are coming increasingly to use the co-operatives, such as the one at Chénas. As far as the wine is concerned, this can do nothing but good. It is a pity, though, that an old order should end.

[1] P. Morton Shand, *A Book of French Wines*, London, 1960.

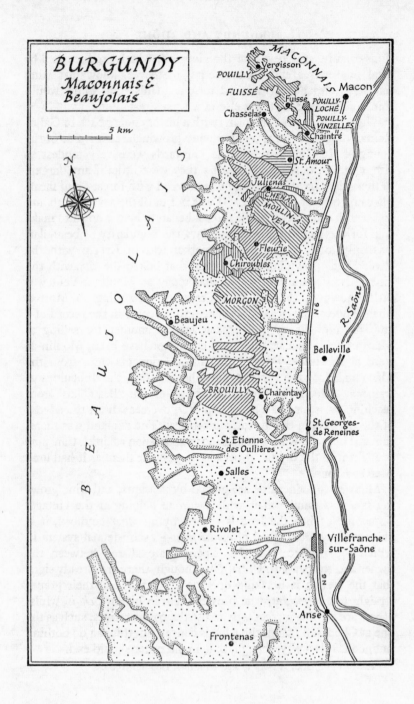

BURGUNDY
Maconnais &
Beaujolais

0   5 km

N

MACONNAIS

POUILLY   Vergisson

FUISSÉ   Macon

Fuissé   POUILLY-
LOCHÉ
Chasselas   POUILLY-
VINZELLES

Chaintré

St. Amour

Juliénas

CHÉNAS
MOULIN-À-
VENT

Fleurie

Chiroubles

MORGON

Beaujeu   Belleville

N 6   R. Saône

BROUILLY   Charentay

St. Georges-
de Reneines

St. Etienne
des Oullières

Salles

Rivolet

Villefranche-
sur-Saône

N 6

Anse

Frontenas

B E A U J O L A I S

Practically all the wines grown in the Beaujolais are red, but there are some whites as well, and these are now becoming more popular in this country. Some of the best are grown in the *commune* of Saint-Amour. In style they resemble the pouilly-fuissés, though they tend to be slighter, and, like the more famous red wines of the area, they are wines to gulp rather than to sip. Perhaps they more than resemble the pouilly-fuissés. In a famous wholesaler's list there is an allegedly single vineyard white burgundy that used, until recently, to be classified as a pouilly-fuissé. Now that white beaujolais is no longer unknown, in his recent lists it has figured as a white beaujolais though the vineyard presumably remains in the same place. It is rather confusing.

Although it is easy to tell where the Beaujolais ends in a southerly direction, as far as the wines exported abroad are concerned, the geography of the shippers is, as usual, both vague and elastic, so that it has spread far down the Côtes-du-Rhône. One often comes across a light rhône being sold as a beaujolais, and I have even come across one rather curious instance of a beaujolais being sold as a rhône. The wine trade is full of surprises. Before the Algerian trouble, it was also quite common for Algerian wine to be blended with the cheaper beaujolais, as it was with the cheaper wines that bore the great names of the Côte d'Or; but this practice is probably more or less at an end, for purely political reasons, and if wines are added from elsewhere they are most likely to come from the Rhône or occasionally from the Languedoc. But the output of genuine beaujolais is large, and such adulterations are probably rarer than they are often made out to be: there is little need of them, especially as beaujolais does not command a high price. Indeed, in comparison with other fine wines, the best beaujolais is often sold far more cheaply than its quality would justify, and there are some very fine wines indeed that find their way to this country only too seldom, simply because the name of beaujolais has become too closely associated with the cheaper growths.

The area may be divided into two distinct parts: the Haut-Beaujolais, roughly north of a latitude passing through Ville-franche, and the Bas-Beaujolais, or Beaujolais-Bâtard, south of the line. The difference between the two is a matter of soil. The finest beaujolais are grown on granite soil north of the line, while the poorer wines are grown on chalk soil in the south and have a rather earthy taste, or *gout de terroir*, that tends to increase as the wine is kept in bottle. These wines should therefore be drunk young; as cheap carafe wines, drawn from the wood in French cafés, they are excellent. The Bas-Beaujolais is essentially a land for quantity rather than quality.

The rise of the Beaujolais during the last two hundred years is really the history of the rise of one vine: the Gamay. In the Côte d'Or, for centuries it has been apostrophized as infamous, and the wines it gives are very poor things. But in the granite soil and hot summer climate of the Beaujolais, it has found conditions which suit it perfectly, and it has become transformed. Perhaps the vine, too, has been improved through the centuries, for only one variety of the Gamay, the Petit Gamay, otherwise known as Gamay-noir-à-jus-blanc, is grown there.

The red wines of the Haut-Beaujolais vary considerably in style. Some, like moulin-à-vent, named after the old windmill that still stands, minus its sails, in the village, are big in body and flavour, needing to be sipped, like the wines of the Côte d'Or. At the other end of the scale comes fleurie, a delicate and beautifully balanced wine that goes down well in great draughts, though it is a wine of quality and it can be appreciated in a wholly different way when it is sipped. Other big-bodied wines include the delicious juliénas (a favourite of the Swiss), saint-amour, and morgon, which has a very individual bouquet and flavour. Chiroubles, though lighter, is still very robust. Brouilly, although robust and strong, generally shows at its best when drawn straight from the cask into a carafe. Lighter still are chénas and thorins, which are comparable to fleurie.

The general *appellation* for the whole of the Beaujolais is, of course, beaujolais. Some individual *communes*, however, known as 'Les Crus', have separate protection. These are: brouilly, chénas, chiroubles, côte de brouilly, fleurie, juliénas, morgon, moulin-à-vent and saint-amour. Each of these names is separately protected and may be used alone or preceded by beaujolais. They have the right, too, to the broader *appellation* of *beaujolais-villages*. As far as the crus themselves are concerned, this alternative is seldom used, but it includes a number of other very worthy if less well-known villages that do make use of it. There is a subtle difference between *beaujolais supérieur* and just plain *beaujolais*, the former having to have a slightly higher alcoholic degree and a somewhat lower yield per acre. *Beaujolais supérieur* can be declassified either as a plain *beaujolais* or as a *bourgogne grand ordinaire*, whilst the latter cannot be declassified further. As with all wines, though, the *appellation contrôlée* is only a part of the story. Much depends on the skill of the grower and shipper. In looking for a wine of the very highest class, it is fair to say that the more details that are given, the better the wine is likely to be. The best wines of all are the single vineyard wines which are at last becoming fairly generally available in this country, though now that the idea has caught on rather too many shippers have chosen to exploit it, so that one doubts the authenticity of some of the wines offered. Nor is a single vineyard wine *necessarily* the best: it depends on the vineyard. Where there is any lack of balance, judicious blending with wine of the appropriate *appellation* is a good thing. To avoid being accused of trading on a gimmick, I know one old-established wine merchant who sells single vineyard beaujolais but refuses to label it as such.

Generally speaking, beaujolais should be bottled early and drunk young, but even then there are exceptions, and the big wines from Moulin-à-Vent or Julienas improve for three or four years in bottle. The humble wines from the Bas-Beaujolais, however, should certainly be drunk young and quaffed rather than sipped. Some people enjoy them when they are slightly chilled. Such simple wines, drunk under the sunshine on a warm summer's day, are a delight. But the finest beaujolais needs and deserves greater consideration. It is by no means a poor relation of the Côte d'Or: the best beaujolais is a proud first cousin.

The Rhône

Lyons is the gateway that divides beaujolais from rhône. Divisions are seldom neat and clear-cut, though, and the city of Lyons is no more than a convenient demarcation: the vines cease because the buildings have usurped their place, not because the ground is unsuitable. In all probability, though, not very much has been lost, and the growth of Lyons has done less damage than that of Bordeaux or of Dijon. It is well to the south of the finest parts of Beaujolais, and even further to the north of the Côte-Rôtie.

Nevertheless wines are still grown there, even in the middle of the city, where there is a spare patch of earth. The people who live in the suburbs just outside the town, such as Sainte-Foy or on the hillside of Saint-Fortunat, have their gardens on vineyard soil that used to enjoy a local fame. Many of them grow some wine for their own use, and what better kitchen-garden could there be?

Rhône wines are grown all the way along the course of the great river, but the best of them, including most of those that are entitled to an *appellation*, grow in two distinct and relatively compact areas. The more northerly of these is of an elongated shape, lying to the south of Lyons and stretching roughly between Vienne and Valence, while the more southerly is more or less square and is centred around the ancient and beautiful town of Orange. The distance from Vienne to Avignon, at the extremities of these two areas, is about 120 miles; and worthy wines are grown further both to the north and south. In the north they grow right into the suburbs of Lyons itself, and in the south they certainly stretch as far as Tarascon before they finally lose the character of the Rhône and take on that of the Midi. The distance between these two towns is over 150 miles, and the river passes through no less than seven different *départements*. It is not surprising, then, that there is variety amongst the wines; the surprising thing is that their family resemblance is so marked. All of them are fine, strong and manly; and they are amongst the most long-lived wines in the world. Even the *vins rosés* improve in bottle.

Their strength and vigour arise directly from the climate in which they are grown. The Rhône valley is even hotter than the Beaujolais. One is approaching the Mediterranean: it is a land of vines, evergreen oaks and olive trees. The river valley, moreover, is far enough inland not to feel the cooling influence of the sea, yet it is not so far south as to become a desert; and the winters can be very cold, so the wines, unlike so many of those grown around the Mediterranean, despite their strength, avoid being coarse. Because of the southerly latitude the vintage is more consistent in quality than that of burgundy, and there are fewer failures. But it is not without its hazards. In 1964, for instance, at the beginning of June, Châteauneuf-du-Pape suffered a tornado. Hailstones, some of them as big as pigeons' eggs, fell so fast that they lay four inches deep in the streets. The hail was followed by a deluge. Well over two thousand acres of vineyards were laid waste and many more seriously affected.

The flavour of Rhône wines, although full, is deep, and they are not lacking in delicacy. In many parts of this vast area, cultivation is difficult. Like the valleys of the Rhine and the Douro, that of the Rhône is often steep and narrow. And in places it is almost as beautiful as the other two. Most travellers to the Riviera, however, rush down the new motorway, as they once rushed down that fast and dangerous road, the N.7. They would do better to take the journey in a more leisurely way, along the right bank of the river; and in doing so, they would pass alongside the greatest vineyards of the Côte-Rôtie.

In Roman days, as it does today, the Rhône valley provided a natural route between the Mediterranean and the north. The Romans used it and had their colonies there. In all their territories they grew vines where ever vines would grow, and this valley was no exception. Pliny praised its wines and so did Martial. It is inconceivable that such viticulturalists as the Romans should have missed the great sites of the Côte-Rôtie and Hermitage, and so it is safe to say that the fine growths of the Rhône are amongst the oldest of wines. In a later age, the popes enjoyed drinking Rhône wines while the papacy was at Avignon, and their successors never lost the taste, for these wines were still being exported to Rome in the sixteenth and seventeenth centuries. Exports to the north, however, were more difficult, and they were virtually unknown in England until the opening of the Midi canal in 1681 gave access to the great sea route from Bordeaux. But although the physical barrier was removed, the trade was not established without difficulty, as the city of Bordeaux chose to exercise some of its ancient privileges in an attempt to prevent any of its valuable trade being taken by wines from elsewhere. Eventually, as has already been related, the Bordeaux merchants seized the trade by subtler means: they themselves became the best customers for Rhône wines and used them for 'improving' their own growths.

Soon other trade routes were opened. Work on the River Loire between Saint-Rambert and Roanne made the river navigable, and from the end of 1709 it provided a new route to Paris. Then came further canals, and eventually the railways. The eighteenth-century pioneer of the export trade was one Mure, of Tain, whose family business was started soon after the route to Bordeaux was opened, and by the middle of the eighteenth century it had become so famous that rhône was sometimes known in England and in Bordeaux as *vin de Mure*. Old Hermitage, and the wines of the Côtes-du-Rhône were held in honour by eighteenth-century British connoisseurs, and reached their peak, both in popularity and esteem, during the nineteenth century. Then they receded in face of the rising tide from Bordeaux, Burgundy and the Beaujolais. Unaccountably they have not made up the ground they lost; at any rate they have not made it up under their own names.

Many grape varieties are grown in the Rhône valley, but the greatest of them, without doubt, is the Syrah. It gives wines that are very hard in style and deep in colour. They last perhaps longer than any other table wines, with great age they tend to lighten eventually taking up that colour known as *pelure d'oignon*. If a lighter style of wine is required, other varieties are grown, of which the most important is the white Viognier. Many of the Rhône wines are made by mixing these two varieties, sometimes with others added.

Although the Rhône valley is such an old wine-growing area, the term *côtes-du-rhône* is a very modern one; and not only is it very modern, it is also very vague, even when the laws of *appellation contrôlée* are strictly adhered to. The term first came into use colloquially in the 1840s when it was used by the local people simply to denote a wine grown anywhere in the valley. It was as vague a description as 'burgundy'. In 1908 it became semi-official when growers from both sides of the river formed themselves into a *Union des Côtes du Rhône*, and it became recognized as an *appellation* in 1937. The official area is shown on the map but the name is sometimes used loosely on wines from even further afield. It includes all the good but less distinguished wines that are grown around the more limited fine wine areas. Thus it is grown behind the Côte-Rôtie, around Ampuis; it continues down the west bank of the river, stretching past Cornas and Saint-Peray; on the west bank it surrounds Tain and its famous Hermitage; then there is a gap until one reaches that big area that is centred around Orange. The *appellation* applies to red, rosé and white wines.

Apart from the general run of côtes-du-rhône, certain *communes*

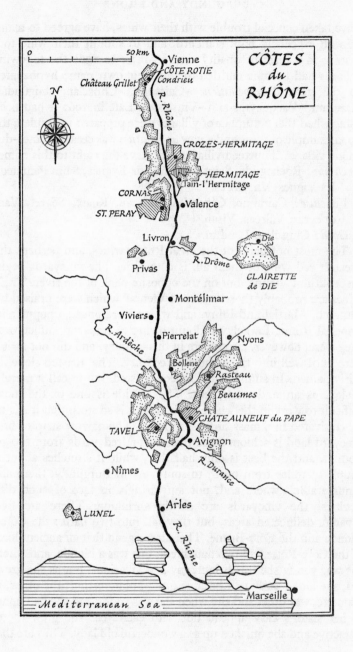

CÔTES
du
RHÔNE

0   50 km

Vienne
CÔTE ROTIE
Condrieu
Château Grillet

N

R. Rhône

CROZES-HERMITAGE

HERMITAGE
Tain-l'Hermitage
CORNAS
Valence
ST. PERAY

Livron
Die
Privas
R. Drôme
CLAIRETTE
de DIE

Montélimar
Viviers
R. Ardèche
Pierrelat
Nyons
Bollene
Rasteau
Beaumes
CHATEAUNEUF du PAPE
TAVEL
Avignon
R. Durance
Nîmes
LUNEL
Arles
R. Rhône

Mediterranean Sea
Marseille

have taken especial trouble with their wines, have agreed to maintain an especially high standard, and to submit their wine to a tasting as a form of quality control. Prior to 1967 the following villages had become entitled to add their own name hyphenated to the general *appellation*: -Cairanne, -Chusclan, -Gigondas, -Laudun, -Vacqueyras and -Vinsobres. Late in 1967 it had been established that a number of villages were prepared to emulate the good example of these and a new *appellation* was created: côtes-du-rhône villages. Fourteen villages now have the right to this name:

Drome: Rochegude, Saint Maurice sur Eygues, Saint Pantaleon les Vignes, Vinsobres.

Vaucluse: Cairanne, Gigondas, Rasteau, Roaix, Segret, Vacqueyras, Valreas, Visan.

Gard: Chusclan, Laudun.

The most northerly of the great Rhône wines, and perhaps the greatest red wine of them all, is côte-rôtie. The vineyards begin just south of Vienne, but on the opposite bank of the river. Their wines are probably those 'wines of Vienne' which were praised by Plutarch, Martial and Pliny, and which were once so popular in imperial Rome. Largely no doubt owing to transport difficulties, they were, however, latecomers in this country, and did not arrive here until well into the eighteenth century. The 'roasted slope' is fairly named. In summer it is indeed roasted, but to call it merely a slope is an understatement. The hillside is one of the most difficult to work in the whole of France: it is so steep that it has to be cultivated in a mass of little terraces. The narrow strip of fine vineyard land is seldom more than a hundred yards from top to bottom, and the best is only half that, while it stretches about a couple of miles from north to south. As in Burgundy, there are innumerable owners and, not surprisingly in face of such difficulties, the vineyards are slowly shrinking. There are five separate delineated areas, but they fall into two parts: the Côte-Blonde and the Côte-Brune. There is a legend that an ancient lord of the Côte-Rôtie had two daughters: one was a blonde, and when she was young she was bright, gay and vivacious, but as she grew old, she faded sadly and became quite uninteresting; the other, a brunette, was quiet and shy when she was young and she had none of her sister's easy appeal, but with each year she grew more attractive and she finished up as a wonderful old lady. Thus are the wines of the Côte-Blonde and the Côte-Brune. This is partly brought about by the nature of the ground, and partly by the choice of vine: the soil of the Côte-Blonde contains more lime and is lighter in colour; and while the Côte-Brune is planted almost exclusively with the Syrah variety, the Côte-Blonde contains a high proportion of Viognier. Nearly all the wine is red, vinified from eighty per cent Syrah and twenty per cent Viognier, though some white is made from the Viognier vines alone. The red wines are magnificent things, and the best balance is achieved by blend-ing from the two slopes. In the old days, the wines were so hard when young that they used to be kept for five or six years in the wood before they were considered fit for bottling. Some are still made that way, but other growers follow the modern fashion, making the red wines rather lighter, so that they can be bottled after three or four years. After bottling, the wines take a corre-spondingly long time to attain full maturity. It is at least twelve years before they are really ready and they are generally still in excellent shape after thirty or forty years. They are then beautiful in colour, and full of body and flavour, with a good bouquet and delightful smoothness. The white wines are fine, strong and fragrant.

Just to the south of the Côte-Rôtie comes Condrieu, where white wines are grown from the Viognier grape. They are very pleasing, with an individual flavour, though some tend, perhaps rather ineptly, towards sweetness. I have tasted superb dry wines, though, which are amongst the very best of the Rhône valley. Within the area of Condrieu, and grown near the village of Saint-Michel, is one of the most remarkable white wines in the whole of France: Château-Grillet. Its production is minute: in 1961 it fell to as little as three casks. The area of the vineyard is correspondingly minute—about four acres. Yet it has an *appellation contrôlée* all of its own; it is world famous; and it commands a consistently high price—when it is obtainable at all. The vineyard is on a steep hillside with a southerly aspect, and the Viogner vines (many of which are very old) grow on minute ledges in black, gritty, granitic sand. The grapes are gathered as late as possible, but the fermenta-tion is complete and any sweetness that is apparent arises from the natural glycerin. This wine, with its indescribable, full and subtle flavour, and a bouquet that is likened to may-blossom, has been grown by the Gachet family for three hundred years: and very understandably they only sell the few bottles they do not require for their friends and themselves. In my own experience the wines of the greater vintages tend to be a bit *too* magnificent—though they would no doubt drink marvellously well given enough age in bottle. One of the most agreeable that I have tried is the 1963. It tastes superb in 1970 but appears still to be improving.

Somewhat to the south of the Côte-Rôtie, and on either side of Château-Grillet, there are some excellent vineyards at Saint-Michel-sur-Loire and at Vérin.

Further to the south, and on the east side of the river, one of the greatest of all Rhône wines is grown: hermitage. The imposing hill, with the hermitage chapel of Saint Christopher on top, after which it takes its name, rises behind the town of Tain, which has now seen fit to call itself Tain l'Hermitage; and hermitage is certainly one of the oldest-established as well as being one of the greatest of French wines. The area around Tain was a favourite of the Romans. They had their country villas there, and archaeologists have unearthed many mosaics and ceramics from nearby. They have also found a store of forty amphoras, which gives some idea of the antiquity of the wine trade there. The story of the hermitage, and of the original hermit who lived there, rests on legend rather than history; and there are many different versions. As a place for religious worship, it goes back further than the Christian era, and in ancient days there was an altar there for the sacrifice of bulls. Morton Shand, who had a profound knowledge of all things French, gave the most circumstantial as well as the most attractive story. According to him[1] the hermit was a knight called Gaspar de Sterimberg, who chose to live alone with his piety on top of the hill when he returned from the Albigensian Crusade in 1224. He was granted a chapel and a vineyard which he tended and enlarged. His good work certainly bore fruit, and although little is known of the wine from his time until the seventeenth century, it was still doubtless grown. The present vineyards are said to have been delineated as far back as the end of the fourteenth century. By the mid-seventeenth century, despite the difficulties of transportation, the wines were sought after by the connoisseurs of

[1] *A Book of French Wines*, London, 1960. This knight is also mentioned by J. L. W. Thudichum, *A Treatise on Wines*, London, 1893.

Paris, and when Louis XIV of France wanted to give Charles II of England a memorable vinous present, he gave him 200 muids (a muid consisted of about eighteen hectolitres) of champagne, burgundy and hermitage. With their wine in regal demand, the growers evidently became desperate when, in 1664, they were attacked by a plague of insects that ravaged the vines, for they petitioned the bishop of Vienne to perform an exorcism.

Despite the royal gift, and no doubt as a result of transport difficulties, hermitage did not become popular in England until somewhat later. Lord Townsend, when he was ambassador at The Hague, bought some in 1710, and the Earl of Bristol was buying it in this country from 1714. As anyone knows who collects old wine labels, from that time onwards it was amongst the most popular of all wines imported here, and it remained so until well into the nineteenth century, when its popularity declined somewhat in favour of claret. But to a lamentably large extent, the new claret was merely the old hermitage sold under another name. Cyrus Redding[1] wrote that four-fifths of the total production in his day was sold to Bordeaux for sophisticating claret. Stendhal related how, in 1837, when the finest vineyards belonged to the Bishop of Valence, he left the task of cultivating them to a company whose obligations included that of providing four hundred bottles of the best wine each year for the bishop's table. The company, in its turn, stipulated that none of the wine should be given away because, wrote Stendhal, 'Doubtless the company was apprehensive of comparisons being made between the episcopal quality and that which was sold to the public.'

The great hill on which the hermitage rests is made of granite with only a very shallow top soil, containing some silicon and calcium; but the composition varies substantially from place to place. The finest of the wines are blended from grapes grown in different areas. Most of the wine grown is red, from the Syrah grape, but there are also white wines fermented principally from Marsanne with some Rousanne grapes. A relatively new variety, the Rousette vine, appears to be replacing Rousanne to some extent; it is a variant on the Marsanne. The red wines generally come from the purely granitic soil and the white from soils containing more silicon and calcium. Red hermitage has been described by

[1] *French Wines*, London, 1860.

the great Professor Saintsbury as 'the manliest of wines', and so it is: vast in flavour, forceful in character, with a purple-red colour that is all its own, a bouquet that has been likened to wild raspberries and gilliflowers, and an over-all magnificence that few wines can rival. It is also amongst the most long-lived of all the table wines. It used not to be bottled until it was four or five years old, and although it is now made lighter, for bottling after two to three years, it still takes even longer to mature than the great wines of the Côte de Nuits. A good hermitage often needs to be in bottle for ten years before it is fit to drink, for when it is young it is so rough and strong that it actually appears coarse, but as it matures its essential balance is revealed in its depth and flavour, while its greatness is shown by its finesse. It is seldom at its best until it is twenty years old. With increasing age, its finesse can become remarkable. Some years ago my father opened an old hermitage to drink with the turkey at Christmas. When he brought the wine up from the cellar I was very doubtful about it, fearing that it would completely overwhelm the flavour of the bird. But I was quite wrong: it was a perfect match. A fine hermitage of a great year seems to last almost for ever: thirty or forty years is common. Morton Shand gives unexpected advice on how an old wine should be treated: 'Red hermitage that has reached its third decade should be carefully filtered and trans-bottled. This imparts a second life, and a wonderful increase of velvetiness and clarity to the colour, and will add years to the wine's natural span.' Such a treatment is distinctly individual, and I have no personal experience of it. Hermitage, indeed, seems to breed eccentricities in its admirers, for Cyrus Redding is no less surprising in his method of assessing its quality: 'If it is bad as hermitage, because it is not the wine in the full extent of the word, it is still an ordinary wine of the greatest worth and distinction. It should be observed that when this wine is most excellent, it will not drink or mix well with water; while, if it be of mediocre quality, it blends well with it. But whether good, mediocre or bad, it preserves its condition, and improves in from fifteen to twenty years, when it changes, slowly or rapidly, according to circumstances.'

White hermitage is amber coloured, dry in that it contains very little sugar, yet rich and mellow in flavour. The whites generally take some ten years to mature, and no doubt if kept long enough they will eventually maderize; but this takes a very long time. In the Paris Exhibition of 1862, some sound wines were shown of the 1760 vintage, and Cyrus Redding, who described white hermitage as the first white wine of France, maintained that it would easily survive for a century. Such longevity as this, though, must be taken as the exception rather than the rule, certainly so far as the wines of today are concerned.

Alas, not all the wines labelled *hermitage* are what they purport to be. Lowly neighbours are ennobled and some of the wine that is said to be genuine does not appear to be well made. A true hermitage is a wine of grandeur, but the fakes are often merely coarse.

While hermitage proper is grown on the southern slopes of the mountain just behind Tain, there is another and much larger area, consisting of a strip of fine vineyards to the north of the mountain of Hermitage and on either side of the village of Croizes-Hermitage, where the wine that bears its name is grown. Croizes-hermitage is no more hermitage than gevrey-chambertin is chambertin, but nevertheless it is a very fine wine, though coarser and less attractive to the nose. These wines are fermented from the same grapes as hermitage proper, though the Rousette appears to be getting a particularly strong hold. Most of them are white, and the wine with the enchanting name of Chante-Alouette is outstanding. This is grown near the village of Mercurol.

Until the end of the last century, the vineyards of Croizes-Hermitage produced a renowned *vin de paille*, but this is no longer made in commercial quantities if it is made at all, and from Cyrus Redding's report in 1860 it is not hard to see why it has disappeared. Even then he could write: 'Little is made, because besides that the price is very high, it is only at long intervals that success attends the operation; a particular maturity of the fruit, and dry weather without cold, are required to prevail while the fruit is spread upon the straw.' Such wines, alas, are clearly unsuited to the Nuclear Age.

Opposite Tain l'Hermitage, on the west side of the river, there is an area called Saint-Joseph. There is no village of that name, but the *appellation* has been devised to distinguish the red and white wines of five villages around Tournon, where vines grow on the granite terraces of precipitous hillsides to give wines that are little inferior to those of Hermitage itself and that are most unjustly neglected in this country. Other wines, mostly red, are sold as *vins de tournon* and *vins de mont fleury*.

Further to the south, and also on the western bank of the river, come the vineyards of Cornas, where fine red wines are grown on the pebbly bed of a dried-up river. The vine is again the Syrah and the wines are equal to those of the Côte-Rôtie. The wines of the next most southerly area—Saint-Péray—are as different from those of Cornas as any wines could be. In the first place they are white, but they are wholly lacking in distinction despite the fact that the grapes are often not gathered until the 'noble rot' has set in. A large part is turned into *mousseux* by the *méthode champenoise*. The trade is almost as old as champagne itself, but the product is not to be sought after.

Die, over to the east on the River Drôme, really hardly qualifies as a Rhône wine at all, but it is in roughly the same area and might as well be included for the sake of completeness. Once it produced a renowned *clairette*. Now it provides frothy, pinkish and negligible *mousseux* with a peculiarly short life. Uninteresting table wines are also grown there.

As will be seen from the map, the next important area lies further south, around Orange, and is crowned by the famous Châteauneuf-du-Pape. But in passing one should mention two sweet liqueur wines: that of Rasteau, and the muscat of Beaumes. They are slightly fortified wines and are inclined to be heavy, heady and uninteresting but may be drunk locally with the dessert and before the siesta. A good example of a muscat de beaumes-de-venise, though, can be magnificent.

Châteauneuf-du-pape is an ancient wine with a modern history; for in between the foundation of the vineyards and their present-day popularity there came centuries of oblivion and neglect. The link with the papacy which the name suggests is by no means a fictitious one. It dates from the fourteenth century, when the popes were at Avignon, but the vineyard was not primarily a papal one. Pope Clement V—the same Pape Clément whose name is still borne by a château at Bordeaux—built a summer palace there. Of this, alas, there remains only a few ruins: it was destroyed by protestants in 1502, during the religious wars. Clement's work was continued by his successor, Pope John XXII, and the vineyard

was established by Innocent VI in the middle of the fourteenth
century. On such a site, and with such owners, great wines must
surely have been grown? But nevertheless, little is heard of them
for many centuries. The Earl of Bristol bought wine of Avignon,
which may well have been châteauneuf-du-pape, in 1704, but this
means very little. At the beginning of the nineteenth century, the
vineyards covered only about a hundred acres. Just before they
were struck by the phylloxera in the 1870s, the figure had risen to
about thirteen hundred acres. After they were reconstituted with
grafted vines, the figure went on rising and by 1913 there were
over two thousand acres.

The revival dates from the middle of the eighteenth century,
when the village was still known by its ancient name of Château-
neuf-Calcernier, on account of the chalk ovens which then provided its principal industry. In 1750, one of the vineyards there
was owned by Jean de Tulle, Comte de Villefranche, and his wine
became so popular amongst his friends that its fame spread and a
demand sprang up. Unfortunately, however, this honourable
demand for an honest wine was supplanted by the demand of the
Bordeaux shippers, who were by far the biggest customers in the
nineteenth century, and who used the wine, like hermitage, for
sophisticating claret. Nowadays large quantities of châteauneuf-
du-pape are bought by Burgundians who use it to contrive those
heady and unnaturally massive wines known as 'shippers'
Burgundies'.

Many vine species are cultivated in the area, but the Grenache
now predominates, and it is this grape that gives the wine its
finesse and softness while the Clairette helps to give it fire. The
Picpoule gives vinosity and bouquet, while the Terret is grown if
quantity rather than quality is required. Other grape species
include the Bourboulenc, the Cinsault, Counoïse, Mourvèdre;
Muscadin, Picardan, Rousanne, Syrah and Vaccarèse. The finest
wines are produced by blending grapes of different varieties from
different *climats* to give the balance that is required. The vines are
planted far apart—there is a gap of five to six feet between them—
and they are cultivated as bushes. The soil is extremely rocky and
infertile, but it is covered with great stones, most of them as big as
a fist and many as big as a man's head. These reflect the hard
sunlight up towards the grapes and help to ripen them.

Both red and white wines are produced. The latter, though, are relatively rare and, although they are more delicate than one might expect, they are not particularly interesting, being outclassed by the white wines from further north. The fame of the district rests entirely upon its red wines. Rather surprisingly these are distinctly lighter than côtes-du-rhône and hermitage; and they mature much more quickly. They can be drunk when only three years old, and they are generally at their best after six to seven years. To get the best results, though, they need longer in cask than burgundies and three to four years is usual. Amongst the leading growths are Château de la Nerthe, Château Fines Roches and Château Fortia or Fortiasse. A favourite in this country is Domaine de Mont-Redon, where over two hundred acres are cultivated by a single tenant who is thus able to provide a wine of very consistent quality. This great, sunny vineyard is a most remarkable sight. It is absolutely covered with rocks and one is amazed that cultivation is possible. Some of the best châteauneuf-du-pape is now domaine bottled.

In the south-west of the area lies a sun-scorched plateau surrounded by hills which are so bleak and baked that one expects at any moment to find oneself in a desert. It is here that the famous tavel rosé is grown: a wine as renowned as it is suspect; for it is generally accepted that much more is sold than is grown. There are one or two substantial growers, but most of the wine comes from the co-operative *chais* in the middle of the vineyards. The real thing is very remarkable: it is one of the few *rosés* that keeps well, and it is only at its best after four or five years in bottle. Its colour is a rather unusual shade of pink, derived from the Grenache grapes. The neighbouring *commune* of Lirac used once to be coupled with Tavel, but the individuality of its wines deserved the separate *appellation* which they have since achieved. It is noted for soft, aromatic wines that are quick to mature.

In considering the vintage years, it would be futile to mention individual wines. It has already been said how drastically the wine of one shipper differs from that of another; and apart from that, this chapter covers wines as disparate as the long-lived wines of Hermitage and the light draught wines of the lower Beaujolais. For example in 1964 I had the pleasure of drinking a Chambolle-Musigny Les Amoureuses 1926, shipped by Prosper Maufoux. It was exquisite, and exactly on top of its form. Another shipper's wine bearing exactly the same label might well have been hopelessly beyond its best. It is probable that no wines from the Côte de Beaune would still be showing so well after such a time. And a beaujolais after nearly forty years would be quite undrinkable. So the vintage years from 1920 onwards will only be mentioned in general terms.

1920: In Chablis this was only an average year. The wines of the Côte d'Or, however, particularly the reds, were excellent; they were beautifully soft and developed well, though the yield was small. The year was also good in southern Burgundy and the Rhône.

1921: In Chablis this was a very great year, though the yield was small. The best wines of the Côte d'Or and those from further south were also exceptionally fine, though many tended to be light and the vintage was rather uneven.

1922: Quite a good year for chablis, and some fair white wines were grown on the Côte d'Or, but there was too much rain and the other districts produced quantity rather than quality.

1923: Everywhere the yield was small, and in Chablis the quality was by no means outstanding. Elsewhere the wines were very good, especially in the Côte d'Or, where the vintage was amongst the best of the century. Some of the wines have lasted very well and are still excellent, but others have faded badly.

1924: This was a fine year for beaujolais and rhône but only moderate further north.

1925: Wines generally very thin, though some were quite agreeable, and the rhônes were best of all.

1926: This was an excellent year throughout the area, though the yield was very small, especially in Chablis. The wines of the Côte d'Or developed more rapidly than expected by those who prophesied a great future for them; but nevertheless they have shown great staying power. At present, wines of this vintage that have survived are speculative: some are delightful, but others tend to be rather hard and uninteresting.

1927: A good year for chablis, and quite good for other white burgundies. Elsewhere it was poor, though a few pleasant wines were produced in the Côte d'Or and Rhône valley.

1928: Very poor in Chablis, but elsewhere a great year giving red and white wines that have lasted well. The yield, however, was small.

1929: A very good year everywhere except in the Beaujolais and Mâconnais, where the wines were too hard. The wines of the Côte d'Or were even better than those of 1928, and the yield was also large. A year to delight growers and drinkers alike. Many of the 1928s and 1929s are still excellent, though unobtainable commercially.

1930: A good average year in Chablis and the Rhône, but elsewhere poor.

1931: A bad year. Some drinkable wines were grown in the Rhône valley, however.

1932: Another bad year.

1933: The yield in the north was only moderate and the quality of the wines was very variable: some of the best were excellent but others tended to be thin and acid. This year seems to have been more appreciated in England than in France. The wines of the Beaujolais and Rhône valley, however, received universal praise.

1934: A large yield was secured, and some *climats* of the Côte d'Or were notable for quantity rather than quality. But others produced very fine wines, and on the whole the vintage was a good one. Good examples of the 1933 and 1934 vintages are still admirable.

1935: Mediocre.

1936: Somewhat worse than 1935 in the north, but a good year for rhône.

1937: A good year, especially for chablis, but the wines of the Côte d'Or, like those of Bordeaux, were too hard and slow to develop; and some of the white burgundies were lacking in character.

1938: An average year in the north, but good for rhône. White wines generally better than reds.

1939: A very poor year in the north, but again good for rhône.

1940: A bad year.

1941: Another bad year.

1942: A good year for chablis and a good average year elsewhere, but the wines in general had little staying power.

1943: By no means outstanding but distinctly better than 1942, especially for white burgundies.

1944: An abundant yield of poor, thin wines.

1945: Severe frost greatly reduced the yield, making it practically zero in Chablis. But elsewhere throughout the whole area, the year was one of the greatest of all for quality. The wines are developing slowly and beautifully. Some of the red wines are still not at their best.

1946: Quite a good year, producing agreeable light wines that developed quickly, but it was completely overshadowed by 1945 and 1947.

1947: A great year throughout the area, both for quantity and quality, though some of the red wines are not lasting as well as was first expected, and others were spoilt by inexpert vinification, as it was very hot at vintage time. Many of the white wines are already becoming maderized.

1948: This was quite a good year throughout the burgundy area, even if not outstanding, but was poor for rhônes. Like the corresponding vintage in Bordeaux, the burgundies have failed to receive their due owing to the excellence of the 1947s and 1949s. Most of the wines are now past their best.

1949: A very great year for the red wines of the Côte d'Or and for chablis. The other white wines were good, though less great, and the rhônes tended to be coarse.

1950: Quite a good year for some white burgundies and for all rhônes, but red burgundies were very variable, and generally light. The yield was large.

1951: As far as red wines are concerned, there was a large yield, though the quality was poor. White wines did not even show a large yield, and that of chablis was very small.

1952: Another very good year in the north, though chablis was not outstanding. Rhône wines tended to be coarse. Most burgundies are now at about their best, though there is no hurry to drink the bigger red wines.

1953: A great year in the north but only mediocre in the Rhône valley. Red burgundies developed rather quickly and most of those from the Côte de Beaune are now tending to be past their best, though the great wines of the Côte de Nuits are still showing well. Some of the white burgundies tended to be dull, though others, including chablis, were good. The yield of chablis, however, was very low owing to frosts.

1954: A mediocre year but some quite good wines were made by those growers on the Côte d'Or who risked picking their grapes late. It was quite good for chablis.

1955: A very good year throughout the area. Most of the wines are ready for drinking, though there is plenty of life left in the best. The yield was not high, and in some areas it was very low, owing to frost and hail. Some of the English bottled red burgundies, however, suffered a malo-lactic fermentation in bottle and were spoilt.

1956: As far as red wines are concerned, in the north there was a very small yield of very poor quality, but the year was quite a good one in the Rhône valley. It was also a good year for chablis and some good white burgundies were grown on the Côte d'Or, though they needed to be selected with great care.

1957: The yield of chablis was minute, owing to frost, but elsewhere the year was a good one, and although some of the wines look as if they will enjoy a long life, most are at least ready for drinking. Some of its red wines were too big and lacking in finesse.

1958: Quantity rather than quality, but some quite good white wines were made.

1959: A great year both for quality and for quantity, though there was so much heat that some of the less skilful growers got into difficulty. The best wines, however, are amongst the best of the century and look as if they will have a very long life. The lighter wines are already mature.

1960: Generally speaking a bad year, though a few drinkable wines were made.

1961: A very good year, and if perhaps not as outstanding as the vintage in Bordeaux, many wines will well repay laying down.

1962: A very good year, both for red and white—marginally better than 1961—but the yield was small.

1963: For red burgundies this vintage was disastrous nor was it good for red rhônes, but white wines were distinctly better and some, especially chablis, were quite good.

1964: An abundant vintage providing good burgundies and very good rhône wines. This vintage is maturing quickly.

1965: Very poor for red burgundies of the Côte d'Or, mediocre for beaujolais. Some acceptable white wines were made, especially in Chablis. About average for rhônes.

1966: This vintage was quite good throughout Burgundy and the Rhône. The production of all burgundies was very high and that of chablis was exceptionally large. Production on the Rhône varied considerably from district to district, following spring frosts, but was generally well above average.

1967: Lighter than 1966 but the best white wines are quite elegant. Production was small, however, and not many really good red wines were grown.

1968: A complete failure, save perhaps for chablis and pouilly-fuissé.

1969: Throughout the whole of the vineyard complex from north to south, the yield was relatively small and the quality about average: rather light wines with the whites better than the reds. Prices were high, though, and burgundy prices astronomical. In such a vintage it only really pays to buy the finest wines as it is absurd to pay fine wine prices for the second rate.

CHAPTER 5

Champagne

~~~~~~~~~~~~~

There is nothing to compare with the sparkle of champagne: it is a metaphorical sparkle as well as a physical one. No other wine is so full of joy. It is the perfect wine for a party, and the supreme aperitif, especially in warm weather. It is wonderfully versatile, too, and tastes well with almost anything. But if it sounds too good to be true, it must be admitted that its gaiety hides one small danger: drink too much, and the hangover is terrible; moreover it brings with it an unquenchable thirst. Not everyone approves of champagne though: there are a few purists who deny that any wine should sparkle, and they dub it the wine of harlots. But if it is, there must be very few of us who are not on the side of the harlots.

The vineyards of Champagne are the most northerly of the great French vineyards, and only those of Germany lie further north in the whole of Europe. To grow wines in such a latitude is hazardous and difficult. It is only worth while owing to their exceptional delicacy and grace, and to the high price that this enables them to command.

It was enterprising, to say the least, for soldiers and colonists, who were used to the heat of Rome and to the strong wines of Tuscany, to think of planting vines so far north in their Empire; it speaks well of them as viticulturalists that the vines flourished and that wine was made; and one wonders what they thought of it when they had made it. For it was the Romans, inevitably, who brought the vine to the forest land of Champagne, after the decree of Domitian was withdrawn by Probus in A.D. 282. But not immediately: there were so many more promising areas that called for their attention. It is likely that about a hundred years elapsed

238

Soissons

R. Aisne

N

• Rheims

VALLÉE de l'ARDRE

PETIT MONTAGNE

• Verzy

MONTAGNE
de REIMS

VALLÉE de MARNE

• Vaudemange
• Ambonney
• Bouzy

Chateau-
Thierry

Epernay Ay

CÔTE de BLANCS

R. Marne

• Chalons-sur-Marne

• Vitry-le-François

R. Aube

R. Seine

Nogent-
sur-Seine

• Brienne
le-Château

• Troyes

Meurville

Bar-sur-Aube

Bar-sur-Seine

CHAMPAGNE

🍇 Main vineyards

0   50 km

before the Champagne vineyards were planted. And although the lightness and delicacy of their new wines might well have surprised them at first, their beauty was soon recognized. Apart from bringing the vine, the Romans did another great work that has proved a boon to modern champagne shippers: they mined chalk, and their ancient workings provide the basis of the great cellars that lie two to three hundred feet deep beneath the city of Rheims. Those of Pommery and Greno, alone, extend for some ten miles.

It almost goes without saying that the earliest of the great wine growers after the Romans were the Church and the Knights Templar. Amongst the greatest of them all was St. Remi, who baptized Clovis at Rheims in 494. His many miracles included one that ranks second only to that of the Marriage of Cana. One day, when he called upon a relation of his named Celia, he found that she was without wine, so he made the sign of the cross over an empty cask and it instantly became filled. He certainly had no need to perform such a miracle for his own benefit: his vineyards were many. And even in those early years wine was being shipped along the rivers to Rouen and overland as far as Flanders.[1]

If the early history is necessarily somewhat sketchy,[2] there can be no doubt that the vine continued to prosper in Champagne. As early as in 1275 King Edward I bought two casks of Rheims wine, and by the beginning of the fourteenth century there were already wine brokers at Rheims. But in the Middle Ages, champagne had no clear and separate identity: it was regarded as part of the wine of the Ile-de-France, and the growths that we now know as champagne were further defined as 'mountain' or 'river' wines. The wines of those days were very different from the sparkling champagnes that we know today: they were still and red, not unlike more southerly wines of Burgundy in style, though lighter both in character and in colour, owing to the more northerly climate. It is not surprising then, that both were often referred to in the same breath, and both 'flowed in rivers' at the coronations of King Charles IV in 1322 and King Philip VI in 1328.

The first Englishmen to drink champagne were the priests and

[1] Roger Dion, *Histoire de la Vigne et du Vin en France*, Paris, 1959.
[2] An exceptionally fine book, Patrick Forbes's *Champagne*, London, 1967, should be consulted for a more detailed account.

the pious, for Rheims was one of the earliest centres of Christianity in northern Europe. The army was not so very far behind, though, as Champagne was conquered by the great Henry V. But although Agincourt was a glorious victory, the king died young and the English rule was short, ill-inspired and unpopular, ending with our expulsion by Joan of Arc. And even when we were rulers of Rheims we made little use of our opportunities, for the soldiery preferred beer, and brewed it there. They thereby evidently ruined the digestions of those locals who took to it, for it is recorded that the apothecaries did a splendid trade in treacle; and the principal use of treacle in those days was to help down the brimstone. If the soldiery spurned the wine, however, their officers became addicted to it and even used it as a weapon. There is a tradition that when Epernay was facing one of its many sieges (and there are few cities with a more turbulent or disastrous history) on a hot summer's day the local commander sent forth a wagon load of wine along the road that led to the safety of Chalons. The French army swooped down on it. Rejoicing in such a delightful prize, they broached the barrels and slaked their thirst beneath the sun. The English gave them just long enough for the wine to do its work, and then the horsemen charged out of the city to gain an easy victory. The French had the last laugh, though, for Epernay eventually fell and they chose to be merciless. When Rheims fell, in its turn, the English retreated with as much wine as they could carry. Rheims had by no means seen the last of English soldiers though. In the Kaiser and Hitler wars we came as friends.

As a Christian centre of the first importance, and then as a scene of battle, Rheims was in a unique position for the fame of her wines to be spread throughout the world. Unfortunately, though, she was also quite landlocked, and being so far from the coast or a navigable river, champagne was at a disadvantage compared with other and lesser wines of the Ile-de-France. These wines, which were sold as *Vin de France*, were certainly imported into England as early as 1200, but it is impossible to say what proportion of them, if any, came from Champagne. Nevertheless there are local traditions that Henry VIII, Charles V of Spain, and François I of France all employed wine brokers at Ay, and that Pope Leo X had his own vineyard: there is still a strip known as Le Léon. Champagne certainly did reach this country, for a letter survives from the

French Admiral Bonnivet to Cardinal Wolsey, advising him of the dispatch of twenty casks of wine from Ay. But it was expensive—partly owing to the high costs of transport—and imports were both few and casual until the seventeenth century.

In 1516, the wine growers became plagued by insects, particularly by varieties known as *bruches* and *éruches*. Finding their simple human methods of pesticide ineffective, they appealed to the church, and the secretary to the Bishop of Troyes signed, in the name of the Lord, an order for the insects to depart within six days, under pain of malediction and anathema. In exchange for this deliverance, the inhabitants were to devote themselves to good works and to pious prayers, to pay their tithes without fraud, and to abstain from blaspheming and from all other sins, especially from public scandals.

An engraving of 1635 shows Rheims as a much smaller and much more beautiful city than it is today. Dominated by its magnificent cathedral, its walls were still intact; they surrounded it completely and were decorated and strengthened with innumerable little towers. The great wine houses were still things of the future but the seeds of their trade had already been sown. Wines from the growers around Rheims, Epernay and Ay were fashionable, and sales were brisk. Champagne was popular with the French court and it was the favourite of King Henri IV (1589–1610). It was he and his courtiers who gave the name *champagne* to the wines of Rheims and Epernay, and so distinguished them for all time from the inferior growths of the Ile-de-France. After his death, its popularity continued, rivalled only by that of burgundy. It had by then become so well established in England that, before the century was ended, it attracted the sincerest form of flattery: when George Hartman published *The Family Physitian* in 1606 he informed the reader how to 'make artificial Champagne comparable with the best of that which is made in that province'. Champagne was worth imitating. With the newly-named wine in immense demand, both in the French and in the English courts, anyone who was able to supply it was sure of his fortune. Prices began to rise dramatically.

To a large extent this popularity stemmed from the good offices of Saint-Evremond. Charles Marguetel de Saint-Denis, Seigneur de Saint-Evremond, was one of the most remarkable personalities of the seventeenth century. Soldier, philosopher, poet, playwright, satirist and courtier, he had originally come to England as a member of the French embassy that was sent to congratulate King Charles II on his restoration. A year later, following the discovery of an unfortunate letter to Charles Créqui—a letter full of wit and sarcasm, in which he attacked Mazarin over the Peace of the Pyrenees—he was banished. He already had many friends in England, though, and he was received here in a manner becoming his rank. His charm, his wit and his wisdom won him the friendship of all the greatest courtiers, scholars and writers of his age, and, as a cultivated Frenchman, he was soon the arbiter of taste. Who better to consult on a matter of wine? And his preference was for champagne rather than for burgundy.

While Saint-Evremond was singing the praises of champagne in England, its greatest champion and grower in France was the Marquis de Sillery. He was blessed with the two things that really mattered: popularity at court and some of the finest wines in Champagne. They were not, however, grown in the village from which he took his title: most of his vineyards were in the parish of Verzenay, where the soil is even better. His holdings, moreover, were large and he could afford to make his wines in the best possible way. Happily, too, he had friends amongst the English aristocracy, such as Lord Crofts, who was also a friend of Saint-Evremond. It was through Lord Crofts that he was able to supply wine to the fifth Earl of Bedford at Woburn Abbey, and it was in all probability his wines, rather than those of the village, that filled the handsome decanters labelled *Sillery* in the seventeenth and eighteenth centuries.

The great wine rivalry of the seventeenth and eighteenth centuries was between burgundy and champagne, both of which had their vociferous and poetic champions. Not only were the wine growers and their laureates involved, but there was also a fierce and lengthy dispute between the doctors of the faculties of Beaune and Rheims on the healthiness of their wines. A friendly rivalry between wine growers never does any harm: it keeps them both up to scratch. But the rivalry between champagne and burgundy was not always so very friendly. Perhaps the wisest poets were those who wrote verses like this:

Bold Burgundian ever glories
With stout Renois to get mellow,
Each well filled with vinous lore is
Each a jolly tippling fellow.

(Anon., tr. H. Vizetelly)

Had champagne not completely changed its style since those days, the controversy might well be with us yet. But it is a pity that it ever began. The more northerly climate of Champagne could hardly hope to produce a red wine to match the strength and flavour of the well-established burgundies. It was a mistake ever to attempt an imitation, and the high prices which fashion had enabled the red wines to command could never have been maintained, save, perhaps, for the greatest growths, which were a small minority of the whole. On the evidence of the few still red wines grown in Champagne that I have tasted, I should back the Burgundian every time. But modern conditions are very different from those prevailing in the seventeenth century. In those days the wines were drunk from the wood, and the ability of burgundy to mature in bottle was unknown and irrelevant. When drunk so young, the lighter and more northern wine may often have been preferable. Moreover the still wines are no longer made from grapes grown on the finest sites.

It may well be that the Champenoises themselves had some doubts. From the second quarter of the seventeenth century they went out of their way to produce new styles of wine that would have an appeal of their own. André L. Simon[1] lists: *oeil de perdrix*, *cerise*, *couleur de miel*, *gris* and *blanc*. *Vin gris*, which was near white, but with a touch of pink, was a novelty in 1660, and wine that was truly colourless did not follow for about another ten years. It was these wines on which the continuing prosperity of champagne depended, and it was these that fetched the highest prices at the beginning of the eighteenth century. The old wines still had their supporters, though. They were particularly popular in the Low Countries, and King William III brought the taste with him when he came to England in 1689.

White wines may have been made from grapes grown in the 'river' vineyards as early as the beginning of the seventeenth

---

[1] André L. Simon, *The History of Champagne*, London, 1962.

century, for those of Ay are mentioned in Estienne and Liebault's
L'Agriculture et Maison Rustique (1620); but it is uncertain just
how white they were and what kind of grape was grown. There is
no reason to believe that they were white wines fermented from
black grapes; and it is wines of this kind that form the basis of the
greatest champagnes today. Most of the wine then grown in
Champagne was still red: the renowned wines of the Montagne de
Reims, which fought for supremacy with those of Burgundy. The
lighter styles of wine, particularly the white wines, did not age or
travel well, and they were shipped young. In that northerly climate,
where cold weather followed swiftly after the vintage, fermentation
was arrested by the cold before it was complete. It was this that
gave the wine its sparkle. When the weather grew warmer again,
the ferments went on where they had left off, and more carbon
dioxide gas was evolved. This can happen with any wine, but with
some wines it happens more easily than with others. Some wines,
moreover, tend to retain their gas and to give it off slowly, keeping
their sparkle for quite a time. Champagne is paramount in both
these respects. According to an Italian writer of the fifteenth
century[1] the strong and foaming wine of Champagne was found so
injurious that Henry V was obliged, after the battle of Agincourt,
to forbid its use in his army, excepting when tempered with water.
In the seventeenth century, Sir George Etherege, in his comedy
The Man of Mode, wrote:

> To the Mall and the Park,
> Where we love till 'tis dark,
> Then sparkling Champagne
> Puts an end to their reign;
> It quickly recovers
> Poor languishing lovers,
> Makes us frolic and gay, and drowns all sorrow;
> But, alas, we relapse again on the morrow.

And George Farquhar, in his first play, *Love and a Bottle*, said of
champagne 'how it puns and quibbles in the glass!'. The only thing
necessary to preserve the sparkle was to bottle the wine at exactly
the right time, during its first or second fermentation, and to drive
home a strong, tight cork.

[1] Titi Livii Foro-Juliensis, *Vita Henrici Quinti*, quoted by Henry Vizetelly,
A History of Champagne, London, 1882.

It is an extraordinary thing that the earliest references to the use of cork to seal wine bottles suggest that the invention might have been English; and it came into use during the reign of Elizabeth I. In 1530, Palsgrave used the phrase: 'Stoppe the bottell with a cork', and by Shakespeare's time it was clearly established. In *As You Like It* the impatient Rosalind says to Celia:

'I prithee tell me who it is quickly and speak apace. I would thou couldst stammer, that thou mightest pour this conceal'd man out of thy mouth, as wine comes out of a narrow mouth'd bottle—either too much at once, or none at all. I prithee, take the cork out of thy mouth, that I may drink thy tidings.'

Cork had been used by the ancient Greeks for stopping their amphorae, but the secret had been lost for centuries, and the value of cork had not been realized by French wine growers, even though the cork oak actually grows in France. They can hardly be blamed, though: with the demise of the amphora, it would have been of little use until the advent of the modern bottle in the latter half of the seventeenth century. Sparkling *vin gris* from Champagne was being drunk in London during the 1660s, and the credit for its effervescence must be given to English vintners, who had corks and who evidently contrived to put them into the bottles at exactly the right time. It was customary for noblemen to have their vast purchases of wine bottled—when they were bottled at all—in their own cellars; and one of the Duke of Bedford's accounts, dating from 1665, shows that bottles and corks were procured in time to bottle some champagne when it was only six months old and still fermenting. Such wines would not have been sparkling in the way that modern champagnes sparkle: there would have been a much lower pressure of gas. They have been described as 'creaming' rather than sparkling. They would have resembled the *vinho verde* of Portugal that is becoming so popular today, or the *pétillant* white wine that is being imported from Luxembourg, save that the champagne wines, with their tendency to a second fermentation and their ability to retain gas, would have shown this creaming quality more markedly. A contemporary report suggests that English vintners actually increased the sparkle of the second fermentation by adding molasses, thereby anticipating the modern process of chaptalization.

By the seventeenth century, then, clear sparkling champagne had very nearly arrived. All that was needed was a man with the genius to take the last leap; and that man was already to hand. Dom Pérignon was born in 1639. He chose to follow a religious life and entered the Benedictine Abbey of Hautvillers, near Epernay. In 1668 he was appointed cellarer. It has often been claimed that he 'put the bubbles in'; but that, of course, is nonsense: they were already there. He did manage to keep them in, though; and he also made better wines, both still and sparkling, than had ever been made before. To keep the bubbles in, he used cork in place of the hemp dipped in oil that had previously given a temporary seal to the bottles, and which naturally let all the gas out. He achieved his quality by selecting grapes from the various vineyards and by combining them to produce a wine of perfect balance. His wine, moreover, besides being without any tinge of false colour, was completely free from sediment. How he achieved this is unknown. Some unscrupulous wine growers claimed to have penetrated his secret and one of them, a M. Bidet, of Ay, published an extraordinary recipe that included the use of sugar candy, peaches, cinnamon and nutmeg. This may well have given a pleasing wine cup, but as a way of making champagne his recipe was a nonsense. Dom Grossard, the last *procureur* of the Abbey before it was secularized at the time of the French Revolution, gave the lie to M. Bidet but he did not disclose the secret:[1]

'You know, Sir, that it was the famous Dom Pérignon ... who discovered the secret of making sparkling white wine, and how to get it clear without having to decant the bottles, as it is done by our big merchants, more often twice than only once, and by us never. Before his time our monks only knew how to make straw coloured or grey wines; and it is also to Dom Pérignon that we owe the cork as now used. To bottle wine, instead of a cork made of cork bark, one only used hemp and after it was dipped in oil it served as a stopper. It was to the "marriage" of our wines that they owed their goodness; and this Dom Pérignon towards the end of his days became blind. He had instructed in his secret of fining the wines a certain Brother Philip. ... When the vintage was near, Dom

---

[1] Letter dated October 25th, 1821, to a M. d'Herbès, of Ay, quoted by Henry Vizetelly, *A History of Champagne*, London, 1882, and by André L. Simon, *The History of Champagne*, London, 1962.

Pérignon would say to this Brother: "Go and bring me some grapes from Prières, Côtes-à-Bras, Barillets, Quartiers de Clos Ste-Hélène, etc." Without being told which were the grapes before him, he would tell the Brother: "These are grapes from such and such a vineyard and they must be 'married'[1] to those of such and such another vineyard." And he made no mistake. . . . I do assure you, Sir, that never did we add sugar to our wines, and you can say so to all whenever you happen to be in company when the subject arises.'

Dom Pérignon had not kept his secret to himself, but had passed it on to his successor. Eventually it had reached Dom Grossard, but as the Abbey was no more, there was no one else to pass it on to, and when the last *procureur* died, it was lost. Its loss, however, was not as tragic as it may sound, for by then the merchants had discovered the modern system of *dégorgement*[2] which worked perfectly. Dom Pérignon first made his great sparkling wine in about 1697, but the exact date is uncertain. He died in 1715, and all who knew him were able to say 'He loved the poor and he made excellent wine.' Has any man a finer epitaph?

Dom Pérignon had the advantage of working in one of the few wine-growing areas where bottles were plentiful and cheap; for wood was used in the making of glass, and there was plenty of that in Champagne. Sparkling wine, of course, *must* be bottled, as wooden casks would let the gas out. But there was one difficulty to overcome: in France it was illegal to transport wine in bottles, as it was thought that this would encourage fraud. This crippled the trade in the new and popular sparkling wine, and in 1724 representatives of the city of Rheims petitioned the government to amend the law. This was done in 1728.[3]

If sparkling champagne was first bottled in the pure and celibate atmosphere of a monastery, it was poured out, as often as not, in a very different atmosphere. It became popular at the Court of the Duc d'Orléans, the dissolute regent of France (1715–1723), and it remained popular when his nephew, Louis XV, came of age; for it was the favourite wine of the king's mistress Madame de Mailly,

[1] In the letters as quoted from the two sources there occurs a discrepancy as to whether the grapes were 'married', or the wines fermented from them. I have not seen the original. Today the wines are blended to make a *cuvée*.

[2] See p. 52.

[3] Roger Dion, *Histoire de la Vigne et du Vin en France*, Paris, 1959.

the predecessor of Madame de Pompadour and of Madame du Barry. Marshall de Saxe was provided with sparkling champagne by his mistress Mademoiselle de Navarre. And so it goes on: always the mistress. It would seem that one can love a wife over a cup of tea, but a mistress demands champagne. In those days, mistresses and champagne had a certain affinity; for both were 'low' and both were fashionable. Wine lovers did not care for the sparkling variety at all. As late as 1775, Sir Edward Barry[1] was able to write of it thus:

'For some years the *French* and *English* have been particularly fond of the sparkling, frothy *Champaigns*. The former have almost entirely quitted that depraved taste; nor does it now so much prevail here. They used to mix some ingredients to give them that quality; but this is unnecessary, as they are all too apt spontaneously to run into that state; but whoever chooses to have such wines may be assured that they will acquire it, by bottling them any time after the vintage, before the month of the next May; and the most sure rule to prevent that disposition, is not to bottle them before the *November* following. This rule has been confirmed by repeated experiments.'

Bertin du Rocheret, who was the greatest grower and exporter in Champagne during the eighteenth century, was no keener on the sparkling variety of his wine. He approved of wine that was *crémant*, but he deplored the craze for a wine that he described as 'frenzied', which was so often made from wine grown in inferior vineyards around Avize and sold for a price out of all proportion to its quality. To him, it was an 'abominable drink': sparkle was a merit only in the least of wines, and more appropriate to beer. He sold it reluctantly, when he had to. Nor were the English wine merchants any more enamoured to it. In 1788, when Messrs. Charbonnell, Moody and Walker, of London, ordered wine from M. Moët they stipulated that 'the wine must be of good quality, not too charged with liqueur, but of excellent taste and not at all sparkling'.

The great sparkling wine that was to delight connoisseurs was clearly on its way; but equally clearly it had not arrived. And it appears that the commercial growers came nowhere near to

---

[1] Sir Edward Barry, *Observations, Historical, Critical, and Medical on the Wines of the Ancients and . . . Modern wines*, London, 1775.

equalling the quality achieved by the great Dom Pérignon. There were many lessons still for them to learn.

It was not, in fact, possible to import sparkling champagne into England in commercial quantities during the eighteenth century, as sparkling wines must be imported in bottles, and, from 1728 to 1802, wine could only be imported in this way with a special permit. Ironically, the English introduced this measure in the same year in which the corresponding French one was repealed. But it did not mean that *no* sparkling champagne was imported. The prohibition was not absolute; the diplomatic bag was notoriously abused; and there was Crown privilege; but the effect of all this was to keep champagne—even had it been cheap and abundant—a perquisite of the rich and fashionable. Nor did the fiscal policies of successive governments do anything to help: the discrimination against French wines, and the official encouragement of the Portuguese, backed by the Methuen Treaty, has already been referred to and will be referred to again. There was no general market in the sparkling wine.

The name of Bertin du Rocheret has already briefly been mentioned: it is a name which perhaps meant more than any other in the champagne trade during the eighteenth century. Adam Bertin, Sieur du Rocheret, was born in Rheims in 1662. He owned vineyards in the valley of the Marne and became a wine merchant at Epernay. Compared with the other merchants and growers, however, he had one great advantage: he was an aristocrat. His position gave him contacts in the French court, in the Army, in England, in the Low Countries, in Germany and even in Russia. And he was a man of enterprise. He made full use of his position to found a business which his eldest son was further to develop. Philippe Valentin Bertin du Rocheret was born in Epernay in 1693 and, like his father, he became in his turn the most important merchant in Champagne. He was the first to have his own agent in England. Although he certainly sold sparkling champagne, he did not approve of it. The wines he sent to England were chiefly those of Ay. He sent them shortly after the vintage and he recommended early bottling; so in all probability, when most of them were drunk, they were *crémant*—continuing the taste of the previous century. It was he, more than anyone else, who sold wine to the fashionable world in London and in the spas of Bath and Tunbridge Wells, where his good wines must have done far more for the health of the wealthy invalids than did the local waters.

At this time the great brand names that are so familiar today did not exist, but they were soon to follow, for several of the great champagne houses were about to be founded; Ruinart Pére et Fils in 1729, Moët and Chandon in 1743, Lanson Père et Fils in 1750 (the name was originally Delamotte Père et Fils but it was changed in 1838), Veuve Cliquot in 1772, and the original firm of Heidsieck, from which the three firms that now bear the name are descended, in 1785. These firms, and others that were founded later, were naturally quick to follow Bertin du Rocheret's good example, and Moët, for instance, sent a traveller to England as early as 1780.

The international trade in champagne had been fairly established, and it was not confined to the Old World; for George Washington himself drank champagne in New York in 1790. Soon the demand boomed, and the merchants were well placed to satisfy it. But before this could happen, the quality of the wine had to be improved. There can be no doubt that *some* first-class wines were already being made—perhaps comparable with those which we enjoy today—but there can equally be no doubt that these were the exceptions: several important advances had to be made before they could become the rule. It is hard to know which was the most important. They all helped, but two of them, perhaps, helped more than the others: chaptalization, and the work of François. Chaptalization has already been described. Briefly, it consists of adding sugar to the must before fermentation, so that the wine has sufficient alcohol even in those relatively sunless years when it would otherwise be thin and lifeless. Champagne, being so far to the north, suffers many such years, and from all accounts the old still white wines, save those of the very best vintages, tended to be green and hard; and they did not travel well. Too many casks 'went wrong', and this, understandably enough, made the wine unpopular with foreign merchants. In Champagne, chaptalization has been practised very successfully since the beginning of the nineteenth century, though it is less used there than in some more southerly districts, as champagne is a blended wine, and the thinness of one can be countered by blending with another of coarser character. In good years this is much preferable to chaptalization and it is the practice. In poorer years, however, chaptalization can be a saviour.

François was a chemist at Châlons-sur-Marne. In 1836 he published the result of some experiments which ended one of the greatest difficulties of the wine shippers: the curse of broken bottles. At the beginning of the century, champagne was made by guesswork. Certainly one can dignify the technique by calling it an art rather than a science; but a science it certainly was not. And getting the right pressure inside a bottle of sparkling wine is an aspect of enology where science is vital. *La casse*, or breakages, seldom amounted to less than ten per cent. Forty per cent was a more usual figure, and sometimes it rose to as much as eighty. It is not surprising that wine shippers regarded the still wines as their staple trade and the sparkling wines as a pure speculation. What is worse, there were most breakages in good years when the wine would have fetched a high price. It was this which gave the clue. As early as in the eighteenth century, growers had begun to realize that there was some connection between the amount of sugar in the wine and the gas evolved. It was not until the work of François, however, that this was evaluated. The growers could then blend their *cuvées* to produce exactly the right amount of gas. Breakages were brought down to manageable proportions and the trade became economically worth while. The final stage came almost a century later, when the mechanically made bottle, with its great strength, cut breakages from five per cent to less than one.

These were great changes, but others also played their part. They included the process of *dégorgement*, whereby the sediment is removed from the bottle. The previous method of *dépotage* consisted of decanting the wine off its sediment and this necessarily entailed a considerable loss of gas. But before *dégorgement* could work perfectly, it was necessary to persuade the finely-divided sediment to cling to the cork. At first the bottles were placed downwards with their necks protruding through holes in a horizontal table. This was not a complete success: the sediment settled loosely and some of it stayed in the wine. The modern method, using A-shaped shaking tables, or *pupitres*,[1] was invented in 1818 by one Müller, an employee of the widow Clicquot. For some

[1] See p. 52.

years she managed to keep it a secret, but eventually it leaked out and now it is used universally. Finally there came the process of *dosage*, following the *dégorgement*, which enabled the wine to be prepared with exactly the right degree of sweetness for each market.

The new wine had its influential advocates, including Lord Byron, who wrote in Canto XV, verse 65 of *Don Juan*:

> And then there was champagne with foaming whirls,
> As white as Cleopatra's melted pearls.

But its popularity with the world at large did not come overnight. The still wine, particularly the red, remained the mainstay of the trade. At about this time, when the shippers were all set to conquer the world markets, there came a disaster which totally disrupted the trade: the Napoleonic wars. The export of wine was cut off and merchants became bankrupt. The Prussians got drunk at Epernay. The Cossacks ravaged the villages of the Mountain and wine that they could not carry off at Sillery flooded the cellars when they staved the barrels. When Napoleon eventually swooped down upon Rheims, the Russian officers were so drunk that they could neither fight nor flee. Cossacks even put champagne in buckets (according to tradition) and shared it with their horses. At the time things looked hopeless, but in the long run this apparent disaster probably did more good than harm; for when the wine was exported again, the invaders remembered it and bought it. The Russian market became one of the most valuable and the wine was specially fortified and sweetened to suit the rigorous climate.

Even so, exports remained inconsiderable for the first half of the century and consisted mostly of the still red wines. As late as the 1840s and '50s, the champagne imported into England was 'rich', and that alone was enough to limit its appeal, though it made life easier for the shippers: to taste well when it is dry, a wine has to be very good, but sweetness will mask its deficiencies. Most of the champagne at that time, moreover, was drunk when it was, by modern standards, very young, and little of it was kept for more than two or three years after the vintage. Some of the rich wines of the great vintages, such as 1834, 1842 and 1846, could and did keep very well; but these were the exceptions. They were notable exceptions, though: in 1871 Moët 1846 fetched 89s. and Clicquot

1846, 86s. a dozen at Christie's. The taste for the rich wines died hard: to this day they remain popular in the northern countries and in France itself. In England, the provinces adopted the new taste for drier wines later than did London. And the sweet wines continued to have their champions. Earlier in the century, before really dry wines had become available, Canning, who was a passionate devotee of sweet champagne, declared that anyone who claimed to prefer the dry wine was an unmitigated liar.[1] 'Dry' champagne was shipped by Clicquot and by Heidsieck in about 1857, but both of these would be considered far from dry today. It was not unil the magnificent vintage of 1874 that most of the leading shippers sold *brut* champagne in this country, and the really dry wine came into its own. The 1874 vintage, which followed some very poor years, was, indeed, perhaps the finest of the century, and the wines, which had an unusually dark colour, sometimes with a slightly pink sheen, became so famous that prices soared up. For instance Pommery's *brut* 1874, the original price of which, in France, was 71s. a dozen, fetched 270s. when sold by auction at Christie's in 1887.[2] It is this slight pink coloration which is said to have made pink champagne fashionable—a whim that still obtains in some circles.

The turning point in the popularity of champagne came in the 1840s: it was then that the still wines became rapidly less popular and the sparkling wines more than took their place. When the change did come, it was rapid: sales increased from less than four and a half million bottles in 1844 to nearly fourteen million in 1869; and most of the increase is attributable to England and the U.S.A. There were three reasons: fashion had changed, the wine had greatly improved, and in 1861 Gladstone finally sealed its popularity by ending the discrimination against French wines. Moreover, once sales increased, the shippers were able to lower their prices very considerably, so that sales snowballed. Despite capricious fashion and grasping chancellors, champagne has never looked back. By 1869 it was so much a popular drink that the great music-hall hit of that year was George Leybourne's *Champagne Charlie*—an immortal song.

Mr. Gladstone's wise budget had made champagne no longer the

[1] Quoted by P. Morton Shand, *A Book of French Wines*, London, 1960.
[2] André L. Simon, *The History of Champagne*, London, 1962.

perquisite of the rich: Mr. Pooter was able to afford his Jackson Frères,[1] and fashion, far from deserting champagne, made it more and more popular in the naughty nineties and in the splendour of Edwardian Europe. Between 1861 and 1890, sales in England rose from three million to nine million bottles, and world sales were not far short of twenty-two million. The greatest age of all for champagne was from 1889 to 1908, for not only was the demand enormous, but there was a succession of fine vintages to help meet it: 1889, 1892, 1899, 1900, 1904 and 1906. Only one vintage proved eccentric: the 1895. There had been some mildew, but the weather was good at the vintage, and the wine seemed to be quite good—at first. But then it went wrong and some of it threw a smoky, blue deposit. The shippers promptly replaced all that had gone out of condition—save one lot. Oscar Philippe, who owned the Cavour Restaurant in Leicester Square, flatly refused to send it back. Instead he sold his '95s in two grades: thick or clear, at the same price. He maintained that the 'thick' tasted just as good, and his customers drank all he had.

Towards the end of the century, though, when trade was the best it had ever been, champagne suffered the scourge that had already affected all the other main wine-growing areas: the phylloxera. It was first noticed nearby at the hamlet of Tréloup in 1890. By 1892, five acres in the Marne had been affected, and slowly it spread: at first very slowly; deceptively slowly. In 1898 there were still less than a hundred acres affected, and perhaps it was this that made some of the peasant growers complaisant and inactive. The more industrious and intelligent of them fought diligently, however, using as their chief weapon carbon disulphide. But this was dangerous to handle as well as expensive. Many of the peasant growers could not be bothered, and it is thanks to their attitude that the phylloxera, when it did begin to spread, spread rapidly. By 1911, about sixteen thousand acres were affected. Had all the growers acted together and at once, it may well have been kept in check as it was in the Rhine valley until the last war. But in the event the stupidity of the peasants made little difference: the campaign would have been lost anyhow when war broke out,

[1] If in fact he was drinking Jacquesson champagne, he was drinking one of the best brands then available. If not, the law of passing off might well have been invoked.

for lack of labour and chemicals. Virtually all the vineyards had eventually to be replanted, using American stocks: only a very few ungrafted vines remain and those only in vineyards on exceptionally sandy soil.

The Kaiser war was disastrous for champagne—as for so many other things. In August 1914 the vineyards were overrun by the Germans, but they did not stay for long, as they were thrust back in the battle of the Marne in September. That first assault caused relatively little damage, but more soon followed. The vineyards were near the front line throughout the rest of the war. Communication trenches were dug through them; they suffered from shellfire and from poison gas; above all they suffered from neglect, for hardly any vineyard work could be done under such conditions, and there was no labour. By the end of the war three-quarters of the best vineyards had been destroyed, and in this country the wine's good name suffered from the importation, at inflated prices, of inferior wines that were never intended for anything but local sale. On the lighter side, a very curious thing happened to the wild boars that used to provide sport in the Montagne de Reims: they disappeared. It is said that they were put to flight by the gunfire, and as soon as peace returned, so did the boars. But no one knows where they were in the meantime.

The task of re-establishing the vineyards was a very expensive one, and then the great slump arrived. To make matters worse, prohibition in the United States and communism in Russia had destroyed two of the best markets. The champagne shippers had a dreadful time and some were ruined. During the 1930s trade gradually improved, but then came the Hitler war. There followed years of occupation, with no export markets save Germany; and there was a dreadful shortage of all materials, such as fertilizers, bottles and corks. A great deal of wine, moreover, was requisitioned. Villainous as this was, though, it was done with some intelligence. One shipper told me that the German officer in charge had himself been in the wine trade, and that before the war he had been German agent for one of the *grands marques*. He was no more disagreeable than he had to be, and when he wanted some wine which was to be sent somewhere where it would almost certainly be ruined—such as to the Russian front—he would say so; and then he did not notice if he was given trash. When it was for the mess, though, it had to be good. Certainly a lot of wine was lost that way, but French cunning managed to hide away a lot more in the vast maze of underground tunnels, and when peace at last came, things were not quite as bad as they might have been. It may be, though, that my informant had an unusually easy time during the war: things were certainly much more difficult for others. Patrick Forbes relates, for example, how the Comte de Vogué was sentenced to death and spent the war years from 1942 in a concentration camp, though the death sentence was never carried out. It is even said that the Germans had the bright idea of blowing all the cellars up when they left the town, but mercifully this was averted by the rapid arrival of the American liberating troops. The recovery after the war was rapid—more so than anyone dared hope at the time, for by the end of the war the champagne houses were desperately short of money as well as of wine, and the political situation was very difficult.

The countryside of Champagne is pleasant enough, but not much more. I cannot agree with André Simon that '. . . nowhere in France, or anywhere else in the world, is there land comparable to that of the old province of Champagne for the variety of its natural beauty . . .'. I would rather agree with Warner Allen that it lacks gaiety and light-heartedness. The landscape is certainly very agreeable in a rather English style; but Rheims, apart from its cathedral and some fine old buildings, is as dull as it is prosperous. It is northern and dour. But my own sympathies are always with the south.

After the French Revolution, the old province of Champagne was divided into four *départements*, and parts of it were also included in four further adjacent *départements*. All of these grow wine, but by no means all the wine they grow is entitled to the *appellation* champagne, which is now confined to certain clearly delimited areas where the soil is suitable. These vineyards are in three *départements*: the Marne, the Aube and the Aisne, but the greatest of all are those of the Marne. The finest soil is generally found about half-way down the slopes of the hills, and it consists of belemite-laden chalk that is covered by a chalky top soil that may be anything from a few inches to several yards deep.

The great vineyards fall naturally into two divisions: those of the mountain and those of the river. The Montaigne de Reims is scarcely a mountain. Crowned with forest—the home of the famous wild boars—it rises steeply from the plain to give a fine panorama; but it does not rise to any very great height. André Simon has likened its shape to that of a flat iron, the point of which faces Châlons-sur-Marne, and I can think of no better simile. Around it, all the slopes are planted with vines, but not all of these give the famous moutain wines: only those on the slopes that face Rheims and the River Vesle. The southern side, facing Epernay and the River Marne, together with the vineyards on the other side of the Marne valley, give those that are known as river or valley wines.

The vineyards are divided into six categories, beginning with the *hors classé catégorie*, then the *première catégorie*, and so on, down to the *cinquième catégorie*. The classification matters greatly to the growers, for at the beginning of the vintage each year representatives of the merchants and growers meet to discuss the price to be paid for the *hors classé*. Then each of the other classes attracts a fixed proportion of this: as much as ninety to ninety-eight per cent for the *première* and as little as fifty to fifty-eight per cent for the *cinquième*. The *hors classé* vineyards are, for the most part, on the Montagne. While many of the great shippers themselves own vineyards, most are still in the hands of small growers: there are fourteen thousand in the Marne, many with less than an acre. The greatest growths of all are those of Verzenay, Verzy, Mailly, Sillery and Beaumont-sur-Vesle, followed by those at Ludes, Chigny-les-Roses, Rilly-la-Montaigne, Villers-Allerand, Villers-Marmery and Trepail. It will be seen from the map that all these are towards the apex of the mountain 'flat iron'. At the tip of the 'flat iron' come the *hors classé* wines of Bouzy, Ambonnay and Louvois. Further back, where the vineyards face Rheims, the quality is less distinguished, and this area is known as *La Petite Montaigne*.

Of the river wines, the greatest are those of Ay, Mareuil-sur-Ay and Dizy, followed by Cumières and Hautvillers. Further to the south, beyond Epernay and across the valley of the River Marne, comes the *Côte des Blancs* which, as its name suggests, specializes in growing white grapes. Its place is an important one, as the lighter wines grown there add much to the elegance of champagne. Its leading growths are found around Cramant, Avize, Oger and

Le Mesnil-sur-Oger, the wines of Avize and Cramant being *hors classé*.

There can be no doubt as to where the great vineyards are, and very little doubt as to the good ones. Only when it comes to the border-line cases—those that are entitled to call their wines champagne, but only just—can there be much dispute. And dispute there has been. It is never easy to draw a line geographically. Notoriously, in all wine-growing countries, local peasants regard their own wines as second to none, and one must always make allowance for those who feel quite genuinely that their thin and wretched wines are equal to the greatest: it is the wine growers' equivalent of poetic licence. But the geographical inexactitude which champagne shippers allowed themselves at the turn of the century went far beyond this. Neither perversity nor ignorance, but only avarice, could explain it. Between 1906 and 1910 there were a series of disastrous vintages and more wine was sold than was grown to an extent, on average, of nearly twelve million bottles a year. Wines were imported from far, far away. Some shippers did not import wines but the actual grapes grown cheaply in the Midi, which were then pressed in Champagne to impart an air of wholly false authenticity. This competition caused the price of the local grapes to fall disastrously, and the small growers, who had counted themselves rich only a few years before, were faced with bankruptcy. The remedy was an obvious one: strict delimitation of the wine-producing zone. This had already been achieved in Bordeaux, despite the opposition of growers in adjacent regions. In Champagne, however, the position was much more difficult. The champagne area was officially defined by decree as early as in 1908, but this proved ineffective. The most reputable houses would only use the finest Marne wines even had they been permitted to use others. But the mushroom firms of no standing, who were profiteering by the fashion for champagne, were not to be deterred by a law which, in the form in which it then stood, could not be enforced; and although ninety per cent of the shippers supported the decree, it was useless without the support of the other ten. The protagonists of the scheme wanted to exclude all save the vineyards of the Marne, but growers from further afield, particularly those from the Aube, protested vigorously. They had been selling their wine as champagne for as long as anyone could remember. It was grown in the old province of Champagne, they argued, and all wines so grown should be entitled to the name. The proposed delimitation would even exclude the old capital of the province— Troyes. It was absurd! In the face of such apparently sane, reasonable, resolute and unanswerable opposition, the government gave up the struggle and, in April 1911, the deputies from the Aube tabled a motion that the delimitation decree be abandoned. It was an ironical situation, for M. Monis, who had been instrumental in securing the delimitation of Bordeaux, was President of the Council.

The difficulties and apprehensions of the government did nothing to appease the wrath of the ruined growers, and they took the law into their own hands. There had already been warnings that they would do so. Following the disastrous vintage of 1909, when some of the peasants had been unable to sell their grapes even at panic prices, there had been angry protests against the 'foreign' wines. In 1910, four hundred growers stormed the Epernay goods yard and staved sixty casks of Midi wine. Two lorries laden with at least five hundred casks of wine were stopped at Hautvillers and the wine was poured on to the road. Another lorry was driven into the Marne. And merchants' cellars had been wrecked. It is therefore not surprising that the imminent abandonment of the decree caused riots to break out. The signal was given by rockets and bells, and the peasants swarmed into Ay, where they laid waste the establishments of the principal offenders, and others who had not offended at all. It was a scene of mob violence, and they did not stop short of arson. Some of the damage, moreover, was quite uncharacteristic of the local people and the shippers claimed that professional agitators had been sent in from the General Confederation of Labour in Paris. For instance no peasant in the wine countries would ever think of attacking the vines: they would as soon attack a child. Yet the rioters destroyed vineyards at Ay; and another at Dizy, which was owned by a famous firm in Epernay, was totally destroyed. It had been protected against late frosts by a covering of straw, and the rioters set fire to this in several places, so that the fire spread throughout it.

Troops who were poured into the area were met with far from passive resistance. Barricades were hastily erected to keep them out, and when they did enter a town, they were welcomed with a shower of bottles thrown from the rooftops. Their intervention caused more misery to the innocent shippers than comfort to the *fraudeurs*. The authorities thought the reputable and respected houses were safe and concentrated the guards on the premises of the notorious; but the mob, deprived of its rightful objective, gave vent to its wrath on the innocent and set fire to their premises. Lamentable though the action of the peasants undoubtedly was, it certainly proved effective. The most urgent reform was to set up *magasins séparés*, in which wine imported from other regions could be kept apart from the true champagne, and this followed in 1912. The delimitation of the new zone took longer. The principle of delimitation was reaffirmed on June 17th, 1911, but the preparation of the final text was delayed by the war and it did not appear until 1927, nor was it completed in its present form until 1942. It is shown in the accompanying map and it has been very strictly adhered to. No wines brought in from outside can be sold as champagne, and the manufacture of *vins mousseux* is now absolutely prohibited.

The effect was immediate and dramatic. In 1910–11, 38,584,402 bottles of champagne were sold. In the following year this figure was reduced to 29,373,899 bottles, but 6,314,115 bottles of *vins mousseux* were also sold. The honour of champagne was satisfied and the livelihood of the growers was secure. But it must be admitted that the new legislation was not entirely without its drawbacks—for there is no law so good that the evil of mankind will not find a way around it. In this instance it was soon found that the increasing demand for champagne could not be entirely met by the vines planted on the finest slopes, and the vineyards were allowed to spread to the areas lower down where the rich alluvial soil was incapable of providing any but inferior wines. It is a pity that such vineyards should exist at all in so fine an area, but the evil must not be exaggerated: there are not so very many of them.

Much of the difficulty of growing champagne arises from the climate; but it is this that also gives the wine its delicacy. The winters are hard, with about seventy-five days of frost, extending from November to March and often for a further month either way. In the spring there is sometimes a veritable return to winter, with black frosts, against which no precautions are fully effective, so that in two years out of three there is relatively serious frost damage. Sometimes, as in 1913 and 1921, it is disastrous. Nowadays naptha burners, automatically actuated by thermostats, greatly mitigate the damage, but they cannot prevent it entirely.

If the winters are harsh, the summers are relatively hot—and it is this that makes wine growing a commercial possibility. Temperatures go regularly into the seventies and sometimes rise to more than a hundred degrees. But in so northerly a latitude there can be no certainty that the summer will be good. And there is always the serious hazard of hail.

The vine that gives the great champagnes is the same as that which gives the great burgundies: the Pinot Noir. But in Champagne it exists in several dozen local variants which arise from selection, assisted by those slight differences in soil and climate which help to provoke mutations. As many as eighty-two variants have been recognized, but there are two basic families: the Plants Dorés and the Plants Gris. It is the former family that gives the greatest wines, and of its members, the Petit Plant Doré is the finest of all. Le Gros Plant Doré gives a greater yield of slightly poorer quality. This has been well known since the beginning of the nineteenth century but during the last hundred years it has lost much ground to the Vert Doré, otherwise known as Plant Jeanson or Plant d'Ay, which gives a wine of similar quality but which is even more productive. The second family, the Plants Gris, must not be confused with the Pinot Gris, which is a white grape. Its best member is the Petit Plant Gris, which is well represented. The Gros Plant Gris, which is also variously called the Plant Gris Renault, the Pinot de Trépail, the Pinot d'Ambonnay and the Pinot de Bouzy, has been known since the end of the eighteenth century and gives a higher yield. The Plant de Vertus is another Pinot of high quality but one that belongs to neither family. The Pinot Meunier is a poor relation that nevertheless has a history going back to the sixteenth century and it is grown extensively in all but the greater vineyards. It gives a wine with plenty of alcohol but one that is deficient in acid and which is short-lived. It has the advantage, though, that it does well in soils that do not suit the Pinot Noir. The white vines grown in Champagne are practically all Pinot Blanc Chardonnay. Other species include the Petit Meslier, which is found mostly around Veneuil, and which gives a very white wine with a characteristic bouquet (it would probably be more widely grown had it taken more kindly to grafting), and the Arbanne, which is found mostly in the Aube, and which gives a good wine, but which is rather vulnerable to disease. The Gamay used to grow in the Aube, where it provided passable table wines, but it was banished from the Champagne district in 1963.

After the grapes have been picked they are examined by a team of women, mostly the older women who are past doing the hard physical work of picking. The bunches are examined quickly and expertly, and any grape that is defective in any respect is cut off with long pointed scissors and thrown away. They may be unripe, or over ripe and mildewed, or else they may be damaged by insects or by birds. Champagne is a delicate wine, as well as a precious one, and no chances are taken. The good grapes are then taken in great osier baskets to the nearest pressing house of the shipper who has bought them, where they are pressed as quickly as possible; for any delay might result in a premature fermentation, with the juice in contact with the skins, and this would cause discolouration. Vast wooden presses are used that can do the work very efficiently, and each lot of grapes is pressed four times: the first gives the *cuvée* pressing that is used for the best wine, the second and third, called the *tailles*, give a perfectly acceptable wine for the cheaper, well-sugared blends. The fourth, known as the *rebèche*, is not used for champagne. The normal full load for a press consists of about 4,000 kilograms of grapes, yielding 440 gallons on the first pressing, 66 gallons on the second, another 66 gallons on the third, and a few more on the fourth.

After the initial tumultuous fermentation is over, the must is taken to the shippers' cellars. Until quite recently it used to be racked in forty-four-gallon oak casks for the journey, but most firms now use tanker lorries. When the must reaches the shippers it is left for eight to ten weeks' slow fermentation and it then becomes new wine. After a few more weeks it is ready to be incorporated into a *cuvée*.

The *cuvée*, or blend, is the secret of a great champagne: each shipper has his own, and it is a closely guarded secret. Writing of the immortal Dom Pérignon, André Simon[1] has described how 'the excellence was due to the art with which he blended the grapes

---

[1] André L. Simon, *Champagne*, London, 1934.

from various vineyards; it was due also to the fact that the Abbey of Hautvillers owned more vineyards and received by way of tithes a greater variety of grapes than any private vineyard owner'. Modern champagne houses can draw upon an even greater variety. The wines from the mountain and from the river each have their own features and merits. Those of Verzenay are noted for their vinosity, those of Ambonnay for their fragrance, those of Avize for their delicacy, and so on. The most balanced wine of all is said to be that from Ay, but even this is seldom, if ever, found alone. Above all, in such a northerly latitude, there is a great difference between the various years. A great year gives a wine that is full and smooth—but perhaps too much so: it may be lacking in natural acidity. A poor year gives a wine that is thin, and perhaps too acid. Thus the *cuvée* is not only a blend of wines but also of years. This even applies to a vintage champagne. The vintage date is that of the year before the bottling, from which at least eighty per cent of the wines must come; but it does not necessarily mean that *all* of them were pressed in that year. The addition of a little older wine produces a character of its own and a proportion of older un-blended wines are held back for this purpose. There must also be a balance between the wines pressed from black and from white grapes. The black grapes give body and vinosity, while the white ones provide delicacy. The proportion is sometimes as high as four-fifths black to one-fifth white, though in some wines a higher proportion of white is used, and some houses specialize in these lighter wines—Taittinger, for instance. The ultimate in this direction is a blanc de blancs, when all the wines come from white grapes, to give a champagne of great delicacy but of slight body—a fine wine for use as an aperitif on a very hot summer's day.

It is always fun to try and discover trade secrets, but the secret of the *cuvée* is impenetrable. Its elucidation would take a secret service agent years of work. Several authors, however, have quoted blends that are probably not far wide of the mark. Thomas George Shaw,[1] writing in 1864, quoted three 'actual instances of *cuvées* of 50 hogsheads', and one of these was quoted by Simon in his recent *History of Champagne* as being not essentially different from the kind of selection used today. They are:

[1] *Wine, the Vine and the Cellar*, London, 1864.

1.	Black grapes	Verzenay	16 hogsheads.
	,, ,,	Ay	16 ,,
	White ,,	Cramant and Avize	18 ,,
			50 ,,

2.	Black grapes	Bouzy	16 hogsheads.
	,, ,,	Pierry	16 ,,
	White ,,	Cramant and Avize	18 ,,
			50 ,,

3.	Black grapes	Verzenay	5 hogsheads.
	,, ,,	Bouzy	5 ,,
	,, ,,	Chigny	$2\frac{1}{2}$,,
	,, ,,	Ay	5 ,,
	,, ,,	Champillon	$2\frac{1}{2}$,,
	,, ,,	Pierry	5 ,,
	,, ,,	Vertus	5 ,,
	White grapes	Cramant and Avize	10 ,,
	,, ,,	Mesnil	5 ,,
	,, ,,	Chouilly	$2\frac{1}{2}$,,
	,, ,,	Crayons de St. Martin	$2\frac{1}{2}$,,
			50 ,,

The last was said to have 'proved exceedingly fine'. These blends are very similar to those given (following Rendu and others) by Louis Jacquelin and René Poulain in their recent *Vignes et Vins de France*[1] and it would appear that the pattern has altered very little for a century. But there are as many *cuvées*, each different, as there are champagnes.

The *méthode champenoise* has already been described.[2] It is the method by which all champagne is made, and although it is used widely for sparkling wines elsewhere than in Champagne, in Champagne it reaches perfection. Champagne is incomparably the finest of all sparkling wines. Others are enjoyable, and even delightful, but champagne stands in a class apart. And because the *méthode champenoise* is so complicated, so lengthy, and calls for so much skill, it is necessarily expensive. When other wines are bottled ready for sale, the work of the champagne shipper has hardly begun. The *méthode* is expensive no matter where it is used,

[1] Paris, 1960; English edition London, 1962.
[2] See pp. 49–53.

though not necessarily quite as expensive in other places as it is in Champagne: some of the lesser wines so prepared are made with less care, and they also mature more quickly; but the cost is still comparable, and because champagne is so undoubtedly the best, it is also the best value.

Since the wine in every *cuvée* is fermented 'right out', little or no sugar remains, and the ultimate sweetness depends on the *dosage*:[1] the final addition of liqueur after the *dégorgement*. The more usual names under which champagnes are sold, indicating the degree of sweetness, are, from sweetest to driest: *doux, demi-doux, demi-sec, sec* or *dry, extra dry, brut* or *nature*. Brut wine has, or should have, no added sugar, though in practice it generally has a little; *extra sec* has one to two per cent of *liqueur*; *sec* has about five per cent; and the ultimate in sweetness, *doux*, has about twelve per cent. It is impossible to be categorical about sweetness, though, as each house has its own rule and tradition. While the sweet wines are popular on the Continent (though the dry wines are rapidly gaining ground), it is those that are dry or *brut* which find the greatest favour in England, and unfortunately they are the most expensive; for sweetness will hide faults, whereas a wine that is dry has to be above reproach. Taking the production of champagne as a whole, though, it is the *sec* that, over the years, has been the most popular individual class, and it is certainly a most agreeable compromise.

Champagne has about it something of an exotic air, earned in the days of the naughty nineties and somehow never lost: an air of high living and of extravagance—even of vice. But if this is true of the white wine, it is even more true of the pink. Pink champagne, like the other and less flamboyant *vins rosés*, can be made in either of two ways: by adding a little of the local red wine, usually bouzy, or by leaving the skins for a short time in contact with the must. Not a little is made accidentally that way. For some unfathomable reason it has a reputation for outstanding excellence. It certainly looks pretty in the glass. But that is all. It remains a mystery why anyone should be prepared to pay extra for a taint of vulgarity.

Champagne is an exception to the general rule of light white wines: it ages well. Even a non-vintage wine improves, in my opinion, for a time with keeping, though I must acknowledge that some of my friends in the champagne trade disagree with me: they

[1] See p. 52.

like their wine fresh, as the shipper sells it. After two or three years in bottle it is distinctly better to my taste than when bought new, and it seldom begins to deteriorate until it is six or seven years old. If kept for too long, however, it coarsens and loses its sparkle. It may even maderize. The same applies to a vintage wine, but here the time taken is much longer. Tastes differ, but few would suggest that a vintage champagne is at its best until it is seven or eight years old. Personally I like it much older. A fine champagne ages gracefully. It loses the brashness of youth. Its sparkle becomes more gentle and more appealing. And it attains a depth of flavour that is wholly delightful. These features appear to perfection when it is from twelve to fifteen years old, and the wine of a great shipper in a fine year may last much longer. We drank the last Louis Roederer 1928 in my family cellar when it was forty years old and in perfect condition. This wine was bought young and kept in ideal conditions. But anyone who wants the joy of drinking old champagne must also face the risk entailed in keeping it. As an example, a friendly wine merchant a few years ago found two cases of 1929 half-bottles which he had overlooked in his bond. They were too speculative a proposition to sell in the normal way of business, so he sold them to my father for a very small sum. We finished them in 1963. When they were opened, it was amazing how consistent the pattern was: of every four half-bottles, one was superb, two were all right, and the fourth had to be thrown away. At such an age, and especially in half-bottles, the wine is very much at the mercy of its corks.

Old champagne used once to be more generally appreciated than it is now. In 1884 Professor Saintsbury found the 1857 Perrier-Jouet 'majestical'. Towards the end of the nineteenth century, vintage champagne became so expensive and sought-after that the wise and wealthy both inside and outside the wine trade used to speculate in it as a profitable change from stocks and shares. André L. Simon,[1] for instance, quotes figures for Bollinger 1884 which show that in 1891 it cost 90s. a dozen and that in 1898 it fetched 245s. He quoted similar figures for other shippers and other years. Today, in contrast, very old champagne tends to be regarded as distressed merchandise; and anyone wishing to acquire some would certainly be well advised to make careful enquiries as

[1] *Champagne*, London, 1934.

to its history: if kept standing upright beneath the stairs, it becomes undrinkable in next to no time. But over-caution can rob one of great joys, and old champagne can often be a real bargain.

In the last few years one great champagne shipper after another has been introducing some special marque of wine made up from their finest *cuvées*, wines such as Moët and Chandon's *Dom Pérignon*, Louis Roederer's *Cristal Brut*, Pommery's *Avize* (a wine derived solely from that district), Mercier's *Réserve de l'Empereur* blanc de blancs and *Cuvée M33*, Heidseick and Co.'s *Diamant Bleu* and Taittinger's *Comtes de Champagne* blanc de blancs. All of these have been admirable and as individualistic in their styles as the shippers who prepared them. One or two of the great shippers, however, notably Bollinger and Krug, have refrained from competing on the ground that their vintage wines are so special that they could not be more so. But in 1968 Bollinger marketed a wine labelled as R.D. 1955. Normally the *dégorgement* is done about six months before the wine is shipped, and the Bollinger 1955 was shipped to this country between June 1961 and the first few months of 1963. The R.D. 1955, on the other hand, was not disgorged until January 18th, 1968, more than twelve years after the vintage. The difference this makes to the wine is an extremely subtle one. In 1968 I tasted the normal and the R.D. 1955 side by side. The former was elegant and exquisitely mature. The latter was every bit as elegant and mature but had a youthful freshness that one normally expects only in a much younger wine. In fact it had *everything*. I wonder whether other shippers will follow Bollinger's example?

As with all wines, the way in which champagne ages depends on the size of the bottle: the larger the bottle, the longer it keeps. The usual bottle is the ordinary wine size: there are six to the gallon. Some wine for England is also shipped in the rather convenient size of the imperial pint, which is just right when half a bottle seems too little and a bottle too much. The magnum holds two bottles, and it it is an admirable measure: in magnum, champagne attains old age with rare elegance. But to drink young wine out of magnums is meaningless, if not an affectation. As wine matures more slowly in such a container, excessive youth becomes even more apparent than it need be, and one is faced, for no possible advantage, with a bottle that is too heavy to manage easily. Even larger is the double-magnum or jeroboam, that contains four bottles; and the same remarks apply, but more so. Other and more exotic sizes are known, but champagne is not matured in them by the shippers, who fill them by decanting the wine from ordinary bottles, so that it is more flat and less good. There is no point in buying wine in such containers except for show. They are: the rehoboam (six bottles), the methuselah (eight bottles), the salmanezer (twelve bottles) and the nebuchadnezzar (twenty bottles). At the other end of the scale there is the nip or quarter-bottle, and the same objection applies to this as to its largest brethren: wine is never matured in such vessels but is decanted from larger ones. A nip is a useful measure for a sick-room but for nowhere else.

Champagne, to be sold as such, *must* be sparkling. The still wines, in so far as they are now made at all, are sold as *vin nature de Champagne*. The authorities and the champagne shippers themselves are very strict about this, for they are determined that nothing shall be allowed to cause confusion in the minds of the public and to detract from the name of champagne. They spare no effort. In 1960 a group of the leading shippers brought an action against the Costa Brava Wine Co. which was shipping a so-called 'Spanish champagne', and obtained an injunction to restrain them from using the name of champagne. One can only regret that shippers of other wines have not, in the past, been so diligent. It is a pity, though, that the shippers' policy has caused the still wines of champagne, which once enjoyed a considerable reputation in England, to vanish almost entirely. No doubt their action has been commercially wise, and there is no denying the fact that the loss of the still wines is as nothing compared with the gain of the sparkling ones. But any loss is to be regretted. Still wines, however, can readily be obtained in Champagne itself and they are worth seeking out, especially the white ones. Henry Vizetelly described the still red verzenay of 1857 as one of the most delicate wines it had ever been his fortune to taste. But this opinion has not been echoed by many who have tasted red still wines of Champagne recently, and it is certainly one that I would not agree with myself. It may be that the grapes that once gave these fine red wines are now all diverted to the more profitable purpose of providing sparkling champagne; or it may be that such wines are still grown but are taken immediately into the most discriminating local cellars. For the red wines that *are* available are thin, rather than delicate: they give one the impression that they would be burgundy if only they could, but that they lack the character and strength. Moreover they travel notoriously badly.

With the white wines it is a very different story. Those that I have tasted have been dry, and the lightness that is unbecoming in a red wine is entirely appropriate to a white. They are utterly delicious. Like the wines of the Loire, they would probably lose some of their freshness after a long journey, but it is inconceivable that all of it would be lost and it is a pity indeed that none of them is exported in commercial quantities.

Since champagne, like port and sherry, is a blended wine, it is the skill of the shipper that determines the quality, and it is the name of the shipper that the buyer must look for rather than that of a vineyard or district. The shipper to choose is purely a matter of personal preference: each house has its own style that is preserved with a striking consistency, and everyone must try them for himself. But in doing so he would be unwise to forget the so-called 'buyers' own brands'. These are the wines that are imported by individual wine merchants who sell them under names of their own devising. Many of them are produced by the smaller shippers who specialize in this kind of trade and who lack the capital or the enterprise to develop a market in their own brands. Until the great names emerged in the latter half of the eighteenth century, all champagne was sold in this way. And most of it was sold under merchants' brands until late in the nineteenth century. It is the way in which all the self-respecting wine merchants preferred to do their business: they had pride in their own selection and their customers trusted them. Happily, despite the big-business methods of the trade today, the tradition has not vanished, and many of these obscure brands afford excellent value. It must be admitted, though, that others—especially the most price-conscious—are pretty poor stuff: wedding champagne. It all depends on the merchant.

The vintage years of champagne must be considered in quite a different light from those of the great table wines. It has already been seen that the *cuvée* is unlikely to consist solely of wine pressed in the year on the label: it will almost certainly contain some proportion of older wine. Moreover, champagne shippers are like port shippers in that they are by no means unanimous in 'declaring' a vintage. For them to do so, two requirements have to be satisfied: firstly the year must be a good one, and secondly there must be a demand that will enable the shipper to sell a vintage champagne. Today, happily, there is seldom any doubt about the second of these, but in the past it has been otherwise. This applied to the 1929 vintage, for example. The 1928 vintage had been a very fine one, and then the great slump of 1929 drastically reduced the demand for vintage champagne. Several houses refrained from shipping a 1929 at all, though the quality was very fine indeed: they thought it would be impossible to sell two such vintages one on top of the other in such circumstances. Most of the good vintages, especially the more recent ones, have been shipped by all the houses, but in considering the following list it must be remembered that there have been many exceptions.

1920: A very good year, but not widely shipped owing to the excellence of the 1921s.

1921: At this time, this year was very highly praised indeed, but the wines were found not to age well.

1922: A large yield, but poor wines. Not a vintage year.

1923: A vintage year of good average quality.

1924: Poor.

1925: Poor.

1926: A very good vintage that was not widely shipped owing to the slump.

1927: Bad.

1928: A very great year. So much so that many of the wines, if kept under good conditions, are still excellent.

1929: The wines were almost as good as the 1928s and the yield was much higher, but owing to the slump the world markets were unable to absorb the *embarras de richesse* resulting from so many good vintages, and some firms refrained from shipping it.

1930: Poor.

1931: Bad.

1932: Poor.

1933: A good year, though most of the wines have long since been past their best.

1934: A great year, and some of the wines, kept under good conditions, still survive.

1935: Rather poor.

1936: Bad.

1937: A very good year but not up to the standard set by 1934.

1938: Average.

1939: Bad.

1940: Rather poor.

1941: Average.

1942: A good year, but most of the wines are showing too much age.

1943: Not unlike the previous year, and most of these wines, too, are showing their age.

1944: Average.

1945: A good year, and many of the wines still taste delightful after twenty-five years.

1946: Poor.

1947: An excellent year. The best wines are still very good to drink now.

1948: Average.

1949: A good year though not quite up to the standard of 1947.

1950: Poor.

1951: Bad.

1952: An excellent year.

1953: An excellent year.

1954: Bad.

1955: An excellent year.

1956: Bad.

1957: Bad.

1958: Poor.

1959: A good year, but perhaps there was too much sunshine, for once: for the wines have more residual sweetness than usual and some even have a suggestion of coarseness, with a lack of acidity. It remains to be seen how they will age, but I have doubts.

1960: Poor.

1961: A very good year, and one that in my opinion will repay keeping.

1962: Another very good year, considered by some shippers to be better than 1961.

1963: Bad.

1964: An excellent year that should age well.

1965: Bad.

CHAPTER 6

The Other Wines of France

The other wines of France are legion. By the Middle Ages the vine was growing everywhere in Western Europe where it would flourish—and that included practically the whole of the area that is now France. Things have not changed much. Some of the unprofitable vineyards that were in the north-west have vanished, as have the many monastic vineyards that were then in England. But others have been planted and there are local wines in all the sunnier parts of the country. Anyone who has had a holiday in France will have tasted some of them; one or two may even have become such favourites that he will go back to seek them out. He may find them mentioned in this chapter—or he may not. Vineyards—even quite good vineyards—come and go. Sometimes they vanish for economic reasons—instances in Chablis and in the Rhône valley have already been mentioned. Sometimes it depends on the taste of the owner. Quite a good bourgeois growth of the Médoc has become a chicken farm. Other fine wines have been destroyed by the growth of towns such as Dijon and Bordeaux. But happily the demand for good wine and the enthusiasm of growers has brought other fine vineyards into being; this has happened, for instance, in Champagne. So this chapter can never be up to date. Nor does it attempt to be complete. To mention all the local wines—admirable though many of them are—would be impossible. Moreover, some of them do not travel well, while others, that do, are not exported because the production is too small. And here it is as well to utter a word of warning: a wine that may taste wonderful with good local food under the relaxed heat of the Mediterranean sun may taste perfectly ghastly when it is drunk with a mutton chop in a London fog. Many a wine merchant

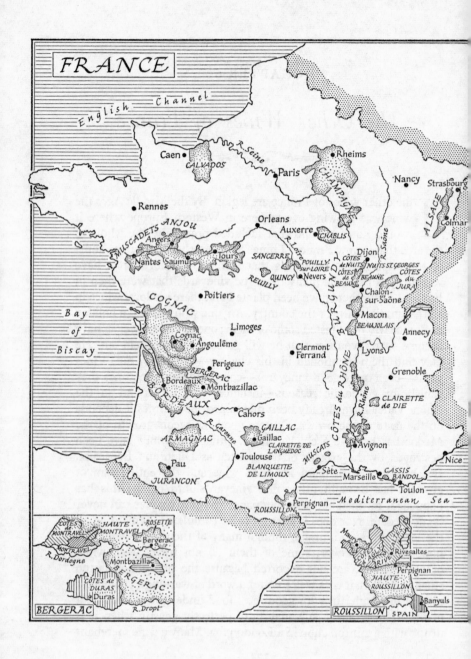

FRANCE

English Channel

Caen
CALVADOS
R. Seine
Paris
Rheims
CHAMPAGNE
Nancy
Strasbourg

Rennes
MUSCADETS ANJOU
Angers
Nantes Saumur Tours
Orleans
Auxerre
CHABLIS
SANCERRE
POUILLY-sur-LOIRE
QUINCY
REUILLY
Nevers
Dijon
CÔTES de NUITS
NUITS ST. GEORGES
CÔTES de BEAUNE
BEAUNE
Chalon-sur-Saône
ALSACE
Colmar
CÔTES du JURA

COGNAC
Poitiers
Macon
BEAUJOLAIS
Annecy

Bay
of
Biscay
Cognac
Angoulême
Limoges
Clermont
Ferrand
Lyons
Grenoble
BURGUNDY

Perigeux
BERGERAC
Bordeaux
Montbazillac
BORDEAUX
Cahors
R. Garonne
GAILLAC
Gaillac
CLAIRETTE DE LANGUEDOC
Toulouse
BLANQUETTE DE LIMOUX
MUSCATS
CÔTES du RHÔNE
R. Rhône
CLAIRETTE de DIE

Avignon

Pau
JURANÇON
Sète
Perpignan
ROUSSILLON
Marseille
CASSIS
BANDOL
Toulon
Nice

Mediterranean Sea

CÔTES de MONTRAVEL
HAUTE MONTRAVEL
ROSETTE
Bergerac
MONTRAVEL
R. Dordogne
Montbazillac
CÔTES de DURAS
Duras
BERGERAC
R. Dropt
BERGERAC

Mau
CÔTES AGLY
RIV
Rivesaltes
Perpignan
HAUTE ROUSSILLON
Banyuls
ROUSSILLON SPAIN

who has specially imported a wine to please a customer, who found it so delicious when he was on holiday, has been landed with a stock of undrinkable and unsaleable bottles. But this by no means applies to all the lesser-known wines. Many of them taste just as delicious here as they do in France. Anyone who spurns them, and who sticks to the great classic wines of Bordeaux, Burgundy and Champagne, misses many very good things, and he absurdly limits the range of styles and flavours that is his to command. With the ever increasing price of the classic wines, the trade is turning more and more to these excellent lesser-known growths; and it is a trend that must continue. There is an immense amount of pleasure to be had from drinking them. It is a pleasure not to be missed.

To classify so many wines in a way that makes sense is not easy, but at the outset, all the wines of France can be divided into three broad categories of class rather than of style: they may be entitled to bear an *appellation contrôlée* (*A.C.*), they may be of the category known as *vin délimité de qualité supérieure* (*V.D.Q.S.*) or they may be one of the wines entitled to an *appellation simple*. The A.C. wines are generally the best ones—though there are exceptions. The V.D.Q.S. wines are generally those of the second flight, though again there are many exceptions that are in no way inferior to the wines bearing an *appellation contrôlée*. These two categories are strictly controlled and are defined according to French law. Anyone wishing to know more of this should refer to Appendix II. Suffice it here to say that the definitions in either instance are primarily geographical; and that if the areas producing the former are more widely publicized and easier to ascertain, those of the latter are no less strict. Moreover, as the V.D.Q.S. wines fetch lower prices, there is less incentive to fraud. A.C. wines must be so labelled, and V.D.Q.S. have a special imprint of their own, about the size of a postage stamp and looking very like one.

Wines of *appellation simple* may lack the purely legal distinction of the others for a variety of reasons. In some instances the growers have not thought it worth their while to secure an *appellation*: where production is small and sales are assured the government red tape that is involved may be thought to outweigh any advantages that may accrue. In other instances an *appellation* has been applied for but its grant has been delayed while the situation is investigated. But there are other instances in which an *appellation* has been positively refused. The still wines of Champagne, although they are certainly worthy of an A.C., are firmly denied one in order to avoid confusion with the sparkling wines, and they must be sold as *vin nature de la champagne*.

Apart from these categories, there are one or two others that may be mentioned in passing but which need not be considered further in this book. There are the *vins de pays*, technically meaning local wines with alcoholic strengths of less than 9·5 per cent, which would be too low to bring them into an A.C. or V.D.Q.S. classification even if they would otherwise be entitled to one. This is confusing, though: in ordinary speech *vin de pays* simply means 'the wine of the country', which may well enjoy the distinction of an A.C. Then there are the *vins de coupage*, or blended wines, which in turn may be *vins de consommation courante* or *vins de marque*. Both of these must have a minimum strength of 9·5 per cent, and the wines in them may come from anywhere, though there are regulations covering certain aspects of their quality, such as acidity. The only difference between them is that the latter are sold nationally under fancy trade marks.

But these legal definitions do not even begin to indicate what the wine will taste like. Some geographical grouping is necessary, and it is not easy. When wines from two adjacent districts of Bordeaux can taste so different, one can hardly expect the country as a whole to be more consistent. But while the adjacent wines are certainly different, they obviously belong to the same family, and their resemblance is far more marked than are their differences. So it is with France as a whole. Some time ago, Mr. Gerald Asher, who is a specialist in the rare wines of France, published a map that divided the country into five parts—which is two more than Caesar managed. One part—the north-west—grows no wine, or none worth mentioning. Another—Alsace—has been deliberately left out of this chapter. Its very nationality has suffered the vicissitudes of Franco-German political fortune. Although it is now firmly part of France, its wines definitely belong to the Rhine valley complex of *vignobles* and they can only be considered in that context.

The largest of the regions is the west, where the climate is Atlantic and temperate. Here the dominating vine for red wines is the Cabernet, and that for the whites is the Sauvignon. The dominant district is of course Bordeaux. Adjacent to the Bordeaux district, and stretching into the Massif Central, come the districts of the Dordogne and Lot. South of Bordeaux comes the Armagnac brandy district, and, further to the south, the wines of the Pyrenean foothills. Immediately to the north of the Bordeaux vineyards, the Cognac brandy area begins, and further still to the north come the wines of the Loire valley.

The great vines of north-eastern France are the Pinot Noir and the Pinot Chardonnay. These are the principal vines of the two great districts of Champagne and Burgundy. The area also includes the important vineyards of the Jura as well as the pleasant wines of the head waters of the Loire and those grown around Clermont-Ferrand, high in the Massif Central.

The area of France that Mr. Asher calls the Rhône Corridor has already been described in the previous chapter. Its vines are not Pinot, and its wines are very different to those of the north-east. The line that Mr. Asher drew on the map is therefore at least as valid as that which I chose to draw in considering the wines progressively as the climate and soils change in a journey down the valley. But although the relationship between the Rhône wines and those of Burgundy is a rather distant one, nevertheless a family relationship does emerge—a relationship that has been artificially exaggerated by the geographical vagueness of the burgundy shippers.

The southern strip of France also includes wines of the Rhône valley that have been described in the last chapter—those of Châteauneuf-du-Pape and Tavel, for instance—wines that become distinctly Mediterranean in character but which still clearly have features in common with their northern neighbours in the valley. The coastal wines are far more obviously Mediterranean. To the east there are Cassis, Palette and Bandol. To the west lie Lunel, Frontignan, the wines of the Languedoc, Blanquette-de-Limoux, and the substantial district of Roussillon.

The West

Dordogne and Lot

The wines of the Dordogne and those of the Lot are not dissimilar to those of Bordeaux—as one would expect from their proximity. When the Bordeaux area was delimited, the principal opposition came from the growers in the Dordogne, who had been accustomed to sell their wines as bordeaux; and until the laws of *appellation contrôlée* came to be enforced the wines from these areas were largely sold to Bordeaux merchants for blending purposes. Both red and white wines are produced in substantial quantities. The principal centre for red wines is Bergerac. They make very pleasant drinking, but no one would accuse them of competing in quality with their neighbours from Bordeaux. They do, however, resemble the lesser growths of St. Emilion. Nice, refreshing little white wines are also grown, that have some character and are distantly related to those of Graves. But despite its agreeable wines, Bergerac is more widely known as the home of Cyrano de Bergerac (though he was born in Paris), a seventeenth-century author who, apart from his literary works, is immortal for the enormous size of his nose, for a lamentable tendency to fight duels, and as the hero of Rostand's play. The area entitled to use the *appellations Bergerac* and *Bergerac Supérieur* is, as the map shows, quite large, but viticulture is far less intensive than in the principal areas of Bordeaux. The soil is silico-argilaceous and the principal vines are the Cabernet Franc, Cabernet Sauvignon and Merlot Noir for red wines; and, for white wines, the Sémillon, Sauvignon and Muscadelle.

Within the larger area of Bergerac, there are several smaller areas defined by the laws of *appellation contrôlée*. The three principal ones are montravel, rosette and bergerac côte de saussignac. These follow the Bergerac style, but the wines have more character. Parts of Montravel form two sub-divisions, each producing a superior wine: haut-montravel and côtes de montravel. There is also a red wine grown on a chalky plateau to the north-east of Bergerac that has the right to a separate *appellation* pécharmant or peycharmant. The wine is good, and though hard when young it has some finesse when mature, but production is very small.

The famous white wine of the Dordogne is monbazillac. The existence of this wine is one of the few benefits wrought by excessive taxation, for until the sixteenth century all the vineyards were on the north side of the Dordogne. Then taxation in that area rose to such an extent that growers decided to clear out and to try the south side. Thus monbazillac came into being. It is grown in a little oasis of chalky soil within the area of Bergerac, and it bears a relation to sauternes like that of white bergerac to graves: the style is recognizably similar but not so good: it is slightly less sweet, less full-flavoured and less aromatic. Although there are a few Sauvignon vines, the grapes generally used consist of a mixture of two-thirds Sémillon and one-third Muscadelle. But the grapes, even if they are seldom Sauvignon, acquire the same *pourriture noble* and, like the fine growths of sauternes in good vintage years, the best monbazillacs age well, deepening in colour and acquiring a distinguished and distinctive flavour. If they fail to achieve the grandeur of a great sauternes, then there is some compensation in that they also fail to achieve the price; and they actually make better drinking with the more delicate desserts that would be overwhelmed by a greater wine. Not surprisingly, then, they have their enthusiastic following; and in particular, they have long been popular in Holland. The connection with Holland goes back a long time: to the revocation of the Edict of Nantes in 1685. The vineyards were then mostly owned by Huguenots, many of whom fled to Holland. From there they used to send ships up the Dordogne to fetch the wines they enjoyed, and the wines they chose are still known locally as the *marques hollandaises*.

There must be few places in Europe that are scenically more delightful than the Lot. It is a land of hills, rivers and vistas, and it enjoys a delightful climate. But nature seldom bestows all her gifts simultaneously, and the wines are generally not outstanding, though there are exceptions. The best of them is cahors—a V.D.Q.S. wine—and a very good red wine it is. Even the humblest growths make excellent luncheon wines, and the best of them are wines of genuine quality, with considerable depth both of flavour and of colour, together with sufficient tannin and natural acidity to ensure that they mature well. Some have a strange, slightly sweet after-taste; which can be so noticeable that I am certain that too much of one example I know would make me sick. The best growths have a remarkable characteristic: they have so much colour that they have long been known as the 'black wines of Cahors'—though this is something of an exaggeration. They are certainly a good deep red, but not much deeper than some of the Rhône wines and nowhere near so deep as some of the wines grown near Alicante. It is almost certain that they were darker in the past than they are today. The modern style is clearly preferable in a world that is anxious to drink its wines at the earliest possible moment, for the old wines needed many years of maturation in the wood followed by several in bottle before they were ready to drink. Most growers now go so far as to use a few white grapes from Ugin Blanc (white Carrignan) or Clairette vines to lighten their wines. This would at once account for their more rapid maturity and for their lack of 'blackness'. It also helps to make up deficiencies in acid. The old black wine was undoubtedly a fine wine, though, and it is a pity to see a fine wine practically disappear.

The best vineyards lie along the slopes of the river valley between Cahors and Puy l'Evêque. The soil, however, is by no means consistent: much of it is clay, but there are some areas with more chalk, and near Puy l'Evêque some of the vineyards are so stony that they remind one of Châteauneuf-du-Pape—and so, to some extent, do their wines. The principal vine is the Malbec, known here as the Auxerrois. It is the varying nature of the soil and the slopes that helps to give to Cahors some of its variety, but apart from this, the wine we know today is probably somewhat different from that of the last century; for in those days the vines were principally planted on terraces carved out of the steep slopes whereas today, although some of them are found in the old places, most of them are on the plateau and in the valleys. It is now economically impossible to work the old terraces.

In the last century, according to Cyrus Redding,[1] a very odd wine was made in Cahors:

'The must and the pellicles are set over the fire, either wholly or in part, in large cauldrons. The whole is left to boil a certain time, and is then flung into the vat, with the unboiled must. It is left in the vat eight or ten days, and then the whole is racked without pressing the murk. This wine is often mingled with a third of the liquor known under the name of *rogome*, made here with the must of the auxerrois grape which is set to boil for five or six minutes, and then brandy ... is added, and the whole barrelled up. Much is sent to Bordeaux to strengthen and colour light wines, or to aid in making *liqueurs*.'

If such wine is made today, I do not know where to find it. To raise the density of a vat by concentrating part of the must is an age-old practice; but this was carrying things to excess.

[1] *French Wines and Vineyards*, London, 1860.

Other V.D.Q.S. wines from the area include côtes de buzet and côtes de marmandais. Both may be either red or white. Côtes de buzet must include at least eighty per cent of Cabernet, Malbec or Merlot grapes for the red, the remaining twenty per cent or less being mostly local varieties, while the white wines are made of Sémillon, Sauvignon and Muscadelle. Both the red and the white wines clearly follow the Bordeaux style. Côtes du marmandais, on the other hand, is made of a mixture of grapes. For the red wines there must be half of local varieties, one-quarter Gamay and one-quarter the classic varieties, while for the white wines, Sémillon and Sauvignon make up seventy per cent, Muscadelle and Merlto Blanc fifteen per cent, and local varieties the remainder. These wines are naturally further from the Bordeaux model, but they are certainly pleasant. It must be admitted, however, that some of the local wines from the Dordogne and Lot are not. I particularly remember one white wine which shall be nameless as it was sold under an impressive château label. Its nose at first reminded me of a farmyard and later of sewage, yet I was assured that there was nothing wrong with it and that it was meant to be like that. I think it must have contained succinic acid. But this happily was the exception: most of the local wines from there are delightful, if small.

Cognac and Armagnac
Where there is brandy, there must first be wine, and these two areas make the finest brandies in the world. Both grow wines— red and white—but the less said the better. They are only of *ordinaire* quality, and are terribly acid to the taste. It is one of the happy chances of nature that such sublime spirits stem from such dreadful wines.

Wines of the Pyrenean Foothills
That enchanting countryside that stretches from Pau into the Pyrenees is perhaps more notable for its landscape than for its wines, but some of them, nevertheless, are worth noting. The most famous wine of the Basses-Pyrénées is the white wine of Jurançon, grown to the south and west of Pau. It is a wine distinguished in the past and practically extinguished in the present: in the mid-nineteenth century there were about seven and a half thousand

acres of vines, and the area has now fallen to about a tenth. When Henri IV of France was born at Pau in 1553, his lips were rubbed with a clove of garlic, and then he was given a sip of the local wine *pour ne pas faire un enfant pleureux et rechigné*. It evidently worked, for he grew up to be a fine imbiber and remained devoted to the Basque wine. During his lifetime it became a European favourite and it was widely exported, but the trade was not a new one: it had been available in Scandinavia during the fourteenth century. In the seventeenth and eighteenth centuries it was quite well known in England under the name of 'Navarre'. Today it is amongst the rare wines, but it is well worth looking for. It has a very fruity flavour with a remarkable, fragrant and subtle bouquet that quite defies description; and it ages very well. In the past it was always rather sweet, but modern growers are tending to produce rather drier wines, though sweet wines are still made, especially in the sunniest years. Personally I like it by itself, well chilled in the middle of the day, rather than with a meal. It is grown from two local vines: principally from the Manseng (which exists in two varieties, Gros and Petit) but also, to a lesser extent, from the Courbu. These vines are grown on very high stakes, rather like those of the Moselle, which is found to protect them from the low-lying frosts that so often descend from the mountains.

Another notable wine of exceptional fragrance is grown nearby around Portet, principally from the Pachérenc vine, which is also known as the Ruffiac. The wine enjoys the startling and un-pronounceable *appellation* of pachérenc du vin bilh. At its best it is good and remarkably fragrant, but it is too often spoilt by bad peasant vinification.

A small amount of red wine is grown at Jurançon, but a better-known red wine is madiran. This gives one the impression of being a wine of unfulfilled promise. The peasants again are to blame, and the Spaniards, in the Rioja area, on the other side of the Pyrenees, do much better. There is a well-known local rosé called rosé de béarn or rousselet de béarn. In its highest form it is known as irouléguy.

Gaillac

The wines of the Tarn were once amongst the most widely exported wines of France, and they were rated amongst the very finest. Alas, gone is the glory! They are now hard to find even in France, and they are practically unknown elsewhere. They were amongst the favourite wines of King John, and they were widely imported into this country for long afterwards. Until the English lost Guienne, their popularity was immense here. It was substantial even as late as the seventeenth century. In the eighteenth they were still known, though they were becoming obscure. With the Methuen treaty they disappeared altogether and have never been seen here since.

To give the detailed history of a wine that is now so excessively obscure would be tedious—interesting though the history is. Indeed there is probably nowhere in the whole of France of which more could be written. In all probability the cultivation of the vine pre-dated the Roman conquest, having spread from the region of Marseilles, where it owed its origin to the Greeks. After devastation by the Saracens, the vineyards were replanted and tended, inevitably, by the Christian orders. Documentary evidence goes back as far as the tenth century, and there are no gaps.[1] But nevertheless it is undeniable that today the wine is of little importance.

The most important wine for export in the past was the 'black' wine—a very dark red, of which the only surviving example produced on a commercial scale in France is that of Cahors. The red wines ceased to be of any importance when the vineyards were replanted after the phylloxera, and the trade today rests almost entirely on the white wines. These were always grown, and they were bought, for example, by King Henry VIII, but they were not then especially esteemed. The best and strongest of them have the *appellation* gaillac premières côtes. The lesser wines are just plain gaillac. Both of these come in every possible degree of sweetness, the sweetest of all being the product of the *pourriture noble*. They are mostly bottled in hock bottles, and the poorer examples taste rather of the laboratory. The district also produces substantial quantities of sparkling wine: gaillac mousseux. This is not made by the *méthode champenoise*, but is a 'natural' wine. It has a tendency to ferment slowly and to retain its gas, so that it can be drawn sparkling from the cask—provided the cask is not kept too

---

[1] For further details see P. Morton Shand, *A Book of French Wines*, London, 1960.

long—or can be bottled at the critical moment while it is still effervescent. To most people's taste, though, it lacks distinction and is spoilt by its excessive sweetness. All these are derived predominantly from local vines—principally Mauzac Blanc, with a small proportion of Lenc de l'El and Ondenc. The Clairette, here known as the Blanquette, is also widely grown, especially for sparkling wines. There is a good trade in sending the young wine in cask, while it is still enjoying the full chaos of its fermentation, to Paris, where it is sold as *vin blanc nouveau*, otherwise known as *vin bourru*, *bernache* or *vin macadam*, after the macadamized boulevards. Much of the wine is made in the Gaillac co-operative, which was founded as long ago as 1903.

Other wines of the district include *vins mutés* or *mistelles*—those wines which have their fermentation stopped with sulphur and alcohol before it is complete, so that they are left with an unnatural amount of sweetness. Villaudric and fronton, or côtes de fronton, are V.D.Q.S. wines that may be red or white.

The Loire

The wines of the Loire make a study in themselves, and a very fascinating one. There are very many of them, and this is hardly surprising, for it is the longest river in France. It rises high in the mountains of the Cevennes at Gerbier-de-Jonc and flows 625 miles before reaching the Atlantic. Vineyards are to be found all along its length, though the wines grown along its upper reaches are only of local interest. But if these can be omitted, the list is still a vast one, for the tributaries have their own wines, some of which are notable.

Amongst the important tributaries is the Allier, and a tributary of the Allier is the Sioule. On this river stands Saint-Pourçain. The town is far removed from the valley of the Loire, and the wine is equally far removed from those of the valley: both geographically and as regards its character it could more validly be grouped with the wines of the north-east. It is worth mentioning if only for the renown it enjoyed in the Middle Ages. It is a dry but fruity wine, made from the Tressalier vine, which is often combined with the Pinot Chardonnay or with the Sauvignon; but despite its ancient renown, it is now seldom seen outside its own area. The reason for this, at least partly, is that its quality steadily deteriorated, reaching

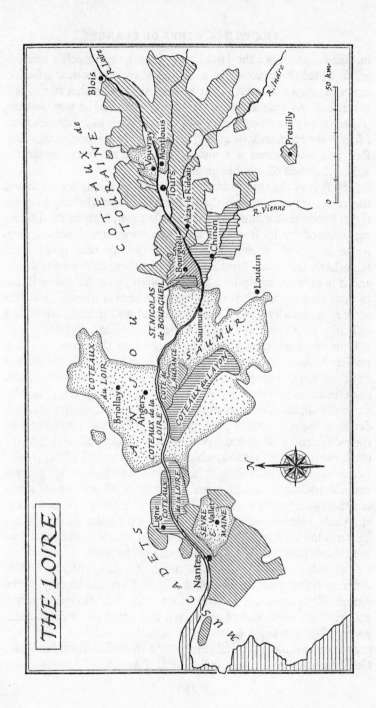

THE LOIRE

50 km

R. Loire
Blois
R. Indre
Vouvray
Montlouis
Preuilly
Tours
C O T E A U X   de
T O U R A I N E
Azay le Rideau
R. Vienne
Bourgueil
Chinon
ST. NICOLAS
de BOURGUEIL
Loudun
COTEAUX
du LOIR
A N J O U
Briollay
Angers
S A U M U R
COTE du
L'AUBANCE
COTEAUX de la
LOIRE
COTEAUX du LAYON
Ligne
COTEAUX
de la LOIRE
SEVRE
&. Vallet
MAINE
C A D E T S
Nantes
M U S C A D E T
N

its nadir just before the Hitler war. It was very much a peasant-made wine: there would be a couple of rows of vines, a field of maize, a couple of cows. . . . It was not surprising that so much of it was bad. As long as the peasant could drink it, he was satisfied. Then, in 1952, a co-operative was set up. This now handles four-fifths of the crop, and the quality has improved beyond recognition. Red and rosé wines are also grown and all come under the V.D.Q.S. when of suitable quality.

The first of the true Loire wines, found on the upper reaches of the river, are sancerre on the left bank and pouilly-fumé on the right. Sancerre is a most delightful little town, high on its cliff and surmounted by its fine château. Both wines are delicious: dry, white and with considerable natural acidity that gives them remarkable freshness. It is this that makes them such a joy to drink; and it is only too easily lost. Sancerre *must* be drunk young if it is to taste its best, and it is often perfect after six months. But this means, necessarily, that it does not travel well in cask, which is a difficulty with many of the Loire wines. Although they are enjoyable in England, they are much more so in their own country. Pouilly-fumé is better than sancerre in this respect. It should not be drunk too young: it is at its best after a year or two years, and it sometimes even develops in the bottle. Pouilly-fumé is also generally slightly the drier of the two. But assuming they are both drunk at the appropriate time, their likeness is more striking than their differences. Both are grown on very chalky soil, and the vine is the same: the Sauvignon, which is known locally in Pouilly-sur-Loire as the Pouilly-Fumé; and both are grown by peasant proprietors, whose holdings are generally small and whose wines are therefore variable. At Pouilly-sur-Loire there are also many vineyards planted with varieties of the Chasselas, which gives a lighter wine with much less character and which is often deficient in acidity. This is sold under the name of the town.

Two other small areas are on much the same latitude but on different tributaries: Quincy on the River Cher and Reuilly on the Arnon. Both areas grow white wines from the Sauvignon grape, and both are fresh and pleasant, but it is essential to drink them young. White reuilly, however, is seen less and less. The local growers find it more profitable to make a rosé wine, from Pinot and Gamay grapes, which they call Coteau d'Aronn.

Once the River Loire reaches Blois, it enters an area of fine viticulture, and there are vineyards all the way to the estuary. They are by no means in an unbroken line, for this is predominantly agricultural country, but throughout the length of the valley they have their place in the scheme of things. It is a valley famous throughout the world for the glory of its châteaux, and it is justly called 'The Seville of France'. The wines are as charming as the place. The first to be reached are those of Touraine, and the names that are familiar to wine drinkers throughout the world follow one after the other. But these more important wines form only a minority of those that are grown. The majority are peasant-grown wines of only local interest: some are good and some are dreadful. The latitude is rather far north: one that enables the skilful grower to produce wines of exceptional delicacy, but if he lacks skill it can be disastrous.

The Touraine grows red, white and rosé wines that are generally light in alcohol. While all can be very pleasant, until one comes to Chinon and Bourgueil it is only the white wines that are notable, especially those grown in the two enclaves of Vouvray and Mont-louis, on either side of the river. In each instance the principal grape is the Pineau of the Loire, usually called the Chenin. These wines, unlike the lesser ones of the area, are by no means deficient in alcohol, especially Vouvray, which, in a good year, can be potent; and in the poorer years it is assisted in this direction by chaptalization. In style and in sweetness, both areas produce wines in great variety, depending on the exact configuration of the vine-yard and on the year: they can be anything from almost bone dry to quite sweet. Generally speaking, the vouvrays are the larger wines and those of Montlouis have less body, less bouquet and develop more quickly, so that they are generally drunk young. In their own country, the Montlouis wines are delicious, with a fine flavour that is slightly reminiscent of Alsace. The vouvrays take longer to develop, and can survive to a considerable age, remaining extraordinarily fresh. They travel a good deal better, but even so the more delicate of them only taste at their best on the spot, where they taste superb—provided one has a good example. Some of the wines from both areas are *pétillant* and others are vinified as mousseux. The former can be delightful, the latter are popular but second-rate. In an exceptional year, vouvray, far from being short-lived, can compete with almost any wine in France. Perhaps the greatest year of all time was 1893—a year enormous in quantity and superb in quality. Wines of this vintage are, of course, unobtainable commercially today, but a few still do survive in private cellars, and their condition is perfect. One might even find the odd bottle in Holland or in Belgium, for, from the fifteenth to the eighteenth century, practically the whole output of Vouvray was exported there. Some of the wine was blended with pedro ximenez from Malaga, to produce a local product that attempted to combine the fragrance of the French wine with the richness of the Spanish.[1]

Next come the fine red wines of the Loire: bourgueil and chinon. The latter is the more famous, but the former is the finer wine. They are grown on either side of the river, where it is broad and tranquil, flowing through gentle and unspoilt country. Chinon owes its fame to history even more than to viticulture, and there is a verse:

> Chinon, trois fois Chinon:
> Petite ville, grand renom,
> Assise sur pierre ancienne,
> Au haut le bois, au pied la Vienne.

It was at Chinon that Joan of Arc met the Dauphin, and it was from there that she set forth for Orléans. It was there, too, that Rabelais was born, and it is said that he owned a local vineyard. He certainly appreciated the wine, and so did his characters. Grandgousier remarked to Gargantua 'Et pas barbe pour un bussart, tu auras soixante pipes, j'entends de ce bon vin breton, lequel point ne croist en Bretaigne, mais en ce bon pays de Véron!' The Breton wine was bourgueil and chinon. Both are derived from the Cabernet Franc, known locally as the Breton. There is some dispute as to why, but the truth is perhaps that there is a twofold reason. In 1631, Cardinal Richelieu (who was born at Richelieu, near Chinon) sent to his manager in the Loire, whose name was the Abbé Breton, several thousand vines from Guienne, and these were planted in place of the local Pineau. It would be a good enough reason for the name, but it will not do, for the wines were so called not only in the time of Rabelais, but as far back as the

---

[1] See Ralph Soupault, *Les Vins de Loire*, Paris, n.d.

THE OTHER WINES OF FRANCE

Middle Ages, when the Bretons provided the main market for the wine.

Bourgueil and chinon can easily be confused with one another, though people who enjoy floral and vegetable similes say that the former has a fragrance of strawberries whilst the latter has one of violets. The lesser growths of both districts can certainly show some of the Loire acidity that ill becomes a red wine, though adding somewhat to its scent. Bourgueil is generally at its best after three or four years in bottle, while chinon, although delightful in its youth, takes somewhat longer to mature. But again there is no rule: both districts include chalky slopes and sandier plains, wines from the former taking longer to develop than those from the latter. The vintage year makes a profound difference, too. A bourgueil of a good year from the chalky slopes often tastes hard when young and is at its best after twenty or thirty years. Amongst the most attractive bourgueils are those from the sub-district of Saint-Nicolas de Bourgueil, and they are well worth looking for, as they are full of flavour. The soil is rather sandy, and the wines develop quickly, having a good bouquet even when young. Some have likened them to beaujolais, and others to claret, but they are really like neither, though they share with beaujolais the unusual characteristic in a red wine that they taste excellent when cold.

Other red wines are grown in the areas known as Côte de Jouélés-Tours, Côte de Saint-Avertin and Coteaux du Loir. The Loir is a tributary of the Loire. There are also several *appellations contrôlées* which travellers in the region may come across, but which are not generally exported, as the wines are not particularly notable. Red, rosé and white wines are sold under the names touraine-amboise, touraine-mesland and touraine azay-le-rideau. Jasnières is well known locally as a white wine.

With Anjou and Saumur one comes to two names that are thoroughly familiar to English wine drinkers. The name of Anjou was even more familiar in Plantagenet times, when the country was under English domination and vied with Gascony to supply us with our wines. After the English were driven out, however, wines from this area practically ceased from being imported, and it was not until this century that they became well known again. Now their popularity is ever increasing, and the most popular of all are the vins rosés, particularly the vins rosés de cabernet. These

289

are grown both in Saumur and in Anjou, though they are generally marketed under the latter name. Their popularity is not at all surprising: they are amongst the best rosés, their price is very reasonable, and an anjou rosé de cabernet is far more likely to be genuine than the even more renowned rosés of Tavel. They are, however, newcomers. The more ordinary rosés of the district—those sold simply as anjou or saumur rosé—are vinified from the Groslot or Gamay vine, while the rosés de cabernet are vinified from the Cabernet Franc or Cabernet Sauvignon. The best of them are grown in those areas where the soil is of sand or of gravel, as clay soil gives a wine that is heady and coarse. The Cabernets were first vinified as a rosé by a M. Daviau-Rozé, of Brissac, as recently as in the second decade of this century. Their qualities were recognized quite soon, but they did not really get under way until the 1950s, when the production rose very rapidly. Their colour is generally very pale, and although some of them are quite dry, most have a considerable degree of sweetness—more, perhaps, than may be apparent, for it is masked somewhat by their good and strong flavour, and by their natural acidity. A good rosé de cabernet will stand up to the flavour and sweetness of strawberries, as well as making a pleasing accompaniment to cold meats. It is therefore an admirable picnic wine, as well as being a popular apéritif. The plain rosés, as compared with the rosés de cabernet, on the other hand, besides being smaller in flavour, are almost completely dry.

If the vins rosés are at present the most popular wines of Anjou, the white wines are nevertheless very noteworthy, and they are now being exported to a greater extent than ever before. They may be found with every degree of sweetness, and in great years, when the *pourriture noble* has done its work, some of them are very sweet indeed. Admirable as the dry wines are, it is the sweet ones which are really worth seeking out—especially those of the Coteaux du Layon, which are amongst the best dessert wines of France.

The Layon is a peaceful little river with an unexpectedly deep valley. It flows into the Loire from the south, and around its banks grows a dessert wine of true grace and quality. Pleasant though the wines of Saumur can be, none can rival those of the Coteaux du Layon. They can hold up their heads in any company, as, apart from their smooth sweetness, they possess their fair share of the characteristic natural acidity that gives the Loire wines their freshness and charm, so that the fine growths of the Coteaux du Layon have an appeal that is all their own; and their sweetness is never cloying. The best are grown on sandy and gravelly soil that is especially good when it is hard. Where clay soil is found, the wine tends to be heavy and dull. It is in the area of Quarts de Chaume, followed closely by that of Bonnezeaux, that the finest growths are found, and from the former perhaps one growth deserves special mention, as it is of the very first quality and is now being imported into this country: Clos Sainte-Catherine.

Saumur was formerly known as Haut Anjou, and it forms a region within the larger region of Anjou: its wines may be sold as Anjou, but not vice versa. The region was once better known than it is now, for it has declined owing to neglect. The still wines of the area, particularly the whites, were very popular on the Continent during the last century, but they never became established in this country, where the name of Saumur has always been associated with the sparkling wine that became popular here in the latter half of the century. It would appear that the wine growers were so prosperous that they chose to rest on their laurels: when the phylloxera hit the area, the vineyards were not replanted with much skill and some inferior vine stocks were used. The area under the vine, too, declined, and it is only recently that things have been put right. The wines are generally dry or fairly dry and the best of them, like most of the Loire wines, are fresh and agreeable. These come from the rather vague area known as 'Coteaux de Saumur' that has never been officially delimited. They have been described as 'manly', and if this term is somewhat fanciful when applied to a wine, it does give some impression of their style; for they are less soft and more vigorous than their neighbours of Layon, and they age relatively slowly. Even when they are not deliberately made into sparkling wines by the *méthode champenoise*, they tend to be distinctly *pétillant*, at least when young. They are grown exclusively from the Chenin vine.

The area known as Coteaux de la Loire lies to the west of Angers on the right bank of the river. Although the wines can be luscious, particularly in great years, they are generally lighter and much drier than the wines of the Coteaux du Layon. They are the biggest wines of Anjou, and in body they can almost approach a white burgundy, whilst still having all the Loire freshness. They are grown from the Chenin grape on soil of partly volcanic origin. They mature gradually and keep very well in bottle. Of the whole of this area, the finest wines are grown in that part delimited as Savennières, and the best of all are in the two sub-areas of Coulée-de-Serrant and la Roche aux Moines. The former has been famous for centuries, but production is minute: the whole vineyard only occupies less than ten acres. The latter, in the twelfth century, was the vineyard of the monks of St. Nicholas of Angers, and in the following century it was the site of the battle in which the future Louis VIII defeated King John. Not many red wines are grown in this area, but some of these are quite noteworthy, having somewhat more body than those of Touraine. The best are grown at Champigny-le-Sec.

Between the Layon and the Loire lie the Coteaux de l'Aubance. The production here is not very large, and the white wines have little of the character of their neighbours of the Coteaux du Layon: they are generally dry, slight and somewhat earthy. While not unrepresentative of the wines of Anjou, they are not noteworthy. The vins rosés, however, are amongst the best, and it was here that M. Daviau-Rozé had his vineyard.

Red wines are not grown in any great quantity in Anjou or Saumur, as the Cabernet Franc and Cabernet Sauvignon vines do not produce good red wines in clay soil, and most of the soils in which they might give good wines are devoted to growing the popular and valuable whites and rosés.

Finally, before the river reaches its estuary, on either side of the town of Nantes, comes the muscadet region. The area is known as the Pays Nantais, and its wines are amongst the freshest, the most delightful, and the most famous of the whole of the Loire. The Muscadet vine, from which the wine takes its name, is none other than the Melon of Burgundy—a variety of the white Gamay. In the soil and climate of the Nantais it undergoes a transformation and produces wines quite unlike those of its native area. The Burgundian vine was introduced on a small scale as early as in the seventeenth century, but it did not arrive in large quantities until 1709, when a great frost destroyed the vineyards and they had to be replanted. Even then, the Muscadet vines were in the minority, most of the area being planted with the Gros Plant, a variety of the Folle Blanche. The Muscadet really gained ascendancy after the vineyards were replanted following the phylloxera. Even then the wine was mostly drunk locally, and this continued until the Kaiser war. It was not until the 1920s that its fame spread; and then it spread rapidly.

Muscadet is remarkably fresh, and it must be drunk young: the younger the better. There is youth in every aspect of the wine. The grapes are picked as soon as they are ripe, and certainly before they become over ripe. It is bottled as soon as fermentation is complete, and it does not enjoy being bottled. It is only at its very best in its own country. In England, some of its delightful freshness is inevitably lost—but by no means all of it. It is the perfect wine for a hot summer's day.

The greatest region for muscadet is Sèvre-et-Maine, both for quantity and for quality. Next comes a part of Les Coteaux de la Loire, where the wines are drier and more acid, which is by no means a fault, as muscadets tend to be deficient in acid. Moreover, the wines from this region tend to survive longer in bottle. But the former, when drunk young, have more delicacy and charm.

The North-East

Auxerrois

Here the great vine is the Pinot, and the two great areas are Burgundy and Champagne. Not far from the medieval town of Auxerre lie the vineyards of Chablis; and these are so surpassingly famous that their neighbours of the Basse-Bourgogne are quite eclipsed, at least in foreign eyes. Nevertheless the latter grow some interesting wines, even if none that deserves exporting. In the Auxerrois, Chablis is so very much the predominant white wine that there are no others worth mentioning. Some quite notable red wines, however, are grown around Auxerre, Cravant and Irancy, but the clay soil gives some of them a very powerful flavour—so much so that they are an acquired taste—whilst others are austere and thin with a dim bouquet and a tendency towards acid. Nowadays more and more of the wine is being vinified as rosé, which is much easier to sell, and some of the Irancy rosé is being exported. Apart from the Pinot Noir, a local vine called the César (which was reputedly introduced by the Romans) helps to give the wines their characteristic flavour. The Tonnerrois, near-by, used to produce red and white wines of comparable quality, but the *vignoble* is now virtually extinct as the last commercial grower died a few years ago. Lesser wines are found around Avallon and Joigny.

The Jura

Travelling east from the Côte d'Or, one crosses over a wide dull plain and then, when the mountains begin to rise again as one approaches Switzerland, one reaches the vineyards of the Jura. Arbois is the ancient city of Franche-Comté where Louis Pasteur was born; and for many of his classic experiments on the chemistry of wine he used those of his home town. The soil is very varied, and several varieties of vine are grown, so that there are red, rosé and white wines, still and sparkling. But the most popular are the rosés, while the greatest are the *vins jaunes*.

The *vins jaunes*, otherwise known as *vins de garde*, are undoubtedly amongst the great wines of Europe. They are quite unlike any other French wines, and the only other wine that comes near to them in character is sherry—way down in the south of Spain. It may be that this resemblance is not purely fortuitous, for the old County of Franche-Comté was for many years under Spanish rule—a domination that only ended in the reign of Louis XIV—and it is more than likely that the Spaniards introduced some of their own methods of enology. These, which are so unlike the traditional ones of France, have certainly proved eminently successful in the Jura. The resemblance between the wines is most surprising when the difference between the soils and the climates is considered. The Jura soil admittedly contains calcium, but not nearly as much as Jerez albariza. And the climate is totally different. That of the Jura is temperate, with plenty of rain and about forty days of snow in the winter, whereas that of Jerez is hot and dry, with no snow at all; even the night temperatures are not expected to fall as low as freezing on more than two or three nights in the year. They could hardly be more different. Yet one of the strangest qualities of the wine is reproduced in the two places: if left alone in cask it grows stronger rather than weaker, whereas wines in other countries tend to grow weaker with increasing age in the wood. The Jerezanos thank their dry climate for this, as the water evaporates more easily than the alcohol under such conditions; but this could scarcely apply in the Jura, where the wine also becomes stronger. The nature of the wine must have something to do with it as well.

The vine that produces *vin jaune* is a local one: the Savagnin, or Naturé. The grapes are picked at the last possible moment—never till November, when they are shrivelled with over-ripeness, and after the first frost has touched them. In Jerez the system is different: the ripe grapes are dried on esparto grass mats beneath the fierce sun; but this would be impossible in the milder climate of the Jura, and the later picking no doubt achieves a similar effect. And whereas in Jerez the fermentation takes place in the wood, in the Jura it takes place in big underground vats. Here a better comparison may be made with the wines of Montilla, near Cordova; and the *vins jaunes* of the Jura may be compared with the montilla-moriles wines at least as validly as with the very similar sherries.

After the fermentation, the wine is left in oak casks to mature for a minimum of six years, and here again the system is Andalusian rather than French, for the wine is left on ullage; that is to say, the casks are not filled, but a substantial air space is allowed to remain over the surface. In the Jura, however, the casks are tight-bunged, whereas in Spain they are left open. Thanks to the air space, a film of yeasts develops on the surface. This film is not the same as the *flor* that distinguishes fino sherries; but it is certainly akin to it, and it brings about similar changes in the wine, giving it a great depth of flavour with that remarkable aftertaste that is so satisfying, and which has so often been described as 'nutty'. But *vin jaune* (like sherry, in its early years) matures in a rather unpredictable way, and by no means all of it is successful. This helps to raise the price to such a level that it can hardly hope ever to become popular in the export markets, where a fine sherry is cheaper, as well as being even more distinguished.

The greatest *vin jaune* of all is château-chalon—which is not a château at all, in the Bordeaux sense: it is the name of a village and that of a whole, rather sparsely-planted district. The area is well worth visiting; for it is remote, peaceful, and incredibly beautiful, with vistas across the hills. These finest of all *vins jaunes* share yet another virtue of sherry: they live almost indefinitely. After forty or fifty years in the wood, their flavour is magnificent; and they go on living for decades, at least, in bottle. As an extreme example, in 1922 the French president was given a bottle of the 1774 vintage. Since I have repeatedly likened them to sherry, it behoves me to say in what way they differ. Certainly they do not in any way resemble an oloroso. They are more like a montilla than a fino or an amontillado; they lack the freshness of a fino, and they are somewhat more obviously acid, while they lack the body of an amontillado. But they do have a very attractive flavour that is all their own, and it is their misfortune that they can be so readily compared with a more popular wine. Unlike sherry, they are not fortified, though their natural strength is such that they can be just as alcoholic. Amongst the many admirers of château-chalon was Prince Metternich, who diplomatically told Napoleon that it was a greater wine than his own Schloss Johannisberger. And he may well have meant it, for he had been importing château-chalon for years.

Vin jaune is the great wine of the Jura, but even without it, the Jura would be an important viticultural district, and it has been so from time immemorial. In the Middle Ages, its wines were invariably listed amongst the favourites of the kings. A story is told that demonstrates the pride that the local people take in their wines.[1] On August 10th, 1595, after the siege of Arbois, the best wines of the district were set before the king, King Henri IV. He was so pleased with them that he asked where they came from. 'From Arbois, of course,' replied a native with more local patriotism than respect, 'where else could they come from?' 'From France,' replied Henri, meaningly. But the Arboisien was not to be intimidated. 'From France!' he retorted; 'devil a wine like that will you find in France.' That diplomatic minister, the Duc de Sully, saw that his royal master was in danger of losing his temper, and hastily remarked: 'Your wine is certainly excellent; no doubt Horace was thinking of it when he said, "vinum addit cornua pauperi" ("wine gives audacity to the poor").' The king's humour changed at once, for he saw an opportunity of making a jest at Sully's expense. 'That certainly,' he exclaimed, 'is the best proof of the excellence of Arbois wine. It makes Sully talk Latin, though he does not know a word of it.'

Jura wines were seldom exported until quite recently when, largely thanks to the efforts of Henri Maire, they were widely

[1] From *The Wines of France* by H. Warner Allen, London, 1924.

promoted. Following the phylloxera there was a disastrous drop in the area under cultivation, and it is still insignificant compared with what it was during the last century. But happily it is rising and the wines are now widely known and popular, especially the rosés.

The two local vines, the Poulsard and the Trousseau, are both members of the Noirien family to which the Pinot also belongs, but unlike the Pinot they have few pigment cells and so the skins can be left in contact with the fermenting must for a relatively long time without its absorbing too much colour. This results in rosé wines of outstanding character. A small proportion of Chardonnay and other varieties are also grown.

The broadest A.C. is simply *Côtes de Jura*. It covers the largest area and also the greatest variety of wines: white, gris, rosé, red, vin jaune, vin de paille and mousseux. The *appellation* Arbois is similar in the varieties it covers, but more limited in area. L'Etoile is a small area for white wines with some vin jaune and vin de paille. Finally, and very properly, château-chalon is a separate *appellation* confined to *vin jaune*. There are also two V.D.Q.S. wines: bugey and roussette de bugey.

The white wines tend to be too thin and acid for my taste, and this acidity is also far too apparent in some of the reds, but others have real character and make excellent drinking, even though they tend to lack subtlety and finesse. Both red and white wines age extremely well. By far the most interesting of the table wines are the rosés, which are amongst the best in France. There is a wide choice of flavour and sweetness; and they vary greatly in colour, ranging from the faint suggestion of pink, that is found in the vins gris, to the very deep pink found in some of the wines that seem unable to make up their minds whether to be enormous rosés or feeble reds. One of the strangest of all the rosé-coloured wines is a *vin de paille*: Grange aux Ceps. It is very sweet and has an immensely powerful and luscious bouquet. It is, in fact, extremely 'interesting', though I cannot imagine what it would taste well with. The sparkling wines lack interest, though some of them are made by the *méthode champenoise*. The most widely advertised of of all is not. This is Henri Maire's *Vin Fou*, which is sparkling through being bottled at the time when the wine is naturally effervescent. It is becoming popular in French cafés, but it is misnamed, for the method of making it is quite different from that of the traditional *vin fou*.[1]

To the south of the Jura lie the vineyards of the Savoy, around the upper reaches of the Rhône and by the lake of Annecy. Both red and white wines are grown, but although the former are pleasant enough, it is the latter that are worth seeking out, especially seyssel and, to a lesser extent, crépy and roussette. The first and second have *appellations contrôlées* whilst the third is a V.D.Q.S. wine. Another V.D.Q.S. wine which is now being imported into this country is apremont: fresh, light, dry and very fragrant, it makes an excellent apéritif or wine for summer drinking. These wines bridge the gap, in character as well as in geography, between those of France and those of Switzerland. They want drinking young, when many will be found to be *pétillant*; others, unfortunately, are deliberately made *mousseux*. They are dry and have considerable *finesse*, whilst by no means lacking body.

The South

It is an old cliché to say that the struggle for survival produces character, but nevertheless it appears to be true, at any rate of wine. Most of the wines in the south of France have no struggle and little character. The vines that yield them are the spoilt children of viticulture. In such a climate they cannot help but grow and flourish, year after year; but such vines seldom give great wines. And it is no easy thing to ferment and to mature a wine perfectly in so hot a climate. It calls for great care, skill and enthusiasm: characteristics that are not ubiquitous. Happily, however, despite these difficulties, a few quite notable wines are grown.

Much has already been written in this book about the influence of Roman viticulture, and there is more to come. The Romans were great viticulturalists, and they did much to improve the cultivation of the vine when they conquered Provincia, which we now call Provence, in 125 B.C. But the vine was cultivated there long before they arrived. It is said to have been brought over from Asia Minor by the Phocaean Greeks who settled in what is now Marseilles prior to 500 B.C. These southern wines are therefore almost certainly the oldest-established in France. It is sad that they are not the best.

[1] See p. 154.

Provence

> O for a draught of vintage! that hath been
> Cooled a long age in the deep delvèd earth,
> Tasting of Flora and the country green,
> Dance, and Provençal song, and sunburnt mirth!
> O for a beaker full of the warm South,
> Full of the true, the blushful Hippocrene,
> With beaded bubbles winking at the brim,
> And purple-stainèd mouth;

Keats knew what he was talking about: his description of Provençal wine is a perfect one—though it is to be hoped that he took great care if he actually bought any. To mature well in such a climate, it needs a cool cellar; and the colour does tend to be purple. One is slightly worried about Hippocrene, since one knows of no wine that has been produced by a stroke of the hoof of Pegasus; and one is far more worried about the 'beaded bubbles winking at the brim'. But a poem is nothing without a little poetic licence. Or if one *must* be scientific about it, it may be blamed on a surface-tension effect after the wine has been rapidly poured, rather than upon an uncontrolled secondary fermentation.

Unfortunately many of the Provençal wines are 'not what they were' fifty or sixty years ago. Two factors are to blame. Firstly the cost of labour, and secondly the tourist trade. Thanks to the former, it is no longer an economic proposition to produce many of the old wines that were grown under conditions of great difficulty and with hard labour on the hillsides; so the vines have descended into the fertile plains. The tourist trade has made it too easy for growers to sell inferior wines—provided the bottle and the label are fancy enough. The growing demand has lessened the real competition rather than added to it.

The two principal vines throughout the south are the Grenache and the Carignan, the former giving a soft style of wine, and the latter, wines that are hard and tough. These are often mixed together to secure better balance, and other varieties are added or are used alone. These include the Mourvèdre—an ancient local strain giving wine with an individual aroma. This vine is particularly prominent in Provence, where the Carignan is not used—at any rate for quality wines. The Carignan is principally found in the Languedoc. In Provence, other popular vines include Muscats,

Malvoisie de Roussillon, Tibouren, Bouteillan, Morrastel and, for rosés, Tibouren and Pécoui-Touar.

The best red wine of the area is that of Bandol—a fine, vigorous red wine, that can be compared with a châteauneuf-du-pape, and which, at its best, is every bit as good, though it tends occasionally to remind one of sunny Algeria. White wines are also grown there, and there are some *blancs de blancs* that are very dry with a very vigorous and full flower, but more famous white wines come from Cassis nearby. These are generally dry, full of flavour and strong. The wine of Cassis must on no account be confused with the alcoholic black currant syrup of Dijon, which has the same name and which enjoys an inexplicable renown as an apéritif when mixed with white wine. Both of these areas are on the coast, to the east of Marseilles. Further along the coast, above Nice, there is Bellet, which principally produces a white wine that enjoys some local esteem. It is well known to those who have taken their holidays in that delightful if over-populated spot. Palette, inland near Aix, provides red, white and rosé wines of considerable reputation of which the best known come from Château Simone. To my own taste, however, they tend to be excessively acid and tannic with insufficient flavour to compensate for their astringency. On the whole, it is the rosé wines of Provence that are most popular. They taste delicious on the spot, well chilled and drunk beneath the sun; and they are now being exported on quite a substantial scale. Most of them are good sound wines and nothing more, but the best of them, which are grown inland on the steep slopes of the granitic hills around Cuers and Pierrefeu, above Hyères, are comparable with any rosé obtainable. Most of them are very dry, and some are enormous in flavour.

The simple but enjoyable V.D.Q.S. wines sold as côtes de provence may be grown in practically the whole of the country lying between Marseilles and the Italian border.

Languedoc and Roussillon

In a book devoted primarily to good wines, the Languedoc need occupy little space; for although the wines are certainly great in quantity, in quality there are few worse; though there is the occasional exception which rises at least to mediocrity. No vines are healthier, and the yield is enormous: so much so that there is chronic over-production, and when two good years follow on top of one another, as they did in 1962 and 1963, the peasants are unable to sell their wine and they try the patience of the government by revolting. The *Guardian* newspaper of August 11th, 1963, gave a graphic picture in a column headed 'Wine growers set roads on fire': 'Liquid fire flowing across country roads in remotest Languedoc, trees felled across the highway, felled telephone and telegraph posts, and a maliciously jammed signal on the railway line from Bordeaux to Marseilles—these are symptoms of the troubles that have called the Minister of Agriculture back from his holiday.' At that time the growers had a surplus of twenty-five million hectolitres of the last year's wine on their hands, and the only solution that could be seen was to distil it for industrial alcohol—though that was not an economic proposition. Most of the wine that had been sold as wine went as *vin de coupage*, which was blended into the cheap table wines that add life if not glamour to the humbler tables of France. A small proportion was blended into greater wines. Roughly half the total wine production of France is concentrated into this area. In the *département* of Gard, which borders the Côtes du Rhône, some quite good wines are grown, and there used to be more, but after the old vines had been destroyed by the phylloxera, the varieties which replaced them were chosen for the quantity of their yield, and the quality was lost. In the *département* of Hérault, wine is mass produced from un-grafted phylloxera-resistant hybrid vines, for despatch by road tankers. Let us say no more of it.

For growing red wines, the Carignan vine is here regarded as the vine of quality, while the principal vine for quantity is the Aramon, and there are several others. For white wines there are the Picpoule, Clairette and Terret Gris, all of which are used to designate the wine they yield.

The best red wines of Languedoc are le minervois and les corbières. Another wine that deserves mentioning is saint-georges-d'orques, for it was once popular in England, and the early nine-teenth-century wine labels engraved with the name of saint-georges were intended to grace decanters filled with this wine, not with nuits-saint-georges. The nearby town of Montpellier, at the beginning of the last century, was as popular a winter holiday resort with the English as Cannes is today, and when war broke out between ourselves and Napoleon, many were taking their holiday there. They were obliged to remain in what was termed 'enforced residence'; but there was none of the brutality of the concentration camp, and no suggestion of barbed wire and wooden huts. They were graciously allowed to lead their normal lives while the wretched war continued. It was a very proper attitude to take towards visiting gentlefolks: they moved in the best society and they chose their own homes. Naturally they grew to know and to like the local wine. And when eventually they were allowed to return, they bore such little rancour that they continued to buy the wine, and they named their new, fashionable squares of Regency houses after the town of their captivity—though they invariably omitted one l in its name. Thus we have that delightful Montpelier Square, then safe in the remoteness of Brompton, but now unhappily surrounded by London; and others were built at Bath, Cheltenham and Leamington. To return to the wine, it is red and fruity; after a few years in bottle it can be quite delicious. One can easily see how the exiles became enamoured of it. Not so far away, by the fascinating old town with the frightening name of Aigues-Mortes, there is the Domaine de Jarras-Listel, where the sandy soil (like that of Colares in Portugal) is resistant to the phylloxera and where ungrafted vines are grown.

There is a wider choice of notable white wines. Lunel and Frontignan produce two of the most delightful muscats of France. Frontignan lies just behind the pleasant seaport of Sète—for it appears pleasant and innocent enough today. In the last century it was the infamous Cette, where it was said that if you went to a wine merchant at 9 a.m. and asked him for fifty pipes of port, fifty butts of sherry, and fifty hogsheads of claret, he would deliver the whole order at 4 p.m.—made entirely out of the local wines. During a recent visit I was disappointed to find no remaining traces of such fabrication. The wine of Frontignan, sold as frontignac, is certainly honourable, and its colour is as pleasant as its flavour: it tends to be a golden brown and sometimes even a reddish brown.

The region of Roussillon is noted for its sweet wines, both red and white. The former are derived from the Grenache grape and come from the areas of Banyuls (on the edge of Spain), Carignan and Maury. The white wines are derived from the Maccabeo,

Malvoisie and Muscat grapes and come from the areas of Rivesaltes, Côte d'Agly and Côtes du Haut-Roussillon. Sweet and coarse when young, all of these can develop considerable finesse and quality with age.

Finally, and some way inland, is found the area of the well-known blanquette de limoux—a sparkling wine, made by the *méthode champenoise*, that is notoriously variable, but which can be very good.

*

Those are a few of the other wines of France; but there are many, many more. And some of those that have been included scarcely deserve their place. Some travel and some do not. But nearly all of them can be enjoyed in their own country: they taste best when they are at home, and the local cooks know how to complement them with their dishes. There is no more pleasant way to spend a holiday than to wander gently around France, drinking diligently all the way.

CHAPTER 7

The Wines of Germany and Alsace

〜〜〜〜） （〜〜〜〜

O f all wines, the German are the most difficult to know well.
The names of the vineyards are as unpronounceable as
they are legion; the nomenclature is long-winded, and at
first appears excessively complex; and the best wines are frighten-
ingly expensive. But in fact things are not as bad as at first they
seem: the names of the districts can be grasped easily enough, if
not those of the vineyards; the nomenclature is easy enough to
understand once the system has been grasped, and its complexity
is justified by its precision, giving a very clear indication of the
style of wine to expect; and if the price is high, the wines are well
worth it. Without these high prices, they would soon cease
from being grown, for in no other country is viticulture so
hazardous and difficult. The study of German wines is certainly not an easy one, but there can be few that are more
rewarding.

The German vineyards are the most northerly, of any importance, in the world. It is all the more surprising that they are
amongst the most ancient. Their origin certainly dates back to
Roman times, and it may even be pre-Roman. Caesar carried his
conquest of Gaul right up to the Rhine, which at first formed the
natural boundary of the Roman territories, though as these were
developed, land on the further bank was brought in. Eventually
almost the whole of the modern vineyard area was under Roman
domination, and the invaders, as ever, needed their wine. The exact
date at which systematic viticulture started remains uncertain: it
could hardly have started immediately—at any rate on a large
scale—and it presumably had to wait until peace was maintained,
in the second century A.D. But one thing is certain, and that is the

304

Cologne

Bonn

R. Rhine

Koblenz

R. Lahn

GERMANY

Frankfurt

MOSEL

R. Mosel

RHEINGAU

NAHE

Mainz

R. Main

FRANCONIA

Würzburg

Trier

R. Nahe

RHEIN-
HESSEN

RUWER

SAAR

Worms

Mannheim

Saarbrücken

RHEIN-
PFALZ

R. Rhine

F R A N C E

0   50   100 km

fact that the Romans cultivated vineyards.[1] Many of their old tools have been found in the Palatinate and may now be seen in the museums. The actual work was mostly done by Gauls whom the Romans had trained.

German scholars have suggested[2] that the vine was already being cultivated before the Romans arrived: the Greeks had brought the vine to Marseilles by about 500 B.C., and their knowledge could possibly have been carried to the north by traders. To support this view, writers have pointed out that vines on the banks of the Moselle are still cultivated in the Greek fashion—up sticks rather than along wires. But there is no archaeological evidence that the vine was cultivated there before the coming of the Romans, and the method of cultivation is more easily accounted for by the physical exigencies of the precipitous river banks than by any historical argument.

What ever the origins of viticulture, by the third century A.D. it was firmly established in the Rhineland and the Moselle. The magnificent Roman gateway at Trier—the Porta Nigra—dates from this time, and at Rüdesheim, Würzburg and Speyer there are fine wine museums with exhibits ranging from the third century to the present day. There used to be another important museum at Trier, but this was unfortunately destroyed during the war.

One of the most beautiful and interesting of the relics is the famous Neumagen Wine Ship, excavated from a Roman tomb. It dates from about the third century and is a sculpture of a great rowing boat, laden with four casks of wine. It was thus that the wine was transported down the Moselle.

After the fall of the Roman Empire, the Rhineland came under the rule of the Franks, and we owe one of the greatest vineyards in the Rheingau to the wisdom of Charlemagne (742–814). From his castle at Ingleheim he watched the snow melting on the opposite bank of the river. In one spot, on a hillside above Rüdesheim, he saw it melting more quickly than in any other; it was so orientated that it caught all the benefit of the sun. He gave orders that it was to be planted with vines, and the Rüdesheimer Berg came into being. Such was Charlemagne's attachment to the vineyards that

[1] See S. F. Hallgarten, *Rhineland Wineland*, 4th ed., London, 1965.
[2] See Alfred Langenbach, *The Wines of Germany*, London, 1951.

there was a legend, for centuries after his death, that when the vines were in flower he left his tomb and wandered along the Rhine, blessing the vineyards.

If the origin of viticulture in the Rheingau was pre-Christian, its development followed the familiar pattern throughout most of Europe, and rested with the Church. The interest of the Church was at first religious: to provide suitable wine for the sacrament. But with the rise of the monasteries, wine growing assumed a commercial scale far in excess of the purely religious requirements. Many of the names that are so familiar to us today were bequeathed by the ancient church. For example, the Archbishops of Mainz owned a hill above Winkel; it was called the Mons Episcopi, or Bishop's Mountain. Then an archbishop gave it to a Benedictine priory, which changed its name to Johannisberg, or the Hill of Saint John. And so it is called to this day: one of the greatest of all the hills of the Rheingau. At the beginning of the twelfth century, yet another Archbishop of Mainz gave a hill called Steinberg to the Cistercian monastery of Kloster Eberbach. The monks cut down the forests that then covered the slopes and they planted vines, to produce another of the greatest growths. And so, gradually, the viticulture of the region assumed its present shape. A similar story could be told of the Moselle and of Franconia.

The monasteries were dominant not only because the monks were good wine growers but also because they had valuable exemption from taxes—a privilege that was also largely shared by the nobles, who were second to them as wine growers. By the ninth century, however, the cities were beginning to compete for the trade. Strasbourg was the first in 825. From the Middle Ages until the seventeenth century, Alsatian wines were sold in England as aussay or ausoye. Worms and Mainz followed the lead soon afterwards. But the Church was still protected by power, wealth, privileged taxation, and above all by its reputation. It was in a position that could not be challenged until well into the thirteenth century. The monasteries, however, enjoyed less of a monopoly in that area which is now known as Rheinhessia, held very little sway in the Palatinate, which was ruled by the Counts Palatine, and were non-existent in the Nahe district.

Viticulture—at any rate on a commercial scale—came to Alsace later than it did to the Rhine. There appears to be no mention of it before the days of Charlemagne, and this may well have been at least partly owing to transport difficulties, as river navigation was difficult beyond Strasbourg. In the twelfth century, however, wine was certainly being grown commercially, though it had little identity of its own, as most of it was at that time exported through the merchants of Cologne. By the fourteenth century production had so far increased that the Alsatian vineyards were the most important in northern Europe.

It is not surprising that the first recorded export of wine from Germany to England came from the Church's vineyards. It occurred in the first half of the eighth century, and was the work of one of the greatest of medieval martyrs: St. Boniface. Born at Crediton, in Devonshire, he was sent to Germany by Pope Gregory II. While carrying the blessings of Christianity to the pagans (who eventually slew him and his followers at Dokkum), he was able to send to his native country the blessing of German wine.

After the good work of St. Boniface there is a considerable gap in the records—a gap that one would expect to find in this period— and it is impossible to say whether or not German wine was being imported into England regularly. In the eleventh century, how- ever, there is a record of wine being sent here from Cologne; and when King John bought 348 casks of wine in 1212, three of them came from Germany. By far the largest number—267—came from Gascony. This would suggest that German wines already had a reputation in England that made them worth seeking out, but that difficulties of purchase, carriage or price kept them a curiosity for wealthy connoisseurs. This is borne out by the record of the following centuries. They continued to be imported, though: on July 24th, 1275, for example, an order was made that one Roger de Greschirche should be paid £10 for two tuns of Rhine wine for King Edward I's use.

Until as late as the seventeenth century, the wines of Germany together with those of Alsace were imported under the vague and all-embracing name 'Rhenish'. The wines of the Upper Rhine and of Alsace were generally considered to be the best, but geographical names were unknown, as were vintage years. The wines were generally imported in *aums*—casks of somewhat variable size, generally holding about forty gallons. A larger cask was the *fatte*, or *vat*, which held either three or five *aums* and largest of all was the *rood*, which held some five hundred gallons. Smaller casks included the *rundlet* of about ten gallons and the *bode* of about four.

During the sixteenth century, the wine growers were less than content. The small growers had for centuries been at a disadvantage as compared to the Church and the nobles, who still enjoyed their ancient tax privileges. They had gained some concessions, but not enough to satisfy them, and in 1525 Kloster Eberbach was attacked and had to hand over at least eighteen thousand gallons of wine.[1] The revolution, however, was disastrous. It was heavily defeated, and in the aftermath conditions were worse than ever before. To maintain discipline, the sale of wine during church hours was prohibited and inns had to close at eight o'clock in the evening. Large parties were forbidden—even at weddings and christenings only eight guests were allowed—and the concessions which had taken so long to achieve were lost. Nothing seemed to go well for the unhappy growers, even in 1582, when the vintage was exceptionally abundant: they did not have enough casks, and the remains of the previous year's vintage had to be poured into the river to make room for the new wine. Despite all this, wine was steadily being exported to England, though the quantities remained small. It had its royal patrons, including Elizabeth of York, the Queen of Henry VII; and in 1543 King Henry VIII placed an order with a Steelyard merchant for supplies on a scale that was altogether unheard of for Rhenish wine at that time. He was to supply 800 *aums* at 30s. each, 400 before Christmas and 400 before the following June; and the wine was to be 'of the best sort, and such as the Emperor, the Duke of Cleves, and other estates use to drink'. In all probability the wines exported were white, but far more red wines were grown then than are today. The principal ports for the trade were Cologne, Frankfurt, Trier and Mainz, but a certain amount was also imported from the Low Countries, notably from Dordrecht and Utrecht.

If conditions were difficult for the growers in the sixteenth century, they were far more so in the seventeenth. In 1618 the

[1] See Alfred Langenbach, *The Wines of Germany*, London, 1951; *German Wines and Vines*, London, 1962.

Thirty Years' War broke out between the Catholics and Protestants in Germany. The Elector Palatine was the focus for
protestantism. His country was the Palatinate, whose vineyards,
together with those of Rheinhessia, were in the centre of the
fighting. They were laid waste time after time. No amount of
pertinacity, courage and skill on the part of the growers could
avert ruin, and many of the great vineyards were totally lost. The
situation was not much better in the Rheingau and Moselle. The
devastation was so dreadful and so far-reaching that viticulture did
not recover until well into the nineteenth century. Throughout
this time, the taste for Rhenish remained unabated, but imports
were never considerable, for supplies were hard to obtain, and far
too much of the demand was met by imitations. Some of these
were manufactured in England, and others were imported from
abroad—notably from France. This did nothing to enhance the
reputation of the genuine wine. In 1614, the Treasurer of the
Exchequer was given power to appoint a commission of four
merchants to taste all wines imported as Rhenish and to take a
bond of wine merchants not to compound any wines to be called
Rhenish within this kingdom. The proclamation makes good
reading:

'Whereas we have lately understood. . . . That some merchants of the
Netherlands have used to buy small French wines at low rates and
drawe the same into buttes and tonns commonly used for Rhenish
wines . . . and sould them in stead of Rhenish wines although at a
lower rate than Rhenish wines can be sould for. . . . That (the farmers
of customs) did find that there were daily brought into this Kingdome
many false and Counterfeit Wines as well as from the ports of Holland
as directly from France and here solde and uttered to our subjects for
right Rhenish Wines . . . whereby our subjects have been deceived to the
prejudice of the health of their bodies by drinking of wines corrupted
with unwhollsome druggs . . . our will and pleasure is that wee and our
subjects may be furnished with right Rhenish wines or ells noe wines
of that nature . . .'

It also showed that several Rhenish merchants were at the time
living in the country. It was a worthy measure, but it is doubtful
whether it worked, for in Howell's *Familiar Letters* (1634) there
was an account of the practice still persisting:

'There is a hard green wine that grows about Rochel, and the islands thereabouts, which the cunning Hollander sometimes used to fetch, and he has a trick to put a bag of herbs, or some other infusions into it (as he doth brimstone in Rhenish) to give it a whiter tincture, and more sweetness, then to re-imbark it for England, where it passeth for good Bachrag, and this is called stooming of wines.'

The wines around Rochelle would presumably be those growths now known as bois-a-terroir which are used for the distillation of cognac, and which do not make good drinking at all. And it is interesting to read of this early reference to sulphuring—a practice which many would think is over-indulged in today by some German growers. As far as the genuine Rhenish wines were concerned, Howell's taste was for wines from 'The Pfalts or lower Palatinate, about Bachrag'—or Bacharach, as it is now called.

Despite the imitations, contemporary accounts of Rhenish are generally favourable, and at last geographical names begin to appear. Thus Gervase Markham in his *English Housewife* (1675) wrote:

'There are two sorts of Rhenish wines, that is to say Elstertune and Barabant; the Elstertune are the best; you shall know them by the Fat, for it is double bard and double pinned. The Barabant is nothing so good, and there is not so much good to be done with them as with the other. If the wines be good and pleasant, a man may rid away a hogshead or two of white wine, and this is the most vantage a man can have by them. . . .'

In 1693 William Salmon wrote of Rhenish in his *The Compleat English Physician*:

'It is a good nephritick and vehemently diuretick, opening all obstructions of urinary parts, and bringing away stones, sand and gravel, and other tartarous matter from the veins, ureters and bladder; it strengthens the stomach admirably, causes a good appetite and a good digestion, and opens obstructions of the lungs. . . .'

It therefore enjoyed a fair reputation with the gastronome and a good one with the physician. The Duke of Rutland knew more of geographical names than did Markham, for Belvoir Castle was supplied with Bacharach, Moselle, Pincair and Hockheim. German wines, too, were supplied for the royal table: in 1673 one hundred vats were bought at Cologne for King Charles II.

As far as Alsace was concerned, the seventeenth century was

disastrous. Following the Thirty Years' War the population was greatly reduced and much of the country was laid waste. Good and careful viticulture practically ceased, and the vineyards did not recover until after the return of Alsace to France after the First World War.

At the beginning of the eighteenth century, the import statistics show that the bulk of wine imports were Portuguese and Spanish. French wines and Rhenish were about equal, but well down. This is partly accounted for by the differential duties, which favoured the Portuguese, but the transport of the wine was very expensive and helped to inflate the price: roads were bad, even where they existed at all, and river transport was made uneconomic by the fees exacted by the riparian owners as the vessels made their way down. Nor can these delays have done anything to improve a notoriously delicate wine. To make matters worse, the quality of the wines deteriorated sadly towards the end of the eighteenth century—the result of over production and bad viticulture. It is the old, old story that has so often been heard: when trade is booming and wine is easy to sell, the growers produce quantity instead of quality and inevitably reaction follows.

It was at about this time, though, that the advantages of late gathering were discovered; and the discovery, as in Sauternes, is attributed to an accident. The Bishop of Fulda, who controlled the vineyards in the Rheingau, omitted to order the start of the vintage, and when at last it was ordered, the monks were in despair, for the grapes were beginning to rot. Happily, however, it was the 'noble rot', and the wine was finer than ever before. It was not for many years, though, that the great dessert hocks that we know today arrived on the scene, and the 'Old Hock' on the Vauxhall Gardens wine list for 1762 was evidently rather sour, for it was available 'with or without sugar' at 5s. a bottle. 'Rhenish and sugar' cost only half a crown. These prices compare with 8s. for champagne, 2s. for port or sherry, and 'Table Beer, a great mug' for 4d.

Alsace is a land that has been much disrupted by war; and war played its part in viticulture there in the last century. Following the Franco-Prussian war, in 1870 Alsace passed to Germany, and it was not returned to France until after the Kaiser war ended in 1918. Throughout this period—almost half a century—the

Alsatian vineyards were regarded as the poor relations of the German ones. Quantity replaced quality and the reputation that they once enjoyed was lost. Nearly all the wine went to the Rhineland, where it was blended with the cheapest hocks. In recent years this policy has been completely reversed, and since the Hitler war, the wines of Alsace have come to be acknowledged as amongst the best.

It goes without saying that the most far-reaching thing that happened in the nineteenth century was the coming of the phylloxera. Noticed for the first time near Bonn in 1874, it spread rapidly. The Germans tackled the problem with unique thoroughness. All vineyards were periodically inspected and the pest was kept under control by the difficult and expensive carbon disulphide treatment. This proved very effective and grafting was little used in Germany until the Hitler war. Then, thanks to the shortage of labour and materials, the phylloxera was released to do its damage. After the war many vineyards had to be replanted with grafted vines, and now it is forbidden by law to plant any vine that is not grafted on to an American root stock. The difference to the taste, however, has been very slight; and this can be seen by direct comparison, for there are many ungrafted vineyards still in Germany. Looked at carefully, the wine from grafted vines is found to be somewhat lighter, which is no disadvantage, as it accords very much with modern taste, and the wines mature somewhat more quickly, though alas they age and die *much* more quickly. In compensation, the yield is about three times as much; and without this increase prices would be even more astronomical than they are. But a few graftings have proved less successful: the style of the American plant shows itself only too clearly; the bouquet is quite spoilt; and the life of the wine is very short.

In the Moselle, in particular, the phylloxera has a hard time of it, as the slate soil is almost as difficult for it to get through as is sand—its only real enemy. Although new vines are all grafted, in accordance with the law, most of the great Moselle vineyards still contain a fair proportion of the old native stock. And certain areas of the Palatinate and Rheinhessia are not affected.

Parallel with the change that is being brought about by the phylloxera, there are others that are even more significant, namely changes in taste and in technology. The change in taste is from the heavy, brownish hocks, which were long matured in the wood, and which found favour at the beginning of the century, to the light, delicate wines that we know today. There are some who still hanker nostalgically for the old wines. Admittedly those that I have myself tasted have been too old—having been too long in bottle— but it is not difficult to imagine roughly what they were like when young; and my own choice would undoubtedly be the modern wines. These have certainly been chosen by the markets, but until recently they could not have been made. Modern technology has brought with it a hospital-like degree of cleanliness and it is thanks to this that wine can be bottled entirely free of ferments so that there is no risk of secondary fermentation even when it retains some of its natural sugar. This in turn makes it possible to bottle the wine earlier, while it still retains its full youthful freshness. The Germans are supreme amongst the wine technologists, and their very skill occasionally brings an undeserved odium, for people claim that too much is left to the chemist and not enough to nature. This is utter nonsense. In the good years the wine is as 'natural' as ever it was. Cleanliness and care in every stage of the fermentation have cut out the misfortunes that made wine making so hazardous in the past and, since all wines can show their best, the occasional products of 'good luck' have now become the commonplace. But it is in the bad years that this modern skill really comes into its own. In 1966 I went round the Moselle tasting wines of the 1965 vintage —said to be the worst since 1922. Those that were made *natur* were so acid that they could hardly be held in the mouth. They were certainly undrinkable and could only be sold soon after the vintage for use in the blends from which sekt[1] is made. Those, however, that had been fermented by skilled enologists, who had chaptalized them, arrested their fermentation by destroying the ferments while a little sugar was left, and then reduced the acids by means of a special alkaline treatment, were more than drink-able: they were positively enjoyable though not, of course, great. And they were perfectly wholesome. Without such wines to stock the local bars, the price of the fine wines would soar far beyond our grasp. And there is no truth at all in the much repeated innuendo that fine wines are 'mucked about with'. The growers and shippers think too highly of their reputations to do any such thing. The

[1] German sparkling wine.

THE WINES OF GERMANY AND ALSACE

Germans are so conservative, indeed, that until about ten years ago chaptalization was little used, and never in the great vineyards. Now they have learnt better, and chaptalization undoubtedly enables quite good wines to be made in poor years. Even the leading growers are now resorting to it, and the supply of fine German wine is happily increased. But in great years, the wines are still most strictly fermented as *natur* wines. The future, however, is in greater doubt. At the time of writing the German wine laws are being revised, and contrary to the trend almost everywhere else, it appears that they are being relaxed. There is real danger that in future wines will be made more artificially attractive by being sweetened. In the long term, if the quality is reduced in this way, there could be disaster.

To approach the classification of the wine of Germany and Alsace logically is not easy. One could start from so many places: from the vines, from the districts, from the vineyards within the districts, from the methods of vinification, even from the vintage years. But the vines are the logical starting point, so let us begin there.

The greatest vine of them all, as far as Germany is concerned (though some would say it only comes second in Alsace), is the Riesling, known in Baden as the Klingelberger; it is undoubtedly one of the great vines of the world. In origin, though, it is German, and it may well be descended from the ancient native vines of the Rhine. Perhaps no other, save for the Muscatel, has spread so widely. No other vine carries its name so proudly on the labels of bottles from so many countries; for the name Riesling is itself a hallmark, and although the style of the wine varies with different climates and different soils, something of the nature of the Riesling grape remains in them all. It has too much character ever to be masked completely. Its berries are well formed, but small—which results in its giving a rather small yield—and they ripen to a rich yellow-brown. It is by far the most prevalent vine in the Moselle and Rheingau, and is prominent in all the great German districts; there might well be room for no other variety, were it not for the fact that the Riesling has some other disadvantages apart from its relatively low yield. In particular, it flowers early and ripens very late, so that it is vulnerable to spring frosts and to wet weather at the time of the vintage; and these are very serious disadvantages in the northern climate of Germany. But the wines it gives are second to none. They mature gently into greatness—and it is largely thanks to them that the German vineyards are counted amongst the greatest in the world.

Next to the Riesling, the Sylvaner is the most famous vine. It is sometimes spelt Silvaner, and is otherwise known as the Franken Traube or Oesterreicher. The former name, which is often used in the Palatinate area, means the *Franconian grape*—and in that district it is particularly popular. The latter means *Austrian,* and some authorities suggest that it originated in the region of the Danube, though this is disputed. The grapes are larger, giving a much better yield, and they ripen far sooner; they will even ripen in places where the Riesling will not ripen at all. It is also less particular as to soil. Because of these advantages it is the most widespread of all German vines. But the wines it gives are not in the same class as those from the Riesling. They are the everyday wines that mature quickly, and provide good value but seldom greatness. They have a less notable bouquet than Riesling wines and are less distinguished generally. There are occasionally exceptions, though, in the Palatinate and particularly in Franconia, where some auslese[1] and even trockenbeerenauslese wines are vinified from this grape, and these can be superb.

The Traminer and the Gewürztraminer are vines of great distinction having a character that is all their own. They give wines with an extraordinarily fragrant and spicy bouquet. The principal difficulty with them is that they ripen even later than does the Riesling. At one time they were quite popular in the area of the Rheinhessia, and although they are now very rare there (having lost ground to the cross-breeds which are mentioned later) they are still occasionally found; and there are even a few in the Rheingau, in the region of Hallgarten. In these districts, however, they are not used alone but their wines are blended with Riesling wines, adding to the intensity of the bouquet. They are more common in the Palatinate and, as far as Germany is concerned, are most popular in Baden. These vines really attain their glory, though, in Alsace, where the soil and climate suit them to perfection, and where the wines they produce are considered by some to be the best of all the Alsatians. Gewürztraminer means *spicy Traminer,*

[1] See p. 320.

and this variety was obtained by selecting from the Traminers vines which gave the spiciest wines. Nowadays all the Traminer vines planted in Alsace are of the Gewürztraminer selection, though wines are still marketed under both names. There is now a different form of selection: that of the wines themselves. Those with the greatest fragrance are taken apart and sold as Gewürztraminer, while the others are sold simply as Traminer.

The two most notable of the crossbred vines are the Müller-Thurgau and the Scheurebe. They were both obtained by crossing the Riesling with the Sylvaner, but it is the former which is vaguely, and often on bottle labels, referred to as the Riesling X Sylvaner. The Müller-Thurgau is named after the Swiss who created it. At first it was acclaimed widely. It ripens early and the yield is large. Its wines are attractive, aromatic and light in body; but unfortunately they tend to be too light. When the vines were first planted it was thought that this lightness would grow less when they were older, but this hope has proved ill-founded: the wines are still light and lack acidity. Although attractive when young, they do not age at all well and need to be drunk after two or three years. On the whole growers are disappointed, and the vine is losing favour though it is capable of producing better wines in bad years than either the Riesling or the Sylvaner. But things are not settled yet: it was successful in 1965 and very successful in 1966. The Scheurebe (or Semling 88, S.88) is a more recent cross, created by one Scheu. The wines produced have a particularly strong aroma that has been likened to that of the Muscatel, and opinions vary as to their merits, though personally I like them. Unfortunately the vine is very susceptible to fungoid diseases, and for this reason its planting is restricted by law. Its future is therefore extremely uncertain, but in some places it has certainly succeeded. Another cross is the Mainriesling, recently renamed the Rieslaner, which has the advantage of ripening earlier than the Riesling and giving wine where the finer vine will not. It is mostly found in Franconia.

Two varieties of Pinot are grown: the Pinot Gris, which is here known as the Ruländer, or occasionally as the Tokaier, or, in Alsace, as the Tokay d'Alsace; and the Pinot Blanc, in Germany known as the Clevner, Klevner or Weissburgunder. The latter, although it gives some very acceptable wines, that are very light in colour, is not widely grown. The former, however, does well on the heavier soils in Germany, and is quite popular in Alsace. It yields soft, well-rounded wines with a heady bouquet and plenty of colour but somewhat lacking in acidity. It is most popular around Baden and in Alsace. In Alsace, various other varieties of the Pinot are also grown.

The Elbling otherwise known as the Kleinberger or Rauschling, or, in Alsace, as the Barger, is rapidly becoming extinct, yet it was once the most popular vine in Germany. Its history may well go back further than any of the others, and it is said to have originated in Italy, its name being derived from the Latin *vitis albuelis*. In the fifteenth and sixteenth centuries it was so popular that the Riesling almost disappeared; yet the quality of wine it produces is of the poorest, and only the yield is good. When the quest for quality reached its full momentum in the last century, the Elbling soon fell into disfavour, and it is now practically eclipsed, though occasionally found in the Upper Moselle, Württemburg and Baden. In Alsace it is no longer tolerated. It has been identified with the Pedro Ximenez of Jerez[1] and one can only say that its performance in the south is very different from that in the north.

Several other varieties of vine are grown in Germany to a lesser extent. The Morio-Muskat is a cross between the Sylvaner and the Pinot Blanc, named after one Morio, who created it. It is occasionally grown on rich soil, where it produces wines of very strong bouquet and intense acidity. These characteristics are so exaggerated that the wines are only used for blending. The German Gutedel is equivalent to the French Chasselas and the Swiss Fendant. The wines it produces are distinctly uninteresting, though in Alsace it yields some quite pleasant luncheon wines.

The Muscat is very uncommon in Germany, but it is otherwise in Alsace, where it produces some of the finest wines. The Alsatian muscats are quite unlike any other, for they are dry, though very fruity.

Of the varieties grown for red wines, by far the most important is the Spätburgunder, which is equivalent to the French Pinot Noir. The Trollinger, which is grown in the area of Württemburg, is none other than the Black Hamburg, which is so well known to those who visit Hampton Court.

[1] A. Massel, *Applied Wine Chemistry and Technology*, London, 1969.

The quest for new varieties is a continuous one, and when I visited the Wine Institute at Geisenheim in 1966 I was shown a great variety of wines vinified from new species, only a few of which appeared at all promising. One that has yielded excellent wine on the Moselle is a cross numbered 133—it is so new that it has not yet been named, nor has there been time to evaluate it thoroughly. Amongst the less recent of the newly-created species, two at least deserve mention—the Würzburger Perle and the Aris. The former is a cross between the Gewürtztraminer and the Müller-Thurgau, and is finding favour in Franconia owing to its ability to withstand the winter cold. The latter has the wild American vine in its ancestry and it is very resistant to disease; but so far it is only in the experimental stage.

After the vines have been grown, the grapes must be picked, and here there is a very real difference between the methods of Germany and those of most other regions; for they may be picked as soon as they are ripe enough—and therefore the vintage is safe, though the wine is likely to be uninspiring—or they may be left to attain a higher degree of ripeness, which gives a richer and finer wine at the risk of the vintage being spoilt by late rains. In so northerly a climate, grapes that are picked too soon tend to be far too acid. The simplest way to reduce the proportion of acid is to add water—a practice which sounds very disreputable but one that is capable of giving a tenth-rate wine from a must which would otherwise give an undrinkable one. Although prohibited in southern countries such as Spain and Italy, and also in the major French districts, this practice has long been tolerated in Germany, though the amount of water that can be added is strictly limited by law. Needless to say, the yield is increased, and tenth-rate shippers specializing in 'bargains' for supermarkets are said to go out of their way to buy the most acid grapes they can get, so as to add the most water, and then to ferment the wine with the aid of sugar. The moral is a simple one: as always with wine, avoid bargains. When the better shippers seek to make a decent wine in a really bad vintage year, such as 1965, when the grapes are hopelessly acid right to the very end, they now use the special alkaline treatment that has already briefly been referred to.

A government organization—the Herbst Ausschluss, which is run by a number of the big growers who are selected for their honesty and intelligence—decides the date of the vintage. With German thoroughness it even decides the hour of the day that picking should start and stop, to avoid picking grapes that are wet with rain or dew: the church bells are rung to signal the beginning and the end of the day's work. Anyone who waits till the end of the vintage period is entitled to call his wines spätlese. But there are also other conditions which must be complied with if this name is to be used: no sugar may be added to the must, and if the grapes are frozen or snowed upon—which is quite a risk so far north—the name is lost. A further refinement, to which the same conditions apply, is to select bunches of over-ripe grapes, when the wine is called auslese. If over-ripe berries are selected instead of bunches, it is called beerenauslese. And finally, if individual berries are picked which are so shrivelled as to be practically like raisins, the wine is a trockenbeerenauslese. Each of these stages represents a further step of richness, and a trockenbeerenauslese is so luscious that it is more like a liqueur than a table wine. One would not wish to drink such a wine every day, nor could anyone save a multi-millionaire afford to, for the price is astronomical; but just occasionally a trockenbeerenauslese can provide a gastronomic treat of a kind that few other wines can approach and none can equal. The fermentation of these wines is also very difficult owing to the high sugar content. It calls for expert knowledge and one very experienced grower told me that one of his casks suddenly ceased to ferment with sad results to the quality of the wine. Necessarily, too, they are extremely expensive, since while a late harvest imparts a unique quality, it also results in a drastically reduced yield, and such wines are hardly ever economic. At best they are a gamble.

These four terms are fundamental in the nomenclature of German wines. A further style of wine has recently sprung into fashion: eiswein. The German vineyards are subject to sudden, intense frosts. If this happens when the grapes are still on the vines, the unripe berries are frozen solid, but those that are ripe are only partially frozen; part of the water separates as ice crystals, leaving the sugar and flavouring matters in greater concentration. To make an eiswein, the grapes are picked at sunrise and are pressed immediately. The first juice from the press comes from the ripest, still-frozen grapes. It is this that is used, and the result is a sweet wine rather like an auslese, but more delicate and having a beautiful, characteristic bouquet. Eisweine, though, are generally less well balanced than auslesen and less long lived. At their best they can undoubtedly be superb: but lately fashion has brought a great demand and some recent examples have been disappointing. They were perhaps once worth their price as rare curiosities but they are now beginning to seem over rated.

Other words used in describing German wines include:

A   abfüllung: bottling.
        abzug: bottling.
        auslese: selected bunches of grapes (see above).

B   beerenauslese: selected berries (see above).
        bestes: best.

C   cabinet, cabinetwein: the best wine produced by the grower concerned.
        creszenz: vineyard the property of the person named. This term may only be applied to unsugared wine.

D   domane: domain.
        durchgegoren: fully fermented.

E   echt: genuine. This term may only be applied to un-sugared wines.
        edelauslese: a noble auslese.
        edelbeerenauslese: see beerenauslese.
        edelgewächs: noble growth.
        edelste: choicest selection.
        edelwein: a noble wine.
        eigengewächs: own growth.
        eiswein: ice wine, when the ripe grapes have been frozen naturally by frost.
        erben: heirs.

F   fass nr.: cask number. This term may only be applied to unsugared wine.
        feine: fine.
        feinste: finest.
        freiherr: baron
        fuder nr.: cask number. This term may only be applied to unsugared wines from the Moselle.
        fürst: prince.

G gebrüder: brothers.

geschwister: literally, brothers and/or sisters; but more loosely, a family business.

gewächs: growth. This term may only be applied to unsugared wine.

goldbeerenauslese: this is not a beerenauslese but an auslese made from fully ripe, golden grapes.

graf: count (as a title).

H hoch: high.

hochgewächs: a noble wine. This term may only be applied to a beerenauslese or trockenbeerenauslese.

hock: a Rhine wine—term used only in English.

IJ jahrgang: vintage.

K kabinett, kabinettwein: the best wine produced by the grower concerned.

kellerabfüllung or kellerabzug: bottled in the cellar named.

kellerei: cellars.

korkbrand: branded cork.

kreszenz: vineyard the property of the person named. This term may only be applied to unsugared wine.

L liebfraumilch or liebfrauenmilch: a term much beloved of the English, but one that is generally to be deplored. It means 'Our Lady's Milk' and was originally closely associated with the vineyards around the Liebfrauen-kirche at Worms. An alternative theory is that it was originally 'Liebfrauminch'—*minch* being ancient German for *monk* and the wines belonging to the monks of the Liebfrauenkirche, which would have given them a larger authentic provenance; but no matter. It is now applied loosely to blended German wines, generally from Rheinhessia. Such wines are commercially popular and invariably pleasant; but they are never great, nor do they provide as good value as those that the discriminating are able to select.

M markenwein: branded wine.

moselblümchen: the moselle equivalent of liebfraumilch.

N   naturrein: as naturwein.

naturwein: a natural wine made without sugaring, and unblended. This is assumed where the wine is spätlese or auslese, but the fact that it is a naturwein may be added for emphasis.

O   original: original. Thus originalwein—original wine; originalabfullung or originalabzug—original bottling; and so on. A wine may only be described as an original bottling if it is unsugared and is matured and bottled in the grower's cellars.

PQ   pfarrgut: an ecclesiastical vineyard.

R   Rein: pure.

S   schlossabfuellung or schlossabzug: bottled at the castle.

schaumwein: second quality sparkling wine. If containing added carbon dioxide, the words 'mit zugesetzer Kohlensaeure' when the new law comes into force in 1971.

sekt: sparkling wine. Under the new law this term will be reserved for wines of the higher qualities.

spätlese: late gathered (see above).

spitzen: of top quality.

spitzengewächs: a noble wine. This term may only be applied to a beerenauslese or trockenbeerenauslese.

stiftung: a charitable trust.

T   trocken: dry.

trockenbeerenauslese: selected very over-ripe berries (see above).

UV   ungezuckerter wein or ungezweckerter wein: a wine without added sugar. The same thing as a naturwein.

verbessert: literally 'bettered'; in fact, chaptalized—that is to say sugar is added to the must to make up a deficiency in the grapes in poor years.

WXYZ   wachstum: vineyard the property of the person named. This term may only be applied to unsugared wine.

wein: wine.

weingut: estate. But this does not mean that the wine is estate bottled.

winzergenossenschaft: co-operative.

winzerverein: co-operative.

Once these terms have been understood the complex German wine label immediately ceases from being incomprehensible; in fact one is struck by its lucidity and pedantic accuracy as compared with the labels from the other great areas. The information is put down in the following order: first the town or village, which generally has the suffix -er added to its name; then the particular vineyard site (the *lagen*); then the grape; then details as to the time of picking, for instance whether the wine was an auslese; then any appropriate details as to the grower, etc.; and then, of course, the vintage. Thus Oestricher Lenchen Riesling Spätlese Cabinet 1959 is a late gathered cabinet wine of the 1959 vintage, grown in the Lenchen vineyard at Oestrich. And so on. All the really fine German wines, coming from leading vineyards, will have the vineyard name specified on the label. The absence of such a name always means that the wine is not in the top class, and usually that it is a blend. But beware of certain vineyard names. Recently the rules have been relaxed, and although the vineyard name still means just what it says on estate bottled wines, on others certain vineyard names no longer have any more than a generic meaning. These have been eliminated from the lists of notable sites mentioned later in this chapter even where mention of them would be justified in relation to estate bottled wines. Under the new German wine laws which will probably come into force in 1971, when a wine is sold under a grape varietal name, it will only have to contain 75 per cent of that variety and the same proportions apply to vintage years and vineyards save that beerenaulese and trockenbeerenauslese wines bearing a site name need only contain 50 per cent of berries picked from that site. These would appear to be retrograde steps but perhaps it would be better to reserve judgment until the new law is finally settled and enforced.

As far as the town or village is concerned, moreover, the use of its name without a specific site name does not mean that the wine has come from the vineyards adjoining the town: the major centres of wine growing are allowed to apply their names to any wine of the appropriate style, quality and value (of which the shipper is the sole judge) grown 'adjacent or near' to them, which in practice means within ten miles. Thus a wine labelled 'bernkasteler' may have been grown up to ten miles from Bernkastel.

In writing of blended wines as I have above, it must not be taken that I disapprove of them: far from it. While they can obviously never be great wines, they are consistent and many of them are good, some very good. It is a blessing that such reliable wines are so readily available.

To take a journey through the German wine lands is principally to explore the banks of two rivers and their tributaries: the Moselle and the Rhine, which join together at Koblenz. The two tributaries of the Moselle are the Saar and the Ruwer. The tributaries joining the Rhine (apart from the Moselle) where it passes through the main vineyards are the Nahe and the Main. The whereabouts of the various districts, along the banks of the rivers and inland, is shown on the map more clearly than it could be expressed in words. It only remains to take the journey, drinking the wines as one goes along. Here the armchair traveller once again finds how inadequate words are to describe flavours. But that cannot be helped. To make the journey in person is far better than to read about it; and no journey could be more delightful. Both valleys in some stretches are comparatively gentle, in others, precipitous, rocky, rugged, and fierce; and the countryside behind the rivers is beautifully varied, from the mountains behind the Rheingau to the quietly rolling countryside of the Palatinate. And all along the way one can stop and taste some of the most delicate and delicious white wines in the world, varying from the dryness and lightness of a Moselle picked early to the lusciousness of a trockenbeerenauslese from the Rheingau or the Palatinate.

The Moselle

Many who like German wines like those of the Moselle best of all. Their appeal is of freshness and delicacy; there is nothing quite like them. The finest hocks admittedly have greater depth and grandeur—though the moselles can have grandeur, too, in exceptional years, when the sun has shone hot and long, so that growers can make rich beeren- and even trockenbeerenauslesen. 1921 and 1959 were two such years. But these exceptional wines are not necessarily those that are most sought after by people who really enjoy moselles. Nor does it look as if the latter vintage, as a whole, will be long lived: there was really *too* much sun. They are curiosities: in acquiring grandeur they lose something of their freshness, and their dignity detracts from their charm. Indeed, to moselle fanciers, the great growths of the Rheingau are tainted by a touch of vulgarity. A woman of perfect taste wears exquisite jewellery discreetly, while a vulgarian will festoon herself with large but imperfect diamonds. But such similes must not be taken too seriously. The hock lover would reply indignantly that the diamonds are far from imperfect, and are by no means out of place on a figure of regal dignity. But whatever one's tastes, it is clear that the great attraction of moselle is its delicacy. It is immensely fresh to the palate—a virtue which stems from that ample natural acidity which also enhances its bouquet to make it one of the world's most fragrant wines. A young moselle is also often *spritzig*, with infinitessimal bubbles that sparkle minutely in the mouth and tickle the palate.

The great vine for moselle is of course the Riesling, which is practically universal throughout the district. As long ago as 1787, the Prince Elector of Trier ordered all other vines to be uprooted and replaced. Not unnaturally this splendidly autocratic edict did not have immediate effect; for one thing there were not enough cuttings. But his wisdom was never forgotten, and what he ordered has now practically come to pass.

The word *moselle* covers the wine grown on the banks of three rivers: the Moselle itself and its two tributaries, forming a district denominated by the composite name Mosel-Saar-Ruwer. The Moselle alone may be considered as three separate districts: the Ober-Mosel, or Upper Moselle; the Mittel-Mosel, or Middle Moselle; and the Unter-Mosel, or Lower Moselle. The first named begins near the border with Luxemburg and continues to the mouth of the Saar. It produces thin, second-rate wines which are seldom if ever exported.

The great vineyards are those of the Middle Moselle. The river winds irregularly through its valley, and vineyards are planted wherever there is a south slope to give sun to the vines—it does not matter on which bank the slope may be. Many of the vineyards are extremely steep, making cultivation difficult, and the soil is full of

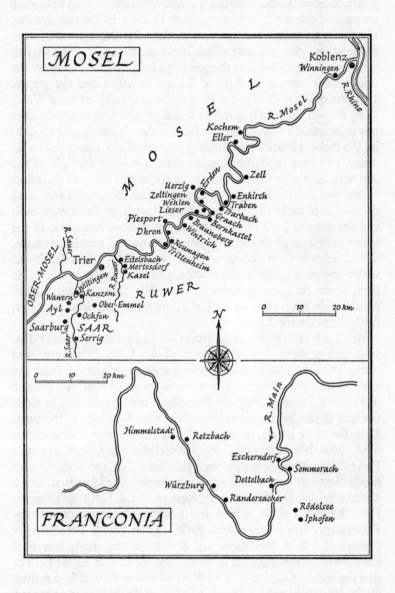

slate, large pieces of it covering the surface. At one time slate quarried from the hills behind the vineyards was broken into small pieces and scattered over the surface to assist in the fertilization, but this is no longer necessary, as modern fertilizers, used in strict moderation, give a better effect much more easily. The surface slate also helps to prevent the soil from being washed away by the rains and it reflects the heat of the sun to help ripen the grapes. Unfortunately, it does not appear to be as durable as hard Welsh slate, though; in time it corrodes and disappears, so that fresh slate has to be quarried from the hills behind the vineyards and brought in. To make full use of the sun's rays is especially important so far north, and here the river plays its part: it reflects the light of the sun and, thanks to the heat stored in the water, tempers the effect of sudden frosts. Recently massive works of canalization were completed to make the river navigable. Two large dams were built and the general level of the water raised, submerging some of the lower vineyards, but happily none that was of any importance. There are now about fourteen locks. The river's greater depth and width appear slightly to have enhanced the quality of the wine from some of those remaining, especially those of the Lower Moselle. It may also, by virtue of its increased heat capacity, further reduce frost risks.

In a book of this size, it is impossible to describe the individual sites and growers. The great sites of the Côte d'Or were hard enough to list. Those of Germany would occupy three times the space. Just a few of the sites, however—the greatest of all—*must* be mentioned. Passing along the Moselle in the direction of its flow, the first of the big names is that of the minute village of Piesport. Here the river bends, in a great, precipitous, south-facing curve. The three best vineyards are Goldtröpfchen, Günterslay and Falkenberg; there are also several others that are scarcely less good. Next one comes to Brauneberg, known until less than half a century ago as Dusemond, a corruption of the Latin *dulcis mons*. Here the south slope is long and straight, the finest sites being Falkenberg, Hasenläufer, and Juffer. Then comes Bernkastel—perhaps the most famous of all. It is an enchantingly beautiful town beside a vast expanse of river. The old houses are so perfect that the whole place looks like a film set, and there is even a ruined castle. Its considerable tourist trade has no doubt helped to spread the fame of its great wines; for great though they are, their fame is perhaps disproportionate. The name of the finest vineyard has also helped—for Doktor is easy to remember, as well as sounding healthy; and the quality of its wines has always been consistently good owing to the meticulous care taken by its three proprietors—Deinhard, Thanisch and Lauerburg—of whom the first two are the largest by far. It is said that the famous Doktor vineyard owes its name to a worthy archbishop of Trier who, in the fourteenth century, lay sick of a terrible fever that no medicines would cure. An old soldier, who was a friend of the bishop's, remembered a similar illness that he himself had suffered from. Resisting all the efforts of the apothecaries, he drunk a great draught of wine, which put him into a deep sleep, and when he awoke he was wholly cured. He went at once to the palace with a keg of his finest wine and, to the horror of the doctors, insisted that the bishop drank deeply until he slept. The next day the bishop woke up feeling perfectly well, and from the depth of his heart he declared the wine to be a perfect doctor. And thus it has been called, from that day to this. Some claim that the wines have a 'smoky flavour' though one suspects that this is in the palate of the beholder. It was, by the way, a favourite wine of King Edward VII. Recently some have suggested that the Doktor wines, exquisite though they are, are over priced, and one can certainly understand the irritation of rival growers whose comparable wines are sold for less. Perhaps there is some justice in this criticism, and one can largely thank the American market for the high prices these wines fetch at auction. For this reason, and so as to be able to supply their old customers at a realistic price, Deinhards have consistently refused to send their wines to auction.

The adjoining Doktor and Graben vineyard is its peer, as is Badstube, and there are several others not far behind, including Bratenhöfchen, Rosenberg, Schwanen and Schlossberg. It is some indication of the care with which the vines are tended that when I went over the Deinhard vineyards I was shown how every single vine was marked and numbered.

The next town is Graach, the finest vineyards being Abtsberg, Dompropst and Himmelreich. Also within the commune, but not sold under the name of the town, is Josephshof. Wehlen is on the opposite, or left bank of the river. Its wines are amongst the finest and costliest of all moselles; but they have not always been so. Until not so long ago they were considered by no means exceptional —of the second flight, even. They have risen into the very first-rank thanks almost entirely to one family—the Prüms—and it shows how much can be achieved, given a good site, by really first class viticulture. The most famous vineyard of all is the Sonnenuhr, or sundial, and it really does have a sundial, enormous and white on a cut-away cliff. Amongst its great neighbours are Lay and Nonnenberg.

Back on the right bank of the river, comes Zeltingen. Its production is vast and the quality of the various Zeltingers naturally varies, but the best are very good indeed, especially Himmelreich, Rotlay, Schlossberg and Sonnenuhr. Uerzig, on the left bank, has its vineyards dramatically carved out of a steep, reddish cliff, the best being Kranklay and Würzgarten. Almost opposite, on the right bank, comes Erden with its fine vineyards of Busslay, Herrenberg, Prälat and Treppchen. With these, the Middle Moselle comes to an end.

The wines of the Lower Moselle are very pleasant, and in a great year they can be excellent, but generally speaking they come a clear second to those of the Middle Moselle, and there is no point in considering individual sites. The dividing line between the two districts occurs shortly after Enkrich, and the next town of any importance is Zell, an attractive place with lots of tourists. Its wines enjoy the generic name—originally a site name—Zeller Schwarze Katz, meaning 'black cat', and are distinguished by having black cats on their attractive labels. Then, between Eller and Kochem the river curves to give a whole series of particularly good sites. Its odd shape at this point is said to resemble a cramp iron, and it is thus called Krampen. Further down the river towards Koblenz, notable vineyards are found at Winningen.

For those of us who remember the war, the name of the River Saar is an ominous one; for night after night our bombers flew over Germany and the Saar was given as their objective. But it was not the peaceful, vine-clad stretch of river that flows into the Moselle just south-west of Trier: the great steel works are further up the valley, by Saarbrücken. The river is the same, but the landscape is very different indeed, and one would never connect the two. Nevertheless, the vines of the Saar valley were greatly affected by the war; for the valley was a battlefield, and many of the vineyards were laid waste. Happily, however, all has long since been put right, for the Germans were indefatigable in working for recovery.

The wines of the Saar valley are often described as 'steely'; and certainly in the past years this hard, almost metallic taste used to give them an austerity which only their most devoted admirers could tolerate, though this has been considerably mitigated by modern cellar techniques. In 1966, for instance, I tasted some very agreeable wines made in that disastrous year 1965. It was said to have been the worst year since 1922, but by then the growers had many more technical weapons, and despite the weather they vinified surprisingly decent wines. The Saar wines are always exceptionally light, and in great years this gives them a unique elegance that is strikingly absent in the bad years. The offer of an off-vintage Saar wine should be regarded with the greatest suspicion: when they are good, they are very, very good, but when they are bad they are horrid; or at any rate they used to be, until modern techniques made them drinkable.

Wiltingen produces some of the very best wines of the area and has been a centre of viticulture ever since Roman times. The most famous vineyard of all is Scharzhofberg, which was planted by the church during the eighteenth century, and soon afterwards, following the sequestration in 1798, came into the hands of the Müller family, where it has been ever since. Other notable growths are Braune Kupp, and Klosterberg, but there are several others not far behind them. Scharzberg is also a very famous growth, but as a geographical name it tends to be abused. In Wawern the finest growth is Ritterpfad, in Canzem (or Kanzem) the leading growth is Altenberg, and in Niedermennig the finest growths are Herrenberg and Sonnenberg. Oberemmel, just to the east, grows wines that are practically as good, fine growths being Agritiusberg and Hütte. Ayl is noted for its Kupp and Herrenberg vineyards, and Ockfen for its Bockstein, Geisberg and Herrenberg. Most of the vineyard holdings in this area are very small. For instance one of the largest proprietors in Ayl is Peter Lauer of the local hotel, and he only owns about five acres. There is a very active co-operative which dates back to 1880.

The Ruwer (pronounced Roover) is the smallest of the Moselle's tributaries—a busy stream rather than a river, and the wines grown on its banks vie with those of the Saar in delicacy; if anything they are even more delicate. Production, though, is very small and only three villages need be mentioned: Mertesdorf, with its Maximin Grünhaus estate; Eitelsbach; and Kasel.

Mittelrhein

Geographically, the Mittelrhein, or Middle Rhine, is logically the next district to consider, for it stretches all the way from Koblenz to the point where the River Nahe joins the Rhine. It is an area of intensely beautiful river scenery, but the quality of the landscape is by no means reflected in that of the wine, which tends to be thin and acid in all save the very best years, when some quite acceptable wines are admittedly grown. In more normal years it is only appropriate for blending into the cuvées from which sekt is made. There is one town, however, on the left bank, whose name is familiar to anyone interested in the history of wine, and that is Bacharach. But its fame was fortuitous, and wholly unconnected with its own wines, which are not noteworthy. Bacharach was the furthest port on the Rhine which big ships could get to. Hence it was the centre for the export trade, and wines from the Rheingau, Rheinhessan and Palatinate were all degraded by being shipped as 'bacharacher'. Just above Bacharach is the Binger Loch, the rapids just by Bingen, which are dramatically visible from the Rüdesheimer Berg and which only small ships can get round.

The Rheingau

Soon after passing Mainz, the Rhine bends, and then it flows just south of a line running due east-west until it passes the junction with its tributary the Nahe, when it bends again, to flow north-west through the mediocre vineyards of the Middle Rhine. It is this east-west section that is the glory of the German wine growers. The right, or northern bank faces almost due south. Behind it, the Taunus mountains provide a natural shelter from the cold north winds. The pebbly soil is quartz stone and slate, which is highly suitable for the great Riesling vine that occupies three-quarters of the vineyards. In fact everything is exactly right. That is the Rheingau. It consists of a single, if much broken, hill-side; and it is so famous that one would hardly suspect it of being one of the smallest of all the German wine-growing areas. But it is.

It almost goes without saying that such a property, in ancient times, was in the hands of the Church. Its wines are amongst the biggest that Germany produces: rich in flavour, with plenty of sugar and ample alcohol. Yet despite their bigness, they have great elegance and finesse. Even in an off-vintage year good wines are produced from many sites, and when the sun shines brilliantly and long, to give a great vintage, the beerenauslese and trocken-beerenauslese wines are the supreme gifts of a rich providence.

Let us continue our tour, but this time against the flow of the river, so as to go on in the same direction, away from the Moselle. The first town is Assmannshausen. Its inclusion within the Rheingau comes rather as a surprise, as it hardly seems to be within it geographically, and it is most certainly not within it spiritually. It produces almost exclusively red wines, grown from the Pinot Noir vine, here known as the Spätburgunder. The Pinot, as we know from Champagne, can produce fine wine in a very northerly climate; but in Champagne the best wines are those vinified as white. In Assmannshausen, the Pinot is, to my taste, a catastrophe. Admittedly the wines are popular locally, nor are they without a certain charm. But they give the impression of aspiring unsuccessfully to be white; their redness is a disguise, worn thinly; they taste rather like a second-rate hock with a dash of burgundy. The best site is the Höllenberg vineyard.

After Assmannshausen, comes Rüdesheim; and that is a very different story. It is an enchanting old town, with steep, narrow streets and, quite apart from its wine, it is a notable tourist centre. High on the hill behind it is the Niederwalddenkmal—a vast memorial commemorating the unfortunate resuscitation of the German Empire. It is worth going up in the cable car just to see the view. The old castle of Ehrenfels is an enchanting ruin, and the most interesting thing of all, for the wine lover, is the wine museum. It is full of beautiful objects, like the three-hundred-year-old carved pillars with a vine motif, from a church altar, seventeenth-century wine glasses, and eighteenth-century masonic firing glasses. There are also many old labels, including one dating from 1775; but the most interesting display of all is the range of old presses, dating from the sixteenth century to the nineteenth, showing how the press evolved. The wines of Rüdesheim, however, are its greatest glory. The story of Rüdesheimer Berg has already been told: it is a massive hill, placed perfectly to catch the sun, and the vines grow all up it in terraces. These wines have one most unexpected characteristic: they seldom show at their best in the very best years. The very feature which is their blessing in second-rate years is their undoing in years of intense heat, for the vines are then so exposed to the sun that they get burnt up, and the soil is too dry, so that the growing grapes are starved of moisture.

The exposed and commanding site of the berg led it to an unexpected fate during the Hitler war: it was extensively bombed. Some of the bombs were actually aimed at it, for it was a perfect and well-used site for anti-aircraft guns and lookout posts; others were aimed at Bingen and missed, falling on the other side of the river. Now it is undergoing a far more drastic change—that of rationalization. Many of the smaller terrace walls have disappeared and the ground has been bulldozed into smooth, more gentle, slopes, while some proprietors have exchanged their holdings so as to have larger and economically viable vineyards instead of small-holdings on different parts of the berg. Such changes are going on all along the Rhine and Moselle, encouraged by the government, and some of the more reactionary wine drinkers, particularly Englishmen, have expressed their forebodings that wine will never be the same again. Nonsense! The German wine trade stands or falls by its quality, and the Germans have more sense than to do anything likely to put this in jeopardy—even though I suspect that one or two of them are trading on the prejudices of an uncritical American market. The gentle slopes will, if anything, give a better exposure to the sun; irrigation will be easier; and it will be possible actually to improve the standard of viticulture. Had the old terraces remained in these days of labour shortage and high wages, costs would inevitably have gone up and quality would have been sacrificed, as the necessary machinery could not have been used. By smoothing the mountain back to its original shape, costs will be reduced and quality increased. Nearly all the best Rüdesheim wines are grown on the berg, and the name of the vineyard is added to that of the hill, to give composite names, like: Rüdesheimer Berg Bronnen. The best sites on the berg are: Bronnen, Burgweg, Dickerstein, Hellpfad, Hinterhaus, Lay, Mühlstein, Paares,

Roseneck, Rottland, Schlossberg, Stumpfenort and Zollhaus. Recently a most damnable sacrilege has been committed on the berg: part of the Hinterhaus vineyard has been turned into a car park. The most famous sites from elsewhere than the berg are Bischofsberg and Schlossberg.

Immediately next door is Geisenheim, which apart from its vineyards has Germany's great school of viticulture and enology. The finest sites are Decker, Hoher Decker, Kläuserweg, Kosackenberg, Lickerstein, Mäuerchen and Rothenberg. Winkel is noted for the fine growths of Dachsberg, Hasensprung and Jesuitengarten; but in the hills behind it are two great schloss where some of the greatest wine of all the Rheingau is grown: Schloss Vollrads and Schloss Johannisberg.

Schloss Vollrads, in the commune of Winkel, is one of the most perfect estates in the whole of Germany, and it has been in the hands of one family—the Greiffenklaus family, and their descendants the Counts Matuschka-Greiffenklaus—ever since the fourteenth century. All its wine is sold under the single denomination, but it is divided into various qualities, distinguished by different labels and capsules. The lowest quality has *original–abfüllung* on the label, and a green capsule—and although it is the lowest, it is still good; then green with a silver stripe; then green with a gold stripe; then comes the red capsule followed by red capsules with silver or gold stripes. Then there is a complete step up. The labels have the word *schlossabzug* with the various green and red capsules as before. No wine is sold as *spätlese*, the Schloss Vollrads equivalent being called *Kabinett*. These wines have blue capsules which may also have silver or gold stripes. Auslese wines have a pink capsule; beerenauslese and trockenbeerenausleses have white ones. But the classification appears to have varied over the years, and it is confoundedly confusing.

Schloss Johannisberg, once a church estate, has been in the hands of the Metternich family since 1816; and there is no more glorious name in German wine lore, though of late its reputation has perhaps not been quite so universally acclaimed as formerly. Sixty-six acres of beautifully kept vineyard enjoy a perfect exposure to the sun on the slope in front of the schloss. Unhappily, during the war it was bombed by the R.A.F.—a single and, it is said, unauthorized incident. Oh, that one could drown the pilot in a butt of riesling! The schloss has largely had to be rebuilt, which has been very well done. The wine is sold under various qualities and with different labels and capsules: red for the lowest quality, then green, then pink. The cabinet wines (which are not necessarily better, though they do tend to be) are sold under a different range of capsules: orange in place of red, then white, and then blue. Beerenauslese and trockenbeerenauslese wines have gold seals. Other notable Johannisberg vineyards include Hölle, Klaus, Klauser Berg and Mittelhölle.

Mittelheim lies between the two better-known names of Winkel and Oestrich. Its best sites include Edelmann and Oberberg.

Oestrich is a pleasant little town with a large acreage of vineyards. Some devotees of the Rheingau suggest that its wines are more notable for their body than for their finesse; but this is merely the sort of carping criticism that emerges when one compares the great with the greatest. The finest sites are Doosberg, Eiserberg, Eiserweg, Kellerberg, Lenchen and Mühlberg.

Hallgarten lies in the hills behind Oestrich between Schloss Vollrads and Kloster Ebebach. Perhaps because the vineyards are high and remote from the moderating influence of the river, the off-vintage wines tend to be disappointing, but those of the great years are amongst the finest of the Rheingau. The best sites are Hendelberg, Jungfer and Schönhell.

Back to the river again, the beautiful little town of Hattenheim and its distinguished neighbour Erbach must be considered together, for most of the greatest vineyards adjoin, forming a strip along the bank. There is one great exception, though: Steinberg, in the hills behind Hattenheim, and belonging to that commune. Between the two villages there is a fine old drinking fountain. It is called the Marcobrunnen, or marking fountain, for it marks the boundary between the two communes. It also gives its name to one of the very greatest sites of the Rheingau—the Marcobrunn (or Markobrunn) vineyard, which belongs to the village of Erbach. An attempt by Hattenheim to append its name to some of the neighbouring vineyards has been firmly fought off and has been declared illegal—a decision that is undoubtedly historically correct. Of the Erbach wines, the marcobrunners are superlative, but there are others that do compare with them, notably Brühl, Hohenrain, Rheinhell and Siegelsberg. Most of the fine Hattenheim vineyards are on the Marcobrunn slope—Engelmannsberg, Hassel, Mannberg, Nussbrunnen, Willborn and Wisselbrunn. But the greatest name of all in this commune is Steinberg. Far from the other great sites, it is high in the hills, adjoining the ancient Cistercian monastery of Kloster Eberbach. Planted by monks, the great vineyard has been kept intact and is now owned by the state, which uses the old monastery buildings (and very beautiful they are) for bottling and storing the Steinberg wines, as well as those from its other properties. Although the vineyard is a single entity, the wine is sold in various grades, and there is often a considerable difference between them. Again, as it is a long way from the moderating influence of the river, the wines in off years tend to be disappointing, hard and harsh. But when the sun has been shining, they are magnificent, regal wines.

There are three more villages amongst the hills: Kiedrich, Rauenthal and Martinsthal. The last named (which used to be called Neudorf) does not grow any really notable wines, but those of the other two are very fine, especially Rauenthal. The best sites in Kiedrich are Gräfenberg and Wasserrose. The Rauenthal Berg is one of the oldest vineyard sites in Germany, and its wines are amongst the best in the Rheingau, so it is surprising that they are not better known in this country. The best sites are: Baiken, Gehrn, Herberg, Rothenberg, Wieshell and Wülfen.

With Eltville one is back on the river. Again its name is surprisingly little known, but its wines are excellent and it is also a commercial centre of the wine trade, with a large Staatsweingut, or state-owned winery. Its best sites are Kalbpflicht, Klümbchen, Mönchhanach, Sonnenberg and Taubenberg.

The wines of the next village—Walluf—are not particularly noteworthy though in good years some fine wines are grown on the Walkenberg site, nor are those of the fine spa city of Wiesbaden, but thereafter the Rheingau reaches its grand finale at Hochheim. That this town should be in the Rheingau at all seems strange, as it is about ten miles from the other main sites and three miles up the Rhine's tributary, the Main. The vineyards even look different, being on flat ground. To my palate they taste rather different, too, though I can certainly accept the universal opinion of the experts that they could belong to no other family than the Rheingau. From the sixteenth century until quite recently Hochheim was the centre where all the Rheingau wines were classed and assessed. The name Hochheimer became synonymous with Rhine wines and it is this, together with the popularity of the wines actually grown at Hochheim, that led to the Rhine wines being known in Britain as 'hock'. When Queen Victoria visited the town one of the vineyards was renamed after her as Königin Viktoria Berg, and it is said that she loyally and regularly imported its wines for her own table. They soon became fashionable, and they still have their followers in this country, but they are not all to my own taste because in the fine vintage years I have found them too big and coarse. The only vintage I have really enjoyed is the off-vintage of 1965. The finest sites are Domdechaney, Kirchenstück, Rauchloch and Stein.

The Rheinhessen

The Rheinhessen lies on the left bank of the river, on the opposite side to the Rheingau, but not directly opposite: if the orientation of the slopes of one bank are perfect for wine growing, it follows that those opposite them will not be. The finest sites of the Rheinhessen lie upstream, between Worms and Mainz, while the section between Mainz and Bingen, opposite the Rheingau, produces, for the most part (but by no means entirely) wines of the second quality. Unlike the Rheingau, the Rheinhessen, as will be seen from the map, stretches quite a long way inland. Its best sites are on the Rheinfront, mostly fairly near the river but slightly inland, following the line of the hills.

The wines, too, differ considerably from their more august neighbours: they are slighter and less subtle. Nor do they last so long in bottle as those from the Rheingau and are often past their best when less than eight years old. This is especially true of the very hot years like 1959. They are very fine wines, though, all the same. The difference arises partly through climate and partly through soil, which sometimes has a slight purple-red tinge from sandstone and slate, but which generally consists of chalk and marl with a top sandstone layer of loess—a fine yellowish-grey loam. In this area, moreover, while the Riesling remains king of the vines and is grown on the finest sites, it by no means reigns alone. The most widely cultivated vine is the Sylvaner. The Müller-Thurgau is also popular and so is the Scheurebe.

The Rheinhessen is inevitably associated with that river of

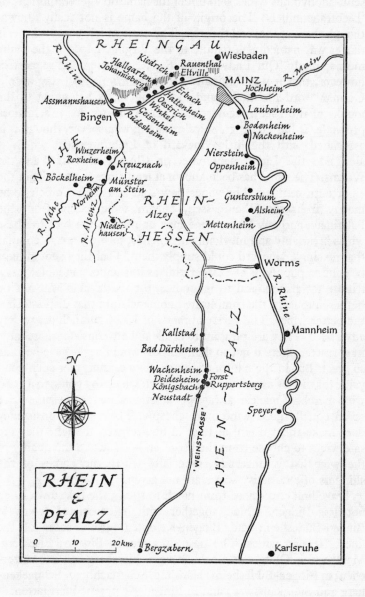

RHEINGAU

R. Rhine

Wiesbaden
Kiedrich
Rauenthal
Hallgarten
Eltville
Johannisberg
R. Main
MAINZ
Assmannshausen
Hochheim
Erbach
Hattenheim
Oestrich
Winkel
Geisenheim
Bingen
Rüdesheim
Laubenheim
Bodenheim
Nackenheim

NAHE

Winzerheim
Roxheim
Kreuznach
Böckelheim
Münster
am Stein
Nierstein
Oppenheim
R. Nahe
Norheim
RHEIN-
Guntersblum
Alsheim
R. Alsenz
Alzey
Nieder-
hausen
Mettenheim
HESSEN

Worms
R. Rhine

Mannheim

Kallstad
Bad Dürkheim
PFALZ
Wachenheim
Deidesheim
Forst
Königsbach
Ruppertsberg
Neustadt

Speyer

N

RHEIN-PFALZ

RHEIN
&
PFALZ

'WEINSTRASSE'

0   10   20 km   Bergzabern   Karlsruhe

semi-anonymous wines sold under the name of 'Liebfraumilch', or 'Liebfrauenmilch'. The origin of the name is not really known, though there are several theories. The most widely accepted one is that it was named as a tribute to the Virgin Mary, for the name means simply 'Our Lady's milk'. S. F. Hallgarten[1] has suggested, however, that it was originally *liebfrauminch, minch* being an old German word for monk, and indicating wines belonging to the monks of the Liebfrauenkirche. This theory sounds much more probable. It has no geographical meaning whatsoever, though it is associated with the little vineyard of Liebfrauenstift which is alongside the Liebfrauenkirche, or Church of Our Lady, at Worms. The name has been known at least since the middle of the eighteenth century. The wines now sold as Liebfraumilch come mostly from the Rheinhessen, but to some extent from the Palatinate, and any Rhine wine may be used in the blend. These wines invariably and inevitably *are* blends, for they are so popular that no single vineyard could supply them. That they should have become so popular is as exasperating as it is understandable: it is a tribute to laziness and to ignorance, for the layman will not be bothered to learn the complicated nomenclature that distinguishes the better wines. The various brands of Liebfraumilch are widely advertised. They are pleasant to drink and are consistently reliable in character; were it not so their success would never have become so great. But in the nature of things, they cannot offer such good value for money as can the lesser-known wines: by going to a good wine merchant one can always get a better wine for the same price or an equally good wine more cheaply. Their sheer consistency does make them useful at least in one respect, though: they are safe wines to choose from the list of an hotel where the quality of the wine list is uncertain, especially where the names of the shippers of alternative wines are not given.

Travelling once more from north to south, the first town to be noted is Bingen, which, together with its associated towns of Bingen-Büdesheim and Bingen-Kempten, grows some of the finest Hessian wines. The best sites are, in Bingen: Eiselberg, Mainzerweg, Ohligberg, Rochusberg, Schlossberg and Schwätzer-chen; in Bingen-Büdesheim: Häusling, Scharlachberg, Schnacken-berg and Steinkautsweg; and in Bingen-Kempten: Pfarrgarten.

[1] *In Rhineland Wineland*, London, 1965.

After Bingen there is a considerable gap where the left bank of the river, opposite the Rheingau, offers the wrong elevation. The next town of note is Mainz, a commercial centre of the wine trade with few vineyards of its own. The vineyards begin at Laubenheim, but the first of any importance are at Bodenheim, where the best sites are Ebersberg, Hoch, Kahlenberg, Leidhecke, Rettberg, Sankt Alban, Silberberg and Westrum. Further along the river comes Nackenheim, a town famous for the quality of its wines, and one in which there is a state-owned vineyard; but unfortunately the quality is not backed up with quantity, and its wines are little known outside Germany. The finest sites are Rothenberg (noted for the redness of its soil) and Fenchelberg.

Next comes Nierstein, a town of resounding fame whose finest wines are second only to the great growths of the Rheingau, and one where the quantity matches the quality. Its best vineyards rise up from the river bank and so benefit from the reflected sunlight and the heat stabilization of the water. The nomenclature of the Nierstein wines is complicated by an attempted simplification. There are eleven collective names, each of which may be coupled with that of Nierstein and each of which embraces a number of vineyards, including some notable ones. The use of the collective name does not preclude the use, in addition, of the vineyard name, though certain vineyards, namely Brudersberg, Glöck, Taubennest and Zehnmorgen are the exceptions to which no collective name applies. The collective names are: Auflangen, Bildstock, Fockenberg, Heiligenbaum, Hipping, Mersch, Oelberg, Paterberg, Rehbach, St. Kiliansberg and Spiegelberg. Notable amonst the many fine sites are: Brudersberg, Fläschenhölle, Floss, Fuchsloch, Glöck, Kehr, Orbel, Pettental and Tal. At the other end of the scale, Niersteiner Domtal does not necessarily come from Nierstein at all: like Liebfraumilch, it is a generic name, but a slightly more precise one, as the wine must come from within ten miles of Nierstein. Much more precise is the name Niersteiner Gutes Domtal, registered by the Nierstein growers in 1959, as an attempt to gain some control over wines sold under their local name. These wines must originate in Nierstein itself.

Oppenheim, the next town up the river, is almost as famous as Nierstein and almost as good. The finest sites are: Kreuz, Sackträger and Zuckerberg. After Oppenheim one finds many excellent vineyards, but no more that are in the truly outstanding class. Finally there comes Worms, more famous for its diet than its vineyards, though it is a notable commercial centre of the wine trade. The Liebfrauenstift vineyard is right inside the city, and whether or not it gave its name to the famous Liebfraumilch, its wines, at any rate in good years, are not sold as such, but rather under its own name.

The Nahe

The River Nahe joins the Rhine at Bingen, and it is at this point that the districts of the Rheingau, Rheinhessen, Mittelrhein and Nahe all meet. The river runs its course roughly parallel to that of the Moselle, and anyone looking at the map might speculate as to the character of its wines. In fact they are as individual as any of the others, but it would not be right to say that they have a character of their own: they have several characters of their own. Many of them subtly combine features both of the Moselle and the Rhine: the delicacy of the former with much of the body of the latter. These are especially delectable. In the upper reaches of the river there is a certain amount of slate, not unlike the Moselle, then there is volcanic soil, sandstone and a certain amount of clay. It is not surprising, then, that the wines offer variety; and they are also of excellent quality. Many of them, moreover, are exceptional value, for the Nahe is less well known than its neighbours. Only about a third of the total area, however, is planted with Riesling.

As a wine-growing area, the Nahe does not begin at Bingen, but further up river, and it is centred around Kreuznach. Although, following the usual pattern, the very finest sites are along the river on the steepest slope, the area stretches some distance inland, where there are some quite notable vineyards. At Roxheim, there are Birkenberg, Höllenpfad, Hüttenberg and Mühlenberg; at Winzerheim there is Rosenheck and others scarcely less good. Travelling up the river, the area of fine wines begins at Bretzenheim, but one must travel as far as Kreuznach before finding the really fine sites. Those at Kreuznach are: Brückes, Kautzenberg, Kronenberg, Krötenpfuhl and Narrenkappe. At Münster-Sarmstein there are Dautenpflänzer, Langenberg and Pittersberg; at Niederhausen there are Hermannsberg, Hermannshöhle and Rossel; at Norheim there are Dellchen, Hinterfels, Kafels and

Kirschheck; at Schloss Böckelheim there is pre-eminently Kupfergrube, a site that did not even exist until the beginning of the century. It was just a steep hillside of desolate scrub land until the state took it over in the 1880s; it was cleared by convict labour in about 1900 and planted out in 1903 as a model vineyard and research centre, growing wines as elegant as the situation of the vineyards is beautiful. The whole place is unique in the perfection of its equipment, including whole cellars that are temperature controlled for carrying out the fermentation in ideal conditions if the weather is hot. With state money one can achieve that sort of thing.

The Palatinate

The name of 'The Palatinate' has a romantic ring about it; for the 'Count Palatine' so often crops up in our history books and even appears in the *Merchant of Venice*. And the wines fully live up to the promise of their name. In Germany the area is known as Pfalz, or Rheinpfalz, and is derived by devious routes from the Palatine hill, in Rome, where the Caesars lived. More immediately, it is derived from the Latin *palatinus*, which signified an officer of the palace. The Elector Palatine was one of the seven original electors of the Holy Roman Empire, but by the fifteenth century the Electorate had already become hereditary. Thus the English name is nearer to the original than the German.

The Palatinate is the exception amongst the great wine-growing districts of Germany in that its vineyards do not line the banks of a river: they follow the direction of the Rhine but are well to the west. It consists of three separate areas: the Unterhaardt, or Lower Palatinate; the Mittelhaardt, or Middle Palatinate; and the Oberhaardt, or Upper Palatinate. In the west it is protected by the Haardt mountains, a continuation of the Vosges range which rise behind the vineyards of Alsace, and its climate is the most pleasant in Germany, with lots of sunshine and limited rainfall, so that semi-tropical plants and trees grow there. It is this climate that gives the wines much of their character, and this is further enhanced by the soil, which is a similar loam to that of the Rhinehessen, but richer. Many of the dry wines seem to me to be rather lacking in delicacy and finesse; they tend to be mellow, full-flavoured, but unsubtle. Nor does one need to be told that one has left the Rhine and is on one's way to Alsace. This applies particularly to those grown from the lesser grape varieties. The Riesling is a vine apart, and on the finest sites of the Middle Palatinate it continues to produce fine-flavoured wines with notable balance, even when they are dry. But the glory of the Palatinate is to be found in its sweeter wines. The spätlese, auslese, beerenauslese and trockenbeerenauslese wines are glorious. The fullness of their flavour well matches their sweetness, and the result is absolutely exquisite.

The Lower Palatinate is the northerly part of the area, extending from Zell south as far as Grosskarlbach. The soil, like that of the Upper Palatinate, is rather heavy, with loam on top and sandstone beneath. The countryside is fairly flat, and so are its wines. Some of these attain mediocrity, but most of them, especially in sunny years, are coarse and earthy *schoppenweine*, which please the local populace but no one else. The best of them appear to be those grown from Gewürtztraminer grapes, and the best of all come from the extreme north, around Zell. The most famous is Zeller Schwarzer Herrgott, which means 'Our Black Lord' and is said to derive its name from a white statue, piously erected in the eighth century, which turned black with age. Or did it take unto itself some of the sins of the world? The impious have suggested that its name was contrived to compete with that well-known moselle Zeller Schwarze Katz. But the wines are as far apart as are the towns.

The wines of real distinction are all found in the Middle Palatinate thanks largely to its lighter loess top soil. The most northerly vineyards are those ranging between roughly Weisenheim am Berg and Dackenheim, but the best sites begin at about Kallstadt, with its Nill and Saumagen vineyards. Ungstein grows quite a lot of red wines, but these are not noteworthy. Its white wines *are*, though, especially those from the vineyards of Herren-berg and Spielberg. Then comes Bad Dürkheim, a charming little spa resort surrounded by vineyards, and an important centre of the wine trade. Its red wines are copious rather than good, while its whites are of good quality.

Going down the Weinstrasse—that delightful main road that passes through most of the wine towns of the Palatinate—one next reaches Wachenheim, where the great wines begin. Its best sites are: Böhlig, Goldbächel, Luginsland and Rechbächel. After that comes Forst, where the very finest wines of the Palatinate are grown. It is no more than a village, but what a village! The soil is remarkable in being basaltic, and it is this that is said to help give the wines their quality. Further basalt is brought in from a quarry in Pechsteinhoff and is spread over the vineyards. The finest sites are: Freundstück, Jesuitengarten, Kirchenstück, Kranich, Pechstein, Ungeheuer and Ziegler.

If the wines of Forst are finer than those of Deidesheim, it is only by a very short head. It were safer to call the race a dead heat. And Deidesheim is a substantial, most attractive town that is the centre of the fine wine trade of the Palatinate. The beerenauslese and trockenbeerenauslese wines grown there in great years are magnificent—second to none. Its greatest sites are: Dopp, Geheu, Grain, Grainhübel, Herrgottsacker, Hohenmorgen, Kieselberg, Leinhöhle, Mühle and Rennpfad. What a mighty collection!

Ruppertsberg, near Deidesheim, but slightly to the east of the Weinstrasse, grows some very fine wines but others, and quite a lot of reds, that are only of average quality. Its best sites are Hoheburg, Mandelgarten and Nussbien. Königsbach lies to the west of the *strasse*, just below the hills, and it is the most southerly town in the Middle Palatinate to produce any quantity of first-rate wines, though it also grows second-rate whites and reds. Its best sites are Bender, Idig, Rolandsberg and Satz. From this point onwards, though the Middle Palatinate extends as far as Neustadt and grows many good wines, there are no more outstanding sites.

Finally comes the Upper Palatinate, extending from Neustadt to the French border. It is a region of quantity rather than quality, and although, of course, some sites on the right slopes are better than others, there is none of sufficient merit to justify singling out. To my own taste (though many German wine growers would hotly deny it) one is now *well* on the road to Alsace. It is a between land, where the delicacy of the Rhine wines becomes lost, while the peculiar charm of the Alsatians is not attained.

Other German Wine-growing Areas

Wine growing is far more widespread in Germany than one might think, and it is particularly creditable that it should be so in a country so far north. For these wines to succeed commercially they must be good enough to command a fairly high price; if they were otherwise, no amount of tariff protection or local patriotism would make them commercially viable. But few of the German growths outside the areas already considered are really in the same class. The other wine-growing areas will therefore not be described in such detail, not even Franconia. And Franconia is the one possible exception, growing wines of international renown. It is said that viticulture was introduced there by the Irish St. Cilian who was martyred at Würzberg in 697.

Franconian wines have their vociferous admirers, and it is said that Goethe preferred them to all others. Geniuses are entitled to their eccentricities; and this must surely be rated as such. The wines have always been popular in their own country but have never been particularly well thought of outside it; and the popularity they do enjoy elsewhere probably stems as much from the beautiful flask-shaped *bocksbeutels* in which they are bottled as from their own merits. This is not to say that they are not good wines: they undoubtedly are. In the best years (which are not always the same years as for Rhine wines) they may even be great. But always they suffer from comparison with Rhine wines. Their flavour is inclined to be rather flat and to lack that exquisite complexity that distinguishes the noble wines of Germany.

They are grown in the valley of the Main, on Keuper soil, which consists principally of clay mingled with chalk. The finest wines of all are derived, as may be expected, from the Riesling grape, but this tends only to ripen fully in the sunniest years, when trockenbeerenauslese wines can sometimes be produced. But the Sylvaner, known locally as the Franken, is grown to a far greater extent, and the Müller-Thurgau is also popular, while the new Mainriesling is gaining ground. Much of the wine comes from small growers, who are organized into well run co-operatives. Franconian wines are often known as *steinweins*, but the term is used far too loosely, and should only be applied to those wines grown in the large and very fine Stein site at Würzburg. The nearby Leisten vineyard produces equally good wines, and there are several others that do not lag far behind.

Ahr is noted almost entirely for its pleasant if somewhat slight red wines. Some of the most attractive of the lesser German wines are those grown around Lake Constance, especially weissherbst— a wine of the palest pink, such as the French would call a *vin gris*, vinified from the Pinot Noir. Baden and Württemberg grow both red and white wines, of which some of the whites are really good. Those Baden wines that are grown between Wiesloch and Weinheim are known as *bergstrasse*, the best of which comes from the Steinhopf vineyard in Heppenheim. So far these are not exported, at any rate in commercial quantities, but Baden, in particular, is on the way up, and it may be that more will be heard of its wines in the future.

Finally one cannot leave the subject of German wines without mentioning sekt: the white sparkling wines, of which there are many producers. These wines are extremely popular in Germany and are becoming more so in the export markets. How exactly they came to be called sekt is a mystery. There is a popular story that the great German actor Ludwig Devrient (1784–1832) who (as did several other members of his notable family) specialized in Shakespearean roles, was accustomed to go with his friends of an evening to his favourite table in a restaurant and call out for sack. He must have known perfectly well that sack was sherry, but he was always served with champagne—real French champagne. By some extraordinary entomological process alleged to be derived from this misunderstanding, German sparkling wine came to be known as sekt. Most of these wines are by-products: grapes are not grown specially for them but are obtained from the poorer sites and from good sites in poor years, while a certain amount of must is imported from France. A few sekts are made by the *méthode champenoise*, and others by the cuves-closes method; that these are as good as they undoubtedly are speaks well for teutonic thoroughness and technical know-how. Others are less good, and I have yet to find in literature any more convincing description of a thoroughly bad wine than that given by Thomas Mann in his last and sparkling novel *The Confessions of Felix Krull*:

'My poor father owned the firm of Engelbert Krull, makers of the now discontinued brand of champagne *Loreley extra cuvée*. Their cellars lay on the bank of the Rhine not far from the landing, and often as a boy I used to linger in the cool vaults, wandering pensively along the stone-paved passages that led back and forth between the high shelves, examining the array of bottles, which lay on their sides in slanting rows. "There you lie," I thought to myself (though of course at that time I could not give such apt expression to my thoughts), "there you lie in the subterranean twilight, and within you the bubbling

347

golden sap is clearing and maturing, the sap that will enliven so many hearts and awaken a brighter gleam in so many eyes! Now you look plain and unpromising, but one day you will rise to the upper world magnificently adorned, to take your place at feasts, at weddings, to send your corks popping to the ceilings of private dining-rooms and evoke intoxication, irresponsibility, and desire in the hearts of men." So, or approximately so, spoke the boy; and this much at least was true, the firm of Engelbert Krull paid unusual attention to the outside of their bottles, those final adornments that are technically known as the coiffure. The compressed corks were secured with silver wire and gilt cords fastened with purplish-red wax; there was, moreover, an impressive round seal—such as one sees on ecclesiastical bulls and old state documents—suspended from a gold cord; the necks of the bottles were liberally wrapped in gleaming silver foil, and their swelling bellies bore a flaring label with gold flourishes round the edges. This label had been designed for the firm by my godfather Schimmelpreester and bore a number of coats of arms and stars, my father's monogram, the brand name, Loreley extra cuvée, all in gold letters, and a female figure, arrayed only in bangles and necklaces, sitting with legs crossed on top of a rock, her arms raised in the act of combing her flowing hair. Unfortunately it appears that the quality of the wine was not entirely commensurate with the splendour of its coiffure. "Krull," I have heard my godfather Schimmelpreester say to my father, "with all due respect to you, your champagne ought to be forbidden by law. Last week I let myself be talked into drinking half a bottle, and my system hasn't recovered from the shock yet. What sort of vinegar goes into that brew? And do you use petroleum or fusel oil to doctor it with? The stuff's simply poison. Look out for the police!" At this my poor father would be embarrassed, for he was a gentle man and unable to hold his own against harsh criticism.

*   *   *

ruin—to express myself metaphorically—knocked with a bony knuckle on our door.

*   *   *

The wine-drinking public had more and more eschewed our brand. Lowering the price (which could not, of course, improve the product) did nothing to allure the gay world, nor did the enticing design produced to oblige the firm and against better judgment by my good-natured godfather Schimmelpreester. Presently sales dropped to zero, and ruin fell upon my poor father in the spring of the year I became eighteen.'[1]

[1] From *The Confessions of Felix Krull* by Thomas Mann, Martin Secker & Warburg Ltd.

The unfortunate Herr Krull's own taste was for finer things, but he was fighting against a national prejudice which at that time caused the Germans to condemn their own sekt. If his was representative, they were justified; but things are very different now, and I doubt whether a wine as bad as *Loreley extra cuvée* could be found. The modern manufacturers of sekt are very good at their job, and their business is booming: between 1950 and 1964 the production of sekt rose from eight million to one hundred million bottles per year. Now it is higher still. Sparkling wines made otherwise than by the *méthode champenoise* are known as *schaumweine*

Alsace

That Alsace should be included in the same chapter as Germany may come as a surprise to some readers. Both the Germans and the Alsatians are full of national pride, and each thinks his wines better than those of the other; while Alsace itself is now proudly French. But throughout this book the problems of drawing boundaries has been a recurrent one. Sauternes, as well as the Médoc, forms part of Bordeaux; Chablis and the Beaujolais both fall within Burgundy; and similarly, in my view, the vineyards of Alsace stylistically form part of that configuration extending through the Palatinate to the valleys of the Rhine and Moselle. Their affinity is more pronounced than their disparity. It has already been seen that in the fifteenth century, Alsatian wines were considered the best in Northern Europe. Then they suffered a sad decline. In recent years, on the other hand, they have been on the up and up. There is no longer any denying that they are amongst the great wines of Europe, even though none of them attain those heights reached by certain quite small vineyards in the Rheingau, or on the banks of the Mosel. But many Alsatian wines are quite able to hold their heads up in such company.

The vineyards are sheltered on the west by the Vosges mountains and extend along the lower slopes in a line from Marlenheim, north-west of Strasbourg, to Thann, north-west of Mulhouse. The most notable town in the area is Colmar, where the annual wine fair is held, and where the Oberlin Wine Institute is situated. Alsace is a most enchanting place to visit: a glorious rolling countryside, with beautiful, ancient villages that look like stage sets for Hansel and Gretel. A journey along the well-signposted *Route de Vin* is an unforgettable experience. And just as it is scenically exquisite, so it is gastronomically superb.

In his book *Alsace and its Wine Gardens*, S. F. Hallgarten lists no less than seven kinds of soil found in the vineyards. Between them they cover the whole range from the lightest to the heaviest. As the vine species has to be selected having regard to the soil, it is not surprising that quite a number of them are grown. Nor is it surprising that Alsatian wines are generally blended, for this enables a perfect balance to be achieved. That the wines *are* blended is also of particular value in a region like Alsace, which has many small growers, though there are very active co-operatives. Single vineyard wines are very rare indeed. In selecting an Alsatian wine, the two most important things to look for are the vine variety and the shipper, for it is the former that determines the style and the latter the quality. Only rarely is a site name used as well, and when it is, it may be taken that it is a particularly good one.

Of the various grape varieties grown, the wine from the Gewürztraminer is often said to be the best: it is certainly the most fragrant and spicy, a unique and estimable wine. That the Traminer and Gewürztraminer are selections from one and the same vine has already been explained. Nowadays the process of selection, as far as the vine is concerned, is virtually complete, and only the superior vines are grown. It is the wine that is selected now, rather than the vine, those casks showing especial fragrance and fruitiness being sold as Gewürztraminer and the remainder as Traminer. Sometimes, in particularly sunny years, there is a trace of sweet in these wines, but generally speaking, like all the wines of Alsace, they are dry.

The Riesling is a universally great vine, and it is certainly great in Alsace. Many prefer its wines to the traminers: they are more delicate, are better balanced, and show finer development in bottle. The Muscat in Alsace gives a wine quite different from the sweet and sticky muscats grown in more southerly latitudes: they are dry and delicate, with a special fragrance of their own. The Tokay D'Alsace is none other than the Pinot Gris; it has been so known locally for centuries, having been imported originally, it is said, from Hungary. The wine it gives is quite different from the

Hungarian Tokay, though: it is dry and fruity. The Pinot Blanc gives a full and slightly hard wine that seems rather lacking in character. The Sylvaner gives a somewhat less elegant wine than those mentioned so far, but it is relatively cheap and very popular.

Those are the noble vines of Alsace, but many excellent wines are derived from other varieties, notably the Chasselas, for good *ordinaires*, the Müller-Thurgau, the Pinot Auxerrois and Knipperle. A wine blended from more than one vine variety, if it contains any proportion of a variety that is not officially classed as 'noble', is sold as a *zwicker*; if it is blended solely from the wines of noble varieties it is sold as an *edelzwicker*, which generally means in practice that it is a blend of Sylvaner and Pinot Blanc.

*

White wines generally do not enjoy the longevity of reds, nor do they improve in bottle to the same extent, but this depends on their sweetness and body. To my own taste a fresh young dry moselle tastes at its best a year or two after bottling. At the other end of the scale, a great trockenbeerenauslese always takes six or seven years to mature before it shows the full glory of its bouquet and flavour, and many take longer. The classic vintage of the century was that of 1921, and some wines of this vintage are still magnificent, but these are exceptions. Wines of other good, or fairly good, vintages such as 1929, 1933, 1934 and 1935 are now mostly just memories, and those that remain forgotten in the corners of private cellars are likely to be well past their best though there are striking exceptions, especially amongst the finest examples of the 1934s, which have retained their freshness to a striking degree. A bottle of Deinhard's Bernkasteler Doktor 1934 that I drank in 1968 was utterly superb: far from being in a decline, it had an indescribably fine bouquet and a magnificent depth of flavour. It was completely fresh and was the finest bottle of moselle I have ever drunk in my life, yet it was not even a spätlese. The oldest vintage likely to be of any general interest, however, is 1937.

1937: A very great year, especially for moselles. Although many of these wines are now hopelessly past their best, the finest of them are still very much alive.

1938: A fair year, but the wines were never exported owing to the Hitler war.

1939: Bad.

1940: Fair.

1941: Bad.

1942: Quite a good year, but the wines are now too old.

1943: Better than 1942, and some beerenauslesen are still excellent.

1944: Fair.

1945: This was a very dry year, though relieved by rain in July, and a small crop of excellent quality was produced in all districts save the Moselle, where the yield was practically zero, thanks to the combined efforts of the weather and the occupying forces. A very long-lived vintage, the better quality wines are now magnificent.

1946: Not quite so good as 1945, and some of the wines were inclined to be too acid, but most were well balanced and good.

1947: A good year, but its initial acclaim has not really been borne out by the longevity of its wines—or at any rate its lesser wines, many of which are deficient in acid and generally lack distinction. Some of those of auslese quality and above are magnificent, though. The vinification presented peculiar difficulties to the growers, as most of the wines went cloudy in bottle. This was found to be due to minute particles of albumen. The wine had to be fined with bentonite and rebottled.

1948: Good both for quality and quantity. A very desirable sort of year which produced many good and some great wines that will go on maturing.

1949: A very good year, particularly for moselles, but most of the wines that remain want drinking. They varied a lot, though, from site to site. Well watered sites gave very fine wines, but there was a lack of rain and those on the drier sites were un-balanced.

1950: Quite good, but there was not enough sunshine, so the wines are a bit disappointing after their illustrious predecessors.

1951: Poor.

1952: Quite good, and would have been very good had the weather held up during the autumn.

1953: A very good year, not unlike 1949, giving first quality, well-balanced wines.

1954: Very bad.

1955: Uneven and generally poor.

1956: Bad, generally speaking, though some good eiswein was made on the Moselle.

1957: Some quite good wines were grown, but unexciting, save for some fine auslese and higher quality wines made on the Moselle.

1958: Somewhat better than 1957, and the same remarks apply.

1959: A very great year, vying with 1921 for the title of greatest of the century. The moselles were enormous in flavour and sweetness—too much so for those who particularly like the delicacy of a more normal vintage, but nevertheless superb in an eccentric sort of way, though it looks as if some of them will be short lived owing to lack of acidity. Some of the Palatinate wines were burnt up.

1960: Fair quality but enormous quantity.

1961: Quite good. There was much less wine than in 1960, but what there was had more body and character. Some eisweine were made.

1962: Quite good, and a frost led to the production of some interesting eisweine, better than those of 1961.

1963: A very large yield of quite good wines.

1964: Excellent moselles and some very fine wines from other regions, but a proportion were rather dull and this is a vintage that needs careful selection.

1965: Climatically as disastrous as 1922 but far better wines were produced, thanks to the skill of the scientists, particularly in Franconia.

1966: A very good vintage, particularly on the Moselle. Though not a year of very hot weather like 1959 or 1964, having a period of bad weather in mid-summer, it provided well-balanced wines that should last well and give great pleasure. Late rains, however, destroyed the prospects of fine beerenauslesen and trockenbeerenauslesen, while late frosts provided eiswein.

1967: By no means a great vintage and a number of wines needed 'helping', as they tended to too much acidity; but some very pleasant wines were made.

1968: Poor, but not as bad as 1965.

1969: The quantity was disappointing but the quality quite good, especially the moselles. Rheingau wines need careful selection as those from the lower lying vineyards were affected by a succession of foggy days just before the vintage.

CHAPTER 8

The Wines of Italy

$\sim\!\!\sim\!\!\sim\!\!\sim\!\!\sim\!\!\sim$

If antiquity marched hand in hand with quality, Italian wines would undoubtedly be amongst the greatest in the world. Although the Italian vineyards are not the oldest—those of the Middle East, Greece and Egypt preceded them—they are certainly amongst the oldest. But antiquity and quality do not always march hand in hand, and even the greatest enthusiast for Italian wines would be bound to admit that their achievement lies in the past rather than in the present—though the present is exciting, and the quest for quality that is now going on augers well for the future.

The Etruscans came to Italy in about 800 B.C. and settled in those areas that we now know as Tuscany and Lazio. They grew vines and it is highly likely that they made wine, but there is no reason to believe that they had any knowledge of scientific viticulture or that their wines were any good. The Greeks came soon after them, though—to Campania—bringing their vines and their knowledge with them. In the course of time, the Greeks conquered the Etruscans and were themselves conquered by the Sabines in the fifth century B.C., but their knowledge remained. Nevertheless wines grown in Greece were thought of more highly than the local ones, and continued so to be until well after the time of Christ.

The wines of ancient Rome are legendary, though; from all accounts they were excellent, and they lived almost for ever. Falernian of the Opimian vintage was served by Pomponius Secundus to Caligula when it was 160 years old, and wine of the same incomparably famous vintage, was specified for Trimalchio's banquet. Of modern wines only sherry, madeira and château chalon can really compete.

354

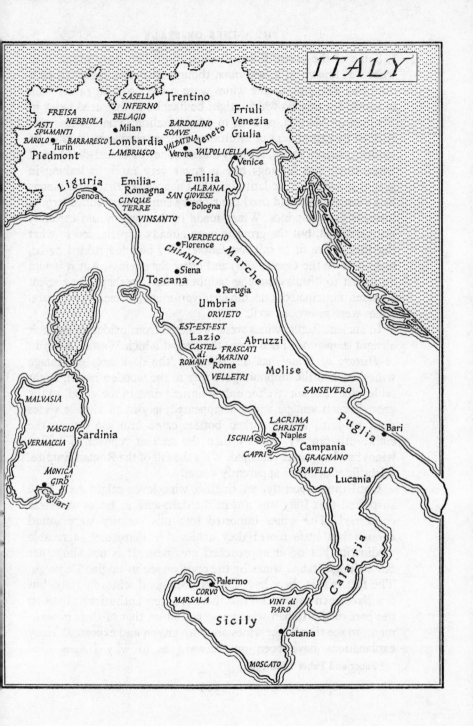

ITALY

SASELLA
INFERNO
FREISA BELAGIO
NEBBIOLA
ASTI Trentino
SPUMANTI • Milan BARDOLINO Friuli
BAROLO SOAVE Venezia
Turin BARBARESCO Lombardia VALPATINA Veneto Giulia
Piedmont LAMBRUSCO Verona VALPOLICELLA
• Venice

Liguria Emilia- Emilia
Genoa Romagna ALBANA
CINQUE SAN GIOVESE
TERRE • Bologna
VINSANTO

VERDECCIO
• Florence
CHIANTI Marche
• Siena
Toscana
• Perugia
Umbria
ORVIETO

EST-EST-EST
Lazio
CASTEL FRASCATI Abruzzi
di MARINO
ROMANI • Rome Molise
VELLETRI

SANSEVERO

MALVASIA
LACRIMA Puglia
CHRISTI • Bari
NASCIO ISCHIA • Naples
Sardinia CAPRI
VERMACCIA Campania
GRAGNANO
MONICA RAVELLO
GIRÒ Lucania
• Cagliari

Calabria

• Palermo
CORVO
MARSALA VINI di
PARO
Sicily • Catania

MOSCATO

Some of the better Roman wines, moreover, were matured in what was known as a *fumarium*, though what this consisted of is doubtful. Presumably the wines were subject to heat rather than to smoke—a process which might be likened to that used today in Madeira or Marsala, or even to pasteurization. The Romans also derived by experiment or intuition a process similar in its effect to modern *chaptalization*, for they added honey or boiled-down must when sugar was lacking; but as sugar very rarely is lacking in grapes grown in these latitudes, the chances are that the Romans had a sweet tooth and used their honey simply to produce strong, luscious dessert wines. Wines made in this way would certainly taste artificial, but the growers were already experienced in what the French see fit to call *bon cuisine*: they blended, added herbs, resin (before the Greeks did) and other flavourings. But it would be unjust to dismiss these as 'adulterations': perhaps the ancient Romans anticipated our modern vermouths. Plenty of natural wines were grown, as well.

In ancient Rome, wines were protected from oxidation by their airtight *amphorae*. Then came the period which Warner Allen in *A History of Wine*[1] has described as 'the dark ages of vintage wines'—when the amphora gave way to the wooden barrel. Light table wines can survive for only a limited time in the wood, so the great Roman vintage wines disappeared, as did all vintage wines until modern, tightly corked bottles came into use during the eighteenth century. But by then the ancient renown of Italian wines had long since vanished. With the fall of the Roman Empire, scientific viticulture apparently ceased.

Until quite recently, an English wine-lover might well have suspected that Italy was *still* in the dark ages as far as wine was concerned. The wines imported into this country were sound enough but little more: they achieved a consistent, agreeable mediocrity but never approached greatness. It is not altogether fair to judge Italian wines by the ones we see in England, though. The fact is that there have always been good wines in Italy, but few have been exported. Now there is a new enthusiasm, both on the part of the Italian wine growers and on that of their government, to see that better wines are both grown and exported. Many explanations have been put forward as to why Italian wine

[1] Faber and Faber Ltd., 1961.

growing is now so dim compared with that of other countries. There is inevitably the influence of the national temperament: Italians are individualists, Italian peasants have been amongst the last to form themselves into co-operatives, and wine growers do not easily unite to promote their wares, as growers in other districts, such as sherry and madeira, have done in the past. And fine wines, being individual things of limited production, do not attract the promotional ability of tycoons, as the Italian motor industry has done. Perhaps the greatest difficulty, however, has been the insular regionalism of the country. Before unification, the small states imposed swingeing duties on their neighbours' goods; and as far as wines are concerned, they looked no further than their own growths. The habit still persists. A wine that is not first renowned nationally is all the less likely to become renowned internationally, while lack of competition from other fine wines within a country leads the peasant growers to opt for the easy way, making lots of poor wine rather than concentrating on quality.

Until recently nearly all the Italian wines exported, and most of those sold by the big merchants on the home market, were products of the blenders' skill: a skill that gives consistently agreeable wines but never great ones. Those delightful straw-covered *fiaschi* labelled *chianti* contained, as often as not, a mixture of the genuine light Tuscan wine with stronger, heavier wines from the south. It is as if wines from all over the Médoc were blended together and a little Rhône wine added to give them strength: the result would be very drinkable, but it would not be Château Latour. Since 1963, however, the Italian wine laws have been greatly tightened, and the effect of this, which has already been felt, is likely to be much more significant in the future.

Wines are to be divided into three categories: *semplice* (unblended), *controllata* (controlled) and *controllata e garantita* (controlled and guaranteed). The first category applies to wines made from traditional vines in a delimited zone; regulations for the second are more stringent and for the third more stringent still. The latter two may also come under the supervision of local voluntary societies which are given statutory recognition. There are penalties, consisting of substantial fines, suspension from business for up to three years, confiscation of stock and closing of the whole establishment for up to a year. The new law is gradually being enforced by decree and should become effective within a decade. Like all laws, though, it is relatively complicated and detailed consideration of it is beyond the scope of this book. A translation of the text will be found in Cyril Ray's admirable *The Wines of Italy*.[1]

Wines are marketed both under the names of the towns around which they are grown and under the names of grape varieties. Sometimes these are confusing; for instance Barbaresco is a village and Barbera a vine, which happens not to be grown there. Generally speaking geographical names are applied to wines grown in delimited areas which enjoy some sort of protection from local associations—a protection that is likely to increase as the wine laws develop—whereas wines sold under the names of grape varieties may come from a very vague area. The latter are quite often as good as the former but rarely, if ever, better. There is one familiar feature, however, that is unlikely often to appear on Italian wine labels, however precise they may become, and that is the vintage year. And with few exceptions, on those occasions when a year has been particularly good or bad for a certain wine, the year is more useful in indicating age than in suggesting the initial quality. On Mediterranean latitudes the consistency of the sunshine does away with many of the differences which, in more northern countries, distinguish one vintage from another. Perhaps the climate over most of Italy is somewhat too healthy to produce wines of the greatest finesse, but consistent wines can be consistently good, as they are, for instance, in the Spanish rioja and Portuguese dão districts. Nor is there any need for chaptalization in Italy, and it is forbidden.

The number of different kinds of wine grown in Italy is bewildering: to name and describe them all would take the space of a very large book, but to taste them on the spot is one of the joys of travelling there. And although France unquestionably leads in the production of quality wines, as far as quantity is concerned Italy and France have long been vying with each other. So it is not surprising that amongst the vast number of Italian wines there are some of real distinction; and now that the Italian growers are at last paying more heed to quality there are likely to be many more.

[1] London, 1966.

Piedmont grows some of the best Italian wines. Many of them may fairly be compared with Rhône wines, which are grown on much the same latitude. Barbaresco is ruby red, dry and has a delicate aroma. Barolo, its near neighbour, and vinified from the same Nebbiolo grapes, is a strongly flavoured red wine that is greatly improved by a few years in a bottle. It is undoubtedly one of the best wines grown in Italy, and to give of its best it should be uncorked an hour or two before being served. The Nebbiolo grape is the aristocrat of vines hereabouts, its name signifies 'mist' and it is said that the grapes need to be enveloped by the mists of autumn if they are to develop their full flavour. Apart from the wines mentioned above, others are sold under the varietal name. Nebbiolo is a red wine that comes in three distinct styles: one is fairly dry but sparkling, a second is still and quite sweet, while the third is still, pretty dry, and rather aromatic. It is this last that is most likely to appeal. Freisa, a light red table wine which is usually slightly sweet with a strawberry-like bouquet, is sometimes vinified to be very sweet and slightly sparkling. Grignolino is a light wine which is now getting rarer owing to the unpredictable yield of the Grignolino vine. Gattinara spanna is a red table wine of excellent quality from the Nebbiolo grape that improves for many years in bottle, as do lessona and barbera, though not for quite so long. Asti is famous for its asti spumante,[1] a sparkling wine made principally from the Moscato (Muscatel) grape, and one that can be very pleasant having a natural sweetness that calls for no *dosage* of sugar. Although a little of this wine is still made by the *méthode champenoise* most of it is now produced by the *cuves closes* process which gives very adequate results more cheaply. The former method, however, is used for making dry sparkling wines from the Pinot grape, but these are only produced on a small scale and only for the Italian market, where they are sold under brand names, as elsewhere they cannot compete with champagne. Moscato d'Asti is another sparkling wine, sweeter than asti spumante, cheaper, and less good. Sweet, still muscat wines are also grown there, as are dry white wines, such as cortese, which comes from the area of Alessandra. The most famous Piedmontese

---

[1] 'Spumante' merely means 'sparkling' and is used in connection with wines from many districts. Some of these are made by the *méthode champenoise*, but others are definitely not.

product, however, is undoubtedly vermouth, which was first made in Turin in 1757. It is prepared by making an infusion of secret herbs into red or white wine, which is nowadays generally imported from areas further south, such as Apulia, rather than grown locally.

Visitors to Liguria—and they are many, for this includes the Italian Riviera—can enjoy a variety of local wines but the best known is the white cinqueterre, which can vary between being fairly dry and very sweet. Grown in those exquisite and inaccessible coastal villages between Levanto and La Spezia, it is of excellent quality, and well worth looking for, but beware of imitations. Campochiesa bianco is a strongly flavoured fairly dry white wine which is said to age exceptionally well in bottle. The best known of the red wines, grown on the French border, is called dolceacqua, though it is not particularly sweet and is by no means water. It is also known as casteldoria and as rossese di Val di Nervia. There is a legend that Napoleon was fond of it.

Of all the Lombardy wines, the one I have most enjoyed has been sassella—a red wine of real distinction. Oddly enough, while sassella is the name of a variety of grape, most of the wine is vinified from the Nebbiolo. Next come inferno—a powerful red wine with far more charm than its name might suggest—and grumello, a red wine with a touch of sweet in it. Both of these are vinified principally from the Nebbiolo grape. Bellagio, quite an elegant red wine that is light in body and vinified from French grape varieties, is well known to holidaymakers, as it grows by Lake Como, while ingana is a good white wine. Lovers of fine wines know the value of the personal touch that springs from the pride of an individual grower, and there is one such in this area who grows all the wines labelled frecciarossa—dry white, medium-sweet white, red and rosé. While all are good, the first named is the most notable.

Trentino and the region of the Alto Adige, with its Alpine climate, grows some wines of real delicacy, often from vines that are more familiar in the north, such as the Sylvaner and the Traminer (indeed the Traminer is said to have originally been a local vine from the village of Tramin), but the wine that is most admired locally is teroldego, a red table wine. Other notable red wines include caldero and santa maddalena, both of which are vinified from Schiava and Schiavone grapes. Rosé wines are also grown.

The province of Veneto grows many interesting wines, especially around Verona, where soave is a dry, white, lightly flavoured wine almost as delightful as its name, and a great favourite of the late Hilaire Belloc. It is vinified from Garganega and Trebbiano grapes. The best red wines, and they are very good, are bardolino, valpolicella and valpatena. These are vinified principally from the Corvina grape, but with some Negrara. Other wines include friularo, which is red, acid and light; and recioto, also red, is vinified from grapes that are subjected to a peculiar treatment: the bottoms of the bunches are cut off and the tops are left to ripen. Sometimes the grapes are then left hanging to dry out and are pressed the following January. It varies between dry and moderately sweet, and there is also a sparkling version.

In Friuli and in the region of Venice pleasant, light red and white wines are grown, known often by the vine variety from which they are vinified—Riesling and Tocai (which has no connection with the Hungarian Tokay) make good white wines, while Cabernet, Merlot and recently introduced Gamay are the vines principally used for reds. A rich, golden dessert wine called picolit used once to be renowned but disease has attacked the vineyards and it is now virtually unobtainable.

A vast abundance of wine is grown in Emilia and Romagna, but comparatively little of it is interesting. This is surprising and unfortunate in an area so noted for its good food. One of the most famous is the red dry, slightly sparkling lambrusco, grown around Modena. In style it is comparable with the red *vinhos verdes* of Portugal, but it lacks their instant appeal and is something of an acquired taste. It should be drunk young. Bologna provides the white albana, which varies between fairly dry and rather sweet, and the red sangiovese, but the latter certainly does not travel well.

From Tuscany comes the most famous of all Italian wines: chianti. Both red and white wines are grown and, when they have not been messed about with, both are excellent, delicate, dry table wines, but only too often those sold commercially, especially for export, have been blended with coarser wines from the south. The best red chianti is chianti classico, which is grown in a delimited area and is matured for three years in the wood before bottling.

Distinguished by a label showing a black cockerel on a gold ground, it is vinified principally from the Sangiovese grape with smaller proportions of Black Canaiolo, Malvesia and Trebbiano.

'Florence wines' were old established on the English market and presumably were the forerunners of modern chianti. W. Salmon in his *Compleat English Physician* (1693) wrote of them that 'Florence, white and red, are both good stomach wines, but the red is something binding' and somewhat earlier, in 1661, Pepys drank Florence at Lady Sandwich's. Other references have been noted (see André L. Simon *The History of the Wine Trade in England*, London, 1906), some of them much earlier, but the wine was scarce until the end of the seventeenth century, when it became a popular drink in the taverns. These wines must have been familiar, too, to all the gentlemen doing the grand tour, for chianti is grown in the exquisite countryside between the sublime cities of Florence and Siena. But these wines were probably very different from the chianti we know today. This was a nineteenth-century creation of Baron Bettino Ricasoli (1809–80) who became dictator of Tuscany and prime minister of Italy. The romantic story as related by Luigi Berzini[1] is thus: it was

'. . . the case of a jealous and moral gentleman, who disliked being cuckolded, but managed to avoid it without harsh words and bloodshed. He was . . . a religious man, dedicated to politics and serious studies in his favourite field, agriculture. He was by no means handsome. In fact, he was extremely cross-eyed, but had a tall and lean figure, and carried himself with a military and proud bearing.

'One night, when he had been married only a few months, Bettino, who had been nicknamed Barone di Ferro, or Iron Baron (such unbending characters are not necessarily admired in Italy, where *souplesse* is prized above all; the sobriquet has a derisive quality it would not have elsewhere), took his young wife Anna Bonaccorsi to a ball in Florence. There the poor lady was briefly and perfunctorily courted by a young man, who danced with her a few times. The husband immediately told her: 'We must leave, my dear.' He escorted her to their waiting carriage, sat down next to her, and told the coachman: "To Brolio." Brolio was the family seat, a lonely and gloomy castle, lost in barren and sterile hills, where none of the Ricasoli had lived for ages. The couple rode in silence through the snow, until dawn, he in his black

[1] *The Italians*, London, 1964, quoted by Cyril Ray in his *The Wines of Italy*, London, 1966.

evening clothes, she shivering in her ball dress. They lived in Brolio for practically the rest of their lives.

'To while away the time he reconstructed the manor, which now looks as if it had been dreamed up by Sir Walter Scott or designed as a background for Il Trovatore. He also experimented with planting different qualities of new vines and producing wines with improved processes. (One must have patience and a firm character for such pursuits. It takes approximately five years for a man to taste the first product of a new combination of grapes he has planted.) The Baron came across a pleasing mixture of black and white grapes, Sangiovese and Malvasia, and a way to make them ferment in two successive waves, which imparted a novel taste to the cru. The wine became popular, was copied by the vineyard owners of the region, the Chianti, and acquired, in the end, a world-wide fame. One of the best chiantis is still the Ricasoli, of which the Brolio Castle is the choice and most expensive variety. Thus the Baron managed to preserve the sanctity of the family, his wife's name and his honour unblemished, to amass a fortune, and to enrich his neighbours, all at the same time.'

Cyrus Redding, writing in 1833, described how chianti was vinified from a creeping species of vine, *vite bassa*, but the Baron discovered that a far finer wine could be produced by blending various grapes. His wine contained seventy per cent Sangiovese, twenty per cent Black Lanoilo, ten per cent Malvasia and Trebbiano; and these proportions, varied somewhat by individual growers, are those used today. Apart from this blending of grapes, one of the features that undoubtedly gives chianti its character is the unusual method of vinification, known as *governo all'use toscano*. The wine is first fermented in the usual way and towards the end of the first year, when the fermentation is complete, a small proportion of sweet must is added, specially made from dried grapes. This provokes a further fermentation that leaves the wine with a characteristic softness. It is the process used for wines that are meant to be drunk young and they are generally bottled in wicker-covered *fiaschi*; and these wines *should* be drunk young. Age withers rather than mellows, and only too often restaurant chianti in England is frankly stale. The *fiaschi*, by the way, hold a litre, so although they cost more than the same wine in bottles, you get more for your money—though generally not that much more. If a chianti is vinified for ageing it is generally in a claret-shaped bottle rather than a flask; and it may or may not have another name apart from chianti on the label, or even instead of it, depending on the whim of the grower.

Although less well known than chianti, brunello di Montalcino is a greater wine. Vinified from the Brunello vine, it is a wine of enormous flavour that needs to be matured for five or six years in cask and then for at least ten years in bottle before it is ready for drinking. It lives for a very long time in bottle and has few rivals amongst the red wines for longevity. In France its nearest rival is probably the black wine of Cahors, though it could also be compared with hermitage. Cyril Ray quotes the firm of Trimani, in Rome, as offering the 1888 and 1889 vintages at about £23 per bottle—a price which a great pre-phylloxera claret could rarely hope to attain. Perhaps because of its high price, very little is exported.

Montecarlo may be red or white; the latter and vernaccia di San Gimignano are amongst the best dry white wines of the area. Vino santo, which is found in other areas as well as in Tuscany, is a particularly attractive, very sweet, white wine made by drying the grapes for some months before pressing and then fermenting very slowly.

Umbria's most famous wine is the white orvieto, which can be dry but which is generally rather sweet—a wine highly praised by Hilaire Belloc. In 1921, writing to Mrs. Raymond Asquith, he said of it: 'The wine is the best in the world. It is white. God, loving Orvieto, has so made this wine that it will not travel. If it could, Orvieto would be ruined and corrupted with Merchants.' In 1934, writing to Duff Cooper, he put it more strongly: 'Orvieto wine—white—*at Orvieto itself, on the hill*, is like a vision of beautitude. A mile away it turns into a lovely woman with a spiteful and insulting spirit, a few miles further it is like an ugly woman with a sour temper and at Rome it is undrinkable. Not so the wine of Frascati at Rome, at the Valle Restaurant. That is quite good.' Like many wines, especially white wines, I dare say that a connoisseur of orvieto would find it tasting best in its own country; but not that much better. Hilaire Belloc exaggerated, carried away by a typically Bellocian enthusiasm. The fact is that although orvieto is not one of the world's great wines, it is a thoroughly good wine, and it tastes well wherever you drink it. The sweeter wine, sold as *abboccato* or *amabile*, is the older established, the dry version being a relatively new thing. Cyril Ray tells of how, when the fifteenth-century painter Pinturicchio was working on his frescoes in Orvieto cathedral, his contract stipulated that he could have as much wine as he wanted of the Trebbiano grape. Orvieto is still made largely from those grapes to this day, together with smaller proportions of Verdello, Malvasia and Grechetto, grown in volcanic soil. The sweetness comes from the noble rot, as with the great sweet wines of France and Germany; but orvieto abboccato is much less sweet than these, and the rot appears in quite different circumstances. Instead of the grapes being left on the vines until they are over ripe, they are picked when ripe and are allowed to develop the rot in open casks before pressing.

Both forms of orvieto are generally bottled in flasks, but smaller ones than those used for chianti, holding-three quarters of a litre instead of a litre. There is also a red orvieto, but it is a wine of no great distinction. Vernaccia di Cannara, in contrast with the wine of that name from San Gimignano, is sweet and red.

Travelling into the Marches, the most distinguished wine is the fairly dry, austere, white verdicchio dei Castelli di Jesi—the wine which Hannibal's army is said to have become drunk on, a fate doubtless subsequently shared by many pilgrims to Rome. Unfortunately it is often sold in dreadful, fancy bottles—an extraordinary indignity to inflict on a wine that is capable of being sold on its merits. Of the various red wines, the best is perhaps montepulciano del Conero, otherwise known as conero rosso or, in its best version, montepulciano piceno.

The province of Lazio grows the famous white frascati, a wine that can be anything from quite dry to very sweet. Quite why its name is so familiar is a bit of a mystery. The wine is good, and of a beautiful, golden colour, but not so good as all that. Perhaps its name evokes the vanished splendour of its namesake the Edwardian restaurant, or perhaps the beauty of the town near where it is grown—a town so close to Rome and yet so individual. To every gastronome its name means something more than the wine, yet one feels that the wine would make the name familiar without any help from outside. Est! est!! est!!! is even more famous. It is grown in two quite distinct styles, the one being pale in colour and relatively dry while the other is golden and sweet. It is vinified from a mixture of Trebbiano, Rossetta and Malvasia Toscana grapes and sold in orvieto-style flasks. The story of how it got its name has often been told: how a bishop on his way to Rome sent his servant on ahead to write 'est!' (meaning *vinum bonum est*) on the door of any inn with good wine. At Montefiascone the servant's enthusiasm so ran away with him that the word appeared three times on one door, and the bishop got no further, drinking himself contentedly into his grave. The good bishop made provision in his will for a barrel of wine to be poured on his grave every year on the anniversary of his death, but this agreeable absurdity was put an end to when the cardinal bishop of Montefiascono decreed that it should be diverted to the use of the local seminary, being of greater use to living priests than to dead bishops.

Some of the best white wines of every degree of sweetness are grown in the large area of some fifty square miles known as Castelli Romani in the Alban hills. The best of the vini dei Castelli Romani also often have village or brand names, and red wines, both dry and sweet, are also grown there but they too are normally sold under local or brand names. Red wines include the agreeable, if very slight, cecubo, which scarcely lives up to its ancient reputation. A local white falernium, or falerno, disputes with the falernos of Campania the honour of being the classic falernian, but is even less distinguished.

In Campania the red and white falernos echo the name of the classic falernian but with none of its renown; indeed the great falernian had already seriously declined by the time of Pliny owing to over production—an oft-repeated history. Around Naples the ischia bianco is a good white wine to drink with fish. Amongst the red wines, aglianico, from the grape of that name, is a strongly flavoured, somewhat tannic, table wine; gragnano is a good quality red wine, dark in colour and light in character; and the ravello rossos are very pleasant, sometimes showing a faint trace of sweetness. The white lacrima christis are more famous and have many enthusiastic admirers, though personally I find them unattractive. Indeed, I have my own theory as to how they got their name. The official story is that when Lucifer was cast out from heaven he took a little bit of paradise with him, and it became the bay of Naples. One day, when Christ saw man sinning even in this earthly paradise he wept, and the wines have flourished ever since, watered by his tears. Personally I suspect that when some English nobleman on the grand tour was offered the local wine his reaction was to mutter 'Jesus wept' and he was misunderstood by the pious and enthusiastic local wine growers. A friend has suggested, on the other hand, that the correct translation should be 'the wine that made Christ cry'. It may be, though, that the ones he and I have tried are not good examples, as the name is so attractive that it is exploited commercially by using it on wines that are fairly near misses geographically and nowhere near the target as regards flavour. Cyril Ray, indeed, describes it as 'dry, delicate, with a hint of sweetness, like a German wine or a dry white Bordeaux, but with a flowery fragrance peculiar to itself'. It is vinified from Coda di Volpe, Greco di Torre and Biancolella grapes grown in an area between Vesuvius and the sea. The red wines sold as lacrima christi are merely local wines with no pretentions as to quality. The red and white wines sold under the name of vesuvio are also of no quality: the better ones are passed off as lacrima christi.

The red, pink and white wines of Capri also enjoy a certain reputation but rather too many of them are said to come from the mainland.

The vast coarse wines of Apulia are notable for quantity rather than for quality. Most of them are used for blending.

In Calabria the wines are also more noted for their sturdiness than for their finesse. Amongst them are the red and white wines of Ciro and the red greco rosso di Pontegrande, while those who like sweet white wines should look out for moscato di Cosenza.

Of all the Sicilian wines, the best known, and perhaps the least typical, is marsala. The name of the town from which the wine in turn takes its name is derived from the Arabic 'Marsh-El-Allah', meaning the Harbour of God, but the wine, far from tracing its origin to Arabic times, came into being through the exertions of a young Liverpool merchant, John Woodhouse, who founded his business in 1773. It is strange how Englishmen take to growing strong wines: beside marsala, sherry, port and madeira all owe a great deal to English growers and merchants. By 1800 he had been joined by his brother William, and in that year they signed one of the most famous contracts in the history of wine: to supply Admiral Lord Nelson with five hundred pipes of marsala for the use of the navy. Further contracts followed, and the navy was well supplied. Rather sadly, it seems that the navy went to Marsala only because they had drunk Naples dry;[1] but many a great discovery is made by chance.

The Woodhouse family had formerly lived in Portugal, and it may well be that the Woodhouse brothers were also familiar with Spain, for the way of making marsala is much like that of sherry. The soil is also somewhat like that of Jerez, having a high calcium content, and so is the climate, but the grape varieties used are different: Insolia, Cotarratto and Grillo. The wines that are made from these vines in the normal way are thin and not very distinguished table wines, though they can attain considerable character with age. Known as *marsala vergine*, these wines are often matured on the solera system. Marsala is produced with the aid of three quite separate processes. Firstly by warming the unfermented must very slowly, so as to produce a concentrate known as *concentrate* or *vino concentrato* comparable with the *sancocho* and *arrope* of Jerez. But instead of being used in blending fermented and matured wine, as happens with sherry, the *concentrate* is added to unfermented must and the combination is then fermented.

Secondly a wine comparable with port and exactly like a Spanish *mistela* is made by adding alcohol to the unfermented must so that the ferments are killed and fermentation stops while some sugar remains in the wine. This is known as *sifone*, as alcohol is syphoned into the must. To produce a richer wine still, *concentrate* is used for making the sifone.

Thirdly, a high proportion of the *concentrate* is turned into a *vino cotto*, or cooked wine, by heating to about 40°C for a month. The wine prepared in this way somewhat resembles madeira.

These wines are then blended with the natural wines in varying proportions, but the following limits give a rough idea of the normal practice:

Vino naturale (marsala vergine)	81–92%
Vino concentrato	3– 1%
Vino sifone	6– 1%
Vino cotto	10– 6%

[1] See T. A. Layton, *Wines of Italy*, London, 1961.

The wine is also fortified.[1] The best wine is then matured for several years in the wood. With age in cask the colour darkens and the sweetness diminishes, producing a deep dry aftertaste. Not all marsala is long matured, however. Under Italian wine law, a wine may be sold as *marsala fine* after four months and *marsala superiore* after two years. There are also special kinds of marsala, such as the popular *marsala all'uova*, which is wine combined with egg yolks to produce something half way between a dessert wine and a liquid pudding. Many of the table wines are unexpectedly delicate for so southerly a latitude. The locals go so far as to liken their corvo di Casteldaccia to claret, but it is really not at all like claret, though strikingly northern in its delicacy. Another very acceptable red table wine is faro. Amongst the better white table wines is taormina, a dry wine, of which more is sold than grown. The best of the sweet white wines is malvusia di Lipari and there are also some good sweet moscatos. Mamertino, a white wine of old renown, varies from fairly dry to very sweet and is vinified partly from the Pedro Ximenez vine, as used for sherry. Some good red, rosé and white wines are also grown around Mount Etna.

The other great island, Sardinia, is a law unto itself. Far off the mainland, it is as different as it is remote. Many travellers regard it as positively un-Italian. Its wines are certainly different. For one thing, the table wines tend to be one shade darker: white wines are *gris*, pink wines are red, and red wines are positively black. They also tend to be several degrees stronger than those of the mainland. The most distinctive wines of all, though, are the apéritif wines which are often likened to sherry: vernaccia is the best and most famous, but there are others such as torbato di Alghero (available as secco, extra and passito, according to the degree of sweetness) and vermentino. Sardinia is also noted for sweet wines such as the red anghelu ruju, which is something after the same style as port and, in contrast, for the drier and very distinctive golden nasco.

There are a great many very good wines in Italy, and part of the pleasure stems from their variety. It is a country full of the unexpected, where famous wines prove disappointing and the unheard of proves to be magnificent. In travelling through Italy,

---

[1] For the above details I am indebted to an article by Colin Fenton, M.W., which appeared in the Winter 1967 issue of *Wine and Food*.

the best way to taste the legion of delightful local wines is to avoid the fashionable hotels and to drink in the little *trattorias*, where the wine will come from the proprietor's vineyard or that of a friend. Many of these little-known wines are delightful. Others, it must frankly be confessed, are not. Only in one place can the traveller taste good unblended wines from all over Italy, and that is in Siena, where there is the Enoteca, or wine library, in the great Medici fortress. Every sort of Italian wine is to be found there from the delicate white wines of the Alps to rich Sicilian marsala, and the variety is astonishing, as is the quality of many of the wines.

CHAPTER 9

Sherry and the Table Wines of Spain

To the itinerant wine drinker, Spain is a most fascinating country. It is also a neglected one—overshadowed by the glory of France. But although the great French wines are in a class of their own, once one goes beyond the vineyards to the cold and grim industrial north, one enters a vinous wilderness with blended wines of the dreariest quality. There is no such wilderness in Spain, for the vine flourishes everywhere, and even though none of the table wines are equal to the classified growths of the Médoc or to the finest wines of the Côte de Nuits, there are nevertheless many well-made table wines that any French *vigneron*, even in the great areas, could be proud of. One Spanish wine stands in a class apart from all the others, but it is not a table wine. It is the world's greatest apéritif: sherry. And it is not only an apéritif, for the same vineyards yield dessert wines of the finest quality.

Sherry

Sherry is grown in the extreme south of Spain, in Andalusia, and it is matured principally in three towns: Jerez de la Frontera, Puerto de Santa Maria and Sanlucar de Barrameda. The most important of these is Jerez, which is some nine miles inland from the sea. The others are on the coast, Puerto being nine miles to the south-west of Jerez and Sanlucar thirteen miles to the north-west. These distances are quite small, but wine is a sensitive, living thing and the slight variations in climate produce distinct differences in the way the wine matures. There is not a great deal of difference between the wines of Jerez and Puerto, though the latter is particularly noted for sherries of the fino and amontillado

371

styles. The wines of Sanlucar, however, are entirely different: all the manzanilla is made there. It has a distinctive, very fresh flavour that cannot be reproduced anywhere else.

Jerez is a very ancient town whose origin is veiled in mystery. Most probably it was founded by the Phoenicians, who moved inland after founding Cadiz in 1100 B.C. After them came the Carthaginians and then the Romans. During the Roman domination the area soon became famous for its good, cheap wine, which was exported in large quantities to Rome, when the policy of *panem et circences* had become so much a part of Roman life that wine had to be imported from the colonies to prevent a rebellion of the plebs. Even in those days it would seem that Spain was a law unto itself, for the edict of Domitian was never enforced.

The Roman supremacy ended with the invasion of the Vandals in A.D. 409, and soon afterwards the Goths arrived. The greatest change of all came in A.D. 711, when the Visigoths were overthrown by the infidel Mussulmans, with their allies the Berbers, at the famous battle of Guadalete, fought very near Jerez. With the victory of the Moors, there rose up one of the most astonishing civilizations in the whole history of Europe. Moorish blood still flows through the veins of the people, and shadows of the past linger in their customs, music, art and the habits of their minds. To see the beauty of their living, one need only go to Granada, Cordova or Seville. During this period, Jerez grew wealthy. It was known as Scheres, a name that was later corrupted to Jerez by the Spanish and to sherry by the English. Even then, despite the Islamic law, the town was surrounded by vineyards, for what nation can remain teetotal in the midst of the most productive vineyards in the world? The Moors certainly could not. To drink wine was the usual custom, and the illegal beverage was even taxed. Wine and women were the inspiration of Moorish poets:

> *Between her white fingers the chalice of*
> *golden wine was a yellow narcissus asleep*
> *in a silver cup*

And Arabic viticulture was first rate.

It was not a peaceful time, though, for the Moors were under constant pressure from the Catholic princes. On October 9th, 1264, the feast of St. Dionysius the Areopagite (of unfortunate literary memory), the Christians under Alfonso X took the town by surprise, and conquered it. Known as Alfonso the Sage, one of the wisest things the king did was to encourage the cultivation of the vine and wine making throughout his territory, and to some extent we owe the modern supremacy of sherry to his enthusiasm. The town never fell again to the Moors, but for the next two centuries it was to be on the border of the Catholic and Moorish kingdoms, and in 1380, King Juan I granted it the privilege of adding *de la Frontera* as a suffix to its name.

As far back as 1485 there is a record of wine being shipped from Puerto de Santa Maria to 'Plemma which is in the kingdom of England'—presumably Plymouth; and foreign merchants were already living in Jerez. They were mostly dealing in wines known as *Vinos de Romania*, or Rumney. Rumney, like Malmsey, is a name that conjures up a glorious past. Originally it came from 'Rumania'—the medieval East Roman Empire—and particularly from southern Greece. The merchants of Jerez had no more right to ship a Rumney than have the growers of Australia or South Africa to ship a sherry. It was not drunk locally, however, which suggests that it was too rich for the hot Andalusian climate. But although there are no clear records of wine from the sherry area having been shipped at an earlier date, there can be little doubt that the trade was already well established by this time, and that it dated from the period of the Moors. The earliest known reference to an Andalusian wine in English literature occurs in the fourteenth century, in Chaucer's *Pardoner's Tale*, in which he referred to the wine of Lepe, which was grown between Ayamonte and Huelva, not so very far outside the sherry area.

By 1517 the English trade was so important that Don Alonso Perez de Guzman, Duke of Medina Sidonia, who was virtually king of the sherry area, conceded special privileges to the English merchants of Sanlucar. This was followed in 1530 by a licence of King Henry VIII establishing the right to elect a councillor, or governor, and twelve 'ancient and expert persons' to be assistants, with 'full power to levy such imposts as shall be thought necessary, and to make ordinances for their welfare'. A meeting held at the colony's newly erected St. George's Church on April 24th, 1539, was attended by eighteen merchants who elected William Ostrich, of Sanlucar, to be their governor.

After King Henry VIII broke with the Church of Rome, the English residents were continually in trouble with the authorities, but trade continued to flourish, and in 1543 forty thousand butts of sherry were exported to England and Flanders. Spanish and Portuguese wines were then being sold in London for a shilling a gallon, whereas those of France and Germany cost eightpence. By Elizabeth's reign, sherry sack was established as a firm favourite, and it was acclaimed by the poets—by Ben Jonson, Marlowe, Raleigh and Spenser, but above all by Shakespeare.

Sir John Falstaff: 'A good sherris-sack hath a two-fold operation in it. It ascends me into the brain; dries me there all the foolish and dull and crudy vapours which environ it; makes it apprehensive, quick, forgetive, full of nimble, fiery and delectable shapes; which deliver'd o'er to the voice, the tongue, which is the birth, becomes excellent wit. The second property of your excellent sherris is, the warming of the blood; which, before cold and settled, left the liver white and pale, which is the badge of pusillanimity and cowardice: but the sherris warms it and makes it course from the inwards to the parts extreme. It illumineth the face, which, as a beacon, gives warning to all the rest of this little kingdom, man, to arm; and then the vital commoners and inland petty spirits muster me all to their captain, the heart, who, great and puffed up with this retinue, doth any deed of courage; and this valour comes of sherris. So that skill in the weapon is nothing without sack, for it sets it a-work; and learning, a mere hoard of gold kept by a devil till sack commences it and sets it in act and use. Hereof comes it that Prince Harry is valiant; for the cold blood he did naturally inherit of his father, he hath, like lean, sterile and bare land, manured, husbanded, and tilled, with excellent endeavour of drinking good and good store of fertile sherris, that he is become very hot and valiant. If I had a thousand sons, the first human principle I would teach them should be, to forswear thin potations and to addict themselves to sack.'

The real Sir John lived long before the days of sack. Be that as it may, sack was certainly a favourite of Shakespeare's, and what character could praise it more appropriately than Falstaff? When Marlowe was killed in a tavern brawl, he was probably drinking it, and I can think of many worse deaths.

The word sack (there is a choice of several spellings) probably originated at the end of the fifteenth century, and is almost certainly derived from the Spanish verb *sacar* (to draw out). It thus signifies any wine for export, and there are many references to Malaga sack and Canary sack, quite apart from sherry sack. Other derivations have been proposed but none is convincing. The frequently repeated derivation from *seco*, meaning *dry*, is almost certainly incorrect, as sack was always classified as a sweet wine. It is difficult to say exactly what this Elizabethan sack was like, but it was apparently something after the style of a modern brown sherry, but with less character, body and flavour.

The reign of Elizabeth was a disastrous one in the history of Anglo-Spanish relations. The Spaniards can hardly be blamed for the animosity they felt against England for her naval activities and for supporting the rebels in the Spanish Netherlands; it must have been somewhat exasperating to have one's Main perpetually harried by knighted corsairs, one's chief seaport sacked, and one's beard singed. Trade between the two countries was, from time to time, banned, but the English government acted generously towards the merchants: they were awarded 200,000 ducats in compensation for the loss of an annual export of 40,000 butts.

The name of Drake became a byword of horror throughout the province of Cadiz, and it still is to this day. He is the local bogy man: when a mother wants to frighten her child into acquiescence, she says, 'El Draque will get you if you're not good.' His most daring raid of all was in 1587. It was the time he 'singed the King of Spain's beard' by setting fire to the Spanish fleet as it lay at anchor in the bay. He remained in Cadiz for three days at considerable risk, and made off with 2,900 pipes of wine. His spoils must have been appreciated in England, as wine imports from Spain had been greatly cut down in consequence of the war. This superb malpractice helped to introduce sherry drinking on a large scale in England, and the publicity was cheap at the price; it has been repaid a million-fold.

After the reign of Elizabeth, trade was somewhat easier. England and Spain were soon at peace again, and sack became so popular in royal circles that on July 17th, 1604, James I was obliged to issue an ordinance:

'Whereas in times past Spanish wines, called Sacke, were little or no whit used in our Court . . . within these late years it is used as a common drinke and served at meales, as an ordinary . . . using it rather for wantonnesse and surfeitting, than for necessity, to a great wasteful expense; We, considering that ... our nobility ... many for their better health desire to have Sacke, our pleasures is, that there be allowed to the sergeant of our seller twelve gallons of Sacke a day, and no more.'

Unfortunately the inevitable happened, and some of the less scrupulous merchants abused their prosperity by shipping very inferior wines. When Roos visited Jerez in 1610, he wrote that much of the sack sent to England was 'sophisticated', and 'of so Churlishe, and unholsome a nature, that no man of honour ... will drinke of it.' The Spaniards marvelled at the poor quality of the wines shipped here, and described them as *vino por borrachos*— wine for drunks. Roos had often heard Londoners boast of how their city was better served with wine than any other in Christendom. They certainly had variety, but in his travels through Spain, France and Italy, he continually heard the growers 'blesse themselves in wondering what Kinde of Creatures those be, which shall drincke those wynes.'

Sack is mentioned frequently in Pepys's Diary. On January 20th, 1662, he and three friends bought two butts of sherry; his was 'put into a hogshead, and the vessel filled up with four gallons of Malaga wine, but what it will stand us in I know not: but it is the first great quantity of wine that I ever bought.' The mixture of malaga with sherry is not as odd as it may seem; the two districts are in the same province and the wines are not all that dissimilar. A hogshead is a large amount for a private person to buy, though; it is equivalent to over three hundred bottles. But Pepys was a canny man, and in August he sold his hogshead to Sir W. Batten— 'and am glad of my money instead of wine.' Whether that were a reasonable attitude would depend largely on the wine.

The sherry trade with Great Britain reached its lowest ebb during the eighteenth century, when imports were fairly steady at about five thousand butts a year. The wine was still greatly praised and esteemed; it remained a favourite with the gentry and with sportsmen; it was drunk regularly by cricketers at the Bat and Ball, Hambledon. But the trade went through a period of stagnation; the potential market was never broached, and the growers were far from prosperous. There are many explanations. Unfortunately England and Spain were involved in a succession of wars that spanned the century and did little good to the trade between the two countries. Some of the Spanish wine trade was diverted to Portugal, and this tendency was encouraged by the preferential rates of duty arising from the Methuen Treaty of 1703. British merchants also began to trade extensively with the island of Madeira. This diversion of trade was used by supporters of the *Gremio*, or wine-growers' guild, of Jerez, to explain away the reduced demand for their wines, but these factors probably did less harm than did the many restrictive practices imposed by the *Gremio* itself.

The Guild was governed by a council of six: two ecclesiastics, two municipal representatives, and two wine growers. These met before and after the vintage to fix the price of grapes and that of the new must; as far as it is possible to calculate such things, based on the relative cost of living then and now, these prices were more than double those of today. When the West Indies fleet was provisioned with wine, this was arranged by a quota system, rather than by free competition. Worst of all, merchants were forbidden to accumulate large stocks; wine was therefore not matured long enough, and trade was lost because lack of stock caused delay in preparing the blends for shipment. The idea behind this extraordinary regulation was that such wine stores would divert profits from the hands of the growers into those of merchants, and that it would encourage speculation. The only large stores of old wine were in the possession of the Church, and in a few private cellars.

These restrictions aimed at making the trade easy and profitable with a minimum of effort and competition, but in fact they had the opposite effect, and sherry shippers were unable to compete with wines grown elsewhere. Malaga, for instance, exported a rich dessert wine not unlike sherry, and it became popular in Britain under the name of Mountain. This captured much of the available market for Spanish wines, and exports from Malaga were greater than those from either Cadiz or Sanlucar.

The restrictions of the Gremio were opposed by a number of merchants, notably by one Juan Haurie. But despite all the efforts of its opponents, the Guild continued until it was dissolved by Royal proclamation in 1834, after a hundred and one years of disastrous existence.

Prior to the eighteenth century the wine trade was in the hands of small individual merchants, and establishments on the scale of modern bodegas were entirely unknown; there was no continuity of name and no records of individual merchants have survived. Only one modern firm—J. M. Rivero—can trace its direct ancestry to an earlier period. This house has been trading at least since 1653. Its trade mark is CZ, and the initials stand for Cabeza y Zarco, the family name of Don Pedro Alonso Cabeza de Aranda y Zarco, who was its founder. Other great names soon followed. The firm of Pedro Domecq traces its descent to an Irish farmer and a wine grower called Patrick Murphy who came to Spain prior to 1730. From him the business passed to Juan Haurie, and from the Haurie family to the Domecqs. Duff Gordon & Company (which trades in Spain under the name of Osborne) was founded by Sir Thomas Duff, then British Consul at Cadiz, prior to 1767; and Thomas Osborne, whose firm later merged with that of Duff Gordon, arrived in Cadiz from Devon in 1781. The firm of de la Riva was in business before 1776 and that of Misa was also in existence by the end of the eighteenth century. William Garvey came from County Waterford in 1780 and his son Patrick founded Garvey & Co. in 1830.

So much for the latter years of the eighteenth century. It was an age of increasing prosperity, stimulated by a new influx of British and French merchants, and interrupted only occasionally by the wars, plagues, upsets and minor disasters to which Spain has always been accustomed.

Of all these troubles, the Peninsular War was by far the worst. Andalusia was a battleground, occupied alternatively by the French and allied soldiers. The armies were relentless in their demands for wine, particularly the French. William Garvey had no time for them at all, and moved with his whole family to Cadiz, which was occupied by Spanish and British garrisons. His account books contain a vivid entry: 'Wine robbed by the French soldiers, 30 arrobas.' Such conduct was enough to make any vintner cross. Sir Francis Darwin described how stores of the finer wines were bricked up, but the French bribed undesirables to show them where these were. Thousands of gallons of sherry were lost, and stocks were seriously depleted, but the fine harvests and abundant yields of the Jerez vineyards soon enabled the growers to recover, when once the war was over and the French expelled. In fact, they more than recovered, and the years following the Peninsular War were the most prosperous and glittering in their whole history.

That the recovery was so rapid was thanks partly to the First Gentleman of Europe, who roundly damned Madeira and swore— by God!—he would drink nothing but sherry. Sherry had 'arrived', and soon a decanter was found on every English sideboard. Jerez had never heard of such wealth. Rich sherry shippers had mansions with gardens planned after the English taste: sweeping lawns of green turf and boxwood hedges, watered continuously from deep wells.

Many of the great sherry shippers began as clerks who left their employers to start their own businesses. John William Burdon originally worked for Duff Gordon, and when he left he soon built up a flourishing business of his own. The last member of the Burdon family died a bachelor and the name has now passed to Don Luis Caballero. The Caballeros were in the wine trade at Chipiona in 1795, and their business as shippers dates back to 1830. The firm of Gonzalez, Byass & Co. was founded in 1835 by Manuel Maria Gonzalez Angel, who took his London agent, Robert Blake Byass, into partnership in 1855. Kenneth MacKenzie came to Jerez to found the firm of MacKenzie & Co. in about 1842. Another clerk who, like Burdon, struck out on his own was Joseph Warter who left Haurie in 1854, and who joined with a Mr. Wisdom to found the house with the striking name of Wisdom & Warter. This firm, in turn, gave rise to another—and one of the greatest names of all. Warter had a clerk called Alexander Williams, a man of great energy who naturally hoped for a partnership. This was not granted—in fact it was refused in very strong terms. In 1877, Williams left, and with a thousand pounds, provided by his father-in-law Mr. Humbert, he founded Williams & Humbert. George G. Sandeman, Sons & Co. began much earlier than this in England, but later in Spain. George Sandeman left Scotland for London in the last decade of the eighteenth century and set up as a merchant, specializing in port and sherry. At first he was agent for Duff Gordon's wines, and then for those of Julian Pemartin. But in 1879, Pemartin, ruined by his extravagant manner of living, went bankrupt, and his agents, who were his largest creditors, acquired his assets. His business had been founded in 1819. Another firm with strong English connections is Wilson & Valdespino, founded by William Wilson, the son of a Derbyshire brewer who spent only a few years in Jerez, returning to England in 1889.

Thus did the great sherry houses come into being. Their histories are intimately tied up with that of the wine: far more so than with table wines, for sherry, like port and champagne, is a blended wine, and it is the shipper who determines its quality. One cannot look for the name of a vineyard, nor for a vintage year. But in listing these great shippers, one has stepped forward rapidly in time, and now one must step back.

By 1840, the fog of Victorian respectability was beginning to descend upon England; everything had to be done properly; there was a new beatitude of bourgeois conventions, and one dictum at least was to benefit the sherry trade for many years before ultimately leading to disaster: it was considered 'correct' to entertain with wine, but the quality did not matter much. Even in humble houses, there was a decanter of sherry with a few biscuits waiting for whomsoever might call.

The demand rose steadily. In the early years of the century, the total export was about eight thousand butts; by 1840, the figure was 17,001 butts; by 1850, 21,457; by 1860 30,725; by 1870, 49,597; and in 1873, sales reached the record of 68,467 butts. In 1864, 43·41 per cent of the total wine imports to Great Britain were sherry. With wine sales soaring, the shippers might well have been sitting back and taking life easily, and some of them doubtless were, but there were many anxious faces: all was not well in the vineyards. In 1855, there was an attack of oidium known locally as 'cenizo', or ash, owing to its colour; there was not another good vintage until 1861. As if that were not enough, there was an attack of pulgon, a repulsive insect that feeds on the vine and finally destroys it. It had periodically devastated the vineyards ever since the Middle Ages and it returned in 1867. It was eventually exterminated, but there was not another good vintage until 1870.

These successive calamities occurring in the vineyards at a time when the demand for wine had reached an unprecedented peak had to be overcome as best they could. There was only one way: must was brought in from outlying districts in ever-increasing quantities. The result was inevitable and rapid: the poorer grades of sherry decreased in quality and increased greatly in price. The situation was made worse by the less reputable British merchants who were determined to maintain the demand by keeping the price steady, and preferred to lower the quality of their wines rather than to add a few pence to the cost of a bottle. On a short-term basis, their policy was probably commercially sound, but nothing could have been more surely calculated to get the wine a bad name.

When trade is booming, it is rather easy to live in a fools' paradise. Even when orders reach new heights, corruption starts to eat away at the foundations of the structure and it is soon ready to collapse. The sherry slump at the turn of the century was brought about by five factors working together: the dreadful imitation sherries or 'horrible mixings' from Hamburg and other places; the very inferior wines made in Jerez itself during the boom years; the ignorant attacks of certain doctors who claimed that the wine was 'plastered', 'goutey', 'full of added spirit', and 'acid to the stomach'; the caprice of fashion; and, lastly, the plague of the phylloxera which for several years made wine-making difficult, unprofitable and heartbreaking. By the late 1870s, merchants all over England were telling the same story: their customers were giving up sherry because 'It is not what it was.' And their customers were quite justified. Wines that were previously 'Shipped off to the leathern-tongued customers of Hamburg or Quebec at £15 per butt' were being sold in England at far higher prices. Members of the wine trade were well aware of the declining quality, and the *Wine Trade Review* put the complaint very clearly, begging that 'the goose which has laid so many golden eggs in the past should not be sacrificed at the shrine of profit'. But the shippers took no heed of the warning.

The medical attack was launched by a Dr. J. L. W. Thudichum. He was a popular and successful doctor, but his attack was based on a series of misconceptions, his chemistry was extremely doubtful, and his quantitative analysis so ludicrously inaccurate that one can only suppose it was guesswork. He was careful to omit details of experiments he had previously performed at Jerez, but Henry Vizetelly, in his excellent book, *Facts About Sherry*,[1] told all about them:

[1] London, 1876.

'In common candour the author of this incredible misrepresentation ought not to have withheld from the public his qualifications to speak so confidently on the subject. He should have told them that he had visited Jerez under the auspices of certain shipping houses to whom he offered, if not to repeat the miracle of Cana, at any rate to produce amontillado by purely chemical agency—that he was provided with considerable funds for the purchase of scientific instruments which he was incompetent to use, and that he resided at Jerez in style for a period of three months at the expense of his principal patron, during which time he lost him half his vineyard's produce through the so-called amontillado which he professed to fabricate turning out such vile stuff that it could only be employed for rinsing casks with, while a further experiment which he made in the bodega of a second shipper resulted in transforming the wine into vinegar.

'The public, knowing nothing of the motive which prompted these attacks upon sherry, naturally grew alarmed, and for a time the subject formed a common topic of conversation at all dinner-tables, where by the lady at your side you found sherry generally declined with thanks. Middle-aged gentlemen, too, perfectly hale and hearty on their daily pint of sherry, fancied that perhaps for them a day of reckoning might be near.'

Eventually the medical profession itself came to the rescue. Doctors were perpetually badgered for information by patients who had read the quasi-scientific attacks on sherry in the press, and they were unable to tell them anything. The *Lancet*, as the leading professional paper, sent a Mr. Vasey as their commissioner to Jerez and charged him to investigate all the complaints. Many stories are still told of the antics he got up to. He was given a free run of all the bodegas and nothing was hidden from him. He would crop up from anywhere, pouncing when least expected from behind a butt of fermenting must, or watching from a concealed place to see the exact amount of plaster added to the grapes. His conclusions were triumphant.

Sherry was exonerated and all the charges of the medical profession were proved false. At a later date, Thudichum's findings were directly contradicted by F. W. Tunnicliffe, M.D. But the damage had been done; the prejudice was already rooted in the public mind and there was no gainsaying it.

To make matters worse, when Queen Victoria died in 1901, Edward VII sold all the surplus wines in the royal cellars and these included no less than sixty thousand bottles of sherry, accumulated through some oversight of the royal bureaucracy, which continued placing orders for wine at the old level although entertaining had virtually ceased with the death of the Prince Consort. Some irreverent journalists also suggested that the state of His Majesty's liver was at least partly responsible for the sales. Sherry had no champions amongst the young, and was drunk indiscriminately with mediocre meals by elderly ladies up for the day from the country. There can be no wonder that sales slumped.

To some extent, it is as well they did. In 1894 phylloxera struck. It had reached Malaga during the 1880s, on vines sent from France. It was brought thence to Jerez by itinerant labourers, and it soon laid waste all the vineyards. It is a blessing that there were vast quantities of wine in the bodegas to tide over the lean years. The remedy here, as elsewhere, was to graft the native vines on to resistant American stocks. Happily the grafted vines have in no way lowered the quality of the wine; in fact the general opinion of sherry shippers who lived through the critical years is that wines from the grafted vines are slightly better, though one particularly attractive style of sherry, called *palo cortado*, has become harder to prepare.

Prosperity had brought new blood and virility, and when the slump came the sherry shippers were not easily defeated. As soon as the vineyards were producing efficiently again, they made every effort to stage a comeback. It was hard going, but in the end they were triumphant. The wines they introduced were altogether better than the majority of those that had been on the market previously and were a delight to the connoisseurs who had affected to scorn sherry; the shippers found, too, that it paid to advertise, and the Spanish houses were also helped by the profitable brandy trade they were building up, principally in the Peninsula and South America. Perhaps the greatest fillip of all that helped to bring about the revival of sherry was a whim of Carl Williams: he gave the first sherry party and the idea caught on. The craze for cocktail parties was just beginning, but the more discriminating began to take sherry instead.

Since 1933 the preparation of sherry has been controlled by the Consejo Regulador de la Denominacion de Origin Jerez-Xérès-Sherry. This corresponds to the French *appellation contrôlée*, and all casks and bottles exported from the sherry area bear the seal of the Consejo Regulador as a guarantee of authenticity. The area of production is carefully controlled and, to ensure that the wine is properly matured, a shipper may only sell a proportion of his stock each year.

*

The sherry vineyards are cultivated on three principal types of soil. Listed in order of quality, these are: *albariza, barro* and *arena*. The albariza soil on which the finest vineyards are grown is found principally to the north and west of Jerez with outcrops in more distant places, notably in Montilla. It also occurs in the immediate sub-soil of the vineyards to the south of the town and is there known as albero. The name *albariza* is derived from *albo*, meaning snow-white, and from a distance the soil does look as white as snow, but when examined closely it is seen to contain many earth-coloured particles. If a handful is dropped into a glass of water, it falls to the bottom, releasing bubbles of air on the way, and then gradually separates into a distinct layer of pasty mud. This mud is so slippery that crossing an albariza vineyard during the rainy season is a very perilous undertaking, an exaggeration of the sort of slipperiness that is well known to those who hike on our own South Downs. When the soil dries out again, though, it turns back into a fine powder; it does not coagulate and there is no trace of the cracks that appear when ordinary mud is dried by the sun. This even texture is extremely important in the climate of Jerez: in February, March and April there are heavy rains which the earth absorbs as if it were a sponge, and when the hot sunshine follows in May, the surface of the soil is baked into a homogeneous and hard layer without any cracks or irregularities. Cool air and water are trapped beneath it to feed the roots of the vines throughout the semi-tropical summer. This soil consists largely of calcium carbonate, or chalk—from thirty to eighty per cent. The remainder, for the most part, is sand and clay, in widely varying proportions.

Alberiza gives wines of the very highest quality, but the yield is small: usually only about three butts per acre during the useful life of the vines, depending on the pruning, and falling to half that quantity in bad years, as in 1945 and 1958, when there had been persistent drought in the three previous years. The Levante wind can also reduce the yield by drying the grapes if it blows for a long time while they are ripening.

Barro soil is darker in colour and gives a rather coarser wine, but the yield is greater—about twenty per cent more than albariza. This soil occurs in the valleys between the hills of albariza and also along the coast from Sanlucar practically to Gibraltar, though only a proportion of this stretch of country is suitable for vines. Like albariza soil, barro is slippery and treacherous when wet and intensely hard when dry, but it contains a lower proportion of calcium carbonate. Iron oxide often gives it a red or yellowish tinge, though the overall colour is brown, and it also contains many fossil shells. Apart from the somewhat inferior quality of the wine produced, viticulture is made difficult in barro regions by wide gaps in the soil which are filled with almost pure sand, and after heavy rain the clay and chalk tend to be washed beneath the surface, leaving a layer of pebbles and sand on top, which makes it hard to see what is good and what is not. Moreover the high fertility causes a prolific growth of weeds, while the heat of the sun dries it unevenly, producing wide cracks.

Arena soil, sometimes known as barro-arena, is very inferior and consists almost entirely of sand with a more marked yellowish-red tinge caused by iron. There is very little of this soil, which was only planted to any significant extent at the end of the last century, as it proved resistant to the phylloxera. It is easy to work and there is little trouble from weeds. The yield is very high—about twice that of albariza—but the quality of the wine is so inferior that the price it fetches is only about half.

The vineyard areas are divided into *pagos*, that may be anything in size from an acre to the two thousand acres of the great Macharnudo district. The most important *pagos* on albariza soil are Macharnudo, Carrascal, Balbaina and Añina, lying to the north and west of Jerez; but Diego Parada y Barreto, writing in 1868, listed 134 pagos in all, each of which he carefully classified. Today there are probably a hundred and fifty.

By far the most important vine is the Palomino Blanco, otherwise known as Listan, Horgazuela, Tempranilla, Palomina, Ojo de Liebra, Temprana or Alban. It produces a must of high quality and is particularly suitable for growing on albariza soil. The grapes are of medium size, tasty and quite sweet; they are pale green in colour but ripen to a translucent golden ochre under the sun.

Next in order of importance comes the famous Pedro Ximenez, which is grown on the lower slopes of the albariza vineyards and produces medium-sized bunches of golden, transparent and intensely sweet grapes. It is particularly noted for making superb sweet wines, but it can also be used for preparing dry sherries of the highest quality, depending on the way the grapes are treated, though for this purpose it is less satisfactory than the Palomino. It has been identified with the German Elbling, but it is clearly more suited to the Spanish climate than to that of Germany.

The Cañocazo, or Mollar Blanco, combines to some extent the properties both of the Palomino and of the Pedro Ximenez; it is a useful compromise between the two, but is gradually falling into disuse, as it is hard to fertilize and there is a danger of the crop failing. The Albillo Castellano, or Calgalon, is also sometimes found on albariza soils; its grapes, which are sweet and juicy, ripen in the second half of September and give quite a good wine, but it is rather vulnerable to insects. It may well be identical with the wine that Columella referred to as albuelis.

All the above vines are also found in barro soil, together with the Moscatel Gordo Blanco, Mantuo Castellano, Perruno and Beba, the last being exclusively for table grapes. The Moscatel is by far the most important of these, and is one of the few vines that can be identified with certainty in the writings of the ancients, including those of Pliny; its name is derived from the Latin *musca*, a fly, because flies are greatly attracted by its sweet grapes. It gives a good crop of large grapes with a very characteristic flavour, rather as if they contained honey instead of sugar. The Moscatel is grown extensively, particularly around Chipiona, and provides a good sweet wine that is used, for the most part, for blending with drier wines to make rich sherries for export.

Palomino and Beba vines are also grown on arena soils, together with Mollar Negro, which is of the family as the Cañocazo, and Mantuo de Pila, otherwise known as Mantuo de Rey, or Gabriela.

The vintage is carefully timed. If the grapes are picked before they are fully ripe, the wine will be weak, and will probably be acid; this is done deliberately at Sanlucar, where the characteristic manzanilla sherries are grown, but it is not desirable for sherries of the normal style.

After the grapes have been picked, rotten fruit is thrown away and the larger stalks are removed; the grapes are then put on esparto grass mats on the *almijar* (a piece of open ground in front of the press-house) to dry in the sun. This reduces the amount of moisture, and hence increases the proportion of sugar, though the actual quantity of sugar is very slightly reduced; it also lessens the amount of malic acid and tannin to some extent. Sunning the grapes is a very old practice and no one knows quite when it began, but it was certainly used by all the sherry growers at the beginning of the nineteenth century. How long the grapes are left in the sun depends partly on the weather and partly on the type of wine that is required. Palomino grapes, for making ordinary sherry, are left out for twelve to twenty-four hours; if a grower wishes to make a high proportion of light fino wines, he may sun his grapes for a shorter time or not at all; but Pedro Ximenez and Moscatel grapes, used for making sweet wines, are sunned for anything from ten days to three weeks, until they look rather like raisins and contain a very high proportion of sugar. At night they are covered with esparto grass mats to protect them from the dew, and they are brought in as soon as possible if there is any sign of rain, as they must be completely dry when they are pressed. Some vineyards are equipped with protective awnings that can be drawn across cane frameworks.

The traditional method of pressing is unique, though alas one should use the past tense, as it has died out as a commercial proposition owing to the cost of labour and is now only occasionally demonstrated as a tourist attraction. It is a delightful sight. When the grapes are ready for pressing, they are carried indoors and put in a *lagar*, or wine press. This is a wooden trough some eighteen feet square and two feet deep; it stands on trestles that raise it two feet off the ground and is slightly tilted so that the juice runs towards the outlet. It holds enough grapes to make a butt of must—about fifteen hundred pounds—and it could hold more, but some room has to be left to prevent the juice from overflowing.

Four labourers, known as *pisadores*, work in each lagar. They are dressed in short trousers and are not barefoot, as in the Douro, but wear special cowhide boots, or *zapatos de pisar*, whose soles are heavily nailed with large-headed tacks driven into the leather at an acute angle. This method of nailing is very important and gives results similar to bare feet but with far less discomfort. The pips and stalks are trapped undamaged between the nails and a soft layer of grapeskins forms over the soles so that the hard pips and stalks of the other grapes cannot be broken. The weight of a man is just right for the work.

The pressing begins in the middle of the night and finishes at about noon the following day, so that the labourers can rest during the hottest hours. Working at night, they are also less troubled by wasps, which find freshly crushed grapes almost as attractive as jam. Quite apart from comfort, pressing the grapes in the cool hours delays the start and speed of fermentation, which is a great advantage, as it should be kept as slow as possible if a first-class wine is to be made.

Before treading is started, the grapes are sprinkled with three to four and a half pounds of gypsum or *yeso*. It is this practice which Thudichum saw fit to attack in the nineteenth century. It does nothing but good. Reduced to simple terms, its action is to convert the cream of tartar in the must into potassium sulphate, calcium tartrate and tartaric acid. The potassium sulphate is a harmless salt; the calcium tartrate is insoluble and falls into the lees of the wine, helping clarification; and the tartaric acid augments the necessary acidity and helps fermentation. It also produces valuable side effects.

The grapes are pressed by foot until they form a pulp, which is then stacked up around a seven-foot-high steel screw that is fixed permanently in the centre of the lagar. The pulp is tapped into place with wooden spades, forming a cylinder with the screw in the middle; this is known as the *pie*, and it has to be very even in shape if the second pressing is to be a success. It is wrapped round tightly with a strong band of plaited esparto grass, five inches wide and eighty feet long, both ends of which are fastened to wooden blocks. One block is attached to the lagar at the bottom of the pie; the other, at the top of the pie, dove-tails with a further piece of wood to fit round the screw, the pair being known as *marranos*, or hogs. These are separated by a metal washer from the big nut which rotates on the screw; this nut is called the *marrana*, or sow, on account of the grunting noise it makes when it is turned. It is fixed to a massive steel handle, more than two yards long from the end to end. As this is turned, the pie is compressed and juice squeezes out through the mesh of the esparto grass band and through the orifice formed by the wooden block at the bottom.

The screw turns quite easily at first, and it is light work for two men, called *tiradores*. It gets harder and harder, though, and after a few turns it has to be worked by four *tiradores*, two on either end of the handle. When the screw is about half-way down it gets so stiff that it cannot be turned continuously, and they press it round in jerks; they even have to tie their hands to the handle, as every muscle is tensed for work and they would probably break a bone or rupture themselves if they slipped and lost their support. Any irregularity in the shape of the pie at this stage produces strong lateral forces on the esparto grass band, and the whole flimsy structure shatters, fragments of pulp flying all over the place.

The must produced by the first pie is known as *de yema* (the bud) and is of first-class quality. It is combined with the foot pressing, and together they account for about eighty-five per cent of the total.

After the first pie, the residue is broken up with the wooden spades. A second pie is then built up. In the olden days, the must from this pressing was mixed with water to dilute the tannin and acid, and it is still known as the *aguapie* although the dilution process has not been used for years. The *aguapie* is of inferior quality and only accounts for about five per cent of the total.

In the smaller vineyards there is sometimes a third pie pressing, known as *espirraque*, but in the larger vineyards the second pie is followed by a hydraulic pressing, known as the *prensa*.

With the growing technology of the nineteenth century, there came an urge for mechanization, and wine presses were installed of the kind commonly found in France. These worked very well, but they were not the perfect solution and it was generally felt that foot pressing remained the best method. By the late 1950s, however, wages were beginning to rise rapidly, with serious economic consequences, and then, at the most opportune moment, the perfect answer was evolved: the German pneumatic and piston presses.[1] These have proved a complete success, and are rapidly coming into practically universal use.

[1] These have already been described. See pp. 34-35.

A few hours after the must has run from the press, when it is safely in casks, the 'tumultuous fermentation' begins, provoked by the natural ferments in the air and in the bloom of the grape skins. The temperature rises rapidly and the must froths and bubbles out from the bunghole of the cask. To keep losses down to a minimum the casks are only filled to seven-eighths of their maximum capacity and a big earthenware, stainless steel, or enamelled funnel, about eighteen inches high and eight inches wide is placed in the bunghole, to give the must room to expand upwards. Even so, it often overflows. To get good wine, the temperature is kept as low as possible, and the butts must always be kept out of the sun.

By the end of September, there are warm butts of fermenting must in every possible corner of the sherry towns, and you cannot walk through the streets for more than a few minutes without coming across the sickly, vegetable smell of fermentation; it is one of the necessary evils.

Tumultuous fermentation is as rapid as it is violent. At the end of three or four days, the heat and turbulence die down and a second fermentation begins. Known as the *lenta*, it is much slower than the first; the wine develops steadily for about a fortnight and then more gradually until December or January, when the opaque must suddenly 'falls bright'. It is still very immature, but it is wine at last.

The technicalities of the bodega may be vital to the sherry shipper, but they mean nothing at all to the casual visitor; all he sees are the great buildings, permeated with the aroma of maturing wine; he steps from the bright, hot sunlight of the patio into the huge, dim nave, where everything is quiet and at peace. Richard Ford likened bodegas to cathedrals, and his simile was so good that everyone who has written about sherry after him has used it. There is something rather awe-inspiring about the sight of so much wine; the buildings are enormous and lofty, and the light is very subdued. But, unlike cathedrals, they are all quite modern and most were built during the nineteenth century. Before that time, much less wine was produced and it was sold when it was only a year or two old. After the Napoleonic wars, the great shipping houses began to accumulate large stocks of old wine and regularly exported better and more expensive sherries than ever before: to store them, they built their great bodegas round the periphery of the town. Structurally, they are all very similar, with thick walls and high roofs to keep the temperature down; the roofs are often insulated with cork sheet and the walls are made with hollow bricks. Small windows protected with iron grilles are set high up in the walls and are left open all the time to let the air circulate freely, but they are covered with esparto grass blinds during the day to keep the sun out. The floors are earth, though the passages between the casks are sometimes paved with oak blocks made from the waste material of the cooperage. Brick or stone is entirely unsuitable. During the hottest and driest months, the floors are sprinkled with water twice or three times a week; it soaks in and evaporates gradually during the next few days, helping to keep the temperature down; it also increases the humidity, and so reduces the rate of evaporation of the wine.

The tall, heavy roofs are supported by rows of square, white-washed columns that help to make the bodegas cathedral-like. The effect is best of all where there is no central row of columns, as in Osborne's beautiful bodega of San José, in Puerto de Santa Maria, which was built in 1837. Some shippers renew their white-wash every year and their bodegas look immaculately clean; others do not bother, and let the cobwebs of ages accumulate; it makes not a scrap of difference to the wine; in fact, one famous shipper told a complaining and hygienic English lady that he would stuff the cobwebs right inside the wine if he thought they would improve it, and gossip says that one of the young shippers, wishing to give an air of antiquity to his buildings, bought cobwebs by the sackful and draped them from the walls. But if cobwebs do no harm, anything evil-smelling, on which bacteria could develop, must not be allowed anywhere near the wine, and any trace of rotting animal or vegetable remains is scrupulously cleaned up. Some shippers go even further and say that pleasant scents are actually good for the wine; for instance, jasmine is trained to grow up the walls of the Misa bodegas.

Sherry is a gift of providence. Everything is exactly right; soil, climate, ferments and fruit. But there is a special gift that is more improbable and more astonishing than any of the others, and that is the sherry flor. *Flor* simply means *flower*, but the sherry flor is not a flower at all: it is a repulsive-looking film of yeast cells that covers the surface of the must in most of the butts some two months after the vintage, though it often does not appear until the following April or May. Its growth is rapid: a month after it first appears it is already about an eighth of an inch thick. It is almost pure white in colour and is a mass of irregular wrinkles; in fact it looks just like a farmhouse cream cheese. Its arrival is spontaneous and natural; it can easily be killed but can never be induced to grow naturally on the surface of wine where it has not appeared of its own accord. Imitators of sherry have taken specimens of flor to South Africa, Australia and California. With great difficulty it has been kept alive and has been induced to grow on the surface of alien wines, but the result has never been quite the same. Chemically its effect is to absorb any remaining traces of sugar and to diminish the quantities of glycerine and volatile acids; at the same time it greatly increases esters and aldehydes. The predominating organisms in the flor belong to the genus *saccharomyces*.

Butts of wine that are kept apart and are not blended with others generally breed flor for six to eight years, but have been known to do so for as many as fifteen years. As the wine grows older in cask, in the dry atmosphere of the sherry towns, it gradually evaporates, but it loses water more rapidly than alcohol, and if it is not refreshed with younger wine it gradually gets stronger and its flavour increases. At the same time, the flor gets thinner and darker, until it eventually sinks to the bottom and disappears altogether when the wine gets too strong. In the scales of a solera, where the old wine is drawn off at regular intervals and replaced with younger wine, it is possible to continue breeding flor indefinitely, and when a butt has been in position in a solera for fifty or sixty years, there is a considerable accumulation of dead cells in the lees. It is largely thanks to the flor that casks of delicate young sherry can be kept loose-bunged and on ullage; for it is a deadly enemy of the *mycoderma aceti*, which produces vinegar, and the flor invariably wins. In fact sherry must not be tight bunged, for if it is, the action of the flor is reversed and vinegar can be formed.

I have seen flor growing in a sample bottle of must, and very unpleasant it looked, though the must was perfectly good underneath when it was shaken off. I have been told of the same thing happening to a bottle of delicate fino in England, and it is partly to prevent this that fino sherry exported to foreign countries is almost invariably fortified.

Nature has been very kind to sherry growers, but such generosity exacts its own price, and sherry is a very perverse wine: until it is fairly mature no one can tell quite how it will develop. It is utterly exasperating. No two butts will turn out exactly alike, even if they have been side by side from the very hour of the pressing. One would expect disparity between the wines of the various vineyards, between wines pressed from different types of grapes grown in the same vineyard, and between similar vines in different areas of the vineyard, but that is only a small part of the story. Even if the must is the same, the oak used to make the casks will never be identical. The exact location of the casks in the bodega may also make a difference. There is no end to the possible variants. If one lot of must is divided between two casks, it is quite likely that one will mature as a delicate, light fino, and the other as a dark oloroso of the coarsest type. There is no rhyme nor reason about it all. There is usually a tendency for a given vineyard to produce a majority of wines of a certain class, but it is never more than a tendency. There is also the influence of sunning and of pruning, which have already been described, but this produces no more than a strong bias as to style. Absolutely anything can happen.

After about six months, the must starts to show its development, and the *capataz*, or head foreman of the bodega, goes round taking samples and putting a chalk mark on each of the casks to indicate the first, rough classification. In tasting musts and young wines, the palate is useless; they invariably taste thin, acid and nasty; moreover, if any is swallowed it deadens the sense of smell to those that follow. It is all done on the nose.

At this early stage, it can only be put into one of four categories, which are distinguished by the following marks:

/ – *una raya*; light and good,
/. – *raya y punto*; slightly less promising,
// – *dos rayas*; musts with less style,
/// – *tres rayas*, or quema; coarse or acid.

Every bodega has its own marks for use at each stage of the

393

classification, but the above are typical. There is, of course, a fifth grade: vinegar, marked *Ve*. This is removed hastily to the vinegar store before it gets the chance to infect its neighbours. The tres rayas is often sent to be distilled.

After the classification, the must is racked off the lees—i.e. it is clarified by decanting it off its sediment. It is then checked for alcoholic strength, which is likely to be between 14° and 16° Gay-Lussac.[1] Any of the first category, that has a good growth of flor, and is likely to develop as a wine of the most delicate style (known as fino) is fortified to 15° or 15·5°, if it is deficent in alcohol; such a slight fortification helps to prevent disease without affecting the quality or style. On the other hand, those of the lower categories, which often grow little flor, and which would normally develop as rather heavier wines (known as olorosos) are fortified to 17·5° or 18° Gay-Lussac. This finally kills any flor that may exist and determines their character once and for all. In this way the shipper can, to some extent, decide what class of wine he is going to make, though he can never increase his supplies of fino by causing flor to grow on wines where it does not appear of its own accord.

After the wine has been racked off the lees and fortified, it is allowed to rest for a week or two and is then classified for the second time as:

γ – *palma*; a wine breeding flor,
/ – *raya*; a rather fuller wine with no flor,
// – *dos rayas*; inclined to be coarse,
– *gridiron*; no good at all.

This classification gives a better indication of how it will develop than does the first, but the wine is still its own master and

---

[1] Gay-Lussac is the French measure of alcoholic strength and is equivalent to alcohol by volume at 59°f. It is the scale most generally used in books on wine and will be adopted in this book though the English scale is in degrees Sikes—named after a customs officer. 25° Sikes is equal to 14·2° Gay-Lussac and 27.5° Sikes is equal to 15·6° Gay-Lussac. Austria, Italy and Russia use Tralles degrees, which are almost the same as Gay-Lussac but taken at 60°F. The German Windisch scale is of per cent by weight, while the United States has its own proof scale and Spain has a hydrometer scale of degrees Cartier. Tables of equivalents are published in wine trade reference books such as *The Wine and Spirit Trade Diary*.

evolves just as it likes—often quite differently from how the capataz expects.

Each cask is matured for anything from nine months to three years as an *añada*. The term is derived from *año*, meaning *year*, and an añada wine is simply a vintage wine. While a young wine is maturing, its development is carefully watched. This rests entirely with providence: there is nothing more to be done. As before, the capataz puts a chalk mark on each cask to define the style, and the following are typical.

γ – *palma*; a fine sherry that is both light and delicate,

 ४ – *palma cortada*; a rather stouter fino, tending towards amontillado,

 † – *palo cortado*; a full-bodied yet delicate wine of particularly good style, not breeding flor,

 | – *raya*; a darker and fuller wine, not breeding flor,

 || – *dos rayas*; a style similar to the above but coarser and less attractive.

I once counted the marks on two sets of eighty-four butts in two separate bodegas at a famous shipper's; the wine came from Palomino grapes grown in the same vineyard, and was two years old. In the first bodega there were five butts of palma, thirty-six of raya, and forty-three of dos rayas, with no palo cortado or palma cortada whatsoever, while in the second there were one each of palo cortado and palma cortada, twenty of palma, thirty-two of raya and thirty of dos rayas. The relative absence of that exquisite wine palo cortado is partly the result of the phylloxera; the old wines gave much more of it. The development is very much of a gamble, especially for the smaller shippers; the larger shippers carry such great stocks of young wine—perhaps as many as four thousand butts of every vintage—that the differences average out. It was to overcome these differences and to produce a sherry of uniform quality that the solera system was developed.

If a cask of young sherry is left to mature and is not tampered with in any way, it will gradually become stronger and its character will steadily develop; it may also evolve subtle distinctions of bouquet and flavour; or it may even change its style completely.

Very often it will become better than its mark would suggest, as every capataz is a notorious pessimist and never spares the chalk, but he will not hesitate to upgrade a wine that proves to be good. At the end of three years, most butts will have settled down and the basic classification will not be changed again, but there are always a few of indeterminate character that remain a law unto themselves and which cannot be classified finally for as many as ten years.

Mature sherry falls into three basic classes: fino, palo cortado and oloroso. Each of these has various sub-divisions, depending on age and quality, and each will be considered separately. This is complicated by the fact that some of the descriptive words used are the same as those used in the earlier classifications, but they do not necessarily have the same meanings. All styles are absolutely dry, as the fermentation is complete and the whole of the sugar is used up. If a sweet sherry is required, it is obtained by blending, at a later stage, with specially prepared sweetening wines.

Except for certain styles of manzanilla, fino is the lightest and most delicate of all sherries. It has a delightfully fresh, slightly piercing, and very clean bouquet, is completely dry, and has exactly the right natural acidity without appearing at all too acid to the palate. It is often described as straw-coloured, though the yellow tinge is so slight that it is really more like hay.

The term *palma* (/) is reserved for finos of the highest quality, with a particularly clean and delicate aroma. As the wine ages, it may become *dos palmas* (⫝̸), *tres palmas* (⫝̸), or *cuatro palmas* (⫝̸), but this classification is purely arbitrary; a shipper may put the dividing line where he likes, so that one shipper's Palma could be similar to another's Tres Palmas. As standards of comparison, such graduations are better ignored except when referring to wines coming from the same source. The term Palma Cortada is used, as in the classification of musts, to denote a stouter fino tending towards amontillado. A fino of little merit, that lacks delicacy, is known as entre fino.

When a fino grows old in cask, any of three things may happen: it may gain in body and develop a new depth of bouquet, becoming first a fino-amontillado and then an amontillado; it may gradually grow stronger in flavour but retain its fino character, becoming that rarest and most wonderful of wines, an old fino; or it may just grow steadily coarser and nastier. As usual, it is a pure gamble, though the dice are loaded in favour of amontillado.

Amontillado is given its name because of its resemblance to wines grown in the district of Montilla, near Cordova. Superficially, the similarity can be striking, though amontillado sherries are more distinguished and have a greater quality of flavour. The term did not come into general use until the beginning of the nineteenth century.

The development from fino is gradual; the points at which a fino becomes a fino-amontillado, and a fino-amontillado becomes an amontillado, cannot be determined exactly: shippers vary in their optimism. The characteristic bouquet of an amontillado has been described as 'nutty'; it is certainly deep, and is completely fresh and clean. The colour graduates from the straw-colour of an amontillado-fino to the amber of a young amontillado, and then to the dark gold of an old amontillado.

Genuine amontillado is absolutely delectable. Ever since I can remember, I have been drinking wine in England out of bottles labelled 'amontillado'; as a boy, I used to laugh at Edgar Allan Poe for making such a fuss about a cask of commonplace sherry, but it was I who was the fool. Most of the 'amontillado' sold in England contains little or none of the genuine wine; it is just bastardized fino. Some of the better merchants do list genuine amontillados, but only at a high price. Since amontillado has, of necessity, to mature in cask for at least eight years, and preferably far longer, and as only a limited proportion of fino develops into amontillado, it is necessarily expensive. Commercially amontillado, like all the other styles of sherry, is matured by means of the solera system, rather than as añada wines, but this makes little difference to the price, as the cost of establishing a solera to produce wine of this style is itself prodigious.

Palo cortado is a rare wine that is the delight of sherry drinkers; it is often classed as a style of oloroso, but this seems very unfair to oloroso. It is similar to oloroso in breeding little or no flor, but in other ways it is a law unto itself. It has a deep and subtle bouquet more like amontillado, and it is clean and crisp on the palate, though it is darker in colour. Since the phylloxera, only a very small proportion of the must develops in this style, and a palo cortado solera is excessively difficult to operate. Apart from the problem of finding sufficient young wine of good quality to supply it, bad mismanagement can result in palo cortado debasing itself and turning into oloroso. According to age, it may be classified as *palo cortado* (ǂ), *dos cortados* (ǂ), *tres cortados* (ǂ), or *cuatro cortados* (ǂ), but as with palma, the classification is purely arbitrary and varies from one shipper to another. Palo cortado in Spain suffers the same indignity as does amontillado in England: most of the 'palo cortado' in the bars of Jerez is nothing of the sort; it is a cheap popular wine of not dissimilar style synthesized out of amontillado and oloroso left-overs. The only way to be sure of drinking the real thing is to get a dos or tres cortados bottled by a reputable shipper. Very little is exported.

Oloroso, in Spanish, means 'fragrant', and the name is said to be descriptive, though personally, I find the virile and piquant aroma of fino and amontillado more memorable than the shallow, broad fragrance of oloroso. This style is darker than the others, even when quite young, and in its natural state it is completely dry although it often has a slightly sweet aftertaste caused by traces of glycerine produced by the oloroso fermentation. When this characteristic is particularly noticeable, the wine is sometimes distinguished by a special mark, converting the raya into a tick: $\sqrt{}$. It is known as *pata de gallina*, or hen's foot, possibly owing to its nutritive qualities. Oloroso has more vinosity than other styles, and blends well with sweet wines to produce the rich dessert sherries that are so popular in Great Britain and Scandinavia. Olorosos that lack distinction and quality are known as rayas; they are used in blending the cheaper sherries for export and are usually stronger than good olorosos of the same age. Wines of intermediate quality are called rayas olorosas. Light rayas are sometimes described as rayas finas.

The account given above may be of some guidance, but it is impossible to describe the aroma or flavour of a wine at all accurately; the only thing to do is to taste and to remember, though Manuel Gonzalez Gordon has invented a graphic and helpful simile by comparing fino to an almond, amontillado to a hazel nut, and oloroso to a walnut.

If the various styles of wine were represented by a family tree, it would look something like this:

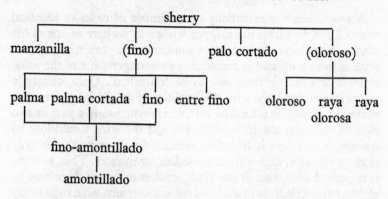

Cowper would have us believe that 'Variety's the very spice of life', and it is partly the great variety found in sherry that makes it suitable for drinking at any time and prevents it from ever becoming monotonous. But the shipper is expected to supply his customers year after year with the wines they like, and the quality must never vary. The traditional way of maturing sherry was to keep it in its separate añadas until it was ready for use, but it developed in all its many styles and shippers could not supply high quality wines in any substantial quantities if the character was to remain unchanged: it is quite easy to blend a wine down to a consistent mediocre standard, but really good wines, especially if they are dry (such as a first-grade delicate fino), need to be shipped in their natural state. If some imaginary and gargantuan shipping house could have ten million butts of añada wine steadily maturing, it would probably be able to find sufficient casks of every kind to satisfy all its requirements, but such an arrangement would obviously be out of the question. It was therefore necessary to devise a way of producing identical wines in large quantities without lowering the quality, and the solera system was invented.

It is one of the convenient, and almost unique, qualities of sherry that if a reasonably small proportion (perhaps a third) of the contents of a cask of superior old wine is withdrawn, and the void is filled with a slightly younger wine of the same style, the younger wine gradually takes on the quality of the older; after a few months, the wine in the cask will be absolutely indistinguishable from what it was before. It is this that makes the solera system possible.

A solera consists essentially of a number of casks of identical wine of a style which the shipper wishes to prepare as one of his standard products. At intervals throughout the year, a quantity of wine is drawn off and is replaced with younger wine of the same style. The solera is then said to be 'refreshed'. Quite clearly, a solera containing wine with the qualities of an añada wine twenty years old cannot be refreshed with añada wines only a year or two old; the contrast would be too great and the wine would lose its quality. The solera is therefore refreshed with wine that is only slightly younger, drawn from a *criadera*, or nursery. This, in turn, is refreshed with wine drawn from another criadera; there may be eight or nine criaderas in all, until the last contains wine sufficiently young in character to be refreshed with young wine (still often, if inaccurately, referred to as must) that may be anything from nine months to several years old.

Each of the stages of development, represented by a criadera or by the solera, is called a *scale*; thus there may be five criaderas and the solera, making six scales in all. The word solera is also used to denote the whole system and, in the above example, the shipper would talk of his solera when referring to all six scales as a single entity. Such soleras are often given fancy names. As all sherry is matured by means of this system, it is clearly absurd to refer to 'solera sherry' as if it were a distinct style, though the term has been misapplied in this way by a number of merchants, who use it to denote a rich dessert oloroso.

Wine that is carefully matured in a solera never varies in quality. It may well be that one or two 'interesting' wines that would develop in the añada system are lost, but the quality of the wines produced by a solera is not one whit inferior to comparable wines matured as añadas; it may even be better, as the wine is improved by its contact with the oxygen in the air as it is moved from scale to scale. Moreover, the sherry towns contain an enormous number of soleras of varying sizes, each of a different style and quality, so there is just as much variety as there was before. The ownership of first-class soleras is the secret of success for a sherry shipper; his whole business depends on their quality and style; they are of incalculable value, and he gives them all the care and attention that is humanly possible.

A popular and erroneous belief held by visitors to the sherry towns is that the scales of a solera are mounted one on top of another, so that wine from the fourth or top tier in the bodega is used to refresh wine in the third tier, but this very seldom occurs in practice. An even and low temperature is vital while the wine is maturing, especially for finos, and the best position is in the bottom two tiers, where the finest finos and amontillados are kept. Olorosos are stored in the third tier, and the fourth tier, when there is one, is used for olorosos and for the sweet and colour wines that are specially prepared for blending. These wines, of course, can also be matured in the lower tiers if there is room for them. The scales of a solera are often separated; they may be in equivalent tiers at various places in the same bodega, or even in entirely different bodegas a mile or two apart. The various scales of important soleras are often divided between the various buildings to minimize fire risk.

Manzanilla appears in the family tree of sherry, and it has already been mentioned elsewhere in this chapter, but it was not described with the other classes of sherry, for it is a thing apart. Manzanilla is the most delicate of all the sherries, with a character and a fragrance that are all its own. Compared with the other styles, it is a comparatively modern wine, for it can only be matured with the aid of a specially regulated solera, and was therefore unknown until the solera system came into being in about 1800. No añada wine ever becomes a manzanilla. There are other differences in its method of growing and of maturation. In the first place, it can only be matured at Sanlucar: attempts to make it in the other towns have only produced some strange finos, and when casks of manzanilla are taken to Jerez, or even Puerto de Santa Maria, they rapidly lose their freshness and delicacy, and turn into rather ordinary finos. After only six or seven months, they are completely spoilt. For the same reason, it does not travel well: when shipped to England, it is often blended with fino, fortified, and even sweetened. It remains an excellent wine, but it retains only a shadow of its natural elegance. This undoubtedly results from the sea air, and the climate, which is more equable than that of Jerez, being warmer in winter and cooler in summer.

There are other differences in the manner in which manzanilla is prepared. The first, and one of the most important, lies in the date of the vintage, which is about a week earlier than for the other styles of sherry—before the grapes are quite ripe. Moreover, the grapes are seldom sunned, so there is less sugar and more acid. The effect is further increased by the method of pruning the vines, which is less drastic than in the other sherry vineyards. All of these things in combination go to produce a wine of exceptional delicacy with an exceptional bouquet.

The fino form of manzanilla, however, called manzanilla fina, is by no means the only one: all the other principal styles—fino-amontillado, amontillado and oloroso—have their manzanilla equivalents, which are basically similar to those of sherry, but each of which has the sharp, penetrating and aromatic character associated with manzanilla. The fino form, however, is by far the most common and the adjective is invariably left out.

As with fino, when manzanilla fina ages, it loses its flor and gains in strength, first becoming manzanilla pasada, which is equivalent to fino-amontillado, and then manzanilla amontillada, when the strength may rise to as much as 20·5°G.-L. These latter wines are prepared by means of successive soleras, each being of greater equivalent age, and the wine in them is moved less often than that in the fina soleras. Oloroso is also made in Sanlucar, using the must that shows no tendency to grow flor. The method of preparation is similar to that of the other towns, but the wine is slightly more piquant.

The origin of the name manzanilla has been the subject of much learned controversy but in all probability it derives from a superficial resemblance to the flavour of *manzanilla*—the common camomile tea that is well known in Spain as a remedy for stomach-ache, and one wonders whether its name was first applied to the newly-invented wine in jest.

When the shipper has prepared his wine and matured it in his soleras, his work has only just begun. The most difficult task of all follows: it has to be blended and prepared for sale.

Just a few of the apéritif finos and amontillados sold in Great Britain are straight solera wines. These are very good, but the market is limited, and they are, of necessity, expensive. Such sherries are absolutely dry, and they are an acquired taste: the palate has to be trained to enjoy their austerity and delicacy. All the sweeter apéritif sherries have to be blended, as do the great, rich, dessert olorosos.

The bases of all blends are the wines from the various soleras, but certain special wines are prepared for adding sweetness or colour. There are four styles of sweet wine: *pedro ximenez, moscatel, dulce apagado* and *dulce de almíbar*. They are quite different in sweetness, flavour, colour and price; each is appropriate to a different style of sherry, and all are essential.

Pedro ximenez and moscatel are rich, sweet wines that are almost like liqueurs. They find great favour with the ladies of Andalusia, but are seldom exported except when blended with drier sherries. Both are extremely expensive, particularly pedro ximenez (or *PX*) which is the traditional great sweetening wine of Jerez. It is prepared from the grapes grown on Pedro Ximenez vines, which are sunned for as long as possible before they are pressed. Stocks of old pedro ximenez are amongst the most valuable assets of the great shippers.

Dulce apagado (quenched sweetness), otherwise known as dulce racimo or mistela, is a cheaper and less distinguished sweetening wine made from grapes grown, for the most part, in the region of Los Palacios, just outside the main sherry area. There is no especial sweetness in the grapes themselves, and the sugar is retained by putting about eighteen litres of *aguardiente*, or wine spirit (which must be entirely free from acid impurities) into the casks that receive the unfermented must; this stops the fermentation before the sugar has entirely been used up. Apart from being cheaper to prepare, dulce apagado has the advantage that it is somewhat lighter in colour than wines made from grapes that have been sunned a long time, and it is therefore suitable for use in wines such as 'medium sherries', which the public expects to be moderate in colour as well as in flavour and in price.

There is a problem with all the above wines: each has its own flavour and colour. This is an advantage in blending rich dessert sherries, but it makes them quite unsuitable for sweetening delicate finos, where they would mask and destroy the flavour of the wine. For this purpose, dulce de almíbar is used. This consists of a blend of invert sugar (which is chemically identical with natural grape sugar) and fino sherry. It is surprisingly expensive.

Very often the natural colour of the wines needs to be augmented, particularly when making a brown or 'Old East India' sherry. This is achieved with *vino de color*—a wine that can have such character that it actually adds distinction to the blend. It is made by concentrating unfermented must over a slow wood fire in a metal cauldron that looks like a victorian washing copper. If the must is reduced to one-third of its original volume, the product is called *sancocho* and if it is reduced to one fifth, *arrope*. Neither of these can be used, however, without further treatment. There are two ways of turning them into vino de color. To make a wine of the finest quality, one or other of them is mixed with unfermented must and the mixture is itself then fermented. To make a cheaper wine, very young fermented wine is used.

The standard shipping butt holds thirty *arrobas* of wine, and all blends are prepared in multiples of that figure. In preparing a blend, one thing is vital: the nose. All blending is done solely on the bouquet of the wine until the very last stage. When a practically perfect match has been achieved, it is tasted, principally to judge the sweetness.

Fino wines in their simplest, greatest, and alas most expensive, form are straight solera wines with no additions whatsoever, and several examples are exported. Others, which are sold in Spain as natural wines, are fortified or sweetened slightly for the export markets although the names are not changed. Most of those sold in the United Kingdom are blended from good basic wines mixed with cheaper wines of less character. A little manzanilla is often added to improve the bouquet, and when manzanilla is exported, it is usually blended with a little fino, which helps it to travel and masks the rapid deterioration that always occurs when it is taken away from Sanlucar. When a delicate fino or manzanilla is sweetened, dulce de almíbar is used, as any other form would darken the colour and mask the flavour. 'Medium' sherries are often very complicated blends that may contain as many as fifteen ingredients.

Something has already been said of the extremely dubious use of the word 'amontillado' when applied to cheaper wines for export; these can only contain a limited amount of genuine amontillado, and consist primarily of anything from fino to oloroso. At best, they are fino-amontillados. Here is an actual example of an 'amontillado' blended for a well-known merchant:

Fino Fuerte	Ro
Amontillado Dolores	5@
MZA Puro	2@
Vino Chiclana Fino	7@
Dulce	2½@

Fino Fuerte is a rather powerful and full-bodied solera fino. MZA stands for manzanilla, and chiclana fino is a cheap fino wine from the neighbourhood of the town of Chiclana. The only amontillado is the amontillado dolores, which, in fact, is not an amontillado at all, but a standard export mark that is available in large quantities; it is made up from several wines of which about half are amontillados. This use of standard blends in preparing special wines is entirely sensible, as it naturally cuts down the work and reduces the price. Carried to its logical conclusion, a special wine for a merchant may consist of nothing more than two or more standard marks blended together, and an example is afforded by a popular 'amontillado' sold by a London merchant. This is the following blend:

Amontillado Dolores	Ro
Oloroso Historico	12@

Ro stands for *resto*—the quantity needed to make the total 30 arrobas.

In preparing top-quality amontillados, palo cortados and olorosos, there is a complication that has not yet been discussed: the oldest wines of these styles are incomparable in aroma and elegance, but they are so highly flavoured that no one can drink them. They are a delight to the nose, but when they enter the mouth it is overwhelmed and shrivels up. When these really old wines are blended with younger ones, their harshness disappears, but all their elegance and maturity shines through, and they irradiate the blend with their goodness. A very small proportion of ancient wine can transform a younger one. If a centenarian oloroso is swirled round a sherry glass and emptied out again, the minute volume that clings to the glass will be enough: when a young oloroso is poured in, its colour darkens, the aroma of the old wine predominates, and the blend has all the character of antiquity. It is thus that the greatest dessert sherries are made: the proportion of old wine need only be small, but its quality must be impeccable. One might have a blend something like this:

Oloroso Viejo	Ro
Oloroso Viejísimo	12@
Oloroso Centenario	½@
PX Viejo	4@

And such a wine would be the climax of a banquet.

The final stage in the blending is to fortify the wine, if necessary, to bring it up to the export strength. This is done with *mitad y mitad* —a mixture of half wine and half alcohol. Wines were fortified originally to stop them turning into vinegar, which was a common calamity before the coming of scientific enology. Above all, it helped them to travel, as the movement and varying temperatures of a journey would easily induce disease in any wine that lacked balance or was weak. At the same time, it coarsened them to some extent, and masked their delicate flavour. There were frequent complaints, particularly in the nineteenth century, that sherry was over-fortified, but this tendency was encouraged by British merchants, who expected it to be spirituous and strong. Quite apart from these considerations, there is, with fino, always the danger that an open bottle will grow flor if it is unfortified, though the risk is not very great and a certain amount of entirely natural fino is already being exported. In future years the proportion will probably increase.

The choice of sherries available is enormous, and anyone should be able to find many that please them. The final choice depends on the time of day, the weather, and the other wines that are to be taken with a meal. Above all, it depends on what one happens to fancy.

For those who enjoy a glass of wine and a biscuit in the morning, any style of sherry is suitable, though the majority prefer a dry wine when the weather is hot and a sweeter wine when it is cold. Likewise a wine that tastes too sweet as an apéritif before lunch may be very acceptable before dinner in the cool of the evening. Very dry sherry has an unaccountable snob appeal, but habitual wine drinkers do generally prefer such sherries as apéritifs; others, who wish to appear knowledgeable, ape them, and often drink very dry sherry at the most improbable times. My own preference is certainly for a wine without the least trace of sweetness, save perhaps in the depth of winter.

A dessert sherry, on the other hand, should generally be more or less sweet: in the British climate, a completely dry wine is seldom appropriate after a meal, save perhaps a dry oloroso after lunch in summer. Such a wine should also have plenty of body, and although I have enjoyed an old amontillado after lunch, palo cortado or oloroso is generally more attractive, especially after dinner.

Such is the story of sherry. It stretches back long into history, and yet it is the most modern of wines—a wine with a universal appeal and one that is unique in its versatility. But a good sherry can never be cheap, and anyone who has read this chapter will know why.

Montilla-Moriles

Until very recently, Montilla was regarded as one of the styles of sherry. Although grown in the middle of the province of Cordova, rather more than a hundred miles from the main area and vinified in a slightly different way, it was so close to sherry in character that it was regularly used in the sherry area for blending. It was also sold, both in Spain and abroad, in its natural unblended state.

That it should have been classed as a style of sherry seems perfectly reasonable. Certainly it is somewhat different from the sherries of Jerez and Puerto, but so are the individualistic manzanillas of Sanlucar. Just as the description 'red bordeaux' covered both the wines of the Médoc and the very different growths of St. Emilion, similarly, the geographical name 'sherry' covered the wines both of the sherry towns and of Montilla. In 1933 this came to an end. The sherry area was then strictly delimited, and the vineyards growing montilla were separately delimited and made into the independent area of *Montilla-Moriles*. This was a decision of extreme purism: the Spaniards, having decided to follow the example of the French and to take geographical names seriously, took them very seriously indeed. Under the regulations of the newly formed *Consejo Regulador*, montilla could no longer be freely used for blending. It was still possible, however, to import wines from Montilla-Moriles into the sherry area when local supplies were insufficient. In the revised regulations of

1964, however, it is envisaged that this will soon cease entirely.

The principal towns of the Montilla-Moriles are Montilla, Los Moriles and Aguilar. Being so much further inland, and far higher, the climate is more continental, with a very hot summer and a cold winter. It is this that principally accounts for the difference in the wine. The soil, however, is very similar to that of the sherry vineyards: a fine white albariza. The principal vine is the Pedro Ximenez, which is pruned very short, though Baladi and Lairén vines are also grown.

Montilla is a charmingly remote, unspoiled, and unaffected little town, living off the vineyards and farms that surround it—a perfect example of an Andalusian hill town. The countryman is a born conservative and if an ancestor fifteen hundred years old could visit the town today, he would see little difference in the way in which the wine is fermented. The Greeks and Romans fermented their wines in great earthenware amphorae; and the growers of Montilla still do so today. The fermentation bodega of a Montilla wine shipper looks like a stage set for Ali Baba and the Forty Thieves. Two or three men could easily hide themselves in each of the great vessels in which the wine is fermented, and it is a beautiful sight to see them all standing there with the *mosto* bubbling at the brim. There is a difference, too, in the pressing of the grapes; yeso is not used, and there is no sunning.

After fermentation is complete, the musts are classified into fina montilla or oloroso, and are then matured in wooden casks, on the solera system, exactly as in the sherry area. When the wine is ready to be shipped, little or no fortification is necessary, as it is by nature stronger than sherry, and some vintages attain the strength of 16·5° Gay-Lussac, unaided.

There is no form of flattery more sincere than imitation, and it is significant that when sherry shippers noticed that when good fino wines matured they took on an entirely different character— deeper in colour, more profound in flavour, and 'nuttier'—they at once noticed the resemblance with the old wines of Montilla, and the word *amontillado* was coined. The Montilla finos have a style of their own. They are light and delicate but with a rather strange bouquet that even seems slightly coarse to one who has been brought up on sherry finos. Others, however, prefer them. When they age, they take on a wonderful character, with a deep and

beautifully balanced flavour. The olorosos, too, are things apart: clearly olorosos, yet equally clearly not from Jerez.

Montilla-Moriles wines are undoubtedly amongst the great wines of the world, and well able to hold their own besides the wines of Jerez—though the latter are, to my own taste, the finer. But although montilla is popular in Spain, it is surprisingly little known elsewhere, which seems strange, and a pity. Its obscurity is a tribute to the commercial acumen of the sherry shippers, who have sold their own wines so much more efficiently; and their proximity to the coast helped them to get a flying start in the days when inland transport was difficult and even dangerous. But the wines of Montilla-Moriles are well worth looking for.

Malaga

The wines of Malaga are now almost completely out of favour in this country and very few are imported, but historically they are amongst the most important in Spain, with the viticulture going back in history to Roman times. In Elizabethan days they were generally known in England as *malligo sack*, and subsequently as *mountain*—as any collector of wine labels will know. In the eighteenth century they were more popular in England than those of Jerez, which were going through their least successful period, and there was a flourishing British colony in Malaga until the end of the nineteenth century. There still is one, but it basks in the sun and is no longer engaged in trade; for Malaga is perhaps the warmest of all the Spanish coastal resorts, and intense sunshine plays an important part in giving the wines their sweet and heady character. Nowadays, by far the most important market for the wine is Germany, with Switzerland coming next, followed by the Scandinavian countries and France.

Some malevolent Jerezanos (who ought to know better) have pointed out that anyone travelling to Malaga sees no vineyards at all, and they then go on to suggest that Malaga wine is really made of dates. This is utter nonsense, and the Jerezanos ought to know better because their own vineyards were almost as elusive before the new by-pass was built round Jerez. Mountain was a very appropriate name as the best vineyards are high in the mountains and scattered throughout the province, though the best of all are in the north around Antequera, Archidona and

Cuevas de San Marcos. By no means all of these vineyards are devoted to wine grapes, though: many table grapes are also grown and Malaga raisins are famous. By far the most important grape variety is the Pedro Ximenez. The Moscatel comes next, followed by Lairén and other varieties such as Vijiriegas, Jaenes and Palomino. A typical malaga is a strong, rich dessert wine not unlike a brown sherry; the strength, though, is natural, there is no fortification. These wines are made from a mixture of grapes, generally about 60 per cent Pedro Ximenez, 20 per cent Lairén, 15 per cent Moscatel, and 5 per cent other varieties. The best are matured by the *solera* system, though the cheaper varieties are bottled after being matured for two to three years in oak casks. But there are many other types of malaga, and strangers to the area seldom appreciate what a wide variety of wine is available. The principal types are as follows:

amontillado: Vinified from Lairén grapes and generally matured for about ten years in the wood before bottling. It is fairly light in colour, and of medium sweetness, resembling some of the cheaper 'amontillados' sold in this country, but very different from the wines of Montilla and from the genuine, dry amontillados of Jerez.

blanco dulce: Golden coloured and very sweet.

lágrima or *lágrima christi*: This is wholly different from the lacrima christi of Italy. It does not pretend to be an imitation, and it is a moot point which came first. The name *lágrima* without the *christi* was originally, at any rate, appropriate, for in ancient days the wines were vinified from juice which fell out of suspended bunches without the grapes being pressed. Such wines must have been very rich and good, something after the same style of Imperial Tokay Essence, but these are no longer made, at any rate on a commercial scale. The name has been debased and is now applied to dark, cheap wines that are very sweet and of no particular distinction.

moscatel palido: Very light in colour and with a pronounced moscatel flavour.

negro: Vinified from Pedro Ximenez grapes, sweet and very dark indeed.

oscuro: Brown and sweet.

seco: Despite its name, this wine is only medium dry, relatively light in colour, and with a distinctive and distinguished flavour having a rather dry after taste which makes it excellent as an apéritif or when taken with a biscuit.

semidulce: Fairly sweet and medium in colour.

In addition to these, several wines are sold under grape varieties such as Pedro Ximenez and Moscatel. With age, malaga becomes extremely distinguished, and some of the finest solera wines are comparable in quality, though not in style, with the rare solera wines of Jerez. In an article in *Wine and Food*, Harry Yoxall described Solera Scholtz 1885 as having 'interesting, almost surprising undertones beneath its unctuous richness, like the dark fires in the heart of a jewel. Just as the touch of something very cold leaves you uncertain whether it has frozen or burnt you, so in the taste of great malagas the sugar is sublimated and becomes almost astringent.' Such wines are great by any yardstick, and it is a pity that the growers of malaga lack the drive of their brethren in Jerez, selling few of their wines to this country and practically none of the best.

The Table Wines of Spain

That wine-growing in Spain is an ancient art has already been shown by the story of sherry, and it is an art that was nowhere seriously interrupted even by the Moors, for it was one of them, the Sevillian arab Ebn-el-Awam, whose book gives details of the Greek methods of viticulture as practised in the Spain of his day. Much of the early history, as everywhere, is tied up with that of the great religious houses, and the more recent history follows the usual pattern: a battle against the phylloxera, followed, in this century, by increased mechanization and improved viticulture and enology.

Of all the countries to wander around, looking for good local table wines, Spain is one of the best, for the vine flourishes almost everywhere, hence the sheer variety is enormous, and many of the wines are excellent. It must be admitted, though, that others are not. The standards of enology in the best-known districts is high, but those of the *vinos corrientes* that are still made by peasants tend to be as unpredictable in Spain as they are elsewhere. These standards are steadily improving, though, while ever more wine is being prepared in well-run co-operatives and in the central press-houses of wine firms. Some Spanish wines, especially those from the extreme north, taste as if they were grown the other side of the Pyrenees; but as a general rule the famous Spanish sunshine brings great ripeness to the grapes, and the wines tend to be strong, hardly subtle in their attractions, and thoroughly southern in character. There is a rather odd thing about wine drinking in Spain: if you want to try the local wines it is as well to avoid the better restaurants, all of which sport fine lists of riojas, with perhaps a valdepeñas or two, and very little else unless you happen to be in a wine-growing city of some note, such as Alicante or Tarragona, where there will, of course, be a selection of the best local wines.

In general terms, then, the wines can be considered as falling within two groups: those of the north and those of the south. But the line is of course an arbitrary one, and it may well be that no two wine lovers would draw it in the same place. No one would dispute that the light white wines of Alella belong to the northern group or that the sturdy wines of Alicante belong to the southern, but what of those in between? If such an artificial line were to be drawn, I should let it begin in the west somewhat lower than the northern line of the Portuguese frontier and passing through Zamora. It would then join the east coast at Villafranca del Panadés, just leaving Valladolid to the north. The Valladolid wines, though, are certainly borderline cases, and other writers might well draw their lines further north, from Vigo. The eastern end, however, is less open to argument: it would clearly have to be north of Tarragona, whose wines are wholly southern in character.

Incomparably the greatest wine-growing area of the north is the Rioja. It takes its name from the Rio Oja, a small river that joins the River Tiron near Anguciana, to the west of Haro, where the Tiron itself joins the Ebro. The Ebro is quite a substantial river comparable, for example, with the Severn at Shrewsbury, and it passes through practically the whole of the best vineyard area from east to west. It can hardly be a coincidence that nearly all the finest vineyards in the world are not far from rivers. Their humidity and heat capacity help to avoid spring frost; their water sinks through the ground to moisten the roots of the vines in times of drought while draining it in times of plenty; and they reflect the light of the sun to help ripen the grapes.

The Rioja is not on any of the popular tourist routes, but anyone bothering to go there will be well rewarded. It is a beautiful piece of undulating countryside, full of enchanting views with mountains on the skyline. The two principal towns are Haro and Logroño. Haro is the Englishman's idea of an unspoilt Spanish town—old, full of departed glory, and crumbling. Logroño is much larger and is generally ignored by guide books, whose authors have probably been put off by the prosperity of the place and by its frankly unpleasant suburbs. Anyone penetrating further will find an agreeable town, with narrow old streets and one fine building—the eighteenth-century church of Santa Maria de la Redonda.

The history of the Rioja as a major wine-growing district is extremely recent. It has certainly grown wines since the sixteenth century, and during the Spanish domination of Latin America its wines are said to have been exported there regularly, but they were not regarded as being at all exceptional. Wine merchants and authors who travelled widely and wrote remarkable books about the wines of Europe during the last century—men like Tovey, Redding, Thudichum, Shaw and Denman—never mentioned them, though they had plenty to say about other Spanish wines. At that time the wines of Valdepeñas were thought to be superior.

The earliest reference to Rioja wines that I have been able to find in the British press was in *The Times* of April 9th, 1850:

THE WINES OF SPAIN—The following appears in the *Clamour Publico* of Madrid of the 38th of March: 'The Duke de la Victoria has for many years past, entertained the patriotic idea of applying himself, whenever he should be able to reside on his property in Logroño, to improve the condition of the Rioja, a province as fertile as it is deficient in capital for cultivating its products, especially as to its wines, which, although the principal wealth of the district, from want to proper treatment have not hitherto been exported. The Duke, during his emigration in London, made arrangements with his friends, Messrs. Ysasi & Co., for exporting the wines of the Rioja, and immediately on his arrival at Logroño he proceeded to carry his plans of amelioration into effect by putting in practice all the modern operations for the more perfect preparation of the wines, which are now fit for exportation, to any country. The Duke has not spared any expense in completing his project and in making known to all the other wine proprietors the improved method of preparation for export. To the public exhibition of the productions of the country, now open in Madrid, the Duke has sent a few bottles as a competitor for the principal prize. The wine is beginning to be known abroad under the title of 'Ebro claret', and there are already large orders for it, which, if they continue, as it is to be hoped, General Espartero will have the gratification of having contributed in his retirement to the prosperity of the province he has adopted, and will secure the lasting gratitude of its inhabitants. The district of Logroño and all the Rioja is likely to become one of the richest in Spain, and the farmers will reap an advantage hitherto unknown to them, since, for the want of a market, they have been often obliged to sacrifice the vintage of a whole year. We have tasted the wine and it has the qualities of a pleasant sort of Bordeaux.'

Ysasi and Co. were a famous firm of sherry shippers.

The duke's efforts, however, did not apparently meet with immediate success. The change came over the Rioja in about 1880, when it remained free from the phylloxera which by then was ravaging the French vineyards. Fearing that their home vineyards would never recover, and finding the markets starved of quality wines, some French viticulturalists recognized the potential of the Rioja and went there to see what they could do. Using Spanish vines, the vineyards were greatly enlarged, cellars and bodegas were built in the towns, and all the know-how of French viticulture and enology were brought to bear so that the wine was rapidly transformed from being a decent *vino corriente* into one of the notable table wines of Europe.

At one time there was a colony of three hundred French living in Haro, but when their own vineyards were replanted and became productive once more, they left, and soon afterwards the phylloxera came. But the Spaniards had by then learnt the lessons of the French growers. They replanted their vineyards and continued to make excellent wine. Now they are so highly skilled that Haro has a famous wine institute and college. The trade with this country, however, did not become important until after the last war, when the prices of French wines had risen so steeply that merchants began to look further afield. Unfortunately, though, the trade is still principally confined to the cheaper growths, and the finer wines are too seldom seen here.

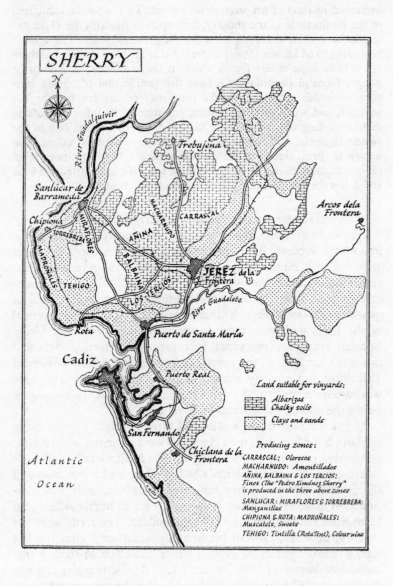

SHERRY

Land suitable for vineyards:

🧱 Albarizas
Chalky soils

⣿ Clays and sands

Producing zones:

CARRASCAL: Olorosos
MACHARNUDO: Amontillados
AÑINA, BALBAINA & LOS TERCIOS:
Finos (The "Pedro Ximénez Sherry"
is produced in the three above zones
SANLUCAR: MIRAFLORES & TORREBREBA:
Manzanillas
CHIPIONA & ROTA: MADROÑALES:
Muscatels, Sweets
TEHIGO: Tintilla (Rota Tent), Colour wine

It is unfortunate that many of these wines suffer from an enforced comparison. Rioja 'chablis', for instance, is nothing like chablis, nor is it anything like so good. For once, the English merchants are not altogether to blame: they followed a custom that was already rife in Spain. It was started by the French themselves who, perhaps with nostalgia, perhaps through insularity, or perhaps through commercial expediency, started to call the wines they grew there by the names they best knew. This does riojas a great injustice, for they can only lose by the comparison. Although they are excellent as wines, they are bad as imitations, as even the finest riojas do not have the subtlety of the best French table wines, though the cheaper riojas are far better than the wretched *ordinaires* grown on the fringes of some of the great French districts.

The Rioja is officially divided into three parts: Rioja Alta (high Rioja), where red, white and rosé wines are grown, Rioja Baja (low Rioja), and Rioja Alavesa (Rioja lying within the province of Alava), the last two divisions growing principally red wines. The first and second divisions lie wholly within the province of Logroño and occupy approximately its northern half. The wines of the three are clearly different in the style and quality; but, since nature does not divide its soils and climates neatly by clearly-drawn lines, there is a fourth area known as the Rioja Media, of indefined and somewhat doubtful extent, but lying around the line that divides the Rioja Alta from the Rioja Baja.

The delicacy of the best riojas is the product, to a large extent, of the district's northern climate, influenced more by the Atlantic than by the Mediterranean. As an indication, in nearby Burgos virtually no wine is grown: it is too cold. In the Rioja Alta and the Rioja Alavesa the spring usually begins quite hot, with warm east winds, but the temperature often falls towards the end of April or the beginning of May, when there are sometimes frosts; the summers, which begin with storms, are sunny with evening breezes; the autumns are long and mild; while the winters are long but not particularly cold, though there are some days of snow and heavy frosts. In the Rioja Baja, on the other hand, the springs are early and hot; the summers are short and very hot, though fairly cool at night; the autumns are short, with extremes of temperature and lots of rain; the winters are long but not particularly cold and with little or no snow. The Rioja Baja is much more arid than the others—as is very clear to anyone driving through, and unlike those of the other two divisions, its wines are by no means delicate. They have all the properties one would expect from such an area: they are very strong, very dark, and highly flavoured, even rather coarse. The best are used for blending while the others are sold in inns, straight from the cask. The Rioja Media produces wines that are intermediate in style. The whereabouts of the bodegas, or headquarters, of the shipping firms, however, is irrelevant to the quality of the wines they sell, as all can buy wine from each district, many of which are grown by small landowners. There are also active co-operatives, particularly in the Rioja Baja.

The area, and its three recognized divisions, is strictly delimited and is under the control of a *consejo regulador*, so all should be well with the labelling of the wines, but in practice I have my doubts. One of my Spanish friends assures me that large quantities of wines from Valdepeñas find their way to the Rioja, and although it does not follow that these are blended into riojas, the chances are that they are. Indeed some of the cheapest wines exported cost so little that one wonders how on earth they could all emanate from one small and good area—a doubt that is reinforced by one's palate. As for vintage years printed on the labels, these are notoriously unreliable. When I was living in Spain in 1956 a Jerezano assured me, somewhat maliciously, that one of the rioja shippers had registered 'Vintage 1929' as his trade mark. I can almost believe it. In practice quality varies little from one vintage to another but it is best to regard the stated vintage as an indication rather than as a firm statement of truth, especially as many riojas are quite legitimately and properly blended wines which may come from two or three vintages.

Many different kinds of soil are found, but the best vineyards grow on rather chalky or slaty, not particularly fertile, and fairly dry soils. The vines grown for red wines are Garnacha (in the Rioja Baja), Tempranillo (the most popular vine in the Rioja Alta), Mazuela (for colour, body and tannin) and Graciano (a noble vine of small yield), while those for white wines are principally Malvasia and Viura (or Viuna), the Catalan name for which is Macabeo. The wines are made by conventional modern methods, and apart from the excellent red and white wines there are mediocre *rosados* (rosés) and not very distinguished sparkling wines which are, however, made by the *méthode champenoise*. As far as colour is concerned, the ascending scale of redness is: *rosado, clarete, ojo de gallo* and *tinto*. The cheapest of all the wines, known as *vinos comunes*, are bottled during the first year. Those somewhat better, that are bottled between one or two years after the vintage, are labelled *cosecha* (vintage) and the year, or alternatively *segundo año*. Those that are kept for a further period in the wood are labelled, for example, *cuarto año* (four year old) or *vieja reserva*, and a vintage year may also be added, though such years should be viewed with suspicion. The fact that an early vintage year is quoted is not in itself, though, suspicious: fine riojas age well and many, happily, are given the chance to do so. The best riojas are powerfully flavoured and need to mature for quite a long time before they are ready to drink, so it is not uncommon to find a good rioja kept for as many as eight years in the wood before being bottled—by which time most French wines would have passed into a decline. Alas it must be admitted that some riojas also pass into a decline before being bottled: they may be left for as many as fifteen years, and even for a rioja that is too long. After ageing in cask they are further improved by being kept a year or two in bottle, and I have tasted red riojas bottled at an earlier stage in their development which would clearly stand bottle age very well. A red *rioja reserva* with fifteen years or so of age to it, divided between cask and bottle, is a fine wine by any standards—a very fine wine, and remarkably cheap for what it is. In fact apart from clarets and burgundies I know of no red table wine with greater potentialities than rioja. These potentialities are now quite often realized, too, and will be more so in the future. The white wines, however, although quite good, are, with a few exceptions, hardly in the same class. Some are bottled in moselle bottles, which makes them look absurd if they are heavy and flabby—as some are; but a few are so delicate as to appear merely somewhat fraudulent. They are vinified in every degree of sweetness from bone dry to very sweet indeed. A very small amount of wine is produced, like tokay essence, from must pressed by the unaided weight of the grapes. Known as *lágrima* or *vino corazón*, it is not available commercially.

Most of the wines are blended and sold under made-up names rather than as the products of single vineyards; and they are none the worse for this, as it is doubtful whether many pearls of individuality are lost, and unquestionably a remarkably high and consistent standard is achieved. It is the technique of the burgundy shippers rather than of the châteaux of Bordeaux, and the wine is blended in Rioja in the same way as it is in Burgundy or Champagne: the solera system is not used. Just occasionally, though, a barrel of specially good wine from a single vineyard and of a single year is kept apart. Such wines are generally found in the proprietor's own cellar, and they are enviable possessions.

Moving eastwards, Aragon grows a great deal of wine but most of it is coarse, strong and red, with little appeal; it is sold to growers further north who use it for blending. The most outstanding area for quality and the only one with a *consejo regulador* of its own is Cariñena. It grows, however, as wide a variety of wines as all the other parts of Aragon put together, ranging from the typical rough blending wines to relatively delicate *claretes*, and white wines named *vino pajarilla*. True white wines are rare, though, but there are some very light-coloured *rosados* which are delicious. The vine variety for red wine is principally the Garnacha, while those for white wines are Macabeo, Mazuela and Blanco Fino. Most cariñenas, however, red or white, are sweet, heavy dessert wines of no especial distinction. The table wines have been described as 'wines to be gulped down', which I think is about fair. Similar wines of even less distinction are found in Navarre.

Catalonia, too, stretching right along the north-east coast, grows a great variety of wines, but an imaginary line passing through Villafranca del Panadés neatly cuts off the southern part. Although the northern part grows a fair proportion of red wine, it is the white wines that are most notable, particularly those of Alella. Although production is quite small, they are considered sufficiently important to have their own *consejo regulador* and these vineyards are undoubtedly some of the oldest established in Spain. They lie not far to the north of Barcelona and are planted on two slopes of granite soil one of which has a rather northern aspect, producing light wines of high acidity, while the other, more southerly, slope yields rather sweet wine of the opposite character. The vine varieties for white wine are principally Garnacha and Picapoll (Picpoule), while for red wine there are Garnacha Negra and Tempranillo. Practically all the wine is made in the local co-operative, which is one of the oldest in Spain, and very well made it is, too. In all there are seven different kinds: marfil blanco, which is slightly sweet and exceptionally pleasing; marfil seco, the driest; marfil tinto, a light red wine; supermarfil, which wine has a deeper colour and the flavour of greater age; lacre gualdo, which is very well matured, old and strong; and lacre violeta, a sweet dessert wine. All of these have very real delicacy with an enchanting, if slight, aroma. Of the wines that are more familiar in this country, perhaps they have most in common with Loire wines, and some admirers have likened them to moselle, but to compare them with anything is to insult them. Marfil blanco and seco are now available in this country, and are worth looking for.

Wines of varying quality are grown all the way up the Costa Brava as far as the French frontier, but perhaps the only ones that call for comment are those vinified in the Castillo de Perelada. These include quite sound white, *rosado* and red table wines, and also a sparkling wine made by the *cuves closes* method. This became the subject of a famous law suit in England—*Bollinger* v. *Costa Brava Wine Co.*—in which an injunction was granted preventing it from being sold under the name of champagne in England. It was a great and brave action. Oh that shippers of other wines had taken similar steps much sooner!

To the south of Barcelona, a good quality dessert wine from the Malvasia grape is grown at Sitges. A little way inland, on much the same latitude, is Villafranca del Panadés. The main road leaves the coast for a while at this point and passes straight through the town, which it inevitably spoils, but behind the dreadful main road it is a quiet and pleasant little place, and it has one especial attraction: the wine museum. This is one of the very best of its kind I have ever been to. Unlike most of the others, it does not confine itself to the local wines, and there are displays showing wine making in all parts of Spain, as well as tableaux showing ancient methods of wine making in Egypt and Rome. After seeing round the museum visitors are finally given a glass of the good local white wine. It is very well worth a visit. The town is roughly in the middle of the Panadés area and this in itself makes nonsense of my line.

The local *consejo regulador* has a rather complicated method of classifying the wines, which includes the strength in degrees Gay-Lussac, and the classification is worth setting out as it shows the considerable extent of possible variation.

blanco panadés corriente	9° to 14°
blanco san cugat	11° to 13°
blanco supermaduro	10° to 13° (with up to 40 grams per litre of sugar)
rosado panadés	10° to 13°
clarete panadés	11° to 13°
tinto panadés	11° to 16°

Quite apart from these table wines, some of the best sparkling wine in Spain is made in this area, particularly in San Sadurni de Noya, principally from the Macabeo grape and using the *méthode champenoise*. It is very good indeed; not as fine as champagne itself, of course, but genuinely comparable.

The principal grape varieties for red table wine are Cariñena and Sumoll, and for white wines are Xarel-lo, Macabeo and Parellada. The vinification of the red wines is entirely normal, but a small proportion of the white wines are matured in a most extraordinary way, by exposure in glass demijohns, or *bombonas*. A bombona is a huge, balloon-like bottle holding about thirty litres of wine. These are sealed by porous corks with metal caps over them to keep the rain out and are left for a couple of years in the open, so that the strong Spanish sun can play upon them—as, indeed, the other elements. At the end of this period half the wine is syphoned off and the bombonas are replenished, as if working an open-air *solera*. The effect, no doubt, would be somewhat like a journey over the equator in a sailing ship. And I wonder whether it was ever more widespread? It could even have been the origin of the *estufas* of Madeira. The wine that has been treated in this way is quite unlike the table wines; known as a *vino rancio* it has a more southerly character altogether, and rather puts one in mind of sherry or montilla. The other white wines are made in the ordinary way and are good table wines with better acidity and balance than have most.

The wines of the Balearic Islands are not at all notable but are perhaps worth mentioning because a certain amount of Majorcan wine is being imported into this country. It must be admitted that most of the local wines served up to unsuspecting visitors in tourist hotels are pretty poor; but there are quite good ones to be had—particularly red wines—if you know where to look for them.

The best have a distinctive, if somewhat coarse character and are to be gulped down under the sun. The strongest are grown around Benisalem and Inca, while lighter ones are grown around Felanitx. There are also some sweet wines from the Malvasia grape grown around Buñols. Apart from several quite substantial private bodegas, there are two co-operatives.

Of all Spanish wines, those of Galicia and the Asturias are the least typical and are also amongst the most delightful. Not surprisingly many of them resemble the *vinhos verdes* of Portugal which are, after all, grown next door, and which are now enjoying a well-merited popularity in this country; but the Spanish wines do not appear to be imported here at all, though according to John Croft's *Treatise* (1788) they used to be imported before the introduction of port—or at any rate the northern Portuguese wines. These Spanish wines are similarly called *vinos verdes*, or alternatively *vinos frios*. Most of the wines of this region are light in alcohol, colour and style, the fully fermented white wines being especially delicate, and delicious with fish, while others are bottled before the fermentation is complete, giving them that pétillance that makes their Portuguese rivals so attractive; and the vines that yield them are similarly trained off the ground, but the wines do not appear to be so well made in northern Spain as they are in Portugal, and are often spoilt by cloudiness. The principal areas of production are Ribero and Valdeorras. The vines for white wines are Albariño, Torrontes and Jerezana, which is the local name for the Palomino, the famous sherry vine, that yields a totally different style of wine in the north; for red wines a great many varieties are grown, but the most popular are Caiño and Brancellao. In addition to the light wines already referred to, sweet, strong, heavier dessert wines are also grown and are known as *tostados* or *tostadillos*. These are obtained from the Treixadura vine.

No one in search of picturesque countryside would choose that which lies roughly on the line drawn westwards from Valladolid to the Portuguese frontier, nor would anyone in his right mind choose to live there, for it is a swelteringly hot plain in summer and is bleakly, bitterly cold in winter. Perhaps it is this latter characteristic that gives the wines an unexpectedly northern character, for some of them are very good indeed, and others could be. They are not unlike those of the Rioja, but are rather fuller in body, and the production of the best is very limited, so they are little known outside their own area. Perhaps this helps to account for the fact that many of them are not at all well made. Or should it be the other way round? At any rate they have the reputation of not travelling and this is borne out by my own experience. Perhaps one of the reasons for this is the odd local practice of adding a little wine to the must, presumably to ensure that the wine is strong, to hasten maturation and to secure a touch of residual sugar. But this is not a good method. The capital of the area is the beautiful cathedral and university city of Valladolid, where the Castilian Spanish pronunciation is a joy to hear. Beginning from the east, one of the very finest red wines in Spain—some might even say the finest—is grown at Quintanilla de Arriba, a little to the west of Peñafiel, on the upper reaches of the Duero. This is called *vega sicilia* and the production is unfortunately minute. A little to the north, an agreeable red wine is grown at Cigales, but some examples are peculiar, being slightly effervescent. To the south-west of Valladolid is Rueda, noted for honest if uninspiring white wines, and further to the west is Toro where a strong red wine is produced. The name of the town has given rise to many jokes about bulls' blood, but its wines are not to be confused with those of Hungary. The principal vines for white wines are the Verdejo, the Palomino and the Albillo, while those for red wines are Tempranilla, Tinta de Madrid and Mencia. In so large a region there are, of course, a great many different kinds of soil, but it is predominantly sand and gravel.

South of the imaginary line the most important vineyards for table wines are undoubtedly those of Valdepeñas. Growers from other areas may well be hurt in their local pride at reading such a statement; but to my mind there is no doubt about it. Valdepeñas is a small, wholly unattractive town on the N.4, the main road that runs from Madrid to Cadiz by way of Cordova, Seville and Jerez. Fortunately for travellers in a hurry, the town is by-passed. They all see the vines though, which grow beside the road in a rich-looking soil of startling redness. All sorts of wines are grown there: deep red, *clarete*, rosé and white, the *claretes* being vinified with a proportion of white grapes. All these table wines are big, vigorous and clearly southern in style, pretending to little finesse, not having a great deal of bouquet, and tending to lack acidity; but they are well made and thoroughly sound. Some *flor* wines are also grown there, which are pleasant enough but bear the same sort of resemblance to a fine fino sherry as do the various Commonwealth imitations. The principal vine varieties are Cencibel (which is similar to the Tempranillo) for red wines and Lairen for whites. The best wines are fermented in vast clay *tinajas*—those vast Ali Baba-like clay jars that are used at Montilla.

If Valdepeñas is the best of the wines of La Mancha, it is very far from being the only one, as vineyards abound in this dry, central plane, producing vast quantities of sound but undistinguished wine that is sold in the bars throughout Spain. More white is grown than red, and some of it—especially that grown around Alcazar de San Juan—is distilled into brandy. It is Don Quixote's country and the wine skin, or *pellejo*, is by no means extinct. For the most part, the wines of this area are dry, but there are also a few sweet white *mistelas*[1] and muscatels, and even a few sweet red wines.

Tarragona is certainly one of the most famous of Spanish wine names, being associated in this country with a sweet red wine often referred to as red biddy, that was a poor man's substitute for port. No one would suggest that it is a fine wine. Tarragona is perhaps the most beautiful of all the cities on the coast of Spain and I have been there several times, enchanted always by everything except its wines. For although it is undoubtedly a major wine-growing area, producing wines of every possible style, I have never found a single one of them that I like. All that I have tried have an unpleasantly earthy taste; they are coarse and give the impression that they are trying to imitate something else. The best is the dry wine labelled Priorato—very strong and almost black. It is vinified from the Garnacha grape grown in volcanic soil. A sweet version of this wine is also made as a *mistela*. One Spanish writer on wine—José Esteve Marti—praises a wine known as rancio de vinebre—a sweet red wine vinified by a special, highly complicated, and age-old method. It might well be worth looking for.

There can be no more agreeable town to stay in than Alicante: it is full of fun, but totally undistinguished. Its wines are in character. Reds, rosés and whites and some sweet muscatels are grown, which tend to be strong and coarse, some being exported to

[1] See p. 403.

France as *vins de coupage*. Some of the reds are so dark in colour as to be almost black. Perhaps the most famous of all the *vins de coupage*, however, is benicarlo: a dark, strong, red wine from around the town of that name further north along the coast. In between, Valencia grows, in addition to table wines, rich dessert wines which are exported in large quantities, especially to Switzerland and Germany. To the south of Alicante, the wines of Murcia, grown around Jumilla and Yecla, are esteemed locally, especially the strong reds. They tend to be rather sweet.

Far to the west, some quite good wines, particularly *claretes*, are made in rather small quantities in Estremadura, along towards the Portuguese frontier, while further south, the wines of Huelva have their own *consejo regulador* and the name *vinos del Condado de Niebla*. Until recently, the white wines from this area, which can be vinified closely to resemble sherry, were largely imported into the sherry area where they were incorporated into the cheaper blends. It speaks much for the acumen of the sherry shipper—or the lack of it in Huelva—that this happened, for the Huelva wines are good ones with a history going back to the eleventh century, and they may well have been imported into England before sherry, as Chaucer, whose father was a wine merchant, mentioned the wine of Lepe. Although a little red wine is grown, most is white and is vinified as a strong table wine with a character somewhat like a light, young fino sherry; and very good it is, too. The principal grape for quality is the Palomino, as in the sherry country, and the Zalema gives quantity. Huelva is also particularly noted for its vinegar. One sherry shipper recently tried the experiment of vinifying some of his wine as table wine: it was quite good, though not of the first rank. As sherry itself is one of the supremely good wines, there seems little point in using any of its grapes for making a second-rate table wine, but the experiment did at least show that a very acceptable wine would result, and one that would no doubt far outshine the experimental cask once the grower has found out how to carry out the vinification to the best advantage. Such a wine, though, will never be more than a curiosity.

CHAPTER 10

Port, Madeira and
the Table Wines of Portugal

Historians seem to be agreed that the grape vine in Portugal is pre-Roman. As in Spain, it survived the rule of the Moors which, in the north of Portugal, was brief. Then, in the twelfth century, Count Henry of Burgundy came. Did he, one wonders, bring any of his vines with him? There appear to be no records. But if the early history of Portuguese wines is rather vague this, in any case, has little bearing on the history of port. The Portuguese are notoriously our 'oldest allies'—a relationship that extends back at least as far as the Treaty of Windsor in 1386, and there had been earlier commercial treaties. It is thanks to later treaties, and to the Anglo-Portuguese Commercial Treaty Act of 1916, that the geographical names of port and madeira have statutory protection in Britain today. These are, alas, the only wine areas to be so protected in Britain. But port is a comparative up-start—a newcomer by the standards of the great wines, with a history only going back as far as the end of the seventeenth century; and it did not become the wine that we know so well today until well into the eighteenth. The earliest wines to be imported on a substantial scale into this country from Portugal were from the Minho area in the extreme north, via the port of Viana do Castelo, where there was an English 'factory'[1] as far back as the sixteenth century. By 1678 there was a sufficiently large English community there to justify the appointment of a consul. Wines

---

[1] The old word for an establishment of factors, thus the term 'Factory House' to denote their headquarters.

from this region in the form of *vinho verde*, are now making very much of a comeback.

We do not know exactly when it was that the Douro wines began to supplant those of the Minho, and Oporto to take over the commercial importance that had formerly belonged to Viana. The process was no doubt gradual and the change happened round about 1700. The boom in Portuguese wines was started off less by the efforts of wine growers and merchants in that country than by those of our own politicians, who chose to be at loggerheads with the French. In 1677 the importation of French wine had been forbidden. The order was, of course, easily circumvented, and a great deal of wine was shipped from Bordeaux to England, some of it via Oporto, but French wine inevitably became scarce and expensive, which gave the Portugal merchants their chance. In the decade from 1678, 75,000 pipes[1] of Portuguese wines were shipped to this country. The figure for port taken separately was, however, lower. From 1678 to 1687 the average export was 633 pipes, the highest figure being 1,610 in 1679 and the lowest 142 in 1681. Between 1688 and 1693 the figure rose from 1,096 to 13,011 and thereafter it fluctuated between 4,000 and 11,000. The agreement which cemented the trade, however, and made it permanent, was not negotiated until rather later: it was the famous Methuen Treaty of 1703, which provided for English cloths to be imported into Portugal and for Portuguese wines to be imported into England, French wines being kept out by a penal tariff. From 1712 exports were consistently in five figures. But the Methuen Treaty pre-dated port wine. During the first part of the eighteenth century the wines shipped from Oporto were rated the cheapest and coarsest of the Peninsula: the table wines shipped through the port of Lisbon fetched higher prices. By the end of the century, in contrast, *The Times* of February 19th, 1798, could print the following anecdote: 'To which University', said a lady, some time since to the late sagacious Dr. Warren, 'shall I send my son?' 'Madam', replied he 'they drink, I believe, near the same quantity of port in each of them.'

The English merchants were, as always in those days, quick off the mark and founded firms that are still pre-eminent in the trade today. But perhaps the oldest of all is of German origin: C. N.

[1] A pipe holds 117 gallons.

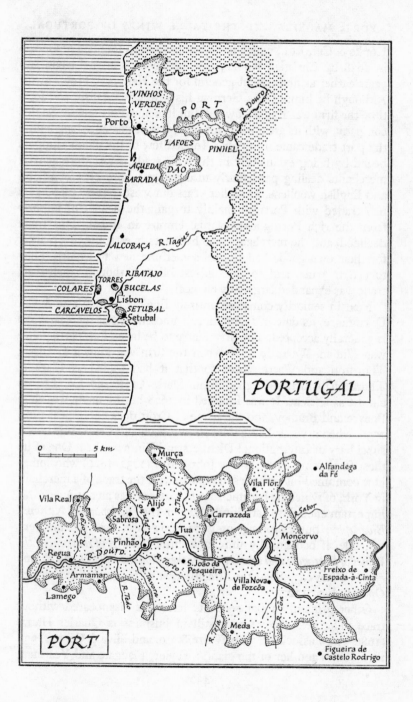

Kopke & Co., Ltd., which is said to have been founded at Oporto in 1638 by Christian Kopke, who had been sent to Lisbon two years earlier as first consul-general for the Hanseatic Free Towns. Although he himself was German his wife was English, and for a time the firm was English owned, but it is now Portuguese. So this company, with its great name for port, was in existence long before the port trade came into being. Indeed few of the oldest shippers began by being exclusively in the wine trade. Most were general merchants dealing particularly in dried cod from Newfoundland and English woollens. In earlier years our west country merchants had traded with Portugal mainly to gain the benefit of imports from the rich Portuguese colonial empire in Brazil. This trade declined, and the merchants who had already established a market for their own goods had to find something new to export. They turned to wine, and so this old-established, though small-scale trade was expanded largely by chance.

Next in seniority comes an entirely English firm, Warre & Co. Once more, its date of foundation is uncertain, but the year 1670 is generally accepted. The first Warre to be taken into partnership was William Warre in 1729 when the firm was known as Clark, Thornton and Warre. Prior to that it had traded as Clark & Thornton, which succeeded John Clark. Croft and Co. Ltd. is almost as ancient. It was founded in 1678 but its name was then Phayre and Bradley, and the name of Croft does not appear until 1736, when it was called Tilden, Thompson and Croft. It is now a subsidiary of International Distillers and Vintners, Ltd. One of its most fascinating partners was John Croft (1732–1820) who some-how combined his activities in Oporto with the trade of a merchant in York, of which he became sheriff. His work as an antiquary was important enough to earn him a place in the *Dictionary of National Biography*, but historians of wine know him best for his very valuable, if occasionally unreliable little book *A Treatise on the Wines of Portugal; and what can be gathered on the Subject and Nature of the Wines etc., Since the Establishment of the English Factory at Oporto Anno 1727.*

Other firms of similar seniority have alas disappeared without trace. The next most senior still in business is Quarles Harris (1680—now associated with Warre & Co. and Silva & Cosens) and then comes another of the giants: Taylor, Fladgate and Yeatman, which dates back to 1692. It may well be, though, that this is the oldest of them all, for the Bearsley family, who founded it, were trading in Viana during the previous century and there is a legend that it is they who discovered the Douro as a wine-growing district. Charles Sellers in his *Oporto, Old and New*[1] gives a list of twenty-one different names under which it has traded. First came Job Bearsley. By 1769 it was Bearsley, Webb and Sanford; in 1813 it was Webb, Campbell Gray & Co.; in 1825 it was Campbell, Taylor & Co.; and in 1844 it became Taylor, Fladgate and Yeatman which it has been ever since.

With the expansion of trade, many more firms were founded: Morgan Bros. (now a subsidiary of Croft's) in 1715, Offley Forrester (now a subsidiary of Sandeman) *circa* 1729, Butler & Nephew (now a subsidiary of Gonzalez, Byass) in 1730, and Hunt Roope (now a subsidiary of a Portuguese house) in 1735. From time to time other great names joined the list, but the greatest burst of energy came at the turn of the following century: Sandeman in 1790, Graham in 1814, Cockburns in 1815, Feuerheerd (now a subsidiary of Barros, Almeida) the same year, Guimaraens in 1822 and, last of the great names, Delaforce (now a subsidiary of Crofts) in 1868. But the Delaforces had been active in Oporto since 1834, and their company had the unique distinction until 1968 that it was still owned by the founder's family, members of which continue the management.

In Portugal, then, as elsewhere, the tendency has been for take-overs and mergers to form larger units, but the individual firms do not lose their separate identities. If they are to continue shipping under their own names the authorities impose a condition that the stocks should be kept apart. Sometimes they are in separate buildings in different parts of Vila Nova de Gaia and when they are adjacent (as for example Cockburns and Martinez Gassiot) only directors have keys of the doors that separate them; and when, for example, port from Martinez is temporarily taken into the Cockburn Lodge to be passed through Cockburn's modern filters, a representative of the official Port Wine Institute has to be there to see that the stocks do not get mixed. Thus the blends retain their individuality and it is not simply a matter of putting alternative labels on the same wine.

[1] London, 1899.

So much for the famous names, or rather for some of them. In a book covering so many wines it is not possible to list them all nor to give a detailed history of any. The most astonishing thing about the port trade remains the dominance of the British, most of whom came from Scotland and the north of England. For countless years we have lived there and run it, including some British families with far from English names, such as Guimaraens, of Portuguese, and Delaforce, of Huguenot descent. Other well-known families have very English names but ones that do not appear on the label of any bottle: names such as Symington, Jennings and Reid— families that have been making port for generations. As a wine district this makes the Douro unique, and there is something remarkably English about its appearance, for many of the houses have sash windows, while the climate of Oporto is almost as detestable as our own, with rain, cold, fogs and heatwaves. Perhaps it helps to make us feel at home there. Whatever the reason, our influence in Oporto and in Madeira is far greater than it is in Jerez, where in turn it is greater than it is in Bordeaux. In the other vineyards it is virtually non-existent.

From the beginning the British Colony did itself proud. In the early eighteenth century many of the servants were American, English-speaking negroes, which must have given the place a positively theatrical atmosphere. But the days of its greatest glory began in 1795, when the Factory House was built: a remarkably English building of austere classic solidity in the middle of a very Portuguese town. John Whitehead, specially empowered by Act of Parliament, organized a levy on the exports of all British Merchants to pay for it, and another levy of shipping freight financed a charity that provided a chaplain and supported the needy. The Factory House was furnished as splendidly as it was conceived. Mr. Thomas Chippendale Junr., according to legend, was specially brought from England to make a set of chairs and sofas which are unique. For my own part I must say that although I have a passion for eighteenth-century mahogany I do not particularly like them: they hark back to the style of Queen Anne and have a solid heaviness about them that is such a contrast with the lightness of rococo. Perhaps even in those days the British colony was staunchly reactionary. The great sets of Coalport and Davenport china are as noteworthy as the chippendale, and the ultimate touch of luxury is the separate dessert room to which the guests can adjourn to take their dessert in a fresh atmosphere. This is still, of course, a custom in Oxford and Cambridge colleges, and for the benchers in the Inns of Court, but I have not found it anywhere else. Every Wednesday there is a luncheon and when I went there on a warm September day in 1965 as a guest of Croft's, I was delighted to be given steak and kidney pudding. What could be more English?

Needless to say, over the centuries we have produced some pretty notable eccentrics as an extract from a letter from the late Mr. Gerard Graham to André L. Simon clearly shows:

'My grandmother's uncle, Mr. Richard Noble, was a great character in Oporto. On one occasion he accepted six challenges to duel in the same week. An attempt was made to conceal this fact from Mrs. Noble, but when that lady heard of it, and had ascertained that his "second" was in every case Dr. Jebb her only comment was, "I could not leave him in better hands!" History does not relate whether any of the duels were actually fought!

'On another occasion my grandfather looked out of the window of Messrs. Graham's offices, which were then in the Rua Nova dos Inglezes, now known as the Rua Infante D. Henrique. The occasion was some civil tumult or other during the troubled period which followed the Napoleonic wars. To his consternation, he saw his Uncle Richard leading the mob with his walking-stick against the troops. On being remonstrated with, his only remarks was "I like to see men! Come on!" He was taken by the authorities and was to have been shot, but was reprieved at the instance of the British Ambassador on the condition that he left Portugal within 24 hours. He was, however, later on allowed to return.

'He was a partner of the firm of Noble & Murat whose successors are the present house of Warre & Co.

'Of my grandfather, John Graham, there are many stories told.

'On one occasion in the early forties he, in the company of a friend, was down in the marshes near Aveiro snipe shooting. As luck would have it, a snipe flew towards a certain bush, and my grandfather firing inadvertently shot a young girl who was lying asleep behind the bush and was entirely hidden from him. Her injuries were luckily very slight, but my grandfather made her what he considered to be an adequate recompense in money and thought the incident closed.

'A few weeks later he happened to go down to the same place once more, and to his dismay found young girls hiding behind every bush and cover hoping to be shot. The money he had given on the previous occasion had been sufficient to provide a dowry and the girl had promptly got married on the strength of it!

'My grandfather when walking home from the Lodges or the office used—when in conversation with anyone—to wave a silk bandana in his right hand. The small street urchins would stand in wait for him, and snatch the handkerchief from his hand when he was in the midst of an absorbing conversation. He seldom noticed this and would walk on, waving his empty hand up and down as though it still carried the bandana! It is said that my grandmother, after a while, used to substitute coloured cotton handkerchiefs—or "Padres" as they were called from the fact that Padres affected them—for the silk ones, much to the disgust of the urchins!

'Another member of my family who was a generation younger than my grandfather but who is still talked of in Oporto as a great character was Robert Graham who flourished in the late sixties and early seventies.

'He used to attend all the village festivals or "Romarias" as they are called, and lead the procession down the village street, decked out with ribbons in his hat, singing and dancing and playing the fiddle!'

The eighteenth and nineteenth centuries, though, were not all comfort. As late as the nineteenth century, in a cold winter wolves would be found by night in the streets of Oporto, taking refuge from the hills. The early part of the century was particularly troubled, when a Spanish invasion was followed by the Napoleonic wars. In 1807, and again in 1809, Oporto was occupied by the French, and the British merchants suffered great apprehension and very real practical difficulties. Some of their property was temporarily transferred to Portuguese trustees. But Marshal Soult was eventually driven out by Wellington, happily on a day when the French chefs had prepared a banquet. Wellington and his fellow officers ate it. The French came back in 1810 only to be defeated once more. All of this must have been very trying for the unfortunate merchants, and the political situation in Portugal was very unsettled. Nor was Oporto such a convenient place to live in in those days; for instance the great bridge over the river, that so dominates the scene today, was not built until 1842, by a French engineer with the startling name of Stanislas Bigot. Before then the merchants had to cross from their houses and from their

Factory House in Oporto to their lodges[1] in the Vila Nova de Gaia by ferry or on a rickety bridge of boats.

The greatest difficulty facing the shippers, though, from the middle of the eighteenth century to the middle of the nineteenth, arose from a long drawn-out dispute with the Portuguese authorities. And despite their indignant protestations, one feels that it was a dispute with right on both sides. That it arose at all was really the fault of the shippers, who tried to take advantage of the Portuguese growers. There was a slight decline in trade. The average export for the years 1749 to 1753 had been 17,800 pipes whereas between 1754 and 1757 it was only 12,800. In 1755—the year of the dreadful Lisbon earthquake—they wanted to buy little or no wine and offered the wretched growers the derisory sum of £2 per pipe. On the other hand they accused the growers of adulterating the wine. The Portuguese appealed to the universal protector—the Marquis de Pombal, the clever and unscrupulous politician who was virtually dictator of Portugal at the time, and a man intensely interested in wine.

To understand the situation one has to go further back, to the end of the seventeenth century, when the valley of the River Douro was principally a grain-growing area. The English merchants thought that its robust wines would appeal to the English taste and the farmers, anxious to benefit from the booming new trade, planted new vineyards; but many of these were not in good places and were planted, moreover, with vine varieties noted for producing quantity rather than quality. These new vineyards gave feeble yet coarse wines quite unlike those that suited the British market, and the growers tried to put matters right by adulterating their musts with sugar and with elderberry juice. It was this principally which led to the crisis more than half a century later. And when the English in 1755 told the Portuguese brokers in far from diplomatic phrases 'That if the Portuguese did not leave off adulterating their wines, the English factory would not buy them'[2] the Portuguese replied that if they were adulterated it was only because the shippers would not buy them otherwise and that it was they who had taught the farmers how to do it, so as to get at the

---

[1] Derived from Portuguese *loja*—a warehouse.
[2] From a letter of Mr. James Croft, dated 1788, and quoted by Geoffrey Murat Tate in his *Port*, London, 1936.

cheapest possible price the strong, dark, heavy wines that their customers wanted. One can only lament. It was the old story of evil leading to greater evil. Whenever, in the history of the wine trade, quality and integrity have been sacrificed, disaster has always eventually followed.

To explain what comes next it should be added that the wines were already being fortified—but not in the way they are today. At the beginning of the eighteenth century—probably in about 1715—someone discovered that port travelled better if a little brandy was added to it. But in those days the brandy was added after the fermentation was complete, not before, as now; the modern method took considerably longer to discover. As late as in 1754 the factors in Oporto called the process—as practised by the farmers—'diabolical'. And perhaps it was—as practised by the farmers. Nevertheless by then it was in regular use, so the growers and shippers needed brandy as well as wine.

The Marquis de Pombal was one of the most effective politicians in Portuguese history; and unlike most statesmen he was noted for vigour, for immediate and clear-cut action. When approached by the growers he acted at once, but perhaps a bit too sweepingly, though there can be no doubt that something had to be done if the trade was to be saved. The English factors had made fools of themselves. It is likely, and indeed natural, that he wanted to use the opportunity to seize some of their power and prosperity for the benefit of the state. He created a new monopolistic company, Companhia de Agricultura das Vinhas do Alto Douro, that had the following rights: to classify and buy all the wines grown in the Douro, to delimit the area in which port wine could be grown, and to hold a monopoly for the distillation and sale of brandy. In the official area it became a felony, punishable with transportation for life and the confiscation of all property, to have a single elderberry[1] tree growing. The object, in the words of its constitution, was 'To uphold the reputation of the wines, the culture of the vineyards,

---

[1] According to John Croft's *Treatise* (1788): 'A Mr. Peter Bearsley, an Englishman, who resided at Viana as a factor was the first who went to Oporto in the view, and for the purpose of speculating in Port Wine; and on the road to the Wine Country at an Inn, he met with an elder tree, whose juice he expressed, and mixed with the ordinary wine, and found it had the effect of heightening and improving its colour.' An unlikely story, but at least it points to the antiquity of the malpractice.

and to foster at the same time the trade of the former, establishing a regular price for the advantage of those who produce and who trade in them, avoiding on the one hand those high prices which, rendering sales impossible, ruin the stocks, and on the other such low prices as prevent the growers from expending the necessary sum on the cultivation of their vineyards.' In theory, it was admirable, in practice less so, hampered by the enmity of the English factors, incompetent technically, hamstrung by inefficiency, and open to bribes. To some extent, too, there was a levelling down, as some of the better growers, in the absence of a competitive market and assured of a safe if mediocre price, did not find it necessary to take so much care. But it did undoubtedly achieve some of the good things that it set out to.

A lengthy correspondence is preserved in the British Museum that passed between Mr. Warre, of the famous port shippers, and Mr. Whitehead, the consul. Mr. Warre's principal complaint was that brandy had become practically unobtainable. In 1799 he was owed seven pipes of brandy that he had paid for six weeks before, and two hundred pipes of port were held up for the want of it. His righteous indignation can be gathered from the first paragraph of a letter he wrote on February 8th, 1800:

'If the Monopoly wine Company is to be supported at all events, in every act of despotism they choose to exercise in direct violation of their own institution, and that their assertions, false, abusive and indecent are to be believed in preference to the just and true representations that the British Subjects find themselves compelled to make, it is time for every prudent man (however inconvenient it may be to him) to seek some other mode of business before he finds himself ruined, by vainly endeavouring to contend against a system which avows the destruction of their trade. The manoeuvres of the Company in the purchase of the wine of the last vintage fully authorize this idea. The Company have no brandy nor is there any reasonable ground to suppose that they can have the quantity necessary and in time.'

Moreover the shippers by then had surely learnt their lesson and the company had ceased to be useful. It was dissolved in 1833, but it was apparently missed, for it was re-established in 1843 only to be dissolved again, as a monopoly, in 1853, though it continued in existence, denuded of its privileges, as a respected independent port shipper.

437

While all this was going on another great change was taking place that brought vintage port into being and which led port from being a despised upstart rival to claret—as it was at the end of the seventeenth century—into becoming acknowledged as one of the greatest wines of the world, as it was less than a century later. This great change was brought about by the development of the bottle. In the first quarter of the century, bottles were pot bellied and broad based: they would only stand upright, as Pepys saw when he visited Mr. Thomas Povy's cellar in Lincoln's Inn Fields. Then the 'bottlescrew' was invented, which enabled corks to be extracted when they had been driven right home; and bottles developed into their modern shape, which could be binned on their sides. For the first time since the days of the amphorae, wine could be matured in airtight containers. Vintage port had arrived. The first acknowledged vintage appears to have been 1775.

Early in the nineteenth century an *enfant terrible* joined the ranks of the English shippers. Joseph James Forrester was a Yorkshireman of Scottish descent. He was born in Hull in 1809, came to Oporto in 1831, and was drowned in the Douro in 1861. His thirty years in Portugal were so full of achievement that the Portuguese created him a baron and at the same time he earned a place in our own *Dictionary of National Biography*. He went out to join his uncle's firm, Webber, Forrester and Cramp (now Offley, Forrester) and soon became popular: he was an excellent linguist and a very competent water-colour portrait artist whose work was much in demand by his fellow countrymen. In fact it is thanks to his efforts that we know what most of them looked like. Above all he did a thing that was unheard of for an Englishman: he got to know the Portuguese farmers really well, explored the valley of the river, made a map of the vineyard area, and conducted a geological survey. These were pioneer works. Unfortunately, though, he saw too much. Despite the ban of the monopoly, elderberries were still being used and so—as was well known— was brandy. He saw these as adulterations, and he condemned them. So far as elderberries were concerned he was obviously quite right, but with regard to brandy he was just as certainly wrong. The English had tasted the naturally-made wine more than a century before and they did not like it, preferring claret. I myself have tasted it and I entirely agree with them. By arresting the fermentation with alcohol before the sugar had all been used up, the growers had hit upon the way of making one of the greatest wines in the world. But in those days no one knew why this happened and one can sympathize with Forrester for holding a reasonable but mistaken view that the alcohol was also an adulteration. Unfortunately he stuck to his view pigheadedly. His first publication on the subject was entitled *A Word or Two on Port Wine*. It appeared anonymously in 1843. In the next year he held a meeting at his firm's quinta[1] up the Douro to launch his campaign. In the following year he published another pamphlet. Unfortunately these pamphlets were quite widely distributed in England and did no good at all to the port trade, creating the impression that all port was in some way adulterated. And to give the baron his due, some of the wines that were being exported to Britain at that time had been fermented right out and, coming from top quality vineyards, they may well have been far better than the table wines which were originally condemned or those that I have tasted. But they were not port as we know and like it, nor were they ever likely to be as popular.

He undoubtedly found many very real abuses to complain of, but unfortunately he persisted in listing the use of brandy amongst them. The result was a pitched battle waged against his fellow shippers for the rest of his life. At best it was misguided, at worst acrimonious, and often downright silly. Fortunately he lost.

His great work, his map of the Douro, was published in 1848. Another of his best enterprises followed shortly afterwards: when the Douro vines were attacked by the oidium in the early 1850s he made a detailed study of the disease and this was instrumental in saving the vines. In 1855, he prepared his '*Second Original Survey of the Bed and Margins of the River Douro, showing the Rapids and the Geological Formation of each Locality.*' Unhappily he was to die in one of the rapids six years later. He was returning by boat with Donna Antonia Adelaide Ferreira, following a visit to her Quinta Vesuvio. Owing to an error of the boatman, the boat capsized and the baron sank like a stone, for it is said that his pockets were full of gold that he was going to use for paying his workers. Perhaps the gold is there still, for the body was never recovered. Or was it an error? Some say the shipwreck was contrived and the gold stolen;

---

[1] Meaning farm, though on the Douro it always means a vineyard estate.

even that the body was later washed up. Certainly the gold was never discovered.[1] Donna Antonia, anyhow, escaped to live for another fifty years, and her escape was a most extraordinary thing: her crinoline billowed out and she floated to safety. Nowadays the Cacho da Valliera, where it happened, is sometimes called by the English 'The Baron's Reach'. I have myself been along it in a rickety boat, and it is certainly a terrifying and exquisitely beautiful place, where the river flows in rapids between boulders at the base of a deep, white ravine.

Baron Forrester would make a wonderful subject for a biography. He must have been a remarkable character, brim full of talent and achievement. There was one sphere, however, which he wisely avoided, at any rate in Portugal: politics. In England he was an active radical, well known in the Reform Club, but in Portugal he avoided taking sides—so much so that when civil war broke out he succeeded in entertaining both the rival generals in his house on the same day, but in different rooms.

At about the time that the Monopoly Company was finally abolished there was a boom in port, with the healthy sign that the prices of fine wines rose while those of poor wines fell. Alas, though, the greatest crisis of the nineteenth century had yet to come. As in all the great vineyards of Europe it was the phylloxera, and it arrived in 1868. By 1872 its effects were becoming noticeable. By 1879 many quintas were ruined. By 1884 grafting was well in hand, and here, as elsewhere, it provided the solution. So far as the vineyards were concerned it may well be that the phylloxera did good as well as harm, for the poorer ones were not replanted while those on the better sites were; and the vast number of vine varieties that had hitherto existed, some of them quite unable to produce top quality wine, at last disappeared and were replaced by those known to be first rate—which still amounted to a considerable number. As far as the wines are concerned, though, there can be no doubt that vintage port is not what it was. Happily the Vanzellers at Quinta do Noval keep one small section of the vineyard planted with ungrafted vines. Known as the Nacional, it gives endless trouble, as the vines are always succumbing to the phylloxera and dying, despite the modern insecticides that are now used in place of the old carbon disulphide treatment. But the wines it

[1] See, for example, Sarah Bradford, *The Englishman's Wine*, London, 1970.

makes are magnificent, though the quantity is too small to be commercial—only 5 to 10 pipes a year. In 1964 I compared side by side the Nacional and normal versions of the 1963 vintage. The former was a much bigger and greater wine, with more glycerine in it so that it stuck to the glass. It would last almost for ever. The difference between two specimens of the 1960s was less marked, with little difference in colour, but the Nacional was again clearly the better, especially on the nose. But in these hurried days the fact that a wine will last for ever has to be weighed against the fact that it will take that much longer to become drinkable. There it is. We still have superb vintage ports and these still take an embarrassingly long time before they are fit to drink, but alas, greater patience can no longer meet with greater reward. A rather odd and fascinating thing that seems to have vanished after the phylloxera is 'bees-wing'—a sort of light, flaky deposit in the wine that decanting did not remove. My old friend the late Warner Allen fancied he saw it in the Quinta do Noval 1931, but that wine was unique in every way.

No sooner had the vineyards recovered from the phylloxera than the unhappy shippers had another crisis on their hands. They dealt with it with ruthless determination but nevertheless it interrupted their trade for six months. It all began in December 1888 when a well-meaning Sr. Pestana, with government backing, attempted to set up another monopoly company. The employers resorted to a lock-out and there was a near riot amongst the workers who wanted to return to work. The Civil Governor was inept and the government was as stubborn as the shippers. But despite the inhuman severity of the shippers' action one cannot help having sympathy with them in view of their unfortunate experiences with the previous monopoly. Anyhow, they won and the lodges were re-opened in the following June.

Despite the general prosperity of the trade at this time, the unfortunate shippers were never without some sort of worry. If it was not one thing, it was another. In 1890, for instance, there was a political dispute between the two countries over their African possessions and it caused considerable ill-feeling in Portugal. The next crisis was centred round London: it was the famous Burnay port sale of 1892. No one has yet quite worked out what happened, for the story is a complicated one. At that time the leading wine auctioneers were Southard & Co., a firm that is still well known in the trade as shippers but which has given up auctioneering. In 1892 a syndicate financed by Count Burnay—a Lisbon banker—bought up the enormous quantity of 17,000 pipes of top quality port and put them up for sale through Southards. This amounted to about half a year's consumption—enough to disrupt the trade completely—and the thought of such a flood of good port suddenly coming on to the market caused enormous consternation to the shippers in Oporto and to the London merchants. To make matters more complicated, just before the Southard sale there was a sale of 1,600 pipes of Croft's port, arranged through Southard's rivals, Restell's (now incorporated into Christie's)—a sale that had nothing to do with the famous Oporto shippers but was arranged by the bankers of their London agents who chose this moment to realize their security. Fortunately each sale was a complete success. Mr. Southard, who from all accounts was a most formidable man and who had apparently thought up the sale, was proved quite right: it did nothing but good. It was so sensational that the publicity it provided for port—and for Southard's—was enormous, and in consequence the demand was such that prices were fully maintained. An enormous gamble came off.

All was not well, though, and something had to be done. Happily the Portuguese authorities, by mutual agreement with the farmers and the shippers, eventually evolved a scheme that was more effective than a monopoly. By the end of the nineteenth century shipments were declining and prices fell so seriously that the Douro farmers once more were unable to make a living. Everyone agreed that the decline had been brought about by competition from other dessert wines, and that the solution was to limit production but to keep the quality up. Once more the growing area was delimited and the new laws prohibited the importation of sweet wines from other parts of Portugal which had hitherto been used for blending with the poorer, rougher, Douro wines.

After the Kaiser war there was a boom in trade again which brought its own penalty in the form of a mushroom growth of small firms, many of which were tenth-rate. When the slump once more followed the boom, there came a spate of price cutting, and very inferior wines were exported—especially to France. To counteract this, the then minister of commerce and agriculture, the very able Sr. Ramirez, introduced legislation which led to the founding of the Casa do Douro—a federation of wine growers with its headquarters at Regoa, and one that had wide powers, including the useful ability to give farmers cash advances, to buy surplus wine for distillation, and to supply brandy to the growers.

The shippers were provided with an equivalent organization—the Gremio dos Exportadores, with its imposing office in Oporto. No one who is not a member can export port, and it acts as a government sponsored trade association, representing the shippers in all trade matters. Amongst its other duties is that of fixing a minimum price for port. Even more important is the Instituto do Vinho do Porto or 'Port Wine Institute' and one of its duties is to control shippers' stocks, ensuring that each shipper has sufficient, in relation to his sales, to maintain the quality. Its officers also taste all wines sold and give a certificate of quality. A sample of each wine is retained and the sight of all the samples for years back in the cellar is a fascinating and impressive one. Amongst its other valuable activities, it does technical work as a viticultural and an enological consultant, maintains a register of trade marks, protects the name port in export markets, issues useful books and advertising material, and so on. No one speaks ill of it, and it certainly does its job. At vintage time its officers arrange patrols at all the critical cross-roads up the Douro to see that no funny business takes place, and their presence is welcomed by growers and shippers alike, while the fact that the world trade is once more expanding is itself a tribute to the Institute's efficiency and emphasis on quality.

More recent history, so far as Great Britain is concerned, has been rather sad, for we seem to have lost our port-drinking habits. Cheap port no longer holds the place that it used to in the pubs, nor as a working-class luxury, while at the other end of the scale life has lost its leisure and the decanter of fine port after dinner is now almost as rare as once it was inevitable. The reasons are complex and a study of changing drinking habits would fill a book in itself. The result at least is clear: this country no longer fills its old place as the pre-eminent country of port drinkers. The only port that is at all hard to come by is vintage port, which cannot be other than rare. At the end of the war the 1942 and 1945 vintages were bottled in Oporto and the British merchants viewed the situation with horror, since vintage port has *always* been bottled in Britain. It had never happened before, so it was obviously wrong. In order to find some rational basis for their denigrations they said that the corks would not last, though why Portugal with its forests of cork oaks should use corks inferior to ourselves, who have no cork oaks, remains a mystery. In the event, the British merchants have been proved wrong. Now they are happy again: they buy their pipes of vintage port and bottle it themselves, though even so things are not quite what they were. In the old days, apart from the vintage ports of the great shippers, some of the finest merchants selected what they thought was the best wine of a given vintage and bottled it under their own names without bothering to mention the shippers at all. The 1912 port in my grandfather's cellar bore the name Sheldon of Shipston, and very good port it was. Nowadays it is only the shipper's name that has any commercial value and it has become sadly rare for a vintage port to be found with a merchant's name attached.

Britain's old position has largely been taken over by France. The French, with their unintelligible taste for sweet apéritifs, have taken to 'Porto' in a big way and drink it before a meal rather than afterwards. In 1963 France, for the first time, imported substantially more than Britain and has kept the lead ever since. For the most part the French buy the cheapest qualities and before the war this market was exploited almost entirely by the smaller Portuguese houses, so it was these that benefited, when, after the war, imports were on a quota basis. Now the larger houses are at last competing, and they have to compete on quality and price, since they do not have the established positions that they have so long enjoyed in this country.

The vineyards where port wine is grown are way up river: none is nearer than forty-five miles from Oporto and some are over a hundred miles away, almost at the Spanish frontier. All are in the region of Trás os Montes y Alto Douro—or the Alto Douro (Upper Douro) for short. The finest wines are grown between Regoa, where the Corgo flows into the Douro, and a point about thirty miles from the Spanish frontier. That is the Alto Douro. Below the confluence the yield is higher but the quality is not so good. It is a wonderful countryside, as dramatic as the Moselle but baked by the southern sun, a land of mountains and gorges, suffused by warmth, music and laughter. It is a delightful place to visit at vintage time, when everything seems to be done to music and with sleepless gaiety. It is a land of passion, too, where simple people think nothing of violence. A friend of mine was annoyed by one of his workmen asking for a day off during the busiest part of the vintage.

'But I must have it off,' he said. 'I have been summonsed to appear before the magistrate.'

'What have you done?'

'A slight argument. Just a little matter of a woman. I knifed my friend.'

'Goodness, did you hurt him?'

'Well, the knife went through and came out the other side. It didn't hurt him, though: it aired him.'

The magistrate fined him, gave him a severe talking to and sent him home. Really there was nothing else he could do: gaol would have helped no one.

The vineyards stretch either side of the river gorge, the width varying between ten and thirty miles. And there is never likely to be the slightest shortage of port as only a fraction of the available good quality sites are planted. The soil is very poor for growing anything other than vines and consists of shist and clay, with a high potassium content, over granite. In some places it is so hard that the ground has to be blasted before vines can be planted. The richer soils are those at the bottom of the valley and the wines grown on them tend to be coarse, while conversely those from the highest vineyards are thin—faults of balance that are corrected by blending. Only a few quintas, such as the renowned Quinta do Noval, are so perfectly sited and so large as to justify marketing a wine from a single vineyard.

Despite the dramatic beauty of the valley it is not a very desirable place to live in: an area of spring thunderstorms, gales, torrential rains, baking sun, enormous hailstones, floods, fogs, occasional snow and frequent frosts in winter, wolves, wild boar, adders and other tiresome things. Even in my own four short visits to the Douro I have come against a fair number of these snags: and I have never been there in winter. The dams built in the upper, Spanish, reaches of the river were supposed to have cured the floods for ever, but it proved wishful thinking. In the winter of

1964-5 there was so much water that the dams had to be opened and the river rose to frightening heights. Friends with quintas overlooking the river (but mercifully above the flood line) told me horrifying stories of houses and furniture rushing past in the swollen waters. And although they knew their own houses were high enough to escape disaster, the incessant roar of the uncontrollable flood gave them unconquerable doubts. Even when there is no flooding, the river flows so fast that it is not easy to swim in; and if you accidentally swallow any water the results can be most trying. I speak from experience.

Although there are now many fewer varieties of grape grown than there were before the phylloxera, there are still a large number, perhaps more than in any other classic wine-growing region. The finest vine of all is the Touriga Nacional, which resembles the French Cabernet. The Souzão yields a deeply coloured wine, while perhaps the most popular vine is the consistent Mourisco Semente. The Tinta Francisca resembles the Pinot Noir, and was imported from France by an eighteenth-century Scot called Archibald who had a hunting lodge on the Alto Douro, occupying the site of what is now Quinta Roriz. The Bastardo, which is sweet and which ripens early, provided those wines which were once, and which are now again, being imported into this country under the name of *brown bastard*—a name liable to misconstruction and giving rise to ill-inspired mirth. Other varieties include:

Alvarelhão (one of the best species, especially in the Lower Douro)
Casculho
Cornifesto
Donzellhino do Castelo (of which there are three variants)
Entreverde
Mourisco Tinto
Mureto
Nevoeira
Peagudo
Tinta Amarella
Tinta Cão
Tinta Castelloa

Tinta Lameira
Tinta Pinheira

All these varieties give red wines. For white port the principal varieties are:

Códega (or Malvasia Grossa)
Dona Branca
Gauveio (said to be the same as the Verdelho of Madeira)
Malvasia (of which there are several variants)
Moscatel (of which there are also several variants)
Rabigato
Rabo de Ovelha (or Estreito)

Many of the finest quintas (and some of them, in their perfect beauty and order, are show places) are owned by the leading shippers in Oporto, but by no means all. Others are owned by large landlords and small farmers. When an absentee landlord visits his quinta for the vintage he receives a memorable welcome: the workers assemble to greet him and honour him by letting off a terrifying succession of dynamite rockets. At the other end of the scale are the small farmers who live in their villages all the year round—villages that seem no doubt very primitive when subjected to a sociological analysis but which perversely remain full of happy people. Sometimes the big shippers buy the grapes off the growers and make the wine themselves in central pressing stations. There are also some well run co-operatives. The larger farmers, however, make their own wine, but there is one small formality that has to be gone through. From long and bitter experience no shipper will let any farmer use a cask for wine making unless the shipper inspects it first. Peasants have a touching way of trusting to providence so that they leave their great fermenting-casks uncared for after they have been emptied when the previous year's wine was delivered to the buyer. Evil ferments and, in particular, *mycoderma aceti* settle in the traces of wine that remain in the wood, and the result can be disaster. I saw one cask which had become so evil that the only hope was to pull it all to pieces and to scrub the separated staves with a strong disinfectant to remove the mould that was growing between them. Every year, just before the vintage, the heads of the various port wine houses go round to all their growers and inspect every cask individually, signing and dating each with chalk if it is deemed to be perfect; nothing less will do. It is a fascinating task and one that I have been privileged to watch twice: in 1962 with Robin Reid of Croft's and in 1965 with Gwyn Jennings of Sandeman's. What is more, they made me do the job myself and made it very clear to me if I slipped up. The tour of the vineyards was wonderful: we went up mountain tracks that could only be driven along in a Land Rover and then up steep paths, miles away from anywhere, that no cart had ever been along. At the top of one of these paths was a beautifully kept little vineyard with immaculately clean buildings where, after inspecting the perfect casks, we were given glasses of 1927 vintage port that had never left the place. It had spent longer in wood than it would have done in this country, so that it was lighter than one would expect, and was absolutely delicious.

Until very recently the Douro was by far the least mechanized and most unspoilt of all the major wine districts: with its primitive peasants and dramatic landscape it was the film director's dream of a wine country. Mercifully the landscape is there for ever, and the peasants show little sign of wanting to become urbanized, but mechanization has already arrived, and wine growing in the Douro will soon be as highly developed technically as it is anywhere. So any intending visitor would be well advised to savour and enjoy it while he still has the chance. The lorry and the Land Rover are now the most common vehicles but one still sees—and hears—the bullock carts, with their primitive axle trees that make deep, screeching groans as they go along—a noise that is actually desired, as it encourages the oxen. In the past it was said to frighten off wolves and even the devil. It certainly gives a useful 'audible warning of approach'.

When the grapes have been picked they are loaded into tall wicker panniers slung over the shoulders, and it is often very hard work carrying them up the precipitous hillside from the vineyard to the press house, so the workmen are encouraged with music: perhaps a single fiddle or even a three-man band. From the press house there is the sound of distant music steadily drawing nearer and then the grapes arrive.

Once inside the press house the grapes are loaded into a hopper and pass to a de-stalking machine, which is usually a modern, electrically driven, centrifugal one. Then, in the traditional method, the grapes are loaded into square granite *lagars*, which are simply pressing troughs about two feet deep. This is done by men for the most part, but also women, with bare feet which are carefully washed beforehand. The first stage is the 'cutting' which is very hard work and is done in silence, the treaders linking their arms to form a chain as they march to and fro over the *lagar*. I have counted seventeen in one *lagar*. After about two hours everything suddenly gets different. At a sign from the leader, the treaders break into a lively song, called *Liberty*, ending with the delightful couplet:

> Long live the girls!
> Long live liberty!

Then the human chain is broken, the band strikes up, and the fun begins. A harvest band may take almost any shape; there is usually an accordian or concertina, with guitars, fiddles, drums, flutes and sometimes even a primitive local form of bagpipes. Everyone joins in, dancing inside the *lagar* and in the yard outside it. Perhaps the most delightful dance of all is one where the people sing extemporaneously, composing insulting and often obscene verses about each other as they go along, and the victim has to reply in verse. One dances way into the night and bed holds no attraction.

Unlike sherry—where the must is run off as soon as it is pressed, so that it can ferment right out in barrels—the port must remains in its *lagar*, fermenting slowly and gathering colour from the grape skins until a certain point is reached when enough colour has been absorbed but when fermentation is still far from complete, so that there is still plenty of sugar left. Then it is run off into casks which already contain alcohol, the proportion being 100 litres of alcohol to 450 litres of must, so that the action of the ferments is suppressed and the wine remains sweet. Sometimes the fermentation is stopped at a very early stage by the use of more alcohol so that the wine remains very sweet. This is known as *geropiga*. It may be red or white and is used for blending. The red version is also sometimes sold as *Lacrima Christi*—a name that is not an Italian monopoly.

White port is made in *lagars* in the same way but using white

EE   449

grapes, and since the colour should be as light as possible, the amount of treading is reduced to a minimum so that the skins are not too broken up. After a certain amount of treading the grapes are packed beneath the surface with *macacos*—devices looking rather like a wooden stool on the end of a stick, such as used once to be used in wash tubs. Some houses also use these for pressing red ports.

That was the traditional method—picturesque, efficient in that it made good wine, but slow, laborious and relying on there being plenty of cheap labour. It could not last. By 1960 labour was already so scarce that the quality of the wine was jeopardized through the pressing not being done properly. Some years ago one or two of the Portuguese houses, notably Kopke, began to experiment with mechanization. When I went to the Douro in 1962 the English houses had begun to follow their example and I was shown the newly installed Sandeman plant at Pocinho, which was then the most complete and up to date there was. By 1964 Croft's and Warre's had similar installations. Soon the traditional method will have disappeared entirely. The change was positively dramatic. After much heart searching and careful experiment, within a period of three years the Douro was transformed from being undoubtedly the most backward of all the great European wine-producing areas to being perhaps the most up to date.

Wine growers are conservative people, and wine drinkers are, if anything, even more conservative, regarding with the deepest suspicion any innovation that the growers may make. But growers and drinkers alike must get used to mechanization in vineyards if we are to continue enjoying fine wines. Nor have they anything to fear. Modern techniques are an age apart from the clumsy efforts of the last century which, in their failure, gave mechanization a bad name. The modern equipment undoubtedly produces wines that are at least as good as those obtained by the traditional methods. Mechanization has arrived. And without it, the shortage of labour is such that the quality of the wine would undoubtedly fall.

The Ducellier system of fermentation is used. It is an improvement over the old *lessivage* system and was perfected in North Africa. A drawing which shows the operation of the fermentation vats will be found on page 123 of Amerine and Joslyn's *Table*

Wines.[1] Explained simply, the grapes, which are already mashed in the normal way, are passed into concrete vats which are not completely filled. On top of each vat there is an open trough, like a traditional *lagar*. A pipe passes from near the bottom of the vat into this trough, so that, when pressure is built up, the fermenting must is steadily forced up and out. When the pressure reaches a certain pre-set level, however, it is released by an automatic valve, and the must in the trough then passes back into the vat by means of a second valve that is so designed that the falling must is made to flow over and through the submerged cap of grape skins. The process then starts all over again. The cycle happens so frequently, though, that it is really continuous. In this way the must has even more contact with the skins than it used to have in the old *lagars*, and the wine has excellent colour. In the most recent installations, such as that of Sandeman at Pacheca Regua, opened in 1969, stainless steel fermenting tanks are used with paddles inside to circulate the must. There are also cooling pipes that can be used if necessary. It is one of those inventions that is so obvious that once someone has thought of it everyone else kicks themselves for not having thought of it sooner.

Whether the wine has been made by the old way or the new it is taken down to the lodges at Vila Nova de Gaia in the spring, after it has fallen bright and has been racked off the lees. Wines that are left up the Douro for too long develop a strange burnt taste, and oddly enough this happens even if they are in bottle. It is probably accounted for by the extremes of temperature. In the olden days it was taken on those beautiful, curious sailing barges that one so often sees illustrated, but these have now practically ceased from being used commercially, though I believe Cockburn's do still use them occasionally. All the other shippers use road tankers or the railway. The two barges moored in the Douro opposite Vila Nova de Gaia are there only for show.

Once the wine has reached the lodge it receives a further slight fortification and it is then left to its own devices for a while. The separate casks develop individually—not so perversely as sherry but still with considerable variations. Unlike sherry, port is not amenable to the discipline of the solera system: it has been tried and has failed. So all the differences have to be taken into account

[1] California, 1951.

when each blend is made, which makes the work even more difficult than it is in Jerez.

The method of storing and maturing wine in lodges, too, is quite different from that used in the bodegas of Jerez. Instead of the casks being only partly filled, so that the wine is on ullage and deliberately kept in contact with the air, port casks are full to the bung and are kept full, following the practice that is universal for table wines. Evaporation, in consequence, is very slight: only about one to one and a half per cent per annum, and this is taken care of in the normal cellar routine, since the wine is racked off the lees three times in the first eighteen months and annually thereafter. The casks are always filled up following the racking and the wine is checked for strength, a little alcohol being added if necessary to see that it remains healthy. As a rule, the various wines are kept in separate vintage *lotes* for at least five or six and sometimes for more than ten years, but thereafter older wines may be refreshed with ones that are a little younger, making a preliminary blend. This calls for considerable skill if the old wine is to be rejuvenated without changing its style, and sometimes it is done in several stages, a younger wine being first blended with an older one and some of the blend added to the oldest. As the wine matures in cask it gets steadily lighter in colour and in body while its acidity rises.

The blending of port calls for great skill, but before describing how it is done it may be as well to mention the various styles of port and what these consist of. First of all, and greatest in renown, comes vintage port. Shippers are hardly ever unanimous in declaring any given year as a vintage year. Sometimes it is a matter of personal good fortune, or ill-fortune. For example when I was up the Douro during the 1964 vintage, vintaging started under ideal conditions, and the quintas low down in the valley, where the grapes ripen soonest, had picked their whole crop, when torrential rains fell for many days, ruining the grapes in the higher quintas where vintaging had not even begun. So some shippers had plenty of good wine and others very little. But that year was not declared as a vintage anyhow. For it to be declared as a vintage two things are essential: firstly the shipper must have enough first quality wine, and secondly the market must be able to absorb a vintage. And for practical purposes the market consists only of Britain,

Belgium and the Scandinavian countries. Thus 1931 was one of the best vintages of the century, but the market was still flooded with the excellent and abundant 1927 vintage and there was a slump in world trade so that there was practically no demand for vintage port. In consequence only three shippers—Burmester, Da Silva and Hooper—declared it. Da Silva's classic Quinta do Noval 1931 fetches fabulous prices whenever any of it comes on the market. Conversely in 1945 there was no great quantity of wine available, but as the quality was good and the markets were crying out for vintage port it was widely declared. So it is not surprising that there is no unanimity between the various houses. For instance some shipped 1934 while others shipped 1935. An enchanting story from an earlier age is related by André L. Simon in his book *Port*.[1]

'The reasons why Messrs. Croft did not ship a Vintage 1868, although every other Port shipper did, is so typical of the old bulldog spirit of most if not all the members of the English Factory at Oporto, that it is well worth preserving. The summer of 1868 was excessively hot, and when the late J. R. Wright, who looked after the fortunes of the House of Croft at Oporto, visited the Upper Douro vineyards, early in September, he found that the little berries were black enough to pick, but so small and parched by the heat of August that they could not be expected to give, either as regards quantity and quality, sufficient and sufficiently well-balanced grape-juice suitable for the making of a vintage wine. Such was his verdict and he let all his friends know, at the Factory, the day he arrived back at Oporto. What Mr. Wright did not know was that from the day, almost the hour, when his mule's ears were cocked in the direction of Oporto and for the whole of the time during which he was leisurely travelling back to town, fine rain had been steadily falling by day and by night up country, the gentle, warm rain causing the grapes to swell and fill out in such a providential—not to say miraculous manner, that the 1868 Port was one of the most perfect vintage wines ever shipped from Oporto. All shippers of port showed and sold a Vintage 1868, all except Croft. Nothing could make old Mr. Wright ship a vintage which he had declared would not be shipped as a vintage by his firm. He maintained that he was not going to break his word for the first time in his life, and he did not. But, of course, he made some excellent vintage port in 1868, like every other first-class port shipper, and his friends wondered what he was going to do with it.

[1] London, 1934.

He did what none of them had expected. He sold it as "1869 Vintage" and he had the field to himself since 1869 was a poor year which nobody except Croft, offered as a vintage.'

When a shipper does decide to declare a vintage he follows the courteous custom of sending samples round to all the other houses, and this no doubt helps to inspire them one way or the other. But no shipper can afford to declare a vintage too often, as the vintage absorbs a high proportion of his first quality wines of the year, and he always needs a big stock of really good vintage wines maturing in the wood so as to maintain the quality of his standard blends.

A vintage port must be bottled within three years of the vintage. Its development then takes place wholly in the bottle and it throws a heavy crust—a sediment of immense weight that clings to the sides of the bottle like an overcoat, and this, despite the sheer quantity of the sediment, makes the wine easy to decant—provided, of course, the bottle is not shaken and the crust disturbed. It is for this reason that old vintage port needs a quiet life. If it is bottled later than that—usually from three to six years—it ceases from being vintage port and is correctly termed *late bottled vintage*. Having had longer in the wood it matures much more quickly than the twenty years or more for vintage port and only throws a small deposit if kept for any length of time in bottle. Such ports were once renowned, and they were widely available in Britain during the last century, but they sank into disfavour until revived once more in the 1950s. The great Professor Saintsbury in his classic *Notes on a Cellar-Book* relates how:

The gem . . . was a '73 which had been allowed to remain in wood till it was eight or nine years old, and in bottle for about as much time before I bought it. It had lost very little colour and not much body of the best kind, but if there ever was any devil in its soul that soul had thoroughly exorcized the intruder and replaced him with an angel. I had my head-quarters at Reading at the time, and a member of my family was being attended by the late Mr. Oliver Maurice, one of the best known practitioners between London and Bristol. He once appeared rather doubtful when I told him that I had given his patient port; so I made him taste this. He drank it as port should be drunk—a trial at the bouquet; a slow sip; a rather larger and slightly less slow one, and so on; but never a gulp; and during the drinking his face exchanged its usual bluff and almost brusque aspect for the peculiar blandness—a blandness as of

Beulah if not of Heaven itself—which good wine gives to worthy countenances. And when he set the glass down he said softly but cordially, "*That* won't do her any harm." But I am not entirely certain that in his heart of hearts he did not think it rather wasted on a lady, in which, as I have said *I* think he was wrong.

In their way these late bottled vintages are very useful wines, having a character somewhat different from most rubies and approaching that of a genuine vintage wine, but they are *not* vintage ports and should never be called such. Some time ago, in a well-known restaurant, I was offered a good tawny port at 2s. 6d. a glass or a vintage port at 7s. 6d. I demanded to see the cork of the vintage port and surely enough it was nothing of the kind but a late bottled vintage port, being passed off as vintage and sold for three times its proper price. These ports are properly classed as wood ports, since they mature principally in the wood rather than in bottle. The misconception that they are vintage ports has brought them into bad odour with many purists, and to make matters worse some of them have been sold as late bottled vintage ports were never vintage ports in the first place, but were full-bodied rubies blended to match late bottled vintages which were popular but unrepeatable. The Portuguese authorities are understandably displeased and are doing their best to prevent it by insisting that all such wines should be bottled in Portugal, have the date of bottling stated on the label, and be matured for a sufficient time. Another designation that displeases the authorities —they 'consider it inconvenient'—is *vintage reserve*, though personally I can see no harm in it: it signifies a rich ruby port of vintage character, and Taylors ship a very fine wine under this name. The authorities do not object to such wines being shipped as *vintage style, type or character* provided that no date is given.

Crusted port is a favourite of those who like a slightly lighter style of wine than a vintage port, who cannot afford a vintage port, or who do not want to wait so long for their port to mature. It is a blend of two or three vintages (seldom more) bottled when sufficiently young to throw a crust, so it has a distinct resemblance to vintage port but is lighter-bodied and has less individuality.

Ruby port means quite simply a young wood port, blended from wines of various vintages which have not been matured in the wood long enough to lose any appreciable amount of their colour. Tawny port, on the other hand, at the highest meaning of this much abused term, is a port that has been so long in the wood that its colour has lightened to a pastel shade, that is soft in flavour and delicate: a port for a summer's day—the sort of port that is always drunk in Oporto. But in the nature of things, if a port has been that long in the wood it must be expensive, and a fine tawny port is very expensive. It is also worth every penny of it. Cheaper versions are blended from younger wine showing less colour, and the cheapest versions of all have white port blended in. They are for the pub trade.

Finally comes white port. Someone or other wisely said that port wine's first duty is to be red, and I entirely agree. White port, made from white grapes in the way already described, is having a minor vogue at the moment, but although not lacking in appeal it seems to me to be a liverish poor relation of sherry and madeira.

Blends are made up in units of one pipe, there being 21½ *almudes* in a pipe and 12 *canadas* in one *almude*. As an example, the following is the blend of high quality tawny port prepared by Croft & Co. for a leading London wine merchant:

Sweetness (Degrees Baumé)	Wine	Almudes	Canadas
3·6	Lote 597 (8 year old)	3	6
2·5	Lote 1025 (4 „ „)	2	—
3·4	Lote 292 (9 „ „)	13	—
6·4	Lote 956 (a geropiga blend 10 years old)	3	—
		21	6

The final degree of sweetness proved to be 3·7 degrees Baumé.

Here, in contrast, are two commercial brands which were prepared on a large scale at the same time (September 1962). The first is a very old blend derived from six different vintage wines:

1934	15 pipes
1935	20 ,,
1936	11 ,,
1938	15 ,,
1941	4 ,,
1950	10 ,,

In contrast, the blend that follows is that of a young, full-bodied ruby:

1958	5 pipes
1959	34 ,,
1960	41 ,,

In addition 2 canadas of brandy were added per pipe.

All the above happen to be blends that I was shown on one of my visits to Croft & Co. A few years ago, serious wine writers in England were invited to attend a tasting by Geo. Idle, Chapman & Co. Ltd., the importers of Dow's ports. In all, seventeen wines were shown, ranging from a sample only eight weeks old to a sample of 'Very Old Blending Port' having an age of thirty-five to forty years, the youngest wine in the lote being of the 1934 vintage. We were also shown how fine wines of varying ages and characters were blended together to produce that admirable tawny, Dow's *Boardroom Port*. In a book of this length it is impossible to describe the character and style of each of these wines, but the exercise showed clearly, just as the Croft's blends had shown, how triumphantly successful blending can be in adding youth to age and bringing out the virtues of each in a perfectly balanced wine. Great shippers have nothing to hide.

The final stage in the preparation of port, as with sherry, is stabilization, and two processes are available: ion exchange and ultra-cooling. In the first the wine is passed through a chemical resin rather like that used in a water softener, but one that works in the opposite way, removing potassium ions and replacing them with sodium ions. Sodium tartrates, being more highly soluble than the potassium compounds, do not precipitate, and hence the wines no longer throw a sediment. This process makes little difference to the flavour and has been used successfully in processing wood ports but it is strongly disapproved of by the Portuguese authorities as it is not 'natural'. Although it has by no means disappeared it is seldom encountered. The alternative, of ultra-cooling, is practised on a large scale and the plants at Sandeman's and at Cockburn's, for example, are vast and very up to date. The wine is cooled to about minus ten degrees centigrade and kept at that temperature for a week or so. Anything that is liable to precipitate in bottle—especially in cold northern climates —separates out. Of course neither process is used for vintage port or for crusted port, both of which *must* throw a deposit.

Port vintages have a unique significance, for there is something of a mystique about them. They are discussed with peppery violence by elderly colonels who cannot be bothered with claret vintages and to whom moselle vintages are a completely closed book. Port is an almost uniquely long-lived wine, too, so that great vintages of the turn of the century are not merely academic wines: many of the old colonels can actually produce a bottle. So it is at least worth mentioning all the vintages of this century.

1900: Although perhaps slightly overshadowed at the time by the 1896, this was very fine and has lasted quite well, despite the fact that it was rather light and delicate. Now generally of academic importance. Declared by most shippers.

1902: Not a very good vintage but a certain amount was shipped.

1904: The yield was so large that some shippers had doubts about the wines but in practice they proved very successful and were declared by most shippers. Despite its age some Sandeman 1904 that I drank in 1965, although admittedly past its best, was still one of the finest ports I have ever tasted.

1906: Wines of rather average quality, but this vintage was declared by a few shippers.

1908: A very fine and long-lived vintage, though now rather old, declared by most shippers. Some Cockburn I had in 1964 showed no signs of decline.

1911: Quite a good vintage in its day but not widely shipped.

1912: A very fine vintage which was almost universally shipped. Bottles are still quite often produced from private cellars and now seem light and mellow—too old, but good.

1917: Quite a good vintage that was widely shipped.

1919: Not a very good year but shipped by seven shippers who were probably carried away by post-war enthusiasm.

1920: Although the yield was not particularly good the quality of the wine was excellent and twenty-two shippers declared it. Some of these wines look as if they will last for ever. The Taylor, for example, shows not the earliest signs of a decline, and the Dow, although perhaps a bit dried up, is still delicious. Many of the later vintages will need to be drunk before this one.

1922: A very good year though not quite up to the standard of 1920. The wines are drinking very well at the present moment. Declared by nineteen shippers.

1923: Not very notable and only shipped by Da Silva and Hooper.

1924: As 1922, with eighteen shippers.

1925: Not particularly good, and only shipped by Offley.

1927: This vintage was universally acclaimed and was shipped by almost everyone. After some forty years considerable divergencies are showing between the individual wines: Cockburn's for example (which was very highly praised) is now just about at its best and wants drinking, while Taylor's seems almost too young still.

1931: One of the greatest vintages of the century, but killed stone dead commercially by the slump and the large stocks of 1927s. Da Silva's Quinta do Noval is legendary. Also shipped by Bermester and Hooper. An occasional case has made its way to this country from other shippers and fortunate is the man who has one.

1934: The 1933 might possibly have been declared by a few shippers had there been more demand and had the 1934s not been obviously better. Although declared by only twelve shippers these wines have lasted well and are admirable.

1935: Marginally better than the 1934s or should it be the other way round? It really depends on the shipper. Of this vintage I have particularly enjoyed Graham and Rebello Valente. 1935 was declared by 15 shippers. The last vintage to be declared before the war.

1941: Although this year is not generally considered to be a vintage at all, I have tasted some Quinta do Noval, bottled in Portugal, which was excellent.

1942: This vintage gave excellent wines and would certainly have been declared widely were it not for the war. As it is, many of the shippers bottled their wine in Oporto and shipped them over afterwards. The wines are now generally slightly past their best.

1945: A very fine year though the quantity was small and the wines likewise were bottled in Oporto. They are still improving and there is no hurry to drink them; in fact this is arguably 'the vintage of the century'.

1947: Quite sound wines but rather light. This was declared as something of a stop-gap vintage but the wines proved better than the shippers expected. On the whole they want drinking now, though. Declared by thirteen shippers.

1948: A fine vintage that is still improving, despite the fact that, probably for economic reasons, it was not widely acclaimed or shipped. Declared by eight shippers.

1950: A good, if light vintage, that already drinks very well. Declared by thirteen shippers.

1954: A pleasant, fairly light vintage for early consumption, though shipped only by Hooper and Offley.

1955: A very good vintage that was almost universally declared, and one that promises very well in the years to come.

1958: A good but not outstanding vintage, declared by five shippers. It may well need drinking before the 1955s.

1960: A good vintage with considerable promise. Declared by seventeen shippers.

1963: In contrast with the disastrous French vintage, 1963 in Oporto was very good and was declared by a large number of shippers. Wines to lay down with confidence.

1965: Again, in contrast with the very poor vintage throughout France, 1965 was good for port and comparable with 1963.

1966: Another good vintage that may well mature comparatively early.

Madeira

Madeira is not, of course, a European wine at all: it is grown and matured in the island of Madeira off the west coast of Africa. Yet no book on the fine wines of Europe would be complete without a description of it: it is European emotionally if not geographically, grown by the Portuguese and by the British in Portuguese territory, and beyond doubt one of our best fortified wines. It is curious how we British are found where ever great fortified wines are grown. Our close connection with Jerez and with Marsala, and our even closer one with Oporto have already been described. Our connection with Madeira is every bit as close as that with Oporto, and it is wonderfully well documented. The whole story is told in fascinating detail by Rupert Croft-Cooke in his excellent book *Madeira*.[1]

By the standards of wine countries, Madeira's history is a short one, for it begins in 1419 when one of Prince Henry the Navigator's captains, João Gonçalvez, known as O Zarco (the Cross-Eyed), landed there and found an uninhabited island covered with trees—hence the name. There is some evidence that the Genoese found it earlier, but if so they evidently forgot it. It was colonized six years later, and the expedition included a Briton: John Drummond, son of 'Sir John Drummond, Lord of Strobhall', who was known as João Escocio ('John the Scot'). So we were in at the beginning.

The colonists must have taken with them all the necessities, and any colonists starting out from Portugal at this time must surely have regarded the grape vine as essential? At any rate, a Venetian traveller visiting the island in 1455 described the vines of Madeira as the finest sight in the world. And where there are vines there is wine. In the sixteenth century one of the great wines of the world was malmsey, grown in Crete, which was then under the rule of Venice, whence malmsey was exported all over Europe. The newly planted Madeira vineyards yielded so rich a wine that it was honoured by the name of (or mis-called) malmsey, and it may well be that the Cretan vine was imported. The Madeira malmseys described as 'malvoisie' or 'see' were exported to England in 1537. In the same century they were also exported to the Low Countries and were found in the French royal cellars. They evidently remained in favour in France as they were included in Louis XVI's cellar in 1782.

Following the defeat of Charles I, Prince Rupert's fleet was harboured by the King of Portugal and Cromwell's government declared war. In 1654, as a condition of peace, the Portuguese were obliged to grant special privileges to English merchants, and by 1658 the English connection with Madeira was sufficiently important to justify the appointment of one John Carter as consul, and within twenty years we had become the leading shippers,

[1] London, 1961. Reference should be made to this book by anyone seeking a complete history, and I happily acknowledge my own debt to it.

though much of the trade was conducted with our North American colonies, where madeira became established as the most fashionable wine, encouraged by the fact that the island was the last port of call for the ships on the American trade route from Europe. After 1663, moreover, madeira was uniquely privileged; for in that year an ordinance of King Charles II forbade the export of any goods to our colonies save in English ships from English ports. But there was one exception: wines could be exported in English ships direct from Madeira and the Azores. This effectively gave Madeira a monopoly of the wine trade with America and the West Indies. The wines were generally sold under the names of their importers and during the eighteenth and nineteenth centuries the bottles were also often labelled with the name of the vessel that carried the wine and the year in which it was imported. Indeed our own taste for the wine may well date from the War of Independence, when our officers drank it in America. These were madeiras such as Nathaniel Hawthorne described in *The House of the Seven Gables*:

'. . . flavoured by a brand of old madeira which has been the pride of many seasons. It is the Juno brand; a glorious wine, fragrant, and full of gentle might; a bottled-up happiness, put by for use; a golden liquid, worth more than liquid gold; so rare and admirable, that veteran winebibbos count it among their epochs to have tasted it! It drives away the heart-ache, and substitutes no head-ache! . . . It would all but revive a dead man!'

Indeed Rupert Croft-Cooke describes how the Boston Tea Party was preceded by a Madeira Wine Party:

'All over British America it had been a recognized practice for the Customs Officers to permit merchants and shipmasters to enter only a part of their imported cargoes in the books of the Customs House, and to land the remainder without payment.

'The Commissioners resolved to put a stop to this, and when the sloop *Liberty*, belonging to Hancock, arrived at Boston laden with Madeira wine, the Captain as usual proposed to the tide-waiter who came on board to inspect it, that part should be put ashore duty free. This suggestion was refused.

'The tide-waiter then became "violent" so Hancock locked him in a cabin and proceeded to land the whole cargo. When the Commissioners heard what was happening they caused the sloop to be arrested, on which the crowd ashore became violent and assaulted the Customs Officers detailed to make the arrest. Next day they smashed the Inspector General's windows, dragged his boat through the town and made a public bonfire of it. The Commissioners and Customs Officers had to take refuge in Castle William.'

The madeira that 'would revive a dead man' was presumably malmsey, but the bulk of the trade in those days was in rather dull, red beverage wines, such as are still grown on the island for local consumption. The general use of fortification probably dates from the middle of the eighteenth century and it was from about this period that madeira became recognized as a great wine.

From the end of the seventeenth century the madeira wine trade is the most perfectly documented of them all and, as usual, we owe a great debt to André Simon, who in 1928 published *The Bolton Letters 1695-1700*. Unfortunately this admirable book was not a commercial success and a projected second volume covering up to 1714 was never printed, but it does exist in cyclostyled form. William Bolton was a merchant, ship-owner and banker of Warwick, and the correspondence begins in 1695 as he was preparing to return to Madeira where he had agreed to act as the agent for Robert Heysham, an important London merchant and banker, to whom most of the letters were addressed. That an English merchant's life was not all peace and prosperity, and that there was even warfare between individual members of the British colony is shown by one of the earliest letters, dated July 6th, 1696:

I am now to informe you of a strang revolution in my affairs.

The first curr[tt], I was seized upon and putt into a wett dungeon with my cheese (chaise) man where we remained 48 hours. The next day following, the Govenor sent a Serjent to notifie me to imbarke from this island in 3 hours. He put a guard upon my house which waxed impatient of my stay, and accordingly because the order was to goe a bord any ship in the roade, I determen'd upon a Flushinger, in order to get a speedy passage for Lis[a].

When we were about half way aborde, the Serjeant was called back to the castel, we still remaining in the boate. He received orders to bring us ashore and carred us to the court of Guards, where we remained some time, and then, with four soulders, carried up through the noted streett round to ye same place, and then shiped us a second time, they accompaining us a borde ye jersey friggatt, and then left us to take passage for the West Indias.

You may guess what a multitude of neggros and Mollottos and rable followed us in the prosession; expected nothing but to have my Braines Beat out and was glad when I got aboard.

Such a sorte of indignity was never put upon any merchant in the world, and at the same time I had 4 ships in ye road wholly consigned to me: your pinke,[1] a small ship of Mr. Renens, a Flusinger and Mr. Halls Briganteen, by whom this goes.

The comander of the Man of War brought me back several Leagues that night, aboard a Flusinger in ye road, where I am privately. Shall sail in a few dayes for Terceira, to gett passage for Lis[a].

After they shiped me of, they seized on all my effects, pretending to be for the King's acc., to whom I am indebted to for custom, but have money enough in the house to pay for it. But what more they intend to doe, I know not of yett.

My wife and sonn are a shore with my famely, which I wish farther of now. Then the first occasion of this was Mr. Halls Briganteen, which lost company of the fleet and, the 30 ultimo, coming of the road, found the winds variable and could not gitt in; whereupon we procured a boat to tow her in, because we had lately 2 Briganteens taken in sight of the Island, and here is a order that noe boat should goe a bord with out asking Lycence; my man went and sued, when, as the Govenor was asleepe, and the rector of the Colledge comming to vezett him awaking, could not be speake with, he left a messinger to receive Lycence and sent of ye boat with ye providores lycence, only upon which we were imprisoned for, the morning following, where we remained as I told you 48 hours.

And then the govenour began to say that he had severall complants against me. One was that I was ye occasion that the fleet maide soe short a stay and took less by 2000 pipes than otherwise they would doe if had stayed longer, whereas som few of the Barbados and Lewerd Islands ships could not take many, and for my owne perticular part, I neather saw nor spoake nor had any communication with the comander of the Barbados convoy, who was the whole occasion of theire going away soe sone.

And that I was the only cause of a Flusinger not going to ye Islands for corne, which is so undoubtedly false, that at the same time and longe before we had concluded upon to goe the voyage, altho he had been arrived but ten dayes, and altho these things, if realy true are not crimes so grevous.

Some person of this place have not been wanting to improve what

[1] The 'Angel Pink' mentioned in several of his letters.

they could by suggestıng and affirming great parte of what hath been said against me, pert
icularly Mr. Miles etc. Such a villainy it is for our owne country men to be the authors of all this mischief by malice which cannot be opposed by vindication of my inocency, because in this arbitrary power they condemne people unhearde'.

The villianous Mr. Miles was no connection of the distinguished family of that name which still lives at Madeira, and happily Mr. Bolton's troubles were eventually resolved; though Mr. Miles, it seems, remained his favourite enemy, and one feels that Mr. Bolton was delighted when he was able to write, during the following year: ' . . . abundance of wines have turned to vinegar, especially of Mr. Miles shipping.' But even when things were going well locally, he was sometimes exasperated by the stupidity of his English principals:

'In ours of the 21st last month, we desired you to send us some hoopes for our owne accompt, in some vessel where freight would cost little, because it is no comodity to sell, but for trimming our casks when they goe aborde ship for their better security. We find you have loaden 30 Mil on the Pink which you send us, but if we pay any more then the first cost we cannot receive them. You may please to be referred to what we writt you under ye 15th May, and 22nd July, that what goods were fitting to send must be Madder Black Colchester Bayes, Kirsies, fine black Sayes, long Ells, etc., and not Butter and cheese and hoopes and Haberdashery and such like Trash, which Masters of ships bring freight free and sell for little or nothing.'

And in 1699 he was reduced to observing that 'When business is at worst, it must be better.' In the same letter he gave an order which reads strangely today: 'Send me Two pair of spectacles of 50 years and Two pair of 55; let them be those that turne one in another with hansom cases.' In a later letter he added: 'Please not to forgett to send me the pair of Pistols wch I desired with the spectacles.' Mr. Miles again? His health, too, sometimes caused him concern: 'Haveing now with much Trouble written the aforegoing—I am to informe you that it hath pleased God to afflict me with a Severe Distemper for three weekes past, being an Impostume upon the Right Side of my Head and Face, for wch I been Nine Times blouded, Twice cupped, and three Times Lanced; my condition was as dangerous as can be supposed, but now, through Gods Mercy, I am very much better then I was, and

I hope, with his assistance, in the Way of Recovery. Excuse my not writeing to other friends, I am: . . .' For the rest, the letters give a very clear, day to day account of a merchant's life and tell of many shipments of wine, with brief notes of the vintage conditions. It is all very much the same today. But there is one interesting note of wine being *imported*: 'One hamper of *Moselle Rhenish Wine*;'—a delightful contradiction—in 1700.

By 1708 the English merchants had established a 'Factory' with similar objects, no doubt, as that of their fellow wine shippers in Oporto, but in Madeira, alas, they did not erect a fine building, and nothing now remains of it, the records having been lost in a flood in 1803. It continued in existence until 1812.

After Bolton a succession of merchants arrived whose names are perpetuated in those of the firms that they founded. The first was John Leacock in 1741 and then Francis Newton, seven years later. The former was the orphaned son of a weaver, who had come to Madeira, after being educated at Christ's Hospital, as an apprentice at the age of fifteen. The latter was a young Scot; he may have been involved in the Forty-Five rebellion, and came as a book-keeper to João José de Camara, a descendant of O. Zarco, who was a landowner. He was also allowed to work on his own account as a trader, and he wrote to his brother asking him to negotiate orders for wine. But from the same letter one gathers that Madeira at that time was not a particularly enjoyable place for a young Scot to live in:

There are no recreations, diversions or companions. The Portuguese are a very sullen, proud, deceitful people and in short there is no such thing as finding one to make a Companion of, very few of them having good education unless the Priests and Collegeans whose ceremonies are so many and conversation so very narrow, being Roman Catholicks that their company is very disagreeable. As for the English here they are much worse, there is nothing but jealousy of one another's correspondents, everybody trying all he can to get another's, that they scarcely speak to one another; if they do it is criticizing and telling stories. This shows how great lengths interest drives people.

Perhaps it was this distrust of the English that kept the two young men apart, and their firms did not come together for two centuries. But in a later letter he explained the prosperity of his fellow traders:

One thing is certain, that no place in the world is more convenient for Business, or quicker to dispatch than this, especially for Englishmen having nothing to divert them from it, as they keep very little company with the Portuguese and are little given to Drinking, so that it is the only pleasure they have. As for the secrets of the trade, one may be master of them in six months time, and am resolved to take my chance here as others have. [I] think there is not a surer trade in the world [there] being very few bad debts, and [I] cannot find it requires stock and with your assistance in London am of the opinion that in a year or two [I] may have as good a business as any in the island, you being well acquainted with most West Indian merchants.

The wines of the mid-eighteenth century were described thus in Savery's *Universal Dictionary of Trade and Commerce*:[1]

Here are several sugar-plantations: the sugar they make is extremely beautiful and smells naturally of violets. This is the first place in the West where this manufacture was set on foot, and from hence it has been carried into America, where they make such vast quantities of sugar that the Portugueze, finding that this trade was not so profitable to them here as it proved at first, have pulled up the greatest part of their sugar canes, and planted vineyards in their stead, which produces excellent wines, and which foreigners come and buy up, and whereby the Portugueze make an immense profit.

There are three or four sorts of these wines.

One sort is of the colour of Champagne,[2] but is not much valued.

The second sort is a white wine, much stronger than the former. The third is delicious and is called Malmsey, being of the same nature with that of Teneriff. The fourth is of the same sort with Alicant wine, but much inferior to it in taste. It is never drank but mixed with the other sorts, to which it gives a colour, and strength to keep.

It is observable of Madera wine, that the heat of the sun improves it much, when it is exposed to it in the barrel, after the bung is taken off.

They make in the whole island about 28000 pipes of wine, 8000 of which are drank there, and the rest exported: the greatest part is sent to the West Indies, especially to Barbadoes.

Towards the end of the eighteenth century there is an interesting reference to that legendary wine Old West India Madeira, for at this time both madeira and sherry were matured by shipping them

---

[1] 1755, quoted by André Simon in *The Bolton Letters*.
[2] The wine of Champagne was at that time not only a still wine but a red wine, similar in colour to the red wines of Burgundy.

over the long sea routes to the East or West Indies and then back to England. In 1799 a convoy of ninety-six ships set sail, bound for the West Indies, escorted by Admiral Sir Roger Curtis, flying his flag on H.M.S. *Lancaster*, loaded with 3041½ pipes of wine. By any standards, that was a very large shipment. Sometimes individuals would arrange to have their wine matured in this way. The following delightful story was told by Lord Eldon of Serjeant Davy and Serjeant Whitaker:

SERJEANT DAVY: Brother Whitaker, how unfortunate we have been in not insuring those pipes of Madeira! The vessel on board of which they were is lost, and our Madeira is at the bottom of the sea, and now you and I have to pay our money for nothing.

SERJEANT WHITAKER: Our Madeira! I don't know what you mean. I have nothing to do with any Madeira.

SERJEANT DAVY: What! You surely don't mean to deny that we were to be joint purchasers of two pipes, which, for improvement, were to go to the East Indies and back, and now to get off paying your half of what we jointly purchased.

SERJEANT WHITAKER: I never entered into such an arrangement.

SERJEANT DAVY: Well, then, I am glad of it. It is the finest Madeira that ever came into the Thames. The ship and wine are safe, and the wine is all my own.

By the end of the eighteenth century, anyone asked to name the Englishman's wine would have said 'madeira' without hesitation. For although port was rapidly taking over, madeira was still esteemed the greater wine. Philip Guedalla, quoting from the Apsley Papers, wrote that the age was one 'when military manners prescribed officially a monthly ration of fifteen bottles of madeira as the bare limit of necessity.'[1]

The nineteenth century began rather dramatically when, in 1801, the island was occupied by the British under the command of Lt.-Col. Sir William Henry Clinton; but they did not stay long and the only effect seems to have been to increase local sales. Our troops came back again in 1806 and stayed until 1814, but the occupation was a friendly one and not an act of war. It may well be that these occupations helped to spread the fame of the wine and to make it popular in England. It was during this period, too, that the trade reached a peak of prosperity to which it has never returned,

[1] *vide* Dermot Morrah, art., Ridleys, March 1970.

for in 1800 exports rose to 16,981 pipes and remained at about this figure until 1825, when it suddenly dropped.

When the troops finally departed, they left behind them a man who was originally their quartermaster and who was to found one of the greatest madeira dynasties. It may well be that he began his dealings in wine while he was still in the army. John Blandy was born in 1783. His descendants are still living on the island and his firm is now controlled by his great-great-grandsons. William Cossart arrived at much the same time, in 1808, to join the firm which Francis Newton had founded and which was then known as Newton, Gordon, Murdoch and Scott. The firm later traded as Newton, Cossart and Gordon, and the name Newton was not dropped until 1861. Another of the great firms was founded during the boom period, in 1814, by William Grant, a Scot. Known originally as Rutherford and Grant, it is now Rutherford, Miles & Co.

In the first part of the nineteenth century, madeira was one of the most esteemed and highly popular wines in the world: of that there can be no doubt. It was also a most 'genteel' drink. When the Forsytes looked back on Superior Dosset Forsyte, who founded their dynasty, they thought of him as 'A hard, thick sort of man; not much refinement about him.' Although they were much in his debt, he was hardly to their credit, but his uncouth nature was mitigated by one glimmering of enlightenment: 'The only aristocratic trait they could find in his character was a habit of drinking madeira.' This was not enough to save the wine from the caprice of fashion, though, for when Henry Vizetelly wrote his *Facts about Port and Madeira* in 1880, he started his chapters on madeira by observing that ' . . . it was a point of curiosity with me as to how so magnificent a wine, once famous throughout Europe, should have gone out of fashion to the extent that Madeira appears to have done.' It may well be that this drop was brought about, at any rate to some extent, by a royal caprice; for madeira had been the favourite wine of the Prince Regent who suddenly changed his allegiance to sherry. Madeira continued to be bought for the royal cellars, though, and a great many bottles were sold off by King Edward VII when he came to the throne in 1901. One can hardly blame him: not even madeira lasts for ever. But what prizes there were at that sale! The explanation favoured by Vizetelly, though—

which is as likely to be right as any other—is that when madeira prices soared, following the oidium, old customers went over to sherry and marsala, and they were never won back. Changing habits of life eventually caused sales of these wines to slump as well. Moreover the valuable Indian market was lost following the dissolution of the East India Company and the opening of the Suez Canal, which cut Madeira off from some of the most profitable trade routes.

The British colony in the island was now in such flourishing condition that it had its own church and chaplain. But—alas!—there was schism, no doubt to the great joy of the local Roman Catholics. One can but imagine the intrigue and hard feelings it must have caused in the colony itself. In 1834 a Mr. Lowe was elected chaplain, and for eleven years there seem to have been no complaints. But then—oh dear!—he developed regrettable High Church tendencies and introduced Innovations. In 1846 a meeting was held and his salary was cancelled, by thirteen votes to five. In the following year, at a very well attended meeting, it was once more voted down by thirty-six votes to twenty. The inhabitants petitioned the Queen for a replacement and the Rev. T. H. Brown was sent out, but Mr. Lowe, who still held the Bishop of London's licence, remained, and the congregation was split in sunder. Even when eventually the unfortunate Mr. Lowe was appointed to a living in London, his chapel continued.

While the British colony was enjoying its petty wranglings over incense and candles a catastrophe was befalling the island that reduced much of the population to penury, caused whole villages to emigrate, and left the wine trade with a wound from which it has still not recovered. In 1852 oidium broke out. It is a scourge that has turned up repeatedly in these pages, but it was particularly bad in Madeira where the climate enabled the fungoid parasite to flourish to a devastating extent in vineyards that, for the most part, were unsuitable for any other crop. Even after the remedy of treatment with powdered sulphur was discovered, it was many years before the vines were yielding well again, and exports slumped, while shippers had to rely on their irreplaceable stocks. A further source of severe loss was the American Civil War (1861–65) which disrupted one of the most valuable markets.

The second plague of the nineteenth century was the usual one:

phylloxera arrived in 1872, just as the growers were beginning to recover from the oidium. The remedy—grafting the native vines on to American root stocks—was of course adopted; and madeira, like sherry, has not been noticeably affected by the change; in fact, as with sherry, the outcome has probably been to improve the wine as the less satisfactory native vines, such as the Bastardo and the Tarrentez, have been eliminated in favour of the better varieties, though the latter was perhaps unsatisfactory commercially rather than aesthetically, as the old wines vinified from this variety that survive have a unique and fascinating flavour; and there is said to be some replanting. This period that contained so many successive bad vintages also led to a change in manner of maturing the wine, for fewer and fewer vintage wines were produced and it became the standard practice to mature the wines by means of the solera system. But some of the vineyards were never replanted and sugar cane took the place of the vines.

In 1896, Blandy's created a great stir and won a noble victory: they secured a court order in France for the seizure of five hundred pipes of wine which they claimed were being sold fraudulently; for at this time considerable quantities of Spanish wine from Tarragona were being sold in France under such names as *Madère de l'Espagne*. It was four years before they got the final judgment but their victory was complete and put a stop to this fraudulent trade.

After the Kaiser war, the shippers suffered a further severe loss, for two of their most important markets were destroyed: Russia and the United States. By then the United States trade had already seriously declined and the disaster of Prohibition was not so serious, but Russia had been a market of the very first importance. The growers were saved by a rapid increase in sales to the Scandinavian countries. In those days, too, France was one of the most important markets, whereas now it counts for nothing, having shifted its allegiance to cheap tawny port. Britain and the United States are, once more, expanding markets, though still by no means large.

*

All who drink madeira will already know the names of the great madeira vines, for the wines are named after them: Malmsey,

Verdelho, Bual and Sercial—though others are grown as well. Two of these names are anglicizations, for in Portuguese the Malmsey is the Malvasia and the Bual is spelt Boal. The Negra Mola, which is akin to the Pinot Noir, used to provide a red wine sold as Tinta, or tent, but although some of this wine is still made and is used for blending—as is the ubiquitous Muscatel—these have totally disappeared as export wines, as have the once-popular Tarrentez and Bastardo. It is said that the Sercial is closely akin to the Riesling, while the Verdelho corresponds to the Spanish Pedro Ximenez. But, thanks to the differences in soil and climate, there can be no comparison between the wines they produce. The vines are not grown in the form of bushes, or trained along wires, as they are in the great European vineyards, but along pergolas, or latadas, and the ground beneath and beside the vines is often used for growing another crop, so the vineyards look, to someone fresh from Portugal, more like the enchanting gardens of the Minho than the well organized vineyards of the Douro. But the untidiness is deceptive: it stems from the prolific growth of the vines rather than from the growers' carelessness. There is drastic pruning every January. This method of viticulture is well suited to the climate, as training the vines high off the ground lessens the effect of the reflected sunlight. In the Minho it results in the acid, fresh *vinhos verdes*, but in Madeira, where the sun is so much more powerful, the wines are as big as can be. Cultivated any other way, one suspects that they would be coarse.

Vineyards are found all over the island, down to sea level and high in the hills, cultivated on carefully-made little terraces, wherever there is any earth to be found. Very little of the island's surface is suitable for cultivation at all, and almost a third of the good soil is planted with vines. With few exceptions the north-facing slopes, although productive, do not yield particularly good wines. The best area of all is that known as Cama de Lobos. Over the island there are, of course, several kinds of soil, the best being *saibro*, formed out of broken-down red volcanic rock. Others include *pedra molle*, from yellow volcanic rock, the strong *cascalho*, and the clayey *marsapes*.

The vintage, owing to the southern latitude, is one of the earliest, beginning in the middle of August, though the vines in the highest vineyards—particularly the Sercials—are not picked until October:

a span of time rivalled only by the great German vineyards. It may come as rather a surprise that the Sercial vine, with its kinship with the Riesling—a vine that ripens in the most northerly European vineyards—should be the last to ripen in Madeira, but the answer lies in the fact that it is grown in the cool heights where it flourishes best. Strangely, in Madeira the vintage is more like that of Jerez than that of Oporto, though the treaders themselves have more of the Portuguese gaiety and abandon than of the Spanish solemn dignity. The *lagars* are similar in size to the Spanish ones and, like them, they have a screw in the middle. The method of treading is just the same, but in Madeira, as in Oporto, bare feet are used rather than nailed boots. And after the treading has been completed, the must is poured into *borrachos,* which are not (as a student of Spanish might suspect) local drunks, but goat-skins that are carried by *borrachieros* to depots where the must is decanted into waiting barrels. The must is then taken by lorry to the shippers' lodges. Before roads were made the barrels were taken to Funchal by sea: they were lowered into the shallow water by the shore and then strong swimmers propelled them to the waiting boats. This picturesque method of transport has quite disappeared, though, save for the sweet wines vintaged early in the off-shore island of Porto Santo. Soon, perhaps, the *lagars* will disappear too, as they already have, to all intents and purposes, in Jerez. Modern mechanical presses will take their place, and it is sad, of course, that the old sights will no longer be seen. But there is no sense in being sentimental about it. Labour costs are increasing in Madeira like everywhere else, and if the price of the wine rises out of proportion to its rivals it will lose its already precarious markets, while there can be no question of quality suffering: the new presses are so good that it will, if anything, improve.

The way of vinifying madeira is also a cross between sherry and port. The dry madeiras—sercial and verdelho—are fermented right out and are then fortified at a later stage, like sherry, while the sweeter madeiras—bual and malmsey—have alcohol added before fermentation so that this is restricted and a high proportion of the natural sugar is retained, as with port. Or at any rate, that is how the higher qualities of the sweet wines are made: the cheap ones are initially fermented right out for reasons that will be explained shortly.

Now comes the process that is unique to madeira: the *estufa*, wherein the wine is first gradually heated and is then equally slowly cooled again. As to how this process originated one can only speculate. The idea of accelerating the maturation of wine was by no means new: it was known in ancient Rome. But there is no reason to believe that the wine growers of Madeira were inspired by classical authors and they certainly reinvented the process even if they were not the first inventors. In all likelihood it was found that wine shipped over the equator had a peculiar elegance and maturity all of its own and the madeira shippers thought that this was brought about by the gradual warming and cooling of the wine in the hold of the ship. Or it could be that someone found that wine warmed by the hot sunlight—wine stored in a conservatory, maybe—was better than similar wine stored in the coolness of the lodge. Or had someone seen Spanish table wines being matured under the sun in glass *bombonas*? It could even be that thoughts running along both these paths converged to evolve the *estufa*.

So far as throwing light on the origin of the *estufa* is concerned, the documentary evidence is very slight. As early as the 1730s the term *vinho do sol*—wine of the sun, or wine treated by sunlight—was in use, and the 1755 edition of Savery's Dictionary already quoted, stated that madeira was improved by exposure to the sun. In 1800, Leacock's built their first *estufa*, describing it, in a letter quoted by Rupert Croft-Cooke, as a 'new Mode of treating Wine', by then used by all the shippers, some of whom hired *estufas*. The letter continues: 'Certainly to those who are not good judges, the new Wine with three months *Estufa* imitates Wine of 4 or 5 years old, and we don't think that the deception will be easily discovered —however the Secret will soon be known abroad and may perhaps prejudice the character of Madeira Wine. In all Hot Climates it improves much quicker than in Cold ones: twelve months in the East or West Indies has more effect than 3 years here, or four or five in England—therefore the Heat must be of Benefit, and we must make a climate.' Two years later John Leacock was writing that the method had become general and in 1804, the Governor of Madeira, in what was no doubt a pious fear of any departure from tradition (the sort of fear that would now banish modern wine presses), attempted—fortunately unsuccessfully—to banish the method. I say 'fortunately' because it was the *estufa*, together with long ageing and fortification, which converted madeira from being merely worthy into being great.

The type of *estufa* constructed by Leacock was clearly one that was heated artificially. In that climate it is not surprising that others chose to use the heat of the sun, and when Henry Vizetelly visited the island an *estufa do sol* was still not an uncommon thing, though these sometimes relied partly on artificial heat. Now they are extinct and all *estufas* are heated by furnaces. Over a period of a month, the wine is gradually brought up to a temperature of about 120°F and it remains at that for three to four months, after which the temperature is gradually lowered again, taking another month. Nowadays the cheaper wines are heated in vast concrete vats holding some 40,000 gallons but the finest qualities are kept in oak casks stored in a room of regulated temperature. Are the casks better than vats? Probably not: at any rate the shippers say that they are not and that they are just used for sentiment's sake. Added to which there is not such a very large quantity of the finest wines, so perhaps concrete vats would not be economic for treating them.

I have already mentioned that the cheapest of all the sweet wines are fermented right out, rather than fortified at the beginning, as the better ones are. The reason for this is that a certain amount of alcohol is driven off in the *estufas*, and if this has to be replaced, it obviously adds to the cost. So the cheapest of all the wines are vinified dry, *estufaed*, and then fortified and sweetened with boiled-down must.

After the *estufa*, what happens to the wine depends largely on its quality and style. The cheaper kinds are left in cask for a few months and are then blended. The better ones are matured by the solera system, just as with sherry. A small proportion of the best of all are set aside and matured to become those rare and wonderful things, old vintage madeiras.

As with sherry and port shippers, blending is, to the madeira shipper, a vital and wholly honourable art. For vintage madeiras are few. Some madeiras are the straight products of soleras, as are some sherries, but these are themselves blended wines, for the solera is really an elaborate blending as well as maturing process. The cheaper qualities contain little or no solera wine and are wholly blends of suitable, relatively young madeiras with blending wines.

Most of the wines, even the expensive ones matured in soleras, are further blended before they are shipped: the products of the various soleras are blended one with another to produce a wine of exactly the style required, and finally specially prepared blending wines may be added. As for the special blending wines, *tinta* has already been referred to: it adds both colour and sweetness. *Canteiro* is a rare and precious wine of great age matured without the *estufa*: it adds a quality of its own. The two cheap sweetening wines are *surdo* and *arrobo* made from boiled-down must, corresponding to the Spanish *sancocho* and *arrope*—honourable enough wines to use, but principally used with the cheapest madeiras. Finally, after the blend, the wine is matured for several months in the cask so that the various parts can 'marry' and the wine settle down.

The four basic styles of madeira are, of course, the four that are named after the most popular grape varieties. Sercial is relatively light in colour, and body, and is comparatively dry; it is principally an apéritif wine. Verdelho is deeper in colour and body, and is sweeter; it is a versatile wine that may be enjoyed before or after a meal. Bual is one stage deeper and sweeter; although some madeira lovers enjoy it as an apéritif it is generally considered to be a dessert wine. Both the last two are, as it were, madeira drinkers' madeiras: they have special subtleties that intrigue as well as satisfy. But the most impressive madeira of all is malmsey: deep and gloriously sweet, the best examples are magnificent dessert wines. Apart from these, some of the blended wines are sold under old-established names like 'London Particular', but two names are so old-established as to call for special comment: Southside and Rainwater. Both of these are found mostly in America—the former almost entirely so—but I remember raising my eyebrows many years ago when offered a glass of the latter in a London wine bar; and I areatly enjoyed it. Southside is a rich blend of wines grown on the southern slopes: the best wines, in fact. Rainwater is a drier blend, mostly from Sercial grapes grown high on the hillsides where there is no irrigation and where the vines have to rely on the rainfall for their water.

Very old madeiras are of course rare and costly, but partly, perhaps, because they are not especially fashionable or popular wines, and partly, perhaps, because very old wines *are* so costly, there is a greater variety of them available than either ports or sherries of equivalent quality. And madeira goes on for ever: no other wine lives so long. In cask it rivals sherry and in bottle it excels port. A madeira old in cask attains the apotheosis of old wine, and in bottle it loses a little sugar to become mild, gentle and glorious. These old madeiras are treasures that are worth seeking out.

Now, happily, madeira seems to be coming into its own again. The shippers have combined together, as the sherry shippers did long ago, to advertise madeira *as a wine*, quite apart from their separate advertisements to publicize individual names. Moreover many of the leading shippers have combined to form the Madeira Wine Association. This is, in effect, a giant co-operative whose members combine to buy, ferment and *estufa* their wines collectively, save for certain individual marks of special quality which are still made as before. The members of the Association who ship to the United Kingdom are:

Blandy's Madeiras Lda.
Leacock & Co. (Wine) Lda.
Miles Madeiras Lda.
Cossart Gordon & Co. Ltd.
T.T.C. Lomelino Lda.
Shortridge Lawton & Co. Ltd.
F. F. Ferraz Lda.
Luis Gomes (Vinhos) Lda.
Freitas Martins Caldeira Lda.

A few well-known firms still, however, remain outside it, including:

Henriques & Henriques
H. M. Borges
Vinhos Barbeito
Marcelo Gomes & Cia Lda.
Veiga Franca & Co. Ltd.

The Table Wines of Portugal

Of all the countries of Europe for a wine lover to wander around, looking for good simple, local wines, Portugal is one of the best. France is of course superb in parts, but the north is dreadful; Italy

477

excels Portugal in range because it is so much bigger, but although it can provide a greater number of pleasant surprises its disappointments are more frequent and more profound; Spain competes, too, and could compete very well if all its wines were as well made as the best, but unfortunately they are not. If any other European country is in the same class, I have not been there. In my own experience, Portugal is the most consistently full of pleasant surprises from end to end and from side to side. I have never had a truly bad wine, even amongst those supplied free of charge at a pensão. Portugal manages to produce this wide variety of good wines thanks to its climate: it is far enough south to ensure fairly good vintages nearly every year, but in winter the mountain vineyards are bitterly cold, while those near the coast are cooled by the influence of the Atlantic, with its mists and cold winds.

The wine growers in all the principal districts are subject to a *designacão do origem* system, comparable with the French *appellation contrôlée*, and this does much to keep the quality up. A traveller will find that, apart from wines from carefully delineated districts, there are also quite good blended wines that are gratifyingly cheap. As far as the district wines are concerned, two words are worth looking out for: *reserva* and *garrafeira*. There is no legal difference between these terms: both mean wines selected for quality and matured in bottle. But in practice the former generally denotes about four years' bottle age, and the latter, eight years'.

Very roughly, the vineyards may be divided into three groups: the northern group, including the *vinhos verdes* and the Douro region; the central vineyards, of which the most notable are those of the Dão; and the vineyards in the region of Lisbon. In the eighteenth and nineteenth centuries, Portuguese table wines were well known in this country—there is many a fine wine label engraved with the name *bucelas*, for instance—but they became completely overshadowed by port, suffered under the phylloxera, and were extinguished by the commercial skill of the French and German wine shippers. Now that the prices of the better-known table wines are rocketing up, though, these good Portuguese wines are coming into their own again. Many of them are already extremely popular.

The wines of northern Portugal were imported into this country by our merchants at Viana do Castelo long before port was discovered. The vineyards of the Minho region are amongst the most enchanting I have ever been to, and they are quite unlike any others. It is a region of gentle hills, charming valleys and small fields, where the peasants grow their vines unkempt on trees and pergolas around the perimeters of their plots, while vegetables grow in the middle. Training the vines so high off the ground prevents the grapes from being ripened by reflected warmth and sunlight, while the long pruning of the vines, and their prolific yield, makes the grapes less highly flavoured, less sweet and more acid, than one could possibly expect from the latitude. Thus the wines—to one who has been brought up on the classic growths of France and Germany—come as a complete surprise: they are fresh, acid, and pétillant from the gas of a malo-lactic fermentation. Although called *vinhos verdes*, they are not, of course, green in colour—most are white, though some are pink or red—but they are green in the sense of being young and fermented from grapes that are hardly ripe. They are consequently light in alcohol. It is their pétillance that gives them so much of their charm, but they met with little favour in this country two and a half centuries ago and one can easily understand why; for they must have lost their sparkle during the long sea journey from Viana, and they probably lost much of their freshness as well. It is impossible to imagine such slight wines 'travelling well' in cask. But in bottle they travel beautifully and are really delightful on a hot summer's day, though for the export markets, they are, unfortunately, usually sweetened, while extra bubbles are also sometimes pumped in; perhaps this is the reason, as much as anything, why they taste even better in Portugal. Personally I prefer the white wines to the pink, and the pink to the red, as red *vinho verde* always seems to me to be some-what emasculated: red wine should have plenty of body and should refrain from sparkling. The red *vinho verde* is altogether odd: dry, astringently tannic and dark, it needs to be matured for two or three years in bottle and then drunk cold. But others may well like it. The area in which these wines may be grown is delimited by law and lies to the north and east of Oporto, the principal centres being Viana do Castelo, Braga and Amarante, while wines of somewhat similar character are grown south of the Douro at Pinhel and Lafões. The principal vine varieties are: Loureiro, Azal Branco, Rabo de Ovelha, Alvarinho and Aresso

479

(white), and Alvarelhão, Bastardo, Verdelho Tinto, Verdelho Feijão, Docar, Casta Borracal, Vinhão Tinto (red). Between the *vinho verde* country and the Douro vineyards a delicious, highly alcoholic white wine known as *entre os rios* is grown from Douro grape varieties and is something like a cross between the two districts in character, having a touch of greenness.

Wines were grown, of course, in the Douro valley long before port was heard of, but these did not find favour in England, and having tasted some peasant-made examples of the local red table wine, or *consumo*, I am not surprised: fermented right out in that hot climate, it can be dry, rough, coarse, astringent, and downright unpleasant. But by no means all the *consumos* are like this. Modern wine growers know far more about enology than their ancestors did, and they are far better at their job. Time and again it has been shown how much better modern wines are than the 'glorious vintages' of the past, and this is most certainly so as far as *consumo* is concerned. Some of the best port growers now also grow a certain amount of table wine for their own consumption, and they grow it very well indeed. Given a few years in cask and a few more in bottle it can be delightful and even delicate. I have also tasted excellent white table wines grown in the Douro. But these Douro table wines are never likely to be sufficiently competitive in price to sell abroad.

It is very much otherwise, though, with the wines grown on the fringe of the port wine region, particularly down river. Some years ago Sacheverell Sitwell wrote in one of his books that he had tasted in Portugal a wine called Mateus Rosé: it was delicious, and why was it known nowhere else? He could hardly write that today! Quinta da Avelada, near Penafiel, is an exquisite estate in the region of the *vinhos verdes* yet not far from the Douro vineyards, and this very well-equipped centre serves the Guedes family as a country headquarters for both kinds of wine. Mateus Rosé is in fact not grown there but higher in the Douro valley, and the bubbles are contrived by the artifice of man rather than by nature, but the result has been a wine of unique popularity.

The greatest of the Portuguese areas for table wines is undoubtedly the Dão, and the journey there is one of the most beautiful imaginable, around the hillsides, through the pine forests, and so to Viseu. An artist would stop a hundred times to capture the view. A wise man with sufficient time would avoid using a car altogether and take to a horse. Viseu, a delightful town, is locally famous as the home of Grão Vasco, a sixteenth-century artist whose works are a source of great local and national pride while the rest of the world remains obtusely unmoved by them. The vineyards are high up—about 1,500 to 2,500 feet above sea level—and vines have been grown there from time immemorial, but the region only began to be of commercial importance towards the end of the last century when improved enology revealed its latent merits. It was officially delimited provisionally in 1908 and finally in 1912. The height of the vineyards provides a cool mountain climate with lots of rain in winter but with a sunny, hot summer. This no doubt helps to give to the finest, but by no means all of these wines, an unexpected degree of delicacy, while the rather infertile soil conveniently exists in two different forms: most of the region is predominantly granite, which is highly suitable for red wines, while some of it, to the west and south, is schistous and suitable for white wines. There are several grape varieties, all of which are grafted on to American roots. For red wines, Tinta Pinheira, Tourigo, Alvarelhão, Alforcheiro Preto, Tinta Carvalha, Baga de Louro, Alvar Roxo and Bastardo are grown; while for white wines there are Semillon, Dona Branca, Barrosa, Assario Branco, Alvar Branco Barcelo, Rabo de Ovelha, Cerceal, Borrado das Moscas and Encruzado. Many of the red wines are vinified with a proportion of about thirty per cent white grapes.

The wines themselves can be excellent and they age well; indeed the finest of them need quite a long time in bottle if they are to show at their best. Although dry, they have a gesture of sweetness about them, thanks to a high glycerine content. When I went there in 1965 I tasted a white wine of the 1957 vintage with six years' bottle age and a red 1954 with nine years' bottle age. Both were bone dry and strikingly good. Some of the cheaper Dão wines now available in this country are remarkably good value: they are massive, hearty things, splendidly robust and not pretending to that delicacy found in the finer and more expensive growths of the region.

To the west of the Dão, in lower country nearer the coast, lie the regions of Agueda and Bairrada. The former grows wines rather after the *vinho verde* style but fuller and less fresh. There is considerable variety, though, some of them closely resembling *vinhos verdes* and others being more like dãos. Bairrada is as yet very little known, but it seems to be a district with great possibilities, growing thoroughly sound red, white, and rosé wines—some of the latter being aerated for the British market but left still for Portugal and the United States. The principal vines grown in this region are Baga and Trincadeira for red wines, Semillon, Pinot and Maria Gomes for whites. There are also some unexpectedly good sparkling wines made by the *méthode champenoise*: they have none of the delicacy and fresh acidity of the French prototype, but they have a strong and agreeable flavour of their own.

The third major group of vineyards is found in Estremadura to the north and east of Lisbon, though one notable area—Setúbal—lies to the south. The most northerly part of this region is the least important: Alcobaca. Its perfectly sound table wines are by no means notable, though any visitor to the exquisite little walled town of Obidos will certainly enjoy them. Passing southwards along the coast, the next area, Torres Vedras, grows wines of similar quality but is of greater interest to historians of battles than to wine lovers. Then comes Colares, and that is quite a different story: it is a complete viticultural anomaly. It is one of the very few vineyards in Europe where the phylloxera causes no trouble, and this itself stems from another aspect of its uniqueness, for it is the only vineyard of any consequence planted in sea sand, through which the wretched vine louse cannot penetrate. The countryside is almost as fascinating as the renowned and romantic Sintra nearby, the vineyards being planted untidily in irregular patches exposed to the Atlantic gales, though sheltered by all manner of barricades. Beneath the sand—sometimes as much as thirty feet down—there is clay, and the vines have to rely on this for their moisture, so teams of men dig great holes or trenches—an occupation that becomes more and more hazardous the deeper they get, so that the man working at the bottom looks absurd, wearing an inverted basket over his head to protect him from suffocation if the wall of sand suddenly falls in. When the clay is reached the vines are planted, and then the sand is gradually shovelled back over a period of months, so that the tips of the vines remain exposed to the sunlight. A small proportion of vineyards are also planted in the clay soil behind the sand, but the wine they yield is distinctly less good and is sold in demijohns for local consumption. These vineyards, moreover, are not phylloxera-resistant and so have to be planted with grafted vines. Their acreage is much less than before the phylloxera, so the quality of colares has actually been improved by the pest. The principal vine in the sandy vineyards is the Ramisco.

The best red colares wines rather put me in mind of a good rhône, and they age extremely well, so that after twenty years or so they can be very fine indeed. Unfortunately, though, true vintage wines are hard to get, and a wine labelled *vendima* or *colheita* need contain no more than a prominent proportion of the vintage indicated. A little white wine is also grown there, but this is to be avoided.

Travelling along the coast towards Lisbon, the next notable area is Carcavelos. Although the vineyards are very ancient they did not expand and grow famous until Marques de Pombal, who had a fine vineyard at Oeiras, brought his influence and enthusiasm to bear. By 1788 John Croft wrote of 4,000 to 5,000 tuns of Lisbon wine being imported annually 'all promiscuously called Carcavelos'. The wine became even more famous following the Peninsular War and remained familiar in England until well into the last century. The best is grown on the small hills known as 'Lombos de Carcavelos', with south-east facing slopes, along the coast; but alas this attractive area is becoming ever more popular with holidaymakers and as a dormitory for Lisbon, so the vineyards grow less every year. Both white and red wines are grown, and the principal vine for the former is Galego Dourado, together with Arinto and Boal. The red wine vines are Trincadeira, Torneiro (or Esadeiro) and Negra Mole. It is the white wines, however, that are most worth looking for: they are fortified to be fairly strong and come in a wide range of sweetness, so one is at once tempted to compare them with sherry; but anyone approaching them and expecting to find a wine like sherry will at once be put off, as they have a character all of their own that is something of an acquired taste, though both their colour and their 'nuttiness' is perhaps somewhat reminiscent of an amontillado—a distinctly sweetened amontillado.

Bucelas also became famous in Britain after the Peninsular War, and was often sold, very misleadingly, as 'Portuguese Hock'. The vineyards lie up river to the north of Lisbon and are planted principally with the Arinto vine (which is said to be not dissimilar from the Riesling) together with smaller proportions of Esgana Cao, Rabo de Ovelha and Boal. It is a light wine, with a fair degree of acidity and an agreeable bouquet that increases with bottle age. To my own taste it is one of the most enjoyable of all Portuguese wines, and it is excellent to drink with shellfish. But it is not at all like hock. It obviously comes from a southern latitude and in fact it rather puts me in mind of a white châteauneuf-du-pape, while Raymond Postgate[1] has likened it to Austrian schluck. It also tends to have a very earthy after-taste.

Travelling northwards, and still inland along the Tagus valley, good red and white wines are grown in the region of Ribatejo. The vineyards span the valley, with Cartaxo on the right bank and Almeirim on the left. In 1966 I tasted some 1954 red and white wines grown in the same locality near Santarém. I was not especially impressed by the white, but the red was an excellent, well-balanced, big-bodied table wine. One of the red vines grown in this area is called the Xerez—improbably, for it is quite unlike anything in the sherry country. It would be interesting to know how it got its name.

To the south of Lisbon lies the last of the truly notable districts: Setúbal. Its best-known wine is the luscious, golden moscatel; and a very fine dessert wine it is, too. The best and sweetest examples become exquisite with bottle age. Various varieties of Moscatel vines are used including the Moscatel de Setúbal (which is the same as the Muscatel of Alexandria), Moscatel de Malaga, Moscatel Romano, Moscatel Roxo, and the Moscatel do Douro (which is the same as the Muscatel of Frontignac). As with port, fermentation is incomplete, being arrested by alcohol. There is also a noteworthy red wine, grown on ungrafted vines in sandy soils like those of Colares, but by no means so hard to work. It is named periquita, after the vine that produces it.

The decline of Portuguese table wines on the British market from their nineteenth-century popularity to their eclipse during the first half of the twentieth century is one of the many odd chapters in the history of taste. No doubt the phylloxera played its part in this, but there can be little question that quite apart from this, the quality of the wines also declined. Probably this was the

[1] *Portuguese Wine*, London, 1969.

result of ineptitude: noting the British taste for strong wines, for example, the shippers tried fortifying bucelas, which must surely have ruined it. And there was no real organization in the Portuguese table wine trade until the major districts were delimited in this century. The labels of wines drunk outside those districts are still frankly suspect, but they are getting more reliable every year, and modern enology has done much to improve the quality of the wines. The sudden and immense vogue for *vinhos verdes* and *rosés* has brought Portuguese wines back in a big way, and good dão wines are now also to be had. It is hoped that the other good Portuguese wines will also come into their own.

A Variety of Countries

〜〜〜〜〜〜〜〜

The leading wine-growing countries, which between them produce nearly all the fine wines of Europe, have been described in detail. If time and space were available I can imagine no task more agreeable than trying to do the same for all the lesser countries. To have to relegate them to a mere appendix is unfortunate, and in some instances—particularly in respect of Hungary with its tokay—it might be regarded as positively insulting. However, the fact remains that the countries considered at length are those which grow the best wines, and to consider the remainder in comparable detail is sadly impracticable.

Austria

Austrian wines have been delighting travellers since time immemorial, but they are relatively new on the export markets, where they are making some headway despite the formidable competition with German wines; for those of Austria are of the same general style, but it must be admitted that they never touch the same peaks. They have a freshness and individualistic style that is all their own, though. They are delightful wines for summer drinking, and the best of them are unquestionably amongst the fine wines of Europe.

The vineyards are older than Austria itself, dating back—as usual—to the days of Probus. As is also usual in European wine history, the earliest enthusiastic and efficient wine growers were the monastic orders. Very little was heard, though, of Austrian wines outside their country of origin, and although there are records of a substantial export trade with the Low Countries in the seventeenth century, most of the wine in the past, as now, was drunk locally. The phylloxera struck early on—in 1872—and in a country largely of peasant growers its effect was especially severe. The vineyards have long since recovered and production is about half that of Germany, eighty-five per cent of it being white. The red wines are of only local interest. Most of the wine is made in co-operatives with a degree of skill quite beyond the reach of the peasants.

Shortly after the phylloxera struck, in 1873, there was a great exhibition in Vienna, and the wine juror for Great Britain was Henry Vizetelly, who put his experiences into an invaluable period piece optimistically entitled *The Wines of the World Characterized and Classed*.[1] This is how he described the Austrian wines of the period: 'The wines of Austria are as diverse as its population. At the extreme south they are so dark and full-bodied that when mixed with an equal quantity of water they are quite as deep in colour and as spirituous as the ordinary wines of Bordeaux, while in less favourable districts they are excessively poor and so sour as to rasp the tongue like the roughest cyder. Many have the luscious character of Constantia and the Muscat growths of Frontignan and Lunel; several, on the other hand, are disagreeably bitter, others, again, are so astringent as to contract the windpipe while swallowing them, whereas a few of the lighter varieties possess the delicacy, if not the fragrance, of certain growths of the Rhinegau. It must be confessed, however, that although the specimens were remarkably varied and numerous, the better qualities were extremely rare.' The variety is still considerable, but the worst were no doubt eliminated in the replanting and there can be little doubt but that the general standard is higher. As compared with German wines, however, those of Austria tend to be unsubtle and lacking in finesse—heavier and inclined to be dull.

Many varieties of vines are grown including the Hungarian Furmint, as well as most of the varieties found in Germany, some of the finest wines being vinified from the Riesling, known locally as the Rheinriesling, the Traminer, and the Sylvaner, while the classic native vine, giving excellent wines, is the Grüner Veltliner. Other native vines include the Rotgipfler and the Neuberger. Wine

[1] London, 1875.

vinified from the Muskat-Ottonel is well worth looking for, and the Müller-Thurgau has been successful.

The vineyards are planted in Lower Austria, Burgenland and Styria. Of these, Lower Austria is the most important, and is divided into seven districts:

Weinviertel: the largest district, planted predominantly with Grüner Veltliner.

Wachau: the vineyards are planted on steep hillsides in the valley of the Danube. The warmest sites are planted with Rheinriesling. Amongst the best of these are Dürnsteiner Hollerin and Dürnsteiner Liebenberg.

Krems: to the east of Wachau. Principally Grüner Veltliner and Rheinriesling. Kremser Kögl, Kremser Kremsleiten, and Kremser Wachtberg are noted sites.

Langenlois: to the north-east of Krems and planted with similar vines.

Donauland: a smaller district on the south bank of the Danube. The same grape varieties.

Baden: outside Vienna and centred on Gumpoldskirchen, near to the Vienna Woods. The climate is warm and the wines are rather full-bodied, vinified principally from the Spätrot, Rotgipfler and Neuberger vines.

Bad Vöslau: mainly red wines of little notability.

Burgenland grows somewhat heavier wines than Lower Austria and is divided into two sections: Rust-Neusiedler See in the north and Eisenberg in the south, the latter growing mostly red wine. Styria is divided into three districts—Weststeirische, Südsteirische and Klöch-Oststeirische—but the wines are not amongst Austria's best, and the area's only well-known wine is a rosé called schilcher.

In all these districts many wines are vinified from the lesser-known grape varieties and are named after them. These are well worth the traveller's while to look for. Nearly all Austrian wine matures quickly and is at its best when fresh and young. The wine terms used on the labels are occasionally somewhat different from those of Germany, an unsugared wine, for instance, being described as *naturbelassen* while a wine vinified from selected bunches of grapes is called *gerebelt*. Most of the German wine terms are used, however, and have the same meanings as in Germany.

Bulgaria

Viticulture in Bulgaria is very ancient but was reorganized completely following the Hitler war and the political upheaval. At present exports are concentrated on cheap wines such as those vinified from the ubiquitous Riesling, though the wines vinified from this grape seem to take on rather an odd local flavour. A pleasant wine is also made from the Red Muscat, called the Misket. The Melnik vine gives a big, dark, heady red wine, often slightly sweet but with a curious, rather bitter after-taste.

Cyprus

Anything written about Cyprus wines at present is likely to be out of date in ten years' time, for recently there have been efforts to recapture their ancient renown. In this respect Cyprus enjoys a practically unique advantage: it has never been invaded by the phylloxera. Its wines, though, have done little to demonstrate this advantage, and for the most part the table wines put one in mind of the undistinguished Greek mainland wines. The red wines, which are strong and heady, include those with the splendid names olympus and othello. A large proportion of the export trade has been in that unfortunate misnomer Cyprus sherry: by no stretch of imagination a fine wine. Now, though, new varieties of vine are being tried, largely thanks to the initiative of the late Fred Rossi who laid the foundations for the new wines as far back as 1956. These vines include the Spanish Palomino, which appears to be eminently suited to the climate, and very good wines may well result: wines good enough to be sold on their own merits without being misdescribed as 'sherry'.

The best of the traditional wines of the island is commanderia, vinified principally from Mavron and Xynisteri grapes: a brown, sweet, dessert wine which can rise to real heights and is undoubtedly a fine wine. It is a wine of great antiquity associated with the Knights Templars.

Czechoslovakia

The Czechs drink more than they produce, so their wines are little known elsewhere, but they are now making some efforts to export them. The white wines are said to be the best, particularly those grown from German wine varieties in Moravia.

Great Britain

In remote times England grew wines that were highly praised,[1] but viticulture died out with the dissolution of the monasteries, assisted by the worsening of the climate through the centuries. More recent attempts include the valiant effort of the Marquis of Bute in South Wales—an effort that might have succeeded had it not been for the Kaiser war. Following the Hitler war interest was revived amongst horticulturalists and vines were planted on a small scale in various areas of England and Wales. At present there are only two commercial vineyards producing wine, and both are in Hampshire: at Hambledon and Beaulieu. Both grow good wine, even though it would be an act of patriotism to call it 'fine'. But the quality is improving as the vines age and the growers gain experience. It could well be genuinely fine eventually, and other promising areas, such as the sheltered south-facing slopes of the chalk downs, remain untried. A third commercial vineyard has more recently been planted in Nottinghamshire.

Greece

If Italian wines fail to live up to their classic renown, then those of Greece are positive non-starters. The Greek viticulturalists, together with those of Rome, were foremost of their age, and Greek merchants helped to spread the vine throughout Europe. But the glory that was Greece is no more; and that applies to the art of making wine just as much as to the fine arts. Greece is a great producer of wine but produces no great wine. It would be pleasant in this chapter to dwell on ancient Greece and the cult of Dionysus, but many a classical scholar has already done so[2] and I shall not write of a remote past that has made so slight a mark on the present. The gods of Olympus drank Nectar, but its secret died with them.

[1] A brief account has already been given, see p. 17.
[2] See particularly H. Warner Allen, *A History of Wine*, London, 1961; Charles Seltman, *Wine in the Ancient World*, London, 1957.

Perhaps one of the ancient wines should be mentioned, though: malmsey. It took its name from the port of Monemvasia, whence it was shipped, but it was one of the first geographical wine names to suffer the indignity of becoming generic, so that it now denotes a style of wine, grown in Greece or elsewhere, rather than any vineyard district.

Statistically, the largest wine-growing areas are Pelopennesos, Sterea Hellas-Euveia, Crete and Macedonia, all four areas growing predominantly red wines save for Sterea. But most of these wines —red or white—are simply beverage wines for local drinking. A few fine wines are grown but these are principally sweet table wines of the kind that are out of favour at the moment. One of the best is the muscat grown in the Peloponnesos and on the Aegean island of Samos, the home of Pythagoras. It is a mountainous island covered with vineyards, most of which are planted with the Muscat vine, and it is this vine which gives to the wines its unmistakable flavour and aroma. The finest are sweet but others are vinified to be medium dry or even completely dry. The latter still retains the muscat nose and is of a very individualistic style—perhaps rather an acquired taste, but one that I feel a wine drinker could easily acquire. This is almost the only Greek wine to be subject to a law corresponding to *appellation contrôlée*, and the production is largely in the hands of co-operatives.

Another well-known dessert wine is mavrodaphne, vinified from vines of that name also grown in the Peloponnesos, in the province of Patras and in the islands of Cefalonia. It has the odd characteristic, shared by tokay, that it need not be chilled. One of the largest growers of this wine is the firm of Achaia-Clauss founded by a German, Gustav Clauss, in 1850, but now Greek owned. The same firm markets pleasant dry red and white wines known as domestica; and saravalle, a sweet red wine of some character. Another good, dry, white, and characteristically Greek, wine from Patras is santa laura.

Perhaps the most famous of all Greek wines, though, is the dry, white, or occasionally pink retsina: the resin-flavoured wine most of which is grown in Attica. It is an acquired taste, and those who have acquired it assure me that it is a wine of which one never tires. Never having acquired the taste I do not know, but I am quite ready to accept that there is no other wine like it. The resin is derived from the sap of pine trees and is added to the must at the time of fermentation. There are two theories as to how this began. Some say that wines of Attica were once stored in pine wood casks and that the growers so liked the flavour these imparted that they cultivated it and added it artificially. Others suggest that resin was first added to the wine as a disinfectant when Athens was infested by cholera. Both theories seem highly improbable, since traces of resin have been found in amphorae and even in wine vessels dug up in Egyptian tombs. It was most probably used because people liked the taste, having found it by chance, or possibly as a preservative or to mask the bad flavours of inept wine making.

Hungary

The reputation of Hungary for fine wines rests entirely with one wine: tokay. It is a wine of legendary splendour: in fact the legend is far greater than the wine justifies, and rests entirely on the renown of imperial tokay essence—an intensely sweet wine that is said to revive the dying when all the doctors fail. I have never tasted any. Those who have, describe it as being honey-flavoured, and delicate in its richness, so that I imagine it as a cross between a trockenbeerenauslese and pedro ximenez. In 1968 some half-litre bottles were sold in Christies, and one of these—of the 1876 vintage from the estate of The Baron Maillot of Tállya-Hegyalja, which had been imported into England in 1938 by Berry Bros. & Rudd—fetched £145. I later learnt that the American bidder had been prepared to go up to £250. In my view no wine can be worth anything approaching this figure, so I shall probably never taste it. But apart from tokay, Hungary grows a wide range of very acceptable table wines, and has done so ever since the days of Probus.[1]

Tokay (or tokai) takes its name from the *Tokaj-Hegyalja* wine growing district—an area which includes about twenty-five villages and which in turn takes its name from the Tokaj hill (1,153 feet) which is the principal hill in the Eperjes-Tokaj range. The wine as we know it today is, like the great sweet wines of Germany and of Bordeaux, the product of the 'noble rot' and, as in

[1] For a detailed history see Zoltán Halász, *Hungarian Wine through the Ages*, London, 1962.

those countries, it was discovered quite by chance, in the seventeenth century, when the vintage was postponed on account of war. From then onwards the fame of tokay rapidly spread, only suffering a setback in the last decade of the nineteenth century, when the vineyards were destroyed by the phylloxera and had to be replanted. Three grape varieties are cultivated: Furmint, Hárslevelü and Muskotály (Muscatel). It is the first two that are attacked by the noble rot. The soil is mostly powdered volcanic rock, and the whole area is extremely sheltered, so that it enjoys a long, hot autumn while the grapes ripen.

The special character and sweetness of tokay is derived from the shrivelled *aszu* which are picked separately from the rest and placed in wooden butts of a local style called *puttonys*, having a capacity of about seven gallons. These grapes are traditionally pressed by foot, but nowadays by machinery—to give a homogeneous, dough-like pulp which is added in varying proportions to the must derived from pressing the normal grapes. The must is then fermented with the dough in comparatively small wooden *gönc* barrels having a capacity of about thirty five gallons. The wine is labelled according to the quantity of dough added to the must before the fermentation. Thus a bottle labelled 'five puttonys' will have the pressed dough from five puttonys added. Very roughly, one puttony approximates to ten per cent of the whole. With each barrel of aszu the richness increases, and all grades are made from one to six puttonys, but in practice one and two puttonys are rare as the wine tends to dry out rapidly in bottle and is not commercially very acceptable, while that of six puttonys is also rarely made, being both too rich and too expensive.

After a day or two, fermentation begins. The barrels are stirred and the liquid is poured into special bags which are then pressed for a second time to produce the aszu must, which is matured for from four to eight years before being bottled. The number of puttonys, however, is by no means the only criterion. As with all sweet wines, much depends on the vintage, and a three puttony wine of a fine vintage may be as rich as a five puttony wine of a lesser one. Once in bottle, a fine tokay lasts almost indefinitely and wines have been tasted after two or three hundred years, acquiring remarkable shades of flavour which have delighted connoisseurs. Unlike most sweet white wines, they taste best at room temperature.

To make tokay essence (which is no longer exported, if made at all) the aszu berries were left in the puttonys and were not pressed at all. The essence was the juice pressed out by the weight of the grapes themselves. It was so full of sugar that the yeasts were inhibited, and even after fermentation the alcoholic strength did not normally exceed eight per cent.

Lastly, and least of the tokays, is tokay szamoradni—literally 'tokay as it has grown'. To make this wine the aszu berries are not separated. As with tokai aszu, it is pressed by a double process, but its quality is far more a matter of speculation, depending on the general quality of the vintage and also on the proportion of the grapes that happen to have been affected by the noble rot. In the best years it approximates to the aszu in quality, but in other years it is dry and not particularly notable.

Tokay is perhaps the only Hungarian wine which ranks with the great European wines; but there are others of a humbler kind which are so popular that they must be mentioned. First amongst these is the bull's blood of Eger (Egri bikavér). Its name suggests a manly sort of wine, and it lives up to it. It is pressed from about seventy per cent Kadarka grapes, twenty per cent Pinot Noir and ten per cent Cabernet Sauvignon. On the whole I prefer to drink it young, before the vigour of youth gives way to a rather dim maturity. Of the other districts, one of the most notable is around Lake Balaton, particularly famous for its Riesling wines, though excellent white wines are also produced from the Furmint grape, while Somló, near the head of the lake, grows a Furmint of very distinctive character that takes an exceptionally long time to mature.

Luxembourg

The Grand Duchy has been growing wine for a very long time, and vintage records are said to extend back to the year A.D. 809. In some respects, however, its history is rather like that of Alsace, for while it was under German domination the vineyards were cultivated only to grow wine of very poor quality which was blended in with German wines to make a poor quality product known as *moselblümchen*. Following the First World War, the wine growers realized that the only hope for survival was to produce a wine of quality, and the vineyards had to be totally re-organized with government assistance. The wines that are now grown are admirable, but only a very small proportion of a small production is exported, so they are necessarily rare. The upper reaches of the River Moselle flow through Luxemburg, so it is not surprising that they have something of a moselle character, but they tend to be thinner, lighter and more acid. The best of them are very good indeed, being particularly fresh and delicate. They are delightful drunk on the spot. A certain amount of the wine is vinified to be pétillant; called *perlwein*, some of this is exported. It is often bottled in moselle bottles with crown corks. A substantial amount of fully sparkling wine is also made. The most widely grown vine varieties are Elbling, Riesling X Sylvaner (Rivaner or Müller-Thurgau) and Riesling. The best wines are sold as *Grand Réserve*, *Réserve*, *Grand Cru*, *Premier Cru* and *Cru Classé*, and to qualify for any of these categories they must be vinified from Riesling, Traminer, Ruländer (Pinot Gris) or Auxerrois grapes. In addition, the words *Marque Nationale* signify that the wine has been passed and approved by a body of tasters.

Malta, G.C.

Malta has a rapidly expanding wine industry. Most of the wine is drunk locally though there are some exports. So far, however, the vineyards have earned praise for their existence rather than for their excellence.

Romania

As with all the eastern Mediterranean countries, wine was grown in Romania from the earliest times, and viticulture owes much to the Greeks. Until recently the export trade was practically non-existent but nowadays it is quite considerable, though British markets have only seen relatively cheap wines intended to compete in that section at present dominated by Yugoslavia. One of the best of these is the sweetish wine sold under the varietal name muscat ottonel. Noted dessert wines include cotnari and chardonnay de Murfatler.

Russia

Russia is a major wine-producing country and, as becomes the leading communist nation, its emphasis is on producing large quantities of standard, consistently good wine rather than on cultivating small vineyards to produce minuscule quantities of the exquisite. Several varieties of wine are now available in Britain at very competitive prices from Armenia, Georgia, the Caucasus, the Crimea and Moldavia, but my impression of them is that they are worthy and dull, not at all good. The Russians are particularly fond of sparkling wine which they make in large quantities. Amongst the best table wines available are the red mukuzani: no. 4 and the white tsinandeli no. 1. Saperavi is an astonishing red wine that is, to say the least, 'full-blooded' and improves vastly after a short time in bottle, astonishingly enough showing a trace of spritzig which seems fascinatingly inappropriate. In so large and scientific a country it would be astonishing if there were no fine wines; but such as there may be do not appear to be exported.

Switzerland

Owing to its high elevation and mountain climate, Switzerland is hardly an ideal country for viticulture, and most of the production simply satisfies local demand. Nevertheless some good wines are grown there and small quantities are even exported. The most important wine-growing areas are the cantons of Valais, Neuchatel and Vaud. The two best-known wines are grown in Valais: the white fendant, vinified from the Chasselas, or Fendant, grape, and the red dole, principally from the Pinot Noir with some Gamay. The wine sold as johannisberg, and which may be said vaguely to resemble a hock, is vinified principally from the Sylvaner, with some Riesling. Neuchatel is principally noted for its white and sparkling pétillant wines. White, red and rosé table wines are also grown. A certain amount of red wine is grown around Zurich from Pinot Noir vines, known locally as Klevener. An interesting red wine, always in short supply, is balgacher schlossberg: from the Pinot Noir grown on the banks of the Rhine in the north-east mountains. White wine is also grown there, and both can be slightly pétillant. Some of the Swiss wines are so light, though, that they rather put one in mind of water.

Yugoslavia

Yugoslavian wines, particularly the rieslings, have been extremely popular in the United Kingdom for many years; they are good, and in terms of value for money they are outstanding. Viticulture has a very long history there. The vine was probably first cultivated by the Phoenicians, then the Greeks cultivated it along the Dalmatian coast, while the Romans cultivated it in the north. The history of this multi-lingual country is extremely complicated and is mercifully wholly beyond the scope of this book: anyone wishing to trace the history of wine alone would have to devote years of research to it. Apart from the combined influence of the Greeks and Romans, in more recent times the Mohammedan Turks occupied parts of the country, during which time wine growing in those areas became virtually extinguished. Little is heard of the wines of what is now Yugoslavia, though, until the country began to enjoy reasonably peaceful conditions at the beginning of the nineteenth century. The first school of viticulture was established in 1872, fortunately fourteen years before the phylloxera struck, and when it did the government was able to help the wine growers. The result, as in so many areas, was an improvement in the quality of the wines, as it gave the opportunity to eliminate unsuitable vine varieties. At this time the northern vineyards were under Austrian domination, and Austrian traditions still maintain there. Ljutomer wines were known as luttenberger, those of Pekre as pickerwein, and those of Halozan as killoserwein: names that are still found in old records and wine lists. Moving on to the present day, wine growing is now highly organized through co-operatives and the wines are sold through state-controlled trading organizations, though most of the vineyards remain privately owned. Nor are the co-operatives communist creations: that of Maribor dates back to 1898.

By far the most important wine-growing province is Slovenia, and the most important area within it is that of Ljutomer, for which most English-speaking wine merchants substitute the more pronounceable spelling *Lutomer*. But there are also four other distinct areas: Maribor, Pekre, Haloze and Radgona. The best vineyards are planted at a high altitude of from 700 to 1,600 feet, but it is impossible to generalize about soil: igneous rock, clay, sand and marl all play their parts. The most commonly found vines are the Riesling, Sylvaner, Traminer, Sauvignon and the indigenous Sipon, a variety of the Furmint. Of those, the riesling is the one most widely exported, and while the lutomer rieslings sold over here are good wines and excellent value, I nevertheless have my reservations about them. Shipped in cask, they are often over sulphured to preserve them on their journey and the riesling character somehow gets lost. Edmund Penning-Rowsell tells me that on a recent visit to the vineyards he tasted rieslings of an altogether superior class that resembled those grown in Alsace, and I hope that such wines will eventually be exported in bottle. As it is, and excellent though they are, it seems to me that the lutomer rieslings do not fulfil their promise. In a tasting of 1958 wines in 1964, the best was undoubtedly a lutomer traminer, which had a beautiful aromatic traminer nose and was very well balanced. A sweet spätlese sold under the name *Tigermilk*, vinified from Ranina grapes in Radgona, came next, followed by lutomer sylvaner, that was slightly sweet, aromatic and rather uncharacteristic of the sylvaners grown further north, and then we put a sauvignon of less distinction, before we placed the riesling.

Although wines are also grown throughout the rest of Yugoslavia, my own experience of these has failed to persuade me that their inclusion would be worth while in this book.

APPENDIX II

Laws of Appellation d'Origine Contrôlée

Laws exist in practically every country of the world save Britain to protect the geographical names of wines. Owing to the malpractices of our wine trade in the past, many unquestionably geographical names such as *burgundy*, *chablis*, *sauternes* and so on have—or are alleged by the trade to have—become 'generic'. In a recent High Court action the name *sherry* was found to be geographical, but owing to its widespread misuse over a long period of time the court was only able to extend a very limited protection to it. As will be seen, the laxity of our own laws (and such that exist are practically unenforceable) leaves a serious loophole that even affects the foreign laws.

All of the wine-producing countries are fortunately more honourably disposed than we British, and each has its own laws relating to the use of the name of the place of origin in relation to a wine. These laws, however, are continuously under review. In recent years those of France have been tightened, those of Italy have been tightened drastically and at last enforced, while those of Germany, which were formerly extremely complicated and strict, have been relaxed to a small extent. The ultimate aim is to arrange for an enforceable set of laws to be universal within the countries of the Common Market, and if Britain is eventually admitted into the Common Market presumably we shall have to conform—and a good thing too. We *can* label our wines honestly when the law demands, as is shown by the observance of the statute implementing the Anglo-Portuguese Trade Treaty, which gives protection to the names of port and madeira; and the name *champagne* which was protected as a result of a High Court injunction when action was taken in time.

The pioneer legislation on this subject is undoubtedly that of France. To be entitled to the name of its place of origin, a wine must in the first place, of course, come from that place. The more geographically exact the description, generally speaking, the finer the wine. Thus all the vineyards within the accepted Bordeaux region are entitled to the general *appellation* Bordeaux; a somewhat stricter, though still very wide *appellation* is Haut-Médoc; a stricter one still is Pauillac; and finally one comes down to a single vineyard such as Château Lafite. The area covered may be anything from the enormous areas of Bordeaux and Burgundy to the minute area of Château Grillet. But whatever its size, it is a defined geographical location. Although fundamental, the geographical requirements are by no means the only ones, though.

The full requirements for any area (and they differ considerably from area to area) are defined by the Institut National des Appellations d'Origine, generally abbreviated to I.N.A.O. Other matters dealt with include the vine varieties permitted; the minimum alcoholic content, which is set at a higher figure for the quality appellations than for those from the wider areas so that a red wine labelled *bourgogne ordinaire* need only have a minimum alcoholic strength of 9° Gay-Lussac, a wine labelled *gevrey-chambertin* must have a minimum strength of 10·5°, a wine labelled *chambertin* must have a minimum strength of 11·5°, and so on; viticultural and oenological practices throughout must correspond to the accepted good practices of the region; and the maximum harvest from any one area of vineyard is also specified. The last requirement is perhaps one of the most difficult. Ideally the yield should be determined simply by the number of vines per acre and the method of pruning, but to enforce such a law would call for an enormous degree of investigation and supervision by the state, and in practice it would be impossible. The yield, too, varies dramatically according to climatic conditions, and in certain prolific years a large quantity of wine can be produced of better quality than that produced in other years, such as the notorious 1956, when frost damage drastically reduced the yield. In the past, when the maximum harvest has been exceeded, it has been the practice to permit only the legal maximum to have the *appellation* and to allow the remainder to be sold without it. It is in this connection that the lack of effective laws in England have helped to ruin the whole system in France. If an English wine merchant is approached by a grower and is told that he can have the wine with or without the *appellation* certificates—and at a very substantial reduction if he has it without—he naturally has it without, since the wine is exactly the same. On the other hand, that leaves the French *négociant* with the appropriate number of *appellation* certificates which he can then apply to any wine, which may not be entitled to the *appellation* at all. This abuse has been substantially reduced of late by a modification in the French laws which has prohibited the export of the more expensive wines without *appellation* certificates. Another useful reform has been to refuse the *appellation* to the whole output when this greatly exceeds the authorized figure until the wine has been tasted to see that it is worthy of its name. In certain instances the *appellation* may be refused to the whole if the output is exceeded.

It seems extraordinary that a high grade *appellation* should ever have been attached to a wine without its having to pass a tasting test, but the institution of such tests calls for considerable machinery. They are now, however, operating in many fine wine areas, and in recent years in Bordeaux many wines—particularly from the Sauternes area—have been denied their *appellation* as a result of having failed the test.

A lesser form of *appellation* is V.D.Q.S., meaning Vins Délimités de Qualité Supérieure, many of which are very good indeed. There are lots of them and most are produced in small areas, or areas of secondary importance, or both; but it would be quite wrong to think that because a wine is V.D.Q.S. it is necessarily second rate or inferior to an *appellation contrôlée* wine. For instance, wines of Cahors are V.D.Q.S. whereas a *bourgogne ordinaire* is *appellation contrôlée*. The degree of control with respect to these wines is somewhat less, but the area, the vine varieties and the minimum alcoholic strength are stipulated, and there is usually a tasting test before the wine is permitted to bear the V.D.Q.S. label.

The above is only a very rough outline of the French system, but all other systems operate on broadly the same principles. In practice the French system has done a very great deal for wine, but of course it is controversial and open to abuse: a dishonest *négociant* can always find highly ingenious and often convincing arguments against a strict form of control. And of course the system, calling as it does for documentation and inspection, is an expensive one to operate: if it operated in this country it would undoubtedly add noticeably to the cost of wine. But similarly the police force adds to the cost of the rates, and I suggest that a purchaser is entitled to buy wine corresponding to the name on the label just as he is entitled to be protected from robbery and violence. It has been suggested, too, that if the laws are enforced in this country the prices of popular wines such as nuits st. georges will rise—and so they will, of course. But there will be the same amount of genuine nuits st. georges and it will fetch the same price at its place of origin. What will happen is that those who want nuits st. georges will get the genuine article and have to pay a realistic price for it, while those who were content with a bogus nuits st. georges will be able to buy the wine they buy now for perhaps a lower price under a brand name. To prevent abuse and at the same time hardship, a certain amount of education of the public will unfortunately be called for. But the wine trade has itself to thank that this should be so, for if it had not permitted abuses in the past the problem would never have arisen. It is now, fortunately, trying hard to put its house in order. And at the same time, alas, it must be admitted that the French house is getting seriously out of order. At the time of going to press there is every sign that the system of *appellation contrôlée* is seriously breaking down, brought about partly by the French tax system. Let us hope that the Common Market will eventually succeed in putting all our houses in order.

Finally, I must emphasize that the above account is both brief and incomplete. To deal with a subject of this complexity fully would call for quite a substantial book; for the history of controlled *appellation* in the various countries is itself a fascinating subject and one that has had many repercussions, while the practical operation of the system is one of great complexity. Nor can one seriously advance or refute arguments for or against the systems as they operate at present, or alternative systems in this or any other country, without dealing with the matter in very considerable detail. In the foreseeable future, though, there can be little doubt that the whole system will be the subject of international treaties and domestic legislation.

Index

INDEX

INDEX

INDEX